P9-AGK-977

MODERN NEWSPAPER EDITING

The Glendessary Press — Berkeley, California

Modern Newspaper Editing

Gene Gilmore
University of Illinois
Robert Root
Eisenhower College

2512 Grove Street, Berkeley, California

Printed in the United States of America
Library of Congress Card Catalog No. 76-142001

First printing January 1971
Second printing March 1971
Third printing August 1971
Fourth printing May 1972

To
Virginia and Christine

Contents

Foreword

I believe any student of journalism will find this book extremely useful. In thoroughly professional fashion it explains with great clarity every facet of modern newspaper editing.

Not only does it cover the technical side of editing, but it thoughtfully discusses some of the ethical and moral questions every editor has to face in appraising the news, in deciding what to print, what to feature, and how to display it. It should be helpful to every young journalist anxious to learn. Even an old-timer like me, with a background of more than forty years of editing experience, found the book stimulating.

Robert Root, one of the co-authors, and I worked together on the *Des Moines Register* and *Tribune* many years ago where we were both beginners in the newsroom. I came to have much respect for his ability and judgment. Bob went on to a varied and distinguished career in journalism and in the academic world. His broad experience superbly equipped him to co-author this book.

News of his recent, untimely death left me very sad. He will be missed by all who love journalism.

Gardner Cowles

Editorial Director, *Look*
President, Des Moines Register and Tribune Co.

Preface

The continuing paradox of the newspaper business is that it must cover an ever faster pace of events with techniques and traditions that change little from generation to generation. At the same time that the newspaper is criticized for slow technical improvement, it has to compete with television in flashing accounts of space flights and wars. So we have been advised by some friends and journalism associates simply to make a better presentation of the "how to" features which have changed little in recent decades. Others have urged that this be a book for futuristic editors with editing consoles and computers. Not without risk, we have tried to solve the dilemma by doing both. The result is a more comprehensive and somewhat thicker volume than most authors of newspaper editing books have attempted the last half century.

The student reader may note a progression from "smaller" concerns to "larger" ones as he goes through the book. Correcting copy and finding the right word for a headline are not really minor, of course, and the early chapters on these topics do touch weightier matters like computerization and international news flow. However, questions of law, taste, theory, research, and policy are treated in detail after the student has got his grounding in basics.

Students and instructors alike may get more out of the volume if they note that certain preconceptions and concerns of the writers emerge again and again through the book. Whatever the technical subject at hand, we have felt it important, where appropriate, to allude to such issues or themes as these: the need for the editor to be concerned about the reader; the nature of the reader today; the goals of a newspaper in a free society; the realistic measures for improvement and reform of the press; the standards of social responsibility and taste; and, especially, the essentials of sound, progressive policy.

So we hope this becomes more than a manual for getting out newspapers the way they were published in the sixties. The student will learn from it what he needs to know to fit in on the copydesk of his hometown paper, however humble, if that is what he wants; but we hope the restive student who imagines greater papers than he has read will be stimulated to create them.

To expand the student's vision, we have devoted considerable space to the problems of news evaluation, going beyond man-bites-dog to standards more appropriate for modern journalism. Ironically, at the same time that the mass media are continually criticized for performance, questions of newspaper morality are seldom considered in either the classroom or the newsroom. So we have given a whole chapter to ethics and taste, and another to related problems of libel and privacy in newspapers.

Still, not to overlook the technical side, the book contains two comprehensive chapters in copyediting technique and a detailed section on good headline writing, with appropriate examples. While many texts handle the problems of typography and photography with a few paragraphs, we have felt it essential to devote a chapter to graphic arts and another to photography and picture editing in order to cover modern presentation.

The impact of new technology, including computers, is discussed in a realistic context. There is a look at the future, with a consideration not only of newer production methods but of more responsible editing. Finally, the book makes a claim to a first by including a chapter on newspaper research with suggestions to the editor for conducting his own studies as well as using the findings of professional researchers.

The focus of the volume is the daily newspaper. The writers are not bemused by the metropolitan press. There are examples from the *New York Times* and the *Los Angeles Times* when appropriate, but there are also illustrations from the middle-size and small dailies which most Americans read. In the framework of a journalism school, the editing course in the newspaper sequence is the natural place for the book. However, many of its lessons on heads, law, style, photography, ethics, and so on are valuable to the study of weekly newspapers, company publications, and even magazines.

No book can offer a whole journalism degree between its covers. Yet we hope, in many of our chapters, to present a summary of several courses in a good school of journalism or communications—typography, photography, communications research, law, etc. Someone considering a career in journalism may find here an illuminating survey. The college student can get both the breadth of a journalism overview and the depth of precise knowledge about newspaper organization, editorial duties, good headlines, and better writing style. Perhaps men and women already working in the media will find here a good review to renew their enthusiasm for newspapering. Younger professionals may discover subjects they have learned little about, and old-timers who have been unable to keep up in some areas will discover information about developments on papers they would like to emulate.

G. G.
R. R.

A postscript of sorrow must be added. Before this book could be published Professor Robert Root died. His early death stunned those who worked with him and who knew of his cheer, his humanity, and his professional goals. He has many monuments. We hope this book is one.

Gene Gilmore

Acknowledgments

We acknowledge with thanks the help of many who have contributed to this book. While assuming full responsibility ourselves for the final draft, we are especially grateful to several colleagues for reading certain chapters: Dr. D. Wayne Rowland, former chairman of the Newspaper Department, School of Journalism, Syracuse University, and now dean of the School of Journalism, Drake University; Dr. Jack B. Haskins, John Ben Snow, Professor at the Syracuse school; Prof. Edmund C. Arnold, chairman of the Syracuse Graphic Arts Department; Profs. Glenn G. Hanson, John Schacht, and W. William Alfeld of the University of Illinois College of Communications; Charles W. Puffenbarger of the *Washington Post;* and Charles-Gene McDaniel, science writer of the Chicago bureau of the Associated Press.

We appreciate also information and suggestions from Robert Kerns, assistant professor of photography, Syracuse; Prof. Roland E. Wolseley, retired chairman of the Magazine Department, Syracuse; Prof. Olin Hinkle, University of Texas; Larry Hale of the *Binghamton* (N. Y.) *Press;* Gerald Bean of the *Rockford* (Ill.) *Register-Republic;* and Vincent S. Jones, executive editor of the Gannett newspapers and past president of the American Society of Newspaper Editors.

The editors of *Editor & Publisher* deserve special thanks for the many articles printed about newspaper editing, which have been invaluable in the preparation of several chapters; the serious professional should keep up with *E & P* in order to get the most out of these pages. He will also find, as we have, that *Journalism Quarterly* and *Quill* publish articles useful to both the scholar and the professional newsman.

Note to the 4th printing

Since the first printing, the salaries of copyeditors have risen dramatically enough to change the discussion on pages 302, 261, and 362. Likewise the increased use of computers is acknowledged in the advice to editors on page 164.

MODERN NEWSPAPER EDITING

1 News editing today and tomorrow

When he was President, John F. Kennedy described what an editor should be. In a speech at the University of North Carolina he said the press needed people "educated in the liberal traditions, willing to take the long look, undisturbed by prejudices and slogans of the moment, who attempt to make an honest judgment on difficult events." Such men, he added, "could distinguish the real from the illusory, the long range from the temporary, the significant from the petty."

These stiff requirements will always mean a shortage of ideal editors. The democratic society, however, to function properly must have a sizeable number of editors who come close to the ideal. Many of the highly qualified professionals of 1980 and 1990 will be men and women who today are journalism students or beginning journalists.

Because journalism professionals rise rapidly, the responsibilities of executive positions may come early. The city editor on a major newspaper can be a man still in his twenties. Sometimes the news editor on a quality, medium-sized paper is barely thirty. Higher administrative positions like managing editor or executive editor often come to men well before middle age. If these journalists are to approach the qualities cited by President Kennedy, they must learn rapidly and well the skills of the reporter and the copyeditor. Rarely can a person leap into an executive position without solid preparation at the typewriter or copydesk. Nor should he.

The ideal editor has been a reporter of various worlds: politics, government, social welfare, labor, and business. He has followed such experience with a period of editing—working to improve the copy of others. Then the young newsman may be ready for the moves to city, state, or telegraph editor; news editor; managing editor; and, eventually, editor.

To grow professionally he must learn each job well. He prepares for the positions that carry even greater responsibility by combining observation, reading, listening, discussion, writing, and introspection. He looks about the newsroom and around the city to see how jobs are done and how they might be done better. He reads about what he cannot possibly observe first hand and seeks fresh insights. He opens his mind by listening to others who report how the job has been done and how it should be done. He sharpens his ideas and challenges his thoughts in discussions with professionals inside and outside of journalism. He examines his concept of himself to recognize and reduce his shortcomings.

Men and women at every level of journalism usually will find satisfaction in helping to inform hundreds or even thousands of people about vital public affairs. Magazines, books, radio, television, and word-of-mouth contribute, but much of what the ordinary citizen knows about current problems he has learned through the work of the editors of his newspaper.

Emphasis changing

To meet this responsibility to the reader, editors at all levels must be thorough and painstaking. This is particularly difficult on daily newspapers or on radio-television news programs because there is little time to examine every issue with scholarly thoroughness. In recent years, however, the better newspapers often have put less emphasis on speed. They have been willing to hold up a story for an edition or two, or even a day or more, until additional facts can be gathered. These papers also make every effort to give reporters time to get the complete story so readers will not be misled by superficial information.

This trend to complete interpretation reflects the modern editor's knowledge of communications. He knows that the public tunes in to radio and television for bulletins and flashes but looks to the newspaper for detail and authentication. To edit an authoritative paper requires not only thoroughness and painstaking attention but sober examination of world events and the editor's community. His sound judgment of the news helps make his newspaper sound.

To keep his newspaper sound the editor must have a sturdy backbone, for he must resist subtle and not-so-subtle political and economic pressures. The power of the press is considerable, and powerful people know it. They try to influence the newsman in subtle ways: dinners, free tickets, gifts, flattery. They can also be more direct: advertising boycotts, organized drives to cancel subscriptions, and vicious whispering campaigns against newspaper employees.

Courage, of course, is a precious commodity. Editors have at least as much as any other professional group, and they need it. To take unpopular positions in public, to dig up information, and to publish stories and editorials against people with power takes a lot of courage.

Editorial courage also can bring economic reprisals and terrifying personal anguish. When the schools in Little Rock were to be integrated, the *Arkansas Gazette* editorialized firmly and almost daily that the courts had ruled in favor of integration and that the community should follow the law. The paper was denounced in vulgar language, the editors were harassed day and night, and an organized campaign cut the circulation more than 10 percent.*

The schools were integrated, but the *Gazette* lost thousands of dollars in revenue and the editors suffered intensely from the insults and harassment. The publisher, J. N. Heiskell, received many awards, including the 1958 Pulitzer Prize for public service. The same year, the editor, Harry S. Ashmore, won the Pulitzer for editorial writing. Though the paper lost money and the staff suffered, perhaps these tributes made the sacrifices worthwhile.

These pressures may seem remote to the young journalist, but he will soon meet them and must prepare himself to react confidently. The beginner practices reporting, writing, and editing, so he might also practice his reaction to a bribe—labeled as a gift. And what would he do if one of his stories lost an advertising contract? What if a group of furious businessmen descended on his office? What if someone called from the White House to complain about an editorial? Unfortunately, most newsmen have not prepared for such occurrences, and the first one can be unnerving. To become a capable and trusted editor, the professional must be able to resist pressures with confidence and skill.

Clarity needed

The conscientious editor makes the whole news picture clear as well as fair. But sometimes the news may not be clear to the editor himself. The reporters may be unable to get complete information, some sources may have tried to mislead the press and the public, and the editor's own background may be inadequate to set the news in proper perspective. No newspaper editor can be sure of the accuracy of all the information reaching him, nor can he usually be certain when attempts are being made to mislead him. And no editor is so erudite that he can grasp the significance of every event or utterance. But he should strive to do the best job possible to make the news understandable. The reader expects and deserves to have events reported to him so they make sense.

The editor's job is to sift and organize the news so the reader does not have to struggle to get information. All kinds of distractions affect the reader. Television, radio, other papers, general noise, and conversation lure his attention. The newspaper editor must make his product easy to read, and worth reading. He does this by an intelligent selection of news, careful interpretation of it, sober but sprightly editorial comment, good writing—and attractive placement of these items on the newspaper pages.

This is creative work, for it requires knowledge, imagination, writing skill, judgment, and an eye for design. An editor who combines these elements can create something significant—a paper that informs the public and thus guides citizens to intelligent decisions.

*Advertising was not reduced, however, indicating that business interests either supported the paper's stand or felt they needed to advertise regardless of the paper's policy.

What about computers?

But won't computers replace human editors and make such idealistic goals passé?

It is true that the computer—and automation generally—will make big headway on newspapers in coming decades as it has in recent ones. The teletypesetter (TTS), which sets type from a perforated tape, has increased the already great influence of the headquarters editor of the new service,* and newspapers have for some time used computers for setting some matter and for billing. In the mid-sixties Dean Wayne Danielson of the University of Texas was already conducting experiments with computer editing of a miniature paper. In view of the magic of many computer-automated industries today, it does not take much imagination to picture a programmed newspaper of tomorrow. The computer would call for a certain mix of stories, direct their lengths, fabricate headlines from the leads, and provide an appropriate percentage of human interest material. The local editors might still do make-up, but even that could be programmed in New York and relayed to local computers, with allowance of certain news holes for local and state stories.

But if newspapers come to that, perhaps the subscriber should have a computer in the home to read the paper! In fact, why print the whole paper at all? Let one computer transmit the file of information, and let the individual subscriber program his computer to print only the news he most needs. Let him also program in approved comics for his children. He can thus produce his own personal newspaper, with only a clerical assist from the local "editor."

Computers in perspective

That dream—or nightmare—is some time ahead. Without being fanciful about 1984, however, the editor of the next few years must come to terms with computers, and four observations appear to be pertinent about them:

Computers are expensive. So are programmers. Cheap programming could no doubt be provided, but it would result in a stereotyped paper, without the depth and sophistication which alert editors can give; because of cost pressures, such low-grade mechanical editing may become a social threat before the century is out. But costs for the continual programming and reprogramming which will match or exceed human editors will be prohibitive, at least for the next several years.

Most newspapers could improve without more machines. Unquestionably, information-retrieval equipment is already at the point where newspapers could amass countless facts instantaneously, but using such machinery would be shipping in an elephant

* In 1958 syndication already threatened to make news more standardized and monotonous: "Syndicated materials will more and more take on the synthetic slickness of the mass-produced. . . . The teletypesetter has already brought us close to the centralized production of newspaper stereotype plates. . . . By 2000 it is very likely that at least several pages of the paper in Los Angeles and another in Minneapolis will be as identical as if they had come from the same New York facsimile transmitter."[1]

to kill a gnat. How many newspapers today make more than a minimal effort to collect facts which are not readily available—or want to spend the money, with present hands and equipment, to really dig for information? In getting full information on a story, newspapers should first spend money and manpower to check their own libraries, phone the public library, interview widely, send queries to press services, and so on. When these elementary methods to retrieve information prove inadequate, more sophisticated (and expensive) retrieval may win a role.

The computer, like the telegraph and the teletype, may well become a great aid for the working editor. If automated machinery is unlikely to emerge soon as the master in the newsroom, it can be a helpful servant. For example, even the experienced human brain is harassed in keeping track of the competing stories on a complex news day. But just as airline and hotel reservations become instantly available now by pressing a computerized button, the whole array of world, national, state and local stories might be quickly recalled for human evaluators. Some experimental tools in machine copyediting are also promising. Development of such aids, however, will be costly.

Human editorial judgment will remain essential to great newspapers. In this generation, it seems unlikely that a robot will be created which can select and display news as well as a seasoned editor. The skill of a computer at chess-playing is limited by the brains of the chess-players who program it. Even if chess-players combine to create a master chess-player, one more skilled than any of them individually, this creation would not completely foreshadow a mechanical super-editor. For editing is less of a science than an art. It might be compared to poetry writing, and the poems and songs produced so far by computers have been remarkable but amateurish. Until computers can successfully make the subtle distinctions in word choice required of poetry, they will not be able to pull together into editorial choices all the variables which, consciously and subconsciously, mold the fine decisions as the editor works at his art.

Goals for newsmen

Even as automation has advanced, so has man's understanding of the complexity of news. Traditionally, the aim of journalism has been expressed in a three-part definition: to inform, to guide, and to entertain. While those goals still serve well enough for quick rule of thumb, any computer programming limited to them would be inadequate for the needs of the modern newspaper reader. In coming years, editors will have to weigh the news with at least nine purposes in mind, giving the edge one time to the serious, another time to the frivolous:

To inform. Transmitting the bare facts to people remains a major goal. They want, as fast as possible and in greater detail than broadcasting can give, the facts of life, like stock quotations, ball scores, election results, and contest winners.

To alert. As watchmen, sentries, and runners have for ages brought vital news to leaders, the media of a democracy today have a role in alerting readers to what they need to know. To assume that the headline-skimmer is uninformed is an oversimplification. For example, over a few weeks a home-owner may note several headlines on house sales or mortgage rates and barely glance at the stories—yet he is alerted to trends which are important if he ponders selling or renting. Even the lack of war headlines from an area may "negatively alert" the reader that "all's well."

To interpret. While the objective newspaper tradition of conveying only facts is still strong, for at least a generation editors have been emphasizing the need for interpretation. The facts alone may lie. Someone must put them into perspective. For example, a Washington reporter may learn that a federal program for the poor has quietly been eliminated. But perhaps its end was contemplated when work was undertaken by another department sometime earlier. What is needed is an interpretation of what all the various departments of government are attempting to do about poverty.

A glance at any newspaper shows that opinion is no longer confined to the editorial page—it shapes many of the most important news stories, sometimes excessively.

To educate. Some editors would argue that education is the same as interpretation, but other old-timers would say newspapering has nothing to do with education.* It is true that many interpretive stories—for example, on urban problems or on measures to overcome poverty—aim to convey an accurate picture of a situation, which is teaching. But many features besides interpretive stories, such as medical columns, science cartoons, and income tax pointers, are printed primarily as education. The "Newspaper in the Classroom" seminars sponsored by universities in cooperation with the American Newspaper Publishers Association underline these educational potentialities. One newspaper critic, W. H. Ferry, goes so far as to suggest that the whole purpose of the press is educational: "My view is that masscomm's social and cultural responsibilities are those of the largest and probably most influential educational system any society has known."[3]

To lead. Newspapers inevitably lead, whether intentionally or not. The presentation of news leads readers to think and act about some things rather than others. A paper which emphasizes crime, scandal, and sex directs the attention of readers to such subjects. A more serious paper, with a diet of more important civic issues, directs community concern by its very act of establishing the agenda

* The mass media in underdeveloped countries, according to Dr. Wilbur Schramm of Stanford University, have three roles: to be watchmen, to be leaders, and to be teachers.[2]

of discussion. Too often newsmen think of their leadership role as confined largely to opinion columns on the editorial page. In fact, headlines probably are more important in making both opinion leaders and ordinary voters sort out the vital issues. The privately-supported Commission on Freedom of the Press—a group of lay intellectuals known as the Hutchins Commission because it was chaired by the educator, Robert Maynard Hutchins—observed in 1947 that one requirement of the press is to present and clarify the goals and values of society.

To persuade. While persuading is of course like leading, there can be static leadership which merely points a direction for concern, as thorough coverage of a pickpocket epidemic would direct attention to solving the problem. But there is also persuasive leadership, which includes arguing and cajoling to get citizens to act. This is a normal function of a good editorial page. When a newspaper crusades, as when it prints numerous items on a subject such as gambling, it is using facts to persuade.

To provide a forum. The letters-to-the-editor page is the most obvious platform for different points of view. But a well-edited paper also has the purpose of seeing that all the important shades of opinion on major issues are aired in the news. One evil of the press in an authoritarian country is that the news presents only the official line, a monolithic view. Most American papers could do a better job than they do of giving a greater range of opinion instead of sticking to the one or two most popular or conventional.

To inspire. A newspaper is not a church, but it can inspire. A good editorial stimulates an almost spiritual thrill of rededication. Even the news sections should contain some stories less important for their information and interpretation than for the bravery, courage, determination, or love they portray.

To entertain. Obviously cartoons and gossip columns provide entertainment, but human interest stories and feature pieces entertain as well as inform. Life is not all drab, as the serious "big bad" news may imply, and editors should give their readers the amusing, the witty, and the whimsical.

Gatekeeping

The editor who puts out a paper which intelligently fulfills all these varied functions is a major figure in his community and in society. The term "gatekeeper" has been coined by some researchers to emphasize the editor's importance at a cutoff point where the decision is made to stop some items, to let a trickle of other news through, or to permit the flow of a story judged as important. In a 1949 study, Dr. David Manning White, now of Boston University, analyzed the reasons a telegraph editor gave for rejecting copy and found them "highly subjective," colored by his personal experiences and attitudes. In later analyses of telegraph editors in the Midwest, Dr. Walter Gieber of San Francisco State College found them making decisions passively under bureaucratic or other pressures. "News," says Gieber, "is what newspapermen make it."[4] We clearly need to know more about what factors influence gatekeepers. And society needs better-trained editors who can attain maximum objectivity and who will know their audiences and facilitate intelligent communication to them.

Newspapers of quality

The emphasis on quality editors may seem to say that a newspaper need only hire competent people and the customers will flock to the newsstands to buy it. That is rarely the case. The production and sale of anything good usually takes time, so much time that the editors of a paper trying to do a conscientious job become discouraged. Its sales may stay small, while a sensational competing paper gains circulation. In other cases a newspaper staff may spend a great deal of energy, resourcefulness, and money to get some outstanding stories, then find that few people bothered to read them.

Rather than get needlessly discouraged, the editors must ask themselves in such cases if they have done as good a job as they thought. Perhaps they had overestimated the reader's knowledge. Were the stories really easy to grasp? Were the editors expecting that a story or two would bring quick reaction in circulation figures? Was the news displayed so the reader could hardly avoid the stories? Or was the paper so deadly serious, so lacking in any humor or sprightliness, that people found it ponderous and tedious?

If the editors with high standards are sometimes discouraged, they are often heartened. Thoughtful people in the community, sometimes called "the creative minority," frequently will praise the coverage of local, national, and world events. Public officials may mutter harsh words, but they usually will work better when aware that what they do is scrutinized carefully but fairly. The business community is especially responsive because advertisers like to put their ads in carefully read newspapers.

What the public wants

Sometimes newspapers employ organizations that survey readership to "find out what the people want." Some successful editors suspect such surveys because people often consciously or subconsciously misrepresent their beliefs on a question. Another reason to be skeptical of surveys is that people tend to like what they are accustomed to. If they have been taking a quality paper for years, they tend to like quality. If they have been handed for years a diet of comics, agony columns, and other fluff, they will find quality hard to digest.*

Editors who have drawn the greatest praise in the nation—men like Joseph Pulitzer, Adolph Ochs, E. W. Scripps—have had concrete ideas on what a newspaper should be. They produced that kind of paper and their kind of journalism was successful, both commercially and professionally.

* Thoughtful research, as discussed in chapter 18, can give editors useful guidance.

Editors who turn out "what the public wants" usually produce an insignificant paper. Believing that the public is bored by anything important, they fill their papers with the trite and the trivial. This formula has been enormously profitable in the past. Circulations skyrocketed at the turn of the century on a news formula of love, lust, and lucre. The technique started to fade in the early thirties and today it is usually the serious, thoughtful, and penetrating newspaper that shows the best gains in circulation, advertising, and influence.

Successful quality

The most spectacular increase in circulation in the last decade has been made by the *Wall Street Journal*, a newspaper with three detailed, socially-significant stories each day, plus several valuable minor stories. The *Journal*, without pictures, comics, sports, or women's pages, has climbed to the second largest circulation in the United States.

The *New York Times* and the *Washington Post*, both serious papers that spend lavishly to get the news, have made remarkable gains. The *Los Angeles Times*, with perhaps more columns of news than any paper in the nation, has soared in circulation to become the dominant West Coast paper.

The more literate magazines, like the *Saturday Review*, the *New Republic*, and the *Atlantic*, have had either steady or spectacular growth. Interest in creative arts, such as painting, music, writing, has burgeoned so fast in the last two decades that the movement is called a cultural explosion. While the extent of this interest may be exaggerated, it should not be ignored. The newspapers of the next decade or generation, to meet public demand, must blend thorough reporting and intelligent commentary with an attractive format.*

These superior newspapers will have imaginative, knowledgeable, and demanding editors who will be looking for young newsmen with a talent for intelligent reporting and editing. They also will be searching for someone to replace them in the future.

It is important that these superior papers not be only the dailies of New York, Washington, Los Angeles, or other huge cities. Dozens of medium-sized or even small papers now do a fine job of reporting the news of their communities and the world, and there is room for many more. These papers also are seeking people who can do the exacting and rewarding job of editing.

Anyone preparing for such a career would do well to consider President Kennedy's ideal newsman, described at the opening of this chapter. One long-time journalist, Walter Lippmann, reinforces Kennedy's concept, noting that the reliable and responsible professional seeks "to bring to light the hidden facts, to set them in relation with each other, and make a picture of reality on which men can act."

*Frothy periodicals may make great gains too, of course, and we do not suggest that quality is measured by circulation growth. Still, strong consumer demand for high quality books and magazines reminds the editor that many of these readers also want a high quality newspaper.

You see here a curious assortment of people. Copy editors. Curious not in the funny sense. Nosey. They ask questions. Sometimes they drive reporters crazy with questions. But because they do—these and the rest of the 75 copy editors on its staff—they make The New York Times just about the most useful newspaper you can read.

Questions. A copy editor starts the minute he picks up a piece of copy. Is this name spelled right? Is that figure correct? Is this the right date? Shouldn't there be a phrase here explaining this fact? Is the meaning of this statement clear? Wasn't someone else involved?

Questions. Copy editors go a little batty themselves sometimes, trying to get all the facts sorted out, all the questions answered. They do this because they have the funny idea that they're not copy editors. *They think they're you.* They're asking the questions they imagine you'd ask. But they ask them before you even think of them so that you won't think of them.

Questions. When they've got the answers to every question they figure you might ask, and maybe even some sneaky ones they think up themselves, they write a headline for the story. The headline tells you what the story is all about. If you're pressed for time, you can get the gist of the story from the headline, read the story later, meantime know what's up.

Questions. Answers. That's what a copy editor's life is all about. No by-lines to gloat over. No public glory to bask in. Only an inner satisfaction to soothe the ulcer. The satisfaction that when you've read a story in The New York Times, your every question will have been answered.

Any questions?

Fig. 2-1. Copy quiz masters. The **New York Times** ran this picture of almost half its copyeditors with an explanation of their work. As pointed out in the ad, a copyeditor is a professional skeptic who tries to see a story through the reader's eyes. He also must be aware of the paper's policies and traditions as he weighs the reporter's words.

2 The copyeditor and copyediting

Newspaper copyeditors have a special place in the newsroom. On the bigger papers they sit at a horseshoe-shaped table, the copydesk, encompassed by paste pots, pencils, scissors, copypaper, and one another. On smaller papers their center is more likely to be a group of flat-topped desks, pushed together so the copyeditors can work efficiently as a team.

The copyeditor's job, of course, is to edit manuscript, or copy. This job, sometimes called simply "editing," is to remove words, alter language, and trim away surplus stories or parts of stories until the finished newspaper product is concise, accurate, factual—and appealing. To be a good judge of copy, the editor needs to combine his interest in the English language with an understanding of reporting, some knowledge of printing processes, and a clear understanding of his own newspaper's policy. (See fig. 2-1.)

The path of copy

The substance of his work is copy—the reporter's manuscript (usually double-spaced on cheap copypaper), which comes to the editor from three main sub-editors.* The city editor sends copy from his city reporters. The state editor provides stories about events from the paper's circulation area outside the city. The telegraph editor delivers copy selected from the wire services. Some papers even have a fourth sub-editor, a suburban editor, who transmits news and features from the suburbs.

The person in charge of the copydesk is the *slot man*, so called because he sits on the inside—in the slot—of the horseshoe desk or its equivalent. His aides, the copyeditors, sit on the outside and so are known as *rim men*, even though occasionally two or three of them will be women. (Copyeditors are also called *desk men* and *copyreaders*.) Figure 2-2 shows a typical arrangement.

* The term "sub-editor" is descriptive but not much used in U. S. newsrooms. In Britain, however, "sub-editor" is common professional usage.

The slot man selects the rim man best able to handle a particular story. He also decides how it should be edited, then writes a curt phrase like "trim," "cut," or "slash" above the story. The slot man may be still more specific. He may write "trim one-third" or may even jot down the number of inches the story should measure when set in type. The copyeditor then understands he must reduce the story to exactly that length. A copyeditor also has some of this executive power. He may cut a story more sharply than ordered or even kill it, but he will probably want to discuss his reasons with the slot man. Others have already planned space for his copy and must know how many column-inches he has trimmed.

Sometimes the slot man will suggest a certain handling of a story. He may write cryptically "Trim out the puffs" or "Bring fire angle to top." But all orders from the slot are not written. Since he is only feet away from his rim men, the man in the slot may shove a story across with "Sharpen up that lead on this stuff of O'Hara's—it's too long. And move it along, ahead of that Latin story."

The notations by the slot man include a symbol to tell the copyeditor what size headline to give the story. It may be simply "C" or "E" or "2/36." Any one of these may mean "two columns of 36-point tempo heavy italic type." The editor knows the shorthand of his paper and can write the head accordingly. (Headlines are discussed more fully in chapter 4.)

Fig. 2-2. Copydesk. The copydesk of the **Binghamton** (N.Y.) **Press** (circulation 78,000) has six copyeditors working under the direction of the slot man. The news editor, standing, normally sits behind the slot man on the rim so he can be in easy communication with the desk chief. The room in the background contains the wire service teleprinters.

This editorial teamwork occurs at a single desk on medium and large newspapers. All local, state, and wire copy crosses this desk. Because stories from all three sources come from everywhere, the desk is called "universal." Only sports and women's news usually are edited at separate desks.

A few metropolitan newspapers receive too much news to use the universal desk system. They divide the flow of news into "city, "national," and "world" operations. Local, suburban, and state copy comes to the city desk, and all wire news and stories from special correspondents go to the world desk. But in this system sports and women still remain worlds apart.

Small newspapers, of course, do not use enough copy to keep a full desk busy, so each sub-editor himself edits the appropriate stories from reporters or wire services. For example, the "city editor" may edit the copy written by one or two local reporters and himself, including sports stories, while a "telegraph editor" may handle international, national, and state news from the wire, as well as copy from correspondents in nearby villages. There then has to be an informal system of consultation so sub-editors know how much copy is flowing and what the top stories are.

No matter how simple or complex the system, an editor must concentrate on improving copy. He tightens, points up, trims, polishes. But he should *not* make over stories by altering every one so it will read as though he wrote it. Reporters seethe when clever phrases are made prosaic or novel leads are made routine. The editor should apply his pencil with care, for he should encourage originality. The best newswriting is sprightly and varied. An editor who makes all copy read alike mechanizes writing; and as Dean Danielson of the University of Texas observed (after working with computers in news research), "If you write like a machine, you can be replaced by a machine."

The nature of desk work

The special qualifications of a copyeditor bring him advantages. In most cases the pay is better. American Newspaper Guild contracts usually set the base pay of editors at least five dollars above the minimum salary for reporters. Since copyeditors are in demand these days, salaries sometimes are pushed above Guild scale and frequently well above the minimums.

The way to promotion most often is by way of the rim man's chair. As copyeditors usually have been reporters, the combination of reporting and desk experience makes a newsman valuable for positions requiring more than one point of view. The first step for a copyeditor usually is over the desk into the slot. But he may be boosted directly from the rim to such jobs as state editor, city editor, suburban editor, telegraph editor, or picture editor. His first promotion may even be to assistant city editor or assistant state editor. These jobs then prepare him to move up to the more responsible and best-paid positions as editor, assistant to the publisher, executive editor, news editor, or even editor-in-chief.

Even at the beginning, in the informal atmosphere of the copy desk, the copyreader is in good company. Most desks are populated by bright men and women with superior wit and humor who appreciate a well-turned phrase. Copydesk wisecracks are told all over the newsroom, and from time to time they show up, without attribution, in a local column. Most of the joking is done during the lulls that occur during the work day, for copy tends to come in spurts. After working at a good pace for an hour or so, an editor can take a few minutes to relax. During these breaks editors often spoof each other, rib the copy boys, or even comment on the boss's foibles. Satirical pokes at local, state, and national stuffed shirts may start a serious discussion of world affairs.

If a young newsman enjoys being up-to-date on current affairs and ideas, he will find the copydesk in the midst of the news flow.* On the small paper editors tend to be better informed on the full range of human events than anyone else in the community and thus have a special responsibility to stay up-to-date. On the large paper the desk man can become expert on a few specialties. Like the professor, he amasses knowledge on a favorite subject or two; but, unlike the professor, he is not pressed to delve for the minutiae and to publish. His scholarship is an avocation. But desk men have written books on their pet subjects and received the acclaim of scholars, and substantial royalties as well.

Though it provides great rewards, copyediting also includes some frustrations. Editing is sedentary, and the lack of physical activity bothers some people.† Egos also get little exercise, since the work is anonymous. The reporter can get a byline, but no one ever sees a story topped "Headline by Joe Guggenheimer." The copyeditor's fame rarely extends beyond the newsroom, so he has to be satisfied in large part by his belief in doing an important job well. Editors find their egos strengthened most by the approving chuckles or praise from their associates or, best of all, from their bosses.

The man who enjoys being out where the news is made and hobnobbing as a reporter with the big names may miss the excitement when he is brought in to the desk. Though writing headlines and reshaping stories has its creative possibilities, the copyeditor who is at heart a writer may be unhappy without the creative challenge of writing news and feature stories. Not all newsmen are cut out for this relatively unspectacular side of the editorial operation.

Perhaps the greatest and most surprising drawback in desk work

*Copydesks once were the preserve of older staff members. Now, because there are more jobs than seasoned staffers, young men and women often are put on the desk right out of journalism school.

† The sedentary aspect of desk work would be no disadvantage for some handicapped persons. Dick Thornburg, editor, *Cincinnati* (Ohio) *Post* and *Times-Star*, has noted that "copyediting offers a useful and reasonably well-paid career for young people—men and women—who are crippled in body, but not in mind or spirit or ambition. . . . A person who showed special talents in newspapering could readily become a city editor or a managing editor, even though handicapped."

is inactivity. While breaks can be stimulating, long slack periods can be depressing. This is particularly true on the biggest newspapers, where there are several editions and the staffs are large enough to cope with almost any emergency. By hard work the first two editions are taken care of, and subsequent editions rarely require many changes. There may be almost nothing to do for an hour or more, yet the editor can't count the time as his own. If a slack period comes at the end of the work day, most slot men let a few copyeditors go home half an hour early. If a rim man can spend his slack times reading magazines or books, he will turn a disadvantage into an advantage. He "gets his reading done" on company time, and the paper gains from his widened knowledge.

Much of the negative side of copyediting can be eliminated by real appreciation from the deskman's editors and colleagues, a good principle for the copyeditor who moves up the hierarchy to recall. Praise when the copyreader has made a complex story readable or turned out an exceptional headline is worth almost as much to him as a raise in pay.

The *St. Petersburg* (Fla.) *Times* underlined the value of accurate editing with a game of "killing enemy errors." "X-act Agent" buttons were distributed to 664 staffers, along with special blue pencils. The paper paid $25 to the one who circled the most errors. Perhaps a corny gimmick, but it showed every reporter and copyeditor that management cared about quality.

Reporters who appreciate the efforts of editors boost the morale of the desk, as an example at the *New York Times* illustrates. A member of the *Times'* Washington bureau wrote a letter to the city room expressing appreciation for checking doubtful points with him. To the amazement of deskmen, a breed accustomed to too little praise, he wrote: "I read my story this morning with just the greatest pleasure, noting where, as always, you had smoothed some lumpy sentences, chopped apart some overly long ones, skillfully made a couple of internal cuts in exactly the right places and, in short, made the story better than the one I had written."

The alert professional

Whether working on small or large papers, editors have to keep tabs on themselves, for they can go stale on the job. A man who develops professional skill remains, it is hoped, a credit to his profession. But a lazy newsman can drift through several years, unaware of changes in newspapers, oblivious to undercurrents in world affairs, and unwilling to prepare himself for more demanding tasks. He goes nowhere.

The editor with the brightest future is a reader. He reads magazines and the best newspapers, and at least skims through the current books, while thoroughly reading some of the old ones. His reading alerts him to change and to ideas. News almost by definition concerns itself with change and ideas, and an editor unfamiliar or uninterested in them becomes ineffective. He will gain neither the responsibility nor the respect of a professional.

Even a competent editor can slip unconsciously into getting careless about the fine points of his job. He may allow slips in grammar because he has let slide the occasional few minutes necessary for review. A well-thumbed book on grammar shows that an editor is concerned with details of quality—and therefore probably concerned with quality in general.

A good desk man can obtain tips for quality writing and editing in three or four minutes of reading every day or so. One of the best sources is *Winners & Sinners*, "a bulletin of second guessing issued occasionally from the southeast corner of the *New York Times* News Room." This one-sheet paper recounts the journalistic blunders and triumphs of Timesmen. The *Cleveland Press* publishes a similar paper called *Tips and Slips*, and a medium-sized paper, the *Wilmington* (Del.) *Journal-News*, turns out *Hits & Misses*. These sheets help greatly in preventing editing mistakes. Books like Strunk and White's *Elements of Style* and Gowers' *Plain Words, Their ABC* (see Bibliography) prod the editor to make sure that his copy uses words correctly and that the language is simple and direct.

The copyeditor takes aim

The goal of the copyreader is to be sure that the stories in the paper are in good, readable, accurate English. He looks at the message and structure of the whole story. But he also fixes all its minute parts. For example, he catches dangling participles. One paper ran a photo of a lost child, with this sentence in the cutline: "Wearing only a diaper and rubber pants, police guessed his age at 12 to 14 months." The copyeditor should have seen that the police were more appropriately dressed.

He also blocks mixed metaphors, such as this quadruple one from a paper submitted by a journalism student: "This then is the key. The potential is pushing at the dam's gates. Given the proper catalyst, we may be on the threshold of witnessing an entire new era of journalism." With luck, maybe the key will keep the flood from getting through the door.

Verne English, long a copyeditor for Syracuse newspapers, kept a file of writers' boners the desk had caught. Here are samples, the kinds of things that the sharp deskman spots:

—Four juvenile boys admitted the theft.

—Dear licenses outsold marriage licenses.

—Passengers were treated to a mid morning concert shortly after noon.

—The General Electric Advanced Electronics Laboratory shot its last employee Saturday as the company's flu vaccination program ended.

—A post-mortem autopsy was performed.

—The hospital reported she was pregnant but the injuries did not effect it.

Copyediting shorthand

A visitor to a newspaper newsroom is often surprised that the paper ever comes out. "How can you keep everything straight?" "Aren't there all kinds of problems that take hours to solve?"

The answer, of course, is that all the jobs mesh. The result is a newspaper with nearly all the words spelled correctly, the main news events reported, all the space filled with a good blend of news, pictures, commentary, and advertising.

One of the reasons so much work can be done in such a short time is that, except in slack times, no one on a newspaper staff spends much time in conversation. On many papers the top editors spend a half an hour a day in conference deciding how the main news of the day will be played. But the rest of the work is a routine with almost no conversation during busy periods. Each man does his job quietly.

That picture may surprise those who imagine the newsroom filled with people screaming orders at one another. Actually the noise level is not much higher than in a bank. The reason for the lack of noise and conversation is that newsmen have a silent language.

The headline order, as mentioned before, comes to the copyeditor in the form of a written symbol. The slot man marks the copy with a string of other cryptic orders, like *kill, add, more,* and *jump.* Other symbols are little more than a scratch of a pencil. The editor uses all this sign language on copy so that the printers will know, without being told orally, what he wants done. The signs he puts on stories are understood in every composing room in the country. The editor uses these symbols unconsciously, just as a touch-typist punches typewriter keys without thinking where his fingers should go.

Symbols in editing

```
          used
the symbols common in every newsroom in the
county may see puzzling to the student at
first but a few hours practice re moves their Mystery
```

Start new paragraph:

```
Jones said he arrived at 10 a.m.  Rogers insisted that
the time was 10:45.
```

Set in lower case instead of capital:

```
The Biology class met outdoors.
```

Capitalize:

```
Los Angeles--President Nixon signed the tax bill.
The supreme court will hear the case at noon.
The supreme court will hear the case at noon.
```

Insert and delete:

He professed a belief in gosts and the conshseus of opinion was that he was sincere.

Insert new word:

The bookkeeper allegdly spent the money at the races.

Separate elements:

Everything had been allright that morning.

Transpose elements:

Albaama

He only won two games.

Close:

He started as a copy reader and worked his way up.

Close, but leave space:

The fourth is freedom of the press.

Connect elements:

He said that he saw the three men enter the building and that the men were injured.

Insert period:

The U S team won the match.

The U S team won the match.

Insert comma:

The tour will include Ireland Scotland and Wal

Insert colon:

Prizes were awarded in three categories fiction, nonfiction and poetry.

Insert semicolon:

The winners were John McIntyre, for fiction Paul Barnes, for nonfiction and William Ellis, for poetry.

Insert apostrophe:

The reporters story was praised.

Insert quotation marks:

The Golden Pheasant is a musical.

Insert exclamation point:

"Oklahoma" was a hit musical.

Insert hyphen:

Police claimed the thief was caught redhanded.

Insert dash (and exaggerate its length or frame it with short lines):

The bill passed 94 to 2 is the first of its kind.

Abbreviate:

Governor Otto Kerner signed the bill.

Spell out:

Wm. B. Zarfoss won the election.

Use figure instead of word:

The group represented twelve states.

Spell out figure:

He had 1,000,000 counterfeit dollars.

(Spelled out it would be one million.)

Let it stand as first written:

stet

He pleaded not guilty.

Indent to left:

(The World Almanac gave the figure as 2.25 million.)

Indent to right:

(The Statistical Abstract of the U. S. listed the number as 28.)

Indent both right and left:

(The Denver Post reported that the lost men were rescued within hours of the disaster.)

Center:

Three Kick Goals

Let capital stand (for marking all-capital copy from Western Union or a news service):

WASHINGTON--SEN. HIRAM FONG, R-HAWAII, INSISTED ON THE CHANGE, AND HE WAS SUPPORTED BY THE UTAH DELEGATION.

Change from tabular to paragraph style:

The decision will give these grants to the following states:

Wisconsin, $14 million;
Utah, $7.4 million; and
South Dakota, $11 million

(Long tabulations require no more than one to two of these connecting lines. Mark the margin "Run In.")

run in

Wisconsin, $14 million;
Utah, $7.4 million;
South Dakota, $11 million;
Ohio, $22 million; and
Kentucky, $14.9 million

Let copy stand as written (if the typesetter may think the copy is mistaken):

ok
The boy's name is Jakque.

The boy's name is Jakque.

("Folo copy" in the margin provides the same instruction.)

Italicize:

The girl said, "Nein, nein."

Set in bold face:

The reporter is a Phi Beta Kappa.

(If possible, hand-print corrections; otherwise clarify ambiguous handwritten letters.)

Underlines

Underline: a, u, w

Overline: o, n, m

The editor's finished work will look like this:

wyeth
hiway
1

The link between Interstate 17 and u.s. 39 in Swampsville will be widened ~~wineded~~ to 4 lanes by ~~under future construction plans of~~ the State Division of highways. The ~~highway~~ program for the year allocates $370,000 $170,000 for acquisition of right-of-way for the multi-million dollar project, which will alter ~~have effects on~~ highway 163 as it enters Swampsville.

Homer C. Keller, highway department engineer enginner for the Central District, said he was not aware ~~of the fact~~ that the Swampsville ~~Seamsville~~ Improvement association had only wanted a 2-lane highway into the city. The Association contends that a four-lane highway is not needed.

The widening ~~of the road~~ should cost about $14 million, keller said, for The distance ~~will be~~ 17.4 miles.

The stretch stretc of new road will go through 3 counties. Keller reported that probably these shares of the cost will be spent in thee three counties:

Adams, $3,142,389, one-sixth;

Vermillion, $2,457,679, one-eighth; and

Van Buren, $8,400,032, the ~~remainder~~ rest

The copyeditor's goals

A practiced copyeditor can flash over copy, flicking his pencil to indicate paragraphs, to cross out occasional waste phrases, and to correct misspelled words. Few mistakes will get by him.

But this kind of editing, after a time, tends to be dull and even sterile. The mediocre editor works mechanically, catching minor errors while failing to detect the big ones, like inconsistencies and omissions of fact.

The excellent editor does not disregard the little flaws. He knows that even a well-written story may have slight imperfections that distract the reader. He not only marks the misspelled word and the redundancy but sniffs the whole story for completeness and accuracy. He questions its news value. Is it worth eight paragraphs as written? Should the story be thrown away as inconsequential? Should it be rewritten for more impact on the reader?

The copyeditor who recognizes that even the best reporter may blunder recognizes that the same thing can happen to him: He may doze off and let an obvious mistake go into print. The editor must not only be skeptical of the reporter's accuracy but skeptical of his own ability to do everything right in what often has to be a hasty reading of a story.

Editing is an intellectual pursuit that requires meticulousness, careful analysis of content, judgment of story value in relation to other news, and a weighing of the significance of all news that gets into the paper. Many newsmen find it satisfying to use their brains and knowledge daily to make the news more understandable for thousands of readers.

3 Copyediting techniques

Copyeditors do uncommon work with common tools: pencils, scissors, and paste pots. Normally the newspaper provides a good stock of round, soft-lead pencils for editing. Ballpoint pens have the advantage of not smearing, but changing their marks on copypaper is impossible. So the realistic copyeditor keeps an art gum eraser at hand to correct his errant pencil marks.

Scissors and paste pots are necessary for *inserts*, pieces of copy to be added to the original story. The editor clips the story in two at the proper spot and pastes the insert to the halves of the original copy. Even without inserts a story may be considerably reorganized by cutting and pasting. Some shops also have the copyeditor paste the pages of each lengthy story together, top to bottom, to make a long, folded roll.

As for editing itself, slot men agree at most points on what they consider good copyediting. They want stories to be "fixed up" but, unless the writing is bad, they don't want them butchered and rehashed. The copyeditor has to learn the technique of the proper amount of editing. He keeps his eye on all the minutiae at the same time he watches to see that the whole story fits and flows together to give an accurate general impression. He combines good English and good sense with the paper's rules and traditions.

The leads of stories deserve particular attention, for a lead can make or break the reader's interest. If the lead doesn't click, the editor certainly should revise it.

A good copyeditor, unless squeezed by a deadline, reads each story at least twice. Often he spots errors each time through, and he should take great care to recheck any of his own rephrasing. The new sentences that he inserts should be read two or three times to make sure that the corrections themselves are not in error.

The editor ought to ask himself finally, "Does this story make sense? Are there any inadequacies? Will the reader have any important questions? Does the story read smoothly? Are all the statements properly attributed? Is there any factual error?"

He should also check to see whether the story rambles on for ten or eleven paragraphs of detail without getting essential information close to the top. This shortcoming often mars stories of strikes. The beginning usually reports who says what and how long the strike has been going on, but what the strike is all about may be buried or ignored.

The copyeditor should make changes that are necessary and quit. This means he keeps his pencil off clear and accurate writing. *Winner & Sinners* has warned editors not to change language for the sake of change. One issue noted:

> Itchy pencil . . . refers to occasional copy desk tinkering with copy for no apparent reason—a practice that sometimes makes the writing inferior, sometimes makes it outright wrong and always baffles the writer. If a hold-up man takes a picture of his colleagues with a Polaroid Land camera and the reporter writes that in that way "he was able to avoid taking the incriminating film to the corner drugstore for developing" what is gained by changing the final quoted phrase to "elsewhere"? There is actually a slight loss in sense.
>
> If a reporter writes about a chimpanzee at the Museum of Natural History that "whizzed across its acres on a red tricycle" why should "acres" be changed to "halls," which loses the idea of vastness? If a correspondent writes that a "betting man could get a dime to a nickel from almost anyone in the Western delegations" about the break-up of the Geneva conference, is there any improvement in making it "could get a wager"?
>
> Although the damage wrought in these instances may seem minor, the reader has been deprived of colorful detail; moreover, the cumulative effect on reporters of such tinkering is discouraging. Changes have to be made in copy, to be sure, but be certain that when you make a change it is definitely a change for the better and not just the work of itchy pencil.

The job of the editor, then, is to go over the copy to correct grammar, to cross out waste words and sentences, and to make the language more graceful. He should throttle clichés. Ambiguous phrasing should be hunted down and corrected.

The probing editor

The editor needs a quizzical, skeptical approach if he is to catch errors. He must keep asking as he reads, "Can this be right?" With this in mind, for example, he will question whether, as the story says, Richard Nixon was born in Massachusetts and the University of Michigan is in Kalamazoo.

Editors must check to see if needed information is omitted. A *New York Times* reporter once sent a note to the desk mentioning an editorial oversight: A story on a supersonic airliner gave only oblique reference—in the eleventh paragraph—to the name of the government agency which received the airliner designs. Knowing this kind of error should be caught by the desk, he wrote (in *Winners & Sinners*), "Every reporter is going to have an occasional lapse in fullest lucidity, and he would like to feel that he is securely backstopped. That, after all, is the copydesk's primary function."

If there is any doubt about the accuracy of his changes in a story, the editor should check with the nearest authority—the writer of the story. He might ask the reporter, "Does this improve the meaning of the story? Have I made it clearer, or have I muddled the facts?" A reporter will be furious, and has a right to be, if his copy is revised into error. It makes him look like a fool with his news sources, and it embitters the staff when an accurate story is distorted by an editor who had no first-hand knowledge of the event.

Where a reporter has used an inappropriate word, the editor should find the right one. He needs to be familiar with semantics to be sure that the words convey the intended meaning. For example, where the reporter has written "statesman," the word "politician" might be better.

There must be a steady watchfulness for libel. Every story that defames anyone—and many stories must defame—should be checked to see if the defamatory phrases can be used safely under law. Chapter 12 discusses in detail the legal pitfalls that always lurk near a copyeditor.

Hoaxes are another thing to contend with. A naive reporter may write a story that sounds like a dandy. The more experienced copyeditor, however, may recall that the same story ran a decade ago and was exposed as a fake. This story needs the oblivion treatment.

Unless editors are careful a single story may get in the paper twice, causing merriment among readers. It is doubly amusing if the same stories get into the paper the same day. Occasionally, different reporters will write essentially the same story a few days apart. The writer of the second story should have read his own newspaper more carefully. But his oversight is no excuse for the copy desk to repeat the error. An alert desk must likewise kill outdated stories which did not make the paper. A story announcing last night's event as "tonight" is bad news for the participants, the frustrated audience, and the newspaper.

Editors also have to watch for advertising that masquerades as news. Since newspapers sell advertising, news stories should mention advertisers only when they make news. For example, if a meeting is going to take place at a hotel, the reporter has to say which hotel. This "advertising" is unavoidable and therefore permissible. Glowing descriptions of the hotel, however, should be crossed out of news copy.

It is even harder but more important to eliminate propaganda. All kinds of people try to sneak their points of view into the paper under the guise of news, and this is most apparent during election time when dozens of events are staged to attract attention. The editor should sift through all the fakery and try to stick to the issues in the reports he prints.

Sometimes an inexperienced reporter will quote a news source too much and let the source misuse the news columns to further himself or his cause. The editor gives this material its proper weight, which is sometimes nothing.

Eight pointers

Double-check names. If the copyeditor has any doubt about the spelling of a name, he should look it up, and he should be sure that a name is spelled consistently through the story. A person should not be Whelan in the first paragraph and Whalen in the second. The editor should watch for a common lapse associated with unusual names: The reporter uses a person's full name in the lead but mistakenly substitutes the first name for the last in the rest of the story. For example, the lead may refer to the president of Harvard University as Dr. Nathan M. Pusey. From then on, however, he is Dr. Nathan instead of Dr. Pusey. The copyeditor should catch this blunder.

Attribute facts properly. Almost anything that cannot be witnessed by the reporter should be attributed to some person. The "almost" is essential to remember because often stories contain facts neither observed by reporters nor found through records, and so there is no attribution. Attribution is unnecessary when the source obviously is telling the truth. For example, it is silly to attribute to a university president the employment of every single faculty member. The university is not going to announce an appointment by a news release and then back out of it, so phrases like "the president announced" are unnecessary.

Produce clean copy. Stories sent to the composing room must be readable. Hurriedly scrawled editorial changes make the printer guess at the scribbles—and make wrong guesses—or force him to throw the story back to the desk. Either way the paper can lose accuracy or time. If the deskman must make complicated handwritten changes, he should type out the most involved ones and paste the retyped material over the messy original.

"Duck it." Sometimes an editor spots a minor misstatement in a story, and the reporter who wrote the story is not around for verification. Any other check might take fifteen minutes. The item is not worth that much time so the editor "ducks it" by omitting the statement. A story may say, "Jones, who moved here in 1953, has served on the county board for 17 years." The copyeditor may trust "17 years" but doubt "1953." How could Jones have won an election so soon? So the editor ducks the problem by changing the sentence to "Jones has served on the county board for 17 years."

Simplify language. Newspapers are not written for morons, but for people who want to get the news and comment in easy-to-read form. Simpler words should replace involved ones like "inextricable," "dichotomy," and "tangential." Language even for an intellectual audience should be precise and readable, not pretentious.

Reporters sometimes get caught up in the special language of the fields they cover. Court reporters, for instance, may write "filed a demurrer," "stayed the execution," or "granted a continuance." Such terms may be hard for a layman to grasp, and the editor who thinks the story should interest the ordinary reader will either change the wording himself or send it back to the reporter for translation.

Recognize your own prejudices. Copyeditors need to double-check themselves to be sure they do not make decisions to chop one story and inflate another because of personal prejudice. Some editors who control newspaper content favor stories that concern their personal hobbies. A man who loves to sail may run an unusual number of stories about boats and the sea. Such prejudices are basically harmless, although they could make the paper look amateurish. Sometimes, however, an editor may intensely dislike a senator or fear that the nation is moving rapidly toward socialism. He may edit the news to make the senator look foolish or to emphasize his own political views. This kind of editing is harmful and unprofessional.

Don't trust your memory completely. A copyeditor is often tempted to pencil into a story a fact that he thinks will improve the article. He should insert these facts, however, only when absolutely sure of them. If he isn't certain, he should look up the information in the clipping file or a reference book.

Be sure copy is fair and tasteful. Balancing objective reporting and interpretation is a continual problem, but even if a story is primarily interpretive it should be fair. Snide, belittling comments should be removed.

Rebuttal from criticized persons should be included or run as a separate story nearby. Copy should also remain in good taste. Taste is difficult to assess, but most editors have a rule-of-thumb: A paper read by all kinds of people, including children, should soften or eliminate the most brutal or intimate details.

While this advice is generally good, it doesn't always work. As an illustration, some papers handle a sex offense by referring to a "morals charge." But such an all-encompassing term actually may be unfair to the accused, because the phrase covers a wide spectrum of sins. In such cases some editors try to be a little more specific without being salacious. Others simply do not print "morals" arrests except in cases when they can't avoid it, as when omitting such news about a public figure might bring a charge of covering-up for him.

Color and completeness

The copyeditor must always be thinking of how to make the news readable for his readers. He points up the local angle whenever possible. He revives listless writing and chops out ponderous language to make the sentences brisk and the story a pleasure to follow. On the other hand, he may have to add a phrase to make the story clearer or to tone down lurid writing. A good slogan is "make copy brisk but not brusque, vivid but not lurid."

The reader in Oshkosh may sit up when he finds a story with an Oshkosh angle in it. Localization can be overdone, of course, like this:

The brother-in-law of a man who lived in Oshkosh in 1929 was arrested today in Dallas on a charge of panhandling.

But if an Oshkosh native wins a Nobel Prize, the Oshkosh paper better have his place of birth in the lead, not in the ninth paragraph as it probably came over the wire.

Localizing often requires some juggling of paragraphs. Sometimes it requires only a phrase inserted high in the story:

(including Peoria,)

Fifteen cities have been awarded million-dollar grants to help relieve poverty.

In other cases it will require restructuring the story considerably, perhaps rewriting the lead or inserting paragraph seven after paragraph one. Feature writers have a habit of writing long introductions before getting to the heart of the story. An editor often can chop out whole paragraphs at the beginning of such pieces, just as he can trim the tail end of many news stories.

Whenever possible the stories should be organized to pinpoint the significance for the reader. Most of us read stories, as Wilbur Schramm has pointed out, because we want to be rewarded: We want to know what will affect our pocketbooks, to know what has happened to our friends and acquaintances, to know what might please us or upset us. The reporter writes his stories with these ideas in mind, and the copyeditor fixes the reporter's oversights:

(property)

School taxes will go up $1.5 million next year, the board of education decided last night. The new rate means that if a resident paid $200 in school taxes this year, he will pay $224 next year.

Because the editor knows that every reader has certain areas of ignorance, he often explains what the reporter thought obvious. "Died of nephritis" needs an explanatory phrase. If the story mentions District IV schools, tell the reader, at least roughly, what District IV covers. If the story mentions Albert Einstein, add an identifying phrase. The story must remind as well as inform readers, and the brightest of them have gaps in their knowledge.

Balancing the reporter's judgment

The reporter, as has been said many times, is the eyes, ears, hands, nose and tongue of the reader. If the reporter does not describe the look, the sound, the feel, the smell, or the taste of something that needs these descriptions, the editor should get him to include it.

But the copyeditor occasionally thinks that a reporter, striving for vividness, has given an incorrect tone. Perhaps the reporter unconsciously chose words the editor thinks will sound snide to the reader. The editors of the *Cleveland Press* once noted that reporters often used the word "peacenik." The editors believed that the word "has a built-in sneer," and pointed out that "there is nothing wrong with being for peace."

Even the context of words may alter the tone of a story. For example, a report of a speech may be filled with attributive phrases like "he roared," "Jackson thundered," and "he shouted." It is possible that the speaker did roar, thunder, and shout. But in print these words make the man sound wild, and he may not have been wild at all. He may simply have had a strong voice or been trying to reach the listeners sitting far behind the reporter's front row seat.

On the other hand, a reporter may turn in a biographical story filled with syrupy phrases that make a rather ordinary person appear to be a saint. The deletion of a half dozen adjectives in these cases usually makes the tone ring true. No one should assume, however, that the tone of stories need always be coldly factual. A funny incident should be reported in a funny way. A story on a political session may be irreverent. And a story on a funeral generally should be dignified and restrained.

The *New York Times* started a story on a St. Patrick's Day parade with: "Irishmen, regardless of race, creed or color, marched down Fifth Avenue today."

In a story on the keynote speech at the Democratic National convention in 1952, Red Smith wrote: "The Democratic party was smitten tonight with the jawbone of an ass."

A somber funeral story might include: "The senator's wife sat dry-eyed through the services, occasionally biting her lip to keep back the tears."

Of course every story should have the essential facts as well as the right tone. The reader is interested in the overall view of an event, but he also expects the story to answer his reasonable questions. If the reporter doesn't have the answer, the story should say so: "Petersen's age was not learned."

Polishing pointers

Sometimes the editor's pencil and willingness to restructure are not enough to revive a story. The sentences are long-winded, the quotes are ponderous, and the story seems to drone on. The copyeditor has to read each paragraph twice to get the foggiest understanding of what the writer was driving at. The story demands rewriting, and it should go back to the reporter or another staffer with specific instructions on how to improve it.

Quotations that look brief in copy take up an alarming amount of space when squeezed into a column width. The copyeditor can boil down long-winded quotations by combining material, omitting by ellipsis, or using partial quotes:

"The dam, which is designed to bring vast blessings to the people of Central Illinois and which will avoid terrifying floods, will cost $8 million and be built within two years," the governor said.

The quote could be paraphrased:

The dam will cost $8 million and take two years go build, the governor said.

Another possibility would be:

"The dam . . . will cost $8 million and be built within two years," the governor said.

Quotation marks do suggest authenticity, but too many of them make the report look patched together. Quotes are the seasoning of the story, not the meat.

Reporters that keep interrupting their own stories put the reader in a coma with the comma. An involved sentence that stitches facts together with commas needs editing:

The Tobiason boy, 8 years old and a fourth grader at the new Leal school, said that his mother~~, the former Ann Davis who was Miss America 14 years ago,~~ had planned to pick him up at 4 p.m. at the school.

The reference to her former title can be inserted elsewhere.

Other reporters string identifications of people throughout a story. This is noted particularly on the sports page. In the first paragraph the football player is simply "a halfback," in the second he is "the native of Florida," in the third "the 205-pounder," in the fourth "the Big Ten's leading ground-gainer," and in the fifth "the junior economics major." Such detailed identification, if used at all, should form a two or three sentence paragraph of background information.

Redundancies are harder to spot than quotes or identification tags, and they are more worrisome. They waste space and bring snickers from readers. Obvious ones like "killed to death" rarely creep into copy, but subtler ones like "widow of the late John Smith" are unsettlingly common. "Autopsy of the body" suggests that autopsies are performed on things other than bodies. "Graves of dead soldiers will be decorated" indicates that some soldiers are buried alive.

The correct use of words can raise interesting problems. A dictionary, of course, is a good guide, but sometimes a "correctly" used word will convey the wrong sense. An editorial writer once referred to a major religious denomination as a "sect." If connotation is ignored, this is a "correct" use of the word. But many readers were incensed, for they viewed the word "sect" as a term for little flocks that convene in abandoned stores.

Six more flaws to fix

Subject-verb disagreement. It is not unusual to see a story with "the council *meet* today at noon" or "the group *is* going to take separate cars to their hotels."

Pronouns. Whenever the copyeditor runs across *he, she, it,* or *they* he should check to see if the right person or thing is identified. If there is doubt, a suitable noun, not a pronoun, should be used.

Illogical dependent clauses. Watch sentences like "A graduate of Harvard, he is the father of eight children." Being a father has nothing to do with attendance at Harvard.

Double meanings. There is always someone around who will spot the secondary—and possibly racy—meaning of a phrase. These double meanings amuse readers, but they detract from professionalism. Even a relatively harmless double meaning embarrasses the parties involved, including the editor. During a presidential campaign, a headline accidentally suggested a domestic problem for Richard M. Nixon's wife, whose nickname is Pat.

Can't Stand Pat,
Nixon Declares

Editorializing. Any trace of personal opinion or a value judgment should be eliminated, unless the story is a feature or news analysis.

Unlikely quotes. Sometimes reporters invent quotes and the unfortunate result is a sentence or two with a hollow ring. A baseball team manager noted for his linguistic errors, for example, may be quoted as saying, "We were in a desperate position in the third inning, but Bocko Jennings, our superlative third baseman, made what must be the best play of the year, allowing us to escape without damage." This unbelievable quote should be scratched and the facts put in as straight news: The manager said Bocko Jennings' spectacular play saved the game.

Occasionally, a reporter writes that more than one person said the same thing: "John Adams and Peter Farrel said, 'I think the foreign policy of the nation is clearly a menace.'" One of them might say it, but not both.

Series. Check a series of several items in one sentence for a surplus verb. "He is a determined golf player, a collector of antique clocks and often reads a detective story at night." To clear up the awkwardness, the copyeditor could change it to: "He is a determined golf player and a collector of antique clocks. He often reads a detective story at night."

Rechecking details

The copyeditor obviously checks spelling and punctuation with particular attention to the placement of quotation marks and apostrophes. *Its* and *it's* always need a second look to see if they have been used correctly. Every possessive must have the apostrophe in the right place. The editor even does a little arithmetic to check totals given in a story. For example, if the reporter's copy states that two objects weigh three pounds and that each weighs eighteen ounces the editor should start asking questions. An editor must not hesitate to ask the reporter to double-check something that looks as though it might be wrong. If the story is from a wire service, a query to the wire service should resolve the doubt.

Saving space

When copyeditors rewrite extensively, they are tempted to pencil whole new paragraphs between the lines of copy. This short cut usually turns out to be the hard way for the typesetter and proofreader. If the copy needs extensive revision, it should be returned to the originating editor for a rewrite. The copyeditor, however, may try to rewrite a few sentences in the story and discover that one new sentence includes the gist of three or four.

Any copyeditor must spend a good share of his time reducing copy—not because he would not like to run more detail but because there simply is no room for it. Editing to save space means applying the scalpel, not the meat ax. Some copy butchers would merely whack off six inches from the story's end and send the remains to the printer. The skillful editor, however, recreates. For example, he takes off the last two paragraphs, removes the fourth, combines two rather long sentences into one of moderate length, takes a phrase from two or three different sentences, and makes a long quotation into a short one. The marked copy below shows how the editor in such condensation leaves as much fact as possible, sacrificing only the least significant details.

The cutting may not seem like much, but it removed about six lines of copy. This means that the story is about an inch and a half shorter in type and may now just fill the allotted space. Furthermore, a dozen stories each shortened that much would make room for another eighteen-inch story.

WASHINGTON-(AP)-The bodies of two crewmen of the U. S. Navy reconnaissance plane shot down by North Korea have been found in the Sea of Japan, informed sources in Japan said Thursday.

A search ~~over thousands of square miles~~ for the plane and its 31 crewmen has been under way since it ~~the four-engine, propeller-driven EC 121~~ was reported missing Monday after North Korea said it had downed the aircraft for allegedly violating its territory.

The massive search, which earlier had turned up only ~~shrapnel-shredded~~ bits of the plane, discovered ~~fuselage and other material, had found~~ no sign of the 29 other crewmen. Officials doubted that any ~~of the men~~ survived.

The sources said they had no information on where the bodies were found. The debris picked up Wednesday was found about 120 miles southeast of the North Korean coast.

The bodies of the two men were clothed in flying suits but not ~~were not wearing~~ life jackets, Japan's Kyodo News Service reported. Kyodo ~~, which did not give its source,~~ also said the bodies were picked up by the U. S. destroyer Tucker.

~~The recovery of the bodies came as the world waited for~~ President Nixon has made no statement about the incident ~~to break the calculated public silence he instituted after North Korea declared it had destroyed the plane.~~

~~Officials indicated Wednesday~~ The President was expected to issue some sort of protest to North Korea, ~~and there has been no evidence of a change.~~ but no decision has been reported about how this would be done.

Every newspaper should have a *style book*. This term does not refer here to a book on writing style but rather to a booklet put out by a newspaper telling how capitalization, abbreviation, and punctuation are handled in news stories for that paper. Reporters are supposed to follow this set of rules, or *style*, but sometimes they don't. The editor must then correct their errors, so he needs to be thoroughly familiar with the style book but willing to look up an obscure point whenever there is any doubt—or argument.

Guidebooks for accuracy

The consistency established by the style book prevents the meticulous reader from being annoyed when a story spells a proper name two or three different ways in as many paragraphs—or abbreviates a word one time and spells it out the next.

If a newspaper does not have its own style book the editors may use a book published by another paper, such as the thorough one published by the *New York Times.* The Associated Press and United Press International have joined forces to publish a widely used style book. Since all copy from AP and UPI coming into newsrooms conforms to this style, it would be wasteful for a paper that used mostly wire copy to make many changes in it.

Accuracy of copy requires several other reference books. Two of them, a medium-sized dictionary and the *World Almanac*, should be at arm's length. The need of the dictionary is obvious. The *Almanac* is the poor man's encyclopedia. It gives an editor quick access to thousands of facts on recent history, dates, biographies, and records. Today a one-volume paperback edition of an encyclopedia is even available to save the editor from getting up to consult the multivolume, recent set that should be nearby.

A good, unabridged dictionary and the city directories should be close by. Most newspapers have such books in the middle of the newsroom where everyone can get to them quickly. In addition, some editors use a thesaurus to help find the right synonym for an awkward word in a headline or story.

The following essential but less frequently used books should be easily accessible in the newspaper's library or reference room (sometimes still called "the morgue").

Congressional Directory
Area telephone books
Various kinds of *Who's Who*, such as *Who's Who in the East*
United States Postal Guide
Blue Book or *Red Book* for every state the newspaper serves—to provide information about state government
Dictionary of American Biography
Current Biography
A grammar, such as E. L. Callihan's *Grammar for Journalists*
Facts on File
A complete, modern atlas, such as the *National Geographic Atlas of the World*
American Labor Yearbook
A geographical dictionary, such as the *Macmillan World Gazetteer and Geographical Dictionary*
New York Times Index, and back issues of *Times* on microfilm
Statistical Abstract of the U. S.
International Motion Picture Almanac
King James and modern editions of the Bible
Poor's Public Utilities
Moody's Railroads
Encyclopaedia of the Social Sciences

Various sports record books and military directories

A book on good usage, such as *Current American Usage*, by Margaret M. Bryant; *A Dictionary of American-English Usage*, by Margaret Nicholson (based on a famous English work by H. W. Fowler); *A Dictionary of Contemporary American Usage*, by Bergen and Cornelia Evans; or *Modern American Usage*, by Wilson Follett

The largest newspapers have even more reference books, and Dr. Eleanor Blum's *Reference Books in the Mass Media*, a paperback, lists all of them. Some are used so rarely that many newspapers don't need to own them. However, a telephone call or a quick trip by a copy boy to a public library can put an editor in touch with almost any reference book.

4 Writing headlines

Headlines have been compared to road signs, advertising slogans, and store windows. All these have in common the task of seizing attention and putting a message across swiftly. That is what a good newspaper head does. The first and most important purpose of a headline is to inform the reader quickly. The well-written head tells him immediately the gist of the accompanying story.

When it is said that we are a nation of headline skimmers, the tone is usually derogatory. The other side of that criticism, however, is that skimming heads is what makes possible our rapid comprehension of the news, since literally no one can read all the stories that are processed each day. If the heads do their most important job—rapid summary—the careful skimmer will get the general drift of events; and yet he can slow up for a story he judges worth more careful reading.

A second important goal of headlines is also related to their billboard function. Headlines must sell. On newstands in competitive cities front page headlines tend to sell one paper instead of another. In monopoly cities they may push a reader to buy a paper instead of skipping it. But on the inside pages of every newspaper, headlines "sell" the reader to start reading a story. Philosophically, the primary function of the free press in a democracy is not to make money but to inform citizens. But in our society the paper must be profitable to remain alive—and lively, so the head that sells is significant.

Related to both informing and selling is a third function: grading, or evaluating, the news. One head shouts that this story is important. Another suggests quietly that this one might be of some interest as well. Even the size and style of type help communicate to the reader the importance and quality of the news—whether it is a cataclysmic disaster or a pleasant afternoon tea. A fuller explanation of how the editor evaluates news appears in chapter 6.

To stimulate the reader's artistic sense is a final purpose of headlines. Dull heads make a dull page. But graphic artistry is much more complex than merely replacing dullness with brightness.

Headlines may add to the clutter of ugly or confusing pages. But when heads are well-written and well-placed in styles that have been thoughtfully designed, the pages are clean and good-looking. Indeed, the whole personality of a paper is set by the consistent use of heads day after day, and a sudden, drastic change in heads may make a subscriber feel he has lost a familiar friend.

Hazards in heads

One of the newspaper's most vulnerable points is the headline. Readers may grumble about the way a paper covers the news but often their complaint boils down to dislike of the heads used.

Simple inattention can make heads which read two ways, sometimes ludicrously. Here are two published examples which seem to speak of mailmen who are stolen and belts which are hurt:

Stolen Postman's Truck
Recovered in N. Jersey

Couple Hurt
Seat Belts Aid
In Collision

More than one reporter has complained that his story was all right—and it was the head on it that distorted. For example, in *Editor & Publisher* James Steed of White Plains, New York, complained: "For too long the reporter has had to explain to the public and his readership that 'someone back on the copy desk' makes up the headlines and if they don't match up with the story there is nothing the reporter can do about it." Steed pointed out that since newspapers print corrections on stories, they should likewise run "a correction when the headline conveys the wrong meaning." He urged that the anonymity and immunity be removed from the headwriter who "messes up a good story by putting the wrong tag on it."

Popular confidence in a newspaper can be seriously shaken by an attack on headlines. For example, at a gathering of the New York State Council of Churches, Governor Nelson Rockefeller criticized a headline on the front page of the *New York Times* for misrepresenting his statement about a state lottery. Rockefeller, who had long opposed such a lottery, said he had explained to a reporter that if the people approved a lottery in a referendum and the legislature then passed a bill, he would study and possibly sign it. The *Times* editor used a short, punchy verb in the head over the resulting story:

Rockefeller Bows
On State Lottery

The secondary head, or deck, on the resulting story did qualify the main head with some of the governor's words:

Would Go Along Reluctantly
With 'Reasonable' Bill

But Rockefeller contended that the main head oversimplified his position and would be all that most readers would catch. Such attacks by public figures erode the public's confidence in newspapers. Admittedly, some headwriters do distort or bias the news, or they editorialize. But there are built-in dangers in headwriting even for the careful copyeditor of goodwill. He has to struggle with the limitations of both space and brief words to convey a fair and accurate impression.

Perhaps oversimplification is the greatest threat in headlines. When the news is complex, the reporter often oversimplifies in writing a tight lead. The copyeditor's job is to polish and tighten that more, if possible. Then he has to condense it still further into a half dozen words or fewer for the headline. The subtleties inevitably get squeezed out, which was at the base of Governor Rockefeller's complaint. All that the honest desk man can do is avoid distortion as best he can, changing the angle if necessary in order to keep from oversimplifying.

A second danger in headlines is emphasis on a minor angle of a story. A common complaint of speakers is that a reporter takes some minor point, even an aside, and builds a big story around it. The fault is compounded if the head plays up this angle, perhaps in oversimplified form. What the speaker and audience both understood as almost a joke may, for example, be blazoned:

Blasts Commie Profs

Readers who were there—and perhaps the speaker's future audiences—will then be re-convinced that newspapers distort and sensationalize.

Distrust of headlines led Mrs. John F. Kennedy, widow of the President, to ask *Look* editors to serialize a book about his last days in not more than two or three installments. Her argument was that critical comments about some prominent persons, including President Johnson, would be fairest in the context of long installments. She feared that if the story came out in small pieces, newspapers would repeatedly pick up minor angles and give them sensational headlines.

Another danger in headlines is overplay. Too much emphasis on a story usually results from a bad choice of type, but vivid headline words may also overdramatize. Another factor is news flow. A story which would deserve a small one-column head inside on an ordinary day may be overplayed under several columns on the front page when news is dull. According to a tradition, which is probably passing, some newspapers run a full-width banner head across the front page every day. (The *banner* is also called a *streamer* or *line.*) This tradition inevitably overplays some stories. A reader might suspect that some of the banners in figure 4-1 distort the news.

Underplay, of course, is also a threat. Admitting that there is no universal standard of correct play, fair-minded editors nevertheless acknowledge that some papers do not give certain stories the space or heads they deserve. This may be the result of policy or simply of ignorance—maybe the desk man does not realize that the coup in such-and-such a country really affects his readers. Some editors knowingly order small heads on racial riots in other communities, on the theory that large heads would "stir things up" at home.

New State Proposal

SALES TAX SURPRISE

The Weather
Bay Area: Fair except for patches of morning cloudiness. High Saturday, low 60s to low 70s.
See Page 27

San Francisco Chronicle

FINAL

105th Year No. 178 ★★★ SATURDAY, JUNE 28, 1969 10 CENTS GArfield 1-1111

New Wales Bombing Raises Tension See Story Column 2

Continued Hot

HOUSTON CHRONICLE

FINAL

10 Cents

Houston's Family Newspaper

Vol. 68 No. 260 MONDAY, JUNE 30, 1969 HOUSTON, TEXAS 77001

Israelis Plunge Deep Into Egypt

WARM

BUFFALO EVENING NEWS

Complete Financial

Vol. CLXXII—No. 121 BUFFALO, N. Y., WEDNESDAY, AUGUST 31, 1966 114 Pages— —8 Cents

Inflation Is Target of Congressmen

City Is Asked to Decide On School Plan in Month

Nun, 85, Wheeled to Safety in Hong Kong

SOARING FOOD COSTS AND INTEREST RATES CAUSING CONCERN

Fig. 4-1. Banners. Though street sales are of declining importance, a number of newspapers still use banner headlines like these, clear across the front page, sometimes with other banners or streamers above or below.

FINAL STOCKS Closing Stocks—Pages 6, 7, 8, 9D Racing News, Page 3B LATE RACING

YEAR'S STOCK TOTALS SUNDAY

CONTINUED SUNNY, WARM

The Hartford Times

WEEKDAYS AND SUNDAYS

NOBODY WANTS JAIL IN TOWN
Editorial, Page 14A

Vol. CXXXI No. 152 Hartford, Connecticut, Thursday, June 26, 1969 TEN CENTS

Parochiaid Faces Court Test

Heads of quality

Notwithstanding criticisms, most newspaper headwriters do a good job, day in, day out. They may often compose routine or dull heads, but they are accurate. Nothing better illustrates such good, ordinary headlines—unimaginative, perhaps, but fair—than the latest edition of any large daily.

Kudos for headwriting usually go to the writers who have a flair for saying the difficult with style. The head which draws the envy of other professionals usually displays unique imagery or wit. The neophyte who wants to distinguish himself as headwriter should try to develop a colorful way of putting things in a few words; he will sometimes write corn, but he may develop a valuable talent. The headwriter should probe nearly every story for something amusing or clever that can be brought up to a headline. In some instances, as for an obituary, it would be in bad taste. But some real effort to be droll or even funny will produce an occasional gem. Here, for example, are several heads which play on words cleverly:

The Mao Clinic: China
Sends MDs to Paddies
To Cure Political Ills

The Reign in Spain Is Plainly on the Wane

Lake Carriers Clear Decks
For Battle with Railroads

Tigers Get 9 Goose Eggs for Easter

Airport in New Zealand
Definitely Isn't for Birds

Heat Turned on Cook
In Very Short Order

Modern head styles

Even before the words of a head are chosen, several other decisions face the copydesk. Normally the slot man or news editor makes these choices almost automatically. Chapter 9 takes up typographic points in detail, but here are some brief guidelines on modern practice.

Type face and size

Modern newspapers use head types which are clean and easily readable, as is apparent in figure 4-3. *Sans serif* types (without decorative lines, dots, and squiggles) are popular; so-called *modern* or *transitional* types—especially Bodoni—also are often employed because their sharp, bold lines are quickly grasped. Condensed type (squeezed so that many letters will fit into a column) was popular a few decades ago, but the trend is to larger sizes. This movement toward display types which are big, legible, and attractive complicates the problem for the writer who has much to say in little space.

Number of lines

The spread of horizontal make-up, which uses multi-column heads almost exclusively, brings wide use of the single line three or more columns wide. But two-line heads are by far the most frequent. Though three lines in major headlines are still common, probably less so than a generation ago, four lines are rare.

Width

Heads are growing wider as "magazine style" becomes more popular. The traditional "Civil War head" of numerous parts was one column wide and, it seemed, almost a column long (fig. 4-2). Today only a few papers still hold to a tradition of frequent one-column heads. Headlines of two, three, and four columns are widely employed on most American newspapers. Use of two and even three heads of six and eight columns on a single page is common.

Style

Aside from the number and length of lines, several other elements set the style of an individual headline.

One factor is arrangement of lines. Should they be even on the left or should they step in on one side? Or should they be stepped in on both sides? The answer will determine how modern or streamlined a head looks. The *stepped* head, in which succeeding lines of about the same length are stepped over to the right, is still used. But the *flush left* head—all lines evened up at the left—has been most popular for decades now, because it can be written more speedily.

If the first line is full and another line or two are stepped in to make a trapezoid shape, the head is called an inverted pyramid. This style is usually used as a subordinate part of a heading, but it sometimes stands alone as the main head.

Lines of varying length are not always set flush left, with ragged right edge; instead, centering each line can make an effective head. This style is not much used in this country but is common abroad, as in the London *Daily Telegraph*.

Stepped Head
Takes Lines of
Equal Length

Centered Head
Finds Little
Editorial Support

Flush Left
Lines Can
Vary a Bit

Inverted Pyramid Style
Rarely Used In
Main Head

Another question of style concerns capitalization. The two older forms are "all caps"—with every letter a capital—or "caps and lowers," the conventional capitalization of book titles. But the *lower case* head, which appears to be growing in popularity because of speed of setting and reading, uses only one capital letter—for the first word. Except for proper nouns, other words are entirely lower case—that is, small letters—for quick reading.

ALL CAPS SEEM
TOO BOLD
TODAY

Caps and Lowers
May Soon Be
On Uppers

Lower case rises
to prominence
in U. S.

The other most obvious variable in determining the shape or appearance of the head is the number of parts. Accompanying the main head may be one or more smaller headings to lead the eye down into the story. These parts of a headline are called *decks* (or sometimes *banks* or *drops*). The strong trend has been towards the single deck, especially in one-column heads. While some papers use three or four decks in a head, two is the maximum on most papers. Typically the story is told in the first part, or *top*, and further detail follows in the second part, which is sometimes called simply *the deck*. (See fig. 4-4.)

As decks have declined in popularity, the *kicker* has become popular. It is a head of from one to several words, frequently with an underlining rule centered above the main head or to the left of it. Writing of decks and kickers will be considered later in this chapter.

In summary, a head in small type, narrow measure, with several decks of stepped lines looks old-fashioned. The modern head tends

Chicago

VOL. XVIII. CHICAGO, SATURDAY, APRIL 15,

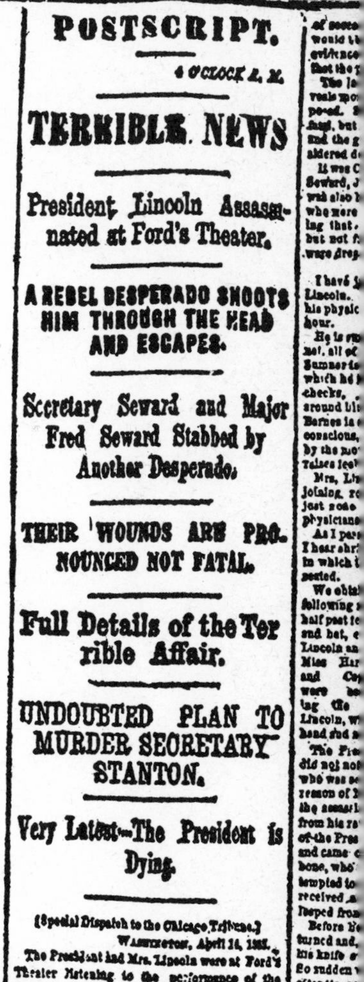

POSTSCRIPT.

4 O'CLOCK A. M.

TERRIBLE NEWS

President Lincoln Assassinated at Ford's Theater.

A REBEL DESPERADO SHOOTS HIM THROUGH THE HEAD AND ESCAPES.

Secretary Seward and Major Fred Seward Stabbed by Another Desperado.

THEIR WOUNDS ARE PRONOUNCED NOT FATAL.

Full Details of the Terrible Affair.

UNDOUBTED PLAN TO MURDER SECRETARY STANTON.

Very Latest—The President is Dying.

[Special Dispatch to the Chicago Tribune.]
WASHINGTON, April 14, 1865.

The President and Mrs. Lincoln were at Ford's Theater listening to the performance of the "American Cousin," occupying a box in the second tier. At the close of the third act, a person

Fig. 4-2. **Civil War head.** It was hard to skim headlines a century ago. To continue past the head into the story took stamina, though no doubt every reader in 1865 continued past the head of this item in the **Chicago Tribune** of April 15.

Fig. 4-3. **Typical headlines.** Ordinary heads from wide variety of papers illustrate the similarity of styles across the country. Note that all are flush left.

Wider Probes Due on UFOs

Astronauts Rehearse Maneuvers

Employe of Hospital Is Held as Suspect In 21 Arson Cases

GOP Watches Activities Of Rival Party

Only Republican Interest Centers on Comptroller

GOP Watches Activities Of Rival Party

Only Republican Interest Centers on Comptroller

Some Fathers Find Loafing Worthwhile

Jobs Pay Less Than Welfare

A Rough U. N. Session Expected

U. S. Diplomats Bracing for Stormy Debate on Viet Nam

Fig. 4-4. Use of decks. Subordinate decks are used in various ways in relation to the main head or deck.

to be in a large and clear face, flush left and several columns wide, in lower case, and accompanied by not more than one subordinate deck.

Head schedules

If the headwriters had to ponder all these decisions for every headline, they would never get out a daily paper. Even on magazines, where longer deadlines permit debate on head decisions, many choices are routinized. On newspapers, the editors select few head styles for regular use and put them into a list or *head schedule*. This listing of headlines facilitates the choice of head and also provides a coding which permits fast communication with the printers. (See fig. 4-5.)

The typical head schedule is a graduated listing of big heads down to little. For example, a 48-point head may be called "A," a 36-point "B," a 30-point "C," and so on. Then the copyreader has only to write the letter to instruct the printer. (A "point" is one seventy-second of an inch. Seventy-two point type, then, is one inch high. Thirty-six point is a half-inch. Other details will be explained in chapter 9.)

With each heading on the schedule—or in the copyreader's memory—must be the "head count," the number of characters or units in a line. Normally this count refers to the maximum number of letters which will fit into one column, and the copyreader writes lines with a count a little below that; if the head is two, three, or more columns, he gets the count by multiplying by two, three, etc. (How copyeditors count fat and thin letters will be discussed later in this chapter.)

Here, for example, is the top of the head schedule for the *Rochester* (N. Y.) *Times-Union*:

Name	*Character Count*	*Type Size Indicated*
No. 2	9	(36-point Bodoni)
No. 3	10-1/2	(30-point Bodoni)
No. 4	11-1/2	(24-point Bodoni)

Fig. 4-5. Head schedule. Chicago Sun-Times "hed sked," typically, gives counts for types ranging from 120-point down to 12.

20 point; count 2½ per column

STRIKE

6 point; count 3 per column

DR. KIN

'2 point; count 5 per column

Water Sho

0 point; count 6½ per column

Depots Destr

2 point; count 9 per column

Hiking Mortgages

0 point; count 11 per column

Law Student Internshi

#43

Britain Defends Pound

#K34

ABSENTEE VOTE

Major Crisis Shakes Little San Marino

#28

Rebels Execute Chief Of Junta, Nigeria Hears

#19

Vatican Raps Speculation On Birth Decisions

#14

Thai Officials Tell Of Foiling Red Plot

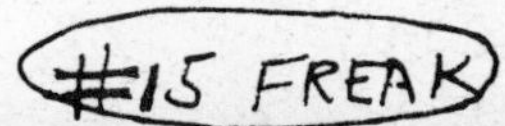

This means that the large No. 2 head permits up to 9 letters and spaces in a column. For two columns the count is obviously 18—perhaps a bit more, because the copyeditor gains the space of the rule between columns. The No. 3 head has slightly smaller type, so 10-1/2 units of this fit into a column. And so on. (On the copy, two lines after the number, like an equals sign, indicate a two-line head, and three lines a three-line head. Thus 4= is a two-line No. 4 head.)

The parenthetical indication of type size in the *Times-Union* schedule is unusual. But even if a schedule does have a reminder of type size, it is important that the copyeditor memorize the faces and sizes of the heads as he then can quickly construct offbeat headlines.

In fact, too often the whole head schedule is not in print. The authors have worked for three large dailies that had no formal printed head schedules. Copydesk men keep the schedule in their heads, and a newcomer must learn the heads and counts from them. The better practice is to have examples of the heads run off on proof paper, distributed to concerned staff members, and posted near the copydesk.

The newcomer to a copydesk naturally learns and follows the heading system in use. To revise the head schedule takes the judgment of newsmen familiar with the personality of the paper; and sometimes typographers may aid in a complete redesigning of the type dress. The general rule is to choose types which harmonize, and that usually means sticking to one family of type. The regular face is used in different sizes, and more variety is introduced by using italic, bold face, ultra-bold, and condensed versions of the basic face. Sometimes a second style of type will complement the basic one, as, for example, sans serif with a modern face. Use of three or more faces leads quickly to chaos.

Too many head sizes also will disrupt the schedule. A dozen probably will suffice for most stories. The head schedule becomes too lengthy and complicated for practical use if jammed with every head ever used. The desk then has to be prepared, and have the liberty, to create different arrangements of type for features and other special needs. Using that *Times-Union* schedule, for example, a copyeditor could write a four-column headline of two lines in 36-point Bodoni, with a 24-point kicker in Bodoni Roman or Ultra. He would simply have to give brief instructions to the printer beyond the head schedule code.

A knowledge of type enables the copyeditor to write offbeat headlines. While he must take care not to introduce confusion and ugliness, the imaginative deskman can create variety and freshness with unorthodox new heads, such as those in figure 4-6.

Basic rules for heads

Label heads

Many of the world's papers have accustomed readers to heads which are mere labels. A London paper, for example, may proclaim in 18- or 24-point type, "Parliamentary Debate" or "Death at Chamonix." Most American readers find such label heads dull, but an editor overseas can argue with some point that they do not give the whole story away. There may even be some tendency in the

The view from above

Water, water everywhere . .

2 Women Try Vainly to Save 3d on IND Tracks

Brooklyn Train Hits Her as She's Almost Pulled Up— 28 Others on Platform

That Station in Wales
(Llanfairpwllewyngyllgogeryc etc.)
Trips Up a Teletypist

At 9:24 A.M. yesterday, the Reuters press agency

Fig. 4-6. Off-beat heads. The copyeditor who knows his head types can create unorthodox headlines such as these, which are probably not on a head schedule.

United States, as newsstand competition diminishes, for the American editor to use more label heads. The well-edited *Des Moines Register*, for example, has recently used a number of verbless headlines like this:

Nuns' China Ordeal:
Tears and Death

Another *Register* example which at first seems to have a verb actually uses a gerund (verbal employed as noun):

Mobilizing of
Guard After
Negro Death

Punchy heads

The main stream of American head-writing, however, emphasizes the punchy, dramatic, summary headline. American readers would immediately sense something wrong if they met this headline:

The Congressmen Were in a Disagreement
On the Housing Legislation

It is wrong because it is past tense; it has no active verb with subject; and it has several articles. Furthermore, most of the words are too long for a conventional head.

An American feels much more at home if he sees the subject summarized this way:

Solons Split
On Race Bill

This head is in the present tense; a concrete noun is followed by a strong, active verb; and the articles have been sliced out. This same example, however, has some weaknesses of headwriting. "Solons" is *headlinese*, or jargon, which many copydesks frown on. "Split" may be read here as a verb in the past tense or an adjective, and it doubtless overstates the debate which the reporter discussed. And while "race bill" has punch, it introduces an oversimplification and perhaps even connotations which the more complex language avoids.

Abbreviating

How does the copyeditor decide what to put in the abbreviated key sentence which is the headline?

As the reporter has tried to get the gist of the story into a lead which summarizes the event, the headwriter now boils that sentence down to fit the count on the head schedule. In theory, at its simplest, he switches the sentence into the present tense and eliminates articles and time-place references. The remaining skeleton is typically subject, verb, and, perhaps, direct or indirect object.

Following the example above, let us say the wire carries this lead:

> WASHINGTON—Congress today launched debate on the controversial bill providing for an expansion of racial integration in housing.

This lead might become a two-line head:

Congress Debates
Housing Bill

But since the second line is a little short, one writer might stretch it a bit by juggling grammar:

Congress Debates
Bill on Housing

Another might prefer to add information:

Congress Debates
Race Housing Bill

It can be objected that this head is rather general and imprecise, but the objection applies to the lead as well. The head properly condenses the lead.

Some slot men would contend that the first words of the head should carry the main punch of the story. "Congress" is dull. So they would ask the copyeditor to substitute a more powerful word:

Race Housing
Bill Debated

But this makes the verb passive, and other editors would argue that the verb must be active.

Rules and reality

This difference illustrates two points about headwriting: (1) "Inviolable" rules sometimes collide head-on, and a choice has to be made as to which is more important; (2) since tastes of copydesk chiefs vary, the headwriter has to be alert to the dictums and prejudices of his boss.

In the American fashion, headlines "give the story away" so the skimmer can decide what he wants to read in detail. But "feature heads," another whole category of headlines, give only a hint of the story. In magazines, of course, these are simply "titles." Such heads do not summarize but rather try to capture interest. They may lack verbs or subjects, as sometimes mere fragments arouse the reader's curiosity.

Traditional headlines usually go on spot news stories. Feature-head treatment best fits material like the human-interest story or the personality sketch. It may pun. It may twist a common phrase or aphorism. It may employ alliteration. As we said earlier, such heads require an imaginative or witty deskman. He can also apply his talent to the occasional straight news story when a traditional summary head doesn't provide insight into the story. A clever, catchy head may do the job. Some editors, to describe this situation, have a slogan: "If you can't tell it, sell it."

Creating the headline

"Almost anything goes" is the motto for the writer of feature heads. But copydesk traditions are quite firm about news headlines. The beginning copyeditor has to have the rules firmly in mind before he can decide which ones may be broken safely.

Cardinal rules

The previous discussion suggests the two cardinal rules of the news headline:

1. State (or imply) a complete sentence in the present tense.
2. Eliminate all articles and most adverbs and adjectives.

The first rule notes that to imply a complete sentence, as with an infinitive or an understood verb, is permissible:

Chancellor to Speak
At Senior Dinner

Guerrillas' Goal
Victory by April

Usually the subject of the sentence is vital to a headline, but sometimes the alert slot man will accept a head that clearly implies the subject. Here are borderline examples:

Discusses GOP
Industrial Plan

Enjoins Strike
In Second Day

Beware of heads that seem to command action from the reader. This one sounds like a plea rather than a report:

Hit Democrats'
Housing Proposal

Some editors, to whom such headlines are anathema, suggest that too much permissiveness may lead to the ridiculous:

Beat Grandma
And 3 Babies

The second rule, banning articles, also has exceptions. Sometimes a head reads and fits better with an article:

Judge Charges Teen-agers
'On the Loose' at Night

Major rules

Beyond these two cardinal rules lie five other guidelines for headwriting. Most of them stem from our discussion of good and bad heads and are given here more or less in descending order of importance.

Be accurate. If necessary, sacrifice color and drama in a headline to avoid leaving an erroneous impression.

Accuracy may force the copyeditor to sift the story for the kernel of the news. Of course if the lead is buried, the good copyeditor revises the story so the major news at the top then draws the head from the revised lead. But an interpretive news story may properly start with a less pointed lead than a spot news story; then the headwriter has to grasp the full meaning of the story and try to summarize that accurately.

Here, for example, is the lead of a story in the *New York Times*:

> ALBANY, April 24—Evidence that the Legislature is embroiled in its adjournment rush is visible and audible this week.
>
> Absent members are being voted "aye" by the leadership to pass favored bills. Legislators cannot get copies of bills even as the bills are being passed, lobbying is rampant and many legislators have dropped all pretense of parliamentary politeness and are literally snarling at each other. . . .

The *Times* copyeditor summarized the whole piece with this head:

Tension Rises as Windup Nears at Albany

Be specific and concrete. "One-eyed thief" is better than "robber" or "man"; "3,000 bales" is better than "cotton." One of the problems in the above illustrations about an interracial housing bill was to be more specific than just "bill." A major headline problem of recent years has been the need to boil complicated civil rights movements and actions down into a single headline word such as "rights." Vague, abstract words make headlines without punch. But blunt words which fit may bias.

Use strong verbs. Avoid jelly words like "discuss" and "indicate" and forms of "to be." As in good news story style, use strong verbs in the active voice—*slash, pinpoint, reveal, assail, hit, kill.* Some otherwise good words have been used so much that good editors avoid or ban their use; these include *rap, sift, probe* and *flay.* Remember that verbs must be accurate as well as active. So perhaps *assail* should be replaced by *criticize*, or *denounce* by *chide.*

Start with the news. The first line of the head should tell the reader what he wants to know immediately. A short noun followed by a short, active verb will usually do:

Pope Decries . . .

Teachers Revolt . . .

U.S. Shifts Lead . . .

Of the five w's used in the lead, the top line of the head summarizes the *who* and *what.*

But sometimes the body acting is less important and newsworthy, at least in a label-word, than is the body acted upon. So, as indicated already, "congress" and "legislature" as the first word of a head probably will have less pulling power than the tag for the legislation passed, as for example *pollution bill* or *teen draft act.* Though such a subject forces the verb into the weaker passive form, strength can still be given, as with *debated, argued,* or *killed.*

Punctuate correctly. Some beginning headwriters mistakenly cut out punctuation marks as well as articles. As figure 4-7 shows, punctuation is the same in heads as other copy, except that the period almost never ends a headline. Commas are often necessary, as in other writing. Semicolons join independent clauses, but a semicolon in the middle of a line splits the reader's attention. To save space and improve appearance, single quotation marks may replace the traditional double ones. The dash has many good head uses, but since words are not split at the end of the line in the heads of the well-edited paper, hyphens appear only between words.

Whether periods mark a head abbreviation is a question of the paper's style; it may be Y.M.C.A. or it may be YMCA. Sometimes a paper will use periods in one group of initials but not in another, according to a tradition which the desk man must learn. Similarly, abbreviation is according to style. *Prof.* without the name, *yr.*, and *Dept.* are typical abbreviations that many newspapers would ban. But *Dr.* and *Rev.* and *Co.* (with appropriate names) or *Pct.* or *U.N.*, would be used without hesitation. Nicknames, like "Rocky" or "Ronnie," as well as first names alone or initials only—like "LBJ," "Spiro," and "Ted"—are taboo on some papers though frequently used by others.

Shot by police, wounded youth faces charge

Mrs. Dittler, 97, Dies in Hospital; Services Monday

SMITH SEES TALKS NEAR 'A CLIMAX'

Jersey Will Spend $30-Million on Rails

Fig. 4-7. Punctuating headlines. Punctuation, as in these heads, follows the conventions of English sentences, without the ending period.

All sorts of other traditions and preconceptions hedge the major rules. One paper may avoid the verb "eye" in heads; another will use names of only the most prominent personages in headlines. But all agree that numerals may be used in heads, even to begin a line. (See fig. 4-7.)

Minor rules

Most editors would further agree on these five minor rules:

Don't split. "Splitting" a head means dividing a natural grouping of words by the end of a line. The most heinous split puts the "to" of an infinitive at the end of one line and the verb on the next:

Mayor Promises to
Study Rent Frauds

Splitting prepositional phrases is almost as bad. But it is also poor practice to sever "have" or "will" from the rest of the verb, or separate an adjective from the noun it modifies. (To keep headline writers sane, editors usually allow splits in decks or between the second and third lines of a three-line head.)

Don't repeat. A good headline, like a good sentence, avoids simple-minded repetition. **Fair Manager Tells Plans for Fair** obviously is awkward. Copyeditors also should eschew awkward repetition of sounds, as in **Legislators Eye New Racing Legislation.**

One of the greatest temptations is to repeat a word from the head in the deck. Even use of a synonym sounds strained, so the deck should usually reveal a second angle.

The subject of the top head may be implied in a deck that starts with a verb. If the subject is omitted in the top, however, it must begin the deck. The following head is wrong because "investigators," not "wild animals," is the subject of "charge":

Charge Cages
Old, Filthy

Wild Animals in Deplorable
Condition, Say Investigators

This head properly handles the omission of subject:

Probers Charge
Zoo Coops Filthy

Claim Wild Animals
'In Deplorable Condition'

Don't overpack. It is good advice to try to get many ideas into a head; good practice avoids padding and thinning. Yet one can cross a line where the head becomes so packed with ideas that the reader has trouble translating it. One of the greatest dangers is in piling up nouns as modifiers. **State police investigators** is clear to most. **State police traffic toll investigators** is more difficult, but **State police major highway traffic toll investigators** is impossible.

Don't use headlinese. Good English is best. As indicated already, headlinese is the language of overworked words. They may be the short, punchy verbs, so some editors object to even *hit* and *gut* as headlinese. Certain nouns, such as *cops* and *tryst*, are overworked and slangy. Stay alert to usage; when a word becomes a cliché, avoid it.

Homely words become headlinese when used for their size and not their sense. One of the most infelicitous such uses is "said" for "termed," "called," or "described as." Those who employ this poor English can argue that it is short for "is said to be," but the mind boggles at fitting in the missing words, as in this head from an Eastern paper:

Red Bloc
Trade Said
Beneficial

Called counts only one and one-half characters more than *said* and in this instance would have fit. (Words like *called* or *labeled* are considered attributive words. They indicate to the reader that someone is making a statement. Without such words the headline would become a flat statement, like **Red Bloc Trade Beneficial**, which would be an *editorial* head appropriate on the editorial page but not over news stories.)

Don't be ambiguous. Mushy words leave mushy meanings. The many legitimate meanings of a single English word make the writer's job difficult. The verb *will*, in faulty context, may appear to be a noun, which one reader may mistake for "determination," another for "legal document," or vice versa. Humor sometimes results from unexpected double meanings.

Roberts Will Suit
Stalls over Horses

Precision is essential in heads, as illustrated by earlier discussion of Governor Rockefeller's reaction to "bow."

Making heads fit

Fitting the letters of a head to a given space is simply a question of figuring out how many of a certain size will go into a line and choosing words with no more than that number.

In the long single line of six or eight columns, this is easy. Here one quickly determines (perhaps by counting heads in old papers) that he can get so many letters in; usually it is thirty-five to forty-five or more, and this means he has six to ten words. He adds, drops, and changes words until he comes out with about the right total. There are enough spaces between words that the printer can fill in with unobtrusive space if the line is a little short.

The problem becomes more difficult when the head must fit the space of only a column or two. The reason is not only that there is room for fewer letters but that letters vary in width; a short space increases the importance of those variations.

Most of the small letters do not vary much in width, of course. So they are simply counted as one character or unit. Some letters are wider, and regardless of the exact variation, this greater width is figured out at 50 percent for counting purposes. The small *m*, for example, is counted as 1-1/2 units, half again as big as an *a* or *b*. On the other hand, some narrow letters—such as *i*—count 1/2. Most punctuation marks also count 1/2.

Capital letters, of course, are generally wider. In the cap-and-lower head which predominates today, therefore, the basic count is 1-1/2 units for most capitals. The wide ones, *M* and *W*, count as 2, and the narrow ones, *I* and *J*, are 1.

A space must of course be allowed between words. It may be counted 1/2. Some copyeditors like to count space between words as 1 because they then feel able to crowd more letters in, since the typesetter can then use less than a full unit of space. But for a tight count, 1/2 is acceptable.

Here is a table for quick reference which shows "the counts" for the characters in a typical case of type:

Lowercase Letters	*Count*
All except f, i, l, m, t and w	1
f, i, l, t (remembered easily by lumping the four letters into the word lift)*	1/2
m and w	1-1/2
Uppercase Letters	
All except I, J, M and W	1-1/2
I and J	1
M and W	2
Miscellaneous	
&	1-1/2
All figures except 1	1
$ % ? " #	1
1 and . , - : ; ! ' ( )	1/2
Space between words	1/2

The counts in this table will work for most head types used by newspapers. The copyeditor new to a paper will find out quickly whether it applies to the faces used there. The *t* may have to be counted 1 rather than 1/2, since it runs wider in some faces. The miscellaneous symbols such as the dollar sign and ampersand may vary from the count given; but they appear in a small minority of heads, and adjustment can be made when they do. Some changes may be made in the table to fit the fonts in use, and other quirks of individual faces can be kept in mind. The *Syracuse Post-Standard*, for example, uses one sans serif type with a very narrow *J* and *r*, so heads which count a shade over the maximum will sometimes, in fact, fit.

* In some faces *j* also counts 1/2.

Note in these lines how the width of the letters actually varies, in spite of identical counts:

MWQ	IJS	mwq	fijlt	Bodoni
MWQ	IJS	mwq	fijlt	New Times Roman
MWQ	IJS	mwq	fijlt	Univers

Awareness of such shades of difference may help a copyeditor, pushed against a deadline, to decide to send a tight head to the composing room with a minimum of fear it will have to be sent back to him for rewriting.

Copyeditors work out their own schemes for rapid counting. Take, for example, this head, used by a Western daily:

Drug Offers
Leprosy Hope

The letters of the first line count this way:

```
  D   r   u   g       O   f   f   e   r   s

 1½   1   1   1   ½  1½   ½   ½   1   1   1
```

The beginner will probably count this simply by adding one number at a time: "1-1/2, 2-1/2, 3-1/2, 4-1/2, 5, 6-1/2, 7, 7-1/2, 8-1/2, 9-1/2, and 10-1/2." But the experienced man knows that a space followed by an ordinary capital counts 2. Two *f*'s can be grouped as 1.

```
  D   r   u   g       O   f   f   e   r   s

 1½   1   1   1   2       1       1   1   1
```

So he can count more rapidly: 1-1/2, 2-1/2, 3-1/2, 4-1/2, 6-1/2, 7-1/2 plus 3 (*e, r,* and *s*), or 10-1/2. Another way is to count all the letters and spaces as one: 11. If the count available is 12 or 13, no further counting is necessary. But for precision, a copyeditor can take the 11, add 1/2 for the capital *D* and subtract 1 for the *f*'s, and he gets the correct answer, 10-1/2.

To mutter "1-1/2, 2, 3-1/2, 4-1/2 . . ." or to make all kinds of marks above or below a head wastes time. It is much quicker to count everything as 1 and then make the adjustments required by the thin or fat letters. In many cases he will note that a fat letter will balance a thin one, leaving the count unchanged. Beginners should learn to count at least by twos and even by fives. "Drug Offers" he can look at and count 5 ("drug" plus a space), 10 (adding "offer"), and 11 at the last letter.

Also, since many names are in the news often, he should glance at the name and know what the count is. For example, "Nixon" and "Kennedy"are frequently in headlines. One counts 5, and the other 7. By adding a count for the space, the editor can add 6 to the rest of a "Nixon head" and 8 to the rest of a "Kennedy head."

The count we have been discussing so far applies to heads that mix caps and lowers. All-cap heads are harder to read but easier to count. The papers that still use them use a different counting system.

An easy rule is: all capital letters except four count 1; *M* and *W* are now 1-1/2, and *I* and *J* are 1/2. Punctuation marks also have varied counts, though most marks are 1/2.

Making heads attractive

Graphically, the phrases of a headline are lines put together in simple designs. Obviously these designs should be chosen to please the eye. Similarity of type is important. For example, lines of very large and very small type clash. The two or three lines of a deck all should be of similar lengths. In the stepped head, for example, lines that vary no more than a unit or two will create the symmetrical design on the left rather than the unbalanced example on the right:

xxxxxxxxxxxx	xxxxxxxx
xxxxxxxxxxxx	xxxxxxxxxxxxxxx
xxxxxxxxxxxx	xxxxxx

The flush-left head was invented to overcome the problems of writing the lines to very nearly the same length, and it is true that attractive heads can be written where the lines in these heads vary three or even four units. Some papers permit more. However, too great a variation makes a flush-left head ugly too. Compare the attractiveness of these two examples:

xxxxxxxxxx	xxxxxxxx
xxxxxxxxxxxxxxx	xxxxxxxxxxxxxxx
xxxxxxxxxxxx	xxxx

Some editors argue that the all-cap line is more attractive than the caps-and-lower because the full-height letters create a clean, straight line on both top and bottom. Most papers still use some all-cap headlines, but they favor mixed upper and lower case letters for legibility because we are accustomed to seeing them mixed in all our reading. To maximize readability the usual practice is to capitalize first words of lines and all other words except articles and prepositions. Admittedly, such lines are ragged on top. Several recently redesigned papers have gone to a head which is mostly lower-case. Whether this very readable style of head is more attractive, because streamlined, than the more traditional kinds is a matter of taste.

While the simple, flush-left head is by all odds the most popular today, newspapers are not completely standardized in the United States. Heads can be pyramids, inverted pyramids, or centered styles. Headwriters, like magazine editors, also create special forms, especially on feature materials. The full-box head is no longer very popular, but the three-quarter box is occasionally used. Sometimes double or shaded rules (Ben Day) are used instead of simply hairlines or one-point rules; frequently words are inserted into the top rule, kicker-fashion. (See fig. 4-8 for examples of box rules and unusual headline shapes.)

In addition to rules and boxes, black-and-white designs or shaded illustrations are often part of standing heads. (See fig. 4-9.) Usually these heads run the same day after day. But space requirements shift, and to adjust a permanent heading a copyeditor must know the type used. The *Rochester Times-Union*, for example, has a daily feature made up of short personality items. Under a three-sided box which may be three or more columns wide is the word "People" in 42 Ultra Bodoni. Each day there is a new 18-point Bodoni head alongside this word, two lines inverted-pyramid style.

Fig. 4-8. Boxed heads. Rules are used in a number of ways to dress up heads, with the three-sided or three-quarter box especially popular for leading the eye into the story. Note the kickers cut into top rules and the varied headline shapes. (The deck of the **Wall Street Journal** head (right) is a hanging indention, a shape now rare on American newspaper pages.)

The Hello Business:
Welcomers Abound
For Moving Families
• • •
But Business, Not Friendship,
Spurs the Visits by Women;
Bargaining With the Milkman

Hijack Plane
18 Invaders Try to Claim The Falklands

Report on Cigarettes
Some Filters Are Branded Worse than the Non-Filters

NEW TESTAMENT EDITION PUT IN SIMPLE ENGLISH

Labor Council Stays Neutral On Governor

Background
Young Red 'Front'
THE W.E.B. DuBois Club was founded on the West Coast in June, 1964, to succeed the Young Communist

Fig. 4-9. Standing heads. Regularly used headings, often with a cut, are kept ready for quick insertion. The bottom ones here guide readers inside. Note that the simple, clean, uncrowded heads are the most atttractive.

ON THE SCENE . . .
In Louisville

Good Morning
News Digest Sunny and Cool

From the bookshelf
Dropping in on the Indians . . . . By Rhea Jane

Easy-to-find . . . Easy-to-read
INSIDE YOUR TIMES-UNION
MAVERICK MILLIONAIRE hurls political charges. Page 9A

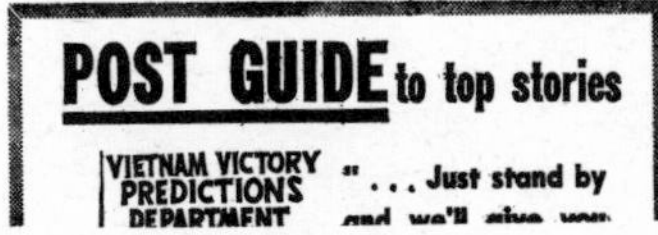

Instructing the printer

Since each paper has its own system for preparing heads and sending them properly marked to the composing room, the new copyeditor has to inquire about local rules. However, certain procedures are the same for all papers.

Heads may be written at the top of copy or on a separate piece of paper, but a newspaper's procedure generally calls for writing the head on the story if the type is small. This is why the reporter has been instructed to start typing his story a third or a half of the way down the first page. If the copyeditor can quickly write the simple head above it, then the compositor can, without changing typesetting machines, set the head at the same time he sets the story. For example, the smallest head on most papers is a single line of the body type set in bold face. It would be foolish to put such a head on a separate piece of paper and make the printers assemble head and story from separate galleys.

Nevertheless, many heads cannot be set on the machine which sets the story. On papers with limited facilities a printer may have to set the big heads by hand; typically, however, a machine specially suited for casting big sizes of type will be used. Either way, the copyeditor must prepare some heads for such necessities.

It is conceivable that, on a slow operation, the stories could all be set and then passed on for the heads all to be set. But it is clearly much faster and more efficient to have men working on the stories and the heads at the same time. For bigger heads, therefore, the copy desk typically writes out the head on a separate sheet of paper. A key word, or *slug*, is given to the story, and this same slug is put on the paper with the head. Finding these slugs in the galleys of type, the printer can assemble the proper head with each story. (The slug line is then thrown into the discard, or *hellbox*, since it has served its communication purpose.)

Aside from the slug, the other main communication to the printer is of course about the style and size of type. Where there is a headline schedule, this information is generally given simply as the head number. For example, a copyeditor might jot "Astro" and "#2" on a story about astronauts. He would write the same coding on the paper with the Number 2 astronaut head he has created. (See fig. 4-10.) The slug on both story and head would then look like this in the proof:

ASTRO #2

Some papers, particularly smaller ones, do not use the slug system to identify copy. They use guidelines, which are the first word or two of the headline itself. For one-edition papers the guideline saves a little time, because the slug does not have to be set on each headline. The Astro story, for example, could have been slugged MOON, CAPSULE, HEIGHT or anything else. But in the guideline system the word ASTRONAUTS would have to be marked on the top of the copy. Note the differences:

ASTRO

Slug system:

2 | Astronauts Soar
To Record Heights

Guideline system:

2 | Astronauts Soar
To Record Heights

When the copyeditor goes beyond the head schedule to create other headings, he must give concise but clear instructions to the printer. If he wants a single, centered line of 24-point Ultra Bodoni, he may write:

24 Ultra Bod. cent.

For two lines of 30-point Cheltenham, flush left, capitals and lower case, in a box made of rules, he may write:

30 Chelt. fl. left c&lc =
3 col. box

or even more simply:

30 Chelt | Astronauts Soar
To Record Heights |

The headwriter can quickly learn the shorthand of different shops. "Ultra" may be enough without "Bod." or "B" because the printer knows that the only "ultra" type used is Bodoni.

Writing a headline

The application of the rules and guidelines may be demonstrated with the handling of an illustrative story. The slot man marks "C" at the top of copy which begins with this lead:

> WASHINGTON—Ardent civil rights backers in Congress are anxiously watching a sharp change in the mood and temper of White America. . . .

The story goes on to point up several recent news items which indicate a turn against further desegregation.

The copyeditor checks the head schedule, unless he has it memorized, to find the requirements of a C head: three flush-left lines with a maximum count of 13-1/2. Mentally he skeletonizes the lead into headline form: "Civil rights backers watch sharp change in mood." But he can be more specific if he notes the direction of the change, so he reframes the last idea as "sharp dip in desegregation zeal" or "sharp rise in resistance to integration." The words are long for the low count, but he can begin:

Civil Rights Backers
Watch Sharp Dip
In Desegregation Zeal

These lines count 18, 15, and 19-1/2—all too long. "In" can be moved up to the second line (creating a split), but the third line remains 3-1/2 counts too long. How about making it "Integration Zeal"? Fourteen, but it might be squeezed in. "Zeal to Change" is only 13 and would be sharper.

The headwriter has to trim, tighten, and re-arrange. If he drops "Civil" in the first line, it fits nicely. The second line can be made to fit by eliminating "Sharp" and by finding a way to get rid of the wide *W* (dips are not watched anyway); so it becomes "Note Dip in" —a bit short, but acceptable. When "Drop" is substituted for "Dip," the head becomes:

Rights Backers
Note Drop in
Zeal to Change

This does the job. But let's say that the slot man wants to get in the idea of "growing resistance" and tosses it back for rewriting. The second line can then become "Note Rise in"—but in what? "Integration Resistance" is much too long and difficult. "Mood to Resist"? That fits, and the head is now:

Rights Backers
Note Rise in
Mood to Resist

This lacks the tone of sharpness which the story attributes to the rise. Some editors would prefer "zoom" to "rise," which fills that second line out a bit anyway; but others would think "zoom" smacks too much of the sports or financial pages. (See fig. 4-10.)

(A metropolitan newspaper which used this story carried this two-column head:

Civil rights
backers note
mood change

The lines fill nicely, though the direction of the change has to be inferred by the reader from his knowledge of recent events. Note the capitalization style.)

Developing the knack

Illustrations can be misleading because they may imply that the creative process is absolutely straightforward. Some headlines come easily and naturally and fit the first time, but often a copyeditor has to ponder several possibilities. He should try to put the whole head together at once and make space adjustments afterward. If he tinkers to make the first line perfect before going on to the rest, he will likely find it impossible to fit other lines to the first line.

Flexibility is most important. The copyeditor should try not to get his mind "locked in" on a particular wording. If a pet phrase doesn't work after a bit of trying, he should stop wasting time with it and use a new approach. He may have to abandon the key statement of the lead and rethink what the story is trying to say.

Three pointers

Here are three pointers on the knack of writing heads, probably in the order the copyeditor will use them.

Try for good short synonyms when the head doesn't fit. Since English has many short verbs, these can probably be juggled more easily than others: e.g., *criticizes, assails, slaps, raps, quits.* Sometimes a slight loss in clarity is unavoidable when substituting, as when "School Superintendent" becomes "School Chief." Initials and nicknames can be used, though good desk procedure requires that they be immediately clear to readers and that they not become too numerous. (Such means may be the only feasible way to distinguish among news figures with the same name; in a city with a mayor named Rudolph Hammerhill, headwriters would use "Rudy," "Ham," "Mayor," and other such codes to communicate the right name quickly.)

Fig. 4-10. Writing a head. The final step in writing the civil rights headline discussed in the text is putting it on copy paper. The example shows the head slugged and marked for a "C" head on the printer's head-schedule.

Reverse the head if the first subject-verb pattern doesn't fit.

Rogers Sees
Venezuela Revolt

will fit if changed to

Venezuelan Revolt
Seen by Rogers

Look for a new angle. In the integration example above, it might have become necessary to try something about Congress pondering news of race developments.

Decks and kickers

To get a little more display than a single two- or three-line head will give, editors sometimes use headlines made up of two decks. A banner headline clearly needs one, two or even more decks to lead into the story. See fig. 4-11.

Television's Trials
TV Industry Is Feeling
Government Pressure,
But the Money Rolls In

Fairness of News Questioned,
Cigaret Ads Face Banning,
Licenses Are in Jeopardy

Station Prices, Profits Rise

CHANGE ON SCHOOL LEVY

Missouri House Approves Proposed Change in Constitution to Aid in Raising Funds—Approval by Voters Is Required Before It Goes Into Effect

WELFARE NOD

Program Clears Legislature, Goes to Governor for Signature

AN EMERGENCY CLAUSE

Tax and Budget Bills Must Be Acted on Before Midnight

Bulletins

Fig. 4-11. Two or more decks. The subordinate unit of the typical two-part head, often called simply "the deck," comes in varied styles and shapes. Though the popularity of heads with several decks has declined over the last generation or two, a few papers still use them.

Traditionally, the lower deck of an ordinary single-column head is two or three lines in inverted pyramid style:

XXXXXXXXXXXXXXXXXXXX
XXXXXXXXXXXX
XXXXXX

Graphically, it is important in the three-line deck to have the lines step in evenly, as in the step head. Head schedules give counts for the full column width, and the top line is written to fill; simply counting letters is usually satisfactory with deck sizes and counts. If the top line is 32, the full count, the second line might be 24 to 26, and the third line should then be 16 to 18. Or the second line could be 20 and the third line 8 to 10. If either the second or third line is too long or too short to provide even steps, the head will be ugly.

Content, of course, is an even more important consideration in the second deck. It should not merely repeat the top. The deck should point up or develop a new angle. The rules for keeping it active and compact are the same as for top decks.

Care should be taken that the headline reads clearly when read straight through. The lower deck may begin with a verb, but the subject then is understood to be the same as that of the top. In figure 4-12 "Mrs. Gandhi" is the subject not only of the top but of the lower deck. A shift to "Gets Offer of Unrestricted . . ." with "Pakistan" intended as subject would be a blooper of the same genre as a dangling participle.

MRS. GANDHI ASKS
PAKISTAN'S AMITY

Offers Unrestricted Travel
and Economic Cooperation

Special to The New York Times

NEW DELHI, Sept. 4—Prime Minister Indira Gandhi tonight offered "economic cooperation" with Pakistan.

In a "person to person" talk, broadcast over the All-India Radio, Mrs. Gandhi also renewed India's pledge "to abjure the use of force in the settlement of differences" between the two nations.

Her conciliatory offer came ter a period of mounting tenbetween the two countries. nt weeks they have ach other of massive d-ups on the bor-

ehensions

Fig. 4-12. Subject of deck. Space can be saved by using the subject of the main head as subject of the deck; here, it is understood, Mrs. Gandhi "offers."

A less common form of deck—the hanging indention—is somewhat easier to write than the inverted pyramid:

XXXXXXXXXXXXXXXXXXXX
XXXXXXXXXXXXXXXX
XXXXXX

The top line fills, and the second line should be two or three characters shorter. The third line then can vary all the way from a few letters to the same length as the second and still be attractive. Otherwise, rules for the pyramid deck apply to this deck.

Since mid-century, the most popular lower deck by far has been the brief, flush-left head. Usually it is two lines, with the right side ragged. Though the number of words available is usually much more limited than in the old-style, inverted-pyramid deck, the content rules are the same for both; the editor constructs it just as he constructs the flush-left head. (See fig. 4-13.)

Fig. 4-13. Popular deck styles. These examples show the popular styles of decks for single-column heads. Pyramid, once the most popular, is now less frequently used than flush-left.

'Hidden'
jobless
on rise
▽ ▽
Rate upsets
labor office

Blast Kills
3 at Toledo
Steel Plant
500 Flee Plant
As Fire Roars

Cost of Living
Up Sharply
During July
Automatic Pay Rises
Increase Concern
Of Administration

SAYS SCHOOLS NOT
FOR SOCIAL CHANGE
Dallas, Tex., Educator Warns
Against Using Them as
Welfare Agency

DISABLED
JET AVERTS
SEA CRASH
Bound For Canada,
DC-8 Lands Safely
In Ireland

Another subordinate head is the kicker, whose growing popularity was indicated above. Almost all newspapers now use this device of a little head above the main head, though research shows that kickers are seldom read. They do, however, provide a ribbon of white space above the head and thus help attract attention. So they should be kept short, to maximize the white space, and their wording should stir interest with a new angle or touch. The words that would make a good, crisp flush-left second deck probably also will make a good kicker, but it should be a little more striking or dazzling than the typical deck. Sometimes dropping the verb will do the trick, for labels are more readily accepted in kickers. A conservative kicker looks like a regular head:

Detectives Spot New Evidence

But a kicker can deliver more punch:

Mysterious Time Bomb

A quote draws attention to the main head:

'I Was Framed!'

To emphasize that not all news is bad, the *Denver Post* regularly employs a little all-cap kicker, "GOOD NEWS," sometimes in red. Papers also use kickers to indicate columns or regular features. (See fig. 4-14.)

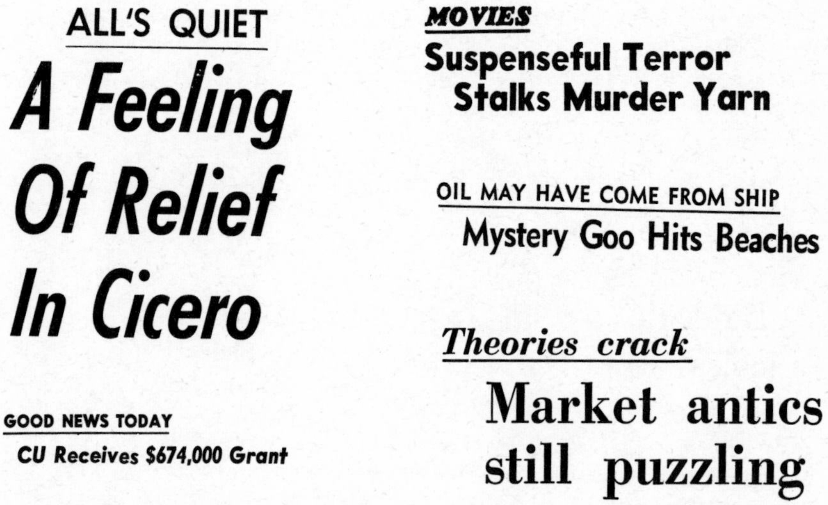

ALL'S QUIET

A Feeling Of Relief In Cicero

GOOD NEWS TODAY

CU Receives $674,000 Grant

MOVIES

Suspenseful Terror Stalks Murder Yarn

OIL MAY HAVE COME FROM SHIP

Mystery Goo Hits Beaches

Theories crack

Market antics still puzzling

Fig. 4-14. Kickers. Typically underlined, the kicker is now widely used by many papers and often replaces the deck. It may give more information in verb–head form or simply add a word or two of identification. Though the type face of the kicker may virtually match the head or be markedly different, it usually represents a shift to italic or caps.

As the flush-left head and kicker have flourished, the crossline has virtually died out. This headline element is a single column-wide line, typically in caps, that appears with four or more decks, usually sandwiched between two inverted pyramids. Copyeditors on the few papers which use crosslines can quickly pick up their rules, but it may be generalized that this form summarizes a new angle with a present-tense verb, just as other subordinate decks do.

Subheads and jumpheads

One form of head, widely used both yesterday and today, is the *subhead*. Ordinarily it is simply two or three words of boldface, the same size as the body type, in the body of a story.

There are two schools of thought about handling the body of a story. One group of editors wants to break it into short "takes" with subheads every three or four paragraphs. The paragraphs not next to subheads may be set boldface and indented. The other school contends that such typographic devices tend to make stories harder rather than easier to read. These editors advocate long, unbroken stretches of body type, with few subheads. The spread of TTS and of horizontal makeup patterns, which reduce the amount of unbroken gray body type, supports the second school. Many papers, of course, will choose a middle ground and use a moderate number of subheads.

Rules for the subhead are much the same as for major heads—present tense, no articles, active voice, and so on. Some papers permit a simple label of two words, because their primary concern is to break up type. Research shows their major practical value is this graphic purpose; still, at least for a minority, well-written subheads can help a reader find parts of a story that stimulate him to read the whole piece.

Except on rare occasions, the subhead should refer to the paragraph immediately following. Few things frustrate a careful reader more than to have curiosity piqued by a good subhead and then have to search down two or three paragraphs to find this angle.

The copyeditor usually writes the subhead right in the copy at the appropriate place. He then marks the margin "sub" or "ffclc" (full face caps and lower case) or simply "BF" (boldface). He may use brackets to indicate centering, but printers usually follow subhead style unless directed otherwise. (See fig. 4-15.)

The declaration contained, apart from the pledge by the two countries to abjure force, various steps toward normalizing their relations.

Peoples Kept Apart

However, except for the withdrawal of troops to positions held before fighting broke out and an exchange of ambassadors, there has been no other significant progress. The peoples of the two nations still live

countries to abjure force, various steps toward normalizing

their relations. Peoples Kept Apart

However, expect for the withdrawal of troops to posi-

tions held before fighting broke out and an exchange of

Fig. 4-15. Subheads. The typical subhead is written into copy this way. A designation such as "BF" or "ffclc" may be used instead of "sub" to indicate boldface is to be used. Illustration also shows how this subhead in the **Times** story on Mrs. Gandhi (cf. fig. 4-12) appears in print.

As type sizes have increased, subheads have grown bolder. Some stories, especially in wide measures, may be broken up with two-line flush-left heads in 12-, 14-, or even 18-point bold italic.

Dingbats—typographic designs such as round dots (bullets) or stars—sometimes accompany a subhead. White space is another important break-up element—around subheads, with dingbats, and sometimes simply by itself. These attention-getters should be used with restraint, for too many will annoy rather than attract the reader.

A number of papers make the first two or three words of a paragraph boldface caps with a break of white space or three bold dots and space just above this paragraph. (See fig. 4-16.) A few papers, in special sections, use the magazine-style printing device of *initial letter* to kick-off major feature stories. This device is a beginning capital several points bigger than the text type and may even be used to start paragraphs in the body of articles, especially on editorial pages.

State Department and White House.

Weary of Work Going for Nought

The arrangement has been zealously adhered to by the President. There has been no break over a fundamental policy issue. Goldberg,

accept offers of help in crossing the border.

*** * ***

One Cuban woman recalled her stay in Mexico City with

descent in the area. Most speak Russian.

Sister Ships at Dock

The Fedor Litke and the Alexy Chirikov are 300-foot sister ships built to

mountaineers, will name nine men.

To Write Constitution

The a s s e m b l y will be charged with turning out a

said the revolutionary teenagers are under direct control of the Mao-Lin faction.

PAPERS BACK DRIVE

It went on to say that "until very recently 'anti-Mao ele-

tion already taken has moderated the growth of bank credit.

ACTION EXPLAINED

"However, in view of increasing pressures on prices stem-

would have to be amended to permit the h i g h -r i s e buildings on the waterfront.

• Jack V. McKenzie, former data processing man-

learned to listen to the strident voices.

NOR DID HE ever manage to convince the black community that he was con-

of advances would be kept to narrow bounds.

THE STRONG performance of blue chips was cited as one of the reasons why

moves with real estate dealers prove unsuccessful.

• • •

KING SCHEDULED a strategy meeting for tonight to evaluate today's activities and

Fig. 4-16. Subhead styles. While the typical subhead is probably still boldface caps and lowers, centered, newspapers use many other devices to break up copy, as illustrated. Some papers are dropping subheads. But where they do, copyeditors must be sure to use horizontal make-up to keep the strips of type short, or to work out other methods to prevent the columns from looking gray, old-fashioned, and forbidding. Note in the bottom row how the importance of division increases, left to right, by the addition of boldface, space, and dingbats.

Stories continued inside the paper need some heading for the continuation, or *jump*. Formerly the *jump head* was the front page head, or very like it. Modifying this tradition, some papers now use a smaller head for the jump. It typically has a "better count" than the one on the front page, and the copyeditor may be able to get ideas and precision here which he abandoned in writing the major head. (A reverse-plate "logo"—white letters on a dark gray background—sometimes helps the eye spot the jump.)

The jump word is often a single key word. It may be employed with a jump head, but more often it stands alone. Like the slug, this word should distinguish the story from all others that day. The jump word is set in larger type or caps; and a box, rules, or white space should make it easy to spot. (See fig. 4-17.)

★ Japanese aim for change
Continued from Page 1

Farmers 'Cleared' In Bread Probe
From page 1A

Storms
From page 1

From Page 1 A

MONKEY

ACTOR YOUNG AND HIS WIFE ARE STRICKEN
Show Goes on with Replacement
[Continued from first page]

Monkey in 2nd Day of Mission
FROM PAGE 1

Prince
(Continued from Page 1A)

RED RAMPAGE
Continued from Page 1

★ Sizzler
(Continued from Page 1A)

Fig. 4-17. Jumps. Editors have developed ingenious heading devices for inside pages to help readers find continued stories. Regular heads are often used to emphasize the news content of these pages. Many editors also use a gimmick, such as a reverse plate, so that the reader's searching eye can spot the jump quickly. A slug word, perhaps with rules, is especially attention-getting, as illustrated by the two bottom rows.

This discussion of headlines has moved from theory to the nuts and bolts of head counts and then to the lowly subhead and jump head. A copyeditor may similarly leave broad principle behind and become involved in the minutiae of quick writing and fast counts—"anything that fits." Professional editing, however, keeps to the high purpose of the newspaper. Even though a head must fit a space and flag attention, its main purpose is to inform quickly and truthfully. And the best headwriter produces such accurate heads so regularly that applying his ethics becomes as habitual and automatic as counting *m* as 1-1/2.

5 Makeup

Good news coverage, news selection, editing, and headline writing are four of the five essentials of an excellent newspaper. The remaining element of excellence is good typographical design—the choices of type and the placement of type and pictures. *Makeup* is the designing process; *layout* and *dummying* are part of makeup but the terms are loosely used to refer to the whole process.

Good design attracts the reader and makes his reading easier. A well-designed newspaper encourages the reader to look through all of it. He will find that his eyes do not have to squint to read the material and that the various blocks of type are arranged in a pleasing way.

There is no set way of doing this, any more than there is a set way of painting a picture. Yet as painters learn to understand form, color, and highlights, designers of newspapers learn the principles of readability and attractiveness. They use findings in art and psychology to test intuitions about what makes pages appealing. Researchers have found that today's reader won't take the time to read small type, so body type sizes have been increased to 9- or 10-point on the better designed papers. Researchers have also discovered that moderately large headlines of both capital and small letters are easier to read than those in all caps. The better papers, then, use headline types that are easy to see, but are not so large they shout at the reader. A few papers, as noted in the previous chapter, have even put all headlines in lower case, capitalizing only the first word and any proper nouns. These moves reflect our total experience with print and handwriting: words are made up mostly of small letters. Designers believe we are more content following familiar patterns.

Modern newspaper designers, in general, have decided that much typographical ornamentation is a hindrance. To separate stories from one another, they reject stars, dashes, asterisks, and cutoff rules in favor of ribbons or blocks of white space. This trend toward "clean" layout has also eliminated most decks from headlines.

The reverse-6

Some researchers have found that the eye tends to scan a page in a line that resembles a reversed number 6. The reader looks toward the upper left of a page first, shifts across to the right, to the lower right, to the lower left, and then loops to the center of the page.

Why, then, do newspapers put their best stories in the upper right, the number two position? Custom, or habit. For years newspapers ran banners on page one. When reading English, people move their eyes from left to right. When they finish reading the banner, their eyes are at the right of the page. Editors argued it was foolish to send the reader back to the left to read the story, so the story "read out" of the banner down the right column. Most papers have nearly given up the banner but still cling to putting the lead story in the upper right. A few have discarded the idea and make up page one with the main story at top left and other strong material at the lower left.

Though many papers cling to the upper right lead, almost all exploit the rest of the reverse-6 findings. Strong typographical display in the lower right and lower left, including the placement of pictures in those positions, support stories with multi-column headlines centered on the page. These stories hold the eye at the end of its sweep around the reverse-6.

Some researchers discount the reverse-6 theory. They contend that the reader starts reading a newspaper page as he starts a book page, at the upper left. His eyes then tend to move diagonally across and down the page until he reaches the lower right, where he expects to turn the page. This diagonal theory assumes that the eye is lured right and left, up and down, to see all parts of the page, rather than moving in a straight line. Defenders of the diagonal theory argue that major headlines or pictures attract the eye out of the diagonal path.

No matter what the theory, all agree that attention should be given to placement of good-sized heads, blocks of copy, and pictures in every section of the page. Generalizations about makeup are usually based on the complicated front page, but they hold good for an inside page, depending on how much space goes to advertisements.

Strengths of horizontal makeup

The grasp of new information about eye movement and design principles led to an introduction of what is called *horizontal* makeup. Previously, blocks of type and headlines invariably moved down a column. Now they can move across the page, sometimes taking up a rectangle of space only three or four inches deep but four, five, or even eight columns wide. This method not only attracts the eye but facilitates the placement of type. Instead of restricting body type to only one column, the horizontal method allows it to be juggled in many different measurements. For example, body type under a five-column head may be two inches deep in the first three columns and four inches deep in the last two. It can even be jockeyed from one column to another so it all fits the page.

The opposite of horizontal, of course, is *vertical*. Most papers a century and more ago ran all stories with single column headlines for reasons related to the fastest presses of that day.* Body type went steadily down under the head to the bottom of the page. When a story ended at mid-page, another single column headline and story began beneath it. A story that reached the bottom of the page with some part left over was continued, or jumped, to another page.

Vertical makeup suited the fast presses but not the reader's eye. The many ribbons of vertical lines made the paper look narrow and skinny. The bottoms of vertical pages looked washed out and dull. Vertical makeup also highly restricted the placement of type as all body type for one story had to go in the one column. If it did not fit, the only solution, except for jumping, was to throw away part of the story.

Horizontal makeup, which is as easy as any to use with modern presses, means a fairly long story can appear complete on one page, without a jump. While the stories often are long, they do not seem lengthy. The few inches of copy in each column encourages the reader to skim the whole story rather than to stop with the first paragraph. The avoidance of jumps is desirable because readers get impatient at having to turn from page one to page twenty-one and back to page one again. Only the most determined readers will make that double jump.

Some years ago newspaper designers took a careful look at the American newspaper and realized that the narrow columns looked jammed with type. The reader had to focus carefully to read the stories. And a rather simple test showed that most readers did not read one line at a time. The narrow, 11- or 12-pica column was a trifle long for one glance and not quite long enough for two. (Since a pica is one-sixth of an inch, a 12-pica column is two inches wide.) So the six-column—or *optimum format*—newspaper was born. The columns widened to 16 picas (two and two-thirds inches), which allows rapid, comfortable reading and permits better head counts—resulting in more accurate headlines.

Two other modern styles increase readability by providing more space between columns. The *W-format* divides the front page into six columns of 11 picas and a seventh of 16 picas. The leftover half column is distributed in white space to divide the columns. Similarly, the *seven format* has seven columns of copy on an eight column page. The extra column allows the news columns to be separated by a full pica of space.

These changes provide more openness on the pages and are in line with the growing tendency of newspapers to report the news in greater detail. Page one of the six-column paper can use two or three

* In 1848 the New York newspapers began using a type-revolving press invented by Richard Hoe. Cylinders with curved iron beds circulated the type itself at high speeds (in anticipation of today's solid stereotype plates). Wedge-shaped column rules held the type in place, and any break in those rules would send the type flying all over the room.

pictures and five or six stories. This method leaves plenty of good stories for the inside. The reader now senses that he is getting a lot of information for his money—and he is. Most users of this format try to put out a newspaper that looks like a big magazine and gives the reader both the news of the *day* and the news of the *times*. That is, he gets, clearly spread out before him, the news of the previous twenty-four hours. In addition, he receives information about trends in local and world events that may have been going on for the last three months or the last three years.

Basic goals of makeup

While *optimum, W-format*, and *seven column* are relatively new terms for makeup, some older descriptive phrases deserve attention. Applying labels is difficult because one category shades into another. Those who actually do the day-to-day job of designing pages may rarely use the names of the categories, if they ever heard of them, for editors make up pages by judgment or "feel," not by labels.

Everyone concerned with makeup does refer frequently to *balance*. The term is so common that it has come to describe a particular kind of makeup. In this system the typographic display on one side of a page balances, or nearly balances, a similar display on the other side. In the early days of newspapers, only the top of the page was balanced, but eventually the whole page fell into this pattern. A picture often occupied the exact center, with headlines of equal size on either side. At the bottom would be a double-column headline on one side and another double-column head on the other. The idea was to achieve perfect symmetry. (See the *New York Times* page, fig. 5-1.)

Perfect balance, however, has serious drawbacks. In judging the day's news, an editor usually decides that one story is clearly better than all others. He wants to say so by giving it the biggest headline. But in *balance* he must give the same headline display to a lesser story.

Strict balance has another shortcoming. The eye finds it hard to focus on anything so exactly proportioned. A balanced page calls attention to a pattern but not a point. Every cluster of type is tempered by another exactly the same. Some critics have contended that looking at a balanced page is a bit like looking at a checkerboard.

For these reasons formal balance has been replaced largely by *contrast-and-balance*, or *imbalance*, or *dynamic balance*. This method of many names includes balance but not exact counterbalancing. A two-column picture may balance a three-column headline in the adjoining quarter page or quadrant. Or a two-column headline may adequately balance a three-column head. In this system, the lead story is clearly the lead, as it has the biggest headline. Most American papers now use this kind of makeup because it provides a certain symmetry, a focal point for the eye, and an opportunity for the editor to give special emphasis to some stories. (See figs. 5-2 through 5-11.)

IN TODAY'S ISSUE: A SURVEY OF AFRICA'S BUSINESS AND FINANCE

"All the News That's Fit to Print"

The New York Times

LATE CITY EDITION

Weather: Cloudy later today; snow likely tonight. Cloudy tomorrow. Temp. range: today 26-15; Thurs. 19-9. Full U.S. report on Page 39.

VOL. CXX....No. 41,278 — © 1971 The New York Times Company. — NEW YORK, FRIDAY, JANUARY 29, 1971 — 15 CENTS

U.A.W. MAINTAINS A JERSEY SUBURB KEEPS OUT POOR

Complains to Rights Division That Members Can't Live Near Ford Mahwah Plant

ONE-ACRE ZONING CITED

National Housing Committee Joins in Class Action—National Impact Seen

By RONALD SULLIVAN
Special to The New York Times

NEWARK, Jan. 28 — The United Auto Workers and the National Committee Against Discrimination in Housing filed a complaint here today charging that local zoning laws are depriving union members—many of them low-income blacks—from living near their jobs at the Ford Motor Company assembly plant in Mahwah.

The complaint, which was filed with the State Division on Civil Rights, represents the first legal challenge in the country by a major American labor union of local land-use restrictions that effectively exclude low-income residents, a committee official said.

The fight to abolish such zoning practices shows every sign of becoming a burning public issue in the nation's suburbs, which face new population pressures and rising local property taxes.

Resistance Expected

Because New Jersey is the most densely populated state and is a microcosm of virtually every form of urban and suburban crisis, state officials and civil rights activists believe that New Jersey will be the country's major battleground on zoning practices.

And because many communities regard families with low or moderate incomes as a financial drain on limited municipal resources, they are expected to oppose any changes that encourage additional population.

In today's complaint, which was filed as a class action in behalf of a number of Ford workers, the auto union and the committee against discrimination charged that Mahwah's one-acre minimum zoning re-

Continued on Page 16, Column 1

9 Banks Agree to Finance Housing Over East River

$72-Million Is Provided for 1,460-Unit Complex Planned on Platform

East River
WATERSIDE
BELLEVUE HOSPITAL
U.N. SCHOOL
MANHATTAN
The New York Times Jan. 29, 1971

By GLENN FOWLER

Nine of the city's largest commercial banks have formed a consortium to provide nearly $72-million to make possible construction of Waterside, the long-delayed housing development for 1,460 families on a six-acre platform over the East River alongside Bellevue Hospital.

The financing arrangement, the first consortium to back middle-income housing here, was concluded after many weeks of negotiations following fruitless efforts by the project's sponsors to obtain money through more conventional means, such as individual banks.

Conceived nearly a decade ago, Waterside wound its way through bureaucratic processes to "final" approval by the Board of Estimate three years ago last month, only to come up against an increasingly tight money market that blocked the start of work until the consortium of banks was persuaded to come to the rescue. Construction is expected to take three years.

Announcing the end of the impasse at a City Hall news conference yesterday, Mayor Lindsay praised the banks for "reaffirming their faith not only in the future of New York City, but also in the capacity of private industry and municipal government to produce together quality housing for families with a wide range of incomes."

Waterside will consist of four towers, three of them 37

Continued on Page 17, Column 2

PRESIDENT URGES MILITARY PAY RISE TO HELP END DRAFT

Asks Congress to Approve $1.5-Billion in Benefits—His Budget Due Today

By ROBERT B. SEMPLE Jr.
Special to The New York Times

WASHINGTON, Jan. 28—President Nixon asked Congress today to approve $1.5-billion in pay increases and other benefits for servicemen to help achieve his goal of ending the military draft by mid-1973.

Mr. Nixon's second legislative message to the new Congress included several proposals submitted but not approved last year. Among them were a request to eliminate gradually the deferments for undergraduates and divinity students and a proposal designed to remove inequities in the lottery system for Selective Service.

The President also asked for a two-year extension of the draft. The current draft law expires July 1, but Mr. Nixon said, "Considerations of national security make it imperative that we continue induction authority at this time."

Target Dates Coincide

The expiration date of such a two-year extension would thus coincide with the July 1, 1973, target that Mr. Nixon has set for establishing an all-volunteer force that would no longer depend on conscription.

At noon tomorrow, President Nixon will formally submit another message to Congress, his budget for the 1972 fiscal year, which begins July 1.

It is known that the budget will propose spending of $229.2-billion and involve a deficit in excess of $10-billion.

The budget and the deficit will, however, be defended by the Administration on the ground that a deficit of this size is needed at this time to stimulate recovery from the economic recession.

50 Per Cent Increase

The President has promised the spending will not exceed the amount the Government would collect in taxes if the economy were operating at full employment. Spending of this amount is not considered inflationary by most economists, in and out of the Administration.

At the heart of the military message was Mr. Nixon's request for $1.5-billion in new funds aimed at "making military service more attractive to present and potential members." The new funds would provide roughly a 50 per cent increase in pay for most enlisted men, and would subsidize

Continued on Page 7, Column 3

United Press International

TESTIFIES ON CAMBODIA: Secretary of State William P. Rogers, left, with Senator J. W. Fulbright of Arkansas, chairman of Foreign Relations Committee, in the Capitol.

ROGERS ASSURES SENATORS ON ROLE IN CAMBODIA WAR

Says U.S. Has No Intention of Expanding the Scope of Its Military Activities

MEETS FOREIGN PANEL

Members Appear Mollified —Plan to Hold Public Hearings Is Dropped

By JOHN W. FINNEY
Special to The New York Times

WASHINGTON, Jan. 28 — Secretary of State William P. Rogers assured a restive Senate Foreign Relations Committee today that the Administration had no intention of expanding the scope of American military activities in Cambodia.

Mr. Rogers also said at a closed meeting of the committee that the Administration did not plan to seek relaxation of the Cooper-Church amendment, which bars the introduction of ground combat troops and military advisers into Cambodia.

[In Pnompenh, official sources said that United States servicemen sent to Cambodia to supervise the use of military equipment would wear civilian clothing and be unarmed. The sources would not rule out, however, the possibility that the men would give some advice to Cambodian troops.]

Senators Seem Reassured

The Rogers assurances to the committee appeared to mollify those members who had been raising critical questions suggesting that the recent expansion of air operations over Cambodia violated the spirit if not the letter of the Cooper-Church amendment, which Congress attached last year to a supplementary military aid bill.

After the hearing, the two co-sponsors of the amendment—John Sherman Cooper, Republican of Kentucky, and Frank Church, Democrat of Idaho — both agreed that thus far the Administration had not violated the Congressional restrictions.

Much of the same opinion was expressed by Senator J. W. Fulbright, the chairman, and other committee members, such as Jacob K. Javits, Republican of New York; George Aiken, Republican of Vermont, and Edmund S. Muskie, Democrat of Maine.

Some Had Been Critical

In the face of the Rogers assurances, given during a three-and-a-half-hour briefing, the committee had clearly retreated from the harshly critical position it had begun to assume toward the Administration on the Cambodian issue.

The committee quietly dropped tentative plans for public hearings. Senator Fulbright explained that Mr.

Continued on Page 2, Column 5

U.S. Warns Newark to Cut Housing Waste or Lose Aid

By STEVEN R. WEISMAN
Special to The New York Times

NEWARK, Jan. 28—A team of Federal housing specialists charged today that the Newark Housing Authority was "top-heavy" with superfluous employes and "wasteful" in its management of the city's public housing and urban renewal programs.

A report by the 40 specialists ordered further that the authority, which is approaching a $1-million debt in its operating expenses, undertake a major reorganization of its personnel or face the loss of continued Federal assistance.

The report was commissioned by the Federal Department of Housing and Urban Development, which had been asked by Congress last year to investigate debt-ridden housing authorities around the country before it approved additional Federal money to meet their deficits.

Newark officials, including Mayor Kenneth A. Gibson, were told of the findings at a meeting this afternoon with Federal investigators and housing officials. The Housing Authority was told to submit proposals for the reorganization by Feb. 22.

Mayor Gibson stated that the report "says many things that need saying." He said he would appoint a committee of representatives from his adminis-

Continued on Page 17, Column 6

SOCIAL-WORK UNIT CHANGING TACTICS

Community Service Society Ends Aid for Individuals —Plans Wider Role

By DAVID K. SHIPLER

The city's oldest private social agency, the Community Service Society, announced yesterday that it would end 123 years of family casework and individual counseling.

The techniques, it said, had proved inadequate for the poor who face overwhelming problems in the slums. Trapped by these larger problems, society officials said, the poor lack the freedom of the middle-class to deal with their own personal difficulties.

The society therefore plans to attack those total problems by working directly with existing neighborhood groups to deliver services, to exert pressure on government agencies and to coordinate existing public and private programs.

While the society is not yet clear about what specific work it will do, officials say that projects might range from bookkeeping services for community groups to setting up day-care centers.

"If you don't deal with the

Continued on Page 46, Column 3

VOLPE ENLARGES RAILPAX SYSTEM

He Issues Final Version of a New Passenger Network —Service to Be Halved

By CHRISTOPHER LYDON
Special to The New York Times

WASHINGTON, Jan. 28—Secretary of Transportation John A. Volpe issued today a final outline of basic rail passenger service to be operated by a quasi-governmental corporation beginning May 1.

The new network significantly expands the Nixon Administration's first proposal, made two months ago, but eliminates about half the passenger trains now running after a decade of heavy attrition.

The major additions to the system, made in response to concerted pressure of passengers, labor unions, and state and Federal regulators, are two long routes now operated by the Southern Pacific Company — between Seattle and San Diego and between Los Angeles and New Orleans.

Other additions to the original network of 16 intercity routes are the route between Norfolk, Va., and Cincinnati; the route between St. Louis and Kansas City, and a spur line to Tampa and St. Petersburg on the west coast

Continued on Page 39, Column 4

Connally Tells Senators Nixon Seeks Tax Reform

By JAMES M. NAUGHTON
Special to The New York Times

WASHINGTON, Jan. 28—John B. Connally Jr. told the Senate Finance Committee today that President Nixon had directed him to develop a broad tax reform program once his nomination as Secretary of the Treasury has been confirmed.

The former Democratic Governor of Texas did not outline the scope of the reform plan, nor did committee members seek details in a swift, friendly examination of Mr. Connally's views that indicated he would receive the committee's approval.

But Administration officials said privately that Mr. Nixon had in mind asking Congress to enact in 1972 fundamental changes in which a value-added tax on goods and services—in effect a national sales tax—would supplant other forms of taxation at Federal and state levels.

Mr. Connally said only that Mr. Nixon wanted the Treasury to examine "any possible tax" and that if the reform should be based on a value-added tax it would be "in lieu of" other taxes rather than in addition to them.

The President is "extremely concerned" about high property and income tax rates "at all levels," Mr. Connally told the committee. He added that Mr.

Continued on Page 12, Column 3

JERUSALEM SLOWS HOUSING PROJECTS

Mayor Says Controversial Plans for Arab Areas Need Further Study

Special to The New York Times

JERUSALEM, Jan. 28—Mayor Teddy Kollek announced today that controversial new Israeli housing projects on the rocky hillsides around Jerusalem would be delayed pending further esthetic and urban-development study.

He denied that there were any political motives behind the slowdown, rejecting suggestions from abroad that Israel should halt construction in Arab sectors while peace talks were under way with neighboring governments.

"It would be a disaster for the city if we would stop building," he told newsmen. "The argument we have is an urbanistic and esthetical argument, not a political argument. To inject a political argument at this stage of town planning is fallacious."

The Mayor called two news conferences, one conducted in Hebrew and one in English for the foreign press, to answer criticism of the development

Continued on Page 8, Column 1

LEFRAK SETTLES U.S. SUIT ON BIAS

Action Dropped After Pact on Renting Procedures

By RICHARD REEVES

The Department of Justice and Samuel J. Lefrak, one of the nation's largest builders, reached an agreement yesterday in which the Lefrak Organization promised to prohibit discrimination in apartment rentals.

It also promised to give the equivalent of a month's free rent to 50 black families to assist them in moving into predominantly white buildings.

In return, the Justice Department agreed to drop its suit against the builder. It had charged racial discrimination in the renting of apartments.

The Lefrak affiliates agreed to the order and contract without admitting any violation of the 1968 law, which was the basis of the Federal charges.

The agreement between the Government and Lefrak associates—formalized in a consent decree signed by Judge Jack B. Weinstein of the United States District Court in Brooklyn — concluded legal action that began last August. The Justice Department at that time charged discrimination in the renting of 21,000 Lefrak-controlled apartments in 150 buildings in Brooklyn and Queens.

The resolution of the case, described by the Justice Department as the largest housing case in its history, was based on two separate agreements,

Continued on Page 16, Column 1

New Setup Is Urged At Juvenile Centers

By MARTIN ARNOLD

In a report replete with details of leaking roofs and dilapidated rooms, of official confusion and of teachers who sometimes refuse to teach, a special panel investigating the city's three juvenile detention centers recommended yesterday that their administration be transferred from the judicial system to the Mayor's office.

In its 87-page report, the court-appointed panel also called for the construction of detention centers and the creation of a city agency responsible for the care of all children who come under the jurisdiction of the city, including those in the detention centers.

Mayor Lindsay immediately hailed the study as an "excellent and important document" and said an "extensive" investigation would be undertaken to

Continued on Page 15, Column 4

Arabs in Israel: Minority Torn Between 2 Worlds

The New York Times/Carol Goster

Israeli Arab women in a part of their Abu Ghosh home that is provided for livestock. Woman photographer took picture—men visitors do not generally see women at home.

By PETER GROSE
Special to The New York Times

ABU GHOSH, Israel, Jan. 28—"As Israeli Arabs, our problem is that other Arabs dismiss us as Israelis and other Israelis suspect us as Arabs."

Speaking in a soft and cultured voice, Dr. Subhi Abu Ghosh, a 42-year-old social scientist thus summed up the identity crisis of 330,000 Arabs who chose, or whose parents chose, to live under the flag of Israel.

These are the more modest families of Palestine who decided in 1948 to remain in their cities, towns, villages and farms within the newly proclaimed country, rather than flee, like the intelligentsia and politically conscious, to become refugees in neighboring Arab countries.

Now an inarticulate minority in an alien society, their plight has political, economic and social aspects. There are no powerful champions of the Israeli Arabs, neither within their own ranks nor in foreign capitals, near or far. No one takes up their cause; they have produced no rebels.

The rest of Israel is bustling and building. The Arab villages remain dusty or muddy, depending on the season, sleepy and crumbling as they have been

Continued on Page 8, Column 1

Council Group Votes Taxi Bill, But Full Passage Is Delayed

A City Council committee yesterday approved a package of taxicab legislation, including a fare increase that would come to $41-million a year and the setting up of a regulatory commission for medallion cabs and for-hire limousines.

Then the Council leadership, unable to muster pledges of the 25 votes needed to speed the plan to immediate passage by the full Council, laid the package over.

When the rules permit it to be acted on next, after eight days, "we have indications it will pass," said the Democratic majority leader, Thomas J. Cuite.

"Tonight the votes were just not available," he said after a two-minute meeting that officially brought the package before the full Council.

The committee package, which can be brought up for passage by a simple majority of the Council in eight days, has two major components:

¶An increase in fares, to 60 cents for the first fifth of a mile and 10 cents for each additional fifth. The present fare is 45 cents for the first sixth of a mile and 10 cents for each additional third of a mile.

¶Establishment of a regulatory commission for limousines

Continued on Page 39, Column 7

NEWS INDEX

The News Summary and Index appears on Page 2; obituary news, Page 40; transportation, Page 39.

Fig. 5-1. Balance. This page is an example of balance makeup, but the **Times** is less balanced than it used to be. Note the good-sized pictures, the Oxford rules, and the near balance of a picture with a two-column headline.

COLDER
Cloudy tonight with possible light snow, much colder, low 15 to 20. Cloudy, colder with snow flurries Tuesday, high in 20s.

KANKAKEE DAILY JOURNAL

New York Times Service · Copley News Service · The Associated Press · UPI Telephoto · United Press International · Newspaper Enterprise Association

118th YEAR · NO. 124 · ALL PHONES 933-7711 · KANKAKEE, ILLINOIS, MONDAY, JANUARY 25, 1971 · SINGLE COPIES 10 CENTS · TWO SECTIONS · 20 PAGES

Injured Girl Taken From Wreckage

Rescue workers carry an injured young girl from the wreckage of a derailed Long Island Railroad train late Sunday. At least one person died, about 40 others were injured and two youths remained trapped in the twisted metal. Police believe that a switch may have been sabotaged. (UPI Telephoto)

Obote's Government Toppled In Uganda

Many Jubilant Africans Join Street Parades

KAMPALA, Uganda (UPI)—Heavy fighting involving tanks and armored cars broke out in Kampala before dawn today, and Gen. Idi Amin, the British trained army commander, said he and E. W. Oryema, chief of the country's police force, had seized power "in the interest of the people."

President Milton Obote was out of the country at the time and was due in Nairobi, Kenya, today on his way home from the British Commonwealth Prime Ministers' Conference in Singapore. Members of his government urged him to remain there until the situation is "clarified."

THOUSANDS of jubilant Africans paraded through the streets of Kampala, celebrating Obote's downfall. A radio broadcast said the new government would "cement" friendly ties with all foreign governments.

News of the coup was broadcast by the official Kampala radio.

Seven persons were reported killed in the predawn fighting in the capital, and a report from Entebbe Airport said a shell exploded at the airport terminal, killing several Africans. Fighting also was reported on the 21-mile stretch of road from Kampala to Entebbe and witnesses said they saw bodies there.

Obote was the second African leader to be overthrown while out of his country. The Ghana army overthrew President Kwame N. Nkrumah on Feb. 24, 1966, while he was paying an official visit to Moscow.

TROOPS WITH armored cars surrounded Parliament and Obote's residence and fired shots into the air to warn people away

The radio announcer, who identified himself only as "a Ugandan soldier," said the army "has taken over the government because it is totally dissatisfied with Obote's economic policies and corruption and tribalism in the government."

Obote, president of the former British protectorate since 1966, was en route home today from last week's commonwealth conference in Singapore. He was scheduled to stop first in Nairobi, Kenya.

The troops who blanketed the area around Parliament and Obote's home fired over the heads of all who approached.

DIPLOMATS said the airport at entebbe, 21 miles south on Lake Victoria, was closed.

The radio announcement declared a curfew from 6:30 a.m. to 5 p.m.

The broadcast did not say who was leading the coup.

The radio bulletin said the new government would seek friendly ties with all foreign governments, but warned other governments to stay out of the Uganda fracas.

The new leader will be "a Ugandan fellow soldier," the announcer said.

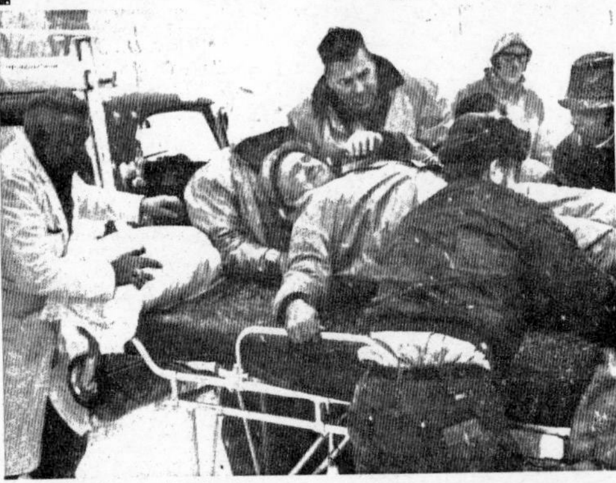

Snow Plow Operator Is Injured

Clarence Watson, 51, is assisted to an ambulance Sunday after being rescued from his snowplow which was buried by a snow slide Sunday near the scene of an avalanche in Washington in which four persons died. (UPI Telephoto)

Apollo 14 Flight Counting Begins

CAPE KENNEDY, Fla. (AP) — Electrical power surged into the Saturn 5 rocket and spaceship today as the launch team began the six-day countdown for the Apollo 14 moon-landing flight.

As the lengthy count got under way aiming for a Sunday liftoff, the three astronauts who will fly the mission underwent their final major physical examination.

TEST SUPERVISOR Charles Henschel gave the signal and the countdown clock started right on schedule, ticking backwards from 102 hours.

The count actually extends over a longer period, but there are five planned "holds" totaling 38 hours 23 minutes to provide any necessary catchup work.

Barring problems, the Saturn 5 will blast away from Cape Kennedy at 3:23 p.m. Sunday to start Apollo 14 on its daring journey of discovery.

The astronauts—Alan B. Shepard Jr., Edgar D. Mitchell and Stuart A. Roosa—planned several hours with doctors today.

PURPOSE OF the extensive examination is to make certain the pilots are physically fit and to provide medical data for in-flight and post-flight comparison.

It was after a similar exam last April that doctors announced all three Apollo 13 crewmen had been exposed to German measles. Tests revealed that one of them, Thomas K. Mattingly, was not immune, and he was replaced on the flight crew by backup command module pilot John L. Swigert.

The astronauts spent a relaxed day Sunday, with their time occupied by a mixture of fishing, flying, televised football and flight plans.

$10 Billion Deficit Seen In Budget

WASHINGTON (UPI)—The budget President Nixon will send to Congress Friday will total a record $229.2 billion — including a deficit of more than $10 billion, White House sources said today.

The $229.2 billion figure compares with a $200.8 billion budget the President proposed one year ago for the current fiscal year. That budget was to have produced a $1.3 billion surplus, but economic conditions worsened and anticipated revenue failed to materialize, forcing Nixon to change his figures in May to about $215 billion, with an expected deficit of $15 billion.

Nixon already has said his budget for the business year beginning July 1 yould be an expansionary one —"One that will help stimulate the economy and thereby open up new job opportunities for millions of Americans."

In his State of the Union address Friday, Nixon said the new budget would call for the government to spend as though the nation had full employment.

4 Killed In Snow Avalanche

WENATCHEE, Wash. (AP) — Four persons died and six were injured when an avalanche crushed one ski cabin and hit another on Stevens Pass atop the Cascade Range in Western Washington.

All but one of the victims were in a cabin that was flattened by the slide Sunday, authorities said.

The other, Peggy Dean, 12, Seattle, died in another cabin when snow filled her bedroom.

Four of the injured, all in one family, were trapped together. They were Mr. and Mrs. Billy 8.

Their third child, Kenny, 9, was among the four killed.

The other two dead, in the same smashed structure, were Mr. and Mrs. Barton Edgers of Seattle.

Another snowslide buried Clarence Watson, 51, when it hit the snow scoop he was operating to clear an earlier slide near the Stevens Pass summit. He was rescued about half an hour after the slide smashed the windshield and filled the cab.

Phnom Penh Under Full Alert; U.S. Forces Leave Road Area

PHNOM PENH (UPI)—South Vietnamese and American forces ended their operation along Cambodia's vital Highway 4 linking Phnom Penh to the sea today, declared the road open and withdrew their forces, military spokesmen said.

Phnom Penh, a city unnerved by three nights of terrorist attacks, was in a state of full alert, with fighting continuing in the surrounding countryside. Communist troops fired a pair of 122mm Soviet-built rockets at Pochenton Airport, blasted by the Communists Friday. The missiles fell short and wounded two villagers.

In Saigon, the South Vietnamese announced they had completed repairs on two bridges south of the Pich Nil Pass on Highway 4 and the road was open. They turned over security to the Cambodians at 7 a.m. and almost immediately the 5,300 South Vietnamese troops were pulled out of the area.

The spokesman said 1,500 Marines returned to their permanent base inside Cambodia at the Mekong River ferry town of Neak Luong, 35 miles southeast of Phnom Penh, and 3,800 rangers and armored cavalrymen drove back to South Vietnamese territory on Highway 3 along the seacoast.

U.S spokesmen in Saigon said two helicopter carriers which had supported U.S. Army AH1 Cobra rocket-firing helicopters making air strikes in direct support of the South Vietnamese and Cambodians during the battle ended their operations today and sailed away from their off-shore stations in the Gulf of Thailand.

It was not known exactly when the American air support began, although officials first acknowledged presence of the two carriers Jan. 17.

A bomb demolished an annex to Phnom Penh's electric power offices Sunday night, injuring six persons. It was the third night of terrorism that started with the major Communist attack on the Cambodian capital's airport early Friday morning.

Military officials ordered the full-scale alert following the blast at the electric annex. Civilians joined soldiers guarding government buildings and heavy military guards were placed at the approaches to Phnom Penh from the south and east, including the two main bridges across the Mekong River.

In Saigon, South Vietnamese military spokesmen said South Vietnam withdrew nearly half of its 5,300-man expeditionary force from the operation to clear Cambodia's Highway 4, the vital land link running from Phnom Penh to the seaport of Kompong Som. It had been closed by Communists Nov. 21 and the joint Cambodian-South Vietnamese expedition succeeded in reopening it Friday aftar a week of bitter fighting.

Three was no indication where the 2,500 South Vietnamese rangers and armored cavalry who left the Highway 4 area were headed.

U.N. Unsafe In New York Says Pravda

MOSCOW (UPI)—The Communist party newspaper Pravda thinks the United Nations should be removed from New York if "hostile hooligans" there continue attacks against Soviet diplomats and offices.

A Pravda story Sunday from New York correspondent Omas Kolesnichenko implied that U.S. authorities intentionally encouraged attacks on Soviet and Arab missions to the United Nations.

"INDEED, WHAT else can explain the fact that American authorities have not taken effective measures to cut short and prevent hostile hooligan actions?

"Now, as the question of construction of new United Nations buildings in New York is being discussed, it is necessary...to give serious thought to the question of whether the United Nations can count on normal functioning in that city."

The Pravda story was part of the continuing Soviet campaign of retaliation against harassment of Soviets in the United States by militant Zionists. The campaign has included intimidaton of American residents in Moscow.

KOLESNICHENKO, in his Pravda article, said "more than once many delegates of the United Nations raised the question of the feasibility of the further locating of the U.N. headquarters in New York, a city that...has become a center of organized crime and gangsterism."

The Soviets repeatedly have insisted the United States has "connived" in attacks on Soviet diplomats by militant Jewish groups.

Groppi Ruling Struck Down In High Court

WASHINGTON (UPI)—The Supreme Court struck down today a Wisconsin law barring a change of venue for jury trials in misdemeanor cases, ruling that the Rev. James E. Groppi was entitled to new consideration at the state level of a conviction in Milwaukee.

Groppi was arrested during several days of demonstrations in 1968 after Milwaukee Mayor Henry Maier issued a proclamation banning night demonstrations. He was convicted by a jury, fined $500 and sentenced to six months in jail.

The case now goes back to the Wisconsin Supreme Court, which upheld the conviction by a divided vote on Feb. 4,1969.

The court agreed today to rule whether a 50-year-old court order prevents the Greyhound Corp. from continuing its control over Armour & Co., the nation's second largest meatpacker.

The Armour case was before the high court in June, 1970, in connection with takeover action by General Host Corp. But the court threw out the case when Greyhound was substituted for General Host, which is in the bakery, convenience grocery and restaurant business.

The Interstate Commerce commission (ICC) which regulates transportation, authorized the Greyhound takeover. The company's interest in the huge meatpacking concern now amounts to 86 per cent.

Wintry Landscape

The last few days have presented spring-like weather, but a few days ago it was cold and the prediction for Tuesday similar. See photos page 8.

Obscene Phone Calls

A telephone company official says a major factor in the obscene call problem is the willingness of some people to lend an ear. See OBSCENE TELEPHONER page 12.

Phosphate Information

The Federal Trade Commission proposes new regulations for the issuance of phosphate information by detergent manufacturers. See FTC PROPOSES page 5.

U. S.-Cambodia Involvement Pursued

WASHINGTON (AP) — United States involvement in Cambodia has "reached the borderline and maybe stepped over" the limitations imposed by Congress, says Sen. George D. Aiken.

But the Vermont Republican, senior GOP member of the Senate Foreign Affairs Committee, was outstripped in his assessment by Senate Democratic Leader Mike Mansfield, who declared the American air support in Cambodia "contrary to the intent and spirit" of the congressional restrictions.

Although a closed meeting of the Foreign Relations Committee was called today, some senators, Mansfield among them, want the panel to hold public hearings on whether Nixon has gone beyond limits put on his action in Southeast Asia last year—the Cooper-Church Amendment.

The amendment—named for sponsoring Sens. John Sherman Cooper, R-Ky., and Frank Church, D-Idaho—bars U.S. combat ground troops and military advisers from Cambodia Eyewitness reports and photographs last week indicated U.S. helicopter crewmen have set foot on Cambodian soil, but White House and Pentagon officials denied they were advisers.

Criticism of American action in Cambodia spread over the weekend. In Sacramento, Calif., Sen. Edmund S. Muskie, D-Maine, said:

"We're just putting our big toe over the treshold. Before we know it, the whole foot and leg are over the threshold . . ."

Muskie, the undeclared front-runner for his party's nomination to the presidency, also is being recommended by the Democratic Steering Committee to be named to the Foreign Relations Committee.

Sen George McGover, the only announced Democratic candidate for the presidential nomination, said Nixon's "failure to pull us out of the Vietnam quicksand promptly and decisively is not an act of strength, but rather reveals a lack of the strength needed to face up to the enormity of our error and the seriousness of our predicament."

McGovern and Muskie both spoke at the California Democratic Convention.

Mansfield suggested Sunday that if the Foreign Affairs Committee doesn't call hearings to consider legislation covering the American role in Cambodia, he will call them himself in his Asian affairs subcommittee.

Aiken expressed reserve.

"I don't think we should continue hearings for the publicity for the Foreign Relations Committee," he said.

"I'm not about to participate in any policy of harassment" against the administration so long as it continues the policy of withdrawal from Southeast Asia, he added.

"If the main objective begins to get closer," he said, "then we have to be a little tolerant."

Secretary of State William P. Rogers said last week the United States will use air power in Cambodia whenever it is felt such action is needed to protect the remaining American troops in South Vietnam

BLOODMOBILE
Herscher — Lutheran Church
1 to 6 p.m. Wednesday
Civic Auditorium
Noon to 5 p.m. Thursday

Fig. 5-2. Splash. Big pictures, sans serif headlines, and elimination of column rules characterize the dramatic front page of the **Kankakee (Ill.) Daily Journal.**

The Weather

Today—Cloudy, rain likely, high in 50s. Monday—Mostly cloudy, chance of precipitation in the morning. Probability of precipitation, 60% today, 30% tonight. Temp.: Today, 38-50; Yesterday, 38-45. Details, D11.

The Washington Post

Times Herald

Index 296 Pages 17 Sections

Table of Contents, Page A2

92d Year · · No. 45 © 1969 The Washington Post Co. SUNDAY, JANUARY 19, 1969 Phone 223-6000 Circulation 223-6100 Classified 223-6200 30 cents Home delivered 35¢

New Law Protects Buyers

Mayor Signs Bill to Prevent Credit Abuses

By Phineas R. Fiske
Washington Post Staff Writer

Mayor Walter E. Washington yesterday signed into law strong consumer affairs regulations designed primarily to eliminate credit abuses affecting the city's poor.

The Mayor formally signed the regulations on the last day he could act, surrounded by eight of the nine City Council members.

The regulations require the licensing of all finance companies and merchants offering credit and full disclosure of the cost of goods and credit. They prohibit such abuses as "small-print" contracts, bar misleading advertising of credit terms, and protect a customer's rights when a purchase is repossessed.

The signing ceremony was set up to counteract any impression of a division between the Mayor and the Council over the Council's interpretation of its powers.

The differences were resolved when Council Chairman John W. Hechinger endorsed amendments the Mayor proposed and said he was "highly optimistic that the proposed changes will be enacted . . ."

The amendments deal primarily with the authority to create city offices and to exercise enforcement powers.

The regulations, as passed by the Council on Jan. 6, seemed to the Mayor to imply that the Council had the power to create an Office of Consumer Affairs and a Consumer Affairs Board. The regulations would also permit the Council to decide if the rules had been violated.

Mayor Washington replied in a letter to Hechinger, prepared late Friday, that the power to establish city offices was his, and that the 1967 Reorganization plan that created the local government did not give the Council enforcement powers.

Hechinger replied yesterday that "Council members view these regulations to be of such importance . . . that no jurisdictional questions should delay or hinder their adoption and implementation."

The Mayor's amendments

See CONSUMER, A23, Col. 4

By Frank Johnston—The Washington Post

Rainy Preview of the Inauguration Site

Two Washington visitors take a look at the Capitol Plaza, scene of Monday's Presidential Inauguration. Yesterday's rain is expected to be gone by the time Nixon takes his oath of office, but cloudy skies are predicted.

Allies and Reds Agree Swiftly on Rules for Talks

First Session On Issues Due in Days

By Murrey Marder
Washington Post Staff Writer

PARIS, Jan. 18 — The opening meeting of the four-way peace talks on Vietnam today reached unexpectedly swift agreement on procedure, clearing a path for substantive negotiations next week.

All initial technical obstacles for the conference either were surmounted or sidestepped by the United States, North Vietnam, South Vietnam and the National Liberation Front (Vietcong). This will enable negotiators of the four delegations to begin grappling next week with the basic questions of peace in Vietnam —possibly as early as Tuesday.

There were smiles of accomplishment all around from the tense adversaries as they emerged from a surprisingly business-like meeting that lasted five hours and ten minutes, with two coffee breaks. But the expressions of self-satisfaction today were counterbalanced by warnings—and evidence—that a prolonged diplomatic slugging match is ahead.

For American negotiators, it was an especially pleasing farewell token in the record of the Johnson Administration, which will hand over the negotiations to a Nixon Administration team next week.

Ambassador Cyrus R. Vance, senior representative at today's meeting, who will stay on in Paris for a month to ease the transition of American negotiators, told newsmen:

"I am happy to report that we have reached full agreement on all procedural questions for the first plenary session, which will take place early next week."

Vance said he was pleased "that we are getting down to the serious business of making peace in Vietnam." The long diplomatic process began here in early May with discussions limited to the United States and North Vietnam.

North Vietnam's spokesman, Nguyen Thanh Le, pronounced today's work "a good result," saying "We consider everything was settled today and are ready for the plenary session."

The NLF and North Vietnam proposed during the meeting that the substantive talks should begin Tuesday, Jan. 21, the day after the Nixon Administration takes office. The United States and South Vietnam agreed to meet as early as possible next week, with American negotiators noting that they want to consult with their new chief of delegation, Henry Cabot Lodge, on his Paris arrival plans.

Lodge replaces Ambassador W. Averell Harriman, who is scheduled to leave Paris Sunday, and, according to Lodge, consult with Lodge in Washington.

Diplomats generally had as-

See TALKS, A22, Col. 1

Negotiators maintain own views of what is going on. Story Page A22.

Associated Press

Cyrus S. Vance, deputy chief of the U.S. delegation, waves as he leaves the International Conference Center in Paris, at the end of the first session of the new Vietnam peace talks yesterday.

Details of Phaseout Not Set, Thieu Says

By Peter Braestrup
Washington Post Foreign Service

SAIGON, Jan. 19—President Thieu today thanked President Johnson for committing U.S. troops to Vietnam and also said allied planning would start on the withdrawal this year of some American soldiers.

"Free Vietnam is today substantially stronger than it was, militarily as well as politically, and we shall not forget that it was mostly thanks to you that we have achieved these results," Thieu told Mr. Johnson in a letter he made public.

But Thieu in a separate statement declined to suggest figures or a timetable for a U.S. troop withdrawal.

"Detailed plans," he said would first have to be developed by Gen. Creighton W. Abrams, the U.S. commander in Vietnam and Gen. Cao Van Vien, chief of the joint general staff of the South Vietnamese forces.

Thieu cited his Dec. 31 speech and prior statements to the effect that in 1969 "the Republic of Vietnam armed forces will share more of the burden of the war so that part of the American troops can return home."

The statement pleased high-ranking U.S. officials here who had privately complained about the spate of newspaper stories, citing South Vietnamese sources, that Thieu planned to suggest publicly a withdrawal of 20,000 to 150,000 American troops this year as a sop to U.S. public opinion.

According to U.S. sources, Thieu discussed withdrawal prospects with U.S. Ambassador Ellsworth Bunker and Abrams Friday for the first time.

Thieu today said he had discussed the problem with Vien

See THIEU, A22, Col. 5

Clifford Sees Missile Lead Ending in '69

By George C. Wilson
Washington Post Staff Writer

A "large increase" in heavily protected ICBMs was "the most significant development" of 1968 in Soviet strategic weaponry, Defense Secretary Clark M. Clifford said yesterday.

In his only "posture" statement on the world military situation and Pentagon plans for dealing with it, Clifford said the Soviet Union will catch up to the United States by the end of this year in ICBMs, with each side having over 1000 buried underground and ready to fire.

While this closing of the missile gap numerically comes as no surprise, the Defense Secretary makes clear in his 165-page valedictory that the Soviets are advancing in quality, too. Also, their ICBM production is continuing while ours stopped at 1054 missiles.

President Nixon will have to decide what to do about it, with his main options being to match the Russians missile for missile or to improve the nu-

See WEAPONS, A6, Col. 1

50,000 Visitors Jam District for Inaugural

By Robert F. Levy
Washington Post Staff Writer

About 50,000 out-of-towners descended on the Nation's Capital yesterday to attend a Presidential Inauguration. They quickly found that while they may be ready for Monday's festivities, the city isn't yet.

Yesterday was a rainy gamut of taxi shortages, traffic snarls, purloined hotel rooms and unavailable tickets. There will be more of the same today, as another 50,000 people arrive, and a worse crush Monday, when 2 million are expected to attend the Inaugural Parade.

You could still obtain a tuxedo, a formal gown or a caterer yesterday for the 50 or so balls on the schedule.

But the city has run out of rent-a-cars, chauffeured limousines and boutonnieres. It might find itself short in a pinch, too, of long-distance telephone operators and hospital beds, spokesmen for those two industries said.

Traffic had already become unusually and ominously heavy yesterday, and many major downtown intersections were choked. Police reported 60 accidents by mid-day, twice as many as usual.

Parking—or lack of it—promises to be the supreme problem. In some sections of

See INAUGURAL, A4, Col. 5

Rules, routes and ritual for Inauguration Day and other Inaugural stories. Page A4.

D.C. Stadium Renamed for R. F. Kennedy

D.C. Stadium has been renamed the Robert F. Kennedy Memorial Stadium, Secretary of the Interior Stewart L. Udall, said yesterday.

"Bob was spartan in his adherence to physical fitness, he loved the out-of-doors, he loved people—and he gloried in the competition of sports," Udall noted in his announcement.

The renaming of the stadium was a joint action taken by the Interior Department, which has jurisdiction over the stadium site, and the D.C. Armory Board, which operates the stadium under a contract with the National Park Service.

Dedication ceremonies will be scheduled later.

'No War' Bible Verse Picked for Nixon Oath

By Carroll Kilpatrick
Washington Post Staff Writer

NEW YORK, Jan. 18—Richard M. Nixon will be sworn into office as the 37th President of the United States Monday with his hand on the Bible verse proclaiming the hope that nations "shall beat their swords into plowshares."

The President-elect, who will leave here Sunday afternoon for Washington, announced that Mrs. Nixon would hold two family Bibles, both open to Isaiah 2, verse 4, when he takes the oath from Chief Justice Earl Warren.

The verse expresses both the President's Quaker philosophy and his determination to bring the Vietnam fighting to an early end.

Mrs. Nixon will hold the opened Bibles, one on top of the other, as the President-elect "swears" to defend and protect the Constitution of the United States. He might have chosen to use the word "affirm" rather than "swear" in deference to his Quaker forebears, but it was announced today that he will use the traditional oath.

The verse on which the next President's hand will rest, one of the most famous in the Old Testament, reads in full:

"And He shall judge among the nations, and shall rebuke many people: and they shall beat their swords into plowshares, and their spears into pruninghooks: nation shall not lift up sword against nation, neither shall they learn war any more."

When Mr. Nixon was sworn in as Vice President in 1953 and 1957 he also had the Bible opened to the verse from Isaiah.

The Bibles to be used have been in the Nixon family for many years. One was printed in 1828 and the other in 1873. Both are bound in brown leather.

The President-elect and his wife are scheduled to leave their apartment here Sunday afternoon for the flight to Washington. They are to arrive at Andrews Air Force Base outside the city about 4 p.m. and from there will motor to the Statler-Hilton Hotel to spend the night.

Their daughters, Tricia Nixon and Julie Eisenhower, already are in Washington.

The President-elect spent his final full day here working alone in his apartment on his inaugural address. Raymond K. Price, who has helped with the drafting and will be a spe-

See NIXON, A5, Col. 1

Arts Patron Mrs. Bliss Dies

MRS. ROBERT WOODS BLISS

By Carl Bernstein
Washington Post Staff Writer

Mrs. Robert Woods Bliss, the benefactress of Dumbarton Oaks and one of the Nation's great philanthropists and patron of the arts, died Friday evening at her Georgetown home. She was 90 years old.

For the past 18 months Mrs. Bliss had been confined by illness to her home at 1537 28th st. nw., where she and her late husband moved after donating the 43-acre Dumbarton Oaks estate to the Federal Government and Harvard University in 1940.

Until she approached her 90th year, Mrs. Bliss continued to regularly visit Dumbarton Oaks, where the United Nations was conceived, where Harvard operates the renowned Center for Byzantine Studies, where a notable collection of Pre-Columbian art is displayed and where Mrs. Bliss created what is perhaps Washington's most magnificent garden.

The life of Mildred Barnes Bliss was closely bound to Dumbarton Oaks, which she and her diplomat husband purchased in 1920.

Largely under her direction, the 169-year-old estate was

See BLISS, A8, Col. 1

Pressure Politics on International Level

'Biafra Lobby' Melds Left and Right

By William Chapman
Washington Post Staff Writer

Patrick J. Frawley Jr. is an ultra-conservative multimillionaire whose corporate profits have supported right-wing, anti-Communist crusades for several years.

Martin A. Peretz is a wealthy Harvard professor whose money has nourished a variety of New Left causes and the political campaign of Sen. Eugene J. McCarthy.

Normally, they have no common interests. But today they support separate organizations with the identical goal of pressuring the U.S. Government to recognize and assist Biafra—the small enclave in Africa engaged in a death struggle with the military government of Nigeria.

The involvement of such opposites as Peretz and Frawley symbolizes the broad nature and growing strength of the "Biafra lobby," one of the strangest alliances of political forces to take shape in recent years.

The alliance embraces the New Left and the old right, idealistic Peace Corps volunteers and Kansas Rotarians, passionate Irish Catholic priests and some militant blacks.

On Capitol Hill, the Biafran cause has enlisted such supporters as Sen. Edward M. Kennedy (D-Mass.), a liberal, and Rep. Donald E. Lukens (R-Ohio), a conservative. Such powerful elders as Sen. Richard Russell (D-Ga.) and House Speaker John McCormack have lent their assistance.

And the White House will be occupied tomorrow by President-elect M. Nixon, who has taken a more vigorously pro-Biafran position than any other major political figure.

The elements of the Biafran lobby have motives as diverse as their origins. Some only want to feed starving people. Others want U.S. air cover for private relief planes. Others want official recognition for a "Republic of Biafra." Others want U.S. arms in Biafran hands. Conservatives, particularly, see Biafra as a block to Communist expansion because it is fighting

See BIAFRA, A14, Col. 1

Fig. 5-3. Capitol dignity. The **Washington Post** maintains a neat, dignified appearance with the restrained use of white space. A modest border of white enhances pictures, and the white left by the indentation of short stories sets them off. Note that some column rules are missing.

Stocks: 20 month high!

Bolstered by the heaviest week of trading in history, the stock market closed Friday at its highest level in 20 months.

The Dow Jones industrial average rose 3.36 points to 868.50. Winners outnumbered losers about 2 to 1.

Volume Friday totaled 20,960,000 shares on the New York Stock Exchange, bringing the total for the week to 100,870,000 million shares. This wiped out the previous one-week record of 92,282,680 shares, set in the week ended last Dec. 4. See Page 25.

$1,100
Mystery jackpot
See if you won, Page 10

Living costs: Up for 14th month

Story in Column 3 below

Colder

Chicago—Windy, much colder, high about 10. **Illinois**—Partly cloudy, windy and much colder, highs around 5 above north to 20s south. See Page 10.

CHICAGO DAILY NEWS

An Independent Newspaper

©1971 by Field Enterprises Inc.

Weekend Edition

96th Year, Number 25 104 Pages in 7 Sections Saturday-Sunday, January 30-31, 1971 25 Cents Phone 321-200 **State**

U.S. judges upset law

Abortions OKd in state

Link truck law, Powell stocks

By John Camper
Of Our Springfield Bureau

SPRINGFIELD, Ill. — In the 1950s, Paul Powell helped push through legislation that put mud flaps on Illinois trucks.

And now the official inventory of Powell's estate has revealed that Powell invested heavily in companies that manufactured the flaps.

As a state representative in

Reveal $150,000 more Powell assets. Page 4.

1955, Powell fought long and hard to ensure passage of a law requiring trucks to use a rigid contour-type mud guard over the rear tires.

The truckers lost a two-year court battle against the law and then tried to get the Legislature to repeal it in 1957.

Powell fought the repeal attempt.

NEWSPAPERS learned that former Gov. John H. Stelle and his onetime purchasing agent, George Edward Day, were stockholders in Contour Truck Guards Inc. which had a cor-

Turn to Page 4, Column 1

Nixon budget goes in red by $11 billion

By Peter Lisagor
Our Washington Bureau Chief

WASHINGTON — President Nixon Friday sent Congress a $229.2 billion budget — $11.6 billion in the red — in which he outlined controversial new departures in turning federal revenues back to states and cities.

The fiscal 1972 estimate of income and outlays was described by the President as

Other budget stories on Pages 2 and 12.

"expansionary but not inflationary" because of the full-employment concept on which it was based.

Under that concept, the President explained, spending

Turn to Page 11, Column 1

Living cost up .4 pct. in Chicago

By Les Hausner

The cost of living in the Chicago area rose for the 14th consecutive month in December, advancing four-tenths of 1 per cent, mainly because of sharply higher food prices.

Nationally, prices rose by five-tenths of 1 per cent last month. The Bureau of Labor Statistics said prices in Chicago and nationally rose by 5.5 per cent in 1970.

That means that in December it took $10.55 to purchase the same goods and services $10 could obtain a year earlier.

THE BUREAU also reported that despite higher paychecks, the purchasing power of factory workers dropped by 2.5 per cent in Chicago and by 1.5 per cent nationally in 1970.

The average weekly paycheck of factory workers rose by $1.03 last month to $122.43. But after deductions for taxes and Social Security and allowing for inflation, the purchas-

Turn to Page 11, Column 1

No mercury, arsenic at Kellogg's plant

WASHINGTON (UPI) — The Food and Drug Administration (FDA) said Friday that an inspection of the Kellogg's plant at Battle Creek, Mich., had revealed no traces of mercury or arsenic in cereal.

The statement came in response to queries by reporters about a request by Sen. William Proximire (D-Wis.) for an FDA investigation into possible mercury contamination of certain food for minks, some of which comes from discarded Kellogg cereals.

A spokesman for the FDA, said the agency had been told through a congressional office last April of possible contamination in the cereals. He said the agency made an investigation in July, taking samples of cereal from the package assembly line and from that which had fallen onto the floor.

"Both were found to be negative for mercury and arsenic," the spokesman said.

Cereal that falls on the floor or is misshapen often is packaged and sold for animal food.

3 of French quints die

GRENOBLE, France (AP) — Two of the quintuplets born Thursday to a 29-year-old schoolteacher died during the night and a third expired Friday afternoon.

They were two boys and a girl. The remaining boy and girl were in incubators. The mother, Mrs. Michele Riondet, was reported in very weak condition.

In The News . . .

Today's chuckle

Why aren't more people happy if ignorance is bliss?
L&N Magazine

A bus driver and repairman work on the engine of a stalled bus that briefly stranded three dozen students from St. Ambrose School, Crest Hill, on I-55 at the edge of Chicago Friday. After the bus was restarted, the young priest in charge said the bus would return home rather than continue on the outing to the Museum of Science and Industry. "I've had about enough of this," said the harried priest. (Daily News Photo/Perry Riddle)

What's a girl like you. . .?

Passersby on Michigan Av. Friday encountered this chain-rattling sight. See story and another picture on Page 6.

3-in. snow blanket gives us zero 'comfort'

By Frank Brennan

Up to three inches of snow blanketed much of the Chicago area Friday before bitter cold moved in for the weekend.

Zero temperatures and powerful winds, gusting to 40 miles an hour and above, were expected to clamp the area in an intense deep freeze by early Saturday.

Travelers' warnings were issued by the National Weather Service, which predicted considerable blowing and drifting snow through the night.

STREETS and expressways were hazardous and often snow-packed in some sections, but salting and snow-removal crews of the state, county and city were out in force to clean thoroughfares before the temperatures dropped.

The heaviest snows of the fast-moving storm were dumped on the Waukegan-Fox Lake-Cary region, where 3 inches and more were reported.

Midway and O'Hare Airports each reported 2 inches of snow. The suburbs of Arlington Heights, Calumet City, Des Plaines, Elmhurst, Evanston, Oak Park, Park Forest, Park Ridge and Winnetka had up to 2 inches also.

THE SNOW, coming at the start of the morning rush hour, triggered minor accidents on streets and highways. State police reported several trucks jackknifed on tollways, and numerous intersections were tied

Turn to Page 11, Column 7

Court cites 'women's rights'

By Ed Kandlik and Lois Wille

A panel of three federal judges ruled Friday that the Illinois anti-abortion law is unconstitutional because it is vague and violates women's rights.

In their 2-to-1 decision, the judges also prohibited the state from prosecuting physicians who perform abortions during the first three months of pregnancy.

JUDGE EDWIN A. Robson said Judge Luther M. Swygert refused a request from an anti-abortion group, the Illinois Right to Life Committee, for an immediate stay of the order prohibiting prosecution.

This means Illinois physicians can perform abortions on women less than three months pregnant without fear of prosecution.

The Right to Life Committee asked for a stay until the United States Supreme Court rules on Fridya's action.

In their decision Judges Robson and Swygert, both Protestants, held that it is unconstitutional to prohibit abortions of women less than three months pregnant if performed by a licensed physician in a licensed medical clinic or hospital.

The majority opinion was written by Swygert, chief judge of the U.S. Court of Appeals.

Judge William J. Campbell, a Catholic, dissented.

"A statute which forces the birth of every fetus, no matter how defective or how intensely unwanted by its future parents, displays no legitimate state interests . . . especially when viewed with regard to

Turn to Page 11, Column 1

Condemned man's tortures

'God saved me in Death Row'

By Edward S. Gilbreth

Religion helped Charles Townsend endure the loneliness and mental torture of nearly 16 years on Death Row, he said Friday.

"I accepted God," said Townsend, whose murder conviction and death sentence were ruled invalid this week.

"I found myself and I promised God I wouldn't be bitter," he said.

Townsend, 35, sat calmly with his hands clasped on his lap as he discussed his Death Row life with newsmen in the

Interview sketches of Charles Townsend appear on Page 2.

chamber of U.S. District Judge Joseph Sam Perry.

TOWNSEND acknowledged that his fate was still in legal dispute because the state is seeking to have the U.S. Court of Appeals overrule Judge Perry's action in freeing him.

"A man born of woman can only withstand so much pressure," Townsend said, in discussing the possibility he may yet be executed in the electric chair.

"A racehorse can only run so far, then the best of him is gone," he added, lowering his eyes. "At the present time, I feel like I've gone as far as I can."

TOWNSEND SAID if the higher court rules against him, he would try to face death in the manner Richard Carpenter did when Carpenter was executed in 1958 for the murder of a Chicago policeman.

"He didn't want any help walking when they came to get him," Townsend recalled. "He walked to the electric chair almost as though he was glad. I think I would feel the same way, relieved that it was finally over."

Townsend said that shortly before Carpenter was executed in the County Jail, Carpenter told him:

"I'll be glad to get it over with . . . I am tired of living. I know that I'm going to die,

Turn to Page 2, Column 3

Fig. 5-4. Black headlines. The **Chicago Daily News** uses special black heads in the skyline and banner to produce a tone that is somewhat shrill. Note the Oxford rules around the story references and the white space around pictures.

THE MILWAUKEE JOURNAL

© 1969, by The Journal Company

ighty-seventh Year — 60 Pages | Monday, January 13, 1969 | Daily, per copy, 10 cents | Latest Edition ††

Johnson Will Urge Retention of Surtax

Washington, D. C. –UPI– ...esident Johnson will recom... nd extension of the 10% in... me tax surcharge for at least ... year, it was disclosed Mon...

Administration sources said ... president would include a ...quest for extension of the ... beyond its June 30 expira... n in his fiscal 1970 budget ...oposal, and that he would ...pose a budget showing a ...all surplus.

The White House announced ...t Johnson would send his ...dget to congress Wednesday ...on. His economic report will ...submitted Thursday.

Johnson will deliver his ...te of the Union address in ...son before a joint session of ...ngress at 8 p.m. Tuesday ...ilwaukee time). It will be ...adcast nationwide.

The White House announced ...t Johnson also would send ...congress later this week a ...ecial message recommend... salary increases for con...essmen and senators to ...ut $42,500. They now re...ve $30,000 a year, and a pro...sal is before congress for a ...000 raise.

The presidential press secre...y, George Christian, de...ned to discuss whether John...n had received support from ...esident - Elect Richard Nix... — which he reportedly re...ested — on his proposal to ...end the surtax.

A congressional source who ...clined the use of his name ...d: "You can assume that there has been agreement between the outgoing and incoming administrations."

Johnson will report a surplus for this fiscal year and will recommend continuation of the surtax in order to have a surplus next year, it was indicated. It has been reported that the surplus will run about $3 billion.

The current year's budget runs about $186 billion. There have been reports that the 1970 budget proposal will go as high as $195 billion.

Sources said Johnson believed the surtax ought to be removed as soon as possible, but that he felt the time was not yet right, because of inflationary pressure.

Humphrey Hints at Future Race

New York, N. Y. –AP– Vice-President Humphrey indicated Sunday night that he was not through with politics yet.

In a speech to 150 musicians, artists and writers at a dinner and reception in his honor, he said: "I feel so healthy, oh so healthy, for a man who's only 57 years old. And you . . . can make your own interpretations what that means."

He left it up to his listeners to decide whether he was referring to the next United States senate race or the 1972 presidential race.

$456 Million Boost in State Costs Likely

'A student lost is a penny saved!'

Needs Cited by Knowles in 2 Areas

By EUGENE C. HARRINGTON
Journal Madison Bureau

Madison, Wis. — State taxpayers will have to provide an additional $190.2 million in revenues to meet the increase in the number of students in state schools and persons in welfare institutions, Gov. Knowles said Monday.

The figure, cited at a meeting of the governor's education cabinet, created the distinct possibility that there will be a state general fund budget of $1.5 billion for the 1969-'71 biennium.

Last week, Knowles said that $266 million additional revenue would be needed to "do exactly what the state is doing now without including any new state programs or services."

The $190.2 million figure would be added to the estimated increase of last week. It would account for increased numbers of students and persons in welfare institutions.

3rd Category Due

The combination of the two — $456 million — would be added to the present state budget for 1967-'69 of $1.1 billion.

The two figures represent all but one category included in the state general fund budget. The third category is that of new programs and services, which still must be dealt with by Knowles.

The budget message to a joint session of the legislature now is planned for Jan. 30. Knowles has leaked the major portions of that budget in his two public statements to date. In the past, governors generally have withheld such information until a briefing for newsmen the night before the budget message is delivered.

State Aid Programs

Of the $190.2 million, Knowles said, $103.1 million would be necessary to provide the current level of services to more persons. In addition, $87.1 million would result from the increase in the persons served through local programs in which state aid is provided.

According to the governor, $55.8 million of the $87.1 million in increased state aids will be needed for aid to additional elementary and secondary school pupils.

The third and still undisclosed estimates on spending for the next two years — that for new programs — is not expected to be large. Knowles and the legislature, faced with a possible deficit of about $26 million at the end of the current two years, are not likely to approve many new programs.

Laird Selects Classmate for Key Post in Pentagon

Journal Washington Bureau

Washington, D. C. – Defense Secretary - Designate Melvin R. Laird Monday announced the selection of Robert F. Froehlke, 46, a Marshfield schoolmate, as assistant secretary of defense for administration.

Related story on page 18.

Froehlke, an executive of Sentry Insurance, was transferred last August from Stevens Point to Boston, where he serves as executive vice-president in charge of Sentry's New England region.

Froehlke was chairman of the Laird for Congress club in seven of Laird's eight congressional campaigns.

Froehlke has been a friend of Laird since their kindergarten days. They were classmates at Marshfield high school, where Froehlke was a member of the 1940 basketball team which was beaten by Shawano in the state tournament finals.

Froehlke had been with Sentry Insurance since 1952. He lives in Winchester, a Boston suburb, with his wife, Nancy, and their four children, Bruce, a sophomore at Haverford (Pa.) college, Jane, Ann and Scott.

He is a graduate of the University ...

Turn to Froehlke, page 3, col. 3

Robert F. Froehlke

CBS Official to Be Next USIA Chief

New York, N. Y. –AP– President - Elect Richard Nixon Monday named Frank Shakespeare, jr., a key campaign adviser and a Columbia Broadcasting System executive, to become director of the United States information agency.

Nixon also decided to fly to Key Biscayne, Fla., Monday night to put the final touches on the inaugural address he will deliver next Monday. He is expected to return to New York Friday.

Shakespeare, 44, is resigning as president of the CBS television services division, which oversees international TV operations for the CBS network. Shakespeare, a New York city native, held various posts with CBS since 1950, including assistant to the president and executive vice-president for CBS-TV. In 1957 and 1958 he was general manager of WXIX in Milwaukee, then a CBS owned television station.

Shakespeare was Nixon's television adviser during the campaign and developed the question and answer format programs which became a fixture of the Nixon vote drive.

Vessel Aground; Has 471 Aboard

London, England –AP– The ...itish liner Carmania with ... passengers aboard ran ...round on San Salvador is...d in the Bahamas Sunday ...ght, the Cunard line an...unced Monday.

The 22,000 ton ship was on a ...uise from Port Everglades, ...a., and most of the passen...rs were Americans, a ...okesman said.

There were no reports of ...sualties or damage.

Tech Union Rejects Truce During Exams

William L. Ramsey, director of Milwaukee Technical college, asked local 212 of the teachers' union Monday to call a moratorium on the teachers' strike so that students' final examinations could go ahead Tuesday as scheduled.

The union immediately rejected the proposal, repeating its position that the teachers would not work without a new agreement on salaries, fringe benefits and working conditions. The old agreement expired Dec. 31.

The union renewed its plea for the college board to resume negotiations, which were broken off Dec. 19 after the board made what it called its last and highest possible offer.

Local 212, which represents the college's 450 daytime teachers, began the strike Jan. 2, the day classes were to resume after the holiday vacation. The college has been operating at about 25% of normal since then, college officials have said.

Final examinations will be held, as scheduled, for students whose classes have been meeting during the strike. The others will be postponed until teachers return to work.

Ramsey said Monday that students who planned to transfer to other colleges at the end of the semester probably could do so, even if their work for the first semester was not completed. He urged such students to contact Jack Gardiner, registrar, to make arrangements.

Ramsey said many colleges were willing to accept transfer students provisionally pending completion of their first semester grade records at the technical college.

Mrs. Ruth Perkins, a part time teacher who has not joined the strike, said a group called Educators for Education had sent a telegram to Gov. Knowles Monday asking him to step into the dispute. They asked Knowles to try to make it possible for all examinations to be held as scheduled, she said.

Stewardess for Delta Locks Out Hijacker

From Press Dispatches

Miami, Fla. – An attempted hijacking of a Delta Airlines jet en route to Miami from Detroit was foiled early Monday when a stewardess disregarded a passenger's shotgun and slammed the cabin door in his face, police said.

The Dade county sheriff's department said local and federal officers arrested Kenneth McPeek, 31, of Orchard Lake, Mich., when the plane landed at Miami International airport. His 3 year old son was taken into protective custody.

Officers said they went to the airport after the plane's captain radioed that he had a man aboard with a shotgun.

Weapon Found

The sheriff's department said McPeek told them he took the shotgun aboard in a duffel bag. The weapon was found under his seat, unassembled and again in the bag, the officers said.

Stewardess Lynne Sargeant of Miami Springs, Fla., said she was accosted by a passenger who placed a shotgun in the pit of her stomach. The passenger told her to tell the captain he was going to Havana.

"Sir, we can't do that, we're in a landing pattern," she said she replied before slamming the door of the cockpit and locking it. The would-be hijacker apparently gave up the idea, officers said.

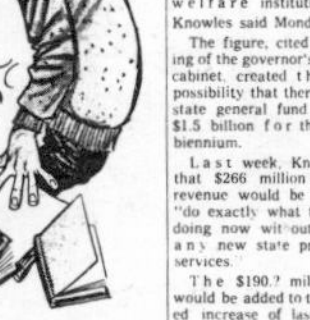

Stewardess Lynne Sargeant

Boeing 707, both bound for Miami.

Capt. George Wagner, 46, of Pompano Beach, Fla., turned the Peruvian jet toward Havana. But a public address system failure kept him from informing his passengers. The plane carried 110 people, including about 80 teen age Argentine students en route to

Turn to Plane, page 10, col. 4

Three times on Sunday, planes swooped into Miami with victims of Saturday's two hijackings. The returning planes carried a band of laughing students, people bleary eyed from loss of sleep and an airliner crew whose captor insisted on a radio message to "tell Fidel Red is coming."

Peruvian, United Jets

The hijackings involved a Peruvian national airlines Convair and a United Air Lines

Milwaukee

McCann's Good Plan for Office Closer to the People

Public prosecutors are ...ometimes called people's at...orneys — representatives of ...e law abiding many ...ainst the lawless few. The ...wly installed district attor...ey of Milwaukee county, E. ...ichael McCann, will at...empt to make his office ...ore like that of a true peo...e's attorney, by emphasiz...g outreach to the people.

His plan to have assistants ...old neighborhood office ...ours, two afternoons a ...onth in each of five loca...ons around the city, would ...e one outreach. Many poor ...timid people may feel they ...ve reason to consult his of...ce but can't or won't seek it ...t in the somewhat awe...me safety building. They ...ay feel freer in their own ...eighborhoods and may also, ...erhaps, find a more at...ntive ear than is always ...ssible to give them in the ...verworked main office.

Another outreach, McCann has announced, will be ...speakers' list that organi...ations and schools may ...raw upon to help fill up ...heir program dates. This can ...elp spread the message not ...nly of law abidance but also ...f what law enforcement ...rocedure is all about and ...spects of the crime problem ...hat need public co-operation ...o deal with.

Manning both the branch ...ffices and the speakers' bu...eau will add a little bit to ...e manpower requirements ...f the office, but mainly a ...arger staff is needed just to ...eep up with the work in the ...ourts. Assistant district at...orneys would have to be in ...wo or three courts at once ...o handle their case loads ef...iciently now and minimize ...ostponements.

This was agreed to in last ...all's campaign by both Mc...Cann and his opponent, Da...id Cannon, but the latter, in ...ffice at the time, did not ...hoose to seek more help in ...he 1969 budget. McCann de...erves strong support in a ...plea for the help now, not ...waiting until 1970.

Sirhan Broods Over Failings of the World, Interviewer Says

© New York Times News Service

Los Angeles, Calif. – Sirhan Bishara Sirhan has been tense and brooding during the more than seven months he has spent in jail. He is distressed by the failings of the world, angered by those who note he is not an American and troubled by his own name.

Such is the portrait drawn in an exclusive article to appear in this week's issue of Life magazine. Sirhan, a 24 year old Jordanian immigrant, is charged with first degree murder in the assassination of Sen. Robert F. Kennedy.

Until recently, the Life article recounts, Sirhan ordered the Los Angeles Times every day. Then he "became depressed by world events" and stopped taking the newspaper.

"It's All Violence"

In the first published interview since his arrest in the serving pantry of the Ambassador hotel where Kennedy lay mortally wounded, Sirhan, who has remained a silent riddle to most of the world, is quoted as having said:

"It's all violence, chaos, unrest. What ever happened to the old days, peace and quiet?"

And the words rang strange. Sirhan has been described by many who know him as the product of an impoverished boyhood in Jerusalem, uprooted from his home by the Palestine war in 1948, with scenes of violence and suffering etched in his young mind.

As a result, friends have said, he was an ardent Arab nationalist, despising Israel and passionately upset because he felt that Kennedy favored Israel over the Arab states.

Angered by Articles

But the Life interview reports that he has become angered in jail upon reading articles that referred to him as

Turn to Interview, page 10, col. 1

Water Drinker Gulps 14 Gallons and Dies

A West Milwaukee man who, authorities said, drank about 14 gallons of water in 72 hours, died of massive ingestion of the water, the medical examiner's office reported Sunday.

He was Henry Paradowski, jr., 37, of 5201 W. Beloit rd. The medical examiner's report said he had been under the care of a psychiatrist for about six months.

Police said the victim's father, Henry Paradowski, sr., came to the West Milwaukee police station Saturday afternoon to report that he and his wife had been unable to stop their son from drinking water. He said his son had been drinking about a glass a minute.

While he was at the station, police said, the victim's mother phoned to say that the son had become ill.

A police ambulance took Paradowski to St. Luke's hospital where he died about four hours later.

No autopsy was planned. Paradowski, who was divorced, lived with his parents and helped his father operate a food market at that address, police said.

Movie Air Collision in Mexico Kills 9

Torreon, Mexico –AP– Two planes engaged in making a Mexican movie collided in the air Sunday, killing all nine men aboard them. A parachutist carrying a manikin representing an actress had just jumped from a Beechcraft C-45. Investigators said the right wing of another plane carrying the cameraman hit the Beechcraft, causing both planes to fall in mountainous terrain.

The Weather

Compiled by US Weather Bureau

Milwaukee — Variable cloudiness and warmer, chance of light snow at times Monday night and Tuesday, low around 15; southeasterly winds 5-15 m.p.h. High Tuesday in upper twenties, southeasterly winds 5-15 m.p.h. Precipitation probabilities: 10% Monday night and Tuesday.

Hour	6	7	8	9	10	11	12	1
Temp	14	14	14	19	21	24	26	27

Wisconsin — Partly cloudy Monday night, not so cold northeast half; lows 2 below to 6 above north, 6 to 12 south. Tuesday, mostly cloudy, highs 15-23 north, in twenties south.

Temperature range Sunday, 13 at 2:30 p.m., 7 at 7:30 a.m.; precipitation for 24 hours ending at 6 a.m. Monday, none

Normal temperature range Sunday, 28 and 13.

Humidity at 6 a.m. Monday, 88%; at noon, 78%.

Sunrise Tuesday, 7:21 a.m.; sunset 4:41 p.m.

Moonrise, 3:51 a.m. Tuesday; moonset, 12:42 p.m. Tuesday.

Weather map, page 8, part 2.

—AP Wirephoto

HELP ON THE WAY – Dennis R. Basney lay on the ice of Black river near Port Huron, Mich., as firemen inched their boat toward him. Basney, 24, awaited rescue for more than an hour after the snowmobile he was riding broke through the ice. A companion, Duane Barnes, drowned. Basney's cries for help were heard by a nearby resident who called police.

Fig. 5-5. Old-fashioned? The **Milwaukee Journal** may look a bit old-fashioned, partly because of the head type face. Nevertheless it is a neat, attractive paper. Note that headlines are staggered, that a political cartoon appears on page one, and that a big picture draws attention to the bottom half of the page.

WEATHER
Cloudy with some drizzle likely Wednesday. High in the mid-30s. See Page 86.

CHICAGO
SUN-TIMES

CIT

Vol. 21, No. 299 Phone 321-3000 WEDNESDAY, JANUARY 15, 1969 100 Pages—

Blasts, Fire Rip Carrie
13 Killed, Scores Injure

Cheering Chicagoans crowd in front of City Hall to give earthy welcome to moon pioneers (circle). (Sun-Times Photo)

'Big E' Repo
Several Miss

From Sun-Times Wires

PEARL HARBOR—Fire and explosio ed Tuesday on the nuclear aircraft ca terprise, the world's largest warship. T reported 13 killed and 85 to 100 injured determined number of sailors were miss

The Navy said the carrier's nuclear reactor was not involved in the tragedy.

The Big E was on maneuvers 75 miles southwest of Hawaii in preparation for deployment to Vietnam for the fourth time.

Cause Not Determined

The fire, followed by about a dozen explosions, burned on the flight and hangar decks. The cause of the blaze and extent of damage were not immediately determined.

A doctor at Tripler Army Hospital in Honolulu said it was preparing to handle at least 100 casualties. At midday, nine men arrived by helicopter in the first evacuation from the ship.

The Enterprise was the third U.S. aircraft carrier to be hit with disaster in recent years.

Nearly 1,000 pers military wives and responded to the N for blood donation rived at Queen's M ter in Honolulu Tripler.

All doctors' a were canceled at treating the Ente tims. The ship, 1,12 has a crew of 4,600.

The Navy called appeal after 200 p donations at Tripl Queens Center. A termed the resp whelming.

Mostly Burn

As the Enterprise Pearl Harbor, mo ters arrived at Trip

Turn

City Pay
Tribute T
Spacemen

Story, Other Pictures

Fig. 5-6. Tabloid style. Page one of the **Chicago Sun-Times,** a six-column tabloid, usually has a full story as well as the big head and big picture typical of tabs. Note the head with a reference to the story inside and the circle in photo drawing attention to space pioneers.

Newsday

THE LONG ISLAND NEWSPAPER

5 CENTS
TUESDAY
JAN. 14, 1969

Soviets Launch Man Into Orbit of Earth

Story on Page 3

Jet Crashes Into Pacific; Many Saved

Los Angeles (AP)—A Scandinavian Airlines jetliner with 45 persons aboard splashed into the rainswept Pacific while approaching International Airport here last night. At least four deaths were reported, and three hours after the crash only 28 survivors were ashore.

The over-the-Pole flight had originated in Copenhagen, Denmark, with a stop in Seattle, Wash. The big DC-8 was still afloat four hours after the crash, the Coast Guard said. The post-crash scene was reported to be one of pandemonium at sea.

The plane's pilot, Kenneth Davies, a Dane, said that at the time of the crash he was making a "routine approach except for some difficulty with the landing gear." He declined to give further details, except to commend the crew and the passengers for "totally heroic and disciplined action" in evacuating the plane and inflating rubber boats. Passengers climbed onto the wings and fuselage, or splashed into the sea through rents in the plane's skin. Many survivors were reported injured.

Radioed reports from the scene indicated a picture of both confusion and heroism: The black of night pierced by passengers' flashlights and searchlights from ships and helicopters. Life rafts bobbing. Small boats and Coast Guard cutters hauling survivors aboard and heading for the nearby Marina Del Rey yacht harbor. From there, survivors, many of them on stretchers, were taken to hospitals.

There was a brisk wind, and both air and sea temperatures were in the 50s. Visibility was good despite a steady rain. The flight was due at 6:05 PM but was running late due to bad weather. Planes normally land at International Airport heading west, toward the sea, but

—Continued on Page 27

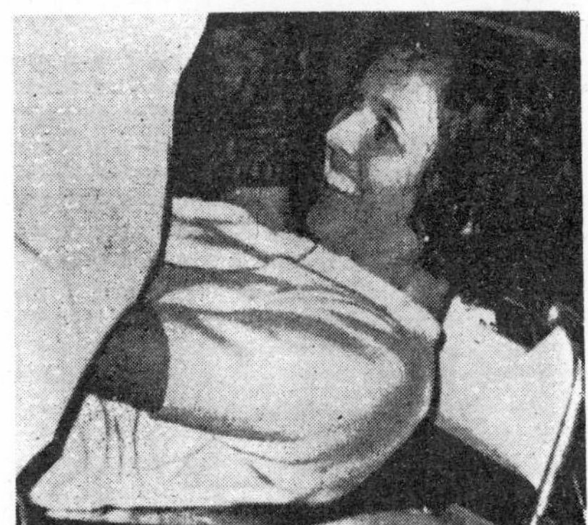

UPI Telephoto

Woman on Stretcher Smiles

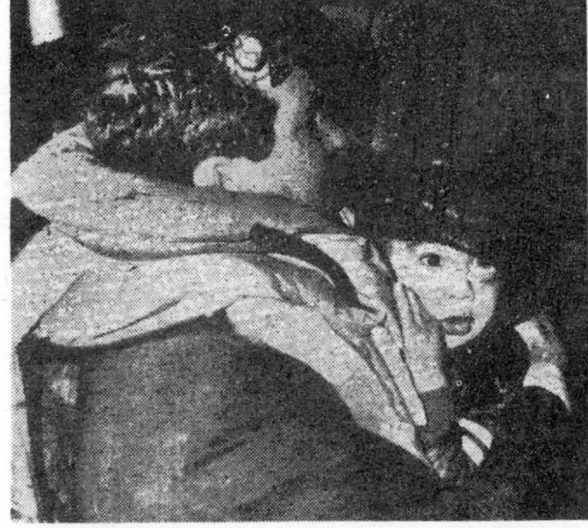

AP Wirephoto

Man and Boy Reach Safety

Fig. 5-7. **Modified tabloid.** To avoid the appearance of sensationalism, the tabloid **Newsday** shifted from old-style tab makeup to a magazine appearance. (Compare to the **Chicago Sun-Times**, fig. 5-6.)

Los Angeles Times

LARGEST CIRCULATION IN THE WEST, 992,075 DAILY, 1,317,220 SUNDAY.

VOL. XC † FIVE PARTS—PART ONE CC TUESDAY MORNING, JANUARY 19, 1971 74 PAGES DAILY 10¢

FLOOD OF 1966

Florence Art Disaster: Some Big Surprises

BY LOUIS B. FLEMING
Times Staff Writer

FLORENCE — The terrifying Florence flood of 1966 may have done almost as much good as it did harm.

Experts will need another 15 years to finish fixing the frescoes, paintings, statues, tapestries and books damaged by the oily waters.

But they can now say with assurance that:

—No work of art was a total loss.

—Some works are better now than before.

—Florence has been established as an international center for the scientific conservation of the art treasures of the entire world.

—New techniques have been found and new financial resources assured that will slow if not halt the deterioration that time works on masterpieces of every civilization.

"The emergency, I can now say, is over," Dr. Umberto Baldini, director of the restoration laboratories, said.

Massive World Support

The miracle was worked with massive support from many nations, including $1.5 million from Americans. So Florence is now planning a "thank you" present to the world: a four-month exposition, beginning next December, which will be combined with a congress of art restoration experts to continue the collaboration which developed during the emergency.

"This is the most important thing that has happened in these four years—the new relationship between persons working in restoring art throughout the world, with Florence the center for the exchange of information and training," Baldini said.

Restoration work in Florence was not born with the flood, however. The state labo t ry has been in operat on for 40 years and at least one of its workers represents the third generation of his family to work at preserving the masterpieces.

'Great Lesson to All'

So the exposition will not be geared to the flood but to 40 years of work "as a great lesson to all and as a warning for conservation," one official explained.

"Many things have changed, including the idea behind our work," Vittorio Granchi, a worker in the laboratory, said. He has been doing art restoration for 37 years, just like his father and his grandfather.

"But my son," he said with a smile, "is not interested. He is a prize-winning abstract painter."

Some of the tools are old. Granchi was using a natural varnish, developed 2,000 years ago by the Greeks, as he worked over one of the greatest treasures in all of Florence, Cimabue's Crucifix from the Santa Croce Church.

But nearby there were tools his father never used: full-spectrum lamps, high-powered double-lens microscopes, hot tables, sealed air exhausts, plastic compounds.

Please Turn to Page 15, Col. 4

OIL SPILL — View looking toward Golden Gate Bridge after collision of two oil tankers in fog. At left is the Oregon Standard, whose tanks ruptured, spilling fuel oil into San Francisco Bay. Not visible is tanker Arizona Standard, which had left scene for dock. Its cargo was not spilled. (AP Wirephoto)

Two Ships Collide in S.F. Fog, Cause Massive Oil Spill in Bay

Estimated 1.9 Million Gallons Lost From Ruptured Tanks; Deposits May Reach Oakland and Berkeley

BY PHILIP HAGER and DARYL LEMBKE
Times Staff Writers

SAN FRANCISCO — Two 17,000-ton Standard Oil tankers collided in heavy fog beneath the Golden Gate Bridge early Monday, spilling up to an estimated 1.9 million gallons of oil in the bay.

A Coast Guard spokesman characterized the oil spill as "the largest here in recent memory" but said preliminary indications were that serious as it was, it would not likely reach the proportions of the Santa Barbara oil disaster of 1969.

Patches of the thick, black substance were sighted on the shore at a number of locations around the bay including Alcatraz, Angel Island, Sausalito, Tiburon and San Francisco's Fisherman's Wharf.

Other streaks of oil were seen moving west under the Golden Gate and out to sea. There was concern late in the day that as the tides changed, oil deposits would move farther east toward Oakland and Berkeley. Some light patches were seen near the Bay Bridge at Oakland.

Standard Oil crews were immediately deployed in an effort to clean up the spill.

Blotting up the sticky mixture was a slow, painstaking process. Vacuum tubes were used both on shore and on the bay to draw oil from the water, and 1,000 bales of straw were spread to soak up the oil on the beaches.

Standard Oil barges salvaged nearly 200,000 gallons before it could leak from one of the severely damaged tankers. State Fish and Game Department officials and volunteers from conservationist groups searched the shores for birds that had been caught in the deposits.

Coast Guard Com. Gordon Dickman estimated spillage at between 500,000 and 1,900,000 gallons. A company spokesman said late in the afternoon: "We just don't know how much was spilled."

The collision occurred at 1:45 a.m. about a quarter-mile west of the Golden Gate Bridge when the bow of the Arizona Standard plowed about 40 feet into the port side of the Oregon Standard. There were no injuries.

The two ships, according to the company, are sister vessels—each 523 feet long, carrying 35-man crews and based in the East Bay city of Richmond.

A Coast Guard spokesman said that both ships, moving in what he called "zero visibility" fog, were equipped with radar and foghorns and that one ship, the Arizona Standard, had been "in contact" with a radar facility that operates at the harbor entrance 24 hours a day.

There was no further explanation from either the Coast Guard or the oil company on what may have caused the crash. A Coast Guard in-

Please Turn to Page 18, Col. 1

N.Y. Tries to End Police Walkout by Ordering Pay Trial

BY JOHN J. GOLDMAN
Times Staff Writer

NEW YORK—A state Supreme Court justice ordered an immediate trial on the thorniest issue in this city's wildcat policemen's strike Monday—a dramatic step which officials hoped would bring the men in blue back to their beats.

Indications were many patrolmen were ignoring the court move and were not hurrying back to their jobs. Instead, the strikers met near station houses and debated what to do.

Late in the evening Edward Kiernan, president of the Patrolmen's Benevolent Assn., wired Mayor John V. Lindsay demanding amnesty from punishment for all his men. Unless this is granted, Kiernan said, "all bets are off."

Meanwhile, order was being maintained by a thin line of tired detectives and police superior officers.

But Police Commissioner Patrick V. Murphy, surveying his skeleton force which had been working 12-hour shifts with no days off, warned he was preparing for the "agonizing decision" of possibly asking Lindsay that national guardsmen be called "within the next two days" to replace striking patrolmen.

The commissioner, who has been working 20-hour days himself, said "the city must be protected. If we have to seek outside help, we'll do it."

The scheduling of a quick trial on the question of parity—pay differentials between patrolmen and ser-

Please Turn to Page 10, Col. 2

U.S. Output Drops; 1st Year Since '58

'70 Report Also Terms Inflation Worst Since '51

BY MURRAY SEEGER
Times Staff Writer

WASHINGTON—The nation's total output of goods and services showed its first yearly decline in 1970 since the 1958 recession, as the auto strike took its toll in the fourth quarter.

The Commerce Department report on "real gross national product," a figure which discounts price increases and thus reflects physical volume of output, also pointed up

Related stories in financial section. See Part 3, Page 9.

the worst inflation since the Korean war year of 1951. The department noted that the prices of all items in the GNP rose by 5.75% over 1969.

With the auto strike now over, however, government officials look for the real GNP to climb significantly in the current quarter. And the Commerce Department issued another report Monday with favorable signs for the economy. That report showed that housing starts jumped 18% in December from the November rate.

Housing industry leaders credited the drop in mortgage loan interest rates and the increased availability of money for the sharp climb, which produced the highest annual rate for starts in a single month for more than 20 years.

As these reports were made public, New York banks again reduced their prime lending rate, the interest rate they charge their best loan customers. It was the second reduction in two working days. The new rate is 6%, a dramatic change from the record 8.5% rate which prevailed less than a year ago.

At the same time the Federal Reserve System board of governors cut the discount rate—the rate banks, themselves, pay to borrow money from the Federal Reserve system—to 5%, the fourth reduction since Nov. 10, when it was 6%.

The reduction in interest rates reflects a lack of demand for loans. And with prices continuing their upward push, the Nixon Administration is left facing the persistent paradox of recession mixed with inflation.

However, in the disagreement

Please Turn to Page 7, Col. 1

BETHLEHEM HALVES PRICE INCREASE TO MEET COMPETITION

NEW YORK (AP)—Bethlehem Steel Corp., backing down under White House and competitive pressure, Monday sliced by nearly half its originally announced price increases on some major steel products.

Bethlehem, the second-biggest steel producer, had announced a week earlier price boosts averaging about 12.5% on steel used in construction.

Monday's rollback trimmed these hikes to about 6.8%, matching the lesser increases announced Saturday by U.S. Steel Corp., the No. 1 steel maker.

President Nixon last week called Bethlehem's increases enormous, and raised the threat of permitting greater steel imports as a means of pushing down domestic prices.

The White House expressed gratification over Bethlehem's pullback to the U.S. Steel range of increases.

"We are pleased Bethlehem Steel

Please Turn to Page 7, Col. 1

U.S. Halts Aid to Ecuador in Reprisal for Tuna Boat Seizures

Exclusive to The Times from a Staff Writer

SAN DIEGO—The U.S. State Department retaliated against Ecuador Monday, banning aircraft sales and ship repair credits for a year, as that Latin American nation seized five more boats of the San Diego tuna fishing fleet.

Secretary of State William P. Rogers summoned Ecuadorian Ambassador Carlos Mantilla-Ortega to his office in Washington and informed him of the action, invoking the Foreign Military Sales Act. It provides that:

". . . no sales, credits or guarantees shall be extended under this act to any country during a period of one year after such country seizes or takes into custody or fines an American fishing vessel more than 12 miles from the coast of that country."

Ecuador, Chile and Peru claim that their territorial waters extend 200 miles to sea and demand that boats fishing within that limit buy licenses. The United States recognizes only the standard 12-mile limit and advises boat owners not to buy the licenses.

Ecuadorian naval vessels plunged into the midst of the San Diego tuna fishing fleet 50 miles off the coast of South America Monday and seized five more boats—bringing to nine the number of such craft taken into custody since last Tuesday.

A spokesman for the American tuna Boat Assn. in San Diego said skippers of other fishing craft radioed that they were being pursued and the spokesman said still more seizures are expected.

It was the most seizures in one day since Ecuador, Chile and Peru began boarding U.S. tuna clippers five years ago.

Ed Silva, vice president of the tuna association said the fishing fleet moved inside the 200-mile limit in pursuit of tuna because "they follow the fish."

Fines levied against seized boats, are set on the basis of tonnage, Silva said, and may run as high as $100,-

Please Turn to Page 3, Col. 3

CIVIC CENTER WARMEST SPOT IN COUNTRY

95 Degrees---Another January Record Melts

BY DICK MAIN
Times Staff Writer

Temperatures climbed to a record January high of 95 degrees at the Civic Center Monday, making Los Angeles the warmest spot in the continental United States.

The peak read'ng at 2:15 p.m. topped previous alltime highs for the month of 90 degrees set Jan. 8, 1923, and on Sunday.

It was the third straight day for high temperature records. Saturday's 84 topped the previous high for the date by 1 degree, Sunday's 90 also was 1 degree higher than the record for the date and Monday's exceeded the date's previous high by 11 degrees.

Two first-stage smog alerts—the first ever issued for excessive carbon monoxide concentrations—accompanied Monday's high temperatures.

The freakish January heat wave was caused by a mild Santa Ana condition with warming northeast winds flowing from the desert tow d the sea. A storm system to the west and north blocked off the normal flow of cold ir or weather front rom the Pacific Northwest.

A slight cooling trend will start today as Santa Ana winds weaken. Increasing clo diness i expected by Wednesday, the National Weather Service said. A Civic Center high of 88 is expected today, dropping to 78 Wednesday.

An extended forecast called for a chance of showers starting Thursday. But more fair weather is expected later in the week, the service said.

Forecaster John Rockey said the extended outlook projections were based on the possibility that a low pressure storm trough about 1,000 miles off the coast will move eastward.

The trough has served as a channel for a series of Pacific storm fronts that have brought rain, snow and dense fog to the Northwest.

The buildup of carbon monoxide was blamed on heavy exhaust discharges of automobiles during morning and evening rush hours under a low temperature inversion.

It was the first time a smog alert had been issued by the Air Pollution

Please Turn to Page 15, Col. 1

Index to The Times

LISTENING — Steven Neumann shows how he detected a defect in his brother's heart. (AP Wirephoto)

HEARS 'SWISHING SOUND'

Boy Reads Book on Hearts, Finds Brother Needs Surgery

WEST BEND, Wis. (AP)—Ten-year-old Steven Neumann became curious about heart beats while reading a book on the subject.

His curiosity led him to compare the heartbeat of 6-year-old brother Jackie and another brother by placing his ear against their chests.

"They don't sound the same," the fifth-grader told his mother, Mrs. John Neumann, a nurse's aide.

She responded that it was Steven's bedtime and urged him to end the game. But he insisted she also listen to the "swishing sound in Jackie's chest."

"It sounded like a wet sponge does when you squeeze it," Mrs. Neumann said of the October experiment. "Steve told me his heart book said the sound was indication of a heart disorder."

The boy's suspicions were confirmed by the family's physician and Jackie underwent a series of tests this month at University Hospital in Madison. He will undergo open heart surgery in a few weeks.

Physicians said the 6-year-old has an enlarged heart, a pinched main artery and a hole between the lower chambers of his heart that should have closed after he was born but did not. The condition went undetected until Steven's curiosity intervened.

THE WEATHER

National Weather Service forecast: Mostly fair today and Wednesday but some increase in cloudiness Wednesday with early morning coastal fog. High today, 88. High Wednesday, 78. High Monday, 95; low, 60.

Complete weather information and smog report in Part 2, Page 4.

Fig. 5-8. Six-column. Like a few other papers that have turned to six-column make-up in recent years, the **Los Angeles Times** gets a clean, attractive look with six columns separated by white space instead of rules. Note the restrained use of heads with decks, the few pictures, and the lengthy stories continued inside.

THE KANSAS CITY STAR

L. 91. NO. 127 MAIN EDITION ★★★★ KANSAS CITY, FRIDAY, JANUARY 22, 1971—32 PAGES For Classified Ads Call 221-5500 To Subscribe Call 421-1200 10¢

Sitting Ducks American made South Vietnamese spotter planes (upper) and Cambodian helicopters and transports (lower) were damaged extensively early today by sneak Viet Cong mortar and rocket attacks. The shells burst among the closely-parked aircraft on the Phnom Penh airport, which apparently had been considered safe from attack. (Wirephotos by radio from Saigon)

Havoc in Airport Raid in Cambodia

Bulletin

Phnom Penh, Cambodia (AP)—Cambodian and South Vietnamese forces joined today on Highway 4 at the Pich Nil pass, a big step in ending the enemy blockade, the government reported. The linkup was three miles from the northern entrance of the pass, which Cambodian soldiers captured yesterday.

Phnom Penh, Cambodia (AP)—Huge fires burned fiercely around Phnom Penh's airport today and explosions continued after a rocket, mortar and commando attack that took a heavy toll of lives.

The raid on the airport and a nearby military camp last night also wrecked Cambodia's tiny air force and overshadowed the army's success in its drive to reopen the highway to the sea.

The casualty count was not available but the number of Cambodian dead and wounded were estimated at more than 100. Only one or two of the attackers were reported killed.

Newsmen were barred from the airport, eight miles outside the city, and no accurate account of the destruction was available. But Cambodian officers said six of their air force's eight helicopters were destroyed and the two others were extensively damaged.

From a nearby rooftop, it appeared that few if any military planes on the field could fly. The military flight line looked like a junkyard.

The destruction of the air force was likely to have little if any effect on the prosecution of the war since most of the air attacks in Cambodia are flown by the U. S. and South Vietnamese air forces. But it was a severe psychological blow to Premier Lon Nol's government.

In the closest enemy attack yet to the center of Phnom Penh, a rocket also landed in a riverside shipyard on the edge of the downtown area. As firemen fought the blaze at the yard, a battle could be seen close to the naval base across another of the capital's rivers, with tracer bullets curving through the night sky and explosions echoing across the waters.

Trucks hauled bodies and scores of blood-spattered women and children into Phnom Penh from the airport and army camp eight miles outside the city.

North Vietnamese and Viet

See RAIDERS on next page

Raid Seen as Reprisal

By George Esper

Saigon (AP)—U. S. military analysts think the attack on the Phnom Penh airport today was a direct response to the widening American involvement in Cambodia.

These analysts noted that the airport has been poorly guarded and an inviting target for many months. But the Communist command did not order the attack until after the United States began providing support for the operation to open Cambodia's highway to the sea and stepped up its airlift of war materials into the Phnom Penh airport.

A News Analysis

Some analysts saw the attack as revenge for the highway operation. It was made less than 12 hours after Cambodian infantrymen supported by American planes and helicopter gunships recaptured the heights overlooking Pich Nil pass, the major enemy strong point blocking the highway.

American experts said the Cambodians probably couldn't have taken the pass without the U. S. air support.

Nixon on Air

President Nixon's state-of-the-Union message will be telecast live at 8 o'clock tonight on channels 4, 5, 9 and 19.

Radio station KBEA will broadcast the speech at 10 o'clock.

Report on Nation By Nixon Tonight

Washington (AP)—President Nixon, his eye presumably fixed on 1972, delivers his state-of-the-Union message tonight, outlining for Congress and the nation "new approaches and new initiatives" he thinks will ease the country's problems.

The traditional message will be delivered live to a joint session of Congress and will be televised and broadcast.

For a brief time, consideration was given to postponing the speech because of the death yesterday afternoon of Sen. Richard B. Russell, Democrat, of Georgia. The White House said it checked with aides to Russell, dean and president pro tempore of the Senate, and with the congressional leadership and was advised Nixon should deliver his address as scheduled.

The focus of the President's remarks will be domestic problems and his prescriptions for dealing with them. Foreign policy questions will be dealt with in mid-February in a lengthy written document informally labeled the President's "state-of-the-world" report.

Because Nixon's state-of-the-Union remarks are aimed squarely at problems at home, all black members of the House announced in advance they will boycott the session. They wrote Nixon: "Your consistent refusal to hear the pleas and concerns of black Americans dictates our decision to be absent."

Sen. Edward W. Brooke (R-Mass.), the only Negro in the Senate, said he will attend the session.

Nixon spent much of yesterday polishing his speech, selecting what he liked from a variety of preliminary drafts prepared under his direction by his chief speech writer, Raymond K. Price. As always, he kept adding some of his own language.

By Nixon's account, work on his 1971 program began in earnest six months ago—long before he set his administration on a new course following what he regarded as a disappointing off-year election showing by some Republicans.

VW Loses Car Safety Suit

efault judgment of liability on a failure to properly r interrogatories was filed in U. S. District court y Judge William H. Beck- inst Volkswagen of Amer- nc., in connection with a ge suit involving a Volks- n.

court's ruling was in a $600,000 damage suit brought by Mrs. Margaret Carroll Bollard, 4036 Locust street, for injuries suffered in a car accident.

Mrs. Bollard was a passenger in a 1966 model Volkswagen that struck a parked car March 2, 1969, at 4320 Rockhill road.

In her petition, Mrs. Bollard said she suffered head and body injuries when her head went through the windshield and then was "violently withdrawn" by the impact. She filed the suit, claiming that Volkswagen of America was negligent in the construction of the car.

The plaintiff's suit contended that the laminated binder between two plates of glass in the windshield was of insufficient thickness and strength to resist breakage. She alleged that the defendants were negligent in failing to warn her of the defective condition and to inspect and test the windshield. She further alleged negligent designing.

See SUIT on Next Page

Pay Raises For Council Appear Out

The council finance and audit committee yesterday recommended that the city council not approve proposals to increase salaries for future council members and the mayor.

The action was taken without notice, apparently after the committee's regular business had been completed.

J. D. Robins, jr., committee chairman, said one proposal would have submitted a charter amendment to the voters March 30 to increase council members' salaries from $4,800 a year to $9,600. The council reportedly had agreed behind the scenes to seek a 50 per cent increase, to $7,200, rather than ask voters to double them.

The other ordinance, which would increase the next mayor's salary to $7,500 from the present $15,000 a year, requires only council approval. However, generally the council follows the recommendations of the committee that has reviewed and studied the ordinances before final action is taken.

Today is the last day council members could approve the proposed charter amendment to seek voter approval of a salary hike for themselves and still have it included on the ballot.

rm Restored to Girl, 6

roit (AP)—Three weeks Marcia Grimm, 6 years old, er arm in a snow blower. she has the arm back tells visitors at Detroit Ford hospital: "I'm go- go home and beat up on ig bad tractor."

ne is in Manistique in gan's Upper Peninsula. s where Marcia's arm ed into the rotating blades snow blower January 3. s snowing heavily, and the was riding her saucer sled while her father, George Grimm, was running the machine.

Grimm stopped the machine and pulled his daughter's arm out, dangling by only two badly stretched nerves. The other major nerve, the bones and all the muscles had been cut through.

Grimm rushed his daughter to the Manistique clinic of the family doctor, Merle Wehner, 56, a general practitioner. He called for an air ambulance and the girl was flown to Detroit.

In five hours of surgery one team of doctors pinned the bone together and a second attached the veins and arteries to get the circulation going again. When the arm bone heals, the surgeons will operate again to splice together the severed radial nerve, which controls finger movement.

"We tagged the nerve end with a tiny steel suture so we can see it on X rays and also a small magnet to trigger a device which will beep when we come near it," explain Dr. Edwin Guise, head of the orthopedic operating team.

Marcia is one of about a dozen persons in the nation who have had severed limbs reattached successfully. Doctors say that perhaps in a year or so she can go back home and hit that "tractor" with either hand.

The Weather

Fair and much colder tonight with lows in the mid-teens and winds of 10 to 20 miles an hour is the National Weather service forecast. Partly cloudy and colder tomorrow with the high in the upper 20s or lower 30s. Chance of precipitation 10 per cent tonight and tomorrow.

Temperatures

Midnight	38	9 a. m.	40
1 a. m.	36	10 a. m.	45
2 a. m.	37	11 a. m.	*46
3 a. m.	35	12 noon	46
4 a. m.	38	1 p. m.	*47
5 a. m.	38		
6 a. m.	38		
7 a. m.	40		
8 a. m.	40		

*Unofficial

Relative humidity, 6 a. m., 67 per cent.

Precipitation in 24 hours ending 6 a. m., none.

Barometer reading 6 a. m. 29.79 inches.

River stage today, 1.1 feet, fall of .0 of a foot.

No Truman Diagnosis

Harry S. Truman was reported in good condition today after a "reasonably restful night" at Research hospital.

John Dreves, hospital public relations director, said the diagnosis of the former President's illness has not been completed. It is not known when he will return to his home in Independence, Dreves added.

Mr. Truman was taken to the hospital by ambulance from his home at 8:30 o'clock yesterday morning. Tests are being made on the 86-year-old Truman, and they are expected to be complete in a few days.

Dreves said he didn't know what kind of tests have been made, that Mr. Truman has received no visitors from outside his family and that "there is no cause for concern at this time."

Mr. Truman slept most of the night, Dreves said. Dreves read the following statement to the 9:30 o'clock hospital press conference this morning:

"After a light supper of tea and soup, he (Mr. Truman) read the evening Kansas City paper, watched television and drank a soft drink before going to bed at 10 o'clock.

"He was sitting up in bed this morning to drink some tea and read the morning paper. There are no plans at this time for the family to come to Kansas City."

Mr. Truman's wife, Mrs. Bess Truman, went home at 4 o'clock yesterday afternoon and returned at 9 o'clock this morning.

The hospital spokesman said flowers and telegrams continue to be received by Mr. Truman and that well-wishers include President and Mrs. Richard Nixon.

Mr. Truman was taken to the hospital because of abdominal pain, and the Research spokesman said the former President experienced some pain yesterday afternoon. Spokesmen said Mr. Truman has been eager to return home.

He has spoken by telephone with his daughter, Mrs. Clifton Daniel, in New York.

Bill Vaughan Says:

His wife says Dick Nixon is a joy to live with. For one thing, unlike so many other husbands, he's not always cussing out the government.

Brief Break In Mail Tie

London (AP)—Hundreds of Britain's striking postal workers returned briefly to their jobs today to pay weekly allowances to mothers and old age pensioners. But union leaders rejected a postoffice appeal to arbitrate the pay dispute.

The government pays pensions and family allowances to mothers with more than two children through the postoffices.

Bay Oil Slick Is Yielding

San Francisco (AP)—After four days of around-the-clock operations, officials say they are beginning to get the upper hand in their battle against a huge oil slick.

On Inside Pages

hat Early Wynn was not voted into base- 's Hall of Fame this year is a black mark the Baseball Writers' Association of Amer- the group that annually votes for candi- s for one of sports most exclusive ors. Joe McGuff, The Star's sports edi- in Sporting Comment points out that the ire of Yogi Berra to be voted in the Hall Fame is understandable because this is first year of eligibility. But Wynn, who missed gaining the required number of es last year, ranks as one of the few major ue pitchers to win 20 games or more seasons. Page 13.

WYNN

Tough Allen J. Ellender takes over as head of the Senate ropriations committee, a powerful post, with the death Sen. Richard Russell. 2.

Kansas City's air is polluted, but many residents do not w who all the polluters are. Carl Potter, the city's director environmental service, is making the list known. 3.

Israel will not accept Egypt's proposal for an international ce force to guard any future border arrangement in the dle East, says Premier Golda Meir. 18.

Friends of James R. Hoffa, imprisoned president of the msters union, reportedly are pressuring the White House presidential clemency or a pardon. 18.

A "very busy year" in labor-management relations is inning to look like the understatement of the year judg- from the number of strikes and strike threats already . 19.

The leading editorial: The crisis in public transit financ- has been brought home with shocking abruptness in the ping of some bus lines and drastic cutbacks in service the others. 28.

The South is rising, writes James Reston, but it's not the one. 29.

PAGE MARKERS

Claim by Scientist

Memory Transfer By New Chemical

Houston (AP—A scientist at Baylor college of medicine says a molecule capable of transferring memory from one rat to another has been synthesized.

Dr. Georges Ungar said artificial reproduction of the memory molecule opens the door to unlocking the complex chemical language of learning.

He said that although he has used the memory transfer method only in rats he is "fairly certain" the same principle will work in man. He said how soon the technique might be applied to humans will depend largely on how rapidly his research team gets "badly needed" funds.

Ungar, 64, a native of Hungary and professor of pharmacology in the anesthesiology department at Baylor, has been working on the memory molecule project almost three years.

He said the artificial substance is identical to a naturally occurring molecule responsible for memory transfer from one animal to another. He said it is less expensive and easier to make than to extract the natural molcue.

In his experiments, Ungar trained rats and mice to fear darkness although they normally seek dark places and are active at night.

This was accomplished by administering an electric shock each time the animals entered a darkened box. After a week of such shocks, Ungar extracted the brains of the animals and isolated the molecule associated with the induced response.

"The substance, injected into the bodies of mice which had never been subjected to such electric shocks, caused them to manifest the same fear of darkness," he said yesterday.

The next step was to produce the substance artificially. He was assisted in this phase by Dr. D. M. Lesiderio, assistant professor of chemistry at Baylor, and Dr. Wolfgang Parr, assistant professor of chemistry at the University of Houston. Parr accomplished the first artificial production of an identical substance last week.

"We hope this discovery will give us insight into the way the brain works and processes all information," Ungar said. "When we learn the rules of the brain's learning code, I think we can apply this knowledge to humans."

Lansing Prison 18 Months Later—Conclusion

An Echo of Barbarism

Strip cells are a form of cruel and unusual punishment, a group of prisoners has charged in a lawsuit against the warden and other Kansas penal officials.

By Stephen Nicely
A Member of The Star's Staff

Lansing, Kas.—The solid steel doors on the two strip cells at the Kansas State penitentiary have been welded shut on order of R. J. Gaffney, warden. Gaffney said he does not believe in them.

The small swinging cover over the "peep hole" on one of the cell doors is frozen shut by fresh paint. The cover on the other door swings aside all right, but there is no light inside to see by. There wouldn't be much to see anyway. Last year Fred H. Kelly, former inmate at the penitentiary, described them this way:

"I've spent seven days in a strip cell. They are barbaric. I would rather be in chains with

See ECHO on Page 8

Legal Opponents A lawsuit over alleged cruel and unusual punishment involving the use of strip cells at the Kansas penitentiary is the subject of a conversation between R. J. Gaffney (left), warden; John P. Biscanin (center), attorney for the prisoners, and John Hazelet, deputy penal director for Kansas.

Fig. 5-9. New format. The **Kansas City Star**, once the most staid-looking big paper in the country, now comes close to circus makeup. Note the cutlines in lower left.

HAWKS TRIP
Atlanta, 104-101
TOUGH PISTONS
See Story on Page 9

THE ATLANTA CONSTITUTION

For 101 Years the South's Standard Newspaper

Cold

HOURLY TEMPERATURES		
4 a.m. 25	Noon 30	8 p.m. 30
5 a.m. 24	1 p.m. 30	9 p.m. 29
6 a.m. 22	2 p.m. 34	10 p.m. 28
7 a.m. 21	3 p.m. 34	*11 p.m. 27
8 a.m. 20	4 p.m. 33	*12 M 26
9 a.m. 21	5 p.m. 34	*1 a.m. 25
10 a.m. 25	6 p.m. 30	*2 a.m. 24
11 a.m. 30	7 p.m. 30	*Estimated

VOL. 101, No. 175 ** P. O. Box 4686 ATLANTA, GA., 30302, SATURDAY, JANUARY 11, 1969 64 PAGES, 5 SECTIONS ***** TEN CENTS

RALPH

McGILL

Look Away, Look Away

If the band master will lift his baton we will get on with the tune—

There now is rather general understanding that the old black-face "darky" minstrel song "Dixie," brought to the South in 1861 by a New York black-face minstrel show cast, is unsuited for sports and other public gatherings which include Negro citizens. Some communities, of course, persist in bad manners by defiant "what-are-you-going-to-make-of-it?" renditions of the admittedly lively and jaunty tune. But even they in time will quietly omit it.

Discussion and controversy, pro and con, stir up the "old South" partisans, especially the professionally unreconstructed. These, by their fervor, seemingly wish the Union had been destroyed and the Confederacy perpetuated. These irrelevancies are amusing and psychologically revealing.

Great Songs

One Confederate asks why not call "Yankee Doodle" bad manners? It is argued that the "Battle Hymn of the Republic" and "Marching Through Georgia" are affronts. "Yankee Doodle" is a rewrite of an old English tune dating back to the time of Oliver Cromwell. It was a popular tune of the American Revolution. "The Battle Hymn of the Republic" is one of the great national songs. It speaks for liberty and freedom and against enslavement of human beings. "Marching Through Georgia" was a song inspired by General William T. Sherman's march from Atlanta to the sea. The song ridicules no one. It celebrates a tremendously successful military operation that helped save the Union and end slavery. It seldomly is played today.

Aficionados of "Dixie" should, of course, feel free to go ahead with the song. They might better enjoy it if they formed "Dixie Minstrel Clubs" and staged black-face programs with soft shoe and buck and wing dances. Only in this manner can they get into the original "soul" of the song. They would, of course, wear preposterous costumes. The original cast of the minstrel show which brought "Dixie" from New York to New Orleans in 1861 for performances in the large river cities, wore long-tailed swallow coats, white pantaloons, gloved hands and tattered shoes.

One of the minor but psychologically interesting bits of history was the South's addiction to the black-face minstrel shows in which white men with blacked faces portrayed the stereotype "darky." He deliberately was made a ridiculous figure, afraid of ghosts, dressed in "cast-off," ill-fitting garments; and he was a foot-shifting, shuffling "yas, suh, boss" fellow who was very good at dancing.

Minstrel Show

In reading diaries kept by civilians in the South during the Civil War one finds frequent references to "going to the minstrel show." Many communities organized their own "minstrels" and white participants would black their faces and give imitations of their concept of the stereotype darky. The South's fascination for black-face minstrels persisted into the 1920s.

It obviously is bad manners to affront Negro athletes, students and spectators with "Dixie," a song historically associated with defense of slavery and ridicule of the Negro by white men in black-face performances. One may be sure that no self-respecting Negro athlete would feel complimented if his school had Confederate flags, Confederate uniforms and a band blaring "Dixie" to remind him of ridicule and slavery. "Dixie" was never a Southern song in origin or intent.

By all means let those who can't do without it continue to have it. I do suggest, however, that only if they black their faces and put on preposterous costumes such as the minstrel show "darkies" wore will they get to the soul of it.

Associated Press Wirephoto

APOLLO 8 ASTRONAUTS WAVE TO CROWD IN PARADE UP BROADWAY
L-R: Capt. James A. Lovell, Col. Frank Borman, Lt. Col. William Anders

Apollo Crew Hailed in N.Y.

By RELMAN MORIN

NEW YORK (AP)—New York swept the crew of Apollo 8 into a wide-ranging orbit of honors Friday, accorded by roaring thousands in the streets and by dignitaries in a round of glittering receptions that lasted from morning to midnight.

Raising a glass of champagne in a toast to the city, Air Force Col. Frank Borman, commander of the moon-circling flight said:

"I only wish each of you could have been with us today. I wish you could have seen the faces, the young and the old, the black and the white."

They all had one thing in common: They were all grateful that this country could achieve the accomplishment of Apollo 8.

"We were only the instruments."

His voice was vibrant with emotion.

Borman spoke at a luncheon in which the city honored him and his companions in space, Navy Capt. James A. Lovell Jr., and Air Force Lt. Col. William Anders.

More than 600 guests attended. In the group were former United Nations Ambassador Arthur J. Goldberg; Floyd McKissick and the Rev. Milton Galamison, civil rights leaders; former tennis champion Billy Talbert, singer Pearl Bailey and other notables.

Borman, Lovell and Anders sat at a table presided over by Mrs. John V. Lindsay, wife of the mayor. The centerpiece was a miniature space capsule orbiting around a miniature moon.

Archbishop Terence Cooke delivered the benediction. He spoke of the astronauts' "courage and unselfishness, their strong faith in You."

The three spacemen wore the medals, presented earlier by Lindsay, on ribbons of blue and gold around their necks.

Lindsay spoke of the "multitudes that lined all of the streets of New York from the Battery to Lincoln Center . . . a glorious sight to see."

The mayor said he had heard someone shout to the spacemen, "Fellas, the next time you go, take Lindsay with you."

When Borman rose to speak

Continued on Page 3, Column 4

The Weekend? Fair and Cold

The weather in Atlanta over the weekend should be fair to partly cloudy and continued cold, the weather Bureau says.

A low of 20 was forecast for early Saturday rising to a high of 40 later in the day. Sunday will be partly cloudy and not quite so cold, ranging from a low of 24 to a high of 46.

Georgia forecast by zones is on Page 12.

Hijacker Returns For Sake of Child

MIAMI (AP)—A U.S. Army deserter who flew to Cuba with his younger daughter in a hijacked private plane last summer returned voluntarily to American soil Friday and was arrested by FBI agents.

Willis Jessie, 27, carried his 2-year-old daughter, Patricia Sue, when he stepped from a Mexican airliner which brought him from Mexico City.

Jessie told newsmen he knew he would be arrested if he returned to this country but he wanted to "insure my daughter's future." He said she had no future in the Communist nation.

He had taken the blonde girl from his estranged wife in West Virginia just a few days before he hijacked the private sightseeing plane that took off from Naples, Fla., last August. He ordered the pilot at gunpoint to fly to Cuba, the pilot said.

Three FBI agents met Jessie here as he stepped off the airliner carrying the girl in his arms. He kissed the girl several time on the cheek as the agents took him into custody.

He was wearing a dark blue pullover sweater and he smiled often as the agents spoke with him.

Patricia Sue wore light blue shorts and a blue and white striped blouse. She seemed bewildered by the popping of photographer's flashbulbs.

The FBI agents whisked him away without allowing newsmen to talk to him.

Earlier Friday, Jessie flew from Havana to Mexico City and was taken into custody by Mexican immigration authorities who placed him aboard the flight to Miami.

Jessie, who has been charged with air piracy was a Vietnam veteran. In Mexico he told newsmen he was returning to the United States for personal reasons.

Policeman Dies In Fiery Crash

KANSAS CITY, Mo. (UPI)—A police helicopter on a training flight crashed and burned Friday, killing one officer.

Police identified the victim as patrolman James William Glenn, 35, an eight-year veteran of the force.

A police department spokesman said Glenn, on a solo flight.

GOP Picks Peake to Raise Cash

By DUANE RINER

Georgia Republicans, $17,000 in the hole after their first statewide primary, Friday named a new finance chairman whose chief responsibility will be to pursue "big money" contributors.

The Republican State Central Committee, meeting at the State Capitol, selected George W. Peake Jr. of Macon, president of Georgia Timberlands, Inc., to head the party's drive for funds. He succeeds Bill Merritt of Atlanta.

President-elect Nixon asks Ray Bliss to continue as GOP national chairman. Page 2.

"Our problem in the Republican party has been that 78 per cent of our financing comes from $10, $12 and $15 contributions," said G. Paul Jones of Macon, state party chairman.

The state party, which spent $132,000 last year for operations — not including campaign expenses — received 22 per cent of its budget from contributions in excess of $50 and only 5 per cent from donations of over $500, Jones explained.

"I feel we've got a good, broad base of ten-dollar small contributors," said Jones, predicting that the party will raise between $50,000 and $60,000 through small gifts in the coming year.

"He (Peake) is going to work on expanding the base and appeal to larger contributors," he said. The small contributors, Jones added, "give us a good political as well as financial base." However, he said the chances of attracting larger donations — "as the Democrats have done in the past" — should be easier with the "added strength" of the state party and a Republican in the White House.

The central committee, meeting behind closed doors, also discussed filling federal patronage jobs now held by Democrats.

Jones specifically mentioned such posts as U.S. attorneys and U.S. marshals in Georgia's

Continued on Page 5, Column 1

Reds Step Up Shelling Pace Across Delta

Allies Count 28 Attacks

SAIGON (AP) — An outburst of enemy shellings dotted South Vietnam's war maps Saturday. Many attacks centered on the Mekong Delta, south of Saigon.

Allied spokesmen said there were 28 overnight attacks by mortars, rockets and recoilless rifles. These included hits on five allied installations, spokesmen said. Most of the attacks aimed at towns and villages were described as light.

The shellings made up the main enemy activity, as they have in the recent weeks but initial reports Saturday indicated the pace of the attacks was being stepped up sharply.

Although there were some sporadic clashes, no major ground fighting was reported.

Early reports show the heaviest casualties in overnight shellings occurred at the Kung Vuong training center on the edge of My Tho some 40 miles southwest of Saigon. Eighty government soldiers were reported wounded but none killed by mortar fire.

Mortar rounds later fell on My Tho itself. Casualties and damage were described as light.

Friday a government report claimed that 191,307 enemy troops were killed in 1968. Another 21,050 were captured and 17,597 defected, the South Vietnamese said.

This period covers the big Tet offensive in February that spread desolation across South Vietnam and includes lesser en-

Continued on Page 3, Column 1

Inside Today . . .

Negroes Mark Time in Worth

By PHILIP GAILEY
Constitution Staff Writer

SYLVESTER, Ga.—Negroes called a moratorium on school demonstrations Friday to await the outcome of a hearing Monday for approximately 80 demonstrators arrested earlier this week.

"What happens to our people in that courtroom Monday will help determine our future course of action," said James Burke, a slender, young Negro representing the Worth County Improvement Association.

"If the results are favorable, then we will be willing to sit down and talk about our grievances."

Burke indicated that if charges against the demonstrators are dropped Negroes will discontinue their demonstrations at the J. W. Holley High School here.

However, Negro leaders said they will continue to protest the sentencing of a 14-year-old Negro girl to a state training center after she was found guilty of delinquency charges arising at her school.

Meanwhile, approximately 60 Negro youths remained in juvenile detention homes in Albany and Waycross. They are expected to remain there until their hearing Monday, according to James Hall, a local Negro leader.

Hall said he and other Negroes Friday attempted to provide collateral bond for those who wanted out, but were told by authorities that all bonds must be in cash.

"We didn't figure on having to make cash bonds," Hall said. "They offered to let us sign the bonds last night, but they apparently decided they wanted cash today."

Roosevelt Cuffie, chairman of the Worth County Improvement Association, said some of the Negro youths placed in the Worth County Public Works Camp complained that the heat in the building was turned up and caused "several cases" of nausea and illness. Local authorities denied the charges.

Some 28 Negro youths and a woman were arrested Thursday for demonstrating at the Negro high school and were taken by school bus to the Worth County camp. The youths were later transferred to the juvenile detention centers.

Wednesday, 47 Negro youths and two women were arrested at the school and charged with disturbing the peace. The school has been the target of Negro demonstrations since last December, when the 14-year-old girl and her sister were arrested.

The older sister, 14, was sentenced to a year in a training center and her younger sister, 11, was released in the custody of her parents.

Negroes say they will continue to demonstrate until the training sentence is revoked and the probation sentence is

Continued on Page 3, Column 4

U.S. Pollution Suit Hits 4 Car Makers

WASHINGTON (AP)—The Department of Justice filed suit Friday alleging that four major automobile producers and a trade association have been party to unlawful agreements that delayed development and installation of anti-pollution devices for motor vehicles.

The civil anti-trust suit was filed in U.S. District Court in Los Angeles. It asked for an end to the arrangement, alleging it violated the restraint of trade section of the Sherman Act.

Named as defendants were General Motors Corp., Ford Motor Co., Chrysler Corp., American Motors Corp. and the Automobile Manufacturers Association.

The suit alleged that the defendants and others have agreed since as early as 1953 to eliminate all competition among themselves in research, development, manufacture, installation and publicity of air-pollution devices and in the purchase of patents and patent rights covering such equipment.

It also alleged that the defendants agreed to install anti-pollution devices only at a uniform date.

Printed for 147 Years, Post Will Fold Feb. 8

NEW YORK (AP)—The Saturday Evening Post, which has focused on the simple delights of American life since James Monroe was President, will expire Feb. 8, victim of changing times.

It lost about $5 million in 1968 and faced a deficit of another $3 million this year, Martin S. Ackerman, president, said.

Ackerman said that after refinancing The Saturday Evening Post Co. with $15 million in new capital, he had assured stockholders and directors that regardless of his personal feelings, The Post would be shut down if it could not return a profit.

"Our editors have been producing for the last year or more one of the finest magazines in America but apparently it was not wanted enough to attract advertising dollars. We just could not sell enough advertising and cut expenses fast enough," he said.

"Apparently there is just not the need for our product in today's scheme of living," Ackerman added.

He blamed the inroads television have made on the advertising dollar for the demise of the magazine, founded in 1821.

He disclosed that the Saturday Evening Post Co. had bought about 80,000 shares of Lin Broadcasting Corp. of Nashville, Tenn., about 4 per cent of the outstanding stock, for $3.5 million.

Ackerman said that with the demise of the Post, Curtis would be close to the break-even point. He said there was $12.5 million in the bank "for worthwhile enterprises," which he said he intended to direct toward the communications field.

Curtis will continue to publish Holiday, Status and Jack and Jill magazines, he said.

The Post, which made Norman Rockwell and Tug Boat Annie household names, had been plagued with financial troubles. It was a major factor in Curtis' estimated $62 million loss between 1961 and mid-1968.

Ackerman took over as president and chief executive officer

Continued on Page 3 Column 5

He'd Revive Trolley Cars

CHAPEL HILL, N.C. (AP) — A University of North Carolina engineer believes city planners in rapidly growing areas should turn an ear toward a sound of bygone days the clang, clang, of the trolley cars.

Dr. Albert C. Stern, a professor of air hygiene in the university's School of Public Health, cited major air pollution problems facing cities. For giant cities in the embryo stage, he said, it may be wise to take a second look at the transportation of the past.

"We have abandoned the trolley cars but they certainly caused no air pollution problem," he said.

Annexation Denied; City's Officials Glum

By ALEX COFFIN

The State Supreme Court's 7-0 rejection of a bid by Atlanta to annex adjacent Fulton County urbanized land came as a bitter blow to city officials Friday.

The decision means city-county consolidation becomes even more important to help prevent the city from losing its traditional leadership and being a haven for the poor, Mayor Ivan Allen said.

Speaking at a Northside Kiwanis Club luncheon, Allen said the only route open is for "the parasites on the periphery of the city to finally realize that the golden egg will be broken unless they come in and take over."

The high court ruling, handed down Thursday, reversed Fulton Superior Court Judge Jack Etheridge's decision upholding the test case of a 1952 state law. That law allowed annexation based on urbanization (density or valuation standards) without permission of the property owners involved.

The supreme court ruled that annexation is a power granted to the General Assembly and can't be passed on.

If the test case involving two land lots had been successful, city officials intended to annex most of urbanized Fulton County.

Allen said that the only way to insure that the city retains some of its traditional leadership is to step up moves toward city-county consolidation.

City Atty. Henry Bowden said he was preparing a request for a rehearing. Because of the unanimous vote, that request has little chance, however.

Asked about the possibility of a request for a new method of annexation from the General Assembly, Bowden said he would have to wait for direction from elected city officials. Allen was out of town late Friday and could not be reached for comment on that possibility.

Earlier, Allen reminded the Kiwanians that the poor, mostly Negro, are moving into the central city, with a simultaneous

Continued on Page 3, Column 2

Fig. 5-10. Southern leader. The **Atlanta Constitution** exhibits a clean and neat, if somewhat conventional, front page. All parts of it have typographical strength. Note that column rules contribute to a crowded look.

THE CHRISTIAN SCIENCE MONITOR

BOSTON, TUESDAY, JANUARY 14, 1969 — An International Daily Newspaper — VOL. 61 NO. 41 THREE SECTIONS — MIDWESTERN EDITION • 10¢

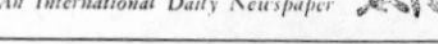

FOCUS on Britain

What's ahead . . .

There is every reason to believe that Britain's rising tide of nationalism will carve out even higher bench marks in 1969.

The year will almost certainly see a start made on restructuring the government and constitution of the United Kingdom of Great Britain and Northern Ireland.

Welsh and Scottish nationalists have notched up considerable successes at the polls. The Plaid Cymru in Wales has widened its hold on the popular vote by 30 percent in two years. A bill now is being prepared for Scottish independence.

Even nationalists in the county of Cornwall—the supporters of "Mebyon Kernow"—are laying plans to put up their own election candidates.

The civil-rights troubles of Northern Ireland, which already has its own Parliament and government as well as representation at Westminster, raise further doubts about the viability of the present UK system.

Liberal and Conservative Parties have taken due note. Both now have reform programs aimed at satisfying nationalist demands while retaining the UK's overall integrity.

Polls show that most nationalist support comes from dissatisfied Labourites. Hence the Labour government feels it must make a move before the next election.

⊕

Britain has had a bill of rights since 1689. Is it time for a new one?

A working group of the organization which ran Human Rights Year (1968) thinks it is.

It proposes that a human-rights commission be set up to handle all complaints from citizens.

This step, the group suggests, should be followed by a new bill which would gather together all rights statutes into a single legal document.

Britain's original declaration and bill of rights include some of what are generally accepted today as basic human rights, but not all of them. And the bill itself is not covered by constitutional guarantee.

Other rights have now been put into law. But, without the protection of the constitution, these also could be changed by parliamentary vote.

Furthermore, the 1689 bill was mainly concerned with protecting Parliament from the sovereign. A new bill would protect the people from the government machine.

Trends . . .

It's been feared that those flareups between Protestant and minority Roman Catholics might make industries shy away from Northern Ireland.

Now that feeling is changing. If the dissension has any adverse effect on the government's program to attract new industries, this, it is believed, will be only temporary.

Why? Nothing succeeds like success. And statistics just released show that output of Ulster firms continues steadily upward.

Estimated gross output of companies employing 25 or more persons rose from £880 million ($2.1 billion) in 1966 to £923 million in 1967—a 5 percent jump.

And this was achieved with a smaller labor force earning wages that grew from £682 to £730 in that 12-month period.

How and why . . .

One of society's contradictions is that law-breakers usually know far more about the law than law-abiding citizens, who rarely if ever see the inside of a court.

Britain's Haldane Society, an association of lawyers, would like to change that. They feel that if a child can be helped to understand the laws that govern his society, then perhaps he will have respect for them.

So the association is proposing that a basic legal education be taught to all children in British secondary schools. The emphasis would be on the nature of law and how it works rather than on its specific content.

The lawyers further suggest that law courses should be made available to adults who don't necessarily have academic qualifications but who want to learn about their country's legal system in their spare time.

Every citizen, says the society, should know about the effect of law on his everyday life.

⊕

For rent: Instant church.

A prefabricated, collapsible, movable building, it's been designed in Britain to serve new housing developments.

With this kind of church building available at a nominal rent, it is hoped that people in housing developments will in time raise enough funds to build their own permanent church.

Then the prefab can be dismantled and transported to some new location in need of a church or community center.

The first of these buildings is expected to serve a new housing area in Sussex.

The idea is quickly spreading. Church authorities across the country are eagerly mulling over its possible uses in their communities.

Where to look

Bundesbildstelle

Joint-operation clouds blur German industrial scene

'Mitbestimmung'

West German industrial future tugged three ways by government, management, unions

By Harry B. Ellis
Staff correspondent of The Christian Science Monitor

Bonn

An elusive concept called "Mitbestimmung" is being tossed about like a political hot potato among political parties and trade unions in West Germany.

"Mitbestimmung" means industrial codetermination, or the sharing of management responsibilities within a firm by employers and workers.

The practice was established in 1951 in the West German coal, iron, and steel industries and the following year was extended in attenuated form to the rest of German industry.

The Federation of German Trade Unions now demands that the coal, iron, and steel model be applied to the 400 largest industrial firms in West Germany.

Management vigorously objects. The political parties, facing a national election this September, are hoping to postpone the issue until a new Parliament is elected.

The Social Democratic Party (SPD), led by Foreign Minister Willy Brandt, gingerly sides with the trade unions—the strongest element of Social Democratic support.

Worker apathy found

Chancellor Kurt Georg Kiesinger's Christian Democratic Union (CDU) is split on the issue, though its sister party — the Christian Social Union (CSU) of Bavaria — comes down squarely on the employers' side.

The concept is elusive, because no one quite knows what the trade-union federation is aiming at or how the system would work.

A public-opinion survey carried out by the Institute for Applied Social Science found that 71 percent of West Germans in principle wanted workers to participate in management decisions.

But workers themselves — as distinct from their trade-union officials — seem apathetic on the question. Many workers queried did not know who, if any, of their representatives sat on boards of directors.

The issue, in other words, currently is being pushed, not by workers en masse, but by their trade-union officials, grouped within the trade-union federation.

Under the 1951 law, each coal and steel company has an 11-man board of directors. Five members represent management, five labor, and the chairman is neutral.

The system has worked generally smoothly. Indeed, it was faster for coal companies

★ Please turn to Page 4

Arab bloc hopeful of U.S. shift

By John K. Cooley
Staff correspondent of The Christian Science Monitor

Amman, Jordan

The Arab world hopes against hope that the anticipated resumption of United States-United Arab Republic diplomatic relations will be a good omen for peace.

The prospect pleases many members of King Hussein's government here. The King, now visiting London, unlike five other Arab rulers, never followed President Nasser's example by breaking with Washington during the June, 1967, Arab-Israeli war.

"Next week [with the inauguration of Richard M. Nixon] just might mean the beginning of many good things," said one Jordanian official. "We hope for a great deal from the new Nixon administration."

This hope has stirred faintly since the Mideast tour last month of William W. Scranton, President-Elect Nixon's special peace emissary.

At the Allenby Bridge between East Jordan and the Israeli-occupied West Bank, where Mr. Scranton spoke his now-famous phrase about the need for a "more even-handed" United States Middle East policy, there was some skepticism.

While two correspondents and a group of

★ Please turn to Page 6

Inside today

Midwinter vacation? Here's a wide selection

Surfing in Hawaii, snowmobile tours to Yellowstone, mountaineering by burro in Jamaica, Motorailroad travel in Britain, chalet renting in the Swiss Alps, air and sea cruising almost anywhere—these are among the travel delights covered in today's Midwinter Vacation Issue.

Second section

U.S. hopes for answers in Soviet Venus probe

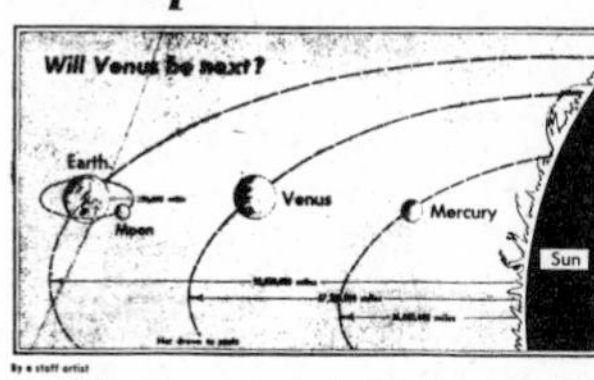

By a staff artist

Needed—measurements of Venus's atmosphere

By Robert C. Cowen
Natural science editor of The Christian Science Monitor

Pasadena, Calif.

American planetary scientists are cheering on the two new Soviet Venus probes with hopes that, this time, the automatic machinery will do its job.

"The thing to hope that the Russians will do is make a really good set of measurements of lower atmosphere composition," explains Dr. Lewis D. Kaplan, planetary atmospheres scientist at the Jet Propulsion Laboratory (JPL) here.

"This was done badly last time," he says. "What we all would like are measurements of things like water vapor or methane in the lower atmosphere and really good measurements of surface temperatures and pressure."

On Oct. 18, 1967, the Soviet Venera 4 reportedly soft landed on Venus. The American Mariner 5 craft, built and commanded by JPL, flew within 6,400 miles of the planet the next day.

The Soviets reported a surface pressure of 12 to 22 times the sea-level pressure at earth. They reported a surface temperature of 536 degrees F. in an atmosphere largely made of carbon dioxide.

Findings conflict

The pressure and temperature data didn't jibe with findings from Mariner 5 and ground-based radar and radio observations. If the Soviets were right, the radius of Venus would be some 30 to 35 kilometers larger than the American findings indicated.

On the other hand, everything matched nicely if scientists assumed that the Soviet data actually referred to a level high in the Venus atmosphere rather than the surface.

Last fall, it turned out that the Soviet probe very likely had failed at high altitude. Its final data appear to have come from a level perhaps 20 miles high rather than from the surface.

This suggests that surface conditions are even more severe than those first reported by the Soviets. An average surface pressure of perhaps 100 atmospheres and average surface temperature close to 800 degrees F. are indicated. The 800 degree temperature would agree with radio measurements made from the ground.

Two probes on way

Now the Soviets have set out to try to get unambiguous data all the way to Venus's surface. The probe Venera 5, launched Jan. 5, is to land on Venus's sunny side sometime next May. Venera 6, launched Friday, reportedly is aimed for the dark side.

"This time," Dr. Kaplan observed, "I think the Russians know what the Venus atmosphere is like and will not underdesign their equipment, as was the case before.

"There may be interesting kinds of clouds lower down in the Venus atmosphere. It's hot enough so that things like mercury and some of its compounds should volatilize. There may be clouds of that there.

"I hope the Russians will take particle samples and analyze them as the probe drops down. They could use a mass spectrometer [an instrument for determining the masses of different particles]. Certainly, we would know how to do this if we had a spacecraft with the weight of the Russian ones."

Its disk shrouded by a perpetual cloud

★ Please turn to Page 3

It's all technology's fault—or is it?

By Florence Mouckley
Staff correspondent of The Christian Science Monitor

London

Technology and the layman are still not speaking to each other.

There was an opportunity for them to kiss and make up at London's current Inventions and New Products Exhibition but the chance was muffed.

It's all technology's fault.

It can't seem to explain itself except in its own complicated terms.

Mental feedback: 'Nil'

True, the LINPEX '69 show—the London International Inventions and New Products Exhibition—is aimed at the engineer, the chemist, the technology expert, and the like. But even more so is it programmed at the nontechnical businessman and ordinary person with some ready money to invest.

There may be a new invention with potential lurking among those on display at LINPEX '69. But the chances are the scientifically unsophisticated investor will pass it right by.

Certainly, if industry, science, and applied technology were "sending," this particular laywoman was not "receiving."

As I read and reread, word by agonizing word, the description of a new computer, the mental feedback I kept getting was, "How's that again?"

The only input I processed was that the maker of this new computer was anti the new decimal system that is coming in in Britain.

The description reads in part:

". . . the . . . computer [is] printed on flexible cheap plastic for shifting the rotor with the left thumb while the stator is held firm and the right hand is free to use the magnifier pencil for extra precision. The existing rigid devices are as unsuited for rapid computing as is the denary (decimal) notation. In scale-16 the L (the symbol re-

★ Please turn to Page 6

By Henry C. Benson, staff artist

Gonks from outer space . . .

2nd Cl Post Pd at Boston, Mass., and add'l offices

Fig. 5-11. White space. The emphasis of the **Christian Science Monitor** on white space and art results in a horizontal makeup with strong overtones of magazine layout. This example has four illustrations, type in five columns, a mixture of roman and italic heads in large sizes, and a big single-word head.

What's Coming Up in 1966 in City and County?

See Page 1B

Colder

U.S. Weather Bureau Forecast

Clearing and colder tonight, mostly sunny tomorrow; the low tonight 20, the high tomorrow 44. (Maps, Page 2A.)

THE TIMES-UNION

48 Pages — Rochester, N.Y., Monday Evening, Jan. 3, 1966 — 10 Cents

What's Ahead in Entertainment — Clip 'n' Save, P. 4C

Suburban News — On Page 8B Today

GIs Invade Delta Area; Pursue Cong

Saigon (AP) — U.S. paratroopers slogged through mud and swamp today in their first big invasion of the Mekong Delta but a large Viet Cong force slipped deeper into the Red sanctuary, eluding their pursuers.

The probe by the 173rd Airborne Brigade, backed by artillery, air strikes and even tanks, began with high hopes of rousing the guerrillas from their stronghold.

Although they offered some sniper fire at the start of the operation on New Year's day, the Viet Cong withdrew into the marshes in the direction of the Plain of Reeds near the Cambodian frontier.

There was only occasional contact with the guerrillas today.

A U.S. spokesman said the 173rd Brigade had killed 111 Viet Cong, captured 7 and detained 502 suspects. Vietnamese troops killed 125 guerrillas in the fighting, their spokesman said.

The U.S. paratroopers had moved westward from Saigon into the sugar and rice fields around Bao Trai, 20 miles from the capital. They captured a large store of rice and other food and some National Liberation Front flags.

By venturing into delta country, the U.S. paratroopers were probing a Communist stronghold that the French were unable to control in eight years of fighting. Government forces have had no more success in recent years.

• • •

U.S. PLANES spared North Viet Nam from attack for the 11th day but B52s bombed jungle targets in Binh Duong Province 40 miles northwest of Saigon.

The Communists attacked a Vietnamese scout company command post with flamethrowers and grenades 12 miles south of Tuy Hoa on the central coast, but were beaten off. Ten Reds were reported killed.

A military spokesman said it was the first time the Communists used flamethrowers.

• • •

TEAR GAS was reported used against the enemy in two instances today.

Associated Press photographer Rick Merron reported from Tuy Hoa, 240 miles northeast of Saigon, that South Koreans discovered a tunnel 1,500 yards long and cleared it with tear gas.

Some Viet Cong were flushed but most of the Vietnamese inside were civilians hiding.

(Hanoi again hits U.S. peace efforts, Page 6A.)

U.S. Will Shift Steel Orders

Washington (AP) — Secretary of Defense Robert S. McNamara directed the shifting of orders for future deliveries of structural steel away from the Bethlehem Steel Corp. and any other firm raising prices.

McNamara issued a statement announcing that he had directed "all defense procurement officials, wherever possible, to shift orders for future deliveries of items of steel on which prices have been raised to companies which have not increased prices."

• • •

JUST AS Asst. Secretary of Defense Arthur Sylvester was reading McNamara's statement to newsmen, the Inland Steel Co. was announcing a boost similar to Bethlehem's $5-a-ton increase in certain types of structural steel.

McNamara ordered that defense procurement officials "take all practicable steps" to insure that defense contractors adopt the same procedures as military procurement officers with respect to their purchases and those of their subcontractors.

The Defense Department uses about 320,000 tons a year of structural shapes and piling. This represents about 5 per cent of total industry output, which has been running at about six million tons a year.

(Other story, Page 4D).

Today's Chuckle

One way to be popular is to listen to a lot of things you already know.

Revolution Topic in Cuba Talks

Havana (AP)—Revolutionists from three continents assembled in Havana to open a nine-day meeting today, increasing apprehension among governments of some of Communist Cuba's neighbors.

"The peace of the continent is at stake," said President Raul Leoni of Venezuela. The so-called Tricontinental Conference of Solidarity is "a new aggression against Venezuela," he said.

Leaders of Brazil, Peru and Colombia were also particularly worried. Each nation has tasted the guerrilla terrorism that the conference delegates favor for the "liberation of the people from oppressive regimes."

Most of the decisions by the approximately 500 delegates from 100 countries will not be revealed. A few open sessions are planned, but they are expected to be filled with long speeches spouting the usual anti-American line.

The real debate and action on the "common struggle against imperialism, colonialism and neo-colonialism" will take place in closed sessions at the former Havana Hilton Hotel in downtown Havana.

• • •

CUBAN Prime Minister Fidel Castro anticipated the "hate-America" mood of the conference in a speech yesterday on the seventh anniversary of his revolution. But most of the speech provided gloomy news for the Cubans.

Castro disclosed that Communist China had broken a trade agreement and would not ship any more rice nor buy any more Cuban sugar.

"We now find we have only half the rice we had in 1964," he said. "We did not grow more rice ourselves because we were concentrating on other agricultural products."

He said China had to stop sending Cuba rice because of stepped up shipments to North Viet Nam, a drop in Chinese production and the need for reserves "in case China is attacked."

Freeman Named Vice Mayor With Support of Gillette

After Councilman Was Stricken

Councilman William J. Malley (right) emerges from Mayor Frank Lamb's office after being taken ill today at Democratic caucus. In front of him is Public Safety Commissioner Harper Sibley Jr.

Lamb Re-Elected Mayor; Malley Ill but Votes

Republican Councilman Hyman B. Freeman was elected vicemayor today with the support of Democrat Henry E. Gillette.

Gillette joined his four fellow Democrats in voting to re-elect Frank T. Lamb as mayor, but sided with the four Republicans to elect Freeman.

Freeman replaces Democrat Mario J. Pirrello as vice mayor.

Gillette has been bitter toward Pirrello since being forced to resign as mayor 2 years ago. His resignation was forced by Pirrello, Councilman William J. Malley and then-Councilman Charles T. Maloy.

Gillette referred to his forced resignation today in voting for Lamb for mayor.

"It is well known that I was hurt by the manner in which I was removed as mayor by certain members of the council," he said.

In voting for Freeman, Gillette said a Republican in the office of vice mayor would result in greater cooperation between the "Democratic" city and the "Republican" county.

Today's meeting, scheduled to start at noon, was delayed about 30 minutes when Malley fainted at a caucus of Democrats in the city clerk's office, just before the council session was to begin.

Malley's head hit a door as he fell. He was revived and walked the few steps to Lamb's office. Dr. Louis A. Cerulli was summoned.

Malley, 49, was able to attend the meeting, but left after the election of Freeman.

Dr. Cerulli said Malley had suffered a "cerebral spasm." He said the councilman was still weak from his bout with pneumonia and pleurisy during last fall's campaign.

FRANK LAMB

FREEMAN, 61, a lawyer, has served on the council since 1955. A 12th Ward resident, he represents the East District.

Lamb, 43, a councilman-at-large, was first elected in 1957. He succeeded Gillette as mayor in 1964.

• • •

BEFORE it was known whether Malley would be able to attend the council meeting, Lamb appealed to Republican minority leader Freeman for GOP support to re-elect Lamb.

Freeman declined, claiming Lamb wasn't pure he had Gillette's vote. Freeman offered to allow indefinite adjournment of the meeting to permit Malley to attend. Under the City Charter, the meeting had to be held today.

HYMAN FREEMAN

In voting for Lamb, Gillette had sharp words for his party.

"Recently," he added, "on the local level, the dominating influence in the Democratic party has been a favored and privileged few who seek special treatment and advance their own interests. . . ."

He said he was voting for Lamb to avoid a council stalemate but served notice he would "vote with the Republicans when I think they are right."

After the meeting, Gillette told a reported he decided to vote for Freeman when the other Democrats refused, at the caucus, to elect Democratic Councilman Raymond J. Lill as vice mayor. Lill was Gillette's choice to replace Pirrello.

Freeman said his election came as "a complete shock."

"I had no notion Mr. Gillette was think in this direction. Wait 'till my wife hears this."

GILLETTE WASTED no time asserting his new power in the council.

Adopted, with the support of the four Republicans, was a Gillette resolution increasing the number of council committees from six to nine. Each councilman will serve as chairman of one committee.

Gillette's fellow Democrats were considering reducing the number of committees from six to five. This would have permitted a different Democrat to head each committee.

For the last two years, when they held a 6-3 margin, Democrats headed all the committees.

Before the Democrats won council control in 1961, there were nine committees. Each councilman, including the minority Democrats, held a chairmanship.

"He (Gillette) brought them (the assignments) in this morning and we didn't agree with them," Pirrello commented later. "It's going to be a difficult time. You'll walk into every council meeting and not know where you're going to be."

Win $1,512

Don't forget the deadline for this week's Puzzle Contest is 1 p.m. Wednesday!

And we have continued the special $500 bonus payable to a winner who is a six-day-a-week Times-Union subscriber. The total jackpot if you meet all the qualifications is $1,512.50.

Thousands Stay Home, Ease N.Y. Transit Jam

New York (AP) — The brunt of a two-day-old transit strike hit New York City this morning, but a major traffic crisis was averted when thousands of workers apparently heeded official advice to stay at home.

The increased flow of cars threatened for a time to overwhelm Manhattan with automobiles, then eased into a flow described as normal.

As traffic had piled up during the early rush hour Mayor John V. Lindsay warned he might be forced to close off the city to any more automobiles.

Lindsay, who took office just hours before the bus and subway workers struck New Year's Day, climbed into a police helicopter for a personal inspection of the choked arteries from the foggy, drizzly skies.

Then, like a breaking fever, the crisis passed and Traffic Commissioner Henry A. Barnes reported traffic in Manhattan was "loosening up."

And the mayor lifted his threat.

By 9 p.m. Barnes said traffic was "about normal now," but urged that no additional drivers head for Manhattan.

He predicted there would be continuous traffic jams in Manhattan throughout the day.

• • •

THE STAY-AT-HOMES, possibly numbering well over a million, may have made the difference between an orderly rush hour and traffic chaos equivalent to that of the Nov. 9 blackout.

Barnes said the city weathered the inbound crush on its roadway, bridge and tunnel system "much better than contemplated." But, he warned, it does not mean the crisis is over.

"We do not know what will happen later today or tomorrow," he said.

Barnes attributed the easing of Manhattan's traffic to the fact that drivers headed for work about two hours earlier than usual. This caused early morning tieups, but eased conditions in the midst of the usual rush hour.

• • •

NEW YORKERS didn't feel the full impact of the strike until today because of the holiday weekend.

Lindsay went on radio and television early today to make a last-minute appeal to commuters not to drive into the city.

The new mayor, setting a brisk pace for newsmen accompanying him, walked 3½ miles from the Hotel Roosevelt to City Hall in 45 minutes.

"Good for the circulation," Lindsay remarked.

ONCE COMMUTERS did get to Manhattan, they still faced walks of varying distances to their places of work—from a few blocks up to seven or eight miles.

Virtually all of the city's 11,772 taxicabs were operating, the Police Department's hack bureau said, and doing a land-office business.

Ignoring the regular rules

Turn to back page of this section

New Yorker 'Fed Up' by Strike, Quits

New York (UPI) — He was tall and wore horn-rimmed glasses, a hounds tooth jacket, tasseled loafers and he was fed up. The transit strike was the last straw.

"Tell them my name is John Petters and I'm getting out," the man told a reporter on route to the airport.

"I've had enough of this town. When you want a taxi there's a taxi strike. When you want to go home the elevator stalls for six hours so the only thing to do is take a plane and get out."

Petters, said his employer had a branch in Miami and he intended to fly there — then call his boss long distance and ask for a transfer.

(New Yorkers use cunning, Page 4A)

Antique Gems Stolen

London (UPI) — Thieves stole antique silverware and jewelry worth about $25,000 from the Mayfair antique shop owned by Denisa Lady Newborough, police reported yesterday. The week-end burglars got into the basement of the house and then chopped a hole in the ceiling to get into the shop above. It was the latest in a spectacular series of jewelry robberies in London this winter.

Sing Sing Prisoners On Strike

New York (AP) — An undetermined number of prisoners at Sing Sing went on strike today in what Warden Wilfred Denno said apparently was a protest against reduction in time off for good behavior.

Denno said there was no violence, but a number of prisoners refused to report for work in the prison's various shops and were "sitting in" on the stands of the baseball field and other sheltered areas.

The warden said he had no control over the "good time" situation, which is in the hands of the legislature.

Fulton County Sheriff Named

Albany (AP) — John Brown of Johnstown is the Fulton County Sheriff, succeeding the late Chris Penchoff.

Gov. Rockefeller named Brown to the post Friday to serve through Dec. 31, 1966. Fulton County voters will choose a sheriff for a regular term in November's election.

Unrest Hits Upper Volta

Quagadougou, Upper Volta (AP) —Police fired tear gas at thousands of demonstrators swarming around the presidential palace today after the government of this West African nation seized emergency powers.

The political climate in Upper Volta has been tense since President Maurice Yameogo declared a state of emergency yesterday.

Easy-to-read . . . easy-to-find . . . INSIDE YOUR TIMES-UNION

★ ★ ★

Getting Your Lumps . . .

IT'S ALL PART of the game in professional hockey. . . .

Read a report of an interview with the Amerks' Brian Conacher by T-U Hockey Writer Frank Cardon. . . . It took place as Brian sat on the training table, the victim of an opponent's skate. . . . It's on Page 8C today. . . .

A THREE-MONTH-OLD BABY steals the show. . . . Read about it in ROCHESTER AFTER DARK, your daily column of night-time doings . . . on the front of your Time Out Section today, Page 1C. . . .

For other easy-to-find, easy-to-read features:

Four Sections

Cut Your Own Taxes

Refunds Returning

This is the first of 14 articles designed to help you save money on taxes.

By RAY DE CRANE
Newspaper Enterprise Assn.

Refunds should be back in vogue again this year.

While filing an income tax return is never an event looked forward to with great expectancy, this year's task should not be the nightmare shared by so many a year ago.

The Revenue Act of 1964 cut the tax rate in two stages. Two-thirds of the cut was effective in 1964; the other third applies to income received in 1965.

And for all of 1965 the withholding tax tables were in complete harmony with the new rates. This was not true in 1964 when the withholding tax cut was too deep to match the tax rate reduction. Consequently, many who had been accustomed to a refund had to make a payment in April 1965 and others found the tax due to be far greater than anticipated.

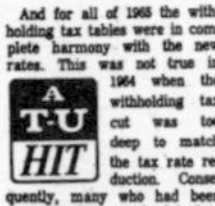

A reduction in the rates—in the lowest bracket the rate has been trimmed from 16 per cent to 14 per cent (a 12½ per cent cut)—is just one of the many changes affecting 1965 earnings.

Persons who have stock investments will find new rules for the accounting of dividends. The first $100 in dividends is excludable from income. If a husband and wife are filing a joint return and each has divi

Turn to back page of this section

Fig. 5-12. **Brace.** In brace makeup, heads and pictures across top and down right form a right angle. The house organ of the Gannett newspapers reproduced this front page of the **Rochester Times-Union** to illustrate handling of holiday news.

SEC Probes Big Stock Volume Story on Page 21, Section C	Frank Shakespeare to Head USIA Story on Page 4, Front Section	Woman Mayor's Record Lauded Story on Page 48, Section F

Wilkins Raps All-Black Study Depts. as 'Jim Crow'

Copyright, 1969, Denver Post-New York Times

NEW YORK — Moderate civil rights leader Roy Wilkins voiced strong opposition Monday to demands by Negro students for all-black studies departments on college campuses.

Wilkins, executive director of the National Association for the Advancement of Colored People (NAACP), said such demands were simply "another version of segregation and Jim Crow."

He said that he not only disagreed with students but added that there was a good chance that the NAACP might test the legality of such departments in court.

In addition to criticizing the idea of black studies departments, Wilkins also rapped students supporting the concept. "They ought to be in the libraries studying and getting degrees so they can do some good," the 67-year-old leader of the nation's oldest and largest civil rights organization said.

Wilkins spoke out at the annual corporate meeting of the NAACP at the Park Sheraton Hotel here.

"We must be for change, yes," he said. "Reform, yes. Sharp alteration in methods, yes. Acceleration, yes. But separatism, no."

Wilkins said that it would be "simple suicide" for a minority as small and as circumscribed as the blacks in America "to talk seriously of separatism, apartheid and going it alone."

He added that "we have suffered too many heartaches and shed too many tears and too much blood in fighting the evil of racial segregation to return in 1969 to the lonely and dispiriting confines of its demeaning prison."

With his plea came the warning to the colleges:

"If some white Americans, torn and confused by today's clamor of some black students, should accede officially to the call for separate dormitories and autonomous racial schools within colleges and universities, there will be court action to determine anyone's right to use public tax funds to set up what are, patently, Jim Crow schools."

TEACHERS, MILITANTS

Groups Outline Changes for Cole

By RICHARD O'REILLY
Denver Post Staff Writer

Two sets of demands—one voted on by teachers and the other drafted by the Denver Black Panthers and other black militants—aimed at making changes at Cole Junior High School, 3240 Humboldt St., were outlined Monday.

Both sets of proposals stem from an attack on two white male teachers Thursday by a group of Negro youths, six of whom were arrested. One of the teachers suffered a minor stab wound. Cole has a predominantly Negro enrollment.

Proposals Considered

The proposals considered by the teachers included a demand that Cole be closed if all other demands aren't met, and consideration of a call for the resignation of the school's principal and assistant principal.

A list of 27 demands was voted on at a meeting of Cole teachers at the school Monday, and, if passed by the secret ballot, could be presented to the Denver Board of Education at its meeting Thursday night. Guy Burrill, a teachers' spokesman, said he doesn't know when the ballots will be counted.

The list incorporates 16 demands previously made of Cole Principal Philip G. Serafini concerning school discipline.

The Black Panthers and the other militants issued their own demands later Monday, after Serafini refused to let a group of Panthers, militants and whites attend the teachers meeting.

Serafini said they weren't allowed to attend, because it was a private meeting and the teachers needed the benefit of their own thinking without outside influence. Serafini said he didn't attend, either.

Generally, the teachers' demands would be aimed at achieving better student dis-

Continued on Page 3.

Educators, Police Study School Strife

Mayor Bill McNichols told the Denver City Council Tuesday that police and school officials have been meeting for the past two days to find a solution for the problems at Cole Junior High School and East High School in northeast and east Denver.

McNichols disclosed that conferences between the police and school officials were taking place after Council President Elvin Caldwell demanded that police protect people and students in the areas surrounding the two schools.

The mayor said, that he, the councilmen and police aren't qualified and don't have the authority to govern what occurs in the schools.

Caldwell said he was more concerned about what is happening in the areas surrounding the schools.

"What can be done inside the schools is problematical," he added.

McNichols told the councilmen he would get in touch with them again after the police and city officials work out a plan to cope with the situation.

GOOD NEWS TODAY

Denver Is 'Assured' On Model City OK

Lee Johnson, director of the Denver Model City agency, said Tuesday that he has been assured Denver's first-year action program will be approved this week in Washington.

Johnson told the weekly meeting of Mayor Bill McNichols and the city council that he was given this assurance in a telephone conversation Tuesday morning with Ralph Taylor, assistant secretary of the Department of Housing and Urban Development (HUD).

Johnson said Taylor, who is in charge of the national Model Cities program, told him that approval of the $29.4 million Denver plan might come as early as Wednesday and would surely come no later than Friday.

The approval of the first-year action plan, consisting of 75 varied projects, carries with it a $5.8 million HUD grant to help pay the local share of the largely federally financed program.

Johnson asked that the councilmen approve a $116,455 appropriation in city funds for administration of the program. He said the appropriation bill would be filed for consideration by the council next Monday night in preparation for the HUD approval of the over-all Denver plan.

The $116,455, representing the city's 20 per cent share of the cost of administration of the program, will pay the salaries of the some 30 people on the Model City staff. They have been paid for the past several months from a $223,000 planning grant provided by HUD.

POST DIGEST OF TOP NEWS

THE SPACE AGE

RUSSIA HAS ORBITED Lt. Col. Vladimire Shatalov in Soyuz-4 in what has been called a "complex, responsible mission." (Page 6)

POLITICS

HISTORY'S VERDICT will be "we tried," President Johnson said in evaluating his White House term at a New York dinner dance. (Page 4)

NEGRO LEADERS have singled out Daniel P. Moynihan, named assistant for urban affairs, in criticism of President-elect Richard M. Nixon's appointees. (Page 6)

NATIONAL

CRUDE OIL from a pipeline leak has forced evacuation of 8,000 persons in Lima, Ohio. (Page 5)

Continued on Page 2.

IN TODAY'S POST

General Information, Sports Scores Dial 297-1521

After 9 p.m. dial 297-1010.

To Place Want Ad—Dial 292-1160

THE WEATHER

'Tis a Privilege to Live in Colorado

The sun rose in Denver at 7:20 a.m.; the sun sets at 4:59 p.m.

DENVER TEMPERATURES FOR THE PAST TWENTY-FOUR HOURS

MONDAY		TUESDAY	
[illegible]	[illegible]	[illegible]	[illegible]

Denver and Vicinity (Radius 20 Miles)—Considerable cloudiness Tuesday night and Wednesday. Chance of shower or light snow Tuesday night and Wednesday. The low Tuesday night, near 30. Mostly west winds 5 to 15 miles an hour Tuesday night. Colder Wednesday, high in the upper 40s. Precipitation probability Tuesday night and Wednesday, 30 per cent.

Colorado—Considerable cloudiness Tuesday night and Wednesday. Snow most mountain areas and chance of rain or snow west Tuesday night, decreasing west Wednesday. Chance of showers spreading east Tuesday night and Wednesday. Chance of heavy snow some high mountains west Tuesday night. Cooler west Tuesday night and most of state Wednesday. Lows Tuesday night, 20 to 30 west, 25 to 35 east and 10 to 20 mountains. Highs Wednesday, 35 to 45 east, in the 30s mountains and west.

U.S. WEATHER REPORT ON PAGE 21.

THE DENVER POST
★ ★ HOME EDITION
Vol. 77, No. 166 — 10 Cents, 48 Pages
The Voice of the Rocky Mountain Empire® Denver, Colo.—Climate Capital of the World—Tuesday, January 14, 1969

Red-Held Peninsula Invaded by Marines

Amphibious Move Biggest Since Korea

SAIGON—(UPI)—U.S. Marines invaded a Communist-held peninsula on South Vietnam's central coast in the biggest amphibious operation since the Leathernecks landed at Inchon 18 years ago during the Korean War, military spokesmen said Tuesday.

Rear Adm. William W. Behrens Jr., commander of the invasion force, said there had been 62 amphibious assaults in Vietnam since 1965, but "none can compare with this." He said many more troops were landed at Inchon in September 1950 in the campaign that drove the North Korean Army out of South Korea, "but this is a far more complicated and far-reaching operation in every other respect."

Communiques said some 3,000 U.S. Marines riding helicopters and landing craft swept into the Batangan Peninsula Monday from the South China Sea. Another 2,000 U.S. and South Vietnamese infantrymen set up a cordon at the neck of the isthmus to block a Communist retreat.

The allied force eventually will total 8,200 men.

Red Soldiers 'Holed Up'

About 1,000 Communist soldiers were believed holed up on the peninsula 300 miles northeast of Saigon. Leaflet drops and loudspeaker broadcasts urged an estimated 5,000 to 10,000 civilians in the area to leave prior to the assault.

The target was an 8-square-mile area heavily fortified with bunkers and tunnels that has been used by the Communists as a staging point for more than 20 years, the spokesmen said. Many of the fortifications were constructed by the Japanese during World War II.

"There are a lot of VC (Viet Cong) in there, and we are sure it will be strongly contested," said Brig. Gen. Howard H. Cooksey of Alexandria, Va., one of the task-force commanders.

Americal Division

Participating in the peninsula drive were elements of the U.S. Army Americal Division, the Marines' 26th Regimental Landing Team and units of the South Vietnamese 2nd Infantry Division.

The same area was the scene of the first major American battle of the Vietnam war in August 1965. Also a seaborne assault, that operation left 56 Leathernecks dead and 150 wounded against 560 enemy killed.

The operation wasn't announced until Tuesday for security reasons. Spokesmen said the advancing troops so far have encountered only light sniper fire, and they speculated it might be some time before the cordon is closed tight enough to force the enemy to fight or surrender. One Marine was killed and six wounded in the early phases.

470 Suspects Held

Military spokesman said 470 suspected Communists had been detained by Marines so far. If past experience is a guide, nearly all will ultimately be released. One woman suspect gave birth to a child in the midst of the roundup and was removed with the baby to a rear area hospital.

Military officials said the cordon won't be pushed too quickly. The area is honeycombed on higher ground with tunnel systems, some three layers deep. Strategists speculate it will take time for guerrillas in these tunnels to run out of food and fresh water, and the allies don't want them popping up behind them with automatic weapons.

Red troops kidnap 40 refugees. Page 5.

You Can Improve Your Reading—See Page 11

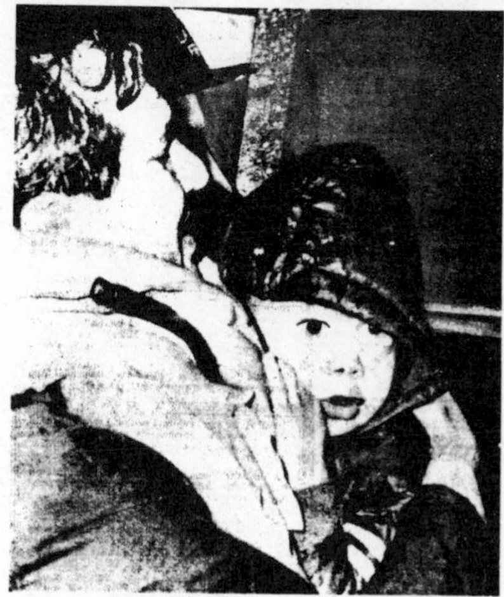

UPI Telephoto

Safe, but Scared Survivors

One of the 30 survivors of the crash of a Scandinavian Airlines jet into the Pacific Ocean near Los Angeles clutches a frightened, soaked youngster as they are assisted ashore at Plaza del Rey Harbor Monday night. Four bodies were found, and 11 other persons were feared killed in the crash of the DC8. The ship plunged into water while making landing. (STORY, PAGE 5.)

Interest in Bull Sold for $45,000

A three-quarter interest in Upstream Dundy 187, champion Hereford bull of the National Western Stock Show, sold Tuesday morning for $45,000—a record price for a bull at the Denver sale.

The consignees, Alfred and Ferrall Meeks of Upstream Ranch, Taylor, Neb., retained one-quarter semen rights.

The buyer was Clarence Cross of Jo-Su-Li Farms, Colquitt, Ga.

An American Hereford Association official said the $45,000 paid for three-quarter interest in the bull places his total value at $60,000.

The previous record bull price—$52,500—was paid for full interest in the champion Hereford of the 1967 show.

On the auction block in the Tuesday sale, which was expected to run through the afternoon, were 76 bulls and 15 females.

See photo on Page 43.

Admiral McCain Stricken

HONOLULU — (UPI) — Adm. John S. McCain Jr., the man in charge of all military operations in the Pacific, was in Tripler general hospital Tuesday recovering from a "mild stroke."

McCain, who will be 58 Jan. 17, was stricken Monday. His condition late Monday was described as "stable."

A spokesman for McCain's headquarters said the admiral suffered a "mild stroke without paralysis."

LBJ Likely to Defer Specifics for Nixon

WASHINGTON — (AP) — President Johnson is expected to outline his analysis of the State of the Union in broad terms Tuesday night and defer recommendations for specific legislation to his successor.

Close associates of the outgoing President say the only exception in his farewell address to a joint session of Congress, and to the nation via television and radio, will be to recommend that the 10 per cent income tax surcharge be extended.

By doing so he can include the $13 billion annual revenue produced by the surcharge in his budget for fiscal 1970, and thus show a small surplus when he sends his last breakdown on government spending to Congress Wednesday.

After it became known Monday that Johnson would recommend continuance of the surcharge, with or without President-elect Richard Nixon's endorsement, he apparently got private assurances of support from Nixon.

Aides of Nixon said in New York that he would make a statement immediately after Johnson's message, and indicated he would endorse the President's decision.

Speech on TV, Radio

President Johnson's State of the Union Message will be televised at 7 p.m. Tuesday over Channels 4, 7 and 9, and at 8 p.m. over Channel 6 in Denver. The message will be broadcast by radio stations KOA, KBTR and KTLN at 7 p.m. and KLZ at 8:30 p.m.

Rain or Snow in Forecast

There's a chance of "a little" rain or snow in the Denver area Tuesday night or Wednesday, according to the Weather Bureau. The precipitation probability for the period is rated at 30 per cent.

If it comes, the precipitation was expected to start in the western valleys of Colorado Tuesday and spread to the eastern portion of the state Tuesday night or Wednesday. It's expected to diminish in the western valleys Wednesday.

The same precipitation pattern is forecast for Wyoming.

It will be cooler Wednesday, with the high in Denver expected to be in the upper 40s. The high Monday was 50, first recorded at Stapleton International Airport at 3:45 p.m. The low Monday night was 30, recorded at 7:30 p.m.

THE PASSES

Loveland—Snowpacked in spots.
Vail—Icy in spots, sanded.
Berthoud—Icy in spots.
Rabbit Ears—Icy in spots.
Monarch—Icy west side, icy in spots and sanded east side.
Wolf Creek—Light snow, snowpacked, chains required.

Fig. 5-13. Post circus. Once the outstanding exemplar of razzle-dazzle circus makeup, the **Denver Post,** whose nameplate always appears on a red-block background, still comes as close to circus as any leading American newspaper. (But note fig. 5-14.)

Mighty Fine
Fair through today. High upper 70s. Low 55-60. S to SW winds, 5-15 m.p.h. Chance of rain in northern areas. Weather maps, data, 2-A.

St. Petersburg Times

Florida's Best Newspaper

VOL. 87—NO. 184 230 PAGES ST. PETERSBURG, FLORIDA, SUNDAY, JANUARY 24, 1971 7 DAYS HOME DELIVERY 85 25 CENTS A COPY

Florida's Courtly Myth: Equal Justice Under Law

By MARTIN DYCKMAN
Of The Times Staff

TALLAHASSEE — Florida courts make a mockery of the motto "Equal justice under law."

Equal justice is a myth, an unfunny joke, to Florida's convicts, as they sit in prisons and compare grossly unequal sentences.

IT'S A MYTH to the black man. His chance of going to prison once the jury says "guilty" is at least twice as high, research indicates, as that of a white man. And the black man's sentence will be longer.

It's a myth even to the prison wardens, counsellors and teachers who compare sentences just as the inmates do.

James Ivey, superintendent at Sumter Correctional Institution, reached into his desk for random contrasts the Division of Corrections has prepared:

✓ Ronald, 18, from Escambia County, a life sentence for an unarmed robbery in which he stole two bottles of whisky; Lucius, 22, Dade County, five years for a gang robbery involving two revolvers and a shotgun. For both men, their first felony convictions.

✓ **ROGER,** 17, from Escambia County, doing 21 years for robbery and attempted breaking and entering, his loot having been cigarettes, candy and a revolver; James, 23, Dade County, three years for a $250 grocery holdup. For both, their first felonies.

✓ Samuel, 25, 20 years for driving the getaway car in four robberies; Larry, 18, four years for strongarm robbery of four people. For both, their first felonies.

"And we're supposed to tell these guys about justice and honesty and truth," Ivey said bitterly.

Theory teaches two sensible reasons for varying sentences: what it takes to protect society from the individual lawbreaker and what it takes to reform him. Those aren't easy judgments under the best conditions; of course, there is no textbook formula for the judge's guide.

WHAT'S WORSE is that 151 different Florida judges have the power to send men, women and children to prison, and the discretion to send them there for a long while, a little while, or not at all.

So Florida's prison sentences also vary:

✓ According to where the lawbreaker broke the law, not simply which law he broke;

✓ According to which judge draws his case, and what the judge's personal prejudices are;

✓ In many cases, according to whether the defendant was foolish enough to insist on his constitutional right to a jury trial.

PRISON OFFICIALS say it's common knowledge that crimes against property are punished more severely in North Florida than in the urban south, and that crimes against persons — assault, for instance provided no robbery is involved — get off lightly in the farmlands and are treated

(See JUSTICE, 20-A)

★

Florida's prison sentences vary:

✓ According to where the lawbreaker broke the law, not simply which law he broke.

✓ According to which judge hears his case, and the judge's personal prejudices.

✓ In many cases, according to whether the defendant was foolish enough to insist on his constitutional right to a jury trial.

On Sidelines, War Is Cause For Cheering

By PETER A. JAY
Washington Post Service

PHNOM PENH — Hundreds of Phnom Penh residents sat on the west bank of the Mekong River Saturday night, listening with evident enjoyment to a battle between Cambodian and Communist forces several miles away.

Monks from the city's largest Buddhist pagoda stood outdoors in the warm darkness listening to distant machine-gun fire and the crump-crump-crump of mortars. Townspeople, like Americans at a country fireworks display, sat in family groups on the river bank and cheered as tracer bullets from a Cambodian navy gunboat in the river arched across the sky.

WHEN AN unidentified aircraft fired a spectacular series of rockets, presumably at Communist positions, there was mild giggling and much nodding of heads.

Earlier in the day, a few wisps of smoke still were rising from what had been a barracks area for soldiers and their families on the grounds of Phnom Penh's devastated Pochentong Airport. Relatives still searched the rubble for bodies.

Across the road, troops wandered through the ruins of an army transport camp, staring at the blackened hulks of scores of trucks destroyed in Friday's massive Communist assault on the airfield and surrounding facilities.

FOR THE first time since the Indochina war began to spread into Cambodia last spring, residents of Phnom Penh could see some of the more grisly effects of that

(See SCENE, 21-A)

U.S. Flies War Supplies Into Battered Cambodia

UPI

American Cobra Helicopters Refuel Near Cambodian Border For Sorties Along Route 4

By The Associated Press

The United States hurried war supplies to Cambodia Saturday, including material for bolstering defenses at Phnom Penh airport, badly battered by an enemy attack.

Two U.S. Air Force C130 transport planes ferried 80 tons of war supplies, including arms, ammunition, spare parts, barbed wire and sandbags.

THE BARBED wire is badly needed. The Cambodians complained they could not provide adequate security at the airport before Friday's attack because they had no barbed wire, even though they expected the attack.

At about the time the airlift was resumed after deliveries were halted for 24 hours by the destructive attack on the airport, a plastic bomb exploded in Phnom Penh at a downtown government office.

Military police said perhaps 10 persons were wounded in the explosion at an immigration service office. They knew of no dead, but said it was possible some bodies may be in the ruins.

The enemy also followed up the airport attack by firing mortar shells into the army's main fuel dump on the outskirts of Phnom Penh during the night but no gasoline tanks were hit.

A government spokesman said an alert Cambodian lieutenant Friday night foiled an attack by saboteurs on an army gasoline dump at Prek Phnoeu, nine miles north of the capital. He reported the officer spotted enemy movement, loosed a rocket flare and in the severe fighting four enemy were killed. Three Cambodian soldiers were killed, he added.

MEANWHILE, a combined Cambodian and South Vietnamese force completed a linkup on Route 4 Friday in Pich Nil Pass, halfway down the 115-mile highway from Phnom Penh to Kompong Som, the deep water port on the Gulf of Siam. North Vietnamese had blocked it for two months.

The South Vietnamese military command announced in Saigon that the 5,300 troops who helped Cambodian soldiers clear the highway would soon be withdrawn. Another 9,000 South Vietnamese troops are operating elsewhere in Cambodia.

"This does not mean they (the Saigon forces) will not

(See CAMBODIA, 21-A)

Tax-Sharing Battle Looms

Times Wire Services

WASHINGTON — President Nixon plans to campaign nationally for broad, bipartisan support for his massive new government reform proposals.

Officials disclosed Saturday that Nixon will make trips to four regional meetings at places not yet determined. The first trip will be in February.

THE PRESIDENT also plans to send Cabinet officers and White House officials on simultaneous satellite trips to other major cities.

As a reflection of bipartisanship, it was learned that steps had been taken, with at least the knowledge of the White House, toward the possible formation of a committee of distinguished former Democratic and Republican Administration officials who support aspects of the new proposals.

The plans for this campaign demonstrate the President's decision to take his case for government reform to the people.

NIXON FACES sure, heated opposition both in Congress and among various interest groups against the proposals, outlined in his State of the Union message Friday night.

The general feeling in Congress, shared by Administration officials, was that the plans would not be approved at this session. Some in the White House held out hope for approval next year.

There are two dramatic components to his call for government reform. One is that $16-billion in federal taxes be shared with state and local governments. This plan includes a major departure — the transfer of $11-billion from

(See Revenue Sharing, 21-A)

Soldiers 3

Abu Nar, Palestinian Guerrilla

Aron Rosenberg, Israeli Army Private

Emad Ismail, Jordanian Army Private

AP Photos by Eddie Adams

There is strained peace in the birthplace of three of the world's great religions. Brother still kills brother, as Jordanian loyalists battle Palestinian guerrillas. And Semite still kills Semite, as Lebanon-based guerrillas attack Israelis. These young men — none of them even three decades old — are dedicated to spilling the others' blood into the ageless, muddy waters of the Jordan.

Modern Children Maturing Earlier

By WALTER SULLIVAN
New York Times Service (c)

NEW YORK — From surveys involving thousands of girls, four generations of Harvard boys, records of the choir of Johann Sebastian Bach and numerous other studies, it has been concluded by researchers on human growth that the rate at which boys and girls mature has been increasing steadily.

Not only are sexual and physical maturity coming earlier, but some researchers have also found a parallel acceleration in mental development.

THE MOST dramatic and clear-cut trend has been in menarche, the first appearance of menstruation in girls. Evidence from many parts of the world shows that the average age of menarche has dropped by at least two and as many as five years.

In the 17th century, according to Quarinonius, a contemporary author, rural girls in Austria rarely reached menarche "before their 17th, 18th or even 20th year." In 1820 working class girls in Manchester, England, did so, on the average, at 15.7 years.

In 1934 a study of 250 girls in a New York Hebrew orphan asylum showed an average age of 13.5 years. The most recent surveys, including one of 6,217 student nurses, show averages in many parts of the world about midway between 12 and 13 years.

HOWEVER, some researchers believe the drop in the age of menarche may be leveling off in the more affluent populations. Dr. Alan E. Treloar of the National Institute of Child Health and Human Development, who has been studying some 1,500 Minnesota women and their daughters, even thinks the trend has reversed.

He says he has "conclusive proof" that, within the last decade, the average age of menarche in this group has risen slightly.

If so, this could mean either that, contrary to the general belief, some factor other than nutrition is at work, or that the nutritional value of some American diets has recently declined.

IN THIS connection, one study by Dr. Isabelle Valadian at Harvard University has led her to suspect that the

(See GROWTH, 21-A)

N.Y. CONN. NEW HAVEN Bridgeport Stamford OIL SPILL IN NEW HAVEN HARBOR Long Island Sound Long Island Patchogue • New York City

AP

Oil Slick Said Moving Into Long Island Sound

L.I. Sound Hit By Oil Spill

A Standard Oil of New Jersey tanker ran aground on rocks at New Haven, Conn., in pre-dawn fog Saturday, spilling 386,000 gallons of heating oil over three miles of Long Island Sound. Hours later a helicopter filming the slick crashed into the frigid water. The accident happened five days after the collision of two Standard Oil of California tankers spread oil in the mouth of San Francisco Bay. (Related story, 18-A.)

on the INSIDE today

Apollo Astronaut In Crash, Safe

Details, 18-A

Reds Expel Protesting Jews

From The Sunday London Times

LONDON — Within the next few days, two of Moscow's militant Jewish activists will arrive, with their families, in Israel. Boris Tsukerman and Vitaly Svichinsky have for several years openly opposed the Soviet government's harsh treatment of Jews.

Their release, at the height of the bitter, worldwide confrontation over Russia's 3.5-million Jews, is the latest evidence of a remarkable exodus which, until recently, the Soviet and Israeli governments had kept a secret.

FOR THE PAST year or more, Russian Jews officially classified as troublemakers — after participation in protests and petitions — have been allowed, even encouraged, to leave for Israel. A new brand of Soviet Zionism has, in fact, become the first dissident movement ever to pester the Kremlin into making concessions. Its success poses a problem for the Israeli government, which has traditionally favored playing the whole thing cool.

Israel's claim that only a "trickle" of Jews are being allowed to leave Russia is regarded by some experts as propaganda. There is evidence that official figures are doctored.

For example, a senior official of the Israeli Embassy in London says that the average monthly flow is only about 30, or 360 a year. Yet the Jewish Agency, a semi-official body which is involved in the emigration sector, has stated that about 1,000 Jews left Russia during 1970. Other estimates go as high as 3,000.

Fig. 5-14. Near circus. Heavy use of pictures, sketches, and big heads make the **St. Petersburg Times** almost circus. Note the two-column boxes, the cropping of pictures, and the lack of column rules.

Pages 4 et 5 : **Le président de la République roumaine** déclare au "FIGARO"...

0,50 F • PETITES ANNONCES téléphonées 256-88-44

LE FIGARO

ÉDITION DE PARIS

144e ANNÉE N° 7.986 depuis la Libération

« Sans la liberté de blâmer, il n'est pas d'éloge flatteur. » BEAUMARCHAIS

Le Gaulois • 14, rond-point des Champs-Élysées, Paris-8 256-80-00

MERCREDI **20** MAI 1970

140e JOUR DE L'ANNEE

Directeur Pierre BRISSON (1934-1964)

Alg. 0,55 din. - Mar. 0,55 dh. - Tun. 53 mil. - Esp. 8 p. - Ital. 120 lir. - Aut. 5 sch. — Belg. Lux. 4,50 fr. - Suisse 0,50 fr. s. - All. 0,70 DM - Gde-Br. 1 sh. - Holl. 0,65 fl.

A L'APPEL DE LA C.G.C.

Les cadres manifestent aujourd'hui dans toute la France

POUR PROTESTER CONTRE LES OPTIONS DU VIe PLAN

(Sécurité sociale et fiscalité)

PAGE 11 : l'article d'André GILLET

M. Edgar Faure élu doyen de Nanterre

M. Edgar Faure a été élu hier soir doyen de la Faculté de droit et des sciences économiques de Nanterre. L'élection a été acquise à la majorité des deux tiers par seize voix sur vingt-quatre.

Une délégation du conseil de gestion de la faculté va se rendre incessamment auprès de M. Guichard.

M. Edgar Faure n'enseignant pas à Nanterre, le ministre de l'Education nationale devra, de toute façon, donner son accord pour que le nom de M. Edgar Faure soit retenu.

(P. 11 : Nos autres informations.)

POUR LE PRÉSIDENT NIXON

L'ENGAGEMENT SUD-VIETNAMIEN AU CAMBODGE facilitera le désengagement américain au Vietnam

• La « joute » indochinoise entre Moscou et Pékin continue

• INTENSE ACTIVITE DU VIETCONG à l'occasion du 80e anniversaire de la naissance d'Ho Chi Minh

PAGE 7 : la dépêche de J. JACQUET-FRANCILLON et nos informations

ROME : Bernard NOËL

L'ITALIE FRAPPÉE DE PARALYSIE PRESQUE TOTALE

Une opération-grève orchestrée par les communistes avant les élections régionales du 7 juin

PAGE 3 : LA DEPECHE de notre envoyé spécial permanent

ROUTE : OPÉRATION LIMITATION DE VITESSE

M. Baumel tire les premières conclusions

• Diminution notable du pourcentage des accidents

• Amélioration de la sécurité

Et pourtant, le bilan de ce week-end : 121 morts 3.743 blessés

PAGE 2 : nos informations

NIXON et ses intellectuels...

LES intellectuels américains aimaient Kennedy. Johnson les rebutait. Nixon les a pris à contrepied, et ils l'acceptent à contrecœur. Mais ils semblent, bel et bien, l'accepter. Peut-être, sous le choc de l'initiative cambodgienne de leur président, les écrivains et les artistes sortiront-ils de leur nonchalance. Il n'est pas douteux que le monde intellectuel est profondément hostile à une reprise de l'escalade dans la guerre d'Indochine. «Mais, comme le note Milton Viorst dans Le Figaro Littéraire*, lors de la manifestation spontanée qui a eu lieu contre le président Nixon à Washington, le 9 mai, le seul intellectuel important que l'on put découvrir parmi les cent mille jeunes manifestants était Allen Ginsberg, le poète lauréat du monde hippie ».*

Sans doute Norman Mailer fit-il acte de présence. Mais il ne fit que passer, en rentrant à New York après avoir purgé une peine de prison à Alexandrie (Virginie) pour avoir manifesté contre le Pentagone. Quant aux autres intellectuels, on ne dit pas où ils étaient.

Le monde intellectuel est peut-être contre Nixon. Il n'est pas encore passé à l'action.

En correctionnelle

TREIZE MOIS DE PRISON FERME POUR L'ÉTUDIANTE ARRÊTÉE CHEZ FAUCHON lors du « raid » d'un commando gauchiste

PAGE 12 : NOTRE INFORMATION

M. ALDO MORO REÇOIT M. MAURICE SCHUMANN... A PARIS

M. Maurice Schumann, M. Jacques Duhamel et M. René Pleven entourent M. Aldo Moro dans les jardins de l'ambassade d'Italie, à l'issue du déjeuner offert par M. Malfatti di Montetretto en l'honneur du ministre des Affaires étrangères d'Italie.

(PAGE 3 : Notre information.)

PRIORITÉ à l'indépendance

par Roger MASSIP

NOUS publions aujourd'hui la première partie de l'interview que M. Nicolas Ceausescu a accordée au *Figaro* à la veille de son voyage officiel en France. Elle concerne plus particulièrement les problèmes au sujet desquels des frictions se sont produites entre Bucarest et Moscou, frictions sérieuses au point qu'au moment de la mise au pas de la Tchécoslovaquie en août 1968 on put se demander si une opération analogue ne serait pas tentée contre les « rebelles » roumains.

Mais s'agit-il bien de « rebelles » ? Comment les Roumains se situent-ils exactement par rapport à Moscou ? Leur vision du « socialisme » peut-elle engendrer des divergences plus graves que celles d'aujourd'hui et mener un jour à la rupture ? Nos questions tenaient évidemment compte de ces interrogations.

L'observation qui doit être immédiatement faite, c'est que M. Ceausescu n'a pas varié dans son comportement depuis qu'à la suite de M. Gheorghiu-Dej il a fait de l'indépendance de son pays le principe essentiel de sa politique. Les Roumains continuent d'opposer à la doctrine de la souveraineté limitée des Etats du monde communiste les droits inaliénables des nations. M. Ceausescu, qui a reçu en août 1969 le président Nixon à Bucarest, sera bientôt l'hôte officiel du président Pompidou à Paris. C'est la manifestation concrète de cette volonté d'être libre.

Liberté sur le plan extérieur donc, et qui va assez loin puisque la Roumanie — qui refuse d'intégrer ses forces dans celles du pacte de Varsovie — a pu se permettre tout récemment de refuser sa participation à la Banque d'investissement du Comecon.

Qu'en est-il sur le plan intérieur ? Ici, M. Ceausescu se montre plus libéral dans ses propos qu'il ne l'est dans son action. Il nous rappelle que chaque peuple doit, pour faire triompher le socialisme, appliquer ses propres méthodes. Mais ce droit qu'il revendique il n'en a jamais beaucoup usé et fort habilement il a su se soustraire aux critiques de Moscou en refusant de s'engager trop avant sur la voie de la démocratisation.

Il faut avoir présentes à l'esprit ces observations si l'on veut comprendre la circonspection avec laquelle M. Ceausescu a répondu à nos questions. Le leader roumain, à la tête d'un pays qui n'a pas de traditions vraiment démocratiques et dont la « libéralisation » éventuelle poserait des problèmes plus complexes encore que ceux auxquels M. Dubcek a eu à faire face, a préféré jouer par priorité la carte de l'indépendance nationale. Ceux-là mêmes qui placent la liberté des hommes avant celle des nations ne sauraient lui reprocher une tactique qui, soyons-en sûrs, a été mûrement réfléchie et adaptée aux conditions mêmes de son pays. Le voyage inopiné du président roumain à Moscou est là pour nous rappeler d'ailleurs combien sa situation demeure exposée.

Roger Massip

Le Comité central du P.C. se prononce sur l'exclusion de Roger Garaudy

PAGE 8 : L'ENSEMBLE DE NOS INFORMATIONS

CAVALIER SEUL

CONCORDANCE

LE nouveau chef du parti socialiste, M. Savary, a déclaré au banquet de clôture des Journées du Sud-Est :

« Le congrès d'Issy-les-Moulineaux a décidé le dialogue avec le parti communiste. J'ai dit que le parti ne faisait pas un préalable de la condamnation de l'occupation de la Tchécoslovaquie par les forces du pacte de Varsovie.

« Mais je précise que l'ouverture du dialogue n'a été possible que parce que le parti communiste avait condamné cette occupation, ce qui mettait ses vues en concordance avec nos positions sur l'indépendance nationale et sur le droit des peuples à disposer d'eux-mêmes. »

M. Savary a une énorme supériorité sur M. Guy Mollet, qui présidait avant lui aux destinées du parti socialiste : il ne lit pas les journaux, pas même l'Humanité, de sorte que rien ne vient entamer sa belle confiance dans les vertus d'un bon et franc dialogue avec ses frères séparés.

En tout cas, qu'il ne se préoccupe pas du procès-verbal des premières conversations.

Le parti communiste amènera son sténographe. Oh ! non pas pour faire de ce compte rendu une éventuelle pièce à charge. Mais non ! Tout simplement pour le relire le soir en famille, et passer un bon moment.

André Frossard

Dessin de Jacques Faizant

• PAGE 25 : Didier MERLIN

Rallye automobile Wembley-Mexico :

LES DEUX CHEFS DE FILE DES ÉQUIPAGES FRANÇAIS sont « tombés » sur la route des Incas

Claudine TRAUTMANN et Colette PERRIER ont triomphé des Andes

• PAGE 26 : « 24 HEURES SUR 24 » par Ph. BOUVARD

UNE JOURNÉE AVEC LE PÈRE DE MAIGRET au cœur d'un univers « siménonisé »

CHRONIQUE

"Vous jeune et moi vieux"

par Philippe ERLANGER

PARMI les interdits, les préceptes, les usages qui depuis la fin du monde païen ont réglé les rapports sentimentaux et physiques entre les humains, à peu près tout a été remis en question. Une seule idée demeure, semble-t-il inattaquable et défie la contestation, peut-être parce qu'elle est ancrée chez les jeunes. C'est celle qui concerne les amours de deux êtres séparés par une grande différence d'âge.

Chacun en tombe ou affecte d'en tomber d'accord : des unions de cette sorte sont étranges, vaguement suspectes, elles frisent à la fois le ridicule et le scandale. En dépit de quoi elles se nouent beaucoup plus souvent qu'on ne veut le penser, elles peuvent apporter un bonheur qui n'ose pas trop dire son nom.

Pourtant les exemples illustres ne manquent pas. Diane de Poitiers, absurdement travestie en courtisane dans l'imagination populaire, n'appartint qu'à deux hommes : au sénéchal de Brézé qu'elle épousa à quinze ans quand il en avait cinquante-six (environ soixante-dix de notre époque) et à Henri II, son cadet de vingt ans.

Chaque fois l'entente fut parfaite, exemplaire. Le sénéchal était de surcroît bossu, les contemporains lui reprochaient sa « vilaine figure ». Cela n'empêcha nullement la radieuse enfant de l'aimer comme ses lettres le prouvent, et de repousser, tant qu'il vécut, toutes les tentations au milieu de la société la plus dissolue du monde. François Ier, qui ne fut jamais son amant, n'en déplaise à Victor Hugo, rendit hommage à sa vertu. Il écrivit sous son portrait : « Belle à la voir, honnête à la hanter ».

Veuve après seize années de fidélité, Diane se montra inconsolable. Contrairement aux usages des cours, elle ne porta désormais que des robes noires, introduisant ainsi chez les femmes de qualité cette mode si seyante. C'est seulement à trente-sept ans qu'elle devint la maîtresse du futur Henri II. Elle en avait cinquante-neuf quand ce dernier signait une de ses lettres : « Celui qui n'a jamais aimé, ni n'aimera jamais que vous ». Mais plutôt que de voir en cette merveilleuse aventure la passion de deux êtres complémentaires, l'histoire et la légende s'appliquèrent à la présenter comme le triomphe de la femme sur son déclin.

Plus tragique devait être le dernier amour de Henri IV foudroyé à cinquante-six ans par Charlotte de Montmorency qui en avait quatorze. On sait comment le Béarnais maria sa belle au prince de Condé dont il surestimait la complaisance, comment le prince ayant emmené de force Charlotte à Bruxelles, il faillit mettre l'Europe en feu pour la reconquérir et comment la fureur du parti espagnol amena en définitive le crime de Ravaillac.

« Troie fut détruite parce qu'Hélène ne fut pas rendue », avait dit Henri IV au nonce. On sait moins que ses sentiments n'auraient pas eu cette violence si Charlotte n'avait brûlé de même. Nous possédons les lettres de l'Hélène du XVIIe siècle. Elle écrivait au roi qui aurait pu être son aïeul : « Aimez qui vous adore ». « S'il m'est chose plus chère que de vivre avec vous, c'est de mourir pour vous. » Exception faite de la Belle Corisande, elle fut la seule femme à aimer sincèrement le Vert Galant.

Et voici qu'apparait un visage imprévu de ce Clemenceau dont nous évoquions récemment la mémoire. Les lettres écrites entre sa quatre-vingt-deuxième et sa quatre-vingt-neuvième année à Mme Baldensperger, révèlent la manière dont le vieux lutteur près de rendre les armes, le prophète en courroux retrouva la joie, la gaieté et comme une fraîcheur d'adolescence au souffle d'un amour partagé. « Vous jeune et moi vieux, je peux vous raconter ma vie et vous, vous me la chanterez. »

Cette victoire sur les années et sur le scepticisme amer qu'elles apportent trop souvent, si elle est miraculeuse, n'est pas exceptionnelle. Des personnes moins illustres que le Tigre ont eu la chance de la remporter. Pourquoi ne pas l'admettre sans rougir et conserver ce tabou alors que tant d'autres, plus respectables, ont été balayés ?

Philippe ERLANGER.

Fig. 5-15. Traditional circus. Some French papers, such as **Le Figaro,** have a helter-skelter approach which is true circus.

Another makeup style is called *focus* or *brace*. The names suggest the heavy focus of attention at the top and the way the big headline at the top is "braced"—or supported—by sizable heads beneath it (fig. 5-12). The big headline and its satellites dominate the page. Few newspapers use this style because it may suggest that, except for the number one story, nothing much is going on. The style also lacks aesthetic appeal, since nothing attracts the eye except the big type at the top of the page.

Circus, the opposite of brace, scatters big headlines all over the page. Its detractors sometimes call circus the "Gee Whiz" method. Half of the front page stories are headlined as though each were an advance on the Second Coming. A few of the heads will even be in color. For years the *Denver Post* had a makeup that might have been considered Seven-Ring Circus, but its makeup has been modified now to only One-Ring Circus. The *Post* still is the leading exponent of circus (fig. 5-13) but occasionally others give it competition (fig. 5-14). Traditional circus is now the province of foreign newspapers (fig. 5-15).

Laying out a circus page is difficult. Any doubters might try to squeeze several stories, most with multi-column heads, on a page with two or three pictures. Since few stories are to be jumped in the circus plan, the problems are evident.

Critics of circus contend that the makeup job is more time-consuming, and therefore more expensive, than other styles, and that the reader becomes jaded to the typographical excitement. They also argue that circus makeup does not jibe with the trend for news detail and that it tends to cram all the good stories on page one, leaving only culls for the inside. The better editors try to draw the reader through the whole paper by putting at least one significant story on each page. For these reasons circus makeup has nearly disappeared from the American newspaper.

Further goals of makeup

While makeup aims primarily to give the reader an attractive newspaper, it has several other functions. One is to reflect the newspaper's personality. The *New York Times*, as a serious paper, would be unwise to adopt a frivolous design. Its makeup has been undergoing liberalization, but the paper still radiates a no-nonsense approach. Much of this serious impression stems from typography, for the type and the layout indicate tradition and formalism. On the other hand, the design of the *Chicago Daily News* suggests not a "paper of record" but a paper filled with alert, lively, clever writing. Newspapers that cling to the policies of Love-Lust-Lucre have page designs to match: headlines and pictures scream for attention.

Another function of makeup is to tell the reader what editors consider the most significant stories of the day. As noted in chapter 4, headline size does most of this job. The bigger the head, the more important the story. But not always. A short story on page one with small but special typography tells the reader that this story is short but important.

Placement, then, cues the reader. A story on page one rates high. On the split page—the first page of another section—it also rates.

But if it is three paragraphs on page sixty-nine, the reader realizes the editor considers the item little more than a space filler.

Makeup should provide other aids for the reader. The various sections—editorial page, comics, sports, etc.—should be in about the same place every day so the reader doesn't have to hunt for them. Related stories, such as reports on state legislative activities, should be grouped. If this is not possible, a "reference," or "refer" (pronounced "reefer"), can be inserted in the story. (See fig. 5-16.)

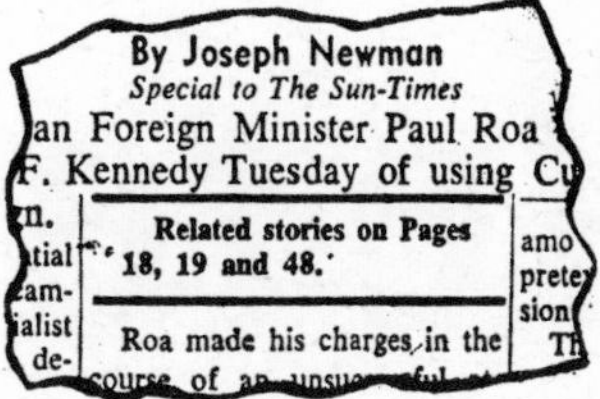

By Joseph Newman
Special to The Sun-Times
an Foreign Minister Paul Roa
F. Kennedy Tuesday of using C

Related stories on Pages 18, 19 and 48.

Roa made his charges in the

Fig. 5-16. Refer. This device in a page-one story alerts the reader to related but secondary stories on inside pages. Note the refer used by the **Atlanta Constitution** in its GOP story (fig. 5-10).

Another goal of makeup is to provide variety. Unless the makeup varies, at least slightly, every day, it lulls the reader into thinking that he saw the same thing yesterday. The main picture may be in the first two columns one day and in columns three to five the next. One day there will be a banner and the next two lines of five-column headline for the lead story.

Typography should enhance the appearance of the paper, but never at the expense of misrepresenting the importance of the story. Readers used to banners that signify nothing will learn to underestimate headlines that are really important. Readers are just as ill-served if a story of considerable significance is underplayed.

Some papers use typographical devices to have fun with the news, if there is anything funny about it. In a way, the makeup in these papers pokes fun at events, and even jabs at the conduct of political and educational figures. The *Chicago Sun-Times* frequently pulls off this kind of humor with its makeup, as shown in figure 5-17.

News before beauty

It is easy for an editor to get so enthusiastic about the design of the newspaper that he lets makeup overshadow content. He concentrates on how the paper looks, not on what the words or pictures tell. His newspaper makes a good first impression. The reader readily picks it up because it looks so delightful. But his delight changes to disgust if he finds the news play clumsy, the stories disjointed, and important items buried or even omitted. An editor infatuated with appearance may refuse to change one day's makeup when a breaking news story demands it. He is so smitten with his page design that he can tolerate no alterations. He may even sketch a design and then look for stories that might match his diagrams.

Makeup should always be an adjunct to news coverage. The editor must first consider the news. After he selects it, weighs its merits, and decides what stories are most important, he decides the typographical display of his most important stories and pictures. No matter how clever his makeup, the editor must be willing to scrap or

WEATHER
Mostly sunny and continued cold Thursday. High 6 to 12. See Page 96.

CHICAGO
SUN-TIMES

FINAL
TURF EDITION

Vol. 16, No. 275 Phone 321-3000 THURSDAY, DECEMBER 19, 1963 120 Pages—7 Cents

We're FrOzen

7 Days Of It; 3 More To Go

A two-dimensional record for a December freeze was set in the Chicago area early Thursday as below-zero temperatures marked the weather's turn from cold to colder.

It was the longest and deepest December freeze in these [illegible], said the weather bureau—seven straight days of zero or subzero temperatures. The previous such record for the month was five straight days in 1945.

With the mercury still on its early morning descent Thursday, the temperature was 9 below at O'Hare Airport and 7 below at Midway Airport, where the official reading is taken. Lower readings were reported in suburbs, where the weather bureau expected the mercury to reach 15 below.

There were prospects that the record might be extended indefinitely.

A long-range forecast envisioned low temperatures near zero for Friday, Saturday and Sunday.

While Chicagoans contend-

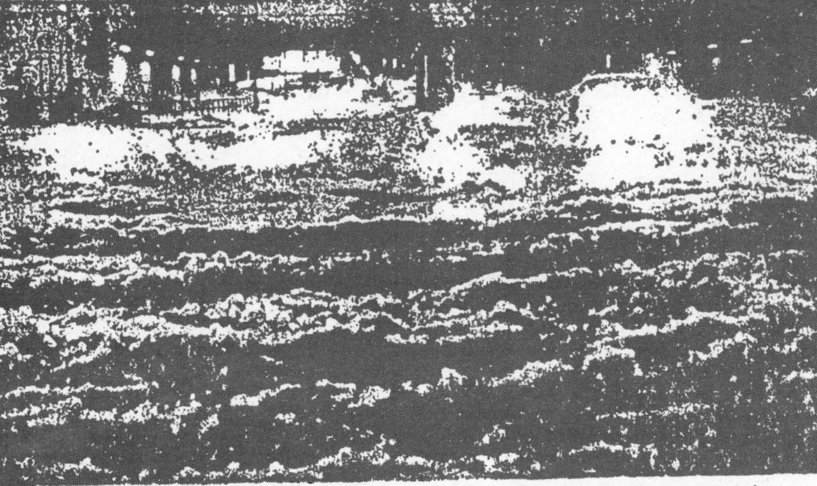

Sea of ice greets motorists on Cicero Av. near 55th after water main break. (Sun-Times Photo by Larry Nocerino)

Other pictures on Page 2

ed with the cold's deepening bite, Muskegon, Mich., struggled through a 24-hour storm that dumped 34 inches of snow and threatened to pile up at least three more inches.

Mountainous drifts rose in near-blizzard conditions to block streets and create emergencies in the Lake Michigan industrial-port city's area of 100,000 residents.

Muskegon Fire Chief Dennis Ward urged special precautions against fire because of the difficulty of moving fire-fighting equipment. Snowplows kept Muskegon's main arteries passable, but few side streets were cleared.

With the storm, Muskegon's December snowfall records for one hour, 48 hours and one week were rewritten.

In the Chicago area, the cold was blamed for the bursting of two water mains.

A break in a 30-inch main under 55th, between Cicero and Laramie caused the Chicago Transit Authority to reroute bus traffic in the flooded area.

Water pressure was reduced in a one-mile radius as city crews sought to repair the break. But no water shortage developed anywhere in the area served by the main, said Thomas Allen, acting assistant

Turn to Page 2

SURPLUS OF MINUSES

Unofficial temperatures in suburban communities early Thursday:

		Harvey	-2	Naperville	-6
Arlington Hgts.	-5	Highland Park	-10	Oak Lawn	-8
Aurora	-6	Hinsdale	-7	Oak Park	-5
Barrington	11	Homewood	-7	Park Forest	-9
Berwyn	-7	Joliet	-10	Park Ridge	-10
Blue Island	-8	La Grange	-10	River Grove	-9
Calumet City	7	Lake Forest	-6	Skokie	-6
Des Plaines	[illegible]	Libertyville	-12	West. Springs	-7
Downers Grove	[illegible]	Maywood	-10	Wheeling	10
Elgin	12	Melrose Park	-5	Whiting	-7
Gary	-8	Morton Grove	-8	Winnetka	-4
Glenview	12	Mount Prospect	-6	Zion	-6

How 'Perfect' Kidnaping Failed

By Sandy Smith
Sun-Times Correspondent

LOS ANGELES—The Federal Bureau of Investigation has learned that Barry Worthington Keenan, 23, planned the $240,000 ransom kidnaping of Frank Sinatra Jr. as a perfect crime.

An FBI probe revealed the abduction was plotted over the last six months by Keenan, son of a Los Angeles stockbroker.

An obsession for money impelled Keenan to polish his plans for the kidnaping until he believed the crime was so perfect that he never would be caught, The Sun-Times learned.

Several times since June, Keenan and his co-conspirators stalked the 19-year-old singer in an attempt to kidnap him.

In one instance, they were prepared to snatch Sinatra when he appeared at a night club here. For undisclosed reasons, their plans went awry.

Keenan finally put his plan into action Dec. 8, kidnaping Sinatra from a motel at Lake Tahoe, on the California-Nevada border.

The abduction showed flashes of cunning but it was far from perfect. The FBI seized Keenan and his partners, Joseph C. Amsler, 23, and John R. Irwin, 42, soon after they collected the ransom from film star Frank Sinatra Sr.

Young Sinatra was released unharmed Dec. 11. Within 48 hours, all of the ransom except $6,000 was recovered, and the three conspirators were jailed on kidnaping charges.

A wrangle among the Sinatra kidnapers over the $240,000

Turn to Page 43

Fig. 5-17. Imagination. An imaginative copyeditor can add zip to the front page with a humorous touch, as when Chicago was hit by ten days of bad winter weather.

revise it whenever news events demand. Revising makeup is itself a skill, and we cover it separately in chapter 11.

Dummying

The process of designing each day's page is called *dummying*. The editor uses a diagram called a dummy to send the printers instructions on where the type and picture are to go. Some papers refer to the dummy as a "map," and the description is apt. The printer is really reading a "map" as he looks over the dummy.

The blank dummy is usually a sheet eight and one-half by eleven inches of columns with measurements, signifying inches, at the sides. (See fig. 5-18.) The news room gets dummies for all inside pages from the advertising department, which has placed the ads in the dummy. The news department fills the remaining space with news and pictures.

The task of dummying is easier if the editor knows almost exactly the length of each story. Many papers have reporters write each line about a certain length so four lines of typewritten copy will equal one inch of type. The number of lines, divided by four, equals the number of inches of type. Headline space is easy to tabulate. If a headline is 24-point, three lines equal one inch. If a story with the 24-point head takes up eight inches the total length, obviously, is nine inches. The editor simply provides nine inches of space on the dummy.

Several editors usually prepare various dummies on a big paper. The sports editor and the women's editor will dummy their pages. The city editor will probably do it for his section. The state and suburban editors will handle a few, and the news editor or slot man probably will lay out page one plus several other pages. On some newspapers the telegraph editor, who handles wire news, makes up page one and other major pages.

The wire service budget, or "news digest," lists the important stories to be filed that day. It gives the editors an early view of what state, national, and world stories will be available. If a newspaper puts any local or regional news on page one—and every paper should—the person dummying the front page will have to confer with the city editor and state editor to see which of their stories may warrant front page play. From the telegraph editor he learns what unexpected stories arriving on the wires are worthy of special attention. He looks over the pictures available, and he notes what pictures might arrive by press time.

The editor then makes a series of decisions almost automatically. He decides the day's best story and assigns a headline to it. In making this decision he compares the merits of the story to top stories on other days. If the story is unusually good, it gets bigger display than an average lead story will receive. If it is less worthy it will draw a smaller headline, and the editor will mumble, "Nothing much going on today."

From then on, the editor quickly sketches where his pictures will go and, holding all the major stories in his mind for comparison, decides which story ranks No. 2. He assigns a head to that story and dummies it—probably near the top and at the left but perhaps under a picture. The "play" of No. 2 depends on how far it ranks in news value behind No. 1 and how attractive the headline on No. 2 will be. No. 3 story may get a three-column head at the lower right. No. 4 may get a two-column head and be placed in the lower left. He makes these decisions while always keeping in mind the total picture he will present.

From then on the priority system is a bit blurred. The rest of the stories he may unconsciously rate "good," "fair," and "expendable." Five stories may about tie for fifth place. The editor may put three or four of these onto page one, until all the available niches are filled. He saves the rest and other good stories for inside pages—and fills holes with "fair" and even "expendable" stories.

The beginner in dummying tends to put all his display at the top. He then methodically marches down the page, filling the space with lesser stories until he hits the bottom. The result is that the top of the page looks good but the bottom looks like the bottom of the barrel: covered with minor, one-column stories.

This tendency of the beginner reveals his limited vision. He works with one story at a time and does not consider or even see the whole news picture as he makes his news selection. He needs to think of *all* major stories together as he sketches the makeup.

The skilled editor looks at the available stories and mentally roughs out the makeup for the front page, putting his key stories at various spots on the page. This means that he places stories with good-sized headlines at the top right, the top left, in each of the lower quarters of the page, and beneath pictures that have been dummied at the top. As a result, five or six important spots are filled and the open space will be blocked out later. While the number of ways the job can be done is not limitless, he guards against having only four or five basic patterns. Like some musical composers, he strives to weave seemingly infinite variations on his basic patterns. The variations can be supplied by several typographical devices.

Typographical devices

Boxes. These can be both ruled and "sideless" (set off with white space only). Boxes can be single-column, double-column, or even eight-column.

Wide measure. This is type set wider than usual, probably one and a half columns to break as two wider columns under a three-column head.

"One-up." Five columns of type go under a six-column head. The extra white space between columns attracts attention. Sometimes the top of the page has a one-up with seven columns of type under an eight-column head.

Headlines with kickers. The extra ribbon of white space above the head makes the headline stand out to attract the reader.

Ben Day borders. These gray strips may go around a whole story or only at top and bottom to call attention to it.

Centered headline. A centered headline in a page of heads set flush left makes an effective contrast.

Art work. A little sketch inserted into stories relieves the monotony of solid type.

Unruled columns. Eliminating the rules between the columns of a story with a multi-column head unifies it.

To supplement these devices, an editor may put a six-column head over a story at the bottom of the page; the next day he may give each lower corner a two-column head. To draw attention to the lower left, he may use a picture some days and a three-column head others. (A wide variety of typographical display appears in the illustrations of front pages.)

The editor does well to dummy his front page with variations in mind. Thus, his tentative sketch of the first five stories in the dummy might look something like figure 5-18. If the dummy of these five is satisfactory, he sifts through his second level stories—the ones that are good but not outstanding—and fills the rest of the space with them. All the type must be arranged so no gaps are plugged with dinky fillers, and there should be few jumps, especially jumps of only an inch or two. If a reader takes the trouble to hunt up a continuation and then finds it is only two sentences, he may be annoyed enough to ignore the story.

Fig. 5-18. Makeup process. The makeup man probably first puts in the main head upper right, then puts another major story upper left. The photo goes between, balanced by the story at lower right.

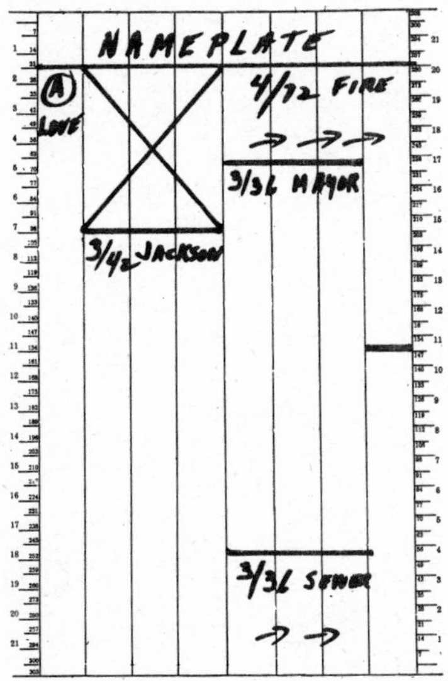

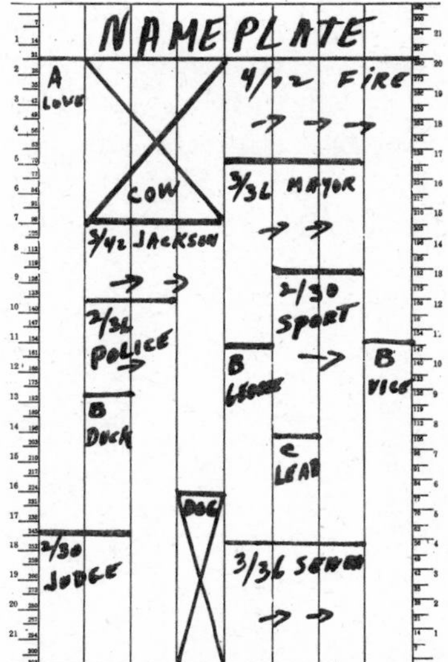

Fig. 5-19. Makeup process. He finishes by blocking in other stories (right) to fill the page and achieve informal balance of elements.

For layouts that neatly fill the page with stories the editor must juggle type, shorten some stories, and move others. Sometimes it means that a story intended for page three must be switched with one planned for page one. If both stories have about equal news value, the transfer is easy. But sometimes the shift forces the editor to alter his original judgment of importance.

Fitting stories to space

Makeup would be easier if there were an endless number of good stories four, seven, twelve, and sixteen inches long. Then the editor could readily choose the right one to fit a certain hole. Now, however, the story he wants for a specific place is almost invariably too long or too short. He then has three choices: select another story, shorten or lengthen the one he has, or shorten an adjoining story to make room for the one he is working with. Though he usually hasn't the time to lengthen stories, the editor can keep shortening, choosing, and juggling until the full page looks like figure 5-19.

The dummy should provide only basic information on picture placement (shown by crossed lines plus an identification word), headline size, slugline or guideline, and how multi-column stories move from one column to another. Any other mark on the dummy will make instructions confusing. For example, it is usually unnecessary to note whether heads are roman or italic type, although good papers do use a mixture of both. It also clutters the dummy to draw all kinds of lines indicating that type goes to a certain point. Under a single-column head, the printer will know that type is to be placed there so it is unnecessary to make any mark in that area. Leave it blank. The little arrows on multi-column stories tell the printer exactly where type is to go.

The job of fitting the copy to the available space in a limited time requires a system. Most papers work the system something like this: Each editor is assigned to fill a certain number of pages. He then reviews the stories that passed over his desk and takes note of the

Copy Control Sheet

Slug	head size	page	length
council	#1	3	8
peace	4/72	1	18
President	3/42	4	12
Gov.	6/42	2	17
goat	# 2	1	4
race	2/36	6	11

Fig. 5-20. Copy control sheet. With a form like this, the copyeditor can keep a list of stories by slug, head size, page placement, and length.

stories expected by deadline. Often he tells reporters what length to write their stories, and they must tell the editor if a story is "running long"—that is, longer than anticipated. Such information enables editors to begin dummying their pages, making minor—and sometimes major—adjustments as the news develops.

When the editor instructs a copyeditor to cut a story to a particular length, he either speaks a sentence across the copydesk or writes the headline size and the desired story length on the copy and simply hands it to the copyeditor. The copyeditor then trims a story by peeling away a few phrases without eliminating the basic information. More extensive cutting will require pulling out paragraphs here and there or perhaps whacking off the last six.

The editor keeps tabs on the stories sent to the composing room by listing them on a *copy control sheet* (fig. 5-20). He refreshes his memory on what stories are still coming by referring to a list of assignments and to the wire service news digest.

Makeup guidelines

Anyone making up pages should keep in mind the knowledge of typography accumulated by researchers. For a newspaper to gain maximum impact with the reader, most experts in typography advise certain guidelines in makeup. Here is a list of negatives:

Avoiding pitfalls

Never let headlines "bump." Heads should be separated vertically by body type so each one stands clearly by itself.

Don't "tombstone." Heads of similar type face side by side resemble grave markers in old cemeteries. (See fig. 5-21.) Even contrasting type faces side by side tend to deaden the page.

Avoid "squint-size" headlines. The reader should never have to squint to read headlines. Twelve-point heads are all right on one- and two-paragraph stories, but a longer story ought to have a bigger head. Multi-column heads should be at least 30-point, unless there is a corner above an ad to fill on an inside page.

Don't restrict the type beneath multi-column heads to neat squares or rectangles. Makeup gains variety if, for example, the body type in column one is four inches, in column two six inches, and in column three three inches. The chance to switch type from one column to another under a multi-column head also makes the job easier. (True, some typographic experts urge that type under heads be squared off. It is not suggested here that makeup men go too far in varying lengths of type under multi-column heads, or do it too often; certainly they should be aware that there is a danger of producing a ragged appearance.)

Never crowd the page. To ensure a fair amount of "air," body should not stand without a subhead every few paragraphs.* Neither should headlines take up every millimeter of space nor cutlines be jammed against their pictures. On the other hand, too much air gives the reader the feeling that he bought a piece of fluff.

* Some papers are dropping subheads because many persons do not read them. But great care must be used to keep strips of type short, by emphasizing the horizontal, if there are no break-up devices.

Stop body type from forming ponderous blocks. Several subheads or some little sketches should break up the gray. Or type should spread over several columns. This way the reader notes only four or five inches of type in each column and doesn't think the reading job will be arduous. Even an editor, when he sees a long story in print, tends to say, "That looks good. I'll have to read it when I have more time." (Then he forgets about it.)

Avoid top heavy or bottom heavy pages. Top or bottom headlines so big that one area overpowers the rest of the page are only appropriate if the paper's policy is to have brace makeup.

No headline should "cry wolf." If a story is of little consequence, let the headline admit it. A reader justly feels cheated if the head grossly exaggerates the story's value.

Repress dingbats. Most stars, asterisks, dashes, and rules can be scrapped. The most typographically advanced newspapers have eliminated column rules and do not end stories with dashes. It is clear to the reader when the stories end, and a little ribbon of white space usually does a better job of separating stories than a rule ever did.

Weatherman Note Challenges the FBI

By Tim Findley

The "Weatherman underground" issued a "third communication" yesterday that disdainfully gave the FBI three clear fingerprints to prove it is not cowed by Federal conspiracy indictments handed down last week in Detroit.

A one-page letter, postmarked in Detroit and sent to The Chronicle, advised United States Attorney General John M. Mitchell:

"Don't look for us, Dog; we'll find you first."

The letter, actually a machine-made duplicate of a typed missive, was signed "For the Central Committee" — "Weatherman underground."

PRINTS

At the bottom were three duplicates of ink-stamped fingerprints apparently intended to be shown to authorities.

The FBI in San Francisco was not able to identify the fingerprints immediately, although FBI experts said two of the prints "possibly" were those of Bernardine Dohrn and Jeff Jones.

Miss Dohrn, 28, one of the best-known members of Weatherman, is being sought on charges that she participated in a Weatherman conspiracy to bomb various public buildings across the country, and on a separate Federal indictment accusing her of participating in a conspiracy to riot in Chicago last October. Jones, 23, is also wanted on that Chicago indictment.

DATES

The letter was dated July 26, but the plain white envelope in which it was sent special delivery was postmarked late July 25.

"With other revolutionaries all over the planet, Weatherman is celebrating the 11th anniversary of the Cuban revolution," the letter said. "Today we attack with rocks, riots and bombs the greatest killer-pig ever known to man — American imperialism.

"Everywhere we see the growth of revolutionary culture and the ways in which every move of the monster-state tightens the noose around its own neck," the letter continued.

"A year ago people thought it can't happen here. Look at where we've come."

SOCIETY

There followed a Weatherman scenario on the state of American society.

"Nixon invades Cambodia; the Cong and all of Indochina spread the already rebelling US troops thin. Ahmed (Evans) is a prisoner; Rap (Brown) is free and fighting. Fred Hampton (Chicago Black Panther leader) is murdered; the brothers at Soledad avenge—'2 down and one to go.' Pun (White Panther Lawrence Plamondon and several Weathermen are ripped (arrested); we run free. Mitchell indicts 8 or 10 or 13; hundreds of thousands of freeks plot to build a new world on the ruins of hank Amerika."

Ahmed Evans is a popular Cleveland black man accused of participating in a 1968 shootout with police in that city and currently facing a death sentence. The other references tied together well-known incidents across the country as part of an over-all "revolutionary" fabric.

NETWORK

The letter appeared to give credence to the Detroit Federal Grand Jury report that Weatherman leaders are moving about the country in

Bombing at B. of A. in New York

New York

A small bomb exploded in the heart of Manhattan's financial district early yesterday shattering windows at an office of the Bank of America.

No one was injured and little other damage was reported.

The bomb was in a small valise placed in the bank's service entrance. Police said it was a pipe bomb six inches long and two and a half inches in diameter, wrapped in red, white and blue cloth.

United Press

Charges in Duchamp Painting Theft

New York

Three Brooklyn men were arraigned yesterday on charges of possessing two stolen Marcel Duchamp paintings and \$200,000 in stolen Treasury bills.

United States Commissioner Max Schiffman set bail at \$10,000 each. The FBI said they were arrested Saturday in a parking lot in Rockville Centre, L.I., where they were allegedly trying to sell the stolen goods.

The two oils by the French artist Duchamp, who lived in New York for years but died in Paris in 1968, were valued at \$95,000.

They were stolen from Kennedy Airport last February while en route from the Philadelphia Museum of Art to the New York Academy of Arts and Letters.

The Treasury notes were part of a \$13-million theft from the Morgan Guaranty Trust Company last October, the FBI said.

Associated Press

Liberated

UPI Telephoto

Two half-brothers who tired of "playing a masquerade" are now sisters after undergoing transsexual surgery at the University of Minnesota Hospital.

In a copyrighted story in the St. Paul Pioneer Press, Lauraine, right, who used to be Cary, and Lenette, who used to be Burt, said they believed themselves the first blood brothers to undergo sex-change surgery.

Lauraine, 28, underwent the surgery two years ago and Lenette, 23, was operated on six months later.

Low-Cost Housing and Palo Alto

The Palo Alto city council was told last night that building "lowcost" housing is becoming a high-cost proposition.

Louis Goldsmith, president of the Palo Alto Housing Corporation, reported that "low-cost" housing development needs some form of subsidy.

He told the council and an orderly audience of 1000 in the Gunn High School auditorium that, even with Federal loans at 1 per cent interest, private developers are unable to construct a unit for less than \$20,000.

With private financing, the minimum figure would come to something like \$38,000, he said.

PURPOSE

The Housing Corporation was organized by the council to involve itself with developers of low-cost housing.

The council is gathering data on low-cost housing, an issue which boiled over into violence in the city this summer.

Activists oppose what they call a growingelimination of low-cost housing for luxury apartments and office buildings in Palo Alto.

MONEY

Goldsmith suggested the council make "seed money" available for various building problems and to help in relocating residents of 112 low-cost units it plans to destroy soon for a freeway.

A spokesman for the Northern California Housing Coalition proposed, however, that the cooncil declare a mortatorium on all development requiring destruction of existing low-cost units.

He also urged the city to buy land and "bank it" for resale later for low- or moderate-cost housing.

Spokesman from the Urban Coalition, AmericanInstitute of Architects, Stanford University and the city's Planning Staff also appeared before the council.

Supervisors Abstain On Parochial Aid

Action on aid to parochial and private schools was tabled by the Board of Supervisors yesterday because the legislation is dead for this session of the Legislature.

Though they have no control over the issue, the supervisors had been asked to take a stand on proposals by State Senator George Moscone (Dem-San Francisco) to provide millions in public funds for the parents of children in private and parochial schools.

Supervisor Terry Francois, who proposed support of the Moscone bills, moved to table them yesterday.

"I'm still in favor, but the bills were killed in the Senate Finance Committee and the question is therefore moot for the time being," he explained.

Francois said the legislation was of vital importance to San Francisco, which has the largest percentage of children attending private and parochial schools in the State.

The only other comment was made by Supervisor James Mailliard, who said he was strongly opposed to the Moscone proposal.

Seven other supervisors at the meeting remained silent and were not unhappy to avoid a vote on such a controversial issue.

Marin Man's Suit to Save His Marriage

A black man married to a Marin county socialite filed a Federal court civil rights suit here yesterday, charging various Marin officials with trying to destroy his marriage.

Moses Harvey Smith III, a researcher at the University of California at Berkeley, charged the officials with trying to break up his marriage to Kathryn Jean Lohmann Smith, 42, of 8 Buckeye road, Belvedere.

Named by Smith were Edward B. Lohmann of Piedmont, his wife's brother; E. L. Nininger, a Marin County Court Commissioner, attorney William O. Weissich and G. T. Ragghianti, a deputy district attorney.

Lohmann is attempting to have his sister's \$200,000 estate placed in his conservatorship, claiming she is unable to care for her property.

This conservatorship is scheduled for a court hearing in Marin on August 11.

UC Band's Rousing Homecoming

The rambunctious University of California Marching Band, fresh from a 32-day tour of Japan, played a sparkling welcome-home engagement at the Opera House last night.

More than 1500 persons, including University of California president Charles Hitch, turned out for the concert — which featured the same program the 110-man band played during the Japanese tour.

Drum major Eric Mart warmly thanked the members of the audience and said they — and many others who contributed funds — helped make "the dream (of the tour) such a beautiful reality."

He said the band, which played several days at Expo '70, at one point performed in a Tokyo baseball stadium and drew the largest crowd the stadium ever had — even larger than the crowd when the San Francisco Giants baseball team appeared there.

Malcolm X Apartments 'Ready to Go'

The Winston A. Burnett Construction Co. said yes-

Two Sleepy Firemen Reinstated

Two Berkeley firemen, dismissed for falling asleep

New 'Christian' School Opening In Castro Valley

A new private school which stresses "Christian truth, high academic standards pure moral values, patriotism and discipline" open in Castro Valley in September.

Called the Redwood Christian School, it will take children from age four through eleven, August Enderlin, administrator said

Homosexual Arrests Lead To Picketing

Macy's downtown store was picketed yesterday afternoon by a group charging the company with illegally trapping and then arresting homosexuals in its men's rooms.

The ad hoc contingent of some 20 persons — mostly male — said in a statement that the store was using

A Mystery Ship Comes Sailing In

The oceangoing tugboat Modoc, which underwent a

Mrs. Thoresen Pleads Not Guilty in Slaying

Fig. 5-21. Tombstones. Putting like heads side by side distracts the reader, as his eyes tend to stray across the column rule. This page has an example of classic tombstoning on each side. The two heads in the center of the page are not true tombstones because they vary in size and one has a rule, but with the two heads to their right they form a shallow staircase that leads the reader's eyes off the page.

Keep a story under its headline. Tucking the last few lines of a story someplace in an adjoining column is sloppy editing. It confuses the reader and makes the type look sidetracked.

Taking positive steps

Other rules accentuate the positive.

Try to put associated stories together. Otherwise insert a "refer" somewhere near the beginning of the major story. This can be a simple statement, such as the "Related stories on Pages 18, 19 and 48" of figure 5-16, or a slug, such as "President Calls Plan Silly. Story on A9."

Liven the corners of the pages. They can look like dead space unless strong typography is planned to give them life.

Choose headline type faces that contrast but don't conflict. Perhaps this harmony of type can be explained by comparing it to harmony of dress. A man who wears a plaid jacket with a horizontally striped shirt and a diagonally striped tie may find his audience turning away because the combination overwhelms the eye. Type faces should impress the reader as pleasantly symmetrical.

Use few type faces. A paper displaying half a dozen different type faces can be as upsetting as a woman wearing an orange hat, a blue blouse, a brown skirt, a purple scarf, yellow shoes, and a green coat. The editors of the *Los Angeles Times* fill that huge paper with only two type faces. For contrast, type varies size and font (roman and italic).

Inside pages

Some editors take pains with front page makeup but throw together the inside pages. The reader may get the impression that the inside is a snarl of words not worth reading. So good editors work nearly as hard on the inside pages as on page one.

Newspapers with good inside pages continue the reverse-6 system, which means that each page has a strong left side with a good-sized headline or a large picture in the upper left. The rest of the page offers such variety that no story, except perhaps a tiny one used as a filler, will be lost. (See fig. 5-22.)

Variety for inside pages follows the guidelines outlined for page one: no tombstoning, a blend of roman and italic heads, a picture or two, and some of those change-of-pace techniques like boxes and Ben Day borders. (See figs. 5-23 through 5-26.)

Most inside pages lack the flexibility available on page one, for ads may fill as much as 90 percent of the space. If copy does not properly fit the news hole of the page, either the story will have to be cut after it has been set in type or two or three shorts will have to be added to make up a deficiency. Such last minute makeup takes time and often cripples a page.

Fitting copy to the news hole on a page can be done quite simply ahead of time. The editor totals the available space. It may come to thirty-two inches and there may be room for a four-column head—that is, ads fill four columns to the top and other ads fill a large amount of the page. The editor may put a four-column head on one

... Moscow Is Talking About ...

Volunteer Police

By David Bonavia
Times of London

Moscow

VOLUNTARY law enforcement squads in Moscow are being reorganized, improved and brought under closer surveillance by the police.

A Moscow evening newspaper has disclosed that the so-called People's Squads (Druzhinniki) are being merged into larger units of 80 to 100 volunteers, while their membership is being reviewed to weed out the weak links.

The report said that the squads would be expected in the future to concentrate their efforts on their own home regions, and give a strict account of their work to the local police headquarters.

* * *

THE DRUZHINNIKI — civilian volunteers wearing red armbands — assist the police in preventing crime, combating hooliganism and drunkenness and controlling crowds. They also guard courtrooms during political trials.

The newspaper said: "The squad is, so to speak, being handed over to assist the district police inspector, and it will work in close contact with him." Until now the Druzhinniki have been mainly responsible to Communist Party organizations.

* * *

THE SQUADS were set up under Nikita Khrushchev, the former Prime Minister, in 1959, in place of the "brigades for assisting the militia," and are believed to number more than 6 million volunteers throughout the country. As a reward for their work, they receive extra rest days and an undisclosed sum of money.

The faults of the system are considered to be the fragmented character of the squads, the loosely defined areas of responsibility, and excessive independence from the police. Reorganization may suggest either that they have exceeded their powers or have not been effective enough. The latter interpretation seems the more likely.

* * *

AS A RESULT of the preliminary reorganization, it is reported, crime and black market trading in vodka have been reduced in two of the more troublesome parts of Moscow. The illicit vodka trade has probably been increased by measures earlier this year to restrict its legal sale.

If Moscow is reorganizing its law enforcement squads, other parts of the country can be expected to follow suit.

Senate Fight On Defense Outlay Starts

Washington

The Senate began a defense spending debate yesterday that may last past Labor Day, and Senator John Stennis cautioned that defeat of the Safeguard antiballistic missile system would be a "clarion message to the other side" of confusion in the U.S. government.

Stennis, chairman of the Senate Armed Services Committee, keynoted the defense debate, insisting the $19.2 billion the bill would authorize in Pentagon weapons spending reflects austerity.

"We are confronted with the grim fact of rapidly increasing Russian strategic forces which could place this country in jeopardy in the years ahead," the Mississippi Democrat said.

OPPOSITION

Senator William Proxmire (Dem-Wis.) asserted the over-all, $72 billion defense budget could be cut by about $10 billion.

"We must reorder our priorities and reduce the excessive claims of the military in order to redress our glaring social needs here at home," Proxmire said.

The military authorization bill includes more than $1.3 billion for the controversial Safeguard program, which passed its first Senate test by a single vote a year ago.

ABM deployment already has been approved at two sites; the expansion in the current bill would add a third, and authorize advance preparation work at a fourth.

REJECTION

The Stennis committee rejected President Nixon's proposal that Congress authorize a more ambitious system designed to protect populated areas against a possible Red Chinese missile attack.

The expansion it approved sticks to the original mission of Safeguard: protection of U.S. offensive Minuteman missile sites.

The defense bill also will be the vehicle for the proposal of Senators George McGovern (Dem-S.D.) and Mark Hatfield (Rep - Ore.) that Congress compel withdrawal of U.S. forces from South Vietnam by next June 30.

Associated Press

Coca-Cola's Labor Camp Admission

Washington

The president of one of the largest orange juice processors, Coca-Cola, condemned his company's treatment of its migrant farm workers yesterday.

He told Senators his company will improve their lot.

The goal, said J. Paul Austin, is to transform the migratory work force into a stable, year-round group with the same fringe benefits as other Coca-Cola employees—health insurance, vacations and job security.

Austin said an NBC documentary last week correctly painted the housing and working conditions of migrants as deplorable.

But he said the farm workers' crusade in California had prompted him in 1968 to investigate Coca-Cola's own Florida workers.

When he found them as bad or worse off than those in California, he ordered long-range plans prepared. He said these will be put into effect beginning in September and be complete in seven years.

The NBC documentary was criticized by a Florida grower, George H. Wedgworth of Belle Glade, and he drew a rebuke from Senator Walter F. Mondale (Dem-Minn.), chairman of the migratory labor subcommittee.

Wedgworth contended the show was biased and that it ignored what he called substantial improvement in the migrants' lot. He also deplored the entrance of outsiders to film the show.

"What kind of help is it when you show someone calling migrants bums?" Wedgworth asked.

Mondale flushed and interrupted.

"In the documentary, wasn't this a young child who said — of himself — he was a bum? What kind of a system is it that produces that reaction?" Mondale asked.

Banging his fist on the table, Mondale told Wedgworth, "That is a child whose life is being mangled — and I'd like to hear some expression of concern from you about that."

Wedgworth said nothing and Mondale continued.

"How do you explain Coca-Cola? They found their own conditions deplorable. Are they outsiders?" he asked.

When Wedgworth still said nothing, Mondale asked if he or the Sugar Cane Growers Cooperative or the fruit and vegetable growers would support unemployment insurance for migrants, or higher wages. Wedgworth said he'd have to look at proposals first.

Wedgworth's own treatment of migrants was attacked by another witness, James M. Pierce, executive director of the National Sharecroppers Fund of New York.

Pierce said Wedgworth provides the celery pickers working for him "a two-story monstrosity which houses over 200 workers during the seven-month cutting season." It was built in 1936, is roach-infested and toilets and running water are outside, Pierce said.

Mondale and the Coca-Cola team disagreed on some points — Austin saying the migrants need more motivation to get better jobs and Mondale saying the laborers probably have more incentive than any work group in the country just to do the job they do — but essentially theirs was a harmonious confrontation.

Austin said the migrants themselves shaped the long-term improvements Coca-Cola will introduce.

Beginning in September, Austin said, the 300 full-time workers will get a 23 per cent pay raise and higher vacation and insurance benefits.

Austin said he didn't pretend his plans would solve the problem of all 250,000 migratory workers in the land, but he said he hopes Coca-Cola will serve as an example of what can be done.

Coca-Cola bought Minute Maid Orange Juice in 1960 and that product along with Snow Crop juices, accounts for $157 million in earnings a year from the Florida fields and groves.

United Press

J. PAUL AUSTIN
Coke president

Kim Agnew, White House Emissary

Taos, N.M.

Vice President Spiro T. Agnew's 14-year-old daughter rode on horseback across rugged mountains yesterday to land, claimed sacred by the Taos Pueblo Indians.

Kim Agnew made the ten-hour trip through the Sangre de Cristo mountains as an official representative of the White House.

President Nixon and Agnew have supported legislation restoring 48,000 acres of land to the Indians. The tribe claims the land and the crystal waters of Blue Lake, lodged at an 11,000-foot elevation in the spruce and fir-studded mountains, hold religious significance.

The Indians often bar visitors from their sacred area, but allowed Miss Angew and Indians Affairs Commissioner Lewis R. Bruce to make the trip.

The Vice President said his daughter was not a typical "blase" 14-year-old, but has "taken more interest in this (the Indians) than anything for some time."

United Press

Deep Probe Preview

The Eerie Times Ahead in Space

By Donovan Bess

Four staunch men, locked in a simulated spacecraft for three months, are drinking only water recycled from their own sweat, urine and exhaled breath moisture. And it's good!

This was asserted here yesterday by Glenn Seaborg, chairman of the Atomic Energy Commission. He said the experiment, under way in Huntington Beach, is an essential of the United States' plans to send explorers far away, as on the planned two-year round trip to Mars.

The Nobel Prize-winning chemist gave a Commonwealth Club luncheon audience a covey of facts and predictions about how extending nuclear energy into deep space will give mankind adventures as eerie as those described in a science-fiction novel like Frank Herbert's "Dune."

The Huntinton Beach experiment, Seaborg said, uses a distillation and vapor filter system "that can produce about one pound of bacteria-free drinking water per hour from perspiration, respiration and urine.

TESTED

"Such water has already been tested to be more potable than ordinary tap water, with no taste problem and no need of chemical treatment."

The system operates from a plutonium - fueled heat source, he said.

He made it clear that he understands that Americans feel queasy at the thought of drinking such water on cosmic trips. He predicted the people of the deep - space age will hesitate to complain in front of their children, to avoid being labeled "embarrassingly old - fashioned."

The AEC chairman said "all effort is being applied" to achieve flight testing of nuclear - powered rocket engines in the late 1970's or early 1980's.

CHEMICAL

They will, he told his Sheraton - Palace Hotel audience, be "second and third - stage rocket vehicles that will be boosted into space by chemical rockets.

"Once in space they can be 'parked' in earth orbit, a few hundred miles up, started up and shut down there, serviced there, and from that orbit used individually or assembled in a variety of clusters, depending on the mission mapped out for them."

He said nuclear fuel is "the only source of energy that is compact and long-lived enough to make feasible extended trips into the incredibly vast environment of cosmic space."

RESCUE

The nuclear rockets "parked" in orbit, Seaborg said, could have diverse uses. Some might be used to operate spacecraft for a "space rescue squad." Others might serve as ferries to take earth tourists on the three-day trip to lunar orbit, where they would board descent craft to the moonport.

The manned mission to Mars, he said, "may be possible sometime in the 1980's."

The AEC chairman said in answer to a question that "if it weren't for nuclear energy, civilization as we know it today would slowly grind to a halt," as fossil fuel sources got used up.

A member of the audience of 500 asked if he thought airplanes could be powered by nuclear reactors. He said he did not think this would be "very sensible" because of the "risk of a crash in an airplane with these radioactive fission products."

Senate Vote On Regents' Terms

Sacramento

The assembly voted yesterday to lower the terms of the University of California Regents from 16 to 10 years and remove the president of the Mechanics Institute in San Francisco from the board.

The proposed constitutional amendment by Assemblyman John Stull, (Rep-Leucadia) was sent to the Senate on a 54-2 vote. It would need approval by the voters in the November general election before going into effect.

The measure would also require gubernatorial appointees to the board to be confirmed by a majority of the 40-member Senate.

United Press

Richmond Wife Cleared On Explosives Charge

San Pablo Municipal Court Judge Wilson Locke dismissed a felony charge of illegal possession of explosives yesterday against Susan Tankersley, an attractive 28-year-old Richmond housewife.

The judge ordered the dismissal of the charge after the prosecutor, Sam Mesnick, and Mrs. Tankersley's attorney, Coleman Sannin, agreed that she had no knowledge of the explosive activities of her husband, Anthony.

The couple was charged after authorities found a large quantity of explosives in their house. The Tankersleys themselves had already left town, and lived for a year in Montreal.

Tankersley, a former University of California student, has pleaded guilty to the possession charge, and to the bombing of a power transmission tower in the Berkeley hills. He is currently undergoing psychiatric testing at the State Medical Facility at Vacaville.

Blacks in Congress Blast Nixon Policy

Washington

Three black congressmen sent a letter to President Nixon yesterday saying his course during the past 18 months "is destined to destroy all possibilities of unity and brotherhood."

Representatives William L. Clay, (Dem-Mo.), Augustus F. Hawkins, (Dem-Calif.), and Louis Stokes, (Dem-Ohio), signed the letter.

They accused Mr. Nixon of failing to make a firm commitment to attaining racial equality.

"Since you assumed office, you have traveled to all corners of the earth emphasizing your concern for many problems and pledging American efforts toward solutions. But you have not come to black America," the letter said.

"If this country is to enjoy internal domestic tranquility, it is imperative that you have an audience with the legitimate and representative leaders of black America to discuss the grievances of 25 million black citizens."

The letter cited Mr. Nixon's failure to meet with nine black congressmen who asked for a meeting with him five months ago. "We were turned away in a manner which showed disrespect for our offices and callous disregard for our views."

"Since April 18," the letter continued, "when we were advised your schedule would not permit your meeting with us, you have issued 19 comprehensive policy statements without touching upon a policy for the improvement of race relations.

Associated Press

Lots of Cells

New York

A human body contains about 50 trillion cells.

United Press

Sale Condemned

Geneva

Dr. Eugene Carson Blake, of the world Council of Churches, issued a condemnation yesterday of the proposed sale of arms by Britain to South Africa.

Associated Press

OFFICE FURNITURE

Fig. 5-22. Reverse-6 inside. The box at the top left of this inside page helps the head and illustration of the Moscow story first attract the reader's eye. The strong head and photo of the Coca-Cola story then draws attention, and the solid arrangement of the left side of the page enables the reader to complete the reverse-6 pattern with the risk of overlooking no more than a filler.

story that will take up seventeen inches. That leaves fifteen. He might place a nine-inch two-column story beneath the four-column and insert a single column story that will take up six inches. The result can be seen in figure 5-27. Note that the four-column story is not "squared-off."

An inside page with a little more space for news can be seen in figure 5-28. To aid in the explanation, we added "roman" and "italic" to the headline symbol.

Defendant Gets Six Terms for Death, Holdups

Court Weighs Case of GI Who Hates War, Wants Out

Wording Called Too Vague

Last of Narcotics Vagrancy Laws For City Found Unconstitutional

Delivery Truckers Up Tight Over Holdups

Vandals Topple War Memorial

Brother Shoots Youth In Neck Accidentally

French Bettors Get Aid

Correction

Additional Automobiles on Page F29

Fig. 5-23. Inside page. The considerable space on this inside page enabled the editor of the **Washington Post** to fit the copy with care, using a big picture to divide two major stories and even putting a kicker on a three-column story.

Pueblo's Mission Low Risk, Navy Says

War Research Sparks Protest By Professors

Anti-Hayakawa Rioters Facing Colorado Charges

Army Lifts Its Curtain On Chemical Warfare

Pompidou Tied To Possible Sex Scandal

Fig. 5-24. Careful layout. On this inside page of the **Louisville Courier-Journal** stories are carefully separated with help from a big picture. Note the blend of roman and italic type.

NEW GOP CHIEF'S VIEW: BE PATIENT WITH SOUTH

By Tom Littlewood
Sun-Times Bureau

WASHINGTON — The new Republican national chairman, Rep. Rogers C. B. Morton of Maryland, can be expected to speak out forcefully within the Nixon administration councils for a go-slow policy on Southern school desegregation.

Before agreeing to succeed Ray C. Bliss as national chairman, Morton asked for and received assurances that he would sit in on cabinet meetings as a representative of the political side.

In recent days he has told associates at the National Committee that he wants to win back recalcitrant Southern Republicans who felt that they contributed to the Nixon victory and then were betrayed by Robert H. Finch, the secretary of health, education and welfare.

Finch ordered federal assistance delayed in some school districts that have not worked out an acceptable timetable for desegregation. Inside the administration, Finch is the foremost spokesman for programs that will attract black votes in the North.

His Concerns Are Different

But the congressman from Maryland, who once worked as a flour salesman in the rural South, has different concerns. He believes that the Republican administration should be patient with the South, listen to its problems and try to reach compromise agreements without using a federal club.

In one recent conversation, Morton said: "This integration route may be a little more difficult to follow. It may take longer in order to preserve the integrity of the education system there and not depress the whole standard of education."

Morton also is prepared to urge that Finch be sure to administer desegregation guidelines strictly within the intent of Congress when the 1964 Civil Rights Act was passed.

It is clear that Morton — unlike Finch and the new chairman's brother, former Sen. Thruston B. Morton of Kentucky — thinks the South is more fertile territory for Republican gains than Northern Negro areas.

Sees Two-Fold Mission

It is equally clear that Morton intends to be · of the first team, acting as an agent for ·l machinery," as he had express-

the mission of the Na-

·cord into
·ing

2 To contribute ideas to cabinet members and other administration leaders who might not be as politically tuned-in as the national chairman.

It is in the latter role that Morton's views may clash with those of Finch, Housing and Urban Development Sec. George W. Romney and some of the other urban-minded officials on President Nixon's staff.

Morton was asked to take Bliss' job in December, on the same day that he had been disappointed by being informed that the post of secretary of the interior would go to Gov. Walter J. Hickel of Alaska. Morton, who was Mr. Nixon's floor manager at the Republican National Convention in Miami Beach, wanted the Interior spot.

Fig. 5-25. **Four column.** The **Chicago Sun-Times** a tabloid, shifted from its usual six-column format to a four-column layout in fitting this special report around ads. The story was of course edited to fill the hole exactly.

Schuetz Raps Red 'Pinpricks'

United Press International

BERLIN — West Berlin mayor Klaus Schuetz said Saturday the communists threatened this divided city "as part of a war on nerves and a policy of pinpricks."

In a television address, Schuetz stressed the importance of President Nixon's recent visit here and said it was of prime importance in deterring the communists.

West Berlin's lifelines to the West were normal Saturday for the first time after a week of communist harassment.

Allied officials said minor communist interference with traffic from West Berlin running through East Germany to the West still might be expected.

But wtih the end Friday of the Soviet-East German military maneuvers, called in reprisal against Wednesday's West German presidential election here, they doubted there would be another total blockade of the highways.

The last of the nine temporary blockades, the longest of which was four hours, occurred Friday on the 110-mile Berlin-Helmstedt Autobahn. The route is the main highway to the West and the only one the Allies may use to supply their West Berlin garrisons.

In his speech, Schuetz indicated he believed the Russians backed down over the Berlin issue in order not to endanger talks with the United States.

Klaus Schuetz
... Russians Backed Down

The mayor said Nixon "not only reinforced the American guarantees of our city and warned against any unilateral measure against Berlin" during the visit but "also marked out the lines within which the United States is prepared to negotiate with the Soviet Union."

The communists objected to the election, which chose Socialist Justice Minister Gustav Heinemann as the country's next president, because they charge any manifestation of a "West German presence" in the four-power city is illegal.

Committee Investigates 'Agitation'

Associated Press

WASHINGTON —A congressional investigation is underway to determine if traveling agitators are trigering college campus demonstrations and it may lead to Senate hearings in May.

Investigators for the Senate headed by Sen. James O. Eastland, D-Miss., are gathering evidence on reports of disturbances which have interrupted classes in a number of universities.

Sen. John Sparkman, D-Ala., applauding this inquiry, said that congressional committees have a mandate to determine whether federal laws against rioting are being violated.

"I think that some of these college campus disorders are being triggered by influences that move from one part of the nation to another," Sparkman said. He added he thinks these "influences" are mostly Communist.

Democratic leader Mike Mansfield of Montana said the federal government should see to it that student subsidies do not go to individuals who participate in violent protests. But he said he doesn't expect Congress to act on any new legislation. He noted there already is a federal law against travel for incitement to rioting.

"Individual colleges should handle these disorders unless there can be found very definitely a criminal act or criminal intent connected with interstate activities," he said.

Kidnaper Gets Life

Associated Press

SANTA MONICA, Calif. — Robert Lee Dacy, convicted of kidnaping the 4-year-old son of a Beverly Hills banker, has been sentenced Friday to life imprisonment without possibility of parole.

Dacy, 40, of Inglewood, a Los Angeles suburb, watched impossibly as the same Superior Court jury which deemed him guilty last month returned the sentence Friday after three hours of deliberation.

Judke Laurence J. Rittenband set April 1 for formal sentencing.

Dacy was convicted of abducting Stanley Stalford Jr. last Aug. 28 by posing as an electrician to gain entry, then tying up the child's mother.

Two days later FBI agents rescued Stalford during a wild auto chase in which gunshots were traded.

Fig. 5-26. **Careful fit.** Dinky fillers are unnecessary when copy fits exactly as on this inside page of the **Charlotte Observer**. Note that an italic head separates two roman heads (one on right, centered).

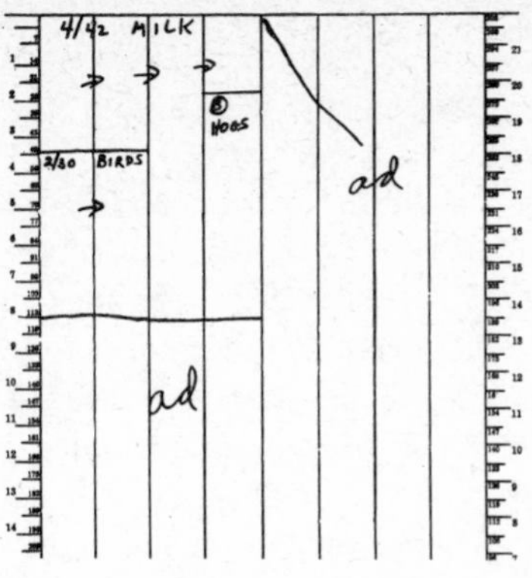

Fig. 5-27. Dummy problem. The ads planned for this page leave little space for news. The copyeditor has fitted three short stories to keep the heads clearly separated.

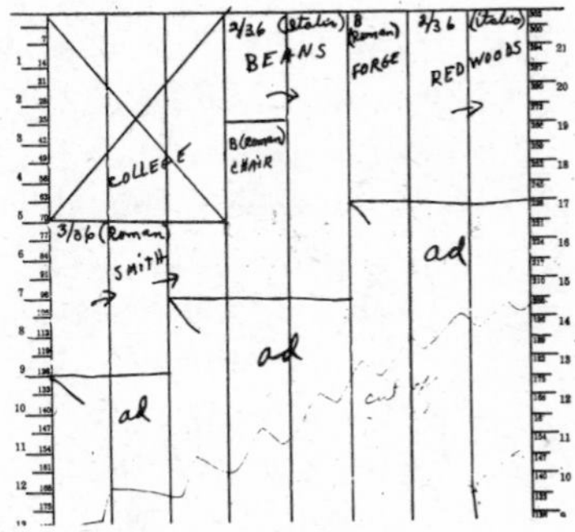

Fig. 5-28. Inside picture. With a big picture and varied heads the editor has moved toward good front-page makeup. He fills the space above the ads on an inside page in an interesting way.

Pictures in makeup

Editors making up pages on a big newspaper usually have a large selection of photos from wire services and from staff photographers. Even if there are only a few really good pictures on a given day, the editor tries to avoid printing any poor art and aims for a large proportion of excellent photographs. He thus keeps the average quality high, even though the number of pictures may have to be reduced some days.

Some papers have a rigid policy on art: There must be a picture on every news page. This restriction frequently forces the editor to use poor pictures. A better policy is to have a picture on every page if a good photograph is available. Some of the better-designed papers that try to mix art and news are not bothered if several pages lack art. Their editors believe that a solid page of type is better than one diluted with a photographic cliché—the presentation of a trophy or the handshake of two grinning men.

Increasingly, editors are willing to print a few pictures that have no direct bearing on the news, pictures published for beauty, not news content. The *Christian Science Monitor* has been a leader in printing this kind of photographs, and nearly every issue has two or three stunning pictures. The handshake shot is dull, but few can overlook a photo of striking beauty.

The makeup editor

The term "makeup editor" may suggest a person who dummies the pages and controls the placing of news. Not so. Although he may make frequent appearances in the news room, his headquarters is the composing room.

The makeup editor makes the necessary little last-minute adjustments that fit all the stories, ads, and photos on each page. Suppose a story planned for sixteen inches really measured sixteen and one-half. The makeup editor then checks a proof of the story to see if four lines can be cut without damaging the story's meaning. He marks these expendable lines, called "bites," and tells the printer, "Bite it here." The printer then throws them in the hellbox.

The makeup editor's biggest job, however, is keeping everything straight in a developing story or during a major change in deadline. In these cases he may cut stories drastically or add material in type that had been set aside. He may have to work with new dummies sent to him from editors in the newsroom. Sometimes the makeup men will have to peer at the type itself to tell the printer where to cut stories and how to juggle the type.

It should be noted that the job of makeup editor varies with the size of the paper. A paper that usually runs less than fifty pages would not have enough work for such a person. And on a big paper the makeup editor usually does not supervise the makeup of special sections. The sports department will send a copyeditor to the composing room for perhaps half an hour to check the makeup on sports pages. Individuals from the financial, women's, and editorial page departments will do the same for their sections. Still the makeup editor on a big paper has plenty to do.

On medium-sized and small papers each sub-editor goes to the composing room to make sure the pages get put together the way he wants them. Each of them may spend no more than thirty minutes at the task. Printers, following dummies, may have the type in the forms by the time the editor arrives. Only a few adjustments may be required or worth the time of both editor and printer. On small papers, the managing editor, who may write editorials as well as manage the news operation, may also be the one who dummies the key pages and supervises their makeup.

Whoever goes to the composing room to make up should remember not to touch type without permission of the printer. That prohibition is a printers' union rule and a reasonable one. An editor would not like a printer messing with his papers, so editors should not interfere with the printer's work.

The person supervising makeup should have proofs of the stories in his section so he can refer to them quickly and mark any changes on them. He also should have a line gauge (a printer's ruler), so he can measure certain news holes for himself. And, most important, he should listen to advice from printers. As most of them are intelligent men who take pride in their craft, they can often suggest ways out of a problem. The makeup editor should accept with thanks the suggestions he thinks are good and reject gracefully the ones he dislikes.

Future makeup

When a newspaper staff decides to try improving typography, it should probably make changes gradually. Readers are creatures of habit who, if confronted by a revolutionized makeup, may rebel. So most papers revamp their makeup piecemeal. The headline type faces are altered, and a few months later the body type is modernized. The nameplate may be next, but each shift comes only after the readers have adjusted to the preceding change.

Staffs of a few papers, however, have decided to make all the changes at once, figuring that the sudden alterations will dramatize for the readers the alertness and modernity of their paper. Each method has its merits, but most editors take the gradual approach. Substantial changes, regardless of how sweeping, should be accompanied by a news story announcing them. The paper may even use pictures to contrast examples of the new and old makeup. The reader then sees the improvement and perhaps will recognize his newspaper as more than a fusty old relic frozen in tradition.

Most typographers look at today's best-designed pages with satisfaction. The type is easy to read, white space separates headlines from stories, and nothing looks crowded. The design pleases the eye.

No one should believe, however, that perfection has been attained. Editors must stay alert to borrow the typographical changes other editors make. They need to find new ways to get the reader to read and to understand what he reads. Of course, what the reader absorbs should be worth absorbing.

Editors must also study the findings of psychologists, communications specialists, and newspaper researchers. While some findings will be of little value, he will find some pearls that will help him help the reader. More thought and study on how human beings respond to the printed page will stimulate hundreds of fresh ideas to help the modern reader both survey and absorb the news.

6 News evaluation

Deep in American folklore is the idea that when a man bites a dog, it's news. The notion accurately emphasizes that the unusual and interesting are one aspect of the news. A small (and probably declining) segment of the press sees only this aspect in its "gee-whiz" evaluation of events. This one-dimensional "definition" of news perhaps subtly influences what American readers expect of their newspapers. Yet how can editors imbued with such a man-bites-dog philosophy consider their periodicals to be bona fide *news*papers?

The bizarre conflict of the mythical man and dog becomes, at a more sophisticated level, the idea that news is conflict. During the last generation editors have given the big play to stories of conflict—the foreign leader threatening the world, the aspiring candidate "flaying" the President, the mayor scrapping with a city councilman.

Front-page headlines tend to make the world look even more belligerent than it is, and yet, in a sense, news interest declines where there is no clash of views or armies. Peaceful government operation, like placid marriages, are considered normal and routine—and dull. If classes go routinely for a college student, he writes home, "No news." But if a professor is fired, or if students demonstrate against a dean, the student's interest perks up, that's news!

Journalism students, many of whom will edit the news the rest of this century, may well ask if the public is jaded with conflict news. Intelligent readers know that a dog fight is not really as important as the medical advances made possible through research with dogs. They have had their fill of conflict in Asia and the Congo and the Mid-East. President Eisenhower was elected after promising to end the Korean conflict, and the 1968 election focused on the means to heal the running sore in Vietnam.

Through habit, some editors make up pages as if bombings and threats of bombings were the most important of news. Certainly conflict is significant; yet readers hunger for news of the relief or end of conflict—perhaps just because peace is uncommon. Journalists, the *Saturday Review* once complained, too often consider only bad news real news, so for a time the magazine ran a column of "good news." Newspaper editors might find a hint here.*

Though sometimes editors act as if the choice of news were decreed by the stars, it is men who make the decisions that make "news." They base their decisions on theories and intuitions which are subject to analysis and criticism. What are these foundations for decisions? Is news the bizarre or the hopeful, the story of conflict or of the meaningful?

What, after all, is news? There is no more critical question for the editor to consider.

The nature of news

News is *current information of interest to readers* (or listeners or viewers). That definition is not meant to be a legalistic pronouncement but a stimulus to thinking about events. The concept "news," like the concepts "mental health" or "spirituality," is more easily recognized than precisely described. That first brief statement is meant to center attention where the editor's attention must be centered: on the reader's concern to be informed more than on the source of information or the incident itself.

The deciphering of an ancient hieroglyphic or the release of secret documents from World War II is clearly news, though the "event" was long ago. The information is fresh and current to the reader today. There has been a tradition of trying to get *today* into the leads of stories about news a day or even a week old: "It was learned today," or "Washington sources said today." But editors are sensibly coming to accept perfect tense forms as equally newsy: "Ancient secrets have been deciphered." If the information is of fresh interest today, it's news to the reader, regardless of the date of the original event.

It may be objected that the definition, by pointing up reader interest, minimizes the significance factor in news. However, we make the assumption that if an item is truly important to a reader, it will interest him. How could it be otherwise? There is no dull significant *news*, there is only dull significant *newswriting*. If an epidemic threatens a reader's town, or if a change in the federal budget affects taxes or services that concern the reader, the medical or fiscal details should be presented in a way that will interest the reader. If an epidemic is far away or if the budget change really will not affect the reader, it does not deserve much of his attention. Why should an editor sweat to interest him in it? We are, of course, not referring to the reader only concerned with himself or perhaps his immediate family. The typical reader, with some concern about the whole nation and the world, must still focus on what is most significant for

* Before Vice-President Spiro Agnew's 1969-70 complaints about the media, former President Lyndon Johnson had complained in print about news evaluations. The "theory on which much of the press seems to operate" was explained to him by an old friend: "When I asked him why the press seldom reported success and seemed to concentrate on mistakes and controversy, this man—a distinguished and experienced publisher—said, 'Mr. President, good news is no news. Bad news is news.'"[1]

him specifically, and the editor should try to help him see and understand that significance.

Where the editor may fail is in taking the easy way out. He knows most readers are interested in the rape-murder—or at least tradition says they are interested—so he prints it. More significant stories tend to be more difficult to work up. The news staff concludes too quickly that the reader has no interest in or concern about a development in foreign aid or a cabinet change in Cambodia. In this age of interpretation, however, the editor's job is often to probe for the relationship of distant or obscure events to the reader, indirect as it may be, and then point that significance up clearly.

This approach to news also helps the editor determine the "size" or importance of a story. Textbooks on newswriting sometimes list qualities which will help the beginning reporter recognize the difference between a big item and a little one. "Proximity" is one, for example; others are "size" and "recency." A flood killing 500 persons is a bigger story than a flood killing 5. Or a wreck killing 5 persons in our own town means more to us than a wreck killing 5 on the outskirts of Cologne. The death of a businessman an hour ago is newsier than the death of a businessman two days ago. All such evaluations are of course made as if all other factors are equal—but usually everything else is not equal in the live news the editor handles. He minimizes the rules and categories and develops a judgment which relates news to the current needs and interests of his readers.

The desires of readers for the superficial as well as the heavy are therefore taken into account. Readers will identify with some stories, and such material—appropriately called "human interest"—will always be used. Reader needs, whether or not the reader recognizes them, are even more important. As pointed out in chapter 1 people have less and less time to keep up with more and more news in a world whose horizons now extend into space; an intermediary must alert them to the news they need. The editor is the man who decides which messages from Asia and the United Nations and Washington and Main Street are important to the busy readers of his pages. His aim is to alert the reader, and this goal, like the other goals of journalism—to lead, to educate, and so on—would not be valid if the editor ignored the readers' needs.*

The evaluation network

Rarely does one man alone decide which stories will reach print. Except with routine local news in small papers, a whole network of writers and editors normally selects stories for the daily press. How vast the problem is can be seen in the fact that the *Chicago Daily News* receives 1.7 million words a day but can print "only" 100,000!

* A hopeful sign that headline appeal and real news significance may not be very far apart in editors' evaluations turned up when UPI asked its newspaper editors to make two lists of the ten biggest news stories of 1967. One list would rate the stories in terms of traditional headline values; the other list would stress long-range importance. Seven stories were common to both lists submitted. Even if the editors fudged a bit to make their head judgments seem significant, the parallels nevertheless emphasize that significant news can also rate good heads.

Suppose, for example, that a snowslide in the central mountains of Switzerland injures several tourists. Depending on such factors as the number of deaths and the prominence of the people, the local correspondent or "stringer" will get the news out. For a wire service the copy would most likely go to Berne or Geneva, probably by telephone. The editors there would doubtless send a full story to a central desk in London. If the dead were Latin Americans, the most complete story might go to South America.

Let's assume a prominent businessman from San Francisco is among the dead. London then sends quite a complete story to New York, and this story goes out on a West Coast regional wire. A much abbreviated item will go to most of the other dailies in the country. Lesser wire-service editors become involved in deciding how much of the story can move to papers under them, and finally an individual news editor or telegraph editor decides how much, if any, of it fits his paper. In San Francisco it is obviously a major story, but editors in many other cities will throw it out.

The fate of this story, moreover, depends on the flow of other news. At each point—Berne, London, New York, and on the telegraph desk—an editor has to weigh the story with other stories that reach his desk at the same time. This variation in the current of news means that one day a relatively small story gets a big play, while another day a significant item is buried.

While the telegraph editor is selecting from the wire, a city editor is dispatching reporters to newsworthy events. Writers on beats are deciding which events they find deserve coverage, and how much. The city editor evaluates the overall flow of city news from these local sources while a state editor weighs copy from the state or region, and a sports editor evaluates sports news. Other editors and writers—the business editor, church editor, and women's editor—survey their fields for news significant to their readers.

But who decides whether the accident in Switzerland deserves more or less space than a local court trial? In part this question is solved or evaded by departmentalization. The city editor, for example, will typically have a page or two for display of local news, and the sports editor and women's editor usually have special sections for their copy.

On the front page, however, the biggest stories from all the channels meet in competition. Here the mountain accident faces the local murder, the bill in the state legislature, the statement from the President, and perhaps a World Series game. The newspaper has to have clear staff organization to decide how the stories should be played.

The managing editor, as his title suggests, is the man responsible; but on larger papers he rarely makes hour-by-hour decisions on all the major stories from varied sources. These routine decisions are left to a *news editor*. (The telegraph editor may in fact fill this role, or the telegraph editor may, as an assistant to the news editor, make most decisions on wire copy.)

On a typical paper, the news editor weighs the space and position requests of the city editor and telegraph editor. Perhaps the state editor, sports editor or other "editors," such as the writers on science or labor, will bid for front-page space too. There may be discussion, and even loud argument, in which the city editor claims that the new break in a murder case deserves "the line" (banner head), while the science editor contends the new break-through on cancer is the best story he has done in a year. The news editor has to decide. Obviously, if he himself does no makeup, he has to work closely with the makeup editor to translate the decisions into type.

On one paper where the authors have worked, four or five of the key editors met in the managing editor's office about 8:30 A.M. for a look at the probable flow of each day's news, and decisions were made by the group. Each evening's makeup was sketched out in committee, as it were. This system lacks the flexibility to accommodate the front page to news that develops around noon. But the plan has the advantage of greater objectivity about the news, for the enthusiasms and foibles of a single editor can be ironed out.

No committee, however, can continuously edit a paper. Individual editors must have the responsibility to make the split-second decisions required by the varied flow of news.

The news flow might be roughly compared to a conveyor belt sending food of all kinds gliding by a person who has to choose the items of his meal quickly, with the need to fit them on his tray hastily, yet with little opportunity to put something back in exchange.

So the telegraph editor has to run his eye quickly down a seemingly endless roll of stories from the wire services. He tears this one off, planning to use most of it. He tears off another and spikes it; and another. He draws a long line to show he is trimming off all but the first two paragraphs of the next lengthy story. The next story that appears may make him alter his previous selections. The importance of experience is obvious, for the telegraph editor has usually no time to ponder relative merits. He has to make quick decisions, drawing on all his understanding of the world, and suspending all his prejudices and personal animosities.

Weighing news values

The men who open and close the gates on the flow of news, we have said, are known as gatekeepers. The many decisions constantly made by writers and editors clearly mean that countless gatekeepers influence the amount and quality of news in every issue of a newspaper. But for the readers of a daily, that paper's most important gatekeeper is the news editor, even though he is virtually unknown to most of them. How does the task of decision look from his chair? How does he choose? How does he rank the stories? How does he modify them?

Significance of a story is the most important consideration on a well-edited paper. Closely related to news importance, as has been argued above, is usefulness to the reader: a story which is not of world significance may nevertheless be highly significant to an individual reader. Other news is printed for its sheer entertainment value, because of its human interest. Each story represents a mix of importance, usefulness, and interest; the biggest stories have the most of each quality. No formula or rule can guide the news editor to infallible choices. Only experience sharpens his judgment so he can produce pages which stand critical examination a month or a year later.

Typically the news editor not only has to choose the news but has to make decisions on treatment. If he has only one wire service supplying him news, he sees only the story filed by that service. But on the larger newspaper he will have to decide whether he wants the Associated Press story or the United Press International version. Or will he ask the desk to combine them? Or does he have copy from a special service which is better than either agency story? Or can he use spot copy from the wire and a backgrounder as a sidebar? In sum, he not only has to decide that a new development in Paris is significant and useful and probably even interesting to his readers, but he has to decide what treatment they will find most meaningful. As he decides the *which* of events, he must also decide the *how* of display. The chapters on headlines and makeup have shown the several ways the editor quickly directs the reader to the major stories and keeps him aware of the minor items.

First, display of the story signals its importance. Position toward the front or near the top emphasizes importance, as does the size of head given it. The typography of the copy itself can likewise increase its display; thus, a story at the bottom of the front page with only a medium-size head gets more attention if set in type six points larger than normal. Similarly, more white space and rules can increase the emphasis given a story. If available, color may also be used to step up display of an item.

Second, the length allotted a story is correlated with the significance it has to the reader. Sometimes a rather short item may be given a large head, as when a story is run a shallow inch or two across two or three columns.

Third, illustration can be used to increase the impact of a story. An imaginative news editor may also vary display with line drawings, charts, cartoons and perhaps such devices as arrows to brighten the presentation of a story.

Finally, accompanying copy may be used to give an event more impact. This additional material may be a bulletin notice from the wire or a small box or table, but it may also range all the way up to a sidebar or lengthy excerpt from a text.

Gatekeeping

In theory, the news editor coolly and objectively decides on the value and display of news, without fear or favor. In fact, he works under varied pressures most of the time. His news sense may be shaped or even seriously distorted by three general kinds of pressure: economic, traditional, and personal.

Economic pressure

"The advertiser made them use that story," one reader observes. "They'll do anything," says another, "to sell papers." Such frequent comments from newspaper consumers point to the supposed influence of profit on news decisions, and the two sources of newspaper income are advertising and circulation.

The threat of the advertiser to full news coverage is exaggerated in the public mind. On the well-run newspaper, the advertising and editorial departments are separate and distinct. Good newsmen would repulse an advertising representative who approached asking favors. In fact, some editors would make a point of doing the opposite of what an ad man asked. There are doubtless cases where a big advertiser asks and gets favors in the news columns, or where a weak editor gives the advertiser free space or kills a story though the advertiser may not even have asked. But toadying is the exception.

One journalistic practice which muddies public thinking in this area is the issuing of special supplements. Since advertising of real estate, resorts, or insurance supports these sections, they are filled with news-like puffs about such businesses. The growing tendency on many papers to stuff regular columns with handouts, not only from charities but from businesses, likewise demonstrates the strength of commercial pressure. Laymen can hardly be blamed if they conclude that plugs can become news if one has money or the right contacts. The objective news editor has to be alert to pressures from advertisers, nevertheless, and resist them.

A greater economic threat to objective news coverage is the publisher's role as capitalist or business leader. Decades ago, the famous editor and political leader from Kansas, William Allen White, spoke of the "country club complex" which publishers and editors develop by mixing socially with the wealthy. Every year rising capital costs of newspapers increase this identification of the press leader with the money or power structure. The newspaper's management and top editorial staffers do not think as blue-collar workers or as union men, or even as teachers and doctors, but as well-to-do business leaders. So a department store owner, for example, may rightly feel he does not even have to mention the ads he buys to get the news treatment he wants. A news editor may have to work consciously to play the news straight when he knows that those above him assess events in much the same way as the more widely feared advertiser.

If purity toward advertisers is easy to sermonize about, the issues involved in keeping circulation up are more complex and more subtle. Everyone on a paper agrees that it has to sell, whether the aim is to make money, to convey news, or to wield great social influence. A paper that does not sell will die. And if it barely sells, neither the business nor the editorial staff is happy. This pressures every editor to print "what the public wants."

Editors who argue that the public wants serious, solid news coverage find many newsmen who say that the public interest is shallow, as shown by the great popularity of comics and sports. That view may be too cynical. The *Christian Science Monitor*, the *Wall Street Journal*, and the *New York Times* are all serious yet successful. We must recognize, however, that in a sense all three are national newspapers. Of the three, only the *Times* relies heavily on a local market, and that market is the nation's largest and wealthiest.

Papers in small cities might break even imitating the *Times*, but the pressure is to build circulation and profit. Circulation can be built legitimately with stories of human interest. Some news editors will go further, giving in to circulation pressure to print a heavy diet of murder, sex scandals, and other sensations. Successful pandering may win a narrow kind of success.

The emphasis on sensationalism, going back to the "penny press" of the 1830s and the yellow journalism of sixty years later, rests on a low opinion of mankind. Perhaps today the masses are more enlightened than when Barnum profited on the theory of a sucker born every minute. If human nature has not improved, at least education has spread. The idealistic editor can point to the error of radio stations which continually play the latest pop music and win great but impecunious teenage audiences which few solid advertisers want. He can also suggest that more serious and less sensational editing may attract the kind of readers that management and advertiser both want.

One pertinent aspect of this argument is the growing monopolization of the press. In the competitive twenties sensation was an important weapon for survival. But publishers of monopoly papers with high home delivery now often argue that they can provide higher quality coverage when they have no competition. A monopoly lifts some of the pressure to strive for sensational headlines that boost street sales.

One of the most difficult aspects of circulation pressure may not be the baseness but the parochialness of reader interests. Cyrus H. Favor, general manager of the International Circulation Managers Association, has suggested that the majority of readers have lagged behind newspaper editors' broadening horizons. He pointed out that the marketing consultant to the Thomson Newspapers in Britain had urged market analysis to create customer-oriented papers.

> Practically, as most circulators see it, this problem is one of balance between local news and the demands for coverage of international and astronautical spheres far out in the universe. Our editors are meeting the challenge on the new frontiers of science and space, as well they might. . . . [But] many would attribute reader turnover to the fact that in many communities the majority of the readers are still stay-at-homes more interested in the PTA, church, Grange and other fraternal groups than in the problems of landing on the moon.

So economic pressure may push the editor to give too much coverage to local trivia as well as to local significance.

Traditional pressure

The pressure of "this is the way it has always been done" pushes the editor to evaluate the news traditionally. For example, newspapers for generations have leaned strongly to government news. As history books have long been bound up with the dates of military and political events, newspapers have traditionally blanketed government offices, from the White House down to the town council. Even now, it is unthinkable that a newspaper would have reporters cover science laboratories as closely as they cover police stations.

There are of course good reasons—in terms of reader interest and concern—for keeping an eye on our political machinery. But suppose a news editor reached the objective conclusion that developments in, say, medicine and education deserved more regular front-page space than did a feud between politicians. He would have to overcome the inertia of his whole profession: City editors habitually have reporters cover government offices, and press services send out daily news budgets heavily weighted with government coverage.

Since a democratic society requires a great deal of government coverage, a still more troublesome tradition is the habit of giving excessive coverage to certain kinds of unimportant and even trivial material. Most papers give sports more space than interest justifies. Heavy coverage, of course, does develop a little more interest in sports news, but there are still frequent complaints that some towns simply will not support this or that sport. All the free publicity fails to spark or to tap deep or widespread interest.

Tradition says also that some kinds of events deserve picture coverage only if the photo can somehow include a pretty girl in shorts and tight sweater. February 2 always has its Ground Hog Day story. Fall and spring bring out a rash of stories about small boys who hate school, apparently because some editor at the time of the Civil War hated school. It is, of course, unthinkable that the authors of such pieces might have enjoyed school writing!

The editor who looks at news in these routine ways would have as much difficulty defending his practice as in justifying that newspapers have for years printed astrological predictions—even during this space age. He is dated, even though astrology has recently become a fad for some. The editor who is modern must look at the news in a different way from half a century ago.

Personal pressure

"The boss" is a near and vital concern of the news editor. The superior may be an absentee owner, the top management man locally, the editor-in-chief up on some higher floor, the managing editor in the next office—or a composite of them all. Usually when one or another of these delivers himself of an opinion, the staff transforms this dictum into dogma. Thereafter *this* kind of story *must* be printed, and that type must *not*—and so the newspaper's sacred cows grow up from calves. *That* boss likes cats, and *this* boss has a feud with a particular politician, so the newsmen open the gates to cat stories and close them to mention of the politician.

Worship of a sacred cow is often foolish, as the presumed need for it and even the boss who created it are long dead. Moreover, sometimes the boss's bias is not dictated; it is simply sensed by the staff. For example, as many Republican papers switched to President Johnson in 1964, a strong pro-Goldwater publisher would have been known to his editors, and they would have been tempted to continue giving Senator Goldwater the news breaks. The same kind of bias is possible wherever a publisher takes a strong position on a candidate or issue. The least a conscientious editor can do is check whether his superiors really insist on a certain handling of certain stories. If they really do, he must decide whether ethics will permit him to go along. If he is a professional, he will resist the personal biases which would distort the news flow—or will look for a job elsewhere.

Research has shown that publishers do become involved in news direction—"interfere with" may be too strong, though so it may seem to the editor. A former news executive of Scripps League newspapers, Dr. David R. Bowers, associate professor of journalism at Texas A & M University, got replies from more than two out of five of all the dailies in the country in a 1967 survey. The 613 responding editors said that the publishers were active in news direction, especially in news jeopardizing advertising and circulation. Significantly, in contrast to popular supposition, publishers interfered less on the big papers than the small. "The closer the geographical proximity of the subject matter, the more active the publisher is in news direction," Professor Bowers concluded. Clearly the publisher has a constitutional and economic right to exert such control, but he can cause the newsroom executives both ethical and practical problems if, trying to usurp their professional functions, he pressures them to act for his business interest rather than the public interest.

Public pressure—the pressure of his readers—may also tend to distort an editor's judgments. If subscribers cancel when reporters delve into some subjects, the editor may soft-pedal these topics. But the pressure may not be this overt. Merely knowing his readers' attitudes may tempt the editor to compromise his judgment. If he knows, for example, that most of his readers are social and political conservatives, he may ignore some news of reform or revolt, or play such stories unsympathetically. Such biasing is unprofessional. To be sure, since we have argued news must interest readers, no wise editor will ignore their wishes. But his goals include leading and educating, not giving into narrow prejudices and preconceptions. Sound, objective news evaluation does not bend before even the tyranny of the majority.

Guidelines of judgment

To avoid pressures that interfere with his good judgment, the editor has several guidelines to help him evaluate the news.

The most obvious guideline is to avoid the "obvious" story.

Events as predictable as the sunrise aren't news. Other obvious stories might be labeled "What-did-you-expect-him-to-say?" The Chamber of Commerce secretary predicts a booming Christmas business. Would anyone expect him to predict bad business? If a President back from a trip announces that he had a "valuable discussion" with the prime minister of Outer Nostrum, an editor probably has to print something because the President spoke officially; but his statement is barely newsworthy because no one would expect him to say anything else. And the only newsworthy prediction by a political candidate about the vote, would be "I'm gonna lose."

The editor should beware of fads. A particular social problem tends to become a national pastime, and the press reflects the current rage by carrying all kinds of stories about it. During one period it may be popular to write at length on juvenile delinquency. It may hold sway for six months or so, then be replaced by drug addiction. Its currency fades after a time and the nation becomes preoccupied with pollution. The next fad might be anything from pre-school education to post-retirement living. All of these subjects are important, but the editor should allow coverage of only major events when the subject has been beaten almost to death.

When an editor decides a subject is good enough for detailed coverage, he applies another guideline: story stamina. Will the issue have long-range interest or will it be forgotten in a few days? Subjects that have had staying power are the perils of cigarette smoking and drug addiction. Some subjects are of continuing interest but their vitality is limited to short bursts of coverage. The ups and downs of the stock market or bank interest may be everyone's concern for a few days, but day after day coverage for weeks on end is too much for the ordinary citizen. A subject with long-term potential may even be killed by too much coverage. Readers can stay interested in stories such as airport development if the major decisions are not lost in complex daily stories.

Bias and business

Critics of the press often have charged that many papers underplay consumer stories. They contend that even health stories which discredit a highly advertised product, like cigarettes, usually are given front page play reluctantly, if at all. Yet, they argue, few stories have more long-range importance than those warning millions of cigarette smokers of their odds with lung cancer or heart disease.

One of the reasons for scanty coverage is that old standby, tradition. Editors did not run many stories in the past on consumer news so they don't do it now. But economic pressures play a role, too. Many editors seem reluctant to publish charges made against business groups by the Federal Trade Commission or the Food and Drug Administration. Hence, the press frequently is criticized for being highly incensed when someone cheats the welfare department out of fifty dollars while saying nothing when a big food manufacturer puts rotten tomatoes in his catsup.

A current example of this tendency to favor business is the coverage of exposés by Ralph Nader. Much of what Nader wrote was first published only in the smaller magazines—those with less than 100,000 circulation. Rarely did a newspaper reprint these articles or create news stories from Nader's facts. The press originally reported his charges on the lack of automobile safety, the filth of some food processing plants, and the perils of pipelines only when they could not avoid it. Many of these newspapers were alert, however, to report stories that countered what Nader had charged, though it must be conceded he got wider coverage once he had become a "big name."

This reticence to criticize business was notable a few years ago when several executives of electrical equipment companies went to jail for price fixing. The fixes had cost private firms and the government millions of dollars in excessive prices. A good many papers did not run a line on the story, although most of them manage to report petty thievery in some detail.

Judging at a distance

News judgment usually is easier when the event is close to home. The facts are clearer and they can be obtained more quickly. The news from far away, however, is much more difficult to evaluate. Who can judge the accuracy or completeness of the information filed by wire services from, say, Ethiopia? How informed is the reporter? Does he know the nuances of politics in the country? Are his news sources adequate?

The editor who judges the merits of such stories has to rely on his experience, of course, but he can take some conventional precautions. The byline is an obvious clue. He may know that the writer is new in the country and therefore inexperienced. The dateline is another obvious clue. Where the story was filed is a guide as to whether the story is a first-hand report or a synthesis of information from second- and third-rate sources. The names of the people quoted in the story can be helpful to the editor as he sniffs for authenticity. If it quotes "reliable sources," he should at least be wary. If refugees are quoted, he should immediately be on guard, for refugees or exiles from any place are hardly objective observers.

If the editor is dubious about the reliability of the facts or the sources in a story, he may edit it carefully to warn the reader of this doubt. A thoroughly suspicious story goes into the editor's wastebasket. Even conscientious editors, however, have bitten hard on a story that should have raised suspicions at a half dozen places. One of the most famous of these blunders was described in the house organ of United Press International:

> This is a footnote on gullibility and sensationalism, how they can prevail for a time over responsibility and common sense, and how newspapers can be imposed upon by a wire service.
>
> Last Friday morning a stranger visited newspapers and wire service Bureaus in Vienna. At the UPI bureau

> he introduced himself as a telex operator in the local Soviet consulate. He said a coded message had come through reporting Premier Khrushchev deposed and under arrest in Moscow. A group headed by Malenkov and Kaganovich had taken over.
>
> Good story—if true. But is this the stuff sensational bulletins are made of? Was there any reason to believe it? Was the stranger a valid news source? Did the fact that a newspaper in Vienna played the story make it authentic? Is the paper known to be sensational or cautious? These are questions a good reporter or editor must answer before filing a story that invites headlines around the world.

Suspecting a hoax, UPI editors used caution. Associated Press filed an early story that included a cautionary sentence: "There was no hint where the rumors originated." Although one Vienna newspaper was mentioned in later versions, AP never mentioned the stranger in Vienna. And a fair number of American papers gave the AP story considerable play. Editors using sound judgment would have spiked such a vague story or at least waited for confirmation.*

Wishful editing

This crucial judgment brings into focus another difficulty that faces the editor—"wishful editing." The editor, like nearly every citizen, has an element of nationalism in his makeup. He wants to report events that he and his government wish would happen. The editors who printed the story from Vienna may have subconsciously wished that Khrushchev would be turned out. This wish might have influenced their judgment. The East-West tension tempts editors to print stories that are perhaps less than "the whole truth," because stories that make the Communists look bad are stories that look good to many Americans.

The danger of wishful editing is that it ultimately betrays the society. American press reports from the Soviet Union for decades demonstrated wishful editing. While some editors got and printed the best information available (and reporters in Russia were always under Soviet restriction), most selected, perhaps unconsciously, "pleasant" news. There were columns of stories that portrayed the Russians as scientific boobs, the state as held together by police threats, and national affairs as hopelessly snarled. It is no wonder that when the Russians lofted the world's first space ship in 1957 the American public came close to panic.

To make good decisions on news play, the editor must be strong enough to take a little time to reflect. Unfortunately, some veteran editors tend to think that decisive editing means fast editing. The best editor, however, knows when decision requires delay. He reads a borderline story two or three times and even discusses it with a

* Historians may someday determine that the threat to Khrushchev was real in 1960. But as he was not actually turned out until 1964, the threat appeared remote at the time of the mysterious stranger's visit.

colleague. The interests of both the newspaper and the reader are best served by an editor who has confidence in his judgment but takes the time to let it operate effectively.

Such an editor recognizes that one of the greatest pressures toward slanted coverage is his own bias. How else can he view the news than through glasses colored by his own opinions and prejudices? Maybe he can see how those under him play to his views on cats or airpower or Agnew. Complete objectivity is impossible, but he can strive for it by regularly analyzing his feelings and checking their influence on his judgments. He can watch the news play in other papers, including great foreign ones like the *Times* of London. Finally, he can check his perceptions by conferring with other staffers.

But even the way his colleagues view the news is not sufficient for the really self-critical editor; colleagues also have their local or national biases. He can try sometimes to imagine how a man in Asia or at the United Nations would view the news. Such regular exercise in trying to rise above his own biases, and even those of his profession and nation, would be salutary for the news editor.*

Professional integrity

These varied pressures on every newsman can distort his evaluations of the news. His integrity, therefore, is the ultimate safeguard of the news stream.

For many Americans, the Golden Rule is the ethical touchstone. Wouldn't a newspaper be ethical if each editor handled the news as he would want news of himself handled? Not necessarily. The principle is not easily applied to the evaluation of news for a large public. Handling news about an individual the way he wants it handled is often not the best from the viewpoint of all the other individuals who make up society. Anyway, the Golden Rule may become very subjective. A managing editor, for example, left out a news item concerning arrest of a prominent out-of-town newsman. "You wouldn't want it put in about you, would you?" he rationalized to fellow staffers, in a subconscious appeal to a Golden Rule for newspapermen. But such a stand of course opens a paper to all kinds of personal pressure. Whether a story sees print then depends on how much pull a person can develop with the editor, since he takes pity on friends. To be an impartial gatekeeper, therefore, the ethical editor in a sense has to be without friends—or enemies.

What news of arrests, suits, bankruptcies, or other unhappy incidents would be printed if the rule were the editor's desire to have

* To see if the attitudes of editors biased their editing of controversial news stories, Guido H. Stempel III, a professor of journalism at Ohio University, set up an experiment with two groups of editing students—those for the draft and those against it. He had them work on a story quoting official Washington sources reporting draft policies. Cognitive dissonance theory, applicable to some communications problems, would suggest that students against the draft would consider the story government propaganda, read it lightly, and catch few errors. Actually, Professor Stempel reported that most of these students did better editing than those favoring the draft. He concluded: "The notion that an editor can't handle a story adequately because he doesn't agree with its content isn't necessarily true."

such news left out about himself and his friends? The printing of most spot news items probably makes someone unhappy, and papers would go out of business if they did not seek a higher principle than saving someone's feelings. Sometimes they must print news which hurts individuals. So they apply a standard of fair-dealing to all alike, regardless of the editor's friendships or compassion.

Sound evaluation of news is bound up in the word professionalism. The professional editor comes to look at his task not as a plumber contemplating a neat fit, important as that is, but as a physician or educator contemplating his role in the improvement of society. Such an editor uses as his frame of reference for decisions, not the personal tastes of advertiser, publisher or himself, but the professional ideals held by the best practitioners of the news profession.

Those ideals can be clarified and firmed up in thought, study and discussion—in talking with colleagues, with professionals at newspaper meetings, with critics of the press, and with teachers and students in good journalism classes.

In chapter 13 we discuss ethical foundations in detail against the background of the book *Four Theories of the Press* by Profs. Frederick S. Siebert, Theodore B. Peterson, and Wilbur Schramm. Books like *Four Theories* can be especially useful in thinking through the ethical problems of news evaluation. Another good one for this purpose is *The Press and Its Problems* by Prof. Curtis D. MacDougall of the Medill School of Journalism at Northwestern University (Dubuque, Ia.: William C. Brown Co., 1964); chapters 9 through 12 are particularly helpful with gatekeeping decisions. Professor Schramm, a prominent communications research leader of Stanford University, also examines the bases of professionalism in his *Responsibility in Mass Communication* (New York: Harper and Brothers, 1957).[2] He points out that the newspaper profession can develop "by asking what kind of behavior is necessary in order to carry out the public service obligations of the craft," and adds:

> The greatest step toward professionalizing the mass-communication industry would be simply to emphasize the *individual* sense of responsibility rather than merely the corporate sense—that is, the responsibility of the communicator as a public servant and a professional, as apart from but not fundamentally contrary to his obligations to the business he works for. . . . Let the employers encourage their employees to behave like professionals, and support them when they do so. Let the employees, on their part, take their own responsibility very seriously and cease to hide behind the fact that they *are* employees and that someone else pays their salary and determines policy. . . . We expect [professionals] to operate somewhere above the level of a pitchman, but somewhere below the level of the angels. We want them to try to live up to the peculiar responsibility of informing free citizens in a free country. (p. 347)

In a free society, few have a professional responsibility which matches the editor's. He must think through his own philosophy of freedom, of objectivity and of responsibility to his community and world. Then hour by hour he must apply his standards professionally by passing, trimming or spiking—weighing the significant against the trivial, the useful against the dangerous.

Chiefs of Associated Press pose with AP General Manager Wes Gallagher in front of the Rockefeller Center office in New York City.

7 The telegraph editor

The person who likes to deal with national and international news often aims for the job of telegraph editor. The telegraph editor's daily responsibility is to take hundreds of news stories from the wire services, select those he considers most significant, and trim them to fit available space. His judgment provides readers with their picture of the world.

To do the job properly the editor needs a good background in world affairs, a fine sense of news values, and an ability to act swiftly when an unexpected development occurs.

The job of being telegraph or wire editor varies tremendously. On a small paper this editor may edit the news, write headlines for the stories he edits, and also report some local news or edit other copy. On papers with circulations of 15,000 to 50,000 he probably concentrates on the wire editing and headline writing. On somewhat bigger papers the telegraph editor probably only skims over the wire stories, selects the ones he wants, and directs copyreaders to edit the stories and write the heads.

On the largest metropolitan papers the wire news may be divided, the city editor or state editor getting the stories that originate close to home, the "world" or "cable" desks getting the rest. There may also be "national" editors or "foreign" editors in charge of a specific division of the news. On the major papers all such editors have plenty of work because a dozen or more teletypes stream out copy at 66 or more words a minute. Papers that print the full daily report on Wall Street transactions, for example, may receive the market prices at 1,050 words a minute. Papers with their own correspondents in the United States or abroad would also get copy from a special teleprinter or from a Western Union machine.

News agencies

The wire services which feed news to the telegraph editor have long traditions.

The first services had extreme difficulties, including low revenues and terrifying transmission problems. Some, more than a century ago, employed carrier pigeons to convey the news, and others used boats or horses in attempts to beat out any opposition. While these struggles were often romantic, dozens of little news-gathering services failed. But they continued to be formed because editors realized that they had to have some kind of cooperative reporting service. They recognized that they could not each afford to have correspondents all over the world and that, if they were to get even minimal coverage of the news outside their own areas, some news association would have to provide it.

After several starts, the first being in 1848 in New York City, the Associated Press formed in 1892. The United Press formed in 1907, and Hearst's International News Service in 1909. INS was sold to UP in 1958, and the merged organizations took the name of United Press International, or UPI.

The AP is a cooperative, with each paper paying for service at a rate determined by a formula that includes its circulation and the population of its circulation area. UPI is a private business and calls its customers "clients," not members. It charges only by circulation.

Because the wires distribute the cost of gathering widespread news, they are a minor expense to newspapers. Their cost will vary from little more than $100 a week for papers with less than 10,000 circulation to several thousand dollars for the metropolitan papers. Even though the total cost for the giants may seem high, no newspaper could afford to duplicate the news coverage of the wire services.

Telegraph editors find that the two major wire services have personalities. AP is known for its reliability, UPI for its bright writing and Latin American coverage. These widely-held impressions were documented in a study of twenty-eight telegraph editors in California, reported by Prof. B. H. Liebes in *Journalism Quarterly* (Autumn, 1966). He found that these wire editors had "distinct preferences for one wire service or the other in different news areas." For example, they preferred AP for Washington coverage but UPI for the White House.

In the last decade the wire services have accelerated the speed of transmission and thereby greatly broadened copy content. Frank McDonald, telegraph editor of the *Winston-Salem Journal*, called the change "a veritable revolution." Because AP and UPI now transmit at about 66 words a minute, 5,000 words can be received in the period formerly used for 4,000 words. McDonald said that when his paper added the *New York Times* News Service, it nearly doubled the incoming words per minute. The extra words broadened the old news budget of politics, accidents, crime, and war to include numerous stories of space, civil rights, and educational reform, and of Africa and Asia.

Wire service executives emphasize their success in bringing more news faster from farther away than ever before. The Saigon news editors of the services are in instant contact with the foreign desk in New York. The 12,000-mile Saigon-New York channel is a combination of radio, cable, and microwave, all linked together as if it were one piece of wire. Transmission has been speeded up, so now a computer can take all-cap copy and convert it into caps and lower case, all hyphenated and justified for the teletypesetter (described later in this chapter).

While AP and UPI are the only services in the United States that try to cover almost all the news of the nation and world, a dozen or more special organizations provide news by wire.

The *New York Times* has its own service and sells it to more than 200 American and Canadian papers. Each subscriber gets almost all the news the *Times* has, except some from New York City. The stories come over a teletype, just as do those from AP or UPI.

The *Washington Post* and *Los Angeles Times* have teamed up to send special articles from their own Washington and foreign correspondents. The *Chicago Daily News* sells its Foreign Service. The *Chicago Tribune*, the *New York Daily News*, and the Newhouse newspapers have wires that can be leased. The British news agency, Reuters, supplies a modest number of American papers. The North American Newspaper Alliance, NANA, also sends feature stories by wire. Many of these wire services use special delivery mail to provide customers with those news and feature stories that need not be speeded to meet a deadline because they are usually timely for a week or more.

Though none of these services provides complete reports, as AP and UPI do, more and more papers are subscribing to them to supplement AP and UPI. Their cost usually is lower, their news selection broader, and their coverage frequently more penetrating than are those of the two all-purpose wire services. (It was Dispatch News Service, run by two twenty-three-year olds, that scooped the big services in November, 1969, to break the My Lai massacre story, which then made headlines for months.) Stories from supplemental services often are slightly editorial, in contrast to the studied objectivity of AP and UPI stories, and some editors think readers find a definite point of view stimulating.

The teletypesetter

Until the early fifties, all wire copy was sent in all-capital letters (fig. 7-1). Editors skimmed the copy, adding a pencil mark under letters that were supposed to remain capitalized. Then the wire services developed the teletypesetter, or TTS, which brought stories to the subscriber's news room in caps and lower case with each line of typed material equal to one line of type (fig. 7-2).

TTS enables the editor to choose his stories as before, but he no longer has to send the copy to the composing room. The wire service feeds stories directly to the composing room on a special perforated paper tape. This tape can be set in type. Simultaneously, the editor receives these stories on an ordinary teletype, reads them to decide which he wants to use, and sends the numbers of the desired stories to the composing room, where the printer snips the tape containing the desired copy and inserts it into a specially equipped linotype machine, which sets stories automatically. The editor sends copy directly to the composing room only if he makes changes in a wire service story.

Fig. 7-1. **All-cap copy.** Before the introduction of the teletypesetter, most wire copy was all-capital and wide-measure. Copyeditors still get some wire copy like this, usually from the paper's own correspondents and local bureaus. Here, the editor has started to mark the copy, underlining letters that are to remain capitals.

EM

285A

WESTING 10/31 PS

URGENT

2ND NIGHT LD WESTING 233A

~~BY WALTER ERDLAND~~

UNITED PRESS INTERNATIONAL

PITTSBURGH (UPI)--A "LAST DITCH" EFFORT TO AVERT A STRIKE AGAINS THE WESTINGHOUSE ELECTRIC CORP. FAILED MONDAY.

THE INTERNATIONAL BROTHERHOOD OF ELECTRICAL WORKERS (IBEW) SAID IT WILL STRIKE AT MIDNIGHT LOCAL TIME AT PLANTS IN 20 STATES.

THE NATIONAL AGREEMENT COVERS ONLY 22 PLANTS BUT MOST OTHER LOCALS WHOSE CONTRACTS EXPIRE AT MIDNIGHT ALSO WILL STRIKE, A UNION SPOKESMAN SAID.

THE IBEW ESTIMATED "CLOSE TO 50" PLANTS ULTIMATELY WOULD BE STRUCK ALTHOUGH A SPOKESMAN SAID AT LOCATIONS WHICH NEGOTIATE SEPARATE CONTRACTS "MONEY IS BEING OFFERED TO BREAK THE STRIKE."

"IBEW LOCATIONS ARE REPORTING THE COMPANY IS NOW MORE THAN WILLING TO END INEQUITIES ON A LOCAL BASIS," HE SAID. ONE OF THE CHIEF ISSUES BLOCKING A SETTLEMENT IS THE COMPANY'S REFUSAL TO NEGOTIATE A COMPLETE CONTRACT COVERING ALL PLANTS.

FEDERAL MEDIATOR WILLIAM ROSE CALLED NEGOTIATORS FOR WESTINGHOUS AND THE UNION TOGETHER AT 2 P.M. MONDAY IN WHAT HE CALLED A "LASTDI

PICKUP 5TH PGH 233A:

FEDERAL MEDIATOR WILLIAM ROSE CALLED NEGOTIATORS FOR WESTINGHOUS AND THE UNION TOGETHER AT 2 P.M. MONDAY IN WHAT HE CALLED A "LAST DITCH EFFORT" BUT WAS UNSUCCESSFUL IN AVOIDING A STRIKE.

PICKUP 5TH PGH 233A: THE MEETING BE

Fig. 7-2. TTS copy. This TTS copy goes to the editor. (We have added the explanation of the wire code.) The story on punched tape goes directly to the composing room. There the printer snips the tape of the copy selected by the editor and inserts it in a linecasting machine, which sets justified lines of type one column wide. (See fig. 7-4.)

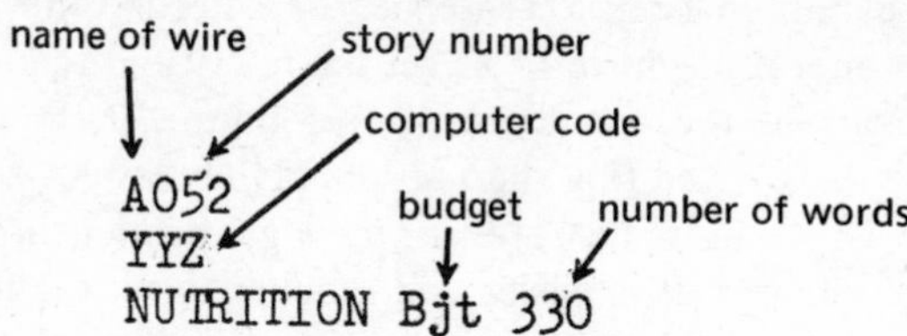

A052
YYZ
NUTRITION Bjt 330

BY ROBERT T. GRAY

WASHINGTON AP - Early findings of a government survey show alarming incidences of malnutrition in America's poverty-stricken groups, the survey director said today.

Dr. Arnold E. Schaefer, director of the 10-state National Nutrition Survey, said in testimony prepared for the Senate Committee on Nutrition and Human Needs "it is unreasonable in an affluent society to discover such signs as those seen to date."

The survey is being conducted by the Department of Health, Education and Welfare. Field teams have reported their findings on 12,000 people in four states--Texas, Louisiana, Kentucky and New York, EXCLUDING New York City.

"It is important to bear in mind and perhaps shocking to realize that

The teletypesetter is a big timesaver, as it sets type about twice as fast as a human typesetter can. But TTS has some drawbacks. The main one is that its time- and money-saving potential quickly dissipates if the editor really operates as an editor—crossing out a word here or there, eliminating a sentence, or altering the wording slightly. Such alterations have to be set manually and the new lines inserted in place of the automatically set lines. So the editor is tempted to do no more editing than absolutely necessary. Most editors handling TTS only reduce stories, having a printer throw away paragraphs set in type. It is easier and quicker to set the full story automatically and then to throw away some of the type than it is to set manually only the part to be used. If the full story is not wanted and no interim editing is done, the tape can be snipped at the last desired paragraph, so only the desired amount is set in type.

A recently invented device has solved one of the difficulties in using TTS. It allows editors to delete paragraphs from TTS copy automatically, thereby speeding up the whole process. The device is called "AP Autotape" by AP and "Autoedit" by UPI. The editor uses a small machine, called a console, to delete certain paragraphs from the TTS tape and to order specific stories into type. This is the way it works: Electric signals that are really stories come from the wire service. The signals are recorded and stored on *magnetic* tape. The editor reads the same copy from an ordinary teletype. He decides which stories he wants to use and whether he wants any paragraphs omitted from those stories. He presses buttons and levers on his console to give orders to the stored tape. The tape then spins out of storage into another machine which perforates a *paper* tape. The new tape contains only the material to be set in type. This revised paper tape, when fed into linecasting machines, sets the type automatically. (See fig. 7-3.)

Fig. 7-3. AP Autotape. This process allows the editor to delete paragraphs from TTS copy. He can use the console at left to cut material and to order specific stories into type. UPI has a similar process called Autoedit.

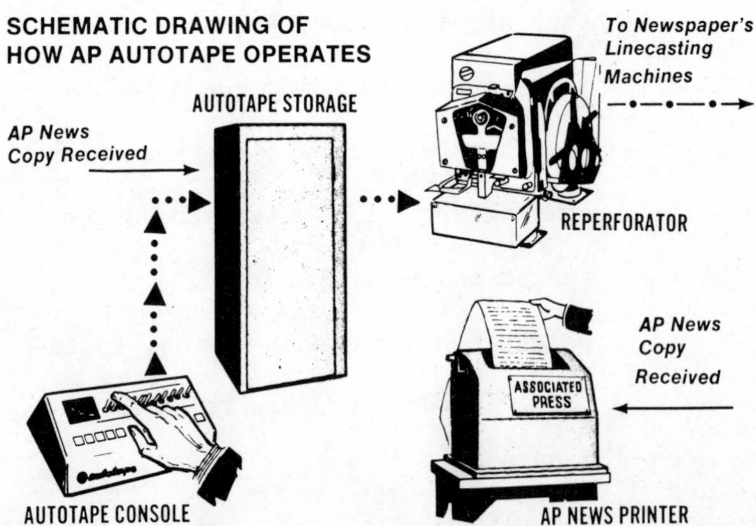

Since this equipment lets a newspaper set only those stories and parts of stories the editor wants, it is obviously a big time and money saver.

Fig. 7-4. "A" wire. The important national and international news goes across the country on the "A" wire. (The "B" wire carries stories that will be important in some areas of the country, minor in others.) This example shows copy as it comes over the wire, to be edited and set by the same procedures used for local copy.

```
48WX
    uivryyr
v for 10 a.m. EST
trition 370
 ROBERT T. GRAY
sociated Press Writer
WASHINGTON AP - Early findings of a government survey show alarming
cidences of malnutrition in America's poverty-stricken groups, the
rvey director said today.
Dr. Arnold E. Schaefer, director of the 10-state National Nutrition
rvey, said in testimony prepared for the Senate Committee on
trition and Human Needs "it is unreasonable in an affluent society
 discover such signs as those seen to date."
The survey is being conducted by the Department of Health, Education
d Welfare. Field teams have reported their findings on 12,000
ople in four states—Texas, Louisiana, Kentucky and New York,
CLUDING New York City.
"It is important to bear in mind and perhaps shocking to realize that
e problems in the poverty groups in the United States seem to be very
milar to those we have encountered in the developing countries,"
haefer told the senators...
```

How services operate

The wire services have a worldwide network, and the operation of transmitting the news, called *traffic*, is enormous. Often men work years for one of the services and still have only a fuzzy idea of how the whole organization works.

The basic operations, however, are not difficult to grasp. The main national and international news appears coast-to-coast on an "A" wire. In slang, often used in messages, it is called the "Aye" (rhymes with "hay") wire. Until 1968 the AP "A" appeared in all-caps on paper eight and a half inches wide but it now is in caps and lower case (fig. 7-4). When reduced to TTS it is called the "TA" wire and appears on paper six inches wide (fig. 7-2). Most large papers and many medium-sized ones get the "A" as it provides a good selection of major news stories and, as mentioned, can be thoroughly edited.

The "B" wire carries stories of interest only to special areas of the country. Such copy is "taken off" the "B" and put on regional wires, which carry news about one state or a few states. For example, if a story from Washington would interest people in Michigan only, it would go out of Washington on the "B." A wire service editor in Detroit would take it off the "B" and send it over a regional wire, one received by most dailies in the state. He would do this because relatively few papers receive the "B," only a small minority of all "B" stories being of interest to them.

The wire services also provide sports wires, which are all TTS. One, called "SB," provides sports stories; the other, called "SA," provides sports statistics. The services also have wires for financial news, and AP has a horse race wire. Regional wires have symbols of their own. For example, Pennsylvania's wire is the "P" wire.

Special wires serve as carriers of messages between the main offices of the services. These main offices are called "control points" or "control bureaus." Usually the biggest city in a state is a control point. But one control may cover several states in the sparsely-settled areas of the West, and Boston is the control for all of New England.

The services operate on two cycles a day, the "AMS" for morning papers and the "PMS" for afternoon editions. Each story is numbered, but the numbering starts anew with each cycle. The PMS cycle starts with the first story of the predawn hours. The AMS cycle starts in early afternoon. The first story of each cycle appears on the "A" with the number A001.

Routing the wire story

One office in the nation, of course, has to run the A wire, to act as a quarterback. The New York office has that job for each wire service. It is guided by a series of messages it receives from control bureaus all over the country. Using a separate wire, the controls send messages to the New York office about any story that might be newsworthy for the A or B wires. The messages usually are one-sentence summaries of the stories, plus the word length.

For example, San Francisco may have a story about a new water supply for Southern California. Washington may have six or eight stories. Chicago may have one about a key speech by a prominent governor. Each control bureau would file its messages, and they would read something like this:

```
    450-BBB-$100 million water system for Southern California
to be opened today.
                    FX July 1  639APD

    600-AAA-President signs bill setting up new air pollution
study.
                    WX July 1  641AED

    400-BBB-Reagan says in speech federal government needs
businesslike administration like his in California.
                    CX July 1  643ACD
```

The opening letters and numbers refer to the wire for which the story is offered and to the number of words in each story. The symbols at the end of each message indicate the control city sending the message, the time, and the time zone. FX means San Francisco, and 639APD means 6:39 A. M. Pacific Daylight Time. WX 641AED means Washington, 6:41 A. M. Eastern Daylight Time. And CX643ACD means Chicago, 6:43 A. M. Central Daylight Time. These examples could not appear consecutively on the wire because of regional time differences.

The New York general desk rates these messages on a priority system. The editor in New York is told when some stories will be ready and whether a story is going to change several times during the day as fresh events occur. With dozens of stories immediately available or scheduled within the next few hours, the editor and his aides draw up a "budget" or "news digest." This is a prospectus telling each editor and the A circuit which fifteen or twenty key stories to expect. Since perhaps 90 percent of news is anticipated, the individual telegraph editor has a good idea of what his news day is going to be like as soon as he reads the budget. (See fig. 7-5.)

If New York decides that the California water story is a good starter, then a teletype operator, called a "puncher," types out "A001FX" and rings a bell. This means that the A wire is about to send its first story (001) and that it is coming from San Francisco (FX). As the San Francisco office has its story already punched on tape, when its bell rings and its call letters appear, a switch closes, and the San Francisco story starts appearing simultaneously in newspaper offices all over the country.

A Washington story may be next, but it has to be identified from among the several Washington stories available. So "A002WX (POLLUTION)" appears on the teletype paper. This refers to the air pollution story, so Washington then sends that story. The identification and sending process is repeated throughout the cycle.

Bulletins and flashes

Important stories have to be hustled onto the wire, sometimes without the prior approval of New York. Stories of special news value are labeled "URGENT" and sent in advance of most others, but an "URGENT" does not have the priority to interrupt a story already being transmitted.

Fig. 7-5. News budgets. UPI Report (left) and AP News Digest (right) indicate major stories each service expects to send on a particular Saturday. Only part of the offering is shown, since each budget lists six or seven major items.

023

zzbylzyr newsked 3-8 gh

EDITORS: the UPI report for Saturday includes:

ABM Washington - With President Nixon's decision on deployment of Sentinel antiballistic missile system due next week, UPI poll shows opponents of ABM within five of a majority in Senate. Should stand.

NIXON Key Biscayne, Fla. -Nixon, armed with pro and con position papers, deciding whether to deploy multibillion dollar ABM system. May be led.

VIET Saigon-Communist

121

lbyl

b53 eg8

AP NEWS DIGEST

For Saturday PMs

NATIONAL

The Apollo 9 astronauts cru[illegible] into the holiday half of the[illegible] mission after proving the[illegible] moonship ready for a moo[illegible] landing.

From Space Center, Houston, prenoon lead at time now ind[illegible] nite, Wirephoto NY2

EDUCATION-CONTROVER-SY

The issue, says the author [illegible] government memorandum on black studies, is clear: ''Y[illegible]

A "BULLETIN" story, which has a higher priority, will interrupt a routine transmission. The story being sent stops usually with the words "BUST IT—BUST IT" or "MORE." Then the bulletin begins. Generally a bulletin consists of three or four paragraphs, with additional material following as "BULLETIN MATTER." Still more is sent later as "URGENT." Three to a half dozen bulletins interrupt every news cycle, as a rule. Figure 7-6 shows the UPI wire interrupted by the bulletin announcing the shooting of President Kennedy.

Fig. 7-6. Wire bulletin. The word "MORE" in the third line of this UPI transmission marks the start of the bulletin on President Kennedy's assassination. (The symbols used to head these fragments have been supplanted in recent years on all copy except radio wires.)

```
NKS." THE DEFENSE HAD IMPLIED IT WILL TAKE THE LINE THAT CAROL'S
ATH AFTER A SAVAGE BLUDGEONING AND STABBING IN HER HOME WAS THE
SULT OF AN ATTEMPTED          MOREDA1234PCS
I   A7N   DA
          PRECEDE KENNEDY
 DALLAS, NOV. 22 (UPI)--THREE SHOTS WERE FIRED AT PRESIDENT KENNEDY'S
TORCADE TODAY IN DOWNTOWN DALLAS.
                              JT1234PCS
I   A8N   DA
        URGENT
 1ST ADD SHOTS, DALLAS (A7N) XXXDOWNTOWN DALLAS.
 NO CASUALITIES WERE REPORTEDZ.
 THE INCIDENT OCCURRED NEAR THE COUNTY SHERIFF'S OFFICE ON MAIN
REET, JUST EAST OF AN UNDERPASS LEADING TOWARD THE TRADE MART WHERE
E PRESIDENT WAS TO MA

ASH

KENNEDY SERIOUSLY WOUNDED
                        PERHAPS SERIOUSLY
RHAPS FATALLY BY ASSASSINS BULLET
                JT1239PCS
```

If the wire service reporter had been immediately certain that the President had been assassinated, the news would be labeled "FLASH." This label is reserved for the most serious or spectacular news events and may not be used for six months or more at a time. When it comes, it comes not as a story or with a dateline. It merely identifies the startling information so that editors can start scurrying to make over front pages to accommodate the monumental news that the wires will soon report in detail.

Wire jargon

The beginner often sees wire copy as a helter-skelter collection of bits and pieces—all kinds of adds, corrections, precedes, subs, etc. The wire services, however, are careful to label everything, so short observation permits anyone to figure out how all the pieces go together. If a "graf" (paragraph) is to be inserted, the copy would say "Insert in A043WX after third graf x x x, President said." The editor merely finds the story labeled A043WX, counts down three paragraphs, notes that the third graf ended with the words "President said," and pastes the insert into the story. The insert will end with "pick up 4th graf, A043WX, x x x he explained." This means that the fourth paragraph will start with the words "he explained." The same system applies to "adds"—portions of copy to be added to a story.

Some stories are "undated" because they have no dateline. Usually they pull together information from several different areas, so that the story has no particular place as its focus.

By United Press International

Fighting broke out in four places in the Near East today apparently for four different reasons. . .

Occasionally, the dateline of a story will change. If a major unexpected event occurs in Lynn, Massachusetts, the first news may be filed from Boston. An hour or so later reporters may have first hand reports in Lynn and can dateline stories from there. The wire service then will write "Precede Boston" on top of the Lynn stories. This simple instruction helps the editor keep the various stories in order.

Once in a while the AP or UPI will decide that papers may not like one particular lead. An "optional lead" is then filed and editors may take their pick.

When a wire service discovers it has made a serious error, one that would cause it great embarrassment or possibly produce a libel suit, the teletype bells ring and a "BULLETIN KILL" goes over the wire. This is an order to kill a certain story or part of one. If the offending story should have happened to get into a few papers, the fact that the service filed a bulletin kill might reduce damages in any libel suit. Introduction of the bulletin kill as evidence in court would indicate that the service made a serious and speedy effort to correct the error.

Less serious mistakes are handled with less drama. A simple "CORRECTION" will be filed, and the editor pastes into a story a new paragraph or pencils the corrected material into the copy.

A "SUB" appears perhaps several times a day. This may be a "sub intro" or "top" of a story—the first few paragraphs—to be substituted for the previous top. The original is not in error; the "SUB" material is more complete, better written, or changes a minor point. More often subs are grafs for the middle of a story to update it.

Editors are assisted through the news cycle by little wire-service notes, called "advisories," that let them know what else to expect. An advisory sent halfway through the cycle may read like this:

All budget stories have been filed. We are topping President's air pollution story (A043). There will be minor inserts or adds to Chicago Reagan speech (A022) and to California water story (A001). We have been alerted that a new Italian government may be formed today. We are watching and will file story if developments warrant.

The AP

1049 aed

Because the system of labeling copy is now being changed, we can expect substantial alterations within a few years. In 1969 AP revised its system to improve editing of copy. Now all the bureaus except Washington send budgeted stories and some other copy to New York on a high speed news collection wire. The copy is edited there and sent all over the country on the A wire, but all major bureaus still can file bulletins or lesser stories directly on the A wire.

This new system does not mean that the bureaus put stories on the collection wire without editing. Stories are edited at the bureau and edited again in New York. Rewritemen in New York, of course, may add a paragraph or a sentence that was not available at the originating bureau.

Regional wires eventually will handle copy in the same way, with a regional desk editing most stories in its territory. AP is making this shift by trying it out first in one region; if it works there, then AP will apply it step by step to the rest of the nation.

Grassroots organization

Regional wires work the same way as the A wire, except that lesser bureaus as well as control points file stories on them. In some areas newspapers themselves may file stories on the AP regional wires. Usually the biggest city in the region is the "New York" of the regional wire. Chicago is home base for the Illinois wire, Philadelphia for the Pennsylvania wire, and Boston, as mentioned, for the New England wire.

Bureaus may exist in other major cities of the region and may consist of one person. University cities, because they generate so much news, often will have a one-man bureau. Most state capitals have a permanent bureau of six or eight employees supplemented by two or three temporary ones when the Legislature is in session.

The editors and writers in bureaus gather much of the news that appears on the regional wires. The AP rewrites carbons of stories written by reporters of member papers. A fair amount of copy, however, comes from "stringers," or part-time correspondents. These persons "string" as a sideline, while working on newspapers or at radio-TV stations. They pick up extra money by filing stories from their areas with a wire service. Often the stringer merely telephones facts to the nearest bureau, where a staffer writes it and puts it on the wire.

With networks of staffers and stringers in nearly every city the wire services cover the whole country, usually reporting events minutes after they occur.

Special messages

A newspaper that telephones or teletypes a bureau or control point is usually asking for information. Such a message, called a "query," often questions the accuracy of a statement or seeks clarification of a point. Unfortunately many papers take no real advantage of this opportunity, accepting without question whatever the service sends them. Wire service reporters can make mistakes, and they certainly can be asked for information. The good telegraph editor will query every day or so, to doublecheck on facts or to request coverage of some event.

His messages, in wire service jargon, are mystifying at first glance. Although most of the terms can be figured out, some need a bit of clarification:

Apc—appreciate.

Pox—police.

Scotus—Supreme Court of the United States.

Ohed—overhead. (The story, sent by Western Union because it will interest no other newspaper, costs extra.)

GN—Good night.

A newspaper in Decatur, Illinois, might query Washington by way of Chicago. The Chicago office would put a message on the wire like this:

WX

Decatur asks story from WX pox on jailing of Elmer Blank of Sullivan, Ill., who freed 2 wks ago in another case by scotus decision.

CX Jan. 25 235CST

The services even subdivide their regional wires by a process known as "splitting." This lets regional wires get news of a sizable area, a state or group of states, plus news of a more restricted region. Pennsylvania, for example, has two major cities, Pittsburgh and Philadelphia, one at each end of the state. Obviously, some news in one section is not news in the other. So sometimes the wire splits —switches are thrown so Pittsburgh files stories about western Pennsylvania and Philadelphia files stories about eastern Pennsylvania. After an hour or so the switch is thrown back, and every newspaper in the state receives the same copy again.

This system is used on what is called the Interbureau TTS. Since the majority of papers are small, they often want only one wire. The Interbureau provides this service by condensing the major national and world news and adding the most important news on livestock, commodity, and stock trading. Sports transmission takes about twenty minutes out of each hour. State and regional news is similarly assigned a chunk of wire time. The AP Interbureau, filed from Chicago, lets the small papers get the gist of the day's news with only one teletype. These papers, to fill page one, a few inside pages, the markets page, and a sports page or two, need all the wire copy they can afford.

Special services

The major wire services provide far more than straight news stories. Both AP and UPI offer columnists. Their work, which appears on the wire when little major news is breaking, includes humor, foreign affairs, business, Hollywood, TV, finance, agriculture, religion —and even oil!

The services also have departments that provide detailed feature stories that may be timely or may be usable for several weeks. Both services file "advance" stories, many for use in Sunday papers. These often are filed two, three, or four weeks in advance of the publication date. Sunday feature stories are in particular demand because most Sunday papers are traditionally bulky, yet little news is made on weekends. By getting such stories early, the newspapers can set them in type during slack periods. The services also mail some feature and "filler" copy.

The radio wires, with news specifically written to be spoken, submit a group of short news items that would take about four minutes to read aloud. With a minute added for a commercial, this becomes the five-minute newscast. A fifteen-minute package also is prepared several times a day. This service has led to the invention of the scornful term "rip and read," as someone unschooled in news can tear off the teletype the latest prepared newscast and go before the microphone to read it. The skilled radio or television newsman, of course, relies heavily on the wire service but adds or subtracts from the summary as his editorial judgment directs.

Both AP and UPI offer full picture services. The latest machines require only twenty seconds to receive and print an eight-by-ten-inch glossy. Papers that cannot afford instant photographs take a slower service or are mailed packets of pictures or mats of pictures. Those who receive the mailings, of course, have to run the pictures a day late.

Special Washington services likewise are available to members or clients. Each wire service has reporters in Washington covering events that are of concern only to regions. If Congress acts on a bill that influences New England, the report probably would appeal only to New Englanders. The New England papers can afford the report because the cost of the services' detailed Washington coverage is shared by all subscribers.

Offset papers can obtain a special wire from which they get copy ready to paste onto a dummy. All that they must do is to write a headline and paste it above the story.

Selecting and compiling

On most newspapers the selection of stories is a major task. Most big papers probably use 10 percent or less of the copy received. The job of sorting and culling takes time, even though the services try to give every possible aid to the editor.

On bigger papers copy boys take the stories off the wires and sort them by subject. If a war is going on, the "book" of war stories may be an inch thick. Although the editor and his assistants cannot possibly read all this material carefully, they do take a quick look at almost everything. Experienced editors make up their minds swiftly, rejecting perhaps half of the material at a glance. They give the rest of the stories a more careful reading, and a few get close attention.

Despite the pressure of time and the flood of news, the better papers encourage the careful reading of the wire copy. A nugget of information may be buried in the next to last paragraph of an otherwise worthless story. When he discovers such tidbits of important information, the editor should slip them into other stories on the same topic or make separate pieces out of them. Local angles to a story may be discovered in close reading.

For example, a newspaper in a university city may note that a former president of the university is mentioned in some detail in the middle of a wire story. The paper probably would want to rewrite the story to emphasize his place in the news.

The following example shows how easily the editor's pencil recasts a national story about pollution to emphasize the local angle:

(including Illinois,) (4)

WASHINGTON-(AP)-Three states have been given $3 million by the federal government to run pilot programs on ending water polution.

(also) (and)

The grants went to Oregon, New Hampshire and Illinois. Each state is to use the funds to see if one small polluted stream can be purified.

Oregon will receive $3.4 million, New Hampshire $5.2 million and Illinois $4.4 million.

Sometimes an editor combines reports from different wire services to make a balanced story. He might lead with the first two paragraphs of UPI, for example, then insert a couple from AP, and close with a half dozen from the New York Times News Service. The job requires a deft pencil to make sure that the language moves smoothly and that essential information has not been left out. When compiling or interweaving wire stories, the editor should be sure to cross out the various wire-service logotypes and write across the top of the patched-together story something like "From our Wire Services" or "Compiled from Wire Dispatches."

In some instances the editor can insert parenthetically a fact gleaned from another service. If the main story is from AP he may strengthen it with a paragraph from UPI:

> (United Press International reported, meanwhile, that the President had decided to stay two more days in Hawaii.)

In this case there is no need to drop the AP logotype.

When an editor rewrites the wire story, he omits the logotype but inserts early in the story a phrase of acknowledgment like "United Press International reported." This phrase informs the reader that the facts came from UPI but now have a different emphasis.

Criticism of wire services

Though wire services provide most of the news in American newspapers, and often are blessed for it, they do have their critics. The alleged shortcomings of AP and UPI have led many newspapers to buy additional services, like those of the *Washington Post-Los Angeles Times* and the *New York Times*.

Editors often complain that too many stories are weakened by mediocre writing and minor inaccuracies, especially the stories filed from the smaller bureaus of the services. The staffs at these bureaus must crank out dozens of stories a day, often based on information from stringers. It is easy for a stringer to forget to include a fact or spell a name when he phones an office staffer—who can easily forget to ask for clarification.

Shallow reporting

The main criticism, however, is that both AP and UPI are fearful of being called politically partisan. Critics say that the services often have avoided real investigative reporting for fear that the facts will embarrass a political party and that party members will cry foul.

The services note that they are under intense pressure to avoid any hint of political partisanship. This pressure comes from members or clients and since they in effect are working for newspapers and radio-TV stations, they write news the way most customers want it. AP and UPI realize that they are prime targets for libel suits, and this perhaps contributes to their being less zealous about doing much investigating except at the national level.

Perhaps for this reason most investigative and depth reporting in the nation, until recently, has been by reporters from individual newspapers, not wire services. While a good many AP and UPI reporters have won Pulitzer Prizes, rarely have the honors come for hidden material painstakingly uncovered.

In the late sixties AP in particular developed a policy of adding much more depth to reporting. Most such reporting had been restricted to AP Newsfeatures, a separate division of AP. (UPI has a similar features division.) To increase coverage in depth, AP instituted what it called an "Enterprise" desk. AP reporters working with the Enterprise editor spend weeks or even months digging up information of great value to the reading public. One effort of an Enterprise team resulted in a penetrating article on the plight of the small American farmer. There is even a special Enterprise force in Washington with carte blanche to uncover issues of national interest. One of the great journalistic coups of the Washington group was its report, in several articles, of widespread corruption in South Vietnam during the war. Another story revealed that tons of American oil intended for the military had been sold on the open market in Thailand. Both of these depth reports had not only national but worldwide impact.

The complaint against wire services for little investigative reporting is also less valid today than it was in the early sixties. The services realize that a reporter who must write several stories a day can do no more than a cursory job on the news. Investigative stories take time, and so do stories that convey real understanding of a major problem. Most observers would say that AP, with greater resources, has moved more boldly into the "enterprise" field than has UPI. The result has been a stronger AP—so strong that some editors and publishers even fear for the survival of UPI. Almost everyone agrees that a nation with only one complete wire service would risk complacent and perhaps biased news coverage.

Uncritical coverage

Another criticism of wire services springs from their extreme objectivity; they tend to report what various officials say, without qualification or interpretation. This objectivity results, occasionally, in the services' being used by government or business figures to disseminate biased information. The reporters, faithfully reporting what the officials say, may then repeat lies or misleading information. A telegraph editor who suspects reported statements should press a wire service to insert a clarification, such as "Three months ago, the secretary said the opposite was the case. . . ." Or he may ask the source for an explanation or request a quote from an opposing source.

An example of thoroughness, plus enterprise, occurred during the escalation of the Vietnam war. Secretary of Defense Robert McNamara had repeatedly said that the war was about over and that American troops would be withdrawn soon. After a long series of these pronouncements AP filed a story simply listing what McNamara had said over a three-year period. The story provided real public service by letting the reader see, in one story, the contradictions in the Secretary's statements.

Problems with pressure

One objection from wire services is pressure from publishers. The editor of one major newspaper whose staff does not belong to the American Newspaper Guild frequently calls up the local AP office to complain that a story written by a Guildsman has a pro-labor slant. Another paper actually requested "as many anti-Red China stories as possible." There are ridiculous and petty complaints, too, like objecting to the use in a story of the word "charged" instead of "said." One wire service staffer equated his job with "having a thousand mothers-in-law."

Nor have wire services always withstood influence successfully. A Texas editor succeeded in getting AP to kill an advance story it had filed on the problems of organizing agricultural workers in his state. The reporter who wrote it quit in anger and disgust.

In other situations the wire services are handicapped by their stringers, who wish to whitewash negative news about their communities. For example, it sometimes may be hard to get the facts about bad weather in Florida. And some small city reporters never tell AP or UPI about a strike in their towns for fear that efforts to attract industry will be upset.

Some wire service sports writers are little more than press agents for certain teams. They so appreciate the coaches and players—or so fear their wrath—that objectivity evaporates. Free lunches, press passes to games for friends and relatives, and special Christmas presents tend to bias all but the most tough-minded reporters.

Nationalistic bias

Wire services can even become nationalistic in reporting foreign affairs. Some coloring of the facts by a reporter's background is natural. But sometimes this coloration severely distorts reality. When foreign dispatches read as though they were written by the State Department, the reader suspects the information. In the mid-fifties some reports of international conferences so strongly supported State Department views that the general manager of AP took pains to remind the whole organization that reporters should strive to report the facts without cheering for one side or the other.

In both hot and cold wars reporters are under pressure, usually unconsciously, to take a nationalistic position. This stance tends to simplify rival ideologies almost the same way that television westerns polarize the good guys and the bad. Ideologies, whether foreign or domestic, are rarely simple, and no reporter should attempt to give them easy labels. For example, calling certain foreign politicians "pro-American" or "pro-Chinese" is convenient but no doubt inaccurate. To say that some of these spokesmen *on a particular issue* support or denounce the American position, however, may be correct and is certainly fair.

It has been too convenient in the years since World War II to describe any opponent of American policy as "Communist" or "pro-Communist." International politics seldom is that simple, and frequently there has to be a big scramble a few weeks or months later to find a different label when events disprove the original assessments. Some leading American diplomats have said cautiously that these simplistic terms often create rigid public attitudes that deprive diplomats of the maneuvering room essential in their work. Telegraph editors with a true national interest therefore must be alert to slants and oversimplified phrasing.

Here is an example of the way questionable editing can expand an adjective into a giant-size stereotype. On the front page of the *New York Times* the story was bland enough:

> WASHINGTON, Oct. 30—Robinson McIlvaine, the United States Ambassador to Guinea, was placed under house arrest this morning by the Guinean authorities in Conakry, a State Department spokesman said.

But the AP version included an innocent-looking characterization of Guinea:

> WASHINGTON(AP)—Guinea's left-leaning government has detained U.S. Ambassador Robinson McIlvaine in his residence in Conakry, in apparent retaliation for an incident in Accra, the Ghana capital, the State Department reported Sunday.

A large Eastern paper picked up the AP's label for a two-column head:

Left-leaning Guinea
Detains U.S. Envoy

Headline skimmers once again see Communists fighting America. But what is "left-leaning"? How many in a government have to be "left" to make it lean? Is the U.S. government "left-leaning" because some right-wingers say so? Or "fascist-leaning" because some Communists say so?

The wire services, in the eyes of many critics, could do a better job of explaining the "why" of an event. The "why" frequently has to be guessed by the reader, or he must look to a columnist for an explanation. Some of the reluctance to explain rests on the fact that often the reporter cannot ascertain the "why." It is difficult in some countries to ask officials the reason for a certain policy. Both editors and reporters should remember, however, that people in most governments think they have perfectly good reasons for the actions they take. It is essential, if people in other countries and cultures are to be understood, that reporters attempt to discover what those reasons are. When reporters find them out, editors should be sure to print the stories.

The AP and UPI are not totally to blame, of course, when significant information does not reach readers. Wire editors and writers know that sometimes the better stories wind up in newspaper office wastebaskets. When a wire service reporter struggles to get the difficult news and finds that editors ignore his stories, he tends to write the easy copy that sees print, even if it oversimplifies or distorts the full picture. This fact should push telegraph editors to use first-class copy even if only a limited number of readers appreciate it.

Another deficiency of wire stories is inadequate backgrounding. When fresh news develops on a familiar event, the background may be so abbreviated that it is inaccurate. Part of this trouble stems from the flaws already mentioned. If the services do less than a first-class job of backgrounding stories, a telegraph editor must keep tabs on what has gone before and be sure that any continuing story refreshes the reader's memory.

Guidelines for novices

These criticisms of the wire services have not been ignored by AP and UPI executives, judging from their public pronouncements and actual changes in coverage. They are aware that yesterday's methods are not always adequate to cover today's news and are taking steps to improve the day's report.

The individual telegraph editor, however, must struggle to give his readers full, accurate, and meaningful news in the limited space of the newspaper pages. He may buy a supplemental service, if the publisher agrees. He should spend nearly an hour a day reading other newspapers to help him understand the news and to help him judge its value. If he works in the East he should read the *New York Times*, the *Wall Street Journal*, the *Washington Post*, and the *Christian Science Monitor*. In the Midwest he should read at least a couple of the Eastern papers, plus Chicago publications and the *St. Louis Post-Dispatch*. In the South he would check the *St. Petersburg Times* and the *Atlanta Constitution*. In the West he would look over the *Los Angeles Times* and the *Denver Post*.

In addition, the good telegraph editor needs to cultivate qualities such as the following:

Knowledge. Keeping up in social sciences, particularly the history of the world during the last thirty years is especially valuable.

Wariness. He tests for news content any story on a fad, whether dope addiction, juvenile crime, or high school dropouts. The editor sees the forest as well as the trees.

Awareness of his goal. His picture of the coverage needed for his paper encompasses tomorrow's world as well as today's.

Alertness. He spots the news that will attain maximum readership in his area.

Organization. Stories need careful placement in the news pages, instead of falling helter-skelter into any hole that fits.

Balance. He should mix major and minor stories effectively and be able to leaven the basic seriousness of the paper with humorous items.

Sensitivity. Planted stories, trial balloons, manipulated press conferences, and calculated leaks should trigger his sham detector.

Top political leaders in the nation, and some of them outside, are masters at these games. Editors should become masters at detecting what game public officials are playing and evaluate the news accordingly.

Creativity. To convey effectively the breadth of an important event, he should be able to inter-weave summaries, associated stories (perhaps bunched on the same page), and an interpretive article.

Flexibility. A story early budgeted for a big play but turning out to be minor should go in the wastebasket or be cut to three grafs and buried somewhere in the first section.

Perspective. Day after day the reader should see continuing stories instead of disjointed reports. And the editor should be checking for tomorrow's big story in today's brief reports.

A telegraph editor who successfully does all these things does what Walter Lippmann suggested in the first chapter: brings the hidden facts to light and sets them in relation to one another. These facts, carefully presented and evaluated, will give, as Lippmann said, "a picture of reality on which men can act."

8 The sub-editors

In addition to the telegraph editor, newspapers have four and sometimes five other sub-editors. Each supervises a staff that may range from one to fifty or more persons, and each is responsible for a certain part of the paper.

The best known of these sub-editors is the city editor, the person who directs a staff of reporters covering the city and, often, its environs. A second sub-editor, the state editor, takes care of a broader area but rarely the whole state because few newspapers sell that widely. "Regional editor" or "country editor" might be a more accurate title than "state editor," because he supervises the collection of news in his paper's circulation area outside the metropolitan district. As a rule state capital reports and most wire service copy belong to the telegraph editor's province, though technically part of the "state" news.

The sports editor cuts across area lines, as he collects sport news from everywhere. He supervises a staff of sports writers, edits their copy, and selects copy from the special sports wires of Associated Press or United Press International.

Like the sports editor, the women's editor collects special news wherever it breaks. That locale used to be exclusive society, but the society page has been democratized. Now most women's pages report more than the social events of the elite. Except on the largest papers, the pages cover nearly everyone's weddings, engagements, and parties, but even these traditional subjects are often secondary to articles on food preparation, art, hobbies, child care, social problems, and education. Some papers have even quit calling this department the women's section and have named it "the family page." The idea behind this name is that the pages should primarily concern families and their problems and activities. The "women's editor," once called the "society editor," may eventually become the "family editor."

Some papers have as a fifth sub-editor the suburban editor. Some newspapers in larger cities without a suburban editor in name usually have one in fact—an assistant city editor assigned to the job.

The task of covering the suburbs has become a difficult one because there often are dozens of little communities, each with its own city government, planning commission, zoning department, school board, etc. It is almost impossible in a city like Chicago, for example, to print any but the most important news from the suburbs. The *Chicago Tribune*, however, makes a good stab at it by putting out, three times a week, a tabloid filled with suburban news. The "tab," inserted into the regular issue of the paper, has separate editions to cover major sections north, west, and south of the city. Other big city papers include strong sections of suburban news because many people in suburbia, who may work in the city, are more interested in their own little towns than in the center city.

The tasks of sub-editors

It would be ideal if every person had a year or more of experience on a desk before he moved up to a sub-editor's chair. Preferably, the experience would be as an assistant to a particular sub-editor. But, except on the biggest papers, this kind of background is usually impossible to get. Often a person will be told one day that he is going to be sports editor (or suburban editor or state editor). He may have only a sketchy acquaintance with editing any copy but his own. He may have had little experience in headline writing and none in makeup. He may also have had no chance to practice the art of supervising the work of others. How can he make the jump gracefully and safely?

A new editor unfamiliar with the job should give himself a cram course. Pumping his predecessor for information and tips, getting advice from the staff, and even soliciting criticisms of his efforts, without indicating a lack of confidence, can help the new editor bolster his talent and experience. He also could check books, pamphlets, and magazine articles to broaden his knowledge.

Directing the staff

The sub-editor should, if possible, delegate a certain amount of responsibility. By doing everything himself, he will probably do nothing well. Nor will he have time to do any kind of long-range thinking about his work and how it will be affected by changing times. Also, by delegation of duties, the sub-editor makes himself available to fill in for the editor when he gets sick or goes on vacation. Should the editor be promoted to another job, the sub-editor will be prepared to take his place.

The sub-editor whose staff can work without constant supervision can set aside a certain time to inspect his territory. Just as it is easy for him to neglect delegating responsibility, it is easy to neglect this requirement. The rigorous demands of his job can pressure the sub-editor into spending all his working time bent over his desk, whereas the sub-editor, especially the city editor, should be out checking new developments in his community, even doing some leg work. He should go to an occasional meeting on a hot local issue to observe first-hand the changes and debates in the town. Traveling his territory will give him a valuable sense of his community, a keen insight into public thinking, and an empathy with his staff.

Empathy is important, as each sub-editor has to direct the operations of reporters and, should they exist, assistant editors. He should direct operations so as to make his section effective, and effectiveness comes with contented, alert, enterprising, cooperative, and professional associates. This is not easy. Some people cannot give orders without being abrasive. Others swing between joviality and gloom. Some editors demand quality one day and forget it the next.

A supervisor ought to be consistent and reasonable with his staff. When he was a reporter or desk man, he certainly wanted congenial surroundings, a dependable and sympathetic supervisor, and a chance to laugh. A sub-editor should at least try to fulfill his own requirements.

But an editor should beware the tangles of doing favors for staffers. A day off given to one man may, because of circumstances, be denied to another. It must be made clear to the second that he couldn't get the holiday because of a scheduling problem, not a personal one. One solution is to give no favors that can't be given to everyone. Yet an editor creates a sense of well-being if occasionally he can let a staffer go home early, or can let him slip out during a quiet period to run a personal errand or to get a haircut. When the sub-editor is both flexible and impartial the staff morale goes up.

Morale improves with other improvements in working conditions. Things like new desks, typewriters, and lights are contributions of management that a persuasive sub-editor can obtain.

Praise and criticism

As we have said before, no editor should overlook the value of praise. Most newsmen are immune to ostentatious flattery—they have seen so much that is phony—but they dearly love a casual sentence of praise from a colleague. A simple "Good story, Charley," or "Nice headline, Liz!" will do more to spark professionalism than any scroll of merit.

Some papers, as mentioned in chapter 2, get out a little sheet that gives credit for work well done. Others post good examples. Some subtle sub-editors might be able to wangle a personal note from the publisher or editor-in-chief to commend the staffer. Discretion here is essential. The minute that an editor hands out laurels insincerely, his whole staff begins to discount his approval.

One of the best ways a sub-editor improves morale, especially if he takes credit modestly, is to get pay increases for deserving staff members. When a requested raise comes through, he can tell the staffer quietly, "Your good work of the last several months means an extra ten dollars a week from now on." The staffer will not only be pleasantly surprised but will realize that his editor went to bat for him.

But what happens when a staffer fails to measure up? In the old days, the editor would probably bellow, "You're fired!" Such abrupt dismissal is rare today because editors realize that it is cruel and that it often loses for the paper a potentially good employee, and because American Newspaper Guild contracts bar dismissal without specific cause.

Instead of muttering deprecations about an inadequate staffer, an editor should do his best to be a teacher. A few minutes spent every day helping the new staffer correct his shortcomings and speaking favorably about his strong points will improve both the newcomer's morale and usefulness to the paper. Sometimes the editor assigns another person to go over a novice reporter's copy, sentence by sentence, to show him how to improve it.

If all efforts fail in getting the staffer to improve, it would be better for the newspaper and the employee if he were urged to look elsewhere for work. If he is not fired outright, he can more easily find another job that he may do well. Any such conversation, of course, should be private. The wise editor, under these circumstances, refrains from suggesting that a person get into another line of work. Many succesful newspapermen have, at one time or another, got such advice and, fortunately, not taken it. But newsmen who recognize they have no talent should quit. They would be only tolerated on any newspaper and would be better off in another business.

Promising reporters and deskmen should be encouraged to attend the increasing number of workshops and study sessions being held throughout the country. They should be urged, also, to take formal courses at local colleges or universities. Some newspapers pay the tuition for such courses if the person completes them satisfactorily. The courses need not be on journalism—almost any knowledge can be valuable to a newsman.

Sometimes even a good reporter or deskman hits a slump. Then his sub-editor should talk with him. Perhaps some personal problem is worrying him, or the job itself has become dull. Talking it out may be just what the staffer needs to regain his former verve and skill. Other times the sub-editor can suggest or even provide solutions to the problem. For example, a man who has worked on the desk for a couple of years and basically likes the work may be getting a little tired of sitting all day long. Couldn't he be a reporter instead? Or have a special reporting assignment once in a while, so he can get out and use his legs occasionally?

A skillful city editor noted that his young reporters often lapsed when excitement in their personal lives overshadowed their work. A young first homeowner or father sometimes dreamed all day of his new acquisitions. Usually, the city editor said, the person came back to earth in a few weeks. If not, a friendly comment, given with a smile, often did the trick. The editor might say, "George, do you believe you could think a little less about that baby and a little more about your job?"

An editor who is critical of a staffer's work should express his criticism out of a concern for the person's welfare as well as the paper's.

It probably will only upset a troubled person more if a critic shows no interest in his problems and only wants to solve his own or the publisher's.

Directing news collection

A sub-editor soon discovers that the efficiency and morale of the staff depend partly on the flow of work in the newsroom. Everyone around a newsroom knows that news comes in spurts. News may be heavy for a week or more, and then for a few days nothing seems to happen. Some of these quiet periods can be predicted. Summer is the calmest season. Schools and legislatures are on vacation, and most community action slacks off as workers prepare for their holidays. The Christmas season repeats this lull in those civic affairs that produce most of the non-spectacular news in a community paper.

In some places local news is heavy a couple of days a week and light on others. The city council may meet Mondays and the school board Tuesdays. Both normally provide several stories. The county board of supervisors, another good news source, also may meet on a Tuesday. If the city planning commission meets Monday night, and the zoning board Tuesday, then local government news may well pile up the first of the week. Unless the sub-editor plans ahead for peaks and slumps, many of his Thursday, Friday, and Saturday pages will be drab and insignificant—not worth reading—and his staff will suffer from being alternately swamped and idled.

During the dull periods the staff should be scratching for feature stories or digging for important information below the surface of events. If it is obvious that the city council will make news early one week about building codes, why not interview the city engineer the week before on new building techniques, or talk to a leading architect on his ideas for the city of the future? On the other hand, if the council makes a surprising or especially significant decision on Monday, the rest of the week provides the time to follow up on the reasons for the decision and its implications.

The ability to create story ideas is one of an editor's greatest assets; the sub-editor must develop it if he is to be more than a person who gives assignments, edits copy, writes headlines, lays out pages, and pats a reporter's back once in a while. An editor may do all his routine work well, but he never will be first-rate without imagination. And since imagination is always in short supply, he should encourage it in his colleagues. The willingness to stimulate story ideas and the "play" of stories is a characteristic that develops a spirited staff. People get excited on a newspaper where the editors listen to new ideas, are willing to experiment, and reward enterprise. Every sub-editor should have a drawer, box, or basket available for staffers to drop suggestions into. But if he is not going to follow a suggestion he receives, he ought to tell the contributor why. An editor who repeatedly ignores ideas quickly freezes the initiative of his staff. He should acknowledge every suggestion and give at least a word of thanks for all that come in.

The city editor

Newspapermen generally concede that the city editor's job is the most difficult of all the sub-editor positions. He has to supervise the biggest staff of full-time reporters, and he must try to fit the talents of these reporters to dozens of jobs. Throughout the work day he has to make alterations and suggestions and give specific directions. The city editor gives assignments to reporters and photographers, sees that the copy is edited the way he wants it, and checks the fit of local copy to the available space.

On smaller papers the job may seem easier but often is not. While the city editor on a small paper may have only a few reporters to supervise, he also has to read all their copy, write headlines, and sometimes produce a few stories himself. He must even dart into the composing room occasionally to oversee the makeup of the pages. Since many reporters on small papers are inexperienced, the city editor must try to make up for their deficiencies with his editing pencil and with some kind of on-the-job training effort of his own. This training, because of a lack of time, often must consist of an over-the-shoulder comment from time to time or some brief instructions on how to get the information for a certain story.

City editors on medium-sized papers will have an assistant or two. One assistant may handle the assignment chore, with the city editor suggesting a special story, and another may edit local pictures. The editor and assistants all will do some editing of local copy and will mark headline size and story length before sending the copy to the universal desk. The city editor will probably lay out the local news pages.

On the biggest papers the city editor has a half dozen aides, each with a specific job to do. The city editor, acting as chairman, checks over the work of others, adding or subtracting copy and accepting or overruling decisions.

This supervisory role gives the city editor the flexibility he needs to handle the day's little or big emergencies. The gifted city editor manages to keep most emergencies in the newsroom from becoming severe because he is prepared and able to move swiftly in crises.

Seeing beyond Now

Preparedness is vital to the smooth operation of a city desk. For a coming election the inept editor fails to prepare for stories that he knows about in advance or expects to happen, whereas the well-organized editor plans who will write the story or stories on state legislative races, who will handle city council contests, etc. He picks someone to funnel the returns from the central counting area to the paper or may even have to plan collection of returns by the paper itself. This work may mean arranging for extra telephones or special lines. All this preparation requires planning, but it means the difference between a confused scramble to get some stories together and the provision of thorough, balanced coverage.

Though an election obviously needs planning if it is to be covered decently, the demands of some events are more subtle. A good instance of how a paper prepared for one such occurred in Rochester, New York. Realizing that the bishop of the large Rochester Roman Catholic diocese was elderly and close to retirement, the city editor had reporters prepare a file so that when the bishop did retire his biography would be easy to get into type. One reporter wrote the basics of the story when he had no spot news to cover, while one or two others hunted for anecdotes or minor incidents in the bishop's life that would make the biographical story alive and appealing. When the bishop did retire, the story was almost ready for the composing room. Even the pictures for a full-page spread were ready to go. With only a little more writing and some editing the retirement story could make the tightest deadline.

In this case there was an unexpected sequel to the resignation: the new bishop was the renowned theological writer and lecturer Fulton J. Sheen. Unless news had leaked in advance, no one could have been prepared for this spectacular development. To cover it the city editor had to move fast. Quickly he conferred with the news editor and managing editor. They decided to charter a plane, in cooperation with a television station, to fly a reporter and a photographer to New York to interview the new bishop.

The city editor then ordered other reporters to pull various kinds of material from library files for sidebar stories on Bishop Sheen's previous trips to Rochester, his speeches in the city, his noted quotations, and his biography. At the same time news from the wire services about the new appointment went to the city desk to be checked for any items the paper had not gathered on its own.

The city editor, had he not prepared for the basic story, would have found the emergency story impossible to handle. But with the spade work already done, the staff could perform an outstanding job.

The press of time

Even when emergencies force a city editor to make quick decisions, he should force himself to pause and ponder: "Are we getting the whole story? Are we missing anything? Are we over-playing? Have we got the right pictures? What's the best layout for all these stories? What must we cut or drop in order to print this hot news?"

To do his job properly, the city editor must be able to grasp instantaneously the value of news, coach the young reporters, juggle his staff to get the best coverage, and inspire respect, if not admiration.

The city editor soon finds that his main concern is the clock. He always has to be checking how much time remains to deadline—to see whether there is time to print any more than the bare facts of a story and engrave a picture to illustrate it.

To keep from being unduly harassed by the clock, the city editor strives to develop top efficiency. He chooses aides who move swiftly to solve the problems that develop. He learns the strengths and weaknesses of his reporters and learns to give the latest story to his fastest writer. He avoids answering the telephone himself, so he is not tied up listening to some complaint that a copy boy could handle just as well. He works to eliminate his own inefficient habits. Since paper usually swirls around a city editor, he is tempted to set some aside to read later. This is usually a mistake. An excellent city editor once remarked that no one should handle the same piece of paper twice. "Read it and decide what to do with it," was his motto. His desk was never a bottleneck for copy, memos, or letters.

The best city editors today keep tabs on more than the city room. In addition to getting around the city themselves, they read up on its history so they can lead their staffs to do sociological articles on the community. Tomorrow's newspapers will almost certainly require such emphasis. They will report such things as the changing political power base, the local developments in mental health, the deep and often hidden frictions behind violence, or a real critique of the local educational system.

Gone are the days when reporters believed that news consisted of the acts of God and politicians. Stories of crimes, accidents, and fires are essential. A few speculative stories still are important, but they have been bypassed for stories that require careful digging and interviewing to help the reader understand his world. Every city editor will have to recognize this change and prepare himself and his staff for the kind of coverage an increasing number of readers demand and all readers need.

The state editor

The work of a state or regional editor often has a direct bearing on a paper's circulation. Many city dwellers will subscribe to a monopoly paper even if its coverage of city news is poor. But often territory in rural or suburban areas can be contested by papers from other nearby cities. For example, counties of eastern Iowa have traditionally been battled for by the *Chicago Tribune* and the *Des Moines Register*, as well as papers of such smaller cities as Davenport, Dubuque, and Cedar Rapids. The *Register* state desk has the same kind of circulation war with Omaha and Council Bluffs to the west. If the state editor slights the news from the outlying areas, the readers there will switch to another paper.

The state editor's chief problem is that his staff never is in the newsroom. He must communicate with his reporters by telephone, teletype, or mail. Frequently his reporters work only part-time for a little extra money and status. Though they usually have serious journalistic limitations, no one else is available who can do the job as well.

Stringers and correspondents

A sizable number of papers have discovered that part-time rural correspondents are, with a few exceptions, not up to modern coverage. These "stringers" often write poorly, miss good stories under their noses, and find it almost impossible to recognize deadlines. As an alternative papers have tried to find professionals who are willing to work the smaller towns. These are persons who not only can report well but have the ability to cover the news of a good-sized region, perhaps a whole county. They can drive over the territory every few days, and, because they get to know the news sources, can also do much spot checking by telephone. Some of these correspondents have teletypes in their homes or some little niche that serves as an office. These teletypes communicate directly with the state editor's desk. Stories from these correspondents usually require little editing or rechecking, and the state editor has less frustration keeping tabs on one efficient remote reporter than on half a dozen incompetent stringers.

Some papers try to solve the problem another way. They use staffers from smaller papers as stringers. A few regular staffers in the "home office" then provide all special coverage. For example, the *Des Moines Tribune* had a strong network of stringers operating under a well-staffed state desk. But to assure stories of interest to readers in smaller communities, the editors pulled one of the top city-side reporters over to state coverage. His task was to drive around the state looking for features and getting pictures. To city-bound reporters, his job looked like a dream, for in two or three days of driving he could collect his material and do nothing the rest of the week but write the five pieces and play golf. In this fashion, he was providing the state desk with a daily, illustrated, by-lined feature from obscure portions of its circulation area. Clearly, the system was great, both for the reporter and the newspaper.

Professionals willing to be correspondents in smaller communities usually are young and at the beginning of their careers. The state editor should coach these beginners into better writing and reporting by writing them notes about their work and, in particular, by urging them to read their copy in print to see how it has been edited. Hopefully, they will pick up tips that will save time for both themselves and the state editor.

Some state editors prefer to send beginners into the field after some specific training. They encourage the managing editor to keep the neophyte in the city for at least a month, where he works under the discipline of the city desk and where his assignments direct him to cover events he soon will be reporting without much direction.

For example, he should tag around with the courthouse reporter for at least a couple of days, soaking up information on the courts and county government. He also should cover a little news of business, police, labor unions, and city government with its main adjuncts: planning, zoning, sewage disposal, parks, revenue, and traffic.

While most such staff correspondents are young, occasionally a highly qualified older person wants to live in a little town. Though sometimes he might be able to hold a key position in the city, he prefers life in a rural community. When a state editor has such a pearl, someone happy in one place and good at the job, he should do everything reasonable to keep him happy. A good salary, frequent bylines, and a note of praise once or twice a year from the editor-in-chief or the publisher are the least a good career correspondent deserves.

But in the main the reporters work in the field for six months or a year and are ready to move. Sometimes there is an agreement that the person from the far reaches of the circulation district will get the first opening on the city staff. Such promises should not be made casually. A young person told that five or six months hard work in Swampsville will earn him a place on the city staff will, as the time drifts on to a year, feel betrayed. If he becomes bitter and quits, suddenly the editor loses not only his coverage but a valuable man. Editors should be honest about future opportunities and keep expectant correspondents informed of any changes in their status.

Of course not all correspondents are in the boondocks. Newspapers in major cities have bureaus in other metropolitan areas, and reporters there can live the city life. Sometimes their lives are easier than the city reporter's because they may have an easier commute than he does.

The *Newark* (N.J.) *News* has such a bureau in nearby Orange, where a staff of eight or ten—a bigger group than the whole staff of some small dailies—covers news of the area. The staff edits copy at the bureau and sends it to the main office by teletype.

Planning state coverage

How thorough should the state coverage be? Obviously, if the state editor covers a sizable area with any kind of depth, he is going to fill many pages. If he only skims the most important news, however, circulation may dip. The solution is to set guidelines on coverage. They should be worked out in conference with the publisher, managing editor, city editor, and other sub-editors. The circulation manager should be brought in, too, of course, because he is the expert on the law of diminishing returns. A town of 1,000 with only twenty-two subscribers will not merit much coverage unless the circulation manager believes its circulation can be built up.

Bigger papers usually restrict news from outlying areas. They may have more than a hundred fairly substantial communities in their circulation area; they can't possibly cover each in detail. Smaller papers, of course, will provide quite thorough reports of the few villages under their circulation umbrella, and some papers will print even columns of personal items mailed in by a stringer. The trend, however, is to reduce trivia.

Once policy has been set on breadth and depth of coverage, the state editor has to struggle with personnel. Sometimes he has to resign himself to stringers and possibly a few full-timers. To make the best of an inadequate situation, the editor should try to give as much instruction as he can to his "staff." Some papers get out a pamphlet or news sheet that explains how to write news and features. These have to be short if the stringers are to read them, and even then the messages don't always get through.

A pamphlet to guide the stringer should be specific:

> We do *not* want accident stories unless someone is killed or seriously hurt or unless there is an unusual angle.
>
> We do *not* want more than three short paragraphs on weddings, unless the mayor is getting married.
>
> We *do* want stories of some breadth, like the amount of school construction planned in your county for the next three years or the plan to clean up Inky Stinky Creek.
>
> We *do* want stories on politics, government, education, and social change.
>
> We *do* want feature stories on funny or peculiar happenings.

The booklet can be supplemented by a mimeographed monthly sheet that praises good work, naming the author, and that criticizes bad work anonymously. This sheet should be written entertainingly and without malice. It should educate, not persecute. Furthermore, if someone does a first-rate job on a difficult task, the state editor should take a few minutes to dash off a personal note. If the work is not so good, the editor should avoid fulminating. He must patiently call the writer, have him collect more information, and have him rewrite the story. If state editors went into a frenzy every time they saw a miserable piece of copy, they would soon be palsied.

The state editor should have the newspaper's librarian maintain a looseleaf booklet of details about the areas that the regular staff as well as stringers report on. Such a booklet would enable reporters to doublecheck all basic information about each town and district, including the spelling of the names of public and business officials.

Editors should make as many calls to get the news or to straighten out inconsistencies as a story warrants. A growing number of newspapers have a contract with the telephone company that provides almost unlimited telephone calls over a large area for a set fee. This arrangement frees editors from having to balance the size of the phone bill against the size of the story.

The women's editor

Over the years the women's pages of the better papers have become a section which is less about the country club set and more about what active women are doing. Consequently, these pages now attract many women besides those fascinated by high society. These women are often more traveled and better educated and have wider interests than women a generation ago. An example of a newspaper's responding to this change was the creation by the *Washington Post* of a new section combining women's news with news of entertainment, culture, and "people."

The cagey editor of the women's pages aims today to attract nearly everyone. The editor should realize that weddings are similar and predictable, so their stories can be told in a few paragraphs.

Breathless reporting of every stitch of the bridal gown appeals to only a few readers and uses up space that deserves news of more general interest. Some weddings have moderately wide interest—at least as wide as some of the other news in the paper—and these stories should cover the essentials of the ceremony and the people involved. Some editors have hit upon the idea of running pictures of the happy couple, in street clothes, instead of only the bride's picture. About twice as many people will recognize one of the two as would recognize only the bride.

All kinds of social items deluge all papers. Medium and small papers especially find that the publicity chairman of every organization mails in or calls in a story every time the organization serves a cup of coffee—and sometimes when it doesn't. In many cases the item could be of interest only to the organization's members, but the members may already know the information. Since many of these items are really announcements, some papers have used a "Community Calendar" to announce in a line or two what organization is going to hear which speaker, where, and at what time. This device saves a galley or two of type a day.

Other papers have a special column for tidbits that may be interesting but not worth a story:

> Ralph Taylor of 1024 Ackerman has been named to the dean's list at Elmhurst College, where his sister Janice was valedictorian last year . . . Their parents are Mr. and Mrs. Homer Taylor.
>
> Mrs. Roger Smythe has been named by the local PTA Council as an alternate to the state PTA convention in Minneapolis.

Condensation of little news items is used on other pages as well, notably sports and business. It saves space, yet allows many marginal items to be read swiftly.

The sports editor

The sports editor has one advantage over the other sub-editors: Almost all his news is expected. He knows at the start of his work day that several games or sports events are scheduled, so the plans for his pages can be seriously altered only by such things as the cancellation of an event, the death of a famed athlete, the highly unexpected outcome of a contest, or the setting of some record.

To offset this advantage he does have some special problems. Some of them stem from the fact that many people find sports and sports stars dramatic and spectacular. Because American sports fans are so intense, sports copy tends to be melodramatic.

The sports editor has to guard against absurdly melodramatic stories. He must keep in mind that victory for the home team really is not the greatest of glories, and defeat is not the greatest of tragedies. The pages should not treat athletes as supermen either, for sometimes off the field they are far from heroic.

Sports writers, often weak in grammar and strong on clichés, need a watchful editor. Sometimes a writer strains to be different and brings forth what amounts to an essay on a game. While this may be a fine piece of writing, too often the writer gets so wrapped up in unaccustomed rhetoric that he even omits the score.

Hyperbole, a characteristic of sports writing, should never replace accuracy. Writers tempted to use superlatives to describe the skill of a rookie, the outstanding ability of a sophomore, and the great prospects for this season's team should remember that often the rookie may soon slide back to the minor leagues, the sophomore to the end of the bench, and the team to the league's cellar.

For years, sports writers covering major league baseball teams in spring training exaggerated the facts so greatly that a substantial number of fans became cynical. Today, these early reports are more restrained. A story from a Florida training camp may say, "The White Sox finished fourth last year, and if there is any change this season it will be for the worse."

Editors also must cool off copy that heralds a forthcoming contest as the "Game of the Decade." If the game is disappointing, the misled fans will feel doubly cheated. A prediction of the "Game of the Century" is even more dangerous. Since there have been several of these already in the twentieth century, it would be wise not to schedule any more.

Sports publicists, like politicians, constantly push reporters and editors to promote their pet topics. So editors have to be sure they are covering, not promoting, a sport. A generation ago, sports pages ran all kinds of stories on professional wrestling, even though it was generally known that most matches were rigged. Finally, a number of editors, deciding not to promote fraud, quit printing stories and pictures about pro wrestlers. The rapid decline of the "sport" suggested that the wrestling promoters depended on the free advertising disguised as news.

Minor league baseball is another sport whose almost tearful requests for promotion must be resisted. In dozens of cities around the country sports editors have been asked to boost the home town team. If they decline, team supporters scorn them as disloyal. Yet most of the teams are owned by private businesses, the major league clubs. By excessive coverage, the newspaper actually subsidizes private business. Such baseball teams often get more stories than any other group in town. No other public performance—movie, play, concert, or opera—ever receives the kind of minute coverage that is given a minor league team that may draw only 500 fans a night.

Sports editors today try to trim coverage of professional and top amateur athletes to make room for unorganized sports. More and more Americans are enjoying sport for its own sake. They sail, ski, surf, hike, camp, fly, shoot, and skin-dive. Because most of these sports, though vigorous, are not competitive, the modern sports editor has to find ways to cover them.

The good editor always has to be attentive to pictures, not only because photography plays an important part in sports, but because today's readers spend more time watching sports on TV, which means that only exceptional pictures are likely to capture their interest. Consistently good photographs are hard to find anywhere, and sports editors usually have the highest proportion of clichés. This means an abundance of photos showing someone sliding into second base or taking a basketball jump shot. Even the most attentive sports fan is going to ignore them.

The sports editor must demand truly extraordinary pictures, ones which illustrate athletic grace, skill, and intensity. Any editor who demands good pictures, of course, must meet the demands of a good photographer—adequate time, excellent equipment, plenty of film, and the promise of seeing his best pictures in print.

Other sub-editing

Aside from the four or five sub-editors of the typical newspaper are several workers who fall into a middle-range category under the managing editor. Some large papers have a foreign editor who directs, at a sophisticated level, a staff of foreign correspondents much as the state editor directs his stringers. Many papers have a "Sunday editor" who may simply put out a weekly magazine section or may be in complete charge of the whole Sunday edition with its magazine and special pages or sections devoted to finance, real estate, books, entertainment, travel, hobbies, television, and so on. Either way, the Sunday editor has a week-long job assembling articles, reviews, and photographs from regular staffers as well as special assistants and part-time writers.

Some "editors" are really specialized reporters. They cover such areas as the arts, education, religion, business, or labor. The term "editor" is perhaps justified for reasons other than status or newspaper promotion, because such a man has more independence than the ordinary writer on general assignment. While the science editor or the music editor usually will direct no staff, he follows the news of his areas in the same way as any sub-editor, selects from the flow of ideas and copy he sees, and assigns himself stories. Some other editor, probably the city editor, is technically his boss, but one who usually defers to the specialized editor-writer's expert assessment of the news.

Papers for many decades now have divided editing responsibilities into sub-editing areas such as city desk and state desk, but better ways can still be found. For example, the *Des Moines Tribune*, after using the standard plan of having a specialized writer travel the whole state, established an effective sub-editorship which combined the jobs of city and state editor. This new man came in very early every morning, surveyed the statewide news situation, and decided on the staff coverage, if any, for points outside the metropolitan area. He could dispatch writers and photographers 100 or more miles away, sometimes by plane.

Recently the *Wilmington* (Del.) *News-Journal* created a new metropolitan desk responsible for coverage in its whole circulation area, which includes the whole state and counties in four additional states. Richard P. Sanger, managing editor, explained that "maintenance of separate city and state desks is an anachronism in this fast-growing and changing area." Commuting, shopping, and problems go across county and state lines, he pointed out. So the city and state desks were consolidated, and the city editor was boosted into the new spot to channel all area coverage through a single desk

The Wilmington experience should be noted by all newspapers as they adjust to changing conditions and changing readership. Sub-editors were named in the past to provide specialized editing and staff direction. They generally provided the kind of coverage the publishers desired. But no one should assume that the organization chart of the 1970s should last forever. State or universal desks, if no longer useful, should be discarded. The growth of suburbs, the shift in public interest, and the increasing specialization of news all force the alert newspaper to examine its operations to see if there is a better way to get the news to its readers.

9 Printing: past, present, future

A girl fresh out of journalism school took a job on a medium-sized daily. On her tenth working day she was told to go into the composing room to see if certain material could be printed. A printer started to give her a long, involved explanation. "Oh, I see," the girl said after a minute, "you mean you don't have the right base to make it type high." He was astounded, and she was treated as a colleague in the composing room from then on.

Like the girl, any copyeidtor ought to be comfortable around most printing operations. He does not have to be an expert, but he should know how to mark copy for the compositor, how long it takes for such routine tasks of makeup as the front page, and what a printer can and cannot do. Otherwise he will mislead—and have to make corrections later. He may send so much copy to be set that the paper will appear hours late. Or he may order the impossible, and so raise the blood pressure of everyone in the composing room.

It is particularly difficult now to be current on printing because changes and innovations come so rapidly. Only an expert can keep up with the latest developments. To cope with this problem some newspapers hire experts to do little more than advise on what kind of new equipment to buy. While the copyeditor doesn't need to know the intricacies of printing machinery, he must grasp the processes his own newspaper uses and how to get the most out of them. This knowledge of familiar printing processes, together with an understanding of the paper's aims, makes an editor ready to move into responsible positions. He is able to understand and assess the advice of the expert. Editors-in-chief and publishers these days spend great chunks of their time examining new printing equipment to see if it can do a better and cheaper job for their paper. Lesser editors who understand the problems can become part of the decision-making team.

Before about 1950 understanding printing processes was relatively easy. Nearly every daily newspaper used the same principle: a raised surface pressed ink on paper—the traditional letterpress method. Stories and advertisements were typically set by a typecasting machine, the Linotype. Engravings, made by etching grooves into a zinc plate, printed pictures. As only minor changes had occurred since 1886 when Ottmar Mergenthaler invented the Linotype, a newsman who understood the basics seemsed to have a life-time knowledge of printing.

Today, however, dozens of major papers have replaced the hotmetal linecasting of the Linotype. These "set" on a strip of film or paper. And pictures may be elctronically engraved on sheets of plastic or metal. The big, heavy plates for the presses often are replaced with thin, light aluminum plates. Sometimes typesetting is automatic. Perforated tape goes to a computer which punches other tape that goes to the typesetting machine. By pushing a switch, an editor can erase part of the tape, producing in type a news story which is at least partially "edited."

Recent developments in mechanization and automation make it impossible to predict the future of newspaper printing. Perhaps today's most modern equipment will be obsolete in ten years. Perhaps a whole new concept of printing will send the equipment that dazzles so many people today to museums.

Dozens of newspapers are part way there now after purchasing electronic editing machines. Copy from wire services or reporters is put on a tape that feeds into a computer. When the copyeditor is ready to edit the story he presses a button and the story appears on what resembles a small television screen. The editor can alter the story by pressing a few buttons or by typing a few words on a keyboard. Another button sends the "copy" to the composing room by wire. Most copyeditors, unless they are resistant to change, learn to run these machines in a few days. The result of the editing, of course, is the same as though the editor were using a pencil. These machines are certain to be used widely within a few years. A Daytona Beach, Florida, editor said that his electronic editor saved him $77,000 a year. Editors and publishers are fascinated by machines that save this kind of money. They will be eager to buy such equipment. This means that the electronic invasion of the newsroom is coming swiftly and journalists will have to adjust to the innovations. An editor who is indifferent or antagonistic to the new machines will be limiting his development.

Letterpress

Letterpress is the "old-fashioned" process. The type, with raised faces like the letters on a rubber stamp, is set by a composing machine such as the Linotype, or it may (rarely) be handset. The type for stories and ads, together with relief plates for illustrations, goes into a rectangular *form* the size of the newspaper page. Ink put on the type comes off in readable form on anything pressed against it. In fact, *proofs* are simply sheets of paper pressed against forms so the type can be checked for errors.

A few weekly papers still print directly from raised type in such flat forms. Ink rolled over them transfers to sheets of newsprint which, after folding, go to the subscriber. This process is called *flat-bed printing*—because the printing is done with the form lying on a flat surface.

This process, however, entails a lot of slow and costly motion for each impression. To speed up printing, almost a century ago the concept of the wheel came into printing with the invention of the *rotary press;* innovators found a way to change the flat horizontal form into something that would rotate. Though this process requires a duplicate platemaking process called *stereotyping,* it more than makes up for that extra step in the speed of printing.

The technique is quite simple. A piece of papier-mâché, called a *matrix* or *mat* (technically a *flong*), is placed on top of the page of type. The whole thing is run through a *mat roller*, much the way wet clothes go through the wringer of an old-fashioned washing machine. The pressure exerted by the roller is intense, and the flong, squeezed hard against the type, takes on a clear, full impression of the page of type. The process thus makes the flong, or mat, into a mold. Anyone can read this mat like a newspaper; the lettering is right side up and the words read from left to right.

It has been necessary that the mat be moderately damp so it will not break under the pressure of the mat roller. Now a man called a *stereotyper* rolls the mat and puts each mat in a special oven for a minute or two to bake out the moisture. He then places it in a curved device and pours molten type metal against it. This metal, mostly lead with a little tin and antimony, hardens in a minute or two into a sturdy, curved plate that works like a big curved rubber stamp.

This *stereotype* is taken to the press and "locked" into position. A row of these plates becomes, in effect, a cylinder. As motors turn this cylinder, rollers spread ink evenly over the raised letters and illustrations. A great roll of paper, or *web*, feeding rapidly through the machine is pressed firmly against the inked surface and becomes a long roll of printed pages. These are automatically folded together in order, cut to separate each copy of the newspaper, routed to a separate room, and bundled for distribution.

Stereotypers also cast ready-made papier-mâché mats. These usually come from advertiser, but some wire service pictures, comics, crossword puzzles, and even copy come to the paper already in mat form. The stereotyper may cast these singly or paste several flat mats together before pouring molten metal over them for a *flat cast.* Such castings, cut apart if necessary, go in the ads or news columns as the flat form is made up. So they are eventually stereotyped again when the whole page goes through the mat roller.*

* Chemical companies here and abroad are attempting to improve the mat-and-metal process of stereotyping by the use of plastics. The Research Institute of the American Newspaper Publishers Association reported optimistically in 1969 on experimental use in newspaper plants of two such new methods: Letterflex, which produces flexible relief-printing plates directly from a photographic negative by etching plastic, and Hylox, which makes a stereotype matrix from plastic rather than papier-mâché.

The Linotype

Since the Linotype casts most of the type used in the letterpress process, it is important to know how it works. The machine has a set of keys much like a typewriter. When the operator taps the keys, he releases brass matrices (molds for letters) which fall into a row where together they become a single mold for a line of type.

What of spaces? The operator taps keys to insert *space bands* between words and sometimes between letters. The space band is shaped like a wedge, and the thin end goes between the words or letters. When the line of brass "mats" is full, the operator presses a lever. Almost simultaneously, the space bands are pushed upward, making the line snug. This motion *justifies* the line—spaces the letter even both right and left with previous lines. (See fig. 9-1.) The molten metal then squeezes through a slot against the line of matrices and fills the little molds; it solidifies almost instantly into a *slug*, or line of cast type.

The inventor of the Linotype also had to solve the problem of getting the brass mats back in proper order at the top of the machine in their storage place, called a *magazine*, ready to be used again.

The problem was solved by notching each mat much as a door key is notched. The A's have one pattern of notches, the B's another, etc. After the line is cast, the machine takes the used mats to the top and back of the machine where they move onto a distributor bar. Hanging by their notches they automatically ride along the bar, which is grooved in as many different patterns as there are channels to store

Fig. 9-1. Line of matrices. A matrix is a small brass mold of a letter. The composing machine assembles these matrices and the longer space-bands (used for spacing between words) in a line, as shown here. It then holds them against a mold into which molten metal is forced and so casts a slug, the metal line of type used in printing.

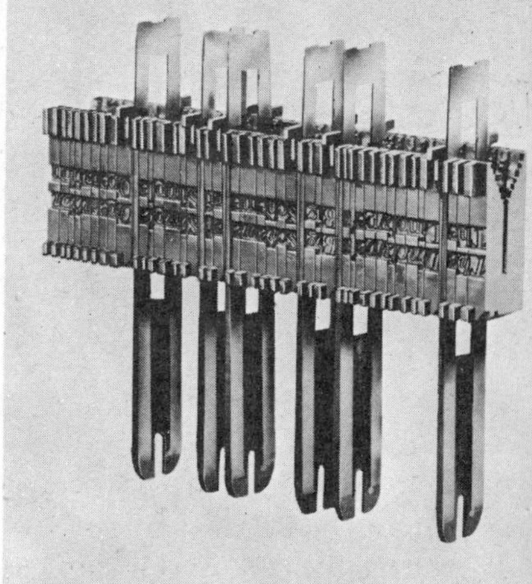

Fig. 9-2. Circulation of matrices. This phantom illustration shows each stage in the movement of the matrix through the Linotype machine. When keys are punched, the matrices drop into line in front of the operator, are cast (at left), and finally are redistributed to magazine (above right).

letter matrices. The A's reach a point where their notches no longer hang onto the bar, and so drop off automatically into their channel of the magazine. The same thing happens to the rest of the letters and symbols so each letter rests in the proper row in the magazine—ready to drop at the touch of its key. (See fig. 9-2.)

About 1945 many papers added an attachment to the Linotype allowing type to be set from a perforated paper tape. The holes signaled for letters, much as an old-time player piano signaled for notes. A person with little more than typing skill can punch the tape by hitting letter keys on a special machine, and the tapes are then fed into the Linotype. (See figs. 9-3 and 9-4.) This automatic typesetting is considerably faster than the old manual way, and most letter-press papers today use some kind of tape perforating system. As we noted in chapter 7, most of them also use tape from the wire services to set wire copy.

Some papers have added computers to typesetting and their number is growing steadily. Though the computer increases efficiency, it does not set type by itself. It receives one tape and produces another. First an employee copies a story by typing on a machine which punches tape. He simply types, using a special key for paragraph indentation, but paying no attention to justifying lines. His tape goes into the computer, which in turn produces a tape to be fed into a typesetting machine. The computer then justifies lines, hyphenates words, if necessary, and even corrects some typographical errors.

Fig. 9-3. Tape perforation. As if sitting at an ordinary typewriter, an operator runs a Swiftape machine to perforate type, which in turn is used in setting type.

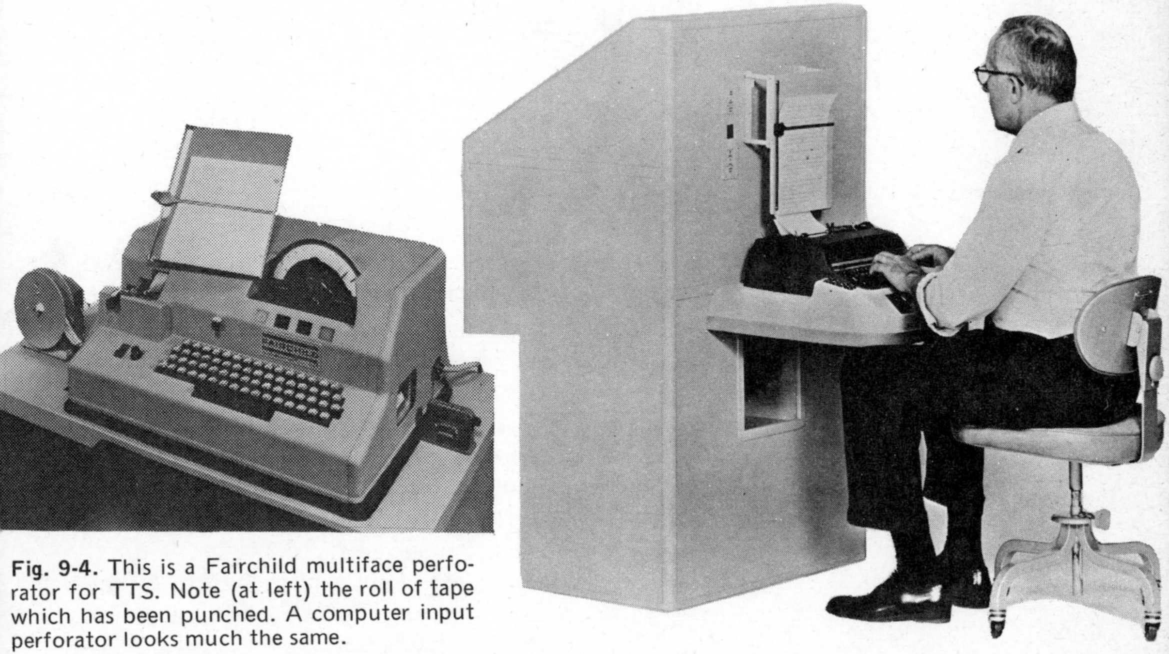

Fig. 9-4. This is a Fairchild multiface perforator for TTS. Note (at left) the roll of tape which has been punched. A computer input perforator looks much the same.

Art by letterpress

Pictures, collectively called *art*, are reproduced either by the conventional process of engraved metal or by an electronic method. In the conventional system acid etches hundreds of little grooves into a plate to produce an *engraving* with a pattern of minute raised dots. These print as tiny points on paper and so produce shades from dark to light. The darkest grays of the picture produce bigger black dots and smaller white areas among them; the lightest grays of course make very small dots against relatively large untouched areas. These massed points of black and white are so tiny, however, that the eye mixes them optically to form the illusion of continuous tones of gray. (See fig. 9-5.)

Fig. 9-5. Halftone screen. This picture, a corner of a large newspaper, employs a gross halftone screen. The dots are magnified for this illustration. To see how the eye blends the dot patterns used in the screens of ordinary engravings, look at the page from eight or ten feet away.

The dots are made by shooting the picture through a *screen*, which thus becomes a kind of measure in engraving. The best printing requires fine screens, which produce very tiny dots, and high quality paper. But coarser screens, with 55 or 65 lines of holes per square inch, are necessary to make cuts which will not blur ink on coarser paper. Newsprint typically requires engravings of 55-line or 65-line screen. The copyeditor ordinarily need not be concerned about screens, except to know that, should he try to introduce different ones, they will print differently, may cause disharmony, and perhaps be worse than those habitually used.

An engraving is also called a *cut*, or *zinc*, and most pictures, made up of varying shades of gray, are called *halftones*, because they are neither solid black nor solid white. When no screen is used and when all background material is removed, only certain lines remain, as for cartoons, fashion drawings, or courtroom sketches. There are, of course, no dots. These *line cuts* produce black on white, or gray if the artist has put black lines close together. (See fig. 9-6.)

Fig. 9-6. Art work. The artist is useful to the newspaper for humor and variety—and for pictures where photographers are barred. This is a line engraving, to be distinguished from a halftone (cf. fig. 9-5). Reprinted with permission of the **Los Angeles Times.**

"I wish they'd let photographers cover these trials -- court artists are sloppy!"

Electronic engraving uses either a plastic or a metal sheet. The picture fits on a drum, revolves, and an electric eye picks up varying light impulses from its varying shades. This eye controls a white-hot stylus above another drum carrying the plastic or metal. Following the shades in the picture, the stylus lightly gouges the plate to convert it to a cut (fig. 9-7). A similar machine with a V-shaped blade literally plows furrows of varying widths into a thin sheet of flexible metal. Parallel lines create the illusion of continuous gray tones.

It is difficult to stereotype the plastic cuts, so many papers simply leave room on the page plate and, with adhesive, stick the plastic to the curved metal just before the presses start to run. Since the metal plates can be stereotyped, they are more popular.

Fig. 9-7. Simple engraving. This Fairchild Scan-a-graver makes quick and inexpensive engravings. Photo or art copy put on the drum at right is engraved on the cylinder at left.

Offset

The *offset* method of printing is much different. Anyone can run his fingers over an offset printing plate and it will feel perfectly smooth. To someone raised in the letterpress tradition, this offset technique of printing from a smooth surface seems magical. Offset works, however, on the well-known principle that oil and water do not mix. So, this process provides that the parts of the offset plate meant to print will receive ink (which is basically oil) while the rest of the plate, taking only water, will reject the ink. But it must be clear that printing is *not* done directly from the offset plate. The plate transmits the image onto a press roller, which squeezes against the paper to transmit, or "offset," the printed impression.

Offset printing can use almost any kind of typesetting method. In fact, whatever can be photographed can be printed offset. This means that an offset newspaper could even be typed or handwritten and then photographed for the press plates.

This possibility has opened the door to "typesetting" methods that do not, in the traditional sense, set type at all. Most offset work uses *cold type* versus the *hot type* of letterpress, which uses the Linotype to cast molten metal. Cold type may be the output of an ordinary typewriter, of a special typewriter that allows varied spaces between words and letters, so the lines can be justified, or of other machines that turn out news stories in neat columns on a strip of film, a method commonly called *photocomposition*.

These columns of type for offset—really strips of paper or film—are pasted onto a sheet of paper the size of the newspaper page. Headlines are set on film by a separate machine and pasted onto a sheet of paper, or dummy, to produce what is called a *mechanical* or *camera copy*. The whole page is then photographed. The resulting page-sized negative is placed on a sensitized aluminum sheet resembling a cookie sheet and light is directed through the negative onto the metal for a minute or two to "burn in" the plate. The latent image of the newspaper page appears on the aluminum. A simple developing process converts the photographic image into an ink-attractive, water-repellent one. The plate, which weighs only a few ounces, then goes on the press and the press run starts.

It is possible to combine hot type with offset printing. The metal slugs are assembled in proper order and a proof is taken on quality paper. This is called a *reproduction proof* or a *repro proof*. Such proofs, pasted onto a dummy and photographed, go through the rest of the offset process. The result can be hard to distinguish from letterpress.

Offset popularity

The shift to offset by American newspapers has been rapid. The first papers to change were tiny weeklies, often with old, worn out letterpress equipment. It was easy to change over such little plants. No agreements were necessary with union printers, and personnel problems usually declined with the move. Women with typing skill could set the type. Though there are some women compositors in the letterpress method, usually men are hired who can repair as well as operate the somewhat complicated Linotype; typists usually are paid much less than such men.

Larger weeklies soon shifted to offset, and within a few years small daily papers joined the move. Dailies in Dubuque, Iowa, and Oklahoma City, Oklahoma, extended offset into the medium-sized field, and the *Sacramento Union*, with about 100,000 circulation, shifted to offset in 1968. One of the giants, the *St. Louis Post-Dispatch*, has started an experiment with offset with special sections. There are now about 400 offset dailies, and a Scripps League executive has predicted that three out of four will go offset before long.

While it is possible that offset will hit the big city, multi-edition newspapers, most of them have decided to stick with letterpress at present; but they remain watchful for labor-saving devices and have adopted many of them.

Big papers continued to use letterpress for several reasons:

1. Until recently, offset presses ran much slower than letterpress, and they are still a little slower.
2. A multi-million dollar investment already has been made in letterpress.
3. The work force is familiar with letterpress operations; retraining would be costly.
4. Type slugs, in contrast to repros, can be treated roughly and used over and over. This is a real aid in changing from edition to edition.
5. Because the actual type is never used on a rotary press, changes in that type can be made while the presses are running.
6. Paper waste is high with offset. Unless pressmen keep a constant ratio between water and ink, sheets come out poorly printed. In letterpress, only ink must be regulated.

Some letterpress operations, nevertheless, use a great deal of cold type. For example, entire ads can be made up with it. The material is photographed and a conventional newspaper engraving is made.

The making of halftones in the offset process is simple. The halftone negative is made as for a photoengraving. Instead of being acid-etched on a plate, the negative is merely pasted into the space left in the full page negative and burned in. When printed the picture appears to be made by a zinc engraving, except that it usually is clearer and sharper. The excellent reproduction of pictures, with 110 to 120 rows of fine dots per inch, is one of the main points in favor of offset (as offset paper can take fine screens). This process also offers benefits with color.

The other advantages of offset are less expensive equipment and usually lower production costs, machinery that is easy to repair, relatively light presses, and flexibility in the use of type.

According to a survey of forty-six editors by the Associated Press Managing Editors Association, editors prefer offset to letterpress once they have changed over. They found the shift less painful than anticipated. A summary of this survey, by D. W. Bowler, editor of the *Billings* (Mont.) *Gazette*, observed that editors have to learn to think offset, and photographers have to learn how to put in the screen as they print pictures. But editors found that it was easier to get fresher news into their pages fast with offset, and they felt that they controlled the offset paper themselves, rather than being at the whim of printers.

Gravure

A third process which has some use on newspapers is *gravure*—also called *intaglio*, from the Italian for "carved in." If recesses are cut into a copper plate and filled with ink, the ink will come off on paper pressed against it. So tiny grooves of different size and depth can be cut by acid to carry different loads of ink. Very fine shading is possible in such printing. *Rotogravure*—sometimes called just *roto*—is a fast rotary-press process popular with magazines and Sunday papers. Fine quality and a variety of colors are possible with roto. Mechanical pasteups are required, so editorial preparation is practically the same for gravure and offset.

Printing measurements

Some printers will say, "Printing is just arithmetic." To some extent this is true. Printers have to measure everything and must calculate how to make the type fit allotted spaces. To give proper instructions to them, the copyeditor needs to know their measuring system.

The two main printing dimensions are *points* and *picas*. In general, a point refers to vertical measure. One point equals one-seventy-second of an inch. Seventy-two-point type, then, is one inch high. Thirty-six-point is half an inch. Twenty-four-point is one-third of an inch. Most *body type*—the type of news stories—is 8- to 10-point.

The measure for horizontal distance is *pica*. A pica is one-sixth of an inch, so a column two inches wide will have type set 12 picas wide. A half-column cut in such a column width would be 6 picas, or one inch.

A few simple problems and answers will help make these measurements clear.

1. If body type is 9-point, how many lines will there be in three column inches?
2. If a cut is three inches wide, how many picas is it?
3. If the body type of a story is nine inches long and the story has a three-line 36-point type headline, what is the total length of story and headline in inches?
4. How many inches of type will eighteen lines of 8-point make?

   The answers: 1. 24; 2. 18; 3. 10-1/2; 4. 2.*

* 1. Three times 72 points gives 216 points for three inches. Divide that by nine to get the number of lines. 2. Since an inch is 6 picas, three times six is the number of picas in three inches. Three lines of 36-point would be 108 points. Seventy-two goes into that one-and-a-half times. So add one-and-a-half inches to nine to get the total. 4. Eight times 18 points gives 144 points. Divide by seventy-two to convert to inches.

A pica sometimes is called an *em*. An em technically is the square of the type. Thus, an em of 18-point type is 18 points square—18 points by 18 points. An em of 12-point is 12 points square. A 12-point em, of course, is also a pica wide, because it is one-sixth of an inch. (The em got its name from the letter M, which usually looks as wide as it is high.)

Careful measurement is necessary because most newspapers fit copy to the available space. For example, if a ten-inch hole exists, an editor will send the composing room a story to fit that space. He can determine the length of the story by counting the number of typewritten lines; or perhaps he has devised a special ruler to measure copy. Four lines of copy often will equal one inch of type. This kind of measure is inexact, so the story may be a few lines too long or a few lines too short. If it is too long, a makeup man will have to remove a sentence or two. If too short, the story can be *leaded* (pronounced "ledded"). This means that thin pieces of type metal, 1 or 2 points in thickness, are inserted between paragraphs to expand it ("lead it out"). If the story has nine paragraphs and 2-point leads are used, the leading will add 16 points to the story, or about two lines in all. This may not be enough to make the type snug in the forms. So leads may be placed to separate the lines of the first paragraph, the lines of the headline, and the space between the head and the story.

The well-edited paper does not use so much lead that white spaces fragment the stories. Neither does it stick meaningless little fillers into the bottom of the page to report, say, on the number of miles of paved road in Sumatra. A good staff can produce quality "shorts" which use space better than remote facts or mere lead.

Leading, of course, is part of the letterpress process. Offset uses a similar technique. Instead of creating space with lead, the person pasting up the dummy will snip a story into paragraphs and paste each paragraph a tiny distance from the one adjoining. The little extra space adds up to the equal of a few lines.

Types of type

Quality newspapers usually spend much effort on the appearance of their pages. Part of this job is the selection of type. At the turn of the century body type was small and crowded. Headline faces were squeezed thin, and there was so much of this type that the reader could hardly make out what was printed. Gradually the 7-point body type was replaced by 7-1/2- or 8-point type, and that frequently gave way to 9. Today many papers use 9-1/2- or 10-point; or they may use 9-point on a 10-point slug—meaning that the type is 9-point with a point of leading. According to the Research Institute of the American Newspaper Publishers Association, the median type size used by U.S. and Canadian papers rose from 7-1/2 point in 1950 to 8-1/2 point fifteen years later, with two out of five papers using 9-point. Most editors in the seventies will probably be working with type of 9-point or larger.

Similarly, the old all-capital headlines, with layers of decks have given way to simple, neatly designed type faces and headline forms that can be read at a glance. The result has been newspaper pages with white space for "air," body type that can be read without squinting, and heads that have clean beauty. (See figs. 9-8 and 9-9.)

1. Text

2. Roman

2a. Oldstyle

2b. Modern

2c. Mixed

2d. Italic

3. Gothic

3a. Sans Serif

3b. Sq. Serif

4. Script, Cursives

5. NOVELTY

Fig. 9-8. Races of type (left). Five major subdivisions, or "races," of type are illustrated. Square serif type, here a subcategory (3b), is sometimes called a race. The fifth race, novelty, sometimes goes by "ornamented" or other names. Most newspaper usage is obviously in categories 2 and 3—roman and gothic. In common backshop parlance "italic" is not a subdivision of roman, as shown, but a slanted, or non-perpendicular, form of roman or gothic faces.

U.S. Plan
May Start
Viet Talks

Tempo bold condensed

Onassis
Airliner
Hijacked

Vogue

A New Moon View

Century

TRAFFIC DEATH
TOLL IS AT 155

Gothic

U.N. Hears
Israel Protest
Arab Tactics

Bodoni face is used by dozens of American newspapers.

KENNEDY GAINING
SUPPORT IN FIGHT
TO DEPOSE LONG

Latin style

Texas Asks
$10 Billion
Water Plan

Cheltenham

Antismoking
Campaigners
See Progress

Century condensed

Fig. 9-9. Headline faces. Races of type (see fig. 9-8) are divided into families. Loosely called simply "faces," they often bear the name of the designer. This illustration shows some of the common headline faces in use. Note that some have serifs and some do not—that, therefore, they are roman or sans serif.

Many papers, however, have a long way to go, and more research on both the readability of type and the techniques of makeup will stimulate further changes. The current shift by many papers from the 11- or 12-pica column to the 16-pica width is one example of typographic change. Another is the *W-format*—six columns set normal width and the seventh set wider. Still another is the *seven format*, which gives seven columns the space normally given to eight. The extra space makes white "rules" between columns.

Headline faces as big as 36-point can be produced for letterpress on a Linotype and for offset on a machine that turns out cold type heads on a strip of film. Both of these methods are fast and flexible. When the page plates have been made, the type for letterpress can be melted for re-use. (The film for offset is thrown away.) For their biggest heads most letterpress papers handset some pre-cast type called *foundry type*, or even wooden type. The printer picks up each letter and puts it in the page form. After the page is stereotyped, he returns each to its bin in the type case. This is a slow process, too expensive to use more than once or twice a day.

Other large headlines and much advertising type are set on a machine called a *Ludlow*. (See fig. 9-10.) A printer picks matrices, similar to Linotype mats, from a case and puts them in a row, then uses the machine to squeeze molten metal against them to produce slugs several inches long. The mats can be redistributed to the case immediately. The slugs are much easier to handle than foundry type because they are big. (When hand-set type such as foundry spills, the resulting mess is *pied* type—past tense of pi.) Ludlow slugs save time and effort another way because they can be melted down once the page is stereotyped, which frees the printer from having to redistribute the type by hand.

Fig. 9-10. Ludlow. From the trays of type (right) the Ludlow operator gets mats which he places in a stick, which the machine (left) casts into slugs of type.

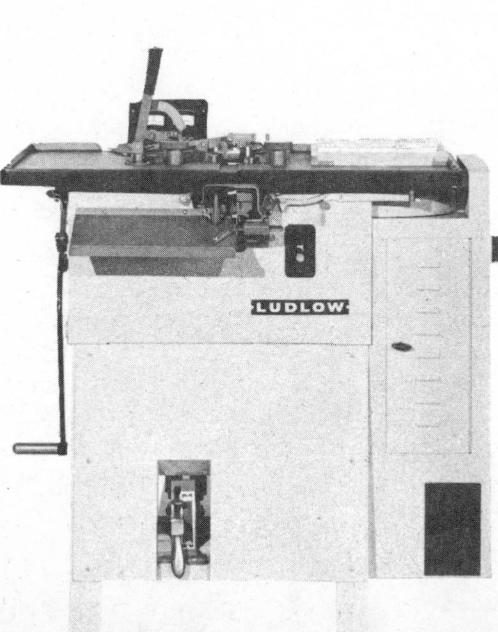

A machine called an *Elrod* is common in letterpress, though it never actually prints anything. The Elrod creates column rules, simple ad borders, leads to separate type, and base material used to raise engravings and castings type high. It is automatic, needing a printer only to change the dies that turn out the various kinds of metal strips and to remove the finished products from the machine.

Format

In a William Allen White memorial lecture at the University of Kansas, Gardner Cowles, president of the *Des Moines Register* and *Tribune* and editorial chairman of *Look*, commented:

> Newspaper pages today—with few exceptions—are made up, or "designed," by an old-time journeyman-printer and a make-up editor who may, or may not, know much about typography and the thousand and one methods for making pages look readable and exciting. On successful magazines, the art director ranks right below the top editor in importance and authority. He has a strong voice in helping decide how a story idea is to be developed. He suggests ways to give it maximum visual impact. He knows how to blend type and photographs so each helps the other. His responsibility is to make each page come alive and intrigue the reader. Newspapers need this kind of talent. Too few have it.

Whether or not it has a regular art director, a newspaper should certainly have expert advice if it plans to change format. The editors then will chip in with their advice, and its usefulness will depend on how much they have kept up on the printing arts. The better papers are ever alert to the possibility of improvement by typographic change. As noted already, the *Louisville Courier-Journal* went to six-column format in 1965. *Newsday*, a Long Island, New York, tabloid, shifted to magazine-style front page and inside makeup in 1968. In 1969 the *Chicago American* changed from full-size to tabloid, taking the name *Chicago Today*, in an effort to keep alive in a city down to four major dailies.

Color

The comic pages of newspapers pioneered color reproduction, but magazines, using higher quality paper, long ago passed the dailies in use of color, and more recently color television has contributed to making the newspaper's gray image look very old-fashioned. The newspaper magazine of the trade, *Editor & Publisher*, has warned against this color competition and in 1955 began an annual special issue on color to promote its use in dailies.

ROP (run-of-the-paper) color is that printed on the paper's regular newsprint, in ads or editorial. SpectaColor and Hi-Fi are trade names for preprinted color, which can be on higher quality paper. "Preprint" refers to the use of a paper roll already carrying full-color printing by roto, or sometimes by offset, which is fed into the presses and folded into the paper along with regular newsprint.

Editor & Publisher says that nine out of ten dailies now offer ROP color. More than half of these provide for *process color*, which uses three colors in addition to black. The eye blends dots of the three primary colors as well as of black to make the different hues and shades of a conventional colored photograph or painting. More papers provide black plus only one or two colors, for *flat color*, also called *spot color*. Red alone, for example, will make a vivid headline or rule. Two ads using flat color won *Editor & Publisher* color contests. One featured a shirt printed flat blue and the other a sporting figure in rose-red behind a black-and-white car.

Color printing requires a separate press plate for every basic color: red, yellow, and blue—with black the fourth color. Other colors are made by overlapping the basic colors. When two color plates are to print overlapping impressions, great care must be taken to get the plates in *register*. This means, for example, that the blue and yellow impressions must coincide exactly to produce a green. Otherwise the printed picture will appear fuzzy. For example, a register only slightly off on the picture of a woman's green dress can give the garment two distinct hemlines, one yellow and one blue.

Register is so difficult that once a color picture or ad is adjusted properly no editor should tinker with it. If, for example, a color picture is running in columns one through four on page one in the first edition, it had better stay there in later editions—unless an editor is willing to argue with an outraged pressman, who probably has a large metal tool in his hand.

Advertising lineage in ROP color has gone up sharply. It increased steadily more than six-fold for fifteen years after 1951, until a slight temporary dip occurred in 1967, according to annual surveys by *Editor & Publisher*. The increasing use of color by newspaper advertisers means that editors can add color more easily to news pages. A press prepared to print colored ads is prepared to print other items in color.

It is perhaps surprising that some of the biggest papers in the nation are not the biggest users of color. Neither the *Wall Street Journal* nor the *New York Times* is equipped to use color in regular news pages. The *Daily News* and the *Post* in New York were late in providing even spot color. But the *Miami Herald* and *Nashville Tennesseean*, as well as the *Milwaukee Journal* and *St. Petersburg Times*, each report use of up to two thousand color pictures a year.

The Associated Press and United Press International distribute duplicate color transparencies on many subjects, but their executives complain that many clients do not use them. In one period the UPI experimented by moving a color photo daily but use was disappointing. This service sent out an exclusive picture of a woman leaping from a brightly burning building. Though more than a thousand papers got it, only one tear sheet, indicating use, came in. UPI, nevertheless, sends three or four color pictures in a typical week.

"It seems," said Charles J. McCarty, assistant general manager of UPI Newspictures, "that every newspaper editor talks about wanting more editorial color illustration but few of them actually use it. We transmit more color now than ever before, but the percentage of use remains the same or less." In 1967 a *Chicago Tribune* executive, complaining that color was still "the exception, not the rule," said that newspapers were still essentially black-and-white products which compared badly with the wealth of color in magazines.

Problems of color

One problem with color is that it takes time. A picture agency must break a color photograph down into its basic colors, so the newspapers can use a different ink with each of them. It formerly took UPI two hours to make such color separations and a black-and-white photo print of each, but the service then developed a Polaroid method which cut the time below thirty minutes. Then recently UPI started sending three color separations on one picture, in twelve minutes, twenty-four minutes less than when three pictures had been sent. Electronic scanners that make plates even as separations are made offer exciting possibilities. The *Sunday News-Journal* of Daytona Beach, Florida, boasted in 1968 that on two successive weekends it ran color photos of sporting events within five hours of the events' starting times. In short, as time problems are solved, editors may use color more freely.

Quality is another problem. Since ordinary newsprint requires a coarse screen, the illusion of solid color is hard to create. Register also may be poor. Indeed, one of the advantages of offset is that it can use finer screens for better color as well as clear photos. After lengthy experimentation with its letterpress color, the *Philadelphia Bulletin*, having won eleven first prizes with its color, claims it has received twice as many ROP color awards as any other American paper—and its color is good. One of its women's pages, for example, features attractive girls garbed in bright red, yellow, and green against a background of natural-looking bricks and furniture. Though the *Bulletin's* ROP uses ordinary newsprint, the flesh tones are truer than those on most color TV sets.

The New York Press Association has taken special note of two small offset dailies with good four-color reproduction of pictures—the *Tonawanda News* (circulation 18,400) and the *Ithaca Journal* (17,200). The *Monterey* (Calif.) *Peninsula-Herald* (28,600) also does a superb job with color.

SpectaColor art—preprinted by either roto or offset on fine paper—is usually thought of for advertising, but it has been used for editorial. The difficulty is that such illustrations have to be planned well ahead. The *Detroit Free Press* introduced editorial SpectaColor in the spring of 1965 with a six-column, front-page picture of a pretty girl and flowers, and since then has regularly planned such art three to six weeks ahead for many events. The enthusiastic response of readers to this high-quality color is typified by the comment by one letter-writer on that first picture: "It is pure sunshine and spring!"

The editor of tomorrow, more than his predecessor, will use pictures and color to make his pages compete more effectively with magazines and TV.

What of tomorrow?

Despite the introduction of color, TTS, cold type, and offset, newspapers still operate pretty traditionally. Vermont Royster, editor of the *Wall Street Journal*, wrote not long ago: "The newspaper industry is about the only one in America that made no important technological progress from about 1880, the date of Mergenthaler's handy-dandy gadget, until the day before yesterday."

Can the newspaper catch up? Royster indicated there would be glorious days ahead if editors learned to use the new tools.

Some prophets foresee the end of the newspaper as it is now known. They expect to see the disappearance of the whole composing and press room sections as newspapers dispense with typesetting and presses. Instead, they believe that each home or business might have its own little news box, out of which would come a paper stream of printed news, editorials, feature stories, pictures, and advertisements. This strip would be perforated about every twelve inches so it could be torn into segments and bound to resemble a modern magazine. Operating all day long, and most of the night, the machine could handle both bulletin news and detailed news analyses. This instrument could provide all the speed of radio-television news plus the benefits of depth reporting that the better papers now provide. Like the newspaper, it would also be a semi-permanent record; any reader could refer to it a week later or ten years later.

Fig. 9-11. Facsimile. The **Asahi Shimbun** of Tokyo recently demonstrated a facsimile receiving set for the home. Like radio and TV, it offers the news rapidly and directly. It has the added feature of giving the subscriber "hard copy" that he can mark, cut, save, or recopy.

Facsimile

This device is no dream. It has been possible since 1940, but no one has had both the nerve and the capital to try it commercially. The system, called *facsimile*, transmits the "newspaper" either by wire or radio. Japanese newspapers are now developing facsimile transmission to homes (fig. 9-11) after having used it to transmit a facsimile, or picture, of each page to a remote printing plant, where plates made from the pictures print the actual newspaper. The *Wall Street Journal* does the same thing by transmitting pictures of some of its editions to other printing plants.

Will facsimile ever replace the conventional newspaper thrown upon millions of porches morning and night? Some think that if facsimile ever comes it will start with the business community. After all, financial needs stimulated the development of telegraphic news services and, indeed, of the newspaper itself. Many offices already have teleprinters bringing them news of the stock market and general business. Dow-Jones, owner of the *Wall Street Journal*, provides this service. But what if Dow-Jones decided to replace the noisy teleprinters, which spew out unattractive type copy, with facsimile? Instead of rolls of wire copy, there could be neat sheets of attractively printed material, including pictures, graphs, and illustrated economic analyses.

If facsimile were accepted in the business community, perhaps some daring newspaper owner would adopt it. Every subscriber, given a little box for receiving the news, would pay a monthly bill for service, like a telephone bill. When his box ran out of paper, he could buy a fresh supply at the supermarket. The great capital outlay of starting such a system is, of course, the major factor blocking it. However, problems of delivery trucks in traffic and getting distributors are a powerful push against this block.

Cable television

The other main possibility for a shift from the traditional newspaper is cable television. When many communities complained about poor television reception, someone hit on the idea of putting up a high tower to receive signals well and then connecting the tower to individual sets by wire. Some of these cable TV firms have permission from the Federal Communications Commission to make special broadcasts, such as high school football games or a hot city council meeting. These same cable TV companies sometimes show news direct from the AP or UPI wires. The TV cameras focus on the copy, and the viewer simply reads the wire report from the screen.

This is already a crude sort of "electronic newspaper," of course, but there is no technical reason why it could not become sophisticated. The wire copy could be typed in a neat, appealing form. Pictures could be interspersed with the text. Editorials, advertising, and comics could appear on the screen. This kind of transmission would require that the subscriber be present to "read" the news. But there is no reason why a paper print could not be made of the newscast by having some attachment on the television set. Or the telecast could be taped and the individual could run the tape through an attachment on his own set whenever he wanted to review the news.

Both facsimile and cable-television newspapers are being considered with some earnestness by big city papers, particularly afternoon papers, which have so much trouble distributing a half million papers through crowded city streets. In New York, for example, it is an ordeal to deliver afternoon papers. Some of the big papers near New York, such as the *Newark News*, have the same trouble. Chicago is not much better. Field Enterprises, which owns the *Chicago Daily News* and the *Chicago Sun-Times*, was so fearful of having the afternoon *Daily News* choked by traffic problems that it set up two suburban dailies in 1966 and another in 1968. The idea was to have a toehold in the suburbs in case the *News* circulation continued to skid. Fortunately for them, the circulation steadied, or another center city daily might have died.

It seems likely that if facsimile or cable-TV "newspapers" develop as general circulation enterprises, they will start in the metropolitan centers. These areas have the potential for subscribers and for investment capital. The start will probably be a small scale experiment launched by an established firm, one with money to risk and with bold executives who can be freed to spend months and even years on development.

Satellite printing plants, pioneered by the big Japanese dailies, may soon solve some problems. The satellite plant can, in some cases, help distribution. The *Los Angeles Times* operates a satellite plant, without using facsimile, in Orange County, south of the city. While this has been working well for the *Times*, it requires an astounding investment in presses and other equipment plus, of course, labor. Satellite plants were considered for the Chicago suburbs by Field but rejected as impractical; the suburbs covered too big an area.

These changes are often considered because they are immediately possible—or nearly so. But some entirely new process may be just over the horizon. The big electronic companies are working in tandem with some of the big publishing houses in an attempt to produce startling changes in printing. They may come up with devices that will truly revolutionize the newspaper business. The inventions may be so innovative, and the output of the new equipment so inexpensive, that the change will sweep the country, as television did in the late 1940s.

The journalism student of today is bound to be plunged into changes. This does not mean that he will have to learn the complexities of new equipment any more than an automobile driver has to know how his newest car operates. The typical journalist, like the typical car driver, needs a basic knowledge of what the machines can do. And he must consider not only how they can work for him, but how they can work in the best interests of the public.

The basics of graphic arts will be important to any conceivable graphic presentation of the future. We have known students who saw no practical use for learning about type and layout, but on the job the background has proved useful in unexpected ways—like making up printed blurbs for TV commercials! Without such knowledge and a continuing interest in the effects of technical change, a copyeditor will fall behind in the task of efficiently bringing the news to his community.

10 Picture editing

The creation of picture magazines in the 1930s compelled newspapers to improve their handling of photographs, and the dailies have been under that competitive pressure ever since. Ironically, one of the magazines, *Look*, was born from a newspaper picture desk. As a result, there has been even in the last decade a "continuing and accelerating revolution in news photography," in the words of *Editor & Publisher*.

As the Speed Graphic replaced the tripod camera and explosive flash powder, the 35 mm. and Polaroid print-on-the-spot cameras are replacing bulky cameras with flash; the bulb is in retreat before natural lighting. Development and printing are becoming automated. The newspaper photographer sometimes produces a photograph as artful as any in *Holiday*. Color photographs, long familiar in the magazine sections of Sunday papers, are becoming common in many metropolitan dailies. An editor who wants a progressive newspaper these days may push the photographers to do more picture stories, to create artistic effects, to think color. But he dare not stagnate.

Management

Picture editing is usually done best by a specialist who is in charge of pictures for news sections. The older way is to let the editor of each department control photographic assignments and select pictures. The newer emphasis on good photography has created specialists designated as picture editors or photographic directors. Sometimes the chief photographer handles the management tasks.

More than anyone except the managing editor and the copy boys, such a supervisor of pictures deals with editorial departments across the board. Even insiders tend to forget just how highly departmentalized the editorial operation of a typical paper is. The news editor himself usually concentrates on the front page. As we saw in chapter 8, other pages fall to several departments or desks—city desk, state desk, women's department, sports department, and so on. Typically, an editor heads each of these divisions, and the picture editor deals with each of these.

At the least pretentious, the picture editor is little more than a technician and go-between. He passes assignments on from the editors to the photographers. He passes pictures back from the dark room and other picture sources to the editors. They decide policy and selection, and then he crops and sizes the photos. This system may be better than having no picture editor at all, because at least the operation is organized. However, the job at this lowest level, sparks little creativity.

The picture editor "must have a voice in how the picture should be used," Harold G. Buell, director of photography for the Associated Press, has argued. Only then can he inspire his photographers to perform with insight. "As long as all that's expected of a picture editor is to find what two-column cut there is available to illustrate a story others have already decided on, and to size it and send it to the engraver, he is only an errand boy. But if he is to do the job intended, he should participate as an equal in status in the editorial planning of any planned story."

The main point of naming a picture editor is to have a man who "thinks pictures" and who has the authority to get the best photographs for the paper. There are various gradations of organization and power to permit this. The papers with the best pictures are likely to have an editor who plans picture coverage, assigns photographers and has authority to hire and fire them, selects pictures or at least has considerable role in selection, makes up a picture page, and directs the artists. The more important the picture editor, the more he must be a manager. He maintains good human relations as well as a workable system for fast production.

Robert Kerns of the Syracuse University School of Journalism recalls that as picture editor for the *Cedar Rapids* (Iowa) *Gazette*, he edited (that is, selected) the Wirephotos and distributed them to the departments. Established next to the city desk, he assigned photographers, created feature ideas, and made up the picture page, including the writing of heads and cutlines. (See figure 10-1.) Kerns, who collaborated on the book *Creative News Photography*, says that as "intermediary between the executives and the photographers" he could appreciate the problems and demands of both

CEDAR RAPIDS GAZETTE
PHOTO ASSIGNMENT (Be There)

Day_____ Date_____ Time_____
Name and Address_____
Telephone No._____
Contact_____
Photos Wanted:_____
Number of Photos_____
Ordered By_____ Dept._____
Date Prints Needed_____
Deliver To_____
PHOTOGRAPHER_____

Fig. 10-1. Photo assignment. A form like this (from the **Cedar Rapids Gazette**) helps the photographer understand the editor's assignments as well as keep track of them.

groups. "Every editor has the right to order what he wants," says Kerns, who was promoted to his editing position from a job as photographer, "but he ought to give the photographer the right to interpret the assignment his own way, and then look at whatever he brings back."

Early in his career, Edmund C. Arnold, the typographic expert who wrote *Functional Newspaper Design* and several other books on graphic arts, was hired as picture editor of the *Saginaw* (Mich.) *News* to revamp its photo coverage. With individual departmental editors making choices, the management believed that less than the best use was being made of photographs. Arnold's job was to work closely with the departmental editors to improve the work, and they stepped coverage up to 300 or more cuts during a seven-day week.

The new system gave Arnold the dummies (blank except for ads) first in the editorial chain, and he chose the art and layout for each page. The section editor could modify details but to change position in the layout or substitute, he first had to consult Arnold. "It's not the right way, but it worked," Arnold recalls. He had "constant liaison" with the editors. Though his office was not in the news room, he had a "squawk box" connection direct to a point between the news editor and city editor. Arnold had to work closely with the city editor, because the paper had a policy of running a local picture on the front page every day. Arnold also went through the early-morning budgets sent out by the wire picture services, showed the best photos to the news editor, and worked out with him which of these should go on front page.

How much should the picture editor know about making photos? Arnold took a few pictures but quit as he fitted into the editing job. "The picture editor should have a photographic background but not be a working photographer," he says. "He gets intrigued with the technical victories—whether it was overdeveloped or underdeveloped, and whether he had to hang by his toes to take it—and it sways his judgment."

A case study

On a Friday in the fall the picture editor of the *Evening News* of Newark, New Jersey, was on the phone to the news room. It was 12:30 P.M., and a radio was monitoring police calls. Tacked on the wall behind the long picture editing desk was a sheet headed, "The Great Reporter." The text began: "I am the news camera . . ."

It was a large room, strangely empty, on the seventh floor. Because it was far from the newsroom, the photo director, Albert C. Beissert, was phoning the desk. The newsroom editor had asked for a three-column picture, and Beissert was arguing that it should be four so the artist could make a better crop. He won, hung up, and called a photographer over to give him a green assignment slip.

Then he sat down to explain how he feels the picture editing operation should be organized. Recognizing the variety of editing practices, he said he likes the concept of a "photo director" who has a picture editor working under him. He is not quite that himself. Instead he doubles as art director and photo editor, supervising a staff of fifteen photographers and seven artists (including two on roto section). The *News* has UPI Telephoto and AP Wirephoto (and receives AP pictures by mail). There are eight telephoto machines in all though obviously some get little use. Despite his involvement in pictures, Beissert says, "I'm a word man really—a reporter." A native of Newark, Beissert was graduated from the Rutgers School of Journalism in 1934 and started as editor of the *Rahway* (N.J.) *Record.* After a stint as sports editor in Stroudsburg, Pennsylvania, he reported on the *Perth-Amboy News*, turning out eight columns of copy a day.

In 1937 Arthur Sylvester, city editor of the *News* (who was to become famous as the controversial public information man at the Pentagon in the sixties) telephoned Beissert and hired him as a suburban reporter. Back in his home town, Beissart shortly moved on to rewrite, then rose to assistant city editor. In 1950, he was chosen for the newly created job of photo directing.

There was talk of calling him "assistant news editor in charge of photography"—which might have been a useful handle in office politics—but Beissert then asked to be simply "photo editor." He learned pictures on the job. Meantime, he took an active interest in press photography and became chairman of the photography committee of the New Jersey Press Association.

Assigning the job

The only blind spot in the twenty-four-hour routine at the *News* photographic department is 4 A.M. to 6 A.M. Two photographers are on the job all night until 4 A.M. Editors are on the news desk all night, however, and photographers are on call from 4 A.M. to 6 A.M. If something big happens in the night, the editors have orders to call Beissert, and he may call four or five photographers out—more if there is an emergency such as the Newark riots of 1967.

PHOTOGS	MORNING						AFTERNOON						NIGHT								
	6	7	8	9	10	11	12	1	2	3	4	5	6	7	8	9	10	11	12	1	2
KEMPER																					
CORBITT																					
CHRISTIE																					
STISO																					
PORTER																					
JOHNSTON																					
TUTTLE																					
DELL																					
LOWEY																					
BAUMANN																					
GEORGE																					
LOWNEY																					
HESS																					
CRYSTAL																					
JONES																					

1		13		
2		14		
3		15		
4		16		
5		17		
6		18		
7		19		
8		20		
9		21		
10		22		
11		23		
12		24		DATE:

Fig. 10-2. From assignment to page. Illustrated here are the steps from photo assignment to printed page (at the **Newark News**). 2B: the record kept on assignments and hourly activities of photographers

Beissert uses a printed daily assignment sheet to guide the photographers (fig. 10-2B). At the side are the names of the cameramen, and across the top are the hours they work; so there is a square in which the number of the assignment each photographer is working on each hour may be entered. There are spaces for twenty-four assignments, and if there are more, the other side is used.

The photographer gets an assignment slip (fig. 10-2A) on which Beissert lists the subject and place, the time, and any additional remarks. There is also space for the name of the editor or department needing the pictures.

PHOTOGRAPHER

Film No.	Names – left to right

Photographer CAR

Subject

Where

DAY HOUR OF ASSIGNMENT

Reporter ASSIGNED—Who?

Editor or Dept.

Remarks

2A: the front and back of the form with the photographer's assignment and space for his notes

Ideas for pictures usually come from the photographers or Beissert, but departments may likewise make suggestions. Most of the society pictures are taken in the newspaper's studio. The sports editor tells Beissert what pictures are needed on his pages, and Beissert assigns photographers to two college games and seven or eight local ones each week, in season.

The weekend of the interview, for example, he was covering the Princeton and Rutgers football games, but he had also sent two photographers to the Army-Navy game. Photographers at these games would send film rolls back by train or bus on pre-game activity. Beissert would use wire photographs of the games themselves in the first Sunday edition, but he would have his photographers' pictures for later editions.

If the city editor has a story requiring pictures, Beissert said, the photographer usually goes along with the reporter. But when Beissert learns quickly of a major event, such as hearing the report of a fire over the police radio, he sends a photographer directly to the scene. He then calls the city desk and says he is covering. (He has direct lines—no dialing—to the city editor, news editor, and composing room.)

No matter what the assignment, *News* photographers no longer use the Speed Graphic. They have shifted to No. 120 two and one-quarter by two and one-quarter inches and 35 mm. film entirely, with growing emphasis on the latter, though the paper is buying a new Rolleiflex (120) every three months.

Editing the pictures

The photographer brings in fifteen or twenty pictures from a job, and editing is then done with the developed negatives. So Beissert spends much of his time examining negatives in the dark room and saying, "Print this—and this." (To reduce dark room labor, the *News* has switched to automatic-printing equipment. However, it retains two well-equipped dark rooms for emergencies.)

When the prints ordered by Beissert are ready, a messenger takes them in envelopes to the appropriate desk: city, feature, sports, state, suburban, society. Messengers run photographs to the engraving department, in a building half a block away, and bring cuts back direct to the composing room. Each envelope has a tag when pictures are enclosed. A red tag signals "next edition." A white tag means that it is to be engraved in early afternoon for the next day, and a black one means it is for overnight.

What happens, for example, to a set of prints on a morning fire? The city editor looks at them and may discuss his choice with the news editor. Exceptional pictures may merit Beissert's attention. Using a black grease pencil, the city editor writes his instructions (such as "3 col." and "Newark fire") on the back of each print (see fig. 10-2E). (The time may also be written on the back. If the fire was at 9 A.M., the city editor may write "11:10" on the back of the print, meaning that the engraver is to have the cut by that time). He may also indicate a desired depth, but Beissert makes the final decision on cropping. The city room then supplies cutlines for the pictures.

2E: the markings on the back of the photo of the boy with his radio (2D), including the correction to two columns by four inches

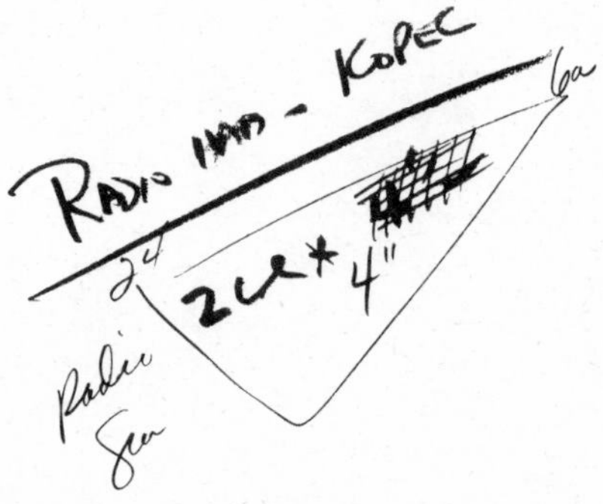

The city editor is also supposed to fill out an engraving order, but, Beissert said, if they are pushed by deadlines, they cut out such paper work. He maintains a "cut list" of engravings for such items as subject of picture, edition, and time received (fig. 10-2C). The cut list is in triplicate, and Beissert keeps one copy for reference.

CUT LIST— ____________________ 19____

ORDERED	EDITION	SUBJECT	Rec'd	Out	In	Cols.	Deep	UNITS	FOR	CHARGE
							TOTAL		TOTAL	

2C: the form for the cut list, to list engravings

The photo editor does not crop the picture himself but tells the artist how to crop it (fig. 10-2D). Proofs of the engravings come back to him (fig. 10-2F), and later he can check the picture in the paper (fig. 10-2G). The news editor may inquire about the depth assigned to a cut in order to work out makeup.

2D: a photograph showing crop marks

2F: the proof of the same picture, one of three made—for editor, artist, and composing room

be presented on Station WCBS' | morial verses by Rabbi William | by Ernest Bloch and per-

With the Radio Amateurs

Chasing 10-Meter DX

By CARL A. ERBACHER (W2EKU)

A 14-year-old youth, Kevin K. Kopec, WB2UGX, is taking advantage of the 10-meter band as it cycles toward its peak performance for DX, and has logged contacts on that band with stations on all continents.

Recently, in a half-hour's time operating from his home in De-Mott Lane, Franklin Township, the youth held a 20-minute QSO with ZS1BV, Capetown, South Africa, and also swapped reports and some conversation

KEVIN K. KOPEC operates ham station, WB2UGX, from his Franklin Township home.

Franklin High School, he is a member of the school radio club. Kevin was introduced to amateur radio by tuning in on a short wave receiver and finding ham signals. One of these he traced to the station of Fred Morehouse, W2GND, New Brunswick, and obtained permission to visit there. A month later, through the aid and encouragement of Morehouse, Kevin obtained a novice class license.

The first contact logged by Kevin was with his mentor. It

few hams that are on the air there.

• • •

Gear used includes a Johnson Ranger transmitter and a Hallicrafter SX140 receiver.

Kevin has become interested in the science of electronics as well as in operating communications, and plans to shape his high school studies toward admission to a college engineering course.

• • •

A hidden transmitter hunt is scheduled for next Sunday, sponsored by the Woodbridge Radio Club, W2ODP. Registration is from 11 in the morning until noon, starting time for the event, at the Civil Defense room, police headquarters, Berry Street, Woodbridge.

Frequencies for the hunt are 146.82 and 146.94 mcs. All mobile operators are invited to participate and additional details can be obtained from Michael Adleman, WB2MVI at 442-3098.

Nutley Meeting

Space communications and communications satellites will occupy the attention of members and guests of the Nutley Amateur Radio Society at their meeting Dec. 5.

A lecture, prepared by the New Jersey Bell Telephone Company, illustrated with slides, recordings and satellite models, will explain how communications satellites are placed in orbit and what types of equipment they carry to relay signals. Included is a demonstration of how the Telstar satellite receives, amplifies and retransmits microwave signals.

The Nutley group invites all interested amateurs to attend

2G: the portion of the page with the photo as it appeared in the News

How are pictures sized or scaled? One of the artists demonstrated the Linkrule—an accordion device like a sliding brass elevator door to measure proportions. On it was a much-used red mark for three-column cuts. (In general, the process was much as described later in this chapter.)

To check the wire pictures, Beissert consults with Alford D. Walling, the news editor. Though Beissert picks the pictures on the inside pages and picture page, Walling makes the decisions on front-page pictures. So he and Beissert are in constant touch, as in their phone discussion of the three-column cut before the interview.

Similarly, Beissert tells the sports editor what size pictures—three, four, or five columns—he is providing each sports page. But if he has one he wants to run six-columns, Beissert discusses it with the editor on the phone. There is a double strength in the *News* system: Photographers and artists have close liaison with the editorial department heads, but responsibility for all art centers in Beissert. As a result, he can gear his staff to produce the quality that the editors want.

The art of quality

Good picture editing starts with high quality photos, which means technical excellence of the negative and superior visualization of the content. Every paper has to print many mediocre pictures and a few poor ones. A family brings in a tinted photograph on soft mat paper to go with an obituary; or a reporter persuades the parents of a kidnapped child to let the paper release a badly-lighted little snapshot of the victim. Such pictures fall short of photographic excellence in several respects, yet they will be published, perhaps even in large sizes; and, amazingly, engraving departments can deliver cuts of fine quality from them, often even better than the original (for example, by improving contrast).

Nevertheless, newspaper photographs should usually be big, shiny-surfaced, and sharp. They are printed in large sizes—typically eight by ten inches, though sometimes larger—on glossy paper. They are not "flat," but well-lighted and "contrasty." The uniform greys of a flat photo make it uninteresting. There must be good definition of tones. (A picture can have too much contrast; in reproductions the blacks go too black with clots of ink, and the whites lose detail.) Usually the newspaper photo is in sharp focus and freezes motion.

From the aesthetic point of view, one of the prime requisites of a quality photograph is a definite center of interest. The photographer eliminates extraneous details so that the viewer's eye goes right to the point of the picture. If the photographer doesn't crop away distracting non-essentials, the picture editor must.

A definite point of view helps the viewer understand the picture's significance. The routine photograph is often shot straight on at eye height. For a fresh approach, the photographer may crouch for a low angle—or go up a ladder for a high one—or walk around somewhere to the side to get an unusual viewpoint. "Photo-letters," a booklet published by the newsphoto committee of the Associated Press Managing Editors Association, illustrates this point with the contrast of two pictures on a stock theme: One is the usual shot of a man giving a plaque to another, and the other, with a rather low angle, shows the winner grinning up on his framed certificate, which has been hoisted to his shoulder. Similarly, another photographer achieved a different angle on former President Johnson by shooting low enough to get into the background a presidential bust above him.

Besides a strong center of interest and a different point of view, good photographers try for appropriate special effects. For example, the illusion of depth comes from using an angle which puts a pertinent subject in the foreground—shooting down a seminar table over the shoulder of a teacher, for example, or including a fireman with hose at the edge of the picture of a building fire. This effort is similar to another useful approach, "framing." Most commonly the frame is produced with a doorway, an arch, or a tree trunk at the edge of the picture (but see figure 10-3). "Photo-letters" approvingly reproduces two "framed" pictures, one showing a library dedication scene framed by books on the shelves, and the other a church dignitary photographed through a cross-shaped hole in concrete blocks.

Fig. 10-3. Unusual framing. The low angle uses the feet of the victim as a frame which, with striking lighting, makes a dramatic photo (taken by Neal Boenzi of the New York Times).

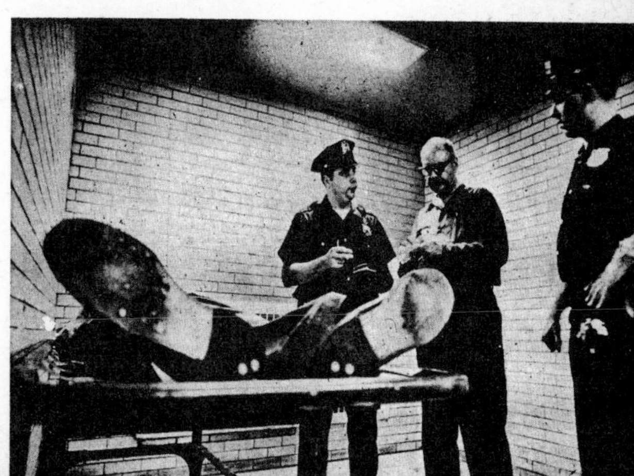

News photographers sometimes strive for artistic patterns in their pictures. These may be rows of bleachers or bottles, lines of fence posts or windows. But highly-patterned backgrounds, that detract from the focal point of interest are avoided. Yet when the best photo artist seeks aesthetic results, he sometimes violates tradition. Fuzziness, at least of some parts of a photo, may create a mood. Since stopping the action can mean a dull sports picture, there may be more drama in the blur of a moving arm or leg, and racing cars with lines of motion may at once seem to whiz and be beautiful.

There is a growing tendency to use natural lighting—so called "available light." Flash bulbs often give a harsh, flat light, though the canny photographer who holds the flash to the side, or perhaps uses two simultaneous flashes from different angles, can get good modeling. Fast film and the small camera have made it common to take quality work even in rather dim rooms without flash.

Essentials of good pictures

Beyond the quality of the technician and the artistry of a creative cameraman, what does the picture editor hope for in the way of content? "The good news picture has two priceless ingredients," writes Dick Strobel, AP newsphoto editor at Los Angeles. "It tells a story. It contains action."

That dictum perhaps focuses too much attention on the melodramatic, unless *action* is broadly interpreted to mean something much more than just the halfback leaping to catch a pass. But Strobel's words describe the content of most good newspaper pictures. They show people, people doing something. Their actions tell the story that the editors want to put across.

Surprisingly, Strobel includes thinking in his definition of action. A study of the photographs in the largest picture magazines, he says, will show two things: Almost all are made with available light, and almost all show people with minds at work. "The subject must be made to think, to react to stimuli while ignoring the camera," he says. "When this is done, the photographer actually *can* photograph the mind at work, and an eye-arresting picture is the result."

As a rule of thumb, pictures without people are dead. Of course there are some good ones with no human face or form, ranging from the great natural disaster to the beautiful lake at dawn, but even these have a kind of human interest. They would have no place in the paper if their terror or beauty did not appeal to the emotions of people. At least nine out of ten published newspaper pictures show people or animals, or both. Of the eighty-one illustrative pictures in "Photo-letters," seventy-four show people. Three others are of animal-life—a lonely cat, gulls in sea spray, a waiting spider. Thus only four show no person or animal, but three of these stand as art pictures—frosty telephone wires; shining leaves above an old barn; a school bus with a plume of dust. The fourth is a junk yard, on which the editors comment, "Ugh!"

As in the theater, props are important to many news pictures. The photo of a man with a telephone may be hackneyed, but it is somewhat better than the mug shot of a person staring into the camera.

So photographers look for pens, notebooks, typewriters, plaques, and baseballs for their subjects to finger, in the hope of creating interest.

It is difficult to get an offbeat picture with such ordinary props, though sometimes they are part of the story. It is easier when the prop is a bit out of the ordinary—a bottle of catsup, a goat, a catcher's mask, an Asian souvenir—or when it is used in an unusual way. A good feature shot shows a little girl trying on hats with a hand mirror. Another shows a wounded G.I. with a tin of rations. Some ground-breaking officials hold shovels like rifles over their shoulders. A politician drinks milk out of a giant bowl. The search for the unusual sometimes lapses into gimmickry and corn, but it can turn up prize winning pictures.

The photographer therefore starts with people, relates them to a prop, and tries to catch them at a unique moment in a natural action. A stereotyped picture is a routine shot of a routine action. Clichés to be avoided include handshaking, the award presenting, ribbon-cutting, gavel-passing, "sunbathing" (of a leggy girl), desk-sitting, proclamation signing, and, worst of all, lining up three or four persons to "watch the birdie."

The way photographers try to break away from the routine is illustrated by an incident when Governor Reagan of California and Governor Romney of Michigan, both being mentioned as possible presidential candidates in 1968, attended a reception in Washington, D.C. A woman who had heard Reagan kept jelly beans in his Sacramento office handed him a glassful. "Hey," said a photographer, "if you start flipping those, you'll be on page one of every paper in the country." Sure enough, a stagy picture of them, mouths open and jelly beans in air, appeared in many dailies the next day.

Judging pictures

A picture editor learns to evaluate photographs as a news editor learns to judge stories—by experience and by observing how other newsmen operate. Some pictures are obviously great, others blatantly dull. But the majority of pictures are in between, and only a fraction of them can be used; those chosen will depend on the day's needs and the editor's personal tastes.

Broadly speaking, most newspaper pictures fit one of two categories, news or feature. As papers use a mixture of news stories and feature materials, they usually want both types of photos.

As indicated already, the choice is easy where the picture portrays a great news event dramatically. Perhaps the only difficulty will be in choosing which of several good shots does the job the best. Aside from the size of the event, the other factors of news judgment, such as proximity of the news and timeliness, come into play in picture selection.

In addition to the unusual news photo which can stand alone if necessary because of its significance, many pictures will be used in tandem with stories, simply as illustrations. They clarify the news account or make it more interesting. Among these are not only the more compelling shots of riot violence and earthquake damage but photos of the President meeting a delegation, a churchman speaking, and a demonstrator painting a protest sign.

Similar to the supplementary news picture is the record photograph. Even papers much smaller than the *New York Times* will use some pictures of low impact simply because they are a part of the historic record—the chiefs of two European nations conferring, the governor signing a law, the mayoral candidates casting their ballots.

Like the news editor, the picture editor chooses these news photos because, like news, they contribute to portrayal of current information which interests readers. The man who selects pictures is under the same pressures as the news evaluator—to choose what will titillate readers and sell papers; what fits newspaper traditions and fulfills reader expectations (that hand-shaking picture again), or what suits his own taste or whim. The good picture editor of course minimizes the effect of these pressures and selects the news pictures that communicate the events most effectively.

Feature pictures are something else again. From the standpoint of hard news values, they would not be given valuable space. But pictures which are simply interesting as pictures, with minimal news values, have the same purpose as comic strips—entertainment. Most of them, like the best of feature stories, have human interest—the baby in a puddle on a hot day, the beauties getting ready for the contest, the puppy with the bandage on his nose.

The better European papers often print a different type of feature picture, the artistic photograph, and some American dailies are tending to use more of these. Art studies are of course familiar in Sunday rotogravure magazines. But in the news pages too the imaginative picture editor may include the well-composed pictures of yachts tied at local docks, of nearby cornfields soft with haze, of a skyline at dawn, or of the cow and kitten wending toward a barn north of town. As the popularity of cameras continues to mount, readers are becoming more sophisticated about pictures and more interested in outstanding photographs with slight relation to the news.

The good picture editor also tries to develop picture stories. The photographs in these probably combine news and feature elements. The pictures—undoubtedly including some posed ones—should have individual feature or artistic value, but they must fit together to tell a story.

By reading newspaper studies, the picture editor can determine what kinds of subjects are of greatest interest to readers. However, just as newspapers cannot finally be edited by polls, pictures cannot be selected by surveys. Ultimately, the picture editor has to understand intuitively what will interest his readers. What will interest him will probably interest the subscribers. If he exclaims, "Wow!" about a photo, it probably means that the reader too will feel it has "impact." So he must learn to understand himself. He will naturally have some enthusiasms, but they should not become hobby horses. Or he may temper his dislike of a certain type of picture because experience teaches him that readers react favorably to it. He gives the reader "what he wants" if, in good conscience, he can; but he usually selects what his judgment says is the best photography.

Ethics of illustration

The tension between what the reader wants and what he should have suggests the problems in ethics which the picture editor also confronts in making selections. Readers may want the macabre or near-pornographic photo, yet may criticize the paper that uses photographs in bad taste. The picture editor must sometimes walk the hazy, wiggling line between the acceptable and unacceptable.

While the movie capitals have long provided hundreds of sexy publicity photos, the picture editor approaches them gingerly. Obviously newspapers are much more liberal in the use of flesh shots than in the pre-bikini, pre-topless era. But the picture editor of a home circulation newspaper, the so-called family paper, makes his judgments with at least one eye cocked toward the junior high readers who sprawl—perhaps on his own living room floor—to peruse the funnies, sports, and whatever cheesecake he purveys.

Pictures of horror have traditionally been prohibited in good newspapers. Any picture of a corpse is normally taboo. If the paper does print a picture of a dead accident victim, the cutlines often suggest that the picture was taken while he still breathed.

One controversial picture showed a lifeguard standing over a drowned child, his arms outstretched in a futile gesture of condolence to the weeping mother. *Editor & Publisher* gave it honors, its editor calling it "tops as a dramatic, story-telling news photo." One editor whose paper ran it on page one, however, came to agree with a reader who questioned it savagely. It tells a story, the editor decided—but what story? What right is there to intrude, he asked, what moral justification? This is no safety sermon. It is the kind of incident which would make a person coming upon it mutter an apology and run. Yet the march of world events regularly provides some of the most horrendous news—and photos. A 1969 cover of *Life* carried a color photo of a boy, wounded in a race riot, lying in blood. Such display makes the newspaper editor less squeamish about distasteful pictures. The usual argument for such display is that the public conscience benefits from confronting the ugly parts of reality.

The Food and Agriculture Organization of the United Nations had a series of pictures of starving children but held back some because they were "too rough" to go with a newspaper series. When *Editor & Publisher* printed some, editors split, some arguing they could be printed. Especially debated was one of a naked baby, emaciated as a baby bird, which the *Journalists' World* in Brussels used in sponsoring an essay contest under the head "Too Gruesome for Use?" The winner, arguing for use of the picture, asserted: "People must face it—hunger has never had a pretty face."

The Associated Press has distributed many pictures of violent horror from the war in Vietnam. Once it sent a package with two pictures of the victims of Viet Cong torture, two pictures of U.S.-

supported troops torturing women Viet Cong prisoners, and a story about both incidents. AP General Manager Wes Gallagher reported:

> Out of 37 papers checked, 19 printed only pictures of the Government troops torturing the Viet Cong suspects, 5 printed only pictures showing Viet Cong torturing victims, 5 presented a balanced treatment, one from each side, 8 published the story only without any pictures. The most used picture of the whole group was the single picture of a government soldier pushing the head of a Viet Cong woman suspect in the river. Now I am sure that our critics would find something sinister in the variety of treatment, but I think it is indicative of a healthy, vigorous attitude on the part of editors who are doing their job according to their own news judgment.

A former editor, James Russell Wiggins, U.S. Ambassador to the United Nations, has called the news camera "a congenital liar." When editor of the *Washington Post*, he recalled, he withheld a photo of President Truman in front of caskets containing U.S. war dead. "What that camera said was that the Korean War was 'Truman's War,' just what thousands of the President's critics were saying. But that was not the truth. It wasn't Truman's war." Similarly, he said, cameras in Vietnam told readers that it was a terrible war but they could not report "the failure to wage it would have resulted in an even more terrible war."

For even the routine events of a city cameraman usually arrive with the police, Wiggins pointed out—"just in time to show the police in the act of apprehension, repression, suppression or ejection from the site." It is possible to say, in words, "that the slight young fellow resisting the police just shot his grandmother, cut his sister's throat, robbed a bank or shot at the mayor, but the photograph is silent on this point." The picture simply says that the prostrate person is the victim of brutal aggression by the cops. As violence goes on in the nation and abroad, and perhaps steps up through the seventies, picture editors will have to take special care that photo coverage tells the truth and does not leave distorted impressions.

Picture pages and stories

Devoting a whole page to pictures has long been popular with daily newspapers. The picture page gives the editor a chance to print excellent photographs which can't be squeezed in on other pages. Here he puts eight to twelve photos in varied sizes, the subjects ranging from the blonde in bikini to the railroad wreck.

Vincent S. Jones, vice president and executive editor of the Gannett newspapers, has long pioneered for a better use of this space. He argues that this variety page or half-page, which just grew, needs planning to be effective. A conglomeration of pictures may stop the reader, he says, but will it hold him? Jones, who became president of the American Society of Newspaper Editors in 1969, says that newspapers used to start all their big stories on page one, but they discovered the jumps to arid inside pages went unread. Using the best pictures all on a single page repeats this error. Usually, he contends, pictures are most effective if they run with, and complement, the news they illustrate.

His suggestion is a picture page made up of related photographs on the same subject, like the series of the picture story. Then the picture page really becomes a display case for the picture story. Limiting the number of photos also makes a better picture page when one is used. Erwin Swangard, the managing editor of the *Vancouver Sun*, a Canadian paper with a reputation for picture excellence, argues for picture pages, saying his paper used thirty-one in a recent year. But the secret is to use photos in big sizes, usually only four pictures to the page, sometimes only two or three. "Make sure your page has a theme and announce it with a 24-point line under the lead-off picture," he advises.

Individual pictures may tell a story, as we have seen. It may be a feature—the puppy covertly munching hot dogs beside the meat counter. Or it may be a news photo—the hard-jawed policeman as he aims a gun at a robbery suspect.

However, the term "picture story" usually refers to a series of pictures which together convey the event. The neophyte may mistakenly think that any collection of pictures on the same subject is a picture story. Sometimes such a collection can make a story—all the striking photographs of an Alpine avalanche, for example, put together so that the reader sees it as a unity. But if neither the photographer nor the picture editor strives for unity, the result will probably not be a story but confusion.

Typically, the photographer imposes a potential unity on several pictures by selecting a common subject, a person, more often than not. *Time* tells a complicated story in terms of a personality pictured on its cover; newspapers often use the case study approach, as when they explain a new medical plan in terms of how it has worked for one elderly couple. So the photographer may choose one person in telling his story—the beauty queen as she goes through the preparations for winning, or the poverty worker as he moves among slum tragedies.

The photographer must take pains to see that the person appears in different poses so the pictures will not all look alike. Most readers can recall picture stories which use six or eight monotonous photographs to tell the tale which one or two could tell. A greater danger for both photographer and picture editor is the ethical one of distortion. Most stories are bigger than one person; the news of a week-long church convention may be more interesting if told as the story of the new president, but no matter how good the photographs of his drinking coffee and fingering the gavel, he cannot embody the whole event.

The editor's job is to get good ideas for stories to be told in pictures, to encourage the photographers to go after them, and to guide them in making the kinds of pictures he needs. With their prints on his desk, then, he must select and organize to give punch to the various stories. He may do this by simple chronology; but he may want to try a magazine format—varied sizes, unusual cropping, and artistic arrangements. Creating a fine picture story can be one of the most creative and exciting parts of the editor's job.

Sources of photos

Agencies

American newspapers get more of their photos from the picture services than any other source. Best known to the ordinary reader is the Wirephoto, a glossy picture which arrives in a flow organized by the Associated Press. Like AP news, scores of these pictures come over the wire from various AP papers and bureaus each day. UPI also has a facsimile machine which rolls a steady stream of photographs into the newsroom on sensitized paper which can be clipped off, perhaps retouched, and used for engravings.

The news services also provide newspapers with mailed packets of eight by ten glossy photos, and they are not alone. The *Editor & Publisher Yearbook* lists twenty-six specialized agencies where editors can get pictures, as well as many syndicates which handle photos among other materials. Many of these provide pictures in special categories. Religious News Service, for example, has about 900 photo correspondents around the world who channel pictures to the New York photo editor and to 100 daily newspapers as well as several religious magazines. The pictures may be hard news, as of clerical protest marches, but they may be inspirational or seasonal (Easter and Christmas). As with other services, editors may get the entire service for a weekly rate based on circulation, see all RNS pictures and pay for those wanted, or buy individual pictures by request.

Smaller papers can also get photos and illustrations in the form of *mats*. Like stereotype mats used in newspaper printing, these are molds made by pressing engravings on a pulpy cardboard, and the purchasing paper simply has to cast them. A shortcoming of both mailed mats and photos is that they lag seriously behind the news, and television is already beating the newspaper pictorially. However, mail is good for feature illustrations. "Although many so-called 'metropolitan' papers scorn mats as beneath the dignity of organizations which can afford real engraving," says an editor of a large Eastern newspaper organization, "we use both NEA and AP mats liberally. They are tops in both editing and reproduction quality."

Local sources

A close competitor of agency pictures, at least on the bigger papers, is the local photographic staff. Syndicated photographs cost less than ones made by the paper but of course can't cover local events. With a single ambitious photographer and a miniature dark room, a paper can have a number of good local pictures for every issue.

In the day of the semi-automatic camera and the Polaroid, some newspapers use reporters as photographers. But the idea of the photo-reporter has never really caught on. A major reason is that many editors contend that a man can't do two things well; he must report and write or he must photograph, and many reporters and photographers will agree on this specialization. Yet some picture editors feel that a reporter who is out on a story might as well have a camera along and shoot some pictures. The *Beverly* (Mass.) *Times*, for example, has experimented with a fixed-focus, automatic-exposure camera using half a frame of 35 mm. film. Reporters can simply shoot away with fast film, getting pictures which are sharp from six feet to infinity. In a little over a year the paper published about one in four of 3,000 pictures made by reporters.

Free-lance photographers place some pictures with newspapers, especially their magazine sections. Many of the most famous news photographs have been taken by amateurs who just happened to be on the spot. Though there would be headaches of organization, newspapers might do much more than they do to buy pictures from free-lances and amateurs.

Many other local pictures are provided by news sources. Families may supply photographs for the obituaries. Brides bring in their pictures for wedding announcements. Sometimes a reporter wangles a portrait from the family of a victim or a suspect. The picture editor must have a good system to return borrowed pictures. Some of this trouble can be avoided if the news subject comes into the paper's studio for a picture; while there is the ever-present danger of stilted photography, this plan works well for such things as awards and some society pictures.

Public relations sources provide many more newspaper pictures than readers realize or most editors would admit. Most of those glamour pictures come from press agents of screen and television celebrities. Photographs in the women's section that feature new fashions, modern interiors, and luscious foods are usually from publicity sources. Local companies provide varied pictures for the business pages. And as publicity workshops never tire of pointing out, the well-planned and well-made photograph from the publicity chairman of even the P.T.A. or hobby group may make the paper.

The daily newspaper has one other important source of pictures—its own library, the one time "morgue." File folders should be established for many subjects and persons that reappear in the news. Many pictures used in the paper, and some which are not used, should be saved, with careful identification. Bigger newspapers also keep in small envelopes the thin metal cuts of potentially reusable pictures. From its files of glossies and cuts, the newspaper can rush into print the photograph of a newsworthy person when he speaks, wins, loses, gets into trouble, or dies. (Only careless editors use old pictures which are obviously ten or twenty years old; however, there are stories—such as the death of a once-prominent tycoon—when an old picture is better than none, but then the date of the photo should be indicated.)

The typical picture editor, in short, has two to twenty times as many photographs as he can use. Still his job is to keep his sources open and maintain a big flow, so that he can pick the best.

Cropping and sizing

The picture editor marks the photos for the engravers. He crops and sizes. Though usually done together, cropping and sizing are two different operations. A photograph must be marked to eliminate unessential material (cropped); it must be scaled to fit into a desired space (sized). Obviously, the sizing problem changes with cropping, and vice versa.

Cropping

Many pictures require little or no cropping, because the photographer has focused on the essentials. Nevertheless, to the experienced editor's eye, some further cropping may be advisable. Or he may want to use only a part of a picture, or to print it in a different shape than the usual 4:5 ratio.

The editor must crop and size in relation to his makeup design, which may require a long one-column cut or a more horizontal picture three columns wide. He also should crop the photograph for maximum communication. He cuts out busy backgrounds, superfluous people and objects, and other distracting matter "to bring the picture out of the photograph." That is, he crops to accentuate the focus of interest—the part of the picture which catches the eye.

Advice on cropping may sometimes seem inconsistent, but the wise editor follows the rules that will make the picture he is working on most effective. He is well-advised to crop ruthlessly, chopping off the top of the head or the legs boldly and letting the reader's

Fig. 10-4. Cropping dramatically close. The high angle in this straight print of the land speed record holder suggests a way to make the picture dynamic.

Fig. 10-5. The result. The crop brings the reader face to face with the record setter and suggests the drama of the speed trial.

imagination supply the missing portions. Yet he should try to retain the essential composition of a good picture. And he should crop only when it is necessary to improve the picture. Bob Kerns suggests cropping to emphasize dominant points of interest (figs. 10-4 and 10-5); yet his picture showing a half-lighted girl at the edge of a stage has much more interest when he crops to retain the "extraneous" footlights and shadows (figs. 10-6 and 10-7). Cropping, too, requires good judgment.

As he crops, the editor should keep these other pointers in mind:

—Look for other than the "obvious" crop, in order to get results out of the routine.
—In head and shoulder shots, leave a bit of space on the side toward which a person faces.
—Similarly, emphasize the action by leaving space before the thrust of an action, whether a racing car or jumping basketball player.
—Avoid spoiling a woman's hair-do or cutting off her legs at the ankle.
—Keep vertical lines vertical.
—Retain horizons for perspective, but be sure they are horizontal.
—Avoid fancy and irregular shapes, unless there is a strong reason for them.
—Experiment.

Fig. 10-6. Cropping to retain drama. The photographer composed this picture with the student thespian looking into space to suggest solitude and, perhaps, dreamed-of glory.

Fig. 10-7. Cropping out drama. The close crop removes the atmosphere, reducing the picture to a routine portrait.

To visualize the picture when cropped, the picture editor often frames different portions of the photograph with a rectangle formed between his extended thumbs and forefingers. The same framing can be done with greater precision if he cuts *cropping L's* from cardboard—two L-shaped tools which he can place like an adjustable picture frame on the face of the photo. L's calibrated in inches will speed up his estimates for the sizing process.

There is no problem of sizing or scaling if the editor simply crops out of the picture an area exactly the size of the required cut; that is, for example, it is no problem to mark an area a column wide and three inches deep. But rarely does the picture fit his engraving needs so exactly.

Sizing

Most pictures used in newspapers are reduced in the engraving process. Tiny snapshots make passable cuts when blown up for engraving, a must when only small pictures of a subject are available. (Engravers prefer that the picture be copied and enlarged photographically before they get it.) Newspapers like to use big photographs because engravings are of better quality when there is reduction, and reduction means that the picture editor has to understand proportion. He faces such questions as, "If I reduce this photograph to three-columns wide, how much space must I allow for its length?"

Mechanical devices, such as sizing wheels or slide rules, or Linkrules, give proportional dimensions quickly and automatically. All the editor has to do is set the desired height or width and he can read off the other dimension of the cut quickly.

The best qualified editor, however, has an understanding of mathematical and geometric proportion. He may almost never use his knowledge in cropping a picture. But being able to deal intelligently with proportion will help him in such tasks as grouping pictures or laying out pages.

The mathematics of photographic proportion are comprised in a simple equation:

$$\frac{w}{d} = \frac{W}{D}$$

Here "w" stands for the width and "d" for the depth of the photograph, and "W" and "D" are the width and depth of the cut.
Now we can translate the formula:

$$\frac{\text{width of picture}}{\text{depth of picture}} = \frac{\text{width of cut}}{\text{depth of cut}}$$

Let's assume we have a ten by eight horizontal photo we want to use, cropped full, and that we want to reduce it to a cut five inches wide. How high will the cut be? The mathematically-oriented may see at once that the answer is four inches. But here is the method:

$$\frac{10}{8} = \frac{5}{D}$$

$$10 \times D = 5 \times 8$$

$$D = \frac{40}{10} = 4 \text{ inches}$$

The same principle of course applies with a much larger picture. It is the same if, for a picture page, we know the finished depth we want and are solving to get width. The formula works equally if we have cropped out a space nine and one-half by seven and one sixteenth inches—though the editor who has to work with mathematical sizing soon learns to keep his measurements more-or-less even!

Some editors may feel more comfortable with arithmetic proportion in which the means and extremes are multiplied. Then the formula may be set up this way:

$$w:d::W:D$$

Figures are substituted in the same way, and we get:

$$10:8::5:D$$
$$10 \times D = 5 \times 8$$
$$D = 4 \text{ inches}$$

The diagonal method is another way of sizing or scaling to determine engraving sizes. A rectangle the size of only the cropped area, is drawn on a sheet of paper. (The size of the photo before cropping should not be used—that size is now immaterial, since part of it is being cropped away.) If the rectangle is drawn using the corner for a 90-degree angle, the job is easier.

Next a diagonal line is drawn from the lower left corner to the upper right. Perpendiculars drawn from any point on the diagonal will, obviously, produce rectangles of the same proportion as the cropped area. A perpendicular for a horizontal of five inches on a ten by eight picture will be four inches, giving the height of the reduced image. But if instead, the perpendicular is drawn at three inches, the height of the cut will be found to be two and four-tenths inches. Naturally this result is the same as if the figures are used in a mathematical equation. (See figure 10-8.)

Fig. 10-8. Reducing with diagonals. The rectangle (ABCD) represents a ten by eight horizontal photo fully cropped. Perpendiculars to any point on a diagonal (AC) drawn on paper (not on the photo!) produce a rectangle of ten by eight proportion. Thus, if a perpendicular is dropped to AD five inches from A, the line X represents the corresponding depth of the cut (four inches). A'B'C'D' represents another ten by eight horizontal photograph, but this one has been cropped on all four sides, leaving only a portion seven inches wide and four inches deep (shaded EFGH). Drawing this seven by four shape at lower right (E'F'G'H') and applying the diagonal method means that a perpendicular dropped to E'H' five inches from the lower left corner makes the line X' the corresponding depth (a bit more than two and three-fourths inches).

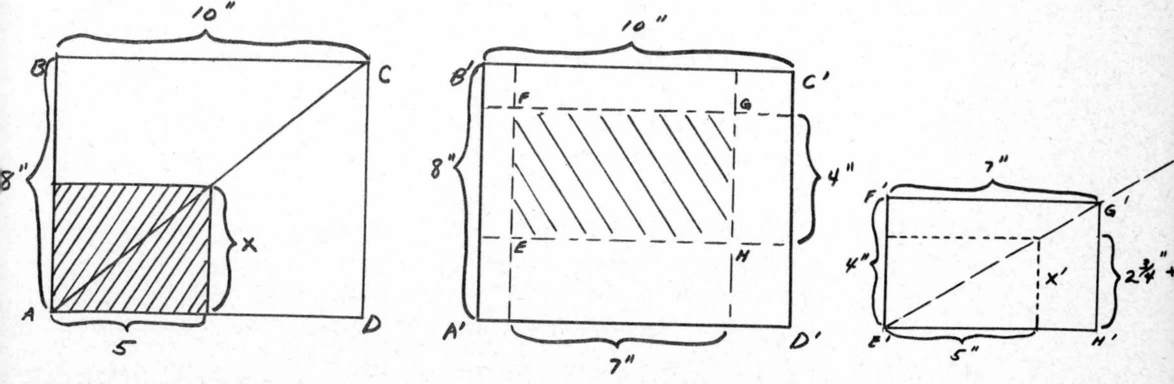

Marking

When the editor has decided just how he wants the photo cropped, he puts *crop marks* on its face with a grease pencil. The mark is simply a line a half-inch long or less at the edge of the picture—in the margin, if there is one, so as to mar the photo as little as possible. The grease pencil marks easily, rubs off with rag or finger, and ordinarily does no permanent damage to the surface of the print.

An overlay of tissue paper, folded over the photograph, may be used in the more precise world of advertising and magazines. In the faster processes of the daily newspaper, there is usually less precise instruction. The editor may put two crop marks on the side, to show top and bottom crops for the cut; puts two at the bottom, to show the left and right edges, perhaps with an arrow between and a notation "2 col." The engraver then knows he is to make a two-column cut, and the height will be worked out mechanically as he adjusts his machine to the side markings. (If there is only one mark, on the side or bottom, the engraver will simply cut from there to the margin.)

The editor writes a slug—like the news story slug— on the back of the photo to identify it in a single word—"touchdown" or "Nixon." If the sizing has not been indicated on the face, it will be marked on the back (width first): "2 col. x 4," perhaps, or "7-1/2 x 5-1/2" (for a picture page). It may also be necessary to mark the edition or the section for which the cut is needed. Craftsmen argue that no one should write on the back of a photo, and hard pencil lead can do damage. In fact, many picture editors do put these marks on the back with a grease pencil taking care that the glossy side is on a clean, flat surface. The only alternative for careful work is to paste instructions on a flap, as agencies and free-lances do, or perhaps to use an identification sticker on the back.

At this point, a retouch artist may work on the photograph. With tiny paint brush or spray, he can heighten the contrast in order to get a better cut. Retouching can tone down busy backgrounds or even delete people. Excessive retouching, however, not only gives the final picture a painted look but raises ethical questions of distorting "reality."

The retouch man also puts in arrows, circles, and the X's which "mark the spot." The popularity of these appears to have declined, but they can still be useful, as in showing where cars have skidded or where a halfback has run.

It is in cropping and sizing that the picture editor has the opportunity to employ the real drama of modern newspaper photography. If the routine method is to reduce everything to two or three columns, he will break away to put his best pictures into sizes six and even eight columns wide, where they can beat the picture magazines. He will also remember to use white space which will set quality pictures of magazine-style.

Writing cutlines

The picture editor must see that every engraving has cutlines (sometimes called *captions* or just *lines*). Sometimes simply the name suffices for the picture with one person, such as the one-column head shot or the bride's portrait (last name only may be used with the half-column cut.) Necessary explanation for a picture should be in short, clear sentences.

The caption-writer should look at the picture carefully to see what the reader needs to be told. Sometimes the press of deadlines requires the photos be sent to engraving early; then the copyeditors write cutlines from notes without seeing the pictures. This is a sloppy as well as dangerous practice, which will inevitably produce errors. The writer should see the action he is describing; he will look for conspicuous objects which need explanation. He should check to see that the number of names in the cutlines is the same as the number of people shown.

Like headlines, cutlines are in the present tense: "Crewmen try to check flames ..." or "Joe Doakes of Middle State hurls javelin ..." Of the five *w*'s usually part of the news lead, the cutlines should include at least the *who* and *where. When* may be appropriate, but most of the *what* is told by the picture itself.

Writers tend to worry too much about *what*. If the picture is good, an unmodified, simple verb is enough. It is amateurish to write "smilingly accepts" or "express delight about." If the girl is gorgeous, that adjective need not be included in the cutlines—let the reader form his own opinions. The expressions "is shown" and "is pictured" waste space. However, if the reason for a smile or gesture is not self-evident, the reader deserves an explanation.

Editorializing is as dangerous in cutlines as in news stories. "Club-swinging policeman" may cast an onus on the officer, but "eyes blazing defiance, the looter" may shift prejudice in the opposite direction. Let the reader make up his own mind from the look of clubs and eyes, unless they misrepresent the full story. Cutlines should be deadpan.

True *captions*—lines above the picture—have pretty well disappeared from newspapers. But some typographical device can well be used to hook the roving eye at the picture. Often this is two or three words of bold-face caps which kick off the cutlines: **CANDIDATES GATHER—Democratic bigwigs of** ... Or there may be a small headline in a larger type than the cutlines:

Candidates Gather
Democratic bigwigs from upstate counties barbecue . . .

Drawing on research with the eye camera, Dr. Chilton R. Bush, retired dean of the School of Journalism, Stanford University, argues for the use of such headings or legends. He cites research by a graduate student, Jack Ling, now of UNICEF, as indicating that readers more often misinterpreted pictures alone than pictures with legends.

In "Writing Captions for Newspictures," a monograph published by the American Newspaper Publishers Association, Bush suggests these guidelines:

> —If the picture is ambiguous, clarify it in the cutlines. For example, a picture of comedian Bob Hope with singers may seem pointless until reader learns it is a Christmas show in Vietnam.

—When the picture is so ambiguous that it does not tell the *what* immediately, write a legend that supplies the central organizing clue to the meaning. Tests showed that a picture of a man standing on a roof baffled many readers; but this event was a suicide attempt, and the legend and cutlines should have made that clear. With a picture of a wreck, "It Wasn't a Drive-In" might be amusing; but "She Pushed the Wrong Pedal" clues the reader into the meaning immediately.

Color photography

Even though amateurs have been shooting color pictures for more than a generation, newspapers have been slow to use color, as we explained in chapter 9. The difficulties of low-grade paper and fast presses are being overcome by printing experts. A recent development facilitating use of color photography for newspapers is a camera that takes three color separation negatives in a single shot. Ordinarily, newspaper photographs come in as transparencies, or slides, requiring special equipment to make separations for printing.

Separation, as used here, refers to the process of using color filters to block out certain colors in an image. For example, if an engraver uses red and yellow filters (or an orange one) in shooting a color picture with blues of sky and sea, he will get an engraving with only those blues. With the appropriate blue ink, that engraving will then reproduce the blues in the original. Similarly he can make separations for the reds and yellows, and the resulting engravings will produce appropriate oranges, browns, lavenders, etc., when printed in combination with the blue plate. The screen is rotated slightly for each separation, so the dots of different colors are close together but not on top of each other. This is *three-color process*. A black-ink plate for grey tones is added for the more realistic *four-color process*.

Other art work

Aside from photographs, line drawings—sketches in black ink on white paper—are the major editorial illustrations used in today's newspapers. Comics and cartoons are the most familiar line drawings, but imaginative editors also use graphs and charts. Line drawings have traditionally headed certain pages and columns, but the modern trend toward clean lines tends to make these look old-fashioned. (See figure 10-9.) Editors must take care that they look sharp and open.

The picture production man on a large newspaper may have a staff of artists able to create various drawings for different departments. Picture editors on more modest papers, however, handle only maps or charts which come in from picture agencies. These reproduce best if made up as line cuts rather than halftones. The editor can even buy drawings ready-made as mats, which syndicates offer to brighten up the news columns.

The halftone process allows the editor to vary illustration with wash drawings or water colors. Fashion drawings, for example, are sometimes halftoned rather than harshly printed as black-white drawings. The artist may get the effect of an unusual halftone by putting lines close, as in cross-hatching, or with *shading sheets.* These sheets are ready-made patterns of dots or lines that can be cut to shade parts of a drawing.

The picture editor may have limited authority to suggest other art work than photographs. On a well-edited paper, however, the staff takes a look at illustration as a whole, so that there is adequate variety and change of pace.

In the future, the picture editor will have to keep up both with technical developments and with new fads and styles in photography and art. The creative individual will welcome the stimulation of such change; in it he will see the opportunity to make his paper more attractive and more capable of competing with magazines and TV in an age when newspapers must be more than black and white to be read all over.

Fig. 10-9. Art. The art department can add variety to the mix of type and photos. But trends in illustration change, so the editor should be alert to art that seems old-fashioned if he wants a light touch. Compare the styles in these sets of illustrations.

11 News crises and edition changes

To many outsiders, the word "newsroom" evokes an image of excited men bellowing at each other, editors screaming at printers and printers screaming at editors, telephones ringing like fire alarms, and copy boys frantically darting from desk to desk. This picture may be great for dramatic presentations, but it would be a horrible way to put out a newspaper. If such turmoil were routine a newspaper could never be printed at all, let alone on time, and the staff would be ready for straight jackets in less than a month.

Newsrooms may not be as serene as libraries, but the noise level is almost always low, shouting seldom occurs, and the staff methodically goes about getting the news into print. The production of a newspaper is a major task, and orderly ways are required to get the job done.

On smaller papers the task is simpler because there is just one edition. Because most papers of less than 30,000 circulation put out only one issue a day, they avoid the emergencies of edition changes. Even so, the staffs of smaller papers are usually kept busy by the problems of a normal news day. In an emergency, they have trouble handling all the extra work. Bigger papers usually can take care of crises more easily because they have enough manpower to cope with late-breaking stories.

Various emergencies can disrupt a newspaper. The press may break down, illness might send home three or four key people, or telephone lines could be knocked out by heavy storms. During the 1965 power failure in New York and much of New England, the *New York Times* staff had to write stories by candlelight, and the printing operations were moved across the Hudson River to Newark, New Jersey. Such emergencies are unusual; the "routine emergencies" come from unexpected news breaks.

If the news is spectacular, as many as a dozen reporters and several copyeditors drop what they are doing to concentrate on the big story. Some reporters handle the main part of the story while others get sidebar material. The editors remake page one, directing reporters and photographers accordingly, and struggle to pull together all the copy into a coherent picture for the reader. If the news breaks shortly before deadline, the reporters and editors will be able to print only sketchy details no matter how quickly they act.

One of the biggest stories in the last twenty years was the assassination of President Kennedy. (See chapter 7, p. 135.) When the wire services flashed the news of that tragedy, every daily American newspaper had to make the maximum amount of room available for it. For afternoon papers, with the exception of those in the Pacific time zone, the news broke when these papers either were on the presses or set in type, so they could carry little more than basic information that the President had been killed. But even the briefest of stories about the death meant that front pages had to be ripped apart and put together again. Some stories had to be thrown away and others shortened to make room for the historic news. Several headlines had to be changed. Because the assassination overshadowed all other stories that day, every editor had to squeeze in as much information about it as possible.

Morning newspaper staffs, by working at a furious pace, managed to report the news with amazing thoroughness. Almost every story in papers of November 23, 1963—from stock market stories to news about cancellation of local events—was concerned one way or another with the death of the President. While doing all this work—gathering, writing, and editing—the newsmen were personally burdened by their horror and grief over the assassination.

Fortunately, there are few such overwhelming crises. Lesser emergencies, however, are frequent. For example, a major decision by the Supreme Court handed down minutes before deadline suddenly becomes the lead story of the day. Or the governor may take an unexpected step involving the city, and the staff must scramble to report all the ramifications. The editor must adjust quickly. One of the ways he adjusts is to expect the unexpected. Each day the editor asks himself the question that he keeps in the back of his head: "What am I going to do if a big story breaks today?" By knowing the available alternatives, he can come up with an emergency plan almost immediately.

Preparation and routines

The well-ordered newspaper, of course, is prepared for all kinds of unexpected news. It has a good library, for one thing, where clippings and pictures of past events can be found in a hurry. Reference books are readily available. One or two reporters can dig out background information from the files while other reporters gather new material and editors juggle stories on page one.

Some papers have material in type ready for a news break involving prominent persons. Using background supplied by wire services, a staff working in slack periods can prepare material and pictures on famous persons who are ill or aged. Some pages may even be made into press plates, ready for the lengthy obituary of a famous person.

To newcomers, writing an obituary before the death may seem grisly. Nevertheless, it enables a paper to cover fully and swiftly the death of someone famous, without taxing the composing room. If two extra pages are necessary, the staff can "jump" the paper's size without difficulty, although few papers increase the number of pages except for a truly monumental event.

In a crisis, staffers should not get so excited that they make the news melodramatic and overplay it. Editors at these times should take pains to double-check their news judgment. The managing editor or news editor might even warn the staff to be certain of the accuracy of information gathered hastily from people whose judgment and powers of observation may be impaired in the excitement.

Editors should consider all the angles that need covering. Should the police be checked? Will comment from the mayor be appropriate or irrelevant? Should the governor be called? Are reporters available to cover not only the main event but also the subsidiary news? While decisions are made on coverage, at least one editor will have to decide what stories to change on page one, and even on an inside page if there is time.

The front page almost always has something expendable: a routine picture, an entertaining but insignificant feature story, a news story that had barely made the front page in the first place. One or all of these pieces could go—or each could be cut from perhaps ten inches to three. Even two or three good but lengthy stories may be reduced to accommodate the emergency coverage. The news editor can sketch a new layout as soon as he knows what new stories are being written. A truly big event displaces the lead story, and space may have to be opened up for two or three sidebar stories. In an emergency the newsroom and the composing room have to cooperate more closely than ever, so printers should be alerted to expect new pictures and copy of a big story.

Everyone's productivity picks up astonishingly at these times. The excitement apparently pumps the adrenalin needed for printers to set type faster, floor men to move type with greater speed, reporters to write more swiftly, and editors to pencil copy at double-time. Everyone relishes the chance to get at least moderately excited, and the experience is undoubtedly one of the attractions of newspaper work.

Lesser crises

In most lesser crises one reporter can quickly write the story. A single editor edits the story and writes the headline. Another editor will juggle something on page one, so the story—in type—slides neatly into the form. The change is almost routine.

The unexpected often results in the changing of a story already in type. In these instances the editor may put a new "top" on the story, add something to it, or insert some new paragraphs. Often the form is already full, so someone has to make room for the new material. The editor usually first tries to throw out a few paragraphs of the original story to open space for the new parts. If every bit of the original story is important, the editor must decide on cutting or killing an adjoining story of less news value to make room for the fresh information.

When a newspaper is locked up and ready for stereotyping, most papers report late-breaking developments as bulletins. If late news changes only the gist of a story already in type, a one or two paragraph bulletin is set bold face, leaded, and indented. The printer quickly places it between the headline and the body of the story already in type.

For example, a story already set may say that the Senate will vote late in the day on a key issue. Suddenly a wire bulletin reports that the Senate voted three hours ahead of schedule. The editor hasn't time to make over the story, so he marks the copy this way:

] BULLETIN [

BF 9/10

WASHINGTON-(AP)-The Senate today voted 55-43 in favor of a stringent auto safety bill. The vote sends the measure to the President for almost certain signature.

The marks at the side mean that the type is set boldface (BF) and leaded (9/10 meaning 9-point type on a 10-point slug). The brackets indicate that the type should be indented one en on each side.

The copy then can be hustled to the composing room, where the editor working on make-up orders an inch and a half cut from some story to make room, and the printer inserts the bulletin. The reader understands that the news broke too late to make over the whole story. Sensing that he is getting last-minute news, he is probably pleased his newspaper took the trouble to squeeze in the bulletin matter.

Some newspapers, in such situations, proceed with stereotyping the original page, put the plate on the press, and start the presses rolling, to meet train or bus schedules or stock trucks headed for the suburbs. In perhaps ten minutes a new headline and a new top for the story are ready. A new plate is made, the presses stopped momentarily, the new plate substituted, and the presses started again. This process means that a few thousand subscribers will not get the late development, but many more thousands will have a complete story and headline.

Not all bulletins, of course, mean changes in stories already set. The news of the bulletin, had it been thirty minutes earlier, might have made the lead story of the day, with banner and pictures. But otherwise the editor may only have time to have the printer yank out a three-inch story on page one and slide the bulletin, bold face and indented, into the vacant space. Or he may remove a double column picture, set the bulletin matter two columns wide—but indented—and drop the type into the hole.

Readers nurtured on old movies may believe that when a spectacular news event occurs, the paper dashes out an extra. If they are young, they overlook the fact that they have never seen a true extra; if they are older they forget that they probably haven't seen one since World War II.

A few papers still will have a type block proclaiming "EXTRA" at the top of page one from time to time, but the editors are only responding to the old urges to use the word. Such an "extra" is really not an extra edition, only a regular edition with news more dramatic than usual. (When Senator Robert Kennedy was shot, in 1968, the *Philadelphia Inquirer*, in the middle of the night, did get out a genuine extra.)

Genuinely startling news is reported almost instantaneously by radio and television. So, except for the treatments described, newspapers have largely conceded the flash and bulletin to radio and TV. The two- or three-sentence reports on the air, however, create a demand for more details. David Brinkley has said that for news coverage the networks aren't even "in the same ball park" with newspapers.

Emergencies of less importance than news crises require other kinds of handling. If a typographical error produces an obscene word, the presses can be stopped and the offending material chiseled off the press plate or even smashed flat with a hammer. These crude techniques, however, never appeal to editors who really care about the appearance of their papers. After all, a headline looks pretty silly with a word or two gouged away or battered into a black smear. The good editor stretches the circulation schedules five or ten minutes to permit the presses to be stopped and the correction properly made. The good editor would also rather delay the paper a little to get real news breaks than print stories that will be made obsolete within a few minutes by radio or TV. So if a good story breaks at deadline or a really important story already in type gets a shift of emphasis, he manages to get the latest into the paper one way or another.

Changing the day's editions

All papers deal with changes, and a bigger paper deals with them constantly as every edition rolls on a different deadline. The number of changes, however, has been declining as most newspapers have reduced the number of editions. Changing editions is expensive. Besides, news simply does not shift a dozen times a day. And most papers now deliver 90 percent or more of their circulation to homes. Though street sales are still valuable, they are far less important than they were thirty years ago. And few home subscribers will buy another edition on the street.

The Washington Post

The *Washington Post*, a morning paper with about half a million circulation, is an example of a big paper with few editions—three regular editions plus a *replate*, an edition created by changing only one or two stereotype plates to include late news. The first edition, reaching the streets a few minutes after 10:00 P.M., sells to people who work nights, to those coming out of theatres, and to tourists and others seeking diversion downtown at night.

The second edition comes out about an hour later with some fresh news and with some stories altered to take account of new developments. In the summer the results of some baseball games can be included. This edition circulates in areas a hundred miles or more from Washington.

The third edition, appearing about 1:00 A.M., is distributed to metropolitan Washington, which includes the District of Columbia and sizable chunks of Maryland and Virginia. This edition has late local and world news, several revamped stories, and final results of baseball games.

The *Post* then replates the third edition by making over page one with the last newest news and few, if any, other pages. In the three editions the *Post* uses either no banner or a restrained one (72-point type or less). The replate edition has a large banner that can be read at a distance, for this edition sells from news stands to people on the way to work in the morning.

Two Syracuse papers

A few papers continue to have many editions because they cover large geographic areas. The morning *Post-Standard* in Syracuse, for example, has seven editions—but Syracuse is uniquely situated to justify them. It is the biggest city by far in a wide section of New York between Canada and Pennsylvania.

Years ago, when newspapers were beginning to expand their territories, the Syracuse papers built circulation over an area about 250 by 100 miles. Habit is important to all readers, and thousands of people in the small towns of the area got into the habit of buying Syracuse papers. To keep these readers, the newspapers have run editions that include local news for each major region: far north, near north, east, south, west, the section nearest Montreal, and Syracuse itself. The edition changes are kept to a minimum as the paper is adapting to readers more than to events.

The *Post-Standard*, except under unusual circumstances, alters page one only once during the evening. Only one inside page, other than sports, is changed from one edition to another. The first edition has a page of news from the area near Montreal. That page is replaced for the second edition by news from an area roughly 100 miles north of Syracuse. The next edition scraps that page for one with news from another section. The process is repeated until the seventh edition arrives. Local news then is put on that changing page and alterations are made on page one.

The afternoon *Syracuse Herald-Journal* operates the same way except that page one changes often because during the day news events occur more often than they do in the evening. The reason for this is that customary newsmakers—presidents, prime ministers, cabinet officials, scientists—make most of their pronouncements during the day. Congress and state legislative bodies rarely meet at night.

The trick in handling edition changes anywhere is to make as few alterations as possible while giving the reader late and significant news. Sometimes news may be fresh but not significant. For example, the wire services may give a string of new leads on one event.

Each new lead tells the latest development, but the last scrap of information may have little significance for the story as a whole. The editor should look over the various leads and be willing to say firmly, "Forget that latest lead. It doesn't give the whole story as well as the one we've got."

The Philadelphia Bulletin

Sometimes enterprising management can help reduce the number of changes. The *Philadelphia Bulletin*, an afternoon paper, has arranged its staff on a twenty-four hour basis of writing and editing so that the flow of copy to the composing room is kept steady to minimize the jam at noon. Managing editor William B. Dickinson claims it "gives us a control of the flow of copy which I have not seen equalled on other papers."

Describing the system in *Editor & Publisher*, Dickinson says that there are a night city editor and a dozen reporters who work up until 2:00 A.M.; their stories are edited and headed in the middle of the night. He continues:

> We also have a man on the telegraph desk at night. Not only does he sort and collate the wire copy so that the early men on the desk will be able to start their work without confusion, but he also edits and heads a number of stories which are not likely to change through the night—such material as we get from the New York Times Service, and the like.
>
> To put the frosting on the cake, we have a news editor who works through the evening. He has dummies of every page in the following day's paper which has news space on it. . . . He dummies most of the inside pages. . . . He is able to gauge the flow of news from both sides, and he knows from his dummies what the news hole will be. The result is that he can and does avoid building up a big overset. The composing room, always busy, is freed from the chore of setting type which will not be used. And the makeup men, when they come in the morning, can go immediately to work on inside pages. . . .
>
> No system is foolproof, and this one can break down on occasion: for instance, when there is a really big story which breaks unexpectedly in the hours from, let us say, 3 a.m. to 7 a.m.—but you don't get many of that kind any more. . . .
>
> Of course, the news department also benefits from this system. Our inside pages are better designed than they used to be.

As Dickinson shows, a well-organized and well-staffed paper finds edition or emergency changes relatively simple.

The developing story

Even if a paper strives to avoid change for the sake of change, there will be much rejuggling on most papers as the editions proceed. Just as some stories have to be lengthened because they have taken on new importance, others must be shortened because they have lost significance. Some can be cast aside because they have been supplanted by better ones or because readers of this edition would find the information irrelevant.

New headlines often have to be written to highlight new material or to fit a different size space caused by makeup shifts. A story worth a three-column head in the first edition may be dropped to a single-column head in the third, or a local story may require a bigger head in the home edition.

Such changes require a precise written code between editors and printers. One technique is to mark each piece of copy with the edition for which it is to be set. A big "2ND ED" may be rubber-stamped or written atop certain stories. The composing room, then, will not set second edition copy so long as there is any first edition material waiting.

Some papers don't require marking of copy for routine editions. Copy is marked if intended for some future publication, like the Sunday edition, but the editors work on this principle: Everything should be set as soon as possible unless otherwise marked.

Sometimes it is convenient to send copy to the composing room without a headline, marking it "HTK" or "HTC"—in either case meaning "head to come." This system is not necessary, however, if the copy is slugged and a carbon or electrostatic copy kept by the copyeditor. A story, for example, may be slugged "PRESIDENT" and sent to the composing room. A couple of hours later, perhaps, the news editor tells the copyeditor what size head to write for the story. If the copyeditor refreshes his memory by reading his duplicate story, he can easily write the assigned head. If the copyeditor normally gets no duplicates, he should make notes on the stories to help him write the heads.

Revising dummies

While editing and headline writing are proceeding, someone—usually the news editor or slot man—will be preparing dummies. As editions change, the dummies have to change, obviously, but the new ones indicate only where new or altered stories are to be placed. After the first edition a complete dummy is unnecessary and actually may be confusing to the makeup man. If three stories are to be changed on page one, the dummy would have to refer only to the three places where something is to be altered. The stories to be altered may be dummied "PRESIDENT—NEW LEAD" or "FIRE—NEW HEAD." Such notations show the makeup man exactly what adjustments are to be made in the stories. (See figs. 11-1 and 11-2.)

As soon as one edition has started its press run, the news editor should send a "kill sheet" to the composing room. This sheet is a copy of the news sections of the paper specially marked to indicate which stories should be killed. The printer, before getting the dummies for the next edition, can lift from the forms the stories to be discarded and thereby prepare for new material. (It might be noted that while printers are instructed to kill type, they rarely throw it

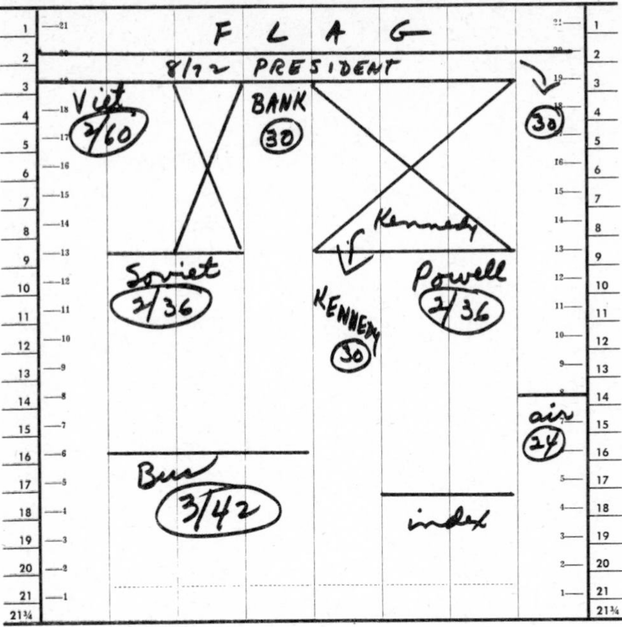

Fig. 11-1. **Complete dummy.** Most of the front page space has been filled with pictures and stories for the first run of the day.

Fig. 11-2. **Revised dummy.** The dummy of figure 11-1 has been changed to bring it up to date. A new banner and a new "Bus" lead have been provided, and "China" substituted for "Soviet."

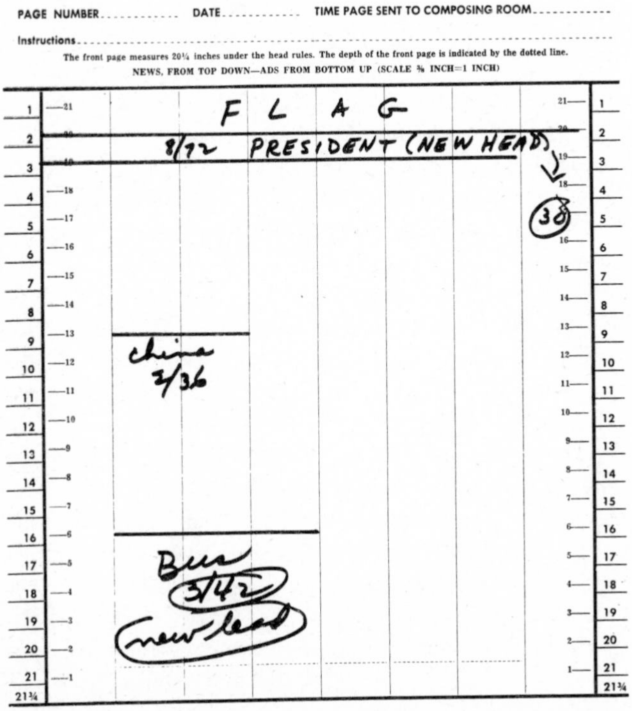

away that minute. They set it aside, remembering the times an editor said to kill something and then changed his mind a few minutes after the type was tossed into the hellbox.)

While great efforts are made to avoid spoken instructions to printers and other staffers, the news editor and the makeup editor may occasionally have brief talks about changes in the dummy. If the paper is small the various editors do makeup as well. To make a last-minute change, they simply walk to the composing room a few feet away and give instructions to the printer about their particular pages. The composing room of bigger papers may be two or three floors removed from the news room, so conversations between a news editor and the makeup editor are usually over inter-office telephone.

Sometimes a story will be dummied in anticipation of getting the facts later, but sometimes the facts don't materialize. An editor has to find a substitute story some place. Many papers have a "bank" of "time copy"—really timeless stories for use in emergencies. The staff adds to the bank in slack periods so the editor always will have a variety of stopgap material available.

Once in a while someone in the advertising department makes a real blunder that confuses the whole operation for several minutes. The ad staff lays out the basic dummy for the paper, positioning the various ads throughout the paper. The editorial staff usually has authority to move ads to facilitate makeup, but only rarely are any but the smallest ads shifted. Sometimes, alas, the ad staff will forget to dummy a major ad. Suddenly the news room editors find that the news hole is, say, 110 inches smaller than they had been told. The opposite can happen, too. The ad staff may dummy the same ad twice. In the one case the editors suddenly have to give up six or eight stories that they had planned to use. In the other they have to scrounge to find six or eight to fill the void.

Revising printed copy

While the composing room prepares for the next edition, the copy desk is working to revise some stories and process new ones. The editors usually work with a copy of the latest edition, which a copy boy has brought to the news room. The system of revision becomes easy to use with a little practice.

Let's assume that the rim man is to revamp that story slugged "PRESIDENT." He clips the story from the latest edition and pastes it on a sheet of copy paper. This sheet then is called a "marker," a "markup," or a "mark." The editor could use a proof of the story, but proofs usually are much harder to find.

On either a proof or a marker the editor writes at the top, preferably with a grease pencil or a crayon, "CX," or "X-correct," or "Krect." The most common is "CX," but all these marks mean *correction*. The printer will know as soon as he sees the marker that he is supposed to correct that particular story.

The editor also crosses out the paragraphs he wants killed. If he wishes to make an insert, he puts an arrow at the point for the first insert and labels it "Insert A." The second insert point is labeled "Insert B," etc. If material is to be added, he puts at the bottom of the marker "TR for add." This means "Turn rule for added copy." When he sees the note, the printer "Turns a rule"—turns over a slug of type at the end of the story—to remind him that one or more adds (additional material) will be coming.

The editor marks the copy to be added or inserted similarly. On the piece to be inserted first he writes "Insert A—PRESIDENT." On the other pieces he writes "Insert B—PRESIDENT," "First add—PRESIDENT," "Second add—PRESIDENT," etc. He may even have a "New lead—PRESIDENT" to prepare. At the bottom of the new lead the editor writes "TR for pickup," which means that the type not killed should pick up with the new lead.

The slug "PRESIDENT" has to be added to all the copy, of course, so the printer will know what story all these new pieces go with. It should be noted, too, that inserts receive *letter* indentification but adds are *numbered*.

The editor, after making all these marks on copy, should check everything to be sure each piece is properly labeled. Then he sends the whole packet—marker, adds, inserts, and new leads—to the composing room via pneumatic tube, and a man called the copy cutter gives the copy to the typesetters and the marker to the floor man. The paragraphs to be killed are put aside. In a few minutes the new type is set and the floor man, using the marker as a guide, pieces the whole story together as the editor directed. The system can be observed in the following examples:

Insert A) (President)

He said that no tax decision would be made until after Congress completes action on all appropriations bills and he sees whether they can be cut.

Insert B) (President)

Mr. Nixon urged the governors Thursday to cooperate in economizing at the state level along lines he is pursuing at the federal level to try to subdue the pressures of inflation.

There was no dissent to the idea from any of the governors.

Add one President

The President did not mention violence and racial disorders in outlining to newsmen what was discussed.

Add two President

On the crime situation, he said he invited each governor to send a representative to Washington in October to discuss implementing recommendations of a commission on crime. He mentioned no date.

Writing backwards

Some unexpected stories can be written in parts—even the last part first. There is a system for handling this kind of story, too. Assume that a gas main explodes at a busy downtown corner. One or two reporters and a photographer would be sent to the scene, another would check library clippings under "Explosions," and others would be telephoning the gas company, police, fire department headquarters, city morgue, and hospitals. Each reporter might gather bits of news that would be worth a couple of paragraphs. But in the confusion no one can be sure immediately whether anyone was killed, how many were injured, what caused the blast, or how much damage resulted.

While attempts are made to find out all this information, it often is helpful to get as much of the story in type as possible. So the city editor directs each reporter to write what material he has and slug it "BLAST." Reporters at the scene telephone the rewrite men as soon as they have any information. The rewrite men pound out the facts as they dribble in, using the same slug. The "top" of the story will be written last, giving the fullest account of the who, what, when, where, and why. The lesser details, gathered earlier, can be on the way to the composing room well in advance of the top. This copy is called "A-matter." The "A" stands for add; in effect, these pieces are adds to a story that as yet does not exist.

To help keep these various adds straight, editors mark the first one "10-add," the next one "11-add," etc. The figure ten is the starter because the lead, which will be written last, may then have as many as nine adds without confusing the numbering system. Ten is safe because a lead almost never has more than nine adds. The adds for the body of the story, then, may look like this:

10-add (Blast)

One witness, Mrs. Carrie Blasingame, 1013 E. Arlington St., said she had just stepped outside Heller's department store when she heard a terrific noise and saw a car flip over less than 75 feet from her. She said that the force of the blast pushed her back against the store front, but that she was not hurt.

11-add (Blast)

The explosion was the first eruption of a gas main in the city since 1927. The blast then killed two persons at Kenwood and Main streets, three blocks south of today's accident.

When the last add is written, the copy should be marked "add all —BLAST." The last add to the lead must be labeled as an add but with the additional mark at the end "TR—pick up 10-add."

If there have been twenty different pieces of copy on the one story, it is unlikely that everything fits together beautifully. The chances are good that the story needs a bit of reorganization. Someone on the desk should recheck the carbon copies of all the pieces (or work from proof) to make sure that the story "reads"—that everything gets in proper order and that the story doesn't have ludicrous duplications or omissions. If possible a second check should be made from proof after all pieces are put together.

Changes ahead

The systems explained in this chapter have concerned letterpress printing only because offset printing has so far been limited almost entirely to those papers with one edition. The reason for this is simple. The letterpress method uses the same type over and over as newspapers change editions. Pages are locked up, stereotyped, torn apart, and reassembled perhaps half a dozen times. The type can be moved easily and treated roughly. In the offset process, however, the "type" actually is a printed strip of paper. It works fine for one edition, but to pull that strip off a dummy, cut it into different pieces, remove some of it, and insert new material before pasting it down again to be photographed for a new plate would be a slow, clumsy process.

No doubt some new development will make this kind of changeover possible for offset papers too. Perhaps an attachment to the machines that "set" type for offset papers could make a neat, clean carbon copy for other editions. Or perhaps the computer that spins out printed matter to be photographed could turn out extra copies.

The editor should look to see which mechanical aids of the future could help him break the time barrier surrounding emergencies and edition changes. The pneumatic tube, the telephone, and even the radio have enabled papers to reduce the time it takes to put an event into print. Perhaps something like a typewriter that prints the spoken word onto a screen where the editor can light-pencil it will make it possible for reporters to spend more time in the field and less at one of the original timesavers—the typewriter. Meantime, editors will use time copy, scissors, and paste to foil emergencies.

12 The law and the copyeditor

The slot man tosses a story about a trial to a copyeditor. Down in the ninth paragraph is this sentence: "When Rogers finished his testimony against the sheriff, Judge Wilson launched into a bitter attack upon the sheriff, calling him a scoundrel, a 'woman-chaser' and a 'lewd, lascivious old man.'" The copyeditor has to consider some important questions: Is it libelous? Will the sheriff sue? If it is libelous and the sheriff sued, how much could the newspaper lose?

Or what if a reviewer says this of a play: "Miss Smith did an adequate job of playing Ophelia, but she might have done better if she had laid off the sauce before curtain time." Is this caustic sentence going to get the newspaper into court?

Suppose a story about the mayor starts: "Mayor Hector Adamson was convicted of stealing a horse in 1919 and served three months in jail for the offense, the Post discovered today." Is it safe to dredge up a story a half century old, even if it is true?

These examples are hardly typical of stories crossing a copy desk, but they show why a copyeditor must be constantly alert to the possibility that, tucked away in an obscure story, is a sentence that will send someone running to a lawyer. That lawyer may decide to call on the newspaper's publisher to see about a tidy out-of-court settlement. He may even reinforce his efforts by stopping off at the courthouse to file a libel suit.

The lawyer may decide to sue the copyeditor, too, since this staffer had a hand in the job. He also could sue the reporter who wrote the story. The working crew rarely gets sued, however; with only a house partly paid for, a three-year-old car, two children free and clear, and $350 in the newspaper's credit union, the newsman would be too small a target. The newspaper is not. Most newspapers, if they had to, could borrow many thousands. In addition, nearly all newspapers have libel insurance, and lawyers know it.

The costs of libel

Back in 1927 Stanley Walker, in his famous book *City Editor*, advised editors to take an occasional risk on a libel suit, because at the worst the paper would lose only a couple of thousand dollars.

That no longer is sound advice. While some libel judgments are for a few thousand, some these days are very large. Imagine what a copyeditor's future would be if he let his paper get socked for a million dollar bill. That award is still almost fantasy, but would any copyeditor feel secure in his future if a blunder on his part cost the paper even $5,000?

The cost of losing a libel suit is not only the judgment handed down by the court. The newspaper has to hire trial lawyers, and good ones do not come cheap. Defense attorneys have to be paid even if the newspaper wins the suit.

Two cases decided in the early sixties reveal the potential size of libel judgments these days. In one, John Henry Faulk was awarded $3.5 million after he sued Columbia Broadcasting System and AWARE, a Communist-hunting organization. AWARE had been instrumental in getting Faulk, a newscaster, blacklisted by CBS and all other networks. The judgment was cut on appeal to $550,000, but to most people, including publishers, that still is a lot of money.

The other case involved Wally Butts, athletic director at the University of Georgia. The *Saturday Evening Post* published a statement that a telephone conversation between Butts and Bear Bryant, football coach at the University of Alabama, revealed that Georgia was going to throw the football game with Alabama. The *Post* story quoted only one witness, who said he overheard the conversation by accident. Both Butts and Bryant sued. At the trial in the Butts case, no one else could corroborate the statements of the sole witness. The witness had also changed his story somewhat and, besides, his reputation was attacked. Butts was awarded $3,060,000, although this was cut to $400,000 on appeal. Bryant settled out of court for $300,000. This was one in a series of mishaps contributing to the death of the *Post*. Obviously libel today is serious, and anyone in the newsroom ought to have a good knowledge of libel law. The copyeditor especially should be as informed about libel law as is a good attorney. If his knowledge tells him something is libelous, he may lean over to the slot man and say, "This looks like dynamite to me." If the slot man agrees, they can rephrase the offending words, remove the dangerous part of the story, or ask the newspaper's lawyer for advice. In most cases the lawyer is not consulted unless the editors, hoping to run the story pretty much as written, want to be as sure as anyone can be that the story will not cost the paper a suit.

What is libelous?

It would be a relief to all newsmen if someone could give them a flat yes or no answer every time something looks libelous, but a lot of cases are borderline. Besides, one never can tell for sure what a jury will decide. When one woman sued a newspaper that reported she had given birth to a litter of pups, almost any libel expert would have said she had a clear case. The jury, however, ruled that everyone knew it was a biological impossibility for a woman to have puppies, so she lost.

Libel is usually defined as *written defamation*, and it applies also to most radio and television programs on the ground that newscasters and performers are reading from a script. But someone is sure to look at the definition of libel and object, "Newspapers and broadcasts defame people all the time." Certainly a story about a man's embezzling $10,000 at the bank ruins his reputation. And a story about a woman's being convicted of running a con game will defame her and keep her from joining the Junior League. Obviously newspapers and newscasters defame people. And they can do it legally because the law provides publishers with defenses which permit printing of certain defamations.

Three defenses

The law provides three main protections for publications printing defamatory information. In general, these legal defenses are the same in each of the fifty states and the District of Columbia. At the heart of the protection is the idea that the public has a right to know many things which are considered defamatory. So papers are given rights, or "defenses," to print such defamation. Theoretically, a person could still sue, but his lawyer would advise him that he could not win because the paper stands behind one of these three protections for the public interest:

Truth. In some states truthfulness alone is a protection. In others it has to be *truth with good motive.*

Privilege. This often is called *qualified* or *statutory* privilege because states let publications print *accurate* stories about the activities of the courts. Newspapers also may report what takes place in public bodies, like Congress or the state legislatures, and may take facts from various public records. Usually privilege does not cover juvenile courts, activities of grand juries, and lesser public bodies like school boards and village councils.

Fair Comment. A newspaper may criticize the activities of public officials and works or performances open to the public and publicly displayed, such as books, art shows, concerts, plays, athletic contests, and night club acts.

These three defenses need to be examined in some depth.

Truth

Truth, under law, is not simply what the newspaper editors believe is the truth or what someone told the newspaper is true. From a legal standpoint truth is what can be proved in court to be true. Occasionally, therefore, a journalist will say, "I know the guy is a crook, but I can't prove it." So the story about him is not printed.

Sometimes a newspaper running an investigation will get someone's promise to testify the truth of a charge in case the story ever comes to court. But suppose the trial date approaches and Mr. Witness is nowhere to be found. Because the truth cannot now be proved, a plaintiff collects a few thousand dollars and the newspaper collects experience. Instead of relying on a witness to appear in a case of libel, many papers take pains to have their sources give them affidavits to be used in case someone sues. The affidavits are sworn statements by the informants that certain assertions made by the paper are true. Newspapers even try to forestall the threat of suit by telling the readers, in effect, that they have the goods: "At least three policemen operate as bookmakers in their spare time, two former policemen *declared in affidavits signed* today." Assuming that the three accused policemen are named later in the story, they and their lawyers are forewarned that the newspaper has sworn statements for court proof.

Something true may still get the newspaper into difficulty. At the beginning of this chapter an illustrative sentence said that the mayor was a horse thief in 1919. Presumably, no reader had known this. If the story is true, one might say that the mayor could do nothing about it. But maybe he could. He could argue that while he had stolen a horse when he was sixteen years old, he had led a respectable life since. The newspaper, he could charge, was being malicious in printing a story that old. (The legal meaning of *malice* is disregard for the rights of others without legal justification.) The newspaper, on the other hand, might argue that the public had a right to know that their mayor had been a horse thief. The case might go either way in court.

Privilege

Since the rights of privilege do not, in all states, apply to *all* courts and *all* deliberations of public bodies and *all* public records, a copyeditor should be familiar with the restrictions in his own state or the states in which his newspaper circulates.

He should be aware that his accounts of committees of Congress and state legislatures are covered by privilege. The protection does not apply to closed legislative committee hearings. However, any publications issued by such committees are covered by privilege, even though the publications may be filled with material that would be libelous if printed by anyone else.

The question of privilege on the floor of the United States Senate got a workout in the early fifties, during the heyday of Senator Joseph McCarthy. The senator often declared in speeches about the country that the government, particularly the State Department, was honeycombed with Reds. On the lecture circuit he always was careful to speak in generalities and never called any government official a Red by name. If he had, he might have been sued for slander, which is oral defamation.

On the floor of the Senate, where he was protected by law, McCarthy called various people Communists. The press was able to report what McCarthy said on the Senate floor without fear of a libel suit because what was said was privileged. Often the named people dared the senator to step outside the Capitol, where his speech would not be protected, and make the same charges. He never took them up on it.

Another situation involving privilege occurred when McCarthy held a Senate subcommittee hearing in New Jersey. The hearing was closed, but afterward McCarthy held a press conference and mentioned names. The papers printed the names and one man sued. The judge ruled that the press conference was an extension of the subcommittee hearing and therefore was privileged. While this was the decision in this one court, the press should be cautious about concluding that all such press conferences would be considered privileged by all judges.

It is always advisable to remember that application and interpretation make the law flexible. The courts may rule at one time that such-and-such is the law. Within five or ten years, with a different political climate and with different evidence, fresh decisions may result in the opposite interpretation. As an illustration, many of the laws made in the forties and fifties to restrict radical political activity were invalidated by the Supreme Court within a decade or two.

Also, like the protection of privilege in many states on juvenile court proceedings, other laws are not clear. The police blotter, or record book, is a privileged document in some states, but in others either it is not or the law on the subject is fuzzy.

Once a law suit has been filed—is in the hands of the clerk of the courts—the contents of the charges are privileged. Some newspapers, however, have declined on ethical grounds to print much of anything on civil charges until the case actually comes into the courtroom. Even then, most newspapers these days print almost nothing on divorce cases. In 1967, for example, the *Louisville Courier-Journal* stopped even listing new divorce actions. There are too many divorce suits to handle, for one thing. Moreover, the angry, venal charges often used in divorce suits seem better left to the quarreling couple and the courts. And it is embarrassing to a newspaper and damaging to the persons involved to print the vile and probably exaggerated charges of one spouse against the other and then, a few days later, have to report that the suit has been withdrawn.

Before filing a lawsuit, an attorney may present *pleadings* to the judge. These are not privileged until they become part of the court record. If the case is dropped or settled in the judge's chambers, they never are opened to the public.

Any part of the trial that is removed from the court record is not privileged. If the judge rules that testimony is "stricken," the protection is taken away. The same applies when the judge "clears the court," for reporters must either leave the courtroom at such times or not print anything that happens in the court after the judge has cleared it.

No story during or preceding a trial should provide any editorial evaluation of the guilt or innocence of the accused. Stories should stick to what has been said for court record. No story should refer to a person as a "killer" or a "burglar" until he has been convicted of such crimes. Obviously, this applies to the headline as well. A person can be an *alleged* burglar, for the word alleged is a synonym for *accused* and should be used accordingly.

Some people have the mistaken idea that if the word alleged is tossed into a story, the newspaper can avoid any libel suit. What if a reporter wrote, "It is alleged that the president of the university, almost immobile from drunkenness, shouted obscenities at the Student Council president yesterday?" There would be no protection unless someone had formally accused the official of this behavior or the newspaper could prove that the report was true.

Reporters often assume that what a policeman tells them is privileged. It is not, although quoting an officer may help prove lack of malice, so any damages assessed may be less. Some papers therefore take chances and tie the phrase "police said" to some defamations.

An arrest, however, is privileged. Nevertheless, it is worth being cautious about. Police may get a little overzealous and arrest people for insufficient cause. So an officer, in the midst of some excitement, may reach out and tell someone he is under arrest. The someone may be the vice president of a university. The newspaper might print a story of the arrest, only to find that while the presses were running the vice president had been taken to the police station and quickly released, with personal and profuse apologies from the desk sergeant, the chief of police, the mayor, and, of course, the arresting officer. The privilege might not hold up now, on the grounds that the vice president was not really considered arrested by the police.

Cautious editors print news of arrests only after an *information*, or preliminary charge, is written out at the police station. This precaution applies especially to mass "arrests" when police will sometimes shove a hundred people into paddy wagons, tell them they are under arrest, take them to a remote police station, and release them. Unless a reporter follows through to see that there is an official record of an arrest, a policeman can deny later, after publication, that a man had been arrested. A denial without a written *information* could leave the paper in a bad spot.

Fair comment

Sarcastic and sardonic play reviews flourished in the thirties and early forties. Reviewers struggled to have something snide and devastating to say about at least one performer, if not the whole cast. That approach to play reviewing spilled over into reviews of books, music, and art. The exaggeration and the strained efforts to be cleverly derogatory may be less common today, but editors still must know where to draw the line.

It is legal to pan a play or performance in exaggerated language. The law provides that anything written about the *performance*, including how the person looked while performing, is protected by what is known as "fair comment and criticism." The only qualification is that the writing not be malicious.

One case that has amused law and journalism students for decades concerned a 1901 newspaper review in Odebolt, Iowa. The reviewer covered the stage performance of a singing trio known as the Cherry Sisters. Since horses were common in 1901, the reviewer chose to use equine terms, knowing his audience would appreciate them:

> Effie is an old jade of 50 summers, Jessie a frisky filly of 40 and Addie, the flower of the family, a capering monstrosity of 35. Their long skinny arms, equipped with

> talons at the extremities, swung mechanically, and anon waved frantically at the suffering audience. The mouths of their rancid features opened like caverns and sounds like the wailings of damned souls issued therefrom. They pranced around the stage with a motion that suggested a cross between the danse du ventre and fox trot, strange creatures with painted faces and hideous mien. Effie is spavined, Addie is stringhalt, and Jessie, the only one who showed her stockings, has legs with calves as classic in their outlines as the curves of a broom handle.

Effie brought suit and lost. As plaintiff (the one bringing the action), she appealed, but appellate court ruled against her: "Viewing the evidence in the light of the rules heretofore announced, and remembering that the trial court had the plaintiff before it and saw her repeat some of the performances given by her on stage, we are of the opinion that there was *no* error in directing a verdict for the defendants."

A copyeditor must make sure, however, that a review does not deal derogatorily with the performer's private life, such as drinking habits, sex life, and political views. These are considered by law to be a person's own business—until he makes them public business by something like getting arrested for drunkenness.

It is almost taken for granted that the press can criticize public officials with impunity. But newspapers cannot report their private lives under the protection of fair comment, so any report on private activity would have to be defended by proof that the report was true. Some public officials, notably the President, have virtually no private life, so criticism of practically anything they or their families do is allowed by custom, though ethics and taste restrain well-edited papers.

The public figure doctrine

In recent years the courts have ruled that certain inaccuracies or falsehoods about *public figures* may be printed safely. The landmark decision on this subject was handed down in 1964 by the United States Supreme Court in *New York Times* vs. *Sullivan*. Some three million dollars in judgments had been assessed against the *Times* in behalf of various Alabama figures, including Governor Patterson and four Montgomery city officials. One of the officials was L.B. Sullivan, commissioner of public affairs and thereby head of the police department. The judgments had been obtained because a full page advertisement, placed by a civil rights group, had appeared in the *Times*. The ad said that during a demonstration at Alabama State College police had "ringed" the campus, student leaders been expelled, the "entire" student body had shown their protest by refusing to register for classes, the campus dining hall had been padlocked.

A substantial number of these statements were not true. For example, nine students were expelled, but for demanding service at a downtown lunch counter. The dining hall never was padlocked, and the police did not "ring" the campus.

The Supreme Court ruling tried the question of malice:

> The constitutional guarantees require, we think, a Federal rule that prohibits a public official from recovering damages for a defamatory falsehood relating to his official conduct unless he proves that the statement was made with "actual malice"—that is, with the knowledge that it was false or with reckless disregard of whether it was false or not.[1]

The *public figure* rule has been decisive in other libel cases. The question that faces editors, however, is what constitutes a public figure. Obviously, the President, a senator, a famous football player, or a noted actor is a public figure. But what about a relatively well-known professor? What about a member of the school board? Are they well enough known to be considered public figures?

There are other tough questions. How incorrect can the news stories be if the public figure defense can be used? How reckless is reckless? Can a newspaper say that Senator Glotzenschlubber beats his wife every other Tuesday? Can a story say that Alderman Leddhedd goes out every Saturday night on a wild binge, when in truth he sticks to sarsaparilla?

No one knows for sure where the borderline is between a public figure and a non-public figure. No one knows how erroneous the stories may be before a newspaper gets in water so hot that the public figure plea won't cool it. Courts define individual, not general, cases.

If a copyeditor sets out to find just where the borderline is, he may find his paper in court. Sticking to the provable facts about anyone is the best way to stay out of trouble. The fact that something is legal is no cause for being sloppy with facts or careless with reputations. A loose newspaper is in no position to recommend virtue to anyone else. If a paper sticks to what the editors think is the truth and makes a mistake, it can use the public figure defense with ethical justification.

Classes of libel

Per se *and* per quod

Libel comes under two main headings: *per se* and *per quod*. Libel *per se* can be translated as "libel on the face of it." To be called a Communist when one is not a Communist has been considered libel *per se* for some years.* The plaintiff would have to bring little into court except the offending newspaper clipping to prove his point. Libel *per quod* is the opposite. One must know the circumstances to determine the defamation. In other words, the plaintiff has to prove that his reputation was damaged. If the court decides that he was defamed, it has to decide how much money he needs to make up for the damage to his reputation.

In two historic cases, the plaintiffs did not want money. All they sought was a ruling by the court that they had been libeled. Theodore Roosevelt settled for a one cent judgment. Henry Ford was less restrained. He took six times as much.

* A federal appeals court in 1966 held that a white businessman was libeled when he was called a "bigot."

Civil and criminal

Libel is almost always a civil dispute. That is, it is a wrong being argued by two people. (Corporations are treated by law as persons.) No jail or prison terms are involved, unless of course the person adjudged guilty of libel does not pay the judgment.

Criminal libel does exist, but it is rare. To get a criminal libel verdict the court would have to rule that a publication has committed a crime *against society.* In such instances, the newspaper story is held to have been so inflammatory that a segment of society riots, storms city hall, or tries to blow up the newspaper plant itself. In recent decades the idea that a newspaper could produce a riot was remote and the threat of this type of libel academic; but if revolutionary ideas gain ground in the seventies, editors may have to take care not to rub the raw nerves of activists of either right or left.

Everything counts

All journalists should be aware that the newspaper is responsible for *everything* it prints: news stories, headlines, features, comics, advertisements, editorials, letters to the editor, and pictures. Aside from the question of malice, quoting someone else on a defamation —such as the superintendent of schools or a policeman—does not enable a newspaper to avoid a charge of libel. It does not save the newspaper any responsibility if it is someone's signed letter in the paper that contains the defamation. Neither is there any help if the libel is in a paid advertisement. It is no relief, either, to have some letter writer say, "I will stand behind it." Don't bet on it. The paper may be assessed, say, $20,000 damages and run up a $10,000 legal bill defending itself. In addition, it may lose the confidence of its readers. Is the letter writer who says he will be responsible ready to cough up $30,000? Editors might cool off demands from hot-headed readers by saying, only slightly facetiously, "Would you put up a $50,000 bond just in case we get sued for libel?" At the mere thought of such a sum most letter writers would throw their libelous prose into the waste basket—or at least cross out the offending phrases.

Editors and reporters are often threatened with libel suits. A news source occasionally will shout, "If you print that, I'll sue you for libel!" Actually it is clear that he doesn't have the slightest idea of what constitutes libel. So the newsman either ignores the threat or gives an ironic rejoinder. If the threats are based on ignorance, as most of them are, the journalist can take a few minutes to explain why the story is either not libelous or not actionable. If this isn't satisfactory, the journalist can suggest that the source consult a lawyer. A substantial number of people assume that they can tell a newspaper what to leave out, or to put in, and successfully sue if the paper disregards their orders.

In any case the journalist is smart to keep calm, although that goes against a long newspaper tradition. To maintain good public relations for the newspaper, staffers should be gentle in handling the irate people who dread exposure in print for their real or imagined sins.

Escape routes

While truth, fair comment, privilege, and, to some extent, public figures are defenses against libel, there are several other ways that a libel suit can be voided.

Statute of limitations. The suit must be brought within a specified time after the offending material was printed. In most states this is one year. If the plaintiff brings suit 366 days after the story appeared, no suit.

Out-of-court settlement. If a newspaper agrees out of court that it libeled someone, and pays a certain sum of money, that act wipes out any chance of a suit.

Consent. This rarely occurs, but if a reporter showed a news source a story or recited to him the facts or charges that were going to be in the story and the source made no objection, the court assumes he "consented" to them.

Once a publication gets embroiled in a libel suit its publisher, editors, and lawyers have to figure how to get out. In many instances there is no real way out. What the publication then tries to do is show that it tried to mitigate the effects of the defamation as soon as it became aware of its error.

The best evidence of mitigation is a *retraction*. The most effective retractions appear in about as prominent a position in the paper as the libel did. If the libel appeared in a banner headline on page one, the retraction would at least have to be in a prominent position on the front page.

These other proofs of the newspaper's good faith *may* help:

—The offending story was omitted or "cleaned up" in later editions.

—An honest effort was made to retrieve the papers which included the libel. For example, if the libel was noticed ten minutes after the press run was started, the paper would have called back the delivery trucks which had left the building.

—The libelous information had been copied by error.

—The information came from a normally reliable source, such as a police chief or a judge.

—The information was "common knowledge." This claim refers to what "everyone knows." As an illustration, a gangster may never have been convicted of anything, but it is "common knowledge" that he is a gangster.

—The newspaper had used normal precautions. This would require evidence that the paper had double-checked the facts before printing them.

—There were persistent and public rumors about the case.

—The staffers were provoked into the publication, or they printed the statement in a campaign so intense that judgment was swayed.

—The plaintiff can be proved to have a bad reputation.

—There was a "prior article"—that is, the story was printed before and the plaintiff had not complained.

Watchwords

Garrett Redmond, an official of a company selling libel insurance, has said that for years the main cause of suits has been careless crime reporting—of names, addresses, or size of crime. So the copyeditor must particularly watch stories involving crime and the courts. As we said earlier, it is easy for a reporter, as mentioned, to refer to "the killer" instead of "the alleged killer"—he is not a killer, legally, until convicted. Sometimes police catch a person red-handed in a criminal act. To be on the safe side the story had better not say, "Joe Johnson was caught breaking into the McTavish warehouse."

The copyeditor must be especially careful when a story touches a woman's reputation. The courts may not be much concerned by a story hinting that a man was philandering. But even though mores are fast changing, to say the same thing about a woman might still get a newspaper into considerable trouble.

Picture cutlines or even placement of pictures can provide grounds for libel. If a sheriff and an alleged criminal are pictured together and the cutlines switch identification, one or both might sue. Also, if a cut runs next to a story so that readers assume they go together, there may be grounds for action.

Implications and insinuations have to be watched with great care. The plaintiff can establish a good case by bringing only two or three people into court to testify that they inferred something defamatory from something the paper printed.

Not naming individuals in stories may be no protection. It is what readers believe is being said that counts. When a column in a college newspaper denounced a football player, but not by name, several readers, at least, thought the column referred to a certain player who had been accused of a serious crime. Actually, the columnist had meant someone else, but the person who some people thought was mentioned might have collected.

As a rule, a group cannot be libeled. It would be hard to convince a jury that something defamatory about a sizable group really applied to every member of the group. A rule of thumb is that the larger the group, the harder to libel. But this depends to some extent on how emotional the public is about the organization. A magazine once implied that University of Oklahoma football players came off the field and squirted dope into their noses. Some of the players sued, claiming that they had shot a peppermint solution into their mouths to relieve dryness. The Oklahoma Supreme Court agreed that the magazine should be relieved of $75,000, which was distributed among some sixty players. The same implications might, perhaps, have been made safely about another large group, say, the

Oklahoma marching band. Because band fans are fewer and less excitable than football fans, a court would probably be reluctant to see such an implication as doing an individual harm.

A few other points on libel should be considered:

The dead cannot be libeled, for the simple reason that they can no longer suffer from slights to their reputations. A suit could be filed by the dead person's heirs, but they would have to prove specific injury to themselves, such as loss of income. It is possible, although unlikely, that criminal libel could occur over defamation of the dead.

The newspaper is safe to print charges once they are actually filed at the courthouse, as they have started through the judicial process. But a story had better not report the gist of written charges casually dropped by a lawyer on a desk in the county clerk's office.

A report on what people told a grand jury would not be considered actionable. But since the operations of the grand jury are secret, the presiding judge might decide the newspaper, or its reporters, are in contempt of court. For that, one can go to jail.

Executive acts are considered privileged, but it is safer to get them in writing than to quote them as given verbally. If the mayor tells a reporter that he fired the police chief "for moral turpitude," it would be helpful if the newspaper could get a copy of the letter dismissing the chief. The copy could be saved, in case the chief sues.

Copyeditors should be suspicious of irony. A story that says, "George Zarfoss went to Boston to visit Mrs. Esmerelda Fisher, a 'friend,'" almost asks for a suit by Mr. Zarfoss or Mrs. Fisher, or both.

Damages

Once a plaintiff wins a libel suit, the court may award one, two, or three kinds of damages:

General. No proof of injury has to be submitted. These are simply presumed, without evidence, to have resulted from injured feelings or humiliation.

Special. The plaintiff proves specific injury. The actual pecuniary loss is assessed. Some statutes refer, in fact, to "actual damages."

Punitive. The court grants a cash award as punishment. Such damages may be quite high, to discourage the editors from libelling again. (Punitive awards, by the way, are taxable. The other are not.)

Privacy

The laws about privacy are fairly new and have not been widely tested in the courts. There has been growing concern, however, about invasions of privacy by the government, particularly with electronic snooping devices. The press has come in for its share of criticism, too, and some of it has been justified. Some newsmen have the idea that anything they want to find or photograph is fair game, never considering if the picture or story could cause unnecessary anguish.

At one time it would have been enough for an editor to remind reporters and photographers to avoid the keyhole and the transom. But now a substantial number of people have begun to file privacy suits over photographs taken almost routinely. Someone who stood still for a picture taken by a photographer who explained that it would appear in a certain newspaper may sue, claiming the paper invaded his privacy in publishing the picture. Many such suits were filed in Appalachia, which in the late sixties was one of the favorite grounds for "depth reporting of social problems" by reporters and photographers. Some poor people thought that the pictures of themselves or their children were unflattering and charged that the photographs held them up to public scorn.

This development caused some newspapers to get signed permission to publish a picture from almost anyone photographed in the area. It is likely that there will be more such privacy suits. Editors must now take special care about pictures that may hurt the feelings of their subjects. Such care applies especially to the posed photograph or the picture taken casually in a non-public place. The law is quite clear that a picture taken at random in public—on the street, at a football game or political rally—does not invade privacy; the individual has already put himself on public display by appearing in public.

Where privacy may be involved, the newspaper editor is wise to focus on newsworthiness, not sensation. Invading privacy simply to entertain or titillate is dangerous as well as unethical. In court newsworthiness is a defense for invasion of privacy just as truth is for libel. News facts from the public record, for example, would be privileged, as would facts about a public figure. These and five similar guidelines are listed by Don R. Pember in "Privacy and the Press: the Defense of Newsworthiness," a discussion useful to the editor desiring more information about this developing body of law.[2] "The press must remember," concludes Pember, "that when it is called into court in a privacy suit it is the judge or jury who will decide what is and what is not news."

As in several other legal problems involving the press, the copyeditor must become reasonably well-acquainted with the privacy laws of his state. His state press association may have the material in booklet form, and a few minutes' reading may save his newspaper thousands of dollars.

Lotteries

Most newspapers mail at least a few copies of every edition and therefore take note of postal regulations. Most important of these for copyeditors is the ban on stories or advertisements about lotteries.

Any newspaper reader can object that he has seen lots of stories about lotteries. True. New York and New Hampshire even have state lotteries, and papers throughout the country have run stories about them.

The post office allows newspapers to cover lotteries if the news value is great enough. Also, the editor can naturally print stories on gambling in home editions which do not enter the mail. So if a nice old lady in town wins a bushel full of money in the Irish Sweepstakes, the paper will probably print the story. But an editor had better not run news about Mrs. Nellie Blotz winning a four-pound chicken at a raffle.

While the post office forbids news or advertising of lotteries, except as noted, in the past, at least, there has been no real penalty if the regulation was violated once. Presumably the post office department assumes—probably correctly—that those who violated the regulation once did so out of ignorance. A letter of mild reprimand is sent to the publisher. It is clear, however, that the post office could and probably would do more if the offense were repeated. To be on the safe side, copyeditors should scrutinize a lottery story to see that it has genuine news value.

Of lesser concern to the editors of family newspapers are the postal regulations that forbid mailing obscene printed material. The drawings and four-letter words that the courts, at least until recently, have ruled pornographic have appeared in books or magazines or "underground" papers. But, by comparison, the content of dailies is mild and not actionable.

Copyright

As the law stands, a published work can be copyrighted for twenty-eight years, and this copyright can be extended for another twenty-eight years. While nearly all books and magazines are copyrighted, few newspapers take the trouble and expense. The copyeditor's concern with copyright is to avoid reprinting copyrighted material without permission from the publisher. Some newspapers, particularly small ones, do often reprint without permission material from copyrighted magazines, books, and other newspapers. In most cases the owner of the copyrighted material throws up his hands and says, "What can I do? It would cost me a thousand dollars of someone's time to get even an apology from the bum. So I'll let it go." Meanwhile, the unscrupulous editor steals editorials, articles, and cartoons without pushing any one source to legal action—and without having the courtesy to tell his readers where he steals them.

It should be noted that relatively few papers indulge in this kind of thievery. Those that do usually pick on the small magazines, ones with no legal staff, time, nor money to fight copyright violation. Thievery from a big magazine, like *Life* or *Look*, is a different matter. Those magazines are able to go to court for copyright violation and get a good-sized judgment, so their articles are rarely stolen. Thieves also know that many people would have read the original article—and thus know that the material was stolen.

A newspaper occasionally will copyright a single story, usually something special like the result of some outstanding investigative work by the staff. The copyright also lets the paper print the story before the news is given to AP, if it is a member. AP or UPI may rewrite the story and, though quoting only a little of the original language, mention the source; then the originating newspaper enjoys the national publicity.

A rule of thumb on reprinting copyrighted material is that 50 words may be quoted directly without getting permission. This is arbitrary to some extent. Obviously, a book publisher would be delighted if a newspaper quoted 300 words—and contributed to the sale of the book. Yet some author may object to the paper's use of 27 words. The best principle is to quote copyrighted material sparingly and always with credit to the author.

Modern copying machines have brought new problems in enforcement of the copyright law. It is easy for someone on a campus, for example, to make bootleg reprints of several pages from a book. It is almost impossible for the publisher to catch anyone at this.

Because of this development, and other problems, Congress has been trying for several years to write new copyright laws. It seems likely that any new law will give greater protection to copyrighted material and provide greater penalties for violation of copyright. The aim, of course, would be to deter bootlegging of copyrighted work.

13 Ethics for newsmen

A rasping voice on the police radio near the city desk announces at 11:38 P.M. that a car has smashed into a utility pole off Hathaway Boulevard. Moments later the sirens of an ambulance from City Hospital scream by below the newsroom. The city editor dispatches a reporter, and within minutes the facts begin to fit into the mosaic of a story. Editors start making decisions, of space, display—and ethics.

The driver, in "critical" condition with a possible concussion, is Oscar Ragsdeal, forty-eight years old, according to the police. His address checks out in the city directory, which lists him as an administrative vice president of First National Bank. Good story. There were two in the car, the second hospitalized in "fair" condition. The police are working on the identification.

So far there appear to be no serious problems. Straight-forward story: serious accident, prominent man, maybe two—probably front page and no argument. But then the ethical complications begin.

The reporter at the hospital calls again with details on the skid and says he is still trying to get the girl's name.

A woman?—probably Mrs. Ragsdeal. Unlikely, the reporter says, because this girl is in her late twenties. Oh yes, he adds, there were a couple of broken whiskey bottles in the wreckage. "Looks like Oscar had something going," says the cynical newsman—but that is his personal, not his professional editorial comment.

The injured woman turns out to be Mrs. Sally Hinslaw, twenty-eight, who has been working in a First National branch since the death of Captain Hinslaw in Vietnam. Ragsdeal is the brother of the Ragsdeal who is advertising manager of the big department store at the corner. The women's editor reminds the city editor that Mrs. Hinslaw is the one who is such a close friend of their publisher's second daughter, in the Junior League and all; yes, these are the Hinslaws of the old mining family who are always in the parties reported on the women's page.

Should the editor print the story?

This fiction brings into focus many of the most important pressures on an editor's ethics: the chance for a big headline and bigger sales. The right of Mr. Ragsdeal and Mrs. Hinslaw to be left alone. The rights of Mrs. Ragsdeal, and of any Ragsdeal and Hinslaw children, to be spared embarrassment. Advertising to be lost from the store and maybe the bank. A segment of the power structure unhappy about the publicizing of social scandal. And not least, the possible displeasure of the publisher himself.

Maybe the editor should forget the whole thing. But what will television do with it? And how will he settle his newsman's conscience, which tells him he lives to print the news, not suppress it?

The intelligent editor must think out a consistent ethical policy to guide him through such thickets. An editor with one policy will see the Ragsdeal piece as a sensational bonanza worth giving the titillating works to the limit of the libel laws. A more moralistic editor might give the story almost as much space and detail, but on an eye-for-an-eye theory that if Mr. Ragsdeal and Mrs. Hinslaw are going to cut capers, they must pay in public. If God made or let the accident happen, who is the editor to interfere with the world's knowing? Still another approach would be to print the news dead-pan, fairly and accurately, and let the reader make his own moral judgments.

One catch-phrase of ethical coverage is "All the news that's fit to print." That slogan was introduced into a front-page ear (upper corner) of the *New York Times* by Adolph S. Ochs, the publisher who brought the *Times* to greatness. It was 1897, when other New York City newspapers were vying in sensationalism, and Ochs used the phrase to emphasize the thoroughness and sobriety of ethical newspapering.

The cynic may say that the slogan should be "All the news that fits"—or that fits the editor's whims. Everyone knows that *all* the news can't be printed. But "all the news" implies a thoroughness which will not omit stories because of laziness or pressure. "Fit" implies that the editors will avoid sensationalism or pandering to low tastes. Yet they should find it fitting for the public to know what happens, however distasteful or terrifying, and regardless of pressures to leave out some events.

Some such principle would guide most good editors in the Ragsdeal accident. Newsmen of equal integrity might disagree about what to say about those whiskey bottles and how far to dig into the time and cause of Captain Hinslaw's death. But they would print a plain, factual account of the crash, the injuries, and the condition of the victim.

Freedom and responsibility

Some editors might say that what they print is their own business and not the province of philosophers. They would be right, in the sense that a free press is guaranteed by the Constitution, and that professional customs in the United States have evolved for handling these ethical questions. Mores probably control more stories than editorial ethics. Yet there are philosophical and even theological bases for the rights of newspapers to operate as they do, and publishers ignore these at their peril. Society has given newsmen wide latitude for their operations and decisions, but what society grants, society can take away. The number of totalitarian countries in this century should be a reminder that press freedom is not automatic.

In the days of medieval kings, there would have been no argument of whether it was right or wrong to publish news of a scandal, even if there had been printing presses and editors. The monarch felt he had authority from God to make such decisions. A long trail of Star Chambers and jailed editors led from such dictatorship to a modern democratic system in which editors, within the framework of law, can print without license or censorship. Men at first argued, as in the Declaration of Independence, that they had such inalienable rights from God; more recently, it is claimed as an essential human right. The willingness of men to suffer and even die for this freedom is still the ultimate test of its survival.

John Milton provided the practical argument for press freedom. In the *Areopagitica* (1644) he argued for the "free marketplace of ideas." If all ideas were freely published, he said, the best ones would win out. It followed that men must have the right to know all the facts and arguments. So he rationalized the editor's freedom as one of the prerequisites for a working democracy. Thomas Jefferson argued for the citizen's right to the truth—being optimistic, like Milton, that a benevolent Providence allowed reasonable and moral men to run their own affairs. His idea of press freedom became one of the guarantees in the Bill of Rights.

But it is a truism that freedom implies responsibility. Those who get liberty must use it responsibly or risk losing it, whether in a developing nation or on a college campus. The grant of freedom to editors to purvey the news necessary to a democratic society carries the implied demand that they will print the news. When the press suppresses or distorts the news, it jeopardizes its claim to freedom. The unwritten expectation of American citizens is that the papers will give "all the news that's fit to print." This is the ethical imperative under which editors work.

Watchwords for ethics

Recognizing these obligations, publishers sometimes proclaim idealistic platforms or policies. At conventions they are especially prone to make the welkin ring with fine phrases. A major statement of high principle became the "Canons of Journalism," adopted by the American Society of Newspaper Editors when it organized in 1923. This code states that the "opportunities [of journalism] as a chronicler are indissolubly linked [to] its obligations as teacher and interpreter." The canons speak of "sincerity, truthfulness, accuracy," of "clear distinction between news reports and expressions of opinion" of "fair play." But they had no teeth and, while mentioned in journalism histories, are now almost forgotten. Few working newsmen could quote a single canon.

The difficulty is that, like democracy, freedom, and responsibility, principles of journalism must be stated as abstractions. Pessimists can readily dismiss pledges of *public interest* or *high trust* as pious hypocrisies. The problem is to relate high-sounding dictums to hard cases; and since no paper and no man is perfect, there are inevitably some tarnishes on the best papers, not to mention the corrosions of the worst.

Still, an effort must be made to set standards for the press. If such moral principles as love, compassion, and kindness are given lip service rather than devotion, they serve still as ideals or goals. Newspapermen need such abstractions to broaden their vision.

Truth is the word that summarizes many journalistic ideals. But what, philosophy has always asked, is truth? The working newspaperman knows well enough what truth means in his situation and doesn't worry too much about Truth. He checks the truth of small details but also the truth of the big picture, so far as he can discover and portray it.

One important facet of truth therefore is *accuracy*. Newsrooms rightly make a fetish of accuracy about names and addresses. But reporters must be at least as careful about accurate quotation, or about the accuracy of the impression which results from the way facts are put together.

Close to accuracy is *objectivity*. The reporter should keep himself out of the story, and the editors should see that he does. The conventional wisdom of the profession dictates that editoralizing will be confined to editorial pages, yet editorializing barbs in stories are always slipping by copydesks. The authors know two or three reporters who produce "stories" that are really editorials, and their editors, with sloppy ethics, by-line them and print them in the news pages. The editor's job is to see that copy is accurate and free of editorial bias, whether it comes from a cub or a Washington or foreign correspondent of a famous press service.

The popular dichotomy of objectivity versus interpretation represents a misunderstanding of the journalist's problem with truth. The short dead-pan news account, the so-called objective story, the feature story, and the interpretive piece are all on one side of objectivity. Opposite them is the subjective story by the reporter who has, knowingly or unknowingly, distorted the news, whether of a minor accident or of international conflict. The sound interpretive story introduces the writer's evaluations (and these are admittedly subjective, with personal coloring), but as fairly and honestly—as objectively—as he can. The corrupt interpretation, by contrast, does not aim at truth but vents the writer's prejudices and slants. (Editorials and editorial-page interpretations are something else again, differing from news stories as oranges differ from apples.)

Intertwined with accuracy and the objective search for it is the concept of *fairness*. Human limitations may prevent a paper's being really accurate and really objective (the words are relative, no matter what grammarians may say), but readers know whether the editors try to be fair. They treat everybody alike. Ideally, they are as gentle with the poor unknown as with the big shot, with the hated political party or enemy nation as with their own faction or country. Perceptive critics of the press see that it is the standard of fairness that is violated when papers blandly print in their news columns accounts which refer to "Huns," "Japs," "Commies," "Birchers," "peaceniks," and so on; the editor may protest that such highly connotative words communicate accurately in some social moods—but are they ever fair?

Keeping the watchwords

Accuracy and fairness are often threatened by pressures on the editor. Pressures from government he understands and can combat. But many critics feel editors are less successful in combatting pressure from advertisers. In an interpretive piece, the *Wall Street Journal* went so far as to say that "many once-principled newsmen have been deeply demoralized by their papers' surrender to advertisers' interest." The paper cited a study by Prof. Timothy Hubbard of the University of Missouri revealing the ideas of 162 business and financial editors who responded to a questionnaire. More than one-fifth of them said that "as a matter of routine they were compelled to puff up or alter and downgrade business stories at the request of the advertisers."

The threat of unequal or unfair treatment is thus often seen as one of special favors to advertisers or establishment figures; so publishers and editors may underscore their pledge to print "without fear or favor" by publishing unfavorable news of themselves. The staff of one newspaper long told how a divorce of the publisher's had been printed on the front page. The staff saw that the standard of judgment was not simply the publisher's or editor's personal attitude toward the news but a standard of fair, full coverage. Similarly, the former publisher of the *Pascagoula* (Miss.) *Chronicle* tells how he finally convinced detractors that his was "an honest newspaper printing the news without favor":

> My son Maybin, 14, ran afoul of the law and was hailed into juvenile court. My practice had been to use the names of juveniles in police stories only if the youngsters were repeated offenders or if their crimes were heinous. My son's offense was minor, but his name appeared in a page-one story I wrote myself. He not only was named but was identified as "son of Ira Harkey, *Chronicle* editor-publisher," so there could be no mistake.[1]

The ideals of accuracy, objectivity, and fairness are all contained in the larger ideal of truth. But are these really phony ideals, used to delude, as hypocrites use flag and motherhood? Some hard-bitten cynics among newspaper editors would doubtless say "yes," and their shoddy papers reveal what happens when principle crumbles. Yet even the most ethical editors tend to be pragmatic about high journalistic principle. Pragmatism is an American philosophy that holds that the best way is the way that works best. Americans are idealistic, but they are also practical. So our editors do not usually mount white chargers. They conform.

When the whole American society preaches that killing is wrong but sends its youth abroad to kill and be killed, when it preaches brotherhood but remains calloused about the hurt suffered by many Negro families, it is not remarkable that this society generates publishers and editors who preach the democratic canons but violate them in practice. They make practical compromises.

The realistic goal for the ethical newsman is to compromise as little as possible, for being pragmatic is not the same as being venal or cowardly. The best editors aim high and therefore hit higher than those who aim low.

Pluralistic foundations

Why is thorough news coverage better than slipshod, or an honest newspaper better than a dishonest one? The answer is self-evident to most of us only because it is woven well into the basic fabric of our philosophical and religious thinking. For there is no more general agreement in America on moral than on political issues. The intellectual problem of ethical journalism is rooted in the pluralistic nature of American society. Some Americans think, at least part of the time, as Christians, others as Jews, a few as Moslems or Hindus, while many eschew religion entirely. Of course some, including certain editors, worship only money or power. What is "right" by one standard is not necessarily right by another.

For example, some church people feel that newspapers should not mention gambling, yet others see nothing wrong if stories promote their bingo parties. One group of Christians wants thorough press discussion on liberalizing divorce or abortion laws; another group deplores it. But the clashes among our pluralistic segments are much more profound than suggested by these so-called moralistic issues. The deep differences among our world views condition the sharp variations in reactions on such questions as America's responsibility to peoples of the world, the proper response to Communism, the sacredness of human life, the relativity of moral values, and the ability of human beings to plan their own destiny. The role of the mass media is not the least of these major issues on which thoughtful Americans can have profoundly different views.

To understand and cope with these differences, we should understand two strands of American thought: first, the religious, or, more specifically, the Judeo-Christian; and second, the philosophical, particularly the pragmatic and utilitarian. We shall then turn to two strands of democratic thought: traditional concern for liberty and individual freedom and this century's growing emphasis on equality and social justice. Throughout, our purpose is to clarify our society's pre-suppositions so that editors may recognize the assumptions behind their practical decisions.

Christian backgrounds

The Puritan roots of American culture suggest Judeo-Christian ethics as an appropriate beginning in consideration of journalistic ethics. The approach can provide insight, even though there is little agreement on what the Judeo-Christian tradition would require. For example, journalistic morality in an Augustinian City of God would be one thing, in Mao's China another. The colonial New England theocracy did provide an official morality, but that church-led day vanished about 1700. The question is whether this strand in pluralistic thought leads to answers for the U.S. press today.

In this context "Christian" goodness may be considered as referring to kindness, generosity, compassion—in a word, love. It is the virtue extolled in the parable of the Good Samaritan and assumed in the Golden Rule. We saw in chapter 6 that editors cannot print the news with a philosophy of doing unto others as he would have done unto him. Much of the hard news in the paper deals with the wrongdoing or tragedy of people, and an editor cannot start leaving it out because he would shrink from seeing his own troubles in print.

An editor sometimes prints unpleasant news about someone by reasoning that he would print the item about himself because society deserves all the significant news. This rationale is close to that of the publishers who print unfavorable news about themselves or their families, in proof of fairness. But with this argument one is moving already from the Golden Rule of Christian love to the toughness of Christian justice.

The Golden Rule has bite because it is highly personal. The philosopher Immanuel Kant extended the Golden Rule to society: act so your actions can become a universal rule. His dictum incorporates both love and justice but diminishes personal involvement. It mediates Christian love to society and therefore helps the decision-making newsman.

Prof. Richard T. Baker of the Graduate School of Journalism, Columbia University, touches on the strand of justice in Christian thought by observing that "even the truth is not enough" for the journalist. Writing in *The Christian As a Journalist*, Professor Baker says:

> You should have extraordinary contributions to bring to your profession as an instrument for a more just society. You should know with precision when and how and where to throw the weight of your journal into the tactical struggles for fairness in human relations. You should not be cynical and defeated by the tragedies of injustice.[2]

The *Christian Science Monitor* takes this challenge seriously. This paper handles the news in a way consistent with its religiously optimistic point of view.

The utilitarian approach

Aside from Judeo-Christian principles, another widely held ethic promotes "the greatest good for the greatest number." As developed by Jeremy Bentham and John Stuart Mill, utilitarianism argues that good conduct is that which produces the greatest happiness for the most people. By dealing in quantities, utilitarianism appeals to the practical-minded. Another advantage of this concept of greatest-good is its democratic flavor. Milton and Jefferson argued for the freedom of the press as aid to the common reason; utilitarianism applies that freedom to the common good. While religious thought has proclaimed the sacredness of the individual personality, here is philosophy that rationalizes majorities and big circulations.

But for newspaper work this ethic, like the Golden Rule, has its difficulties. There is a practical problem in deciding what really is good for the most people. Can one be sure that the value to the public in printing the name of a rape victim is greater than the hurt to the girl—or vice versa? How, in fact, do you weigh such things? Yet an editor can feel "greatest good" does help him weigh.

This suggests a perhaps still greater problem: the tyranny of the majority. Do the masses, just because they possess numbers, have an inalienable right to news whose publication will hurt a smaller group? Or, on the contrary, would a majority "vote" for suppression of news justify keeping the facts from a minority, simply because less good (arithmetically figured) appears to be involved?

Editors who print news of wrongdoing as well as progress, who publish a lot of comics and sports, and who perhaps circulate sensational accounts of sex and violence can rationalize that they are utilitarian. In fact, when they are criticized, the reflex of many editors is utilitarian; they say they are giving the public (presumably, the greatest number) what it wants. The very self-righteousness of such contentions, however, underscores the limitation of this philosophy: editors adhering to it too literally may slight the good of the cultured minority with higher taste than the masses, of the politically sophisticated minority jaded by the banalities of mass campaigns, and of the intellectual minority needing the free exchange of ideas and contributing to the real good of society.

To apply utilitarian theory most usefully, therefore, editors must consider the "greatest number of people" not as stupid, faceless masses but as groups of important, reasonable, individuals. Then the editor may justify overruling the restraints of religiously-motivated goodwill and print what he feels serves the greatest social good.

Rights and responsibilities

The Golden Rule and the rule of greatest-good do not exhaust the list which could be developed in a pluralistic society. Nor is balancing these two the only way to deal with the ethical problems of newspapering. If we approach the problem now from different theoretical vantage points, we get new slants on the tensions and balances ever present in editorial decisions.

The authors of *Four Theories of the Press* construct a framework important to any modern consideration of journalistic ethics.[3] The two most pertinent concepts for us are the libertarian theory and the social responsibility theory. (The other two theories are the authoritarian and the Communist, which bear only indirectly on our discussion of American journalism.)

Libertarian theory

Libertarian theory emphasizes the freedom of the newspaper editor. As we have said, this concept, developed by such men as Milton and Jefferson, opposes the autocrat's power to license and censor. It holds that editors should have liberty to print what they please (restrained only by such necessary laws as discussed in the chapter on press law). The assumption is that one journalist or another will dig out and print what the people ought to have.

The optimism of this theory may seem naive because of the horrible events of the last century and pessimistic intellectual trends since Darwin and Freud. Can men really discover through reason what is best? Many youth today, however, are starry-eyed about man's nature and here, curiously, go along with the assumptions of many of their elders. It is no doubt this tradition of hopefulness about men that most American editors embrace. They oppose government interference and control in the hope that common men will find the truth in what is printed.

This libertarian concept has its aspect of social good, a fact that is often overlooked. Selfishness is not part of the theory but part of the men who work under the theory. Editors—sinful, or at least as limited, as other men—have often abused this freedom; they have printed scurrilous political attacks, exaggerated and faked the news, scandalmongered, and pandered to the cheapest tastes. Before he died Jefferson himself was strongly impelled towards second thoughts about the virtue of editorial freedom. Yet according to the theory, out of the welter of what editors print will emerge the knowledge John Citizen needs for intelligent action. To work today, the theory requires reasonable printing costs and competition unrestricted by press monopolies. Then even those who are most hard-headedly realistic about the difficulties of opening the market-place to all ideas may still logically contend that the libertarian theory offers the brightest hope of good for society.

The theory of social responsibility

This social strength of libertarian theory is worthy of consideration because the rival theory of social responsibility, as its name suggests, tends to assume all claim to social good. Its advocates accuse newspapers of social irresponsibility and call for social instruments to see that the press fulfills its social responsibilities.

The authors of *Four Theories of the Press* trace the roots of this theory to the 1947 report of the Commission on Freedom of the Press, issued as the book *A Free and Responsible Press*. Known often as the Hutchins Commission—because it was chaired by

Robert M. Hutchins, then chancellor of the University of Chicago—this group criticized press performance and listed several demands which society makes on the press. Among its suggestions was "establishment of a new and independent agency to appraise and report annually upon the performance of the press."[4]

Such suggestions and proposals have been increasing since World War II. In Britain royal commissions made blistering comments about the press, and since 1953 the British Press Council has monitored performance. On the ombudsman pattern, Sweden has a "court of honor" (*Pressens opinionsnamnd*) to adjudicate complaints against the papers. Harry S. Ashmore, executive committee chairman of the Fund for the Republic (and former editor of the *Arkansas Gazette*) has urged a similar body for this country. At a meeting of Sigma Delta Chi, Barry Bingham, Louisville publisher, urged that communities have citizens' groups to evaluate the efforts of their papers. But almost all American editors have shouted down suggestions like those of the Hutchins Commission as the worthless ideas of eggheads who "don't know anything about newspapers."[5]

Increased pressure to make newspapers more responsive to the needs of the people, however, was almost inevitable from the days of the New Deal, if not from the muckraking period early in the century. In the thirties social control moved from its previous domain of international trade (tariffs) and monopoly (trust laws) to wages and hours, unemployment and old-age benefits, and agricultural supports. Not the least of the intellectual pressures behind these moves were those religious and philosophical concepts of the Golden Rule and utilitarianism.

Conservatives dug in their heels, but greater government regulation has marched into such areas as health and medicine. Many corporation presidents and doctors have repeatedly warned that other businesses and professions would be next. Radio and television had faced regulation from their beginnings, and movement on to other areas of communication was theoretically inexorable. To some, religion or philosophy demand it. So far, the Constitution has protected the press. But basic laws can be modified or ignored. For a generation voters have endorsed numerous steps toward greater control in the name of the public welfare. A social-responsibility theory of the press would naturally garner wide support on similar grounds.

Pragmatic considerations

Pressure for the press to be socially responsible, in line with this theory, is real and recent. In a 1967 congressional poll reported by *Editor & Publisher* 91 out of 155 representatives and senators said they would favor a code of ethics for newsmen assigned to congressional galleries. The other 54, perhaps recalling that many congressmen want no code for themselves, were opposed or had no opinion. (One factor in the heavy vote was doubtless that 40 respondents said newspaper coverage was only fair or poor, and 15 said

said news coverage of Congress was "seldom" or "rarely" accurate!) In the *Harvard Law Review* of June, 1967, Jerome A. Barron, an associate professor of law at George Washington University, contended that the First Amendment imposes on the press an affirmative responsibility to publish minority views. He argued that judicial remedy or legislation might guarantee the public limited access to press columns, as in the letters-to-the-editor section.

In one form the concept of social responsibility is familiar to all working newsmen. Chambers of Commerce, city officials, businessmen, and professionals may all argue to leave out, or at least "modify," some stories so they will not hurt the community. One graduate student came back from interning on a Midwest paper, for example, to say that it published *no* news which might be considered harmful to the community.

Advocates of social responsibility theory have several problems in explaining how it would operate. What kind of sanctions will restrict irresponsible newspapers? And if the teeth in controls are real, can the press still be called truly free? What watchdogs will watch the watchdog press? The journalistic battle of the young Ben Franklin against the ruling Mathers in colonial Boston is a bleak memory for the advocates of society's control, however high-minded. Many liberals who are disturbed with press performance would be outraged if society were controlled, as is likely, by the industrial-military complex. Venal politicians, perhaps representing the least educated segments of the electorate, could be even worse. Would a cure by social control be worse than the disease of irresponsibility?

Editors nurtured on libertarian ideas tend to see all proposals for outside checks as revival of Star Chambers and censors. What is the practical difference, they argue, between a monarch like King George, a dictator like Hitler, a government agency, and a fancy social-control council? They all want to interfere with printing the truth. Prof. John C. Merrill of the University of Missouri is an authority on the foreign press who has argued that authoritarian regimes use the claim of public interest to censor their press.

> The only way a "theory" of social responsibility could have any significance in any country is for the government power elite to be the definer and enforcer of this type of press. Since in any country the organization of society—its social and political structure—determines to a large extent what responsibilities the press (and the citizen) owe society, every country's press quite naturally considers (or might logically consider) itself as being socially responsible.
>
> Assuming that a nation's socio-political philosophy determines its press system, and undoubtedly it does, then it follows that every nation's press system is socially responsible. For example, the Marxist or Communist press system considers itself socially responsible, and certainly it is responsible to its own social system. . . .

> The same thing might be said of the so-called "authoritarian" press system, exemplified in Spain.[6]

Society will want to move slowly in changing a system which has served American democracy for almost two centuries, however badly at times. If editors don't want this change, they relax in the hope that change will be glacially slow. A major part of their ethical and moral responsibility today is to develop instruments of self-control, whether codes or councils within the industry, to obviate the need for outside enforcement of social responsibility.

The libertarian theory is most popular among journalists and publishers, but all its advocates are not within the Fourth Estate. For example, from a perhaps unexpected source, Germany, Karl Jaspers, the famous existentialist philosopher, offers a view of the press quite similar to the views of Milton and Jefferson:

> What we call publicity today is more especially the world of speakers and writers, of newspapers and books, of radio and television. This publicity is not the proclaiming ground for a single truth, but *the battleground for all truth.*
>
> Writers are *the third force between the government and the people*, between the actions of politicians and the inarticulateness of the people. They create the communicating language. But this third force is significant *only if it is independent.* [Emphasis supplied][7]

In this decade libertarian press theory clearly has the edge from tradition, but the concept of social responsibility remains in conflict with it. The authors do not insist on a choice. Nor is America likely soon to make a clear decision between the theories, any more than it has chosen between those other similarly disputed abstractions "free enterprise" and "the welfare state." As the nation appears to be settling for a mix of "capitalism" and "socialism," it may settle too for a mixed theory of the press, with maximum liberty and responsibility for all.

Editorial balance

From the discussion thus far, it becomes apparent that much of the editor's ethical problem is one of balancing. He must weigh the importance of pressures to distort or omit the news against the demands of his own conscience to be thorough and fair. At the same time he must counterbalance the frailty and limitation in his own freedom with the need to be socially responsible. He must put the individual's right of privacy in the balance against the public's right to know, and he must weigh the religious demand for compassion against the utilitarian requirement to do what is best for the most.

Editors, however, are not systematic philosophers who worry much about complete consistency. Pragmatically, and perhaps too hastily, they make a decision, and then another and another. This is journalistic life, and editors have to live with the results. Day to day editorial work focuses on three issues of press ethics. Each of them combines the tensions of different ethical problems, and the editor must develop attitudes on each of the three which harmonize satisfactorily with his whole philosophy of newspapering and life.

Good taste

Taste in journalism as elsewhere is a subtle quality that must be learned. In some cultures a hearty belch after a meal is considered a compliment to the cook, but in the United States a child has to learn that "it isn't done in polite society." A boor never learns this lesson; and if he gets into an editorial chair, his crudity may come out in print. But, still reacting against Victorianism, even cultivated editors hesitate to argue for good taste lest they be considered square. Frankness is "in" throughout our culture. As a result, the level of taste in newspapers today has doubtless settled much lower than during the yellow journalism of the nineties and the jazz journalism of the twenties which today's critics still ridicule.

The popularity of bad taste

The pressures for bad taste in print have increased in the last half dozen years. Illogically reasoning that two wrongs make a right, young radicals have attacked "obscenities" in society by using obscene words. When their use of these words becomes news, editors must decide whether to print them. When a federal report on political violence at the 1968 Democratic convention in Chicago went out, the AP sent a customary warning flag that some members might find objectionable material in it. A.I. Goldberg, editor of the *AP Log*, checked eighty-seven papers and found only fourteen used part of the text. He added on changing taste: "Several newspapers, however, used in their own or combined stories the phrase 'Get the bastards.' Thirty years ago the word bastard would be represented by a dash or, at the most, a 'b----.' . . . Freely quoted in most newspapers was the police officer who cried, 'For Christ's sake, stop it!' This was another phrase that before World War II would have been considered blasphemous." (In 1969 the *San Rafael* [Calif.] *Independent Journal* experimented with using xxx's for vulgar words spoken at school meetings. The idea was to give a more accurate account of the rhetoric than would a bland summary.)

Community standards

Though the public may revolt against excessively bad taste, looser standards promise to give editors headaches for years to come.* Indeed, editors of the next generation may feel socially responsible for cultivating higher standards of public taste if they believe politeness and "breeding" are still essentials of civilization.

Newspapers of course must keep their standards somewhere near the levels of popular taste in their communities, and many factors

* Taste in newspaper ads has obvious relevance here. A 1968 survey of fifty daily advertising managers showed that they felt movie ads were getting progressively more distasteful, and 95 percent believed the paper "has a moral obligation" to control such ads. Paul Rand Dixon, chairman of the Federal Trade Commission, has praised papers which "had the guts to stand up for principle" and reject dubious advertising. By 1970, many newspapers were simply refusing x-rated ads.

have been pushing these down. Some put most of the blame on liberalized rulings by the Supreme Court. But the Court too tends to follow popular trends, and the many depressing influences on these include: the debauchery of several wars, the degeneration of the plays and novels, the popularity of the sexy paperbacks and sensational magazines, proliferation of "adult" motion pictures, and the strains of living in a mass society.

The need to maintain standards in "a family newspaper" sometimes is cited to avoid the worst excesses in the press, but families already find it more and more difficult to prevent the erosion of taste in their children. One of the most important influences on family taste, of course, is television. Even more than the newspaper, TV brings into the family circle a vivid portrayal of what was once scandalous. Motion pictures exhibited with "adults only" signs a few years ago are now available to children in the living room. It takes a quick parent to keep ahead of society in "educating" his child, who may pick up on TV while he is preschool age what appropriately might be left until his teens. Many will not blame the newspaperman if, like the tired parent, he gives in.

The contexts of bad taste

While they have followed established positions on taste, editors generally have been horrified by foul words in print but blasé about foul living conditions in town. The press—and society—have been indignant about an unmannerly act but casual about reports of people slaughtered, maimed, or scorched in a war. Press and society may be outraged by unconventional dress but only mildly distressed when commercial interests desecrate a place of beauty. Yet at this point we are discussing taste, not morals, and even if all the evil that men do were to be abolished, editors would still have problems with the good manners of print.

The problem of taste in newspapers is not, as many suppose, wholly one of restraint about vulgarity, profanity, and sex. There can be bad taste in political writing. In the partisan-press days of the early Republic, editors scurrilously attacked political enemies. During the depression of the thirties, newspapers indulged in excessive calumny, and in recent years the issues of Vietnam and civil rights have triggered a barrage of bad taste.

Such issues bring up the difficulty of reporting violence with good taste. Riots and war-time killings must be reported to the public with the graphic aid of pictures where possible. Once newspapers avoided publishing pictures of dead persons. But if for comprehensive coverage present-day editors must use these pictures of the dead from riots and war, why not of the dead from disasters and accidents? Yet a line must be drawn to exclude the macabre and the gory.* Newspapers were within bounds when they reported that

* Alert to criticism of the media and violence, several editors in 1968 dropped Dick Tracy and other cartoon strips with guns. At about the same time, irate readers in Ohio assailed UPI for several stories publicizing "the barbarous activity of bullfighting."

actress Jayne Mansfield was decapitated in an automobile accident. News pictures showed the crumbled car and even the sheet-covered body. But the *Chicago American* went over the line of good taste in a caption: "White area on the hood of the car is Miss Mansfield's blonde head."

As the chapter on picture-editing indicates, the problem of taste is particularly acute in art work. Restraint must be shown with photographs of cheesecake and gore, and what television may use cannot be the criterion. The fleeting quality of pictures on the screen may lessen the objection to some material on television, but there is a permanence about the printed picture which can make it more titillating or repelling, the factors which come into play in judgments of taste.

So the editor must strike balances. He must satisfy the public's need for the facts, but he must also recall the high professional obligations of a free press in the area of taste as elsewhere. He will not let fears of the Nice Nellies keep him from portraying realistic aspects of the cruel and vulgar world as they are. But in an era when public taste has been cheapened and hardened, his greater concern will be to view the press as an instrument to maintain culture and even civilization itself.

Respect for the individual

The pressure of the age is to make us all faceless fragments of mass society. Names become numbers. We are zip-coded, IBMed, and computerized. College students complain that they are processed like punched data cards, and old people say that they are just Social Security numbers. The press can join the trend by treating people as chaff for the news machines, or it can stand against dehumanization by recognizing and preserving the integrity of individual human personality.

The right of privacy

The right of privacy is a delicate thing. From the legal side, as we saw in the last chapter, the newspaper can probably get by if its publication of personal matter is closely related to news events, but privacy is more than a question of law. Sometimes press ethics may halt an invasion of privacy which law would permit.

Since much of their most significant work is always close to invading someone's privacy, newspapermen may have to remind themselves not to be too hard-boiled on the question. Ordinary persons, as distinguished from politicians and celebrities, have great sensitivity about "undue publicity." In an actual case a mother was incensed because the media printed and television carried the news that a teenager had shot her passing car with a BB-gun. As a misdemeanor, the shooting became a public record, and a newsman could see plenty of reasons for printing the news: The public could judge whether juveniles are delinquent, whether the neighborhood had gangs, whether the police were doing their job, and whether guns should be controlled. The mother could appreciate none of these arguments. She saw no reason why her age should be printed; and she feared that the teenager, knowing her name, would take reprisals against her or her children. Silly? From the editor's point of view, yes. But from the point of view of privacy and her feeling about press invasions, it was her own business whether she was shot at. She wanted to be more than grist for "a couple of grafs." Newsmen have to be sensitive, at least, that ordinary citizens have such "unreasonable" feelings.

Mass labeling

Another level of respect for individuals is in news about whole masses of people, as in wars and urban violence. Communist newspapers incline to dismiss our millions with the stereotype of "imperialistic warmongers." But our press easily slips into such dehumanizing labels too. In World War I we made the enemy an inhuman mass with the word "Huns." Then in World War II it was "Japs." In more recent years those who fight against the United States are often lumped as "Communists," even though it would usually be difficult to prove there was a card-carrying Red among them. It is much the same when reporters write loosely of "black rioters" or "Negro hoodlums," leading white readers to react against a whole Negro community that may in fact be more than 99 percent non-rioting and non-hoodlum.

With a little care about such issues as privacy and mass labeling, the press can be a good influence in maintaining respect for individuals. This is an area of the newspaper's greatest strength. When focusing on the individual because of honest human interest, journalism can repulse the dehumanizing forces of mass society.

The effects of news

The libertarian editor who says he prints "without fear or favor" is emphasizing his objectivity. He overrides pressures to print or not to print. And he learns to overlook the consequences of his decisions, for editorial action is paralyzed or biased if an editor worries about how an item is going to affect the co-worker or mother or girl friend of a person in the news.

There is a running debate whether newspapers have much effect anyway. Editorials have been discounted as political factors for decades. Civil libertarians contend that publication of pornography does not increase sex aberrations: "No girl was ever ruined by a book." Communications researchers have been able to demonstrate few clear effects of simple reports and have drawn back from trying to analyze really complex but important problems such as how newspapers influence the vote for President.

Yet if the influence of newspapers cannot be pinpointed, can the effects of home or school or church be proved any more convincingly? Are they any less real for that? Would anyone seriously hypothesize that the media have less effect than parents or teachers? The person involved in the news does not doubt that the paper has an effect. The college football star knows that sports reporting influences his ability to get dates and a pro contract. The embezzler recognizes that at the very least news stories about his deeds can wreck his credit rating.

The editor too knows that newspapers have an effect from the actions of publicity seekers asking space and acquaintances phoning to try to suppress news. He hopes that the effect is good, and one of his strongest arguments for press freedom is that full reporting has a beneficial effect on the democratic process. He likes to point to times his coverage has led to ouster of public chiselers and his crusades have brought civic improvements. The development of social responsibility theory urges him to be even more concerned about his paper's effect on society.

Chain reactions

As news of one suicide in a mental hospital gets around, other patients sometimes make suicide attempts. From that observation psychiatrists move on to the conviction that news accounts of suicides tend to trigger other suicides. Some of them argue that accounts of a dramatic, "mad" killing, like the 1966 murders by the sniper in a tower at the University of Texas, stimulate others to attempt such killings. The argument is plausible, since it is obvious that "good" ideas for communities and business catch on because they get press notice. But can an editor start holding back "bad" news lest it stimulate readers to try the same misdeed?

Suicide is normally played down in papers, since usually the person who kills himself is not of great news importance. If a celebrity commits suicide, that fact can hardly be ignored. Many newspapers have followed the practice of giving few details on the method of suicide. They may omit the name of a poison, for example, on the theory that other depressed persons may want to take the same "out."

Other anti-social incidents are not so difficult to handle. The ordinary burglary hardly attracts others to the craft, nor does a speeding conviction encourage others to speed. In fact, news of frustrated or punished crimes is considered a deterrent.

The problem is touchier where mass emotion is involved. During widespread economic depression, milk-dumping reported in one agriculture center may set it off in another, and violence in one strike may touch off violence in another. News of violence and rioting in recent years, whether started by whites or blacks, whether by students or nonstudents, seems to create a mass psychology which brings rioting in other cities and schools.

Newspapers can contribute to widespread panic. If the wire services carried news that an incurable flu had hit several West Coast cities, the whole nation could be panicked overnight. A similar and actual mass phenomenon was the spontaneous flaring up of "hippy" philosophy in many cities at once. While it can be argued that like social causes ignited all of this, it appears that the quick communication of youthful ideas by the media was a major factor, though television was probably more important to this than the press.

The editor's dilemma

The ethical editor, then, has to consider the effects of his paper on the individual and on the society. He must print, without malice or prurience, the necessary news of individuals. The truth will probably hurt less than wild rumors spread by word-of-mouth. One journalism professor advised students to act so that they would not be afraid to have their actions published under headlines on the front page. It is a salutary moral dictum. Yet if they believe that their acts won't make headlines, they should realize that wrong-doing inevitably gets around among those who count. The editor with a sensitive conscience cannot forget that. The problem of the effect of news on society is much stickier. The editor hates to print the news that bad conditions in his community lost it a government contract or news that might spread a riot. But he must be accurate and complete; otherwise he blunts his claim as defender of the public's right to know. Practically, he will find that others disagree about his evaluation of what should be kept from the people and accuse him of venality. The editor weighs and balances his values and may at times have to compromise a rigid application of personal principles when the public interest is at stake.

Some common problems

Underlying the discussion in this chapter is the assumption that the newspaperman will live up to the ethical standards of the community. As we assume that cashiers will not dip into the till and that government officials will not take bribes, we assume that editors should be honest. They will not accept gifts which will color their judgment, will not take money to leave news out, and will not promote a pet cause in order to win favors or preferment. But such general principles are more more easily stated than practiced. There are puzzling decisions to be made when the newsman gets down to concrete cases.

In instances of obvious pressure from advertisers or the subtle influence of the "country club complex," it is usually assumed that the corrupted figure is the publisher or a top executive. Such convenient goats do not deserve all criticism, however, for pressures to conform afflict the whole newspaper staff. A reporter may say, "I knew the druggists would be sore if I wrote that kind of a story so I put the angle on something else." Or a deskman may say, "Man, if we printed that we would lose all the car dealers' advertising!"

Personal favor

Reporters, in particular, move among sources who may offer gifts. In most cases the gift is merely a token: a necktie or some handkerchiefs at Christmas, a lunch, or a ball point pen. But sometimes the gift is not a token, but a bribe. For example, reporters covering a professional football team were each given a quality electric portable typewriter at the end of the season. A reporter who accepts a $200 gift can easily slip into softening or eliminating any critical stories about the football team or its management. But wasn't that the purpose of the gift?

As we pointed out in chapter 2, gratuities to newsmen are usually far more subtle. An invitation to a special cocktail party, a fancy dinner, or a plush weekend sometimes sways a newsman into thinking that the merchant in trouble with the Federal Trade Commission is too charming to expose. The reporter's copy reflects this appraisal. Sometimes reporters have been flattered to the point of being obsequious when a President or a governor asks them for advice. Others can succumb to flattery coming from a much lower level.

Newsmen, like everyone else, want to be liked and it bothers some journalists to play the role, even occasionally, of the curmudgeon. Perhaps the best advice is that the journalist should at these times ask himself, "What is more important, my ego or the public's right to know the facts?"

Thoughtful reporters in Washington sometimes admit that an invitation to the home of the Secretary of State for a "not for attribution" press conference causes them to crawl at least a little way into the Secretary's pocket. After all, only about fifteen reporters are so honored. What reporter would not be a bit dazzled if he lunched at the White House? For weeks after the newsman can drop into all conversations, "When I was lunching with the President . . ."

Public duty

Other governmental pressures have ethical overtones. A reporter or editor who criticizes the military is apt to be considered disloyal or at least "not on the team." A dissenter from American foreign policy may be reminded sternly that "dissent stops at the water's edge." In one case, a famous columnist critical of a past administration was subjected to a whispering campaign to discredit him as senile. The critic of hometown business operations may be denounced, in public, as a "carping critic who is bringing scorn to our fair city." These pressures, often not expressed so bluntly, are hard to combat because they are subtle. Also, the person who is pressured enjoys being praised by the rich and powerful as a person who "has helped our town a lot." What they probably mean is that the journalist has been a faithful puppet of the elite—a mouthpiece for a few rather than a spokesman for the many.

One of the toughest ethical problems facing newsmen is when to be silent. All kinds of responsible people—police, industrialists, city officials—will ask the press to withhold information. The reasons are various, but at the highest levels the customary reason is "the national interest." The best known instance of silence in the national interest was President Kennedy's persuading the *New York Times* to kill a story revealing that the United States was planning to invade Cuba. Later, when Clifton Daniel was managing editor of the *Times*, he said Kennedy had admitted that the paper should have printed the story—it would have saved the nation the humiliation of the Bay of Pigs fiasco.

There are times, of course, when the press is quick to withhold information in the public interest. If the police are about to raid an unlicensed bar or are ready to make an unexpected arrest, the facts are withheld until after the police do their work. But the "interest" had better be clear. Otherwise, the press will not be serving the public, only those who wish to operate in secrecy. Nothing so damages a newspaper's reputation and more encourages rumor than the public's realization that it omits news or favors the police, the mayor, or the manager of the town's biggest industry.

Political involvement

Another practical ethical consideration for an editor is whether to run for public office or to head a special committee. It inflates anyone's ego, of course, to be asked to run; but as a candidate or an elected official, the newsman puts the newspaper in a position either to be partisan or to be accused of partisanship. The decision becomes acute when the journalist, being as objective about himself as he can, believes that he is the best qualified person for the office.

One newspaper editor became chairman of a civic committee to investigate new water sources for the city. It was an important job and a position he could fill capably. But the findings of his committee became controversial and the key issue in a mayoral campaign. Much of the public thought that the newspaper was acting as a mouthpiece for the editor's own views on water sources. The newspaper's standing in the community declined even though no bias was ever proved.

It would be unwise to suggest that no newspaperman ever take public office. Many editors have been good public officials and their papers good public servants as well. But no journalist should take such a position without thorough consideration of the perils and a couple of pledges that his newspaper never will sound like his press agent.

Using freedom responsibly

The ethical newspaperman, then, must face honestly the basic questions of business integrity and the special moral problems of the news industry. Beyond that, within the ethical considerations of this chapter, the editor must use freedom of the press responsibly. And his best guide to printing a responsible paper is to print the truth.

Accuracy is one facet of truth. The paper gets the facts straight. But accuracy refers to more than the news story. Headlines, photographs, and even editorials have an obligation to be truthful and accurate. The concept of objectivity is a part of accuracy as is the concept of balance. An accurate reflection of the community and world includes good news as well as bad.

Another facet of truth is completeness. Information can be accurate but incomplete, and then facts add up to a half-truth. Thoroughness is an editorial virtue. The editor is not swayed by political, economic, or other pressure. He is fair to individuals and to movements. Fairness requires that he clearly label editorializing and opinion. As monopoly newspapers take on the coloration of a public utility, the concept of completeness and fairness no doubt means that even on the editorial page the editor is obligated to give attention to varying views. He must be fair even to the parties, persons, and ideologies he hates.

Finally, newspaper responsibility means allegiance also to values which make the ethical problem very complex. An editor must have compassion and must respect the sacredness of individuals. He must have a proper concern for the effects of its publication in society. And he must print within the limits of good taste. Yet where a balancing of values becomes necessary, even these virtues are in the second order for a free press in a free society. An editor must be careful lest he use "kindness" or "my responsiblity to the town" to be weasel-word covers for his cowardice. Truth must, ultimately, be the lamp which guides him.

14 Imagination in news editing

> An editor must have his own profound vision of things. He cannot seek to fill his newspaper with what the reader wants for the simple reason that no editor *knows* what the reader wants. The editors I have admired have known, however, and quite clearly, what *they* wanted to put in their newspapers, what *they* thought belonged there. And they didn't get their ideas from readership surveys; they got their conception of the *good* newspaper from their own education and interests and understanding and instinct—in short, their own imagination.
>
> —Tom Wicker, *New York Times*

One paper is routine; another impresses its readers as fresh, dynamic, and challenging. The difference is imagination. An editorial team, given the freedom to use its creative powers, can generate new and improved newspapers, in the same way as other professionals discover new methods to save hearts or make homes more livable.

Imagination is needed in many details of headlines; story structures, and display. But this chapter will consider imagination in three major aspects of newspaper operation: excellence of product the progress and reform of the community, and the people's right to know.

Imagination and excellence

Too often excellence is thought of merely in terms of preserving and imitating what is good. American editors never tire of asserting, somewhat chauvinistically, that they produce the best papers in the world. It may seem to them logical that all they have to do is keep on doing the job they've been doing. The challenge, however, should be to make the newspaper of 1972 better than that of 1971, and that of 1980 even better.

True, if there is a better newspaper in a rival community down the freeway or in a city a thousand miles away, the editor can copy its superior features and, using his imagination, learn and adapt from other editors. But the real challenge of editing is to create and test new concepts and forms of newspapering.

Imaginative editing, by definition, can't be frozen into a textbook of rules, for it is impossible to anticipate the freshness and creativity that the working editor must discover in himself. Still we can give some hints for applying editorial imagination to problems of modern coverage and the use of specialized writers, editors, and critics.

Creative thinking

The key to creative newspaper work is the editor's ability to generate imaginative story assignments. It is easy to assign a reporter to cover a city council meeting, a school bond referendum, or an explosion at the popcorn factory. The editor can sharpen his imagination in assignments by constantly asking himself about whatever he reads, hears, and sees, "Is there a story in this for our paper?" In most cases there is not. But perhaps once in twenty or thirty times there is. Articles from magazines like *Harper's, Commonweal*, the *New Republic,* or *Nation's Cities* offer information and insights about problems of general interest, and the creative editor should always be thinking how these articles could apply to home base.

A few years ago the big circulation magazines like *Life* and *Look* were of little use to the serious newspaper editor, but today they offer solid reporting as well as entertainment. The smaller magazines mentioned previously, however, are better sources of insight about trends in social change. Scholarly magazines, too, are filled with articles that, although sometimes stiff and dry, contain fresh and even startling ideas. News assignments on politics, foreign policy, economics, sociology, and other topics spring from these articles to the mind of an alert editor.

The same potential lies in current books. An editor need not read them completely to get practical ideas. First chapters, for example, can often be skipped or skimmed. Tables of contents usually give clues to important chapters, allowing an editor to pick and choose the material he wants and thereby review some books in an hour or two. Obviously, there are volumes that deserve careful attention, but a good editor identifies them quickly and gives them extra time.

Creative assignment

Having found an idea for a story, the editor must ask himself where his staff can obtain necessary information. Will a state official have a few facts? Will someone in city hall be able to add a few details? Is there an expert in the community who could supply more information? Could he direct a reporter to other sources? Is there someone who knows the practical difficulties? Do staff reporters have clues about where to find information?

After an editor clarifies his ideas on how to get the facts, he should make his assignment to the reporter in detail. A mere "Get a little story on pollution of Hickory Creek" produces "a little story" with few facts. That article will bounce off the reader, and the next day concern for Hickory Creek's foul condition will evaporate. Rather, a written note should describe the idea carefully, in such clear detail that the reporter can have no doubt that a thorough story is desired and that certain sources are probably most promising.

It is important, too, that the editor assign the story to a reporter who is interested in the subject. A writer who is unconcerned about an issue—and unable to get concerned—will do a poor job and may even consciously or unconsciouly sabotage the whole idea. But the editor should not expect a reporter to signal his interest. Sometimes the quiet fellow sitting in the corner is itching to dig into a serious and important subject.

Creative encouragement

In a creative newsroom, ideas for stories will come from staff members as well as editors. Some city desks have a suggestion box where reporters, photographers, and copyeditors can drop notes proposing stories. As noted in chapter 8, this source will dry up in a hurry if the editor pays no attention to the suggestions. When he uses a tip, he should thank the person who presented it. When he is unable to use it, he should tell the author why. Some papers can even give a small bonus to a staffer for an unusually good idea, and magazines pay well for story tips.

A word of praise for a professional piece of reporting is also helpful. So is posting a good story on the newsroom bulletin board. Mention in a staff publication of outstanding work stimulates more exceptional reporting, as does a ten-dollar bonus.

If an editor takes the stories as they come, never suggesting changes or seeking more information, the imagination of his reporters will wilt. If he never shows enthusiasm, if he is as unconcerned about the discovery of a new cure for cancer as he is about the Cub Scout cookout, he will drive away good reporters and encourage the mediocre to imitate his dubious success.

Insightful coverage

Good papers today offer depth coverage. The superior ones of the future will search for significance with even more imagination and care. They will seek to discover trends, strive for insight into complex issues, and explore ways to relate their findings to reader concern and interest. Consequently, leading editors will turn more and more to subjects that have not been covered and are not easily accessible. Recognizing the difference between imagination and imitation, they will resist following "news fads." Few editors today are so perceptive. They think they are being imaginative when they run stories about a current social problem that has seized the general attention of the moment. Such subjects come and go, like women's fashions. For a time, the papers are full of stories on juvenile delinquency, drug addiction, or school dropouts. The subjects are in the spotlight for a year or so—lighted only on their surfaces—and then they fade into the background. A few years later they may again take center stage. The better editors go after subjects, not because everyone else does, but because of their own thoughtful judgment of significance.

Widespread, stereotyped reporting of social and political problems was noted in a criticism of special television news shows. The critic said the networks use and reuse the same material: Space, Race, Reds, and Feds. That criticism is harsh, but it suggests that the networks cover only obvious subjects. They fail to dig into material that promises discovery of unrecognized problems and fresh information for old concerns. The same criticism could be made about newspapers.

Though little is new under the sun, institutions change and novel events occur. It is the job of the journalist to observe these changes and events, even those that may be barely distinguishable, and to identify them in ways that make sense to the reader.

Not only do the media neglect some changes and events until they explode into spot news, university specialists sometimes fail to grasp what is happening under their noses, and often political leaders badly misread public moods and attitudes. Because of man's insensitivity to change, many problems are full-blown before they are recognized. To some extent this is inevitable. Humans seem almost incapable of paying attention to minor problems. Only when they become gigantic—and almost impossible to solve—are they tackled. Even then, it is tempting simply to reduce rather than eliminate them.

Examples are everywhere. Air pollution is dismissed as an irritant until it kills large numbers of people. Nothing serious is done about water pollution until our Great Lakes become cesspools. Mental health is little more than an unmentionable subject in a family until nearly every member realizes that one of them is in torment. Even when the ills of society are obvious, many people ignore them, apparently assuming that they will go away.

Fusing interest and importance

It is difficult under these circumstances for an editor to print the news his readers need if they are to act as responsible citizens. Criticize an editor for not printing much of anything about Africa or South America, and he may reply sadly, "I printed stories about Africa, and a readership survey showed that only 6 percent paid any attention. The same thing happened to our South American articles. I can't fill up the paper with stories that only 6 percent will read."

Though his argument sounds irrefutable, there is a flaw in it. The editor is right in implying his paper must print what readers want if it is to survive. But he is wrong in suggesting that everyone has to be interested in everything in the paper. Most items must appeal to large groups of readers, but this principle leaves room for some material that will be read by a minority, even a small one. Of the solid, important story, the editor should say, "The public needs to know this, even though many readers will not read it. So I am going to print it. If the majority of readers skip it, they will still find plenty of other items to interest them."

The editor has to keep in mind *why* people read newspaper

stories. Wilbur Schramm, the communications researcher, argues that people read because they expect a reward. They find information satisfying even when it may be "bad news" because it provides a negative reward. College students avidly read about a tuition increase. Motorists read with satisfaction about the elimination of a dangerous stretch of highway, but they also read with concern about the closing of a shortcut. Young people read about the possible bad effects of "The Pill." And older people carefully follow the obituaries. Probably none of these readers, however, will pay attention to an election in Uruguay or a disease in Tanzania. Such subjects are too remote from their own interests.

The task of the editor, then, is to attempt to link these socially and politically important subjects to the legitimate interests and concerns of his readers so that they anticipate—and find—some reward. This is not easy. The editor, working with the reporter, photographer, and artist, must plan with care and imagination, striving for a compelling blend of copy and art. In some ways, the task is easier today than even a decade ago. More readers have attended college; more have travelled, read, and broadened their awareness through television news reports and documentaries. Also the political and economic involvement of the United States with the world has brought a greater public consciousness of that world. So more people are interested in Uruguay and Tanzania than used to be.

It is easy, however, to exaggerate the increase of interest in peripheral subjects. College does not always educate. Almost everyone knows college graduates who are narrow, ignorant, and scornful of intellect. And many who have traveled extensively are less enlightened about foreign culture than the faithful reader of the *National Geographic*. So the alert editor must search for relevance, attempting to make the readers, through their self-interest, aware and concerned.

Presenting news imaginatively

Good reporting must be supported by imaginative presentation. To write a story and slap on a two-column head is not enough. Major pieces deserve major treatment. They require striking pictures or art work. They must jolt the reader's interest by presenting the drama of the facts themselves.

Ideas for good visual presentation can be obtained from newspapers that consistently do a good job of combining words and art. Some Sunday magazines published by newspapers manage this effectively. Their small format helps, for if two facing pages offer type and art work, the reader's eyes will have no distractions from the spread. The *National Observer*, the *Chicago Daily News*, the *Minneapolis Tribune* and *Star*, and the *St. Petersburg Times* are among the papers that cleverly present major stories. Magazines like *Fortune* and *Look* consistently offer dramatic presentations. Any editor who actively examines their layouts will discover ideas for exceptional visual presentations that can be adapted to the needs and character of his own paper.

Interpretive pieces need not be lengthy. It has become fashionable in recent years to run "The Depth Story," in which a reporter writes and writes about every facet of one problem in a single report. By itself, the report may be outstanding. But an editor should worry that well-intentioned readers may become overwhelmed and put it aside, saying, "I'll have to read that when I get time." Others may go through the whole thing but forget the single impact after a few days. Because memory must be refreshed, continuing problems need big, medium, and small stories every week or so. They also need display that demands attention.

This kind of presentation is not cheap. It may take capable, well-paid reporters, photographers, and artists days or even weeks to do a short series. This sometimes means an expenditure of several thousand dollars, which only the wealthiest dailies can afford. But smaller papers can do excellent work a little less elaborately. The pictures can be good, if not superb. The writing can be colorful and thorough. The material can be put together in an attractive way, by using devices of makeup mentioned in chapter five, such as boxes, Ben Day borders, white space, little sketches, copy set in wide measure, and a little extra space between columns.

All this takes additional time and money—but it is well worth it if the reader lingers longer with the paper. It may even be financially profitable in the long run: advertisers should prefer a paper that people spend twenty-five or thirty minutes with to one that is skimmed through and tossed aside.

Trends to specialization

The specialized writer has only come into prominence since World War II. Specialization probably will continue and spread beyond reporting. In the past, for example, most copyediting "specialization" was done helter-skelter. If a copyeditor had a sailboat, he was given stories about the sea. If he had played a violin in the high school orchestra, he read the music critic's column. This has worked moderately well on some desks, but on better newspapers today it is simply inadequate. Most copyeditors, as an illustration, usually do not try to work over science news because they are afraid to. This means that science news often is not as lucid as it should be. Increasingly, however, copyeditors who specialize in sciences and medicine, or in urban affairs, education, space technology, the arts, and dozens of other areas, are appearing in major newspaper offices. The American newspaper is generating specialists on the desk as well as in the field.

The team of specialists

More and more, perhaps, a copyeditor will work with a team of reporters and photographers on special stories. Suppose that the top editors decide on thorough coverage of the housing needs of the community. The copyeditor will be in charge of the team. The staffers will map out what information they intend to get: the number of substandard houses, the need to mesh housing developments with transportation, the cost of decent housing, and proposals for cuts in building costs. The copyeditor, striving for display that assures maximum readership, will talk to photographers and artists about effective illustrations. All of these journalists—reporters, photographers, an artist, and the copyeditor—may spend several hours or days reading and talking about the problem before anyone leaves the office.

The reporters will go out and dig up information. The photographers will take pictures to tell part of the story pictorially. An artist may add cartoons, sketches, and graphs. The copyeditor will work and rework the copy into a series, a full page layout, or part of the front page plus some inside material. Thus, the whole issue of housing will be thoroughly covered—yet the writing can be lean and precise, taking up relatively little room. All those who took part in the reporting and editing, meanwhile, have become somewhat expert on the community's housing problems, which will be useful when later specialization is needed.

The future, if this kind of team reporting and editing becomes at all common, will put a premium on planning. The copyeditor in charge of such a team must analyze a problem and set about methodically to investigate it, a task blending imagination and organization.

The generalist

Though specialization is the trend, the generalist remains immensely valuable. A copyeditor who can do a good job of editing copy about an uprising in Bucharest because he is fairly well-informed about Eastern Europe and who can also handle a story about heartburn because he knows quite a bit about medicine is good to have around. Besides, some specialists get into the bad habit of writing only for other specialists. They gradually take on the jargon of the specialty and sometimes become part of the speciality's establishment. Well-informed generalists can help the paper minimize such dangers of over-specialization.

A generalist, even a new reporter, may be able to spot a story that the expert overlooked because he was too close to the scene. A few years ago, for example, the medical writer for the *Washington Post* went on vacation. His substitute, Morton Mintz, ran across the thalidomide story—which actually had been available to science writers for months. He found that a tranquilizing drug called thalidomide, given to pregnant women, caused deformities in their babies. The story he broke produced worldwide concern, and led to closer testing of drugs as well as the elimination of thalidomide. Apparently the specialists had all been too close to this news to see it.

Imaginative coverage of the trends, nevertheless, usually requires specialists. Expert coverage has been long established in two journalistic fields, sports and business. For decades no editor would have dreamed of sending a football writer to cover the stock market or a society writer to cover the World Series. It is perhaps some kind of wry commentary on American culture that experts have been demanded by only our sportsmen and businessmen. More and more, however, the educational level of our culture now demands expertise in the coverage of such areas as science, health, labor, religion, education, and the arts.

It is no longer thinkable, as Scripps believed, that a diplomatic conference can be covered by a police reporter or a church editor—even though both may have expert knowledge of human nature. The foreign affairs expert who writes on international conflicts, the education editor who writes on changes in schools, and other such specialists are positioned to spot the vital trends of war, of student unrest, of cancer breakthroughs, strike threats, aesthetic revolutions, moral upheavals, and the rest. At their best, they are experts strategically placed.*

The critical function

To many, critical writing about music, drama, and other arts is simply a form of news coverage. Some critics, however, see their work as another art, as comment upon a presentation which will not only guide ticket-buyers but help shape taste. But whether it is art or news, criticism is an aspect that the imaginative editor has to ponder how he can improve—or inaugurate.

Again we must consider that newspapers often have done the job inadequately, and realistically ponder how they can improve. Most often, outside of cities such as New York and Los Angeles, editors have found a music teacher or a reporter who likes movies to review everything from a high school production of *South Pacific* to the local appearance of the Ballet Russe. The practice is not necessarily deplorable. Almost any criticism is better than none at all, and with guidance the amateur critic may become a fine professional one.

The culture boom

Nevertheless, for some years the bigger and better papers have supported full-time specialists in criticism. Culture has come to "the provinces." Theatrical performances in Houston and symphonic programs in Minneapolis can equal those of Paris or Prague, and our affluent society can support local appearances of artists from not only New York, London, Tokyo, Bombay, Israel or Mali. These performances deserve more than a public relations handout. By publishing criticism, the newspaper helps its readers check their own impressions, guides them to more sensitive appreciation, and stimulates them to awareness of how their tastes differ from others.

The culture boom means also that local presentations are at an all-time high. Appreciative coverage is needed for community drama, local art shows, local museum exhibitions, university dance presentations, community orchestra concerts, church pageants, and photographic shows. In any city of 50,000 or even fewer, one man could be kept busy most of the time covering cultural events, and even if he were only semi-expert, the growing number of educated readers would find the local paper more vital for his coverage.

* The *Chicago Tribune* assigned an education specialist, Casey Banas, to work six weeks researching and writing a series "with a fresh perspective" on the Chicago police department, which had received nationwide criticism in 1968. The paper headed a front-cover ad in *Editor & Publisher*: "We assigned the biggest police story of the year to our education writer."

This observation especially pertains to the motion picture. If attendance is a criterion, the movie houses are the local institutions most deserving critical coverage. Traditionally, papers print puffs about movies in return for ads and perhaps "comp" tickets. The system is unfortunate, for the paper gives away valuable space and the film business encounters a generation of people who don't believe what they read about the pictures. We sense a trend toward better cinema criticism in small and middle-sized as well as large communities. While honest and objective reviews may cause some turkeys to lose money, they may contribute to the success of good films. Sound criticism in newspapers around the country might much improve the motion picture industry.

Newspapers hold the same potential for television, though syndicated criticism makes it more difficult for the local TV critic to contribute meaningfully. By the time the television show is over, who cares about critical reactions? Some viewers want to know what others thought, just as they do when they bring the subject up at the coffee break the next morning. Some spot-criticism of bigger shows would be appropriate, just as some local editorializing on global issues is. Where local television shows do something out of the ordinary in documentaries or entertainment, the newspaper ought to take critical note, for the other media will. Probably the greater opportunity for TV criticism in most cities, however, is to criticize, from a local perspective, what networks, producers, or certain shows are attempting to do over a period of time. For inspiration, editors might turn to Robert L. Shayon's long-range interpretations in the *Saturday Review.*

The search for critics

Imaginative criticism in the future probably will be handled either by full-time writer-editors or by groups of part-timers. The full-time man will have to develop in the same way as any other specialized writer or editor. The part-timer presents the editor with an even bigger challenge. First, recruiting must be careful. The temptation to take just "anyone" should be resisted; men and women with both aptitude and interest should be sought out with care. The fledgling critic, then, should prepare for professional work by reading a book or two on criticism. Tuition for one or two courses in a nearby school might be supplied. Courses in literature, history, music appreciation, and drama might all be appropriate. The reporter who acted in college plays might take a course in Greek tragedy, and the school music director who wants to try her hand at criticism might take a journalism course.

Finally, the recruit should be assisted to see and hear as much as he can, and not always as an assignment. Here he must know what area he will work in. It is as important for the part-time critic to know he is to deal only, say, with music and dance as for any other specialized writer to know the limits of his field. Then he can read, study, and observe with a focus. Like writing, the way to learn to criticize is to criticize. "The one indispensable requirement for such work is taste," says Walter Kerr, drama critic for the *New York Times*, "and taste is formed, I am convinced, only by maximum exposure to a field."

Book reviewing also deserves the attention of imaginative and creative editors. Today, few papers offer more than token news and criticism of books. There is syndicated criticism, of course, but that puts the newspaper into competition with the more thorough presentation of magazines. More important, the reaction of a local reviewer may be more interesting and useful to many readers than the criticism ground out in Manhattan.

Here the editor may follow the tack of specialization or not. Often local intellectuals who write with grace can review books for general reading. Or the newspaper can find, as do many magazines, an expert to review a book—an engineer at the local plant to comment on the book about scientists in government, and the clothing shop owner to review the volume on fashion history. Admittedly, heavy editing and rewriting may be necessary, but the possibilities are wide if imagination is used to find specialized reviewers. The mayor may review a book on politics, or a school board member may handle a book on education. Publishers provide free copies of the books, and many reviewers are delighted to have the book, a byline, and nothing more.

In all types of criticism, the newspaper has unusual opportunities to develop a role in a field that is free of competition. For more than a generation we have heard how broadcasting pushes newspapers to wider and deeper interpretation. Extrapolating this trend, we are suggesting that editors use imagination also to criticize culture in ways only newspapers can. National media can't localize as the paper can, and local television appears unable or unwilling. The field is free; the gates are wide open.

Progress and reform

Imagination should be used both in reforming the paper and in reforming the community. Traditionally the good newspaperman has served as messenger, watchdog, and crusader. As editorial emphasis moves from deadpan objectivity to depth reporting it also advances leadership and guidance. What values are behind interpretive articles, what standards and goals are being suggested by the very fact of their appearance? The imaginative editor goes beyond the search for internal excellence to visualize, plan, and help build a better community.

Watchdogging power

Crusades seem to have gone out of fashion. It is true that many papers are fat and complacent; they don't make waves. But the fact remains, as the annual awards of Pulitzer and other prizes testify, that some newspapers still campaign for progress and reform.

Crusading often means bucking the powerful men of the community. Wealth means power, and more often than not political leadership is tied with that power. The newspaper publisher and his chief managers are probably close to the Establishment men of the community—meeting on committees with them, golfing, dining and cocktailing with them. It is not easy for a paper to break with and confront this aggregation of power, which provides much of its own economic energy. Picking at the petty politicians may not be difficult, and may even be a pleasant sort of sport; but hitting at the real political, social, and economic power of the city takes more nerve.

Peter B. Clark, president and publisher of the *Detroit News*, views the problem of power structure in a somewhat different way. In a Journalism Day address reported by *Editor & Publisher*, he pointed out that "the writings of most American journalists are informed by explicit or implicit criticism of powerful men and powerful institutions." But:

> In the last two decades, some of the wrong men and institutions have been labeled powerful, while some really powerful ones went unnoticed. We have missed real targets as we flailed away at stereotypes. . . . The professor, the journalist, and the bureaucrat have gained moral influence while the formal church has lost it. Taken as a group, the men of new power establish the fashions in ideas. . . . We are all, to some extent, more likely to criticize strangers than friends. All college-trained journalists (myself included) are far more likely to have professors, government employees, or other newsmen as close personal friends than corporate presidents, labor leaders, generals, or police chiefs.
>
> The new professions are far more like each other than like the old professions. Our backgrounds, educations, experiences, life-styles, tastes, and basic values are more like those of the new men of power than the old. Thus, we write favorably about our friends (or their friends) but we pick away at the men of old power—armed perhaps with tips, leaks, and insights provided by our friends, the new men of power.

Clark's emphasis on finding real power and watchdogging it is appropriate. We doubt, however, that the power shift has been so great. It is true that powerful trustees sometimes have been unable to control students. It is also true that President Johnson was forced to "abdicate" because of the critical power brought by "some professors, some students, television people, and some newspapermen." These examples seem to us noteworthy precisely because power so rarely operates that way. But whether Clark's vision, or ours, or another is accurate, the task of the imaginative newsman is to seek significant information. Editors, journalism educators, and would-be newsmen should investigate and debate where power lies, watch for its misuse, seek progress and reform, and crusade where necessary.

Clark Mollenhoff, an outstanding veteran reporter of the Cowles newspapers, has argued that a reporter tracking down corruption "should follow the dollar." At times people engage in shady practices to gain power, to keep power, or to help their friends. But most often money is behind corruption. Editors, without becoming manic about the subject, should routinely check to see whose pocket might be lined as a result of an important proposal, act, or deal.

Editors must, at the same time, realize that there are altruistic people who work hard for changes that offer them no financial rewards whatever. They toil only for what they consider will make a more pleasant or just world. Among these people are those who work for preservation of green space, recreation, family planning, safer highways, improved education, political reform, and dozens of other worthy goals—and even the goals the editor himself considers mistaken. These people also make news—news of progress. One satisfaction of newspaper work is observing up close a spectrum of the human race, from scoundrel to saint. The editor should not assume, despite confirming evidence on certain days, that everyone is a scoundrel. Imaginative editing includes also the search for "good news" of change.

Challenging prejudice

Impressions, not necessarily accurate ones, are picked up by people from their papers. These impressions are the result of hasty reading, poor memories, and habits of noting only what bolsters their prejudices. A good newspaper should challenge such impressions by printing, from time to time, the cold facts of a situation. For example, every year or so it may be necessary to recap the concrete actions concerning school integration in a community or state. Not everyone will read such facts, of course, but some will, and perhaps by steady effort the myths, half-truths, and incorrect assumptions can be given a decent burial.

Political figures and others who frequently make public pronouncements often only repeat what is common prejudice. In some instances prejudices are studiously promoted by certain people or groups, and the newspaper must convey the correct information. A sizable proportion of the public, for example, has accepted the idea that everyone on welfare is a loafer. It is commonly said that women on welfare have babies so they can get more money. The editor should check these common impressions. How much more does a woman on welfare get if she has another child? How much does a welfare family get? If a person on welfare got a job for one day, would his income be deducted from his welfare check—and thereby encourage him not to look for part-time work? The truth would make a story.

Another example is the impression in recent years that United States Supreme Court decisions have turned loose hundreds of criminals on silly technicalities. Unfortunately, many of these impressions were supported by editorial positions in carelessly edited newspapers. An imaginative editor, however, can take the impression and run what amounts to a box score on the Supreme Court's criminal decisions in the last half dozen years. What were the results? Who was released? Was anyone? Or, simply, was a new trial ordered? Did the decisions really hamstring the police? Or have some policemen used that story as an excuse for mediocre police work? And what of the courts closer to home? Might there be a box score on their activities?

Dozens of other illustrations could be cited. While these are examples of national impressions, in most towns at least a few local misconceptions are bandied about without correction. A good editor will do his best to get at the truth, even though he may suspect that most subscribers would rather read editorials and stories that reinforce their incorrect impressions.

It is helpful also to consider whether a person making a proposal has a concealed axe to grind. This does not mean that the editor must always suspect evil motives. But he should be skeptical. A senator once introduced legislation which would forbid imports of foreign firearms. This sounded like good news to those who supported gun control legislation. But there was a joker in the proposal: The senator came from the state that produced the most firearms in the nation. A ban on foreign weapons presumably would endear him to home industry and the home work force.

Covering varied viewpoints

Good newspapers pride themselves on giving "both sides"—the pros and cons. William F. Buckley, Jr., is put to bed next to Max Lerner, amid columns that are pro-Democratic as well as pro-Republican. Better papers have their own strong editorial voice, but they open their letters column to replies which rebut and even insult them.

Actually, complex issues have more than just pro and con sides. There are various angles which a newspaper has an obligation to cover in both its news and editorial pages. A major criticism of newspapers is that they present a narrow range of opinion. As presidential candidates and voters tend to cluster to the middle of the road on issues, so do newspapers. There have always been a few right-wing columnists, from Westbrook Pegler to David Lawrence to Henry J. Taylor, but columnists much to the left of center have been harder to find. For a time, Norman Thomas, perennial Socialist candidate for President, wrote a column for dailies, but his pieces were never widely used. On the Vietnam issue, the aging Walter Lippmann led the radical opposition, though for most of his days as columnist he was a centrist. Dick Gregory launched a column which might be called "radical black." But one of the major challenges to imaginative editors today remains that of finding and developing columnists who can go beyond regurgitating the conventional wisdom and present fresh and stimulating ideas and viewpoints. They may infuriate hidebound readers, but even optimists agree that the country's survival requires creative thought which will jog us out of old ruts.

Imaginative editors also could turn up local writers who would present strong viewpoints. That happens, but, in a quite human way, the editor too often prints or reprints "a terrific piece" which is terrific only because it endorses his views. Alert editors should also go after articles from the sociologist who wants a much more basic attack on ghetto problems, the minister who opposes a war (or endorses it), and the teachers' union president who feels a strike may be necessary next fall.

Some dissenting comments will come automatically to the letters column, of course. The editor takes particular care to print those which intelligently present views different from his own. Some editors try to print at least the nub of argument in every letter received. Others pride themselves—wrongly—in throwing away those from their opponents. Every paper receives a certain percentage of "nut letters" which deserve little space, but nothing angers the readership more than knowing that they have no chance to get their arguments into a paper, especially if it enjoys monopoly status through the support of their subscriptions! Publishing the full range of opinion in a community is survival insurance for a paper at the least, but at the most it demonstrates the highest responsibility to the community.

In broadcasting, regulations supporting the right of reply have been formulated, although the networks are contesting them in court. As it has worked out, the equal-time doctrine for political news has hampered the best coverage—yet some important people would like to have such regulations applied also to newspapers. The American Civil Liberties Union, for example, has contemplated a series of lawsuits to get court support for letting readers have a reply right in the paper. This raises important questions of press freedom—does the citizen's right to present his views outweigh the right of the editor to run his paper as he pleases? And what are society's rights? Taking a tip from this controversy, the editor might improve his paper's handling of opinion (and forestall government regulation) by encouraging replies. Too often an editor is content to give a maligned figure a paragraph or two of denial deep in a news story. Some news personalities fear how the reporter may handle their words. Then why not give them some space to state their side? How about a "combat page" where those involved in controversy can slug it out?

Why have there been so many demonstrations, marches, strikes, and riots in recent years? One explanation is that there is widespread feeling that only by such dramatic actions can ordinary citizens get media attention for civil rights or student gripes or peace or the high price of groceries. The difficulty is that news feeds on violence and unusual costumes. The pros and cons of the issues which have these citizens (and readers) agitated are glossed over or forgotten. The alert editor identifies the ferment, creating interest in his paper and contributing far more than the confused TV shots of moiling figures. Why not provide some columns of dissent? The Establishment—white or military or university or labor or corporate—has ways of getting its messages out. The newspaper might provide space for "the little guy," and let the powerful make their case too. People might stop saying that the newspaper is dull, that "there's nothing in it," if there were more real opportunity for clash of ideas. Editors might, indeed, raise the whole level of public controversy above the mindless level of recent combats.

Imaginative editing, in short, must challenge every group—the Establishment, the "silent majority," the radicals, conservatives, and so on—and seek new ways to involve ordinary citizens in improving our society.

The right to know

In their running battle with government, newspapermen for some time have emphasized the people's "right to know." Embedded in our constitutional law is the idea that citizens must be fully informed to participate intelligently in government. It is not surprising that in recent years Washington officials have been attacked first for "news management" and later for "the information gap."

Editors must remember, however, that their own job involves "managing the news," as the title "managing editor" suggests. Understandably, some citizens who are skeptical of Washington management are cynical, too, about the editor's management. They feel he leaves gaps in his reports, and they might insist to him, too, upon their "right to know." Far from quarreling with their ideas, a good newspaperman could only hope that more readers would insist on higher quality news work. Their demands might make it easier to get a better budget, hire more and better staffers, and put out an improved paper.

Emphasis on the reader's right to know brings us back to the subject of attaining excellence considered at the beginning of this chapter. There discussion was on internal organization and planning for improvement. The subject is further illuminated by considering excellence in light of what the reader needs to know.

The reader's needs

In some ways the flaws of the newspaper are the flaws of the modern university. The student picks courses in history, political science, economics, and literature. Unless he is unusually sharp, he may not see how economics affects politics and how history affects literature. Some educators and some students would like to figure out how to mesh these subjects, so as to provide an understanding of the world we live in, the world we used to live in, and the worlds we may live in.

The newspaper provides a similar smorgasbord. There are stories about politics, economics, social movements, education, and conservation, but there is little effort to interrelate them. Editors, if they think of it at all, apparently assume that the reader will put all these subjects into some loose order. It is quite an assumption, for most of the nation's editorial pages reveal that editors themselves are not particularly gifted in catching the ties between all the subjects they cover.

Many editors, of course, are concerned about this fragmentation and try to relate one piece of news to another, so perhaps it is a safe prediction that more and more newspapers will try to help the reader understand the interlinking of events that pass before him. Today, we are limited to grouping of associated news events, an occasional news analysis, and a boldface insert directing the news reader to check an editorial on the subject on page 22. Good as this is, it is not good enough. Part of the solution may be in the blend of the visual and the written word, as already discussed.

Not long before his retirement as executive director of the American Press Institute at Columbia University, some of the things that the modern reader has a right to expect from his paper were outlined by J. Montgomery Curtis. Subscribers are better educated and have much wider interests than they used to, Curtis pointed out, but "they also need leadership as never before." So he spoke of these "hard challenges" which readers present to the editor today:

> —to know simply and factually what our readers want and need most in their newspapers. *(Are you using your best reporters to let you know what non-newspaper people are talking about?)*
> —to report thoroughly on developing situations, whether there is news in them at the moment or not.
> —to report the truth about the quality of education in our communities.
> —to report thoroughly on that subject which probably is of more concern to our readers than any other—the matter of how to make a successful living, how to build a successful career, how to conduct a successful business in this world with ever-increasing automation. *(Are there more jobs in your community or are there fewer as a result of automation?)**
> —to help our readers to live in a world of inflated prices. *(Can you serve women by giving them news of prices and trends in food, clothing, etc.?)*
> —to report the truth about economic conditions in your cities. *(Are retail sales up or down? Why? Do you really know?)*
> —to protect the consumer from fraud. *(How about that door-to-door roofer—and is the truth-in-lending or truth-in-labeling law working out in your town?)*

The reader's nature

Perhaps the ideal editor would be one who is pushing constantly to get his readers to attend to the serious events and trends of their time. Without such an editor, the newspaper is little more than an entertainment sheet. The job of prodding and luring the reader requires subtlety—and patience. A reader will not get interested in Africa or even air polution by reading one story. William Rockhill Nelson, founder of the *Kansas City Star*, talked about the need for patience by citing his paper's campaign for a new bridge across the

* During the Depression, a neophyte pollster, George Gallup, told Columbia journalism students that the newspapers were missing a real bet in failing to give news about where job opportunities were. Papers are still missing that bet.

Missouri River. For years, he said, his paper ran news stories, feature stories, editorials, pictures, and cartoons about how the bridge was needed, how it would be needed even more in the future, how commerce would be assisted with a new bridge. The effort paid off. The bridge was built—but only after an editorial campaign that lasted ten years.

Such hammering at the public consciousness must be done if the citizen is to grasp the significance of what is all around him. To accomplish this hammering, without boring or irritating the reader, requires imagination. The editor must be able to present this information in dozens of different ways and, in most instances, in ways that the reader will think give him reward.

The most obvious play of imagination comes in the selection of stories. Problems never will be acute to the reader unless they are brought close to home. Even a newspaper in Phoenix should report that Lake Erie is so polluted that it has almost no marine life in it. The public needs to know that. But a reader in Arizona is not going to be as concerned about Lake Erie as a resident of Ohio. The editor must take the shocking story of Lake Erie's pollution and tie it to conditions at home.

It takes no great imagination to do this. Water pollution in one's own area can be checked. How pure are the streams nearby? How about the lakes? Is the supply of pure water in any danger? What would happen to the water supply if the area's population doubled within twenty years? How can the present pollution be shown graphically, with words and pictures? What is the state water control board doing about polluters? Scolding them? Fining them only $500?

The stories that result from investigation should not be pelted at the reader. A story today may be followed up in a couple of weeks. An editorial or a cartoon could be run from time to time. More ideas might be produced. Is there a conservation group? What does it propose? What is being suggested in other areas? Would those suggestions apply here? These local stories can be reinforced with national stories about water pollution. In so selecting and highlighting vital issues, the editor meets the real needs of readers.

The paper's teaching role

The newspaper of tomorrow may set aside certain sections for unabashed teaching. A generation or more ago newspapers ran serialized novels each day. Some even published a short novel in the Sunday supplement. To this day, papers run crossword puzzles and bridge columns. Why not a learning column?

With the superior color printing already available there could be a series on the history of art, with a text of perhaps 1,000 words under a four-column cut of a famous painting. A little quiz could be printed, for self-grading, every few days. Readers probably would not immerse themselves in the subject the way they would if they were taking a formal course in art history. But perhaps they would learn something about art and so appreciate it more.

The art course might run a month and then there could be a shift to economics, or a study of the short story, or geography, or transportation. Perhaps even serious non-fiction could be serialized. Rachel Carson's *The Sea Around Us*, for example, would have been an excellent book to serialize for a month. It would be possible that the "learning column" could always appear in a corner so the reader could clip each piece and put all of them into a folder.

Other instructional stories could be presented. The workings of the court system baffle many people, and yet news stories about the courts rattle off such words as appellate, mandamus, stay, and tort, as if anyone past the sixth grade were familiar with them. The series could tell the process of arrest, arraignment, the setting of bail, indictment, and trial. Another series could report on the history of the Bill of Rights, explaining in detail why the grand jury system was implanted there or why a person could not be accused twice of the same crime.

Already newspapers sometimes republish a series of articles or special layouts, such as housing stories, in a booklet. Such booklets are sold or given away as newspaper promotion. This practice will probably spread even to medium-sized papers. The booklet preserves the reporting beyond the admittedly short-lived newspaper story, helps promote the paper, and, best of all, serves as a reference work on the topic.

It is even possible that a newspaper might use the pictures and stories for a documentary film. This could be done inexpensively, with a stream of pictures (more than were used in the newspaper) serving as a backdrop to the words being spoken by a narrator. The film could be loaned or rented to interested schools and organizations. Again, the material would be excellent promotion for the paper.

This kind of enterprise was displayed when the famous Tokyo newspaper *Yomiuri Shimbun* sent a team of nine experts, journalists and scholars, to mainland China. After talks with officials and ordinary villagers, they produced a series of articles which was published in the United States as *This Is Communist China.*

A few American newspapers have published books. Many of these have been "instant books," in which several reporters each swiftly wrote three or four thousand words on some part of a big story. Copyeditors quickly read copy and a printing firm did the rest at breakneck speed. An illustration of this process occurred when Pope Paul VI visited New York. The *New York Times* staff, unoccupied at the time because of a strike, put together a book within twenty-four hours ready to deliver in Rome by the time the Pope arrived home.

The *Wall Street Journal* has put out a half dozen books, and the Associated Press published books soon after the murders of President John Kennedy and Senator Robert Kennedy. Today only a few big newspapers have the staff and money to attempt book publishing, but probably more will make the effort in the remaining years of the century. Perhaps eventually the books will be filmed and the reader, instead of holding a book in his hand, will project the words, in 72-point type, onto the wall. Books, or filmed books, will require the services of good editors, some of whom will be pulled off the copydesk to do the job.

There are schools with classrooms. There are schools of the air. As the imaginative editor fulfills the challenge of meeting the readers' right to knowledge, he can create a school of newspaper print.

15 The editor and journalistic writing

Editors on newspapers deal with writers and their writing in a number of ways, the most obvious being copyediting. The first three chapters covered problems of correcting and improving news stories; now we focus on more theoretical or philosophical problems. Copyeditors and other influential editorial employees must develop a philosophy of newswriting style, inculcate their ideas in their writers, and guide them toward the production of better writing.

Team leadership

The relationship of editor and writer may be on a one-to-one basis. Traditionally, the city editor assigns a reporter to a story and then sees that he does the job well. But as newspaper journalism becomes more and more thorough, an editor plays the role of a good athletic coach or committee chairman. A sub-editor, perhaps in consultation with the managing editor, decides whether to put two or three reporters on a series covering an important subject, or to organize a team for a complete investigation. Then he provides the leadership for the creation of the copy until it is finally edited and published.

As discussed in chapter 14, an editor should recognize and develop good ideas for major stories. Sometimes a subject is a natural because an alert reporter brings in a tip from some contact, and the appropriate editor simply has to give him the green light for time to dig into the question. The assistant city editor may hatch the idea for a great series while he is driving to work. Some of the best ideas may develop as a few editors and reporters are lunching, or perhaps talking shop at a picnic.

But as newspapers move to develop more and better interpretive and specialized pieces, editors have to set aside time to be creative and work out ideas. The newspaper office has traditionally been too hectic for other than the obvious ideas to be recognized. While some newspapers show initiative, in the last decade or two it often has been the magazine editor or the producer of an occasional TV documentary who has launched the really penetrating studies on subjects like violence or poverty. To be similarly effective, the newspaper editor must seek the quiet to ruminate about his community and trends and the problems of his neighbors and himself, and so discover what his readers need to know more about. The idea for an investigation of teen-age use of a new drug will probably hit any editor in the eye. But some knowledge of social developments and some pondering probably are necessary to recognize the need for a series on abortions among the community's women, changing rates of illegitimacy, or the fate of adoptable babies.

Perspective reporting

It can be argued that interpretive reporting is just good reporting. It is true that "in-depth" or "enterprise reporting" or "backgrounder" may simply be a fancy title for the old-fashioned digging which was a part of any good newswriting any time. Yet the complexity of modern issues and the social need to understand them require more resources, more reporters, more thought, and more leadership. Wes Gallagher, general manager of the Associated Press, has pointed to the shift toward investigative reporting and what he calls "perspective reporting."

"Today's problems are much more complex and investigation of them takes a lot more time and effort," he said in a William Allen White Memorial Lecture. "It is a rare case when one reporter can gather enough facts in a short time and come up with a story that will be authentic enough to convince and hold the attention of our new readers. . . . We can convince only by the most detailed presentation of facts, for facts alone have the ring of truth." It took months, he said, for the AP to develop a story of graft in Vietnam which ran on most of the front pages of the U. S. While the main job was done by two men, many others had a part. He continued:

> The other great weapon that we have is perspective reporting that can and must be used on the daily flow of news. . . . Perspective reporting is presenting news in its proper relationship to the whole and in relation to other news in its own time. Perspective reporting dissects the situation today and compares it with the past. . . . Perspective reporting requires a cold, logical approach to the news. It requires dogged pursuit of facts until the writer is convinced that he has everything he can possibly dig out. The facts must then be sorted and logically presented.

A sample investigation

Gallagher complained, for example, that the federal government was simply too big to be covered. There were 1,222,000 employees in the Department of Defense, he said, 80,000 in Agriculture, and so on. To deal with that coverage problem, the AP established a Washington-based group of ten top reporters, called the Special Assignment Team. Its head, Ray Stephens, a man in his forties with about two decades of AP experience, says its job is to ignore deadlines and look for "the submerged dimension" of the federal government. Its stories have made nation-wide headlines, such as "U.S. Military Fuel Stolen in Thailand" and "Study Shows Waste by Pentagon." Team members get leads to such stories by reading government reports or sometimes by tips from highly-placed friends. Then, like police investigators, team members conduct lengthy interviews and check published materials. In one instance, two members spent five months digging, which included line-by-line reading of fifteen volumes of hearing transcripts.

Under the direction of the metropolitan editor, four writers for the *New York Times* produced a 30,000-word report for the paper on a scandal in the city's Human Resources Administration. Some three months of work began on an October 18 when Metropolitan Editor Art Gelb wrote a memo telling Richard Reeves, city hall bureau chief, to take a look. A tip from Reeves and a word dropped from a city official to a magazine writer persuaded him that the anti-poverty program was in a "ghastly mess." Later, Gelb added Barnard L. Collier to the job. By mid-December there was considerable material, and Gelb deployed Richard Phalon from the city financial beat and Richard Severo of criminal court beat to join the team.

In early January Gelb told the foursome to get out of the office and not come back until ready to write. Five days later, after midnight, the four phoned Gelb from a Chinese restaurant in New Jersey that they were ready and had to see him right away.

> "Right away" turned out to be dinner that night at the Gelbs' apartment when Barbara [Gelb] joined a support team that finally included Beverly Collier and Carol Reeves—whose homes were invaded by the strangest men—Barbara Campbell, who shifted our phone calls from the office to a dozen weird places and then held us together for the first week of writing, Linda Lake, our blushing researcher who learned words they don't teach in Library Science, George Barrett, who read and reread every one of our 30,000 words, John Darnton and Jim Sterba, who did some fine reporting, Marty Tolchin, who faithfully recorded every nasty thing the mayor and Mitch Ginsberg (HRA administrator) said about us, and Steve Roberts, who was followed by Los Angles police as he tracked down a West Coast lead. The L. A. cops faithfully reported to New York authorities that Steve was staying at a "motel" with a woman "unknown locally." It was his wife, Cokie.
>
> There were also honorary team members in the highest and lowest places who might be embarrassed, fired, or indicted if we revealed what they told us or did for us.

Gelb moved the team into a conference room next to the sports department and set the clock half an hour ahead each afternoon to get copy moving earlier. He talked the other editors into allotting more or less unlimited space. It appeared that part of the scandal involved a plot to embezzle a million dollars and transfer it from city accounts to a bank in Zurich, so the *Times* pulled its foreign desk into the story. "There was something satisfying about working on an investigation and having some of the best professionals in the law enforcement business calling you for information. And that's the way it was on the Swiss bank caper." (The team won the 1968 Byline Award of the New York Newspaper Reporters Association.)

Investigative leadership

The editor's role in such investigative or interpretive reporting is that of any good team leader. He goads, he persuades, he inspires, he pushes. He supervises the collection of data, on the theory that two or more editoral heads are better than a single reporter's. He works over drafts to see that there are no holes—and no libel. He asks the questions that even the best team of investigators may not think of. The editor puts together his own experience in reporting and editing and his knowledge of the community to make sure the staff has done its best.

Sometimes the editor must use a firm hand to get the production the community deserves. In one middle-sized city the social welfare reporter got the go-ahead to do a series on Negro employment in local business and industry. He was so thorough that he conducted scores of interviews over several weeks. As time passed, the information in the early interviews began to get stale. The paper's interest flagged, perhaps in part because the lengthy investigation brought worried inquiries from industrial leaders. When the brief series finally appeared, it was weak—much weaker than if done with more dispatch. Perhaps the city editor should have assigned a second reporter to help collect information. Perhaps the editor should have told the reporter at a certain point, "You've got enough material. Write it!" In any event, firm and courageous editorial leadership was missing.

Aides of the team

Editors also have leadership roles with various non-staffers. As indicated in chapter 8, the state editor may have to teach the country correspondent the basics of straight writing. Steady, clear communication is essential to lead a team of part-time stringers. Similarly, a good foreign desk provides leadership for its foreign correspondents—staff and stringer. One of the major complaints of reporters who write abroad is that the home office does not communicate but leaves them too much on their own.

Free-lance writers and photographers also can be valuable. They should be treated courteously even if the paper can use only a little free-lance work, and they should be encouraged and guided if the quality of work is poor but promising.

Amateurs should be given pointers about producing the articles or pictures the paper can use. The roto magazine of the *Houston Chronicle* has a form that explains its needs in subjects, pictures, manuscript preparation, and deadlines, and its method of payment. Queries on ideas should be answered, not ignored. Rejected material should be sent back promptly, even if the editor is busy and overburdened, and checks ought to be mailed quickly for accepted material. The smart editor supplements his regular staff operation when he provides effective leadership for the part-timers and free-lances.

The editor as teacher

More advanced editors in various slots must serve as instructors in English and journalism, especially with greener reporters. At worst this teaching is hit or miss; at best it must be sandwiched into the few moments that editors and writers can find together in their busy schedules.

The editor first of all has to be clear what his goals are for good writing. Does he want thoroughness, brightness, or both? Then, in countless observations, corrections, criticisms, and sermonettes, he shows his writers how they are, and are not, measuring up.

Outlines and structures

Every journalistic neophyte soon learns, if he does not already know, that news stories are constructed on the pattern of the "inverted pyramid." The most important facts go into the first paragraph, or lead, and other information follows in short paragraphs of less and less importance so the pattern can be diagrammed as a triangle standing on its point, a two-dimensional inverted pyramid. The perceptive editor discovers soon enough, if he has not already learned it as a reporter, that this pattern applies only to the simplest news items, unless "inverted pyramid" is understood in the most general terms, as different stories require different forms.

Traditionally, the feature story has always been an exception. The writer can start a feature with a question or an anecdote or a quote, among other devices, and he may write chronologically or according to some other non-triangular logic. Sometimes features are diagrammed as pyramids sitting on their bases, but this schematization is no more applicable universally than the triangle is to news stories. An editor who started to revise a feature to fit any such preconceived pattern would soon stop, frustrated and foolish.

What, then, *can* an editor discover about the structure of complicated stories, and what can he hope to teach his advanced reporters?

In his popular English textbook, *The Practical Stylist*, Prof. Sheridan Baker of the University of Michigan argues that the writer should find a *thesis* to begin his piece. A thesis can be stated as a debate resolution, "Resolved that . . ." When the writer thus clarifies his aim, he finds that the supportive information falls into logical order, into an outline.

This approach has some validity for most news stories, since the beginning states the point of each piece (though not argumentatively as the word *thesis* implies). The concept is most applicable to the work of the editorial writers when they attempt persuasive editorials, but in the newsroom Baker's thesis on theses is generally valuable. It reminds editors to look for clear exposition of the main point close to the top of a story.

Another rhetorical tradition classifies writing forms, such as the essay, into a natural (and obvious) pattern of three parts—beginning, middle, and end, standing like three rectangular blocks piled one on another. The middle block might be subdivided into several flat rectangles (or paragraphs) of development. The bottom block is conclusion. This plan fits nicely with Baker's, if the top block contains the statement of thesis.

This tripartite form again may seem more suited to essays for the editorial page than for front-page news accounts. The shift toward more and more interpretation, however, makes this observation less and less certain. What is a series of articles but a number of blocks? And as background, depth, and perspective become the writer's watchwords, he is less concerned with the first-paragraph punch of the inverted-pyramid and more concerned with the clarity emphasized in the beginning-middle-end structure.

Complex patterns

Analysis of news stories over many decades shows that actually they are not simple triangles. Usually they are a number of triangles on a string, like fish. The story unfolds in two or three paragraphs, then recaps with more detail, explains at length in a third triangle, and perhaps adds minor detail and color in still another. Consider the story of a major fire in three or four buildings. The first section quickly recounts the deaths and damage. The next section reveals how it started and spread and how fire-fighting forces were marshalled. The next triangles tell who discovered it, of the efforts to confine it to the first building, and of a call for outside help. There may be a snippet about two suburbs that sent equipment and men. A block of type may inquire into insurance. Then in more leisurely fashion the writer may present the whole chronology again, quoting the passerby who thought he saw smoke, the watchman who opened the inner doors and discovered the blaze, or the woman who threw her baby into the fire net.

The story may form a more complicated pattern than even a series of triangles, as figure 15-1 suggests. A triangle that tapers off to the inconsequential point would bore a reader. Rather, each triangle becomes blunt-bottomed. Some are hardly triangles at all. Can a chronological account be called a triangle, since start, middle and finish are equally essential to the tale? Is a list of injured a triangle? Blocks and wedges are more appropriate to clear portrayal of the way a long story is put together.

The copyeditor who sees news articles in some such schematic fashion will understand better how they can be tightened and rearranged. Perhaps the inner logic requires that a paragraph or two near the end be moved up to a higher position, even though these sentences are in themselves quite trivial. Or perhaps cutting a minor detail in the heart of the story will strengthen the whole.

An editor able to analyze advanced writing can quickly show reporters where their work is solid and where it is loose or rambling. His analytic skill is especially useful in working with an investigative team. Structuring the long series becomes like outlining a lengthy magazine article or the book. Formal logic has to be related to the likelihood that a reader's interest will wane, and to the technical demand that the individual pieces be a certain length. "Can we shift this block into the first article in the series, and can we give the third piece some punch by building up this anecdote?" Sometimes these deceptively simple questions lead his writing team into a type of outline they hoped to have left in Freshman English.

It may be useful to think of the modern news story not as a triangle but as a freight train: The diesel supplies the power and the pace, and a series of boxes follow with the information. More than other types of writing, news stories have minimal transitions and internal references. With little concern, a copyeditor can shift paragraphs around. The building blocks of many stories seem almost interchangeable. To the extent that the news fits this train pattern, writer and editor both can shunt the box cars in and out of the line, pushing those with the less important freight to the end, where an editor or printer can uncouple the last few.

Fig. 15-1. Story patterns. These patterns are a more realistic picture of complex news stories than the traditional inverted pyramid. The more complex the story, the more likely it is a combination of triangles, wedges, and rectangles. Copyeditors who recognize these variations will be able to reshape a story effectively.

Whatever the pattern, the story must be logical. That logic need not be of the I, II, III type. It can be chronological or it can be psychological, in the sense that the reporter moves the reader from one point of interest to another. The chief sin is rambling. It is "circling and droning, reminiscent of buzzards hovering, swooping over a victim until he drops," in the words of a prominent magazine editor and no mean writer himself, Norman Cousins, of the *Saturday Review*. Good organization of thoughts is the key to good written or oral communication, says Cousins, adding: "The prime element in this process is sequence. Ideas have to be fitted together. The movement of a concept or an image from the mind of the speaker to the mind of the listener is retarded when words become random chunks rather than sequential parts of an ordered whole."

Both reporters and editors rarely think of the most effective ways to structure their accounts. They play by ear and do the job as newsmen have for decades. Therefore, the editor-teacher must jog both writers and copyeditors to strive for patterns that will communicate best in today's paper.

More should be done on newspapers to discover fresh, new ways to present material related to a central story, but more variations could be explored. Instead of one long story, why not five short stories which are sidebars to each other? Why not play three or four related stories, perhaps with a box or editorial to explain their common theme?

Magazine editors appear more ambitious in developing new patterns of presentation. They have tried boldface summaries, like precedes, at the top of articles in trade magazines. They have boldfaced the first paragraph of new sections. Some have tried narrative, near-fiction techniques; others have paired two pieces, one light and illustrated, the other serious and editorial. Newspapermen may find stimulating ideas of writing patterns and related graphic displays in the best-edited magazines.

The meanings of style

"Style" is used by newspaper editors in at least two senses. The uniform system of spelling and capitalization is called style, as we discussed in chapter 2 on copyediting, but the form and presentation of newspaper prose are also style.

Good journalistic style is not florid, not ornate, not rhetorical. The late journalism dean Frank Luther Mott used to say, the best journalism is also good literature, as clearly demonstrated in the reporting of Ben Franklin, Stephen Crane, and Ernest Hemingway. English professors have long contended that good prose is usually plain and straightforward and therefore clear. "The approach to style is by way of plainness, simplicity, orderliness, sincerity," says William Strunk, Jr., and E. B. White's *The Elements of Style*. And so it is to good newspaper style too.

Effective prose communicates ideas and information. It might be argued that some English is used to convey an ambiance or feeling without presenting much fact. But such usage in news reports is rare.

Journalistic style has to be functional. The need to quickly convey ideas from one mind to other minds underlies the need for simple, clear writing.

What language scholars call "standard English" is appropriate to newspapers. Neither the formal English of the academic book nor the "non-standard" or colloquial dialect of folksy talk has much place in newspaper pages. For most purposes, reporters and editors should choose their words from the broad range of language understood by most moderately educated people.

Standard English is threatened on the one side by jargon and gobbledegook. Reporters close to many professions may fall into legalese, academic pudder, or bureaucratic gibberish. On the other side is a threat from what has traditionally been known as slang —faddish talk. Noting the likenesses between the academicians and the hip talkers, the editing authority on the *New York Times*, Theodore Bernstein, has pointed out that both groups substitute their own redundant words for normal English. Both have some intent to be secret and so obscure to those not of the in-group. Newspapers must abjure both kinds of fringe English if they are to communicate across the strata of a diverse readership.

Advocates of plain, simple style sometimes face the objection that this kind of writing is dull and lifeless. It need not be. Concrete nouns and strong verbs close to human experience can make a simple sentence vivid and lively. Yet sometimes even a good writer will fill a story with the stereotyped and obvious until it shrivels and dies.

"Over the years, wire service reporting had gotten flat, had leveled off to an efficient but uninspired pattern," said Roger Tatarian, UPI editor, to explain why UPI was shifting its attitude about news presentation to stress readability. To help make its style more human UPI introduced a category, "Personal Report," to personalize stories traditionally done impersonally. Reporters were instructed to write first-hand pieces and even use "I." In a staff memo Tatarian said: "The use of the *I* can be effective only if it is not overdone, and if it is done logically and naturally. There should be enough of it to give the flavor of a letter to the folks at home, but not so much as to make the writer hog the center of the stage."

Other editors might adopt this view as they try to develop reporting styles which are at once simple, lively, clear, readable, and communicative.

The sources of style

An editor's examination of style comes down to his analysis of the grammatical ingredients of the story. As the physicist probes molecules, atoms, and electrons to try to understand matter, the editor digs into paragraphs, sentences, and words. Admittedly, there is a mystic quality in the overall effect of writing, for the whole somehow turns out to be greater than the sum of the parts. Still, some of the mystery can be penetrated by looking at the individual blocks and the ways they fit one another.

Paragraphs

In most writing the paragraph is an obvious fundamental block. The formal outline of an essay or a book divides into topics, subtopics, and sub-sub-topics; each sub-sub-topic may be treated as a paragraph. Such a unit will have a topic sentence (actually a sub-sub-topic sentence) supported by five or a dozen or more sentences. With proper transitions, such paragraphs clearly reveal the structure and movement of the work.

Such paragraphs set in column widths, even the new-fashioned six-column pages, might each run four or five or even ten inches. Even set in the wider measure used for editorials, they would look forbidding. So newspapermen, including editorial writers, use shorter paragraphs, often only one or two sentences long.

Copy is not effectively formed into short paragraphs by haphazard chopping, as some reporters and copyreaders apparently suppose. Nor is simply breaking most stories into one-sentence paragraphs enough, as it once was in more sensational papers. The best procedure is to search the "normal" paragraph of the topic-sentence variety for the clusters of ideas within it. Thus a twelve-sentence unit may prove to be made up of four to six smaller pieces. Each piece then may become a newspaper-type paragraph, and each may run one or two, perhaps three, sentences, but rarely more. In type the paragraph will be a horizontal rectangle or a square rather than a formidable, vertical oblong. At the same time, if the writer sees the relation of these shorter paragraphs to the overall pattern, he is able to write in a more logical style.

Sentences

A paragraph should rarely run over fifty words. In typescript, a paragraph of four or five lines is beginning to run too long. If such a paragraph has even two or three sentences, they must obviously be short—perhaps an average of fifteen words, though no such figure should be taken arbitrarily. Length is thus one criterion of the good sentence, and newspaper sentences are usually short compared to those in books or scholarly magazines.

Sentences also should be straight—that is, clear and to the point. "English is going to pot, and one of the reasons it's going to pot is the way it's taught," complained Dr. Don Cameron Allen, professor of English at Johns Hopkins University. "I teach students to write a straight sentence. That's what English is all about. You will find excellent examples of good straight sentences in good American newspapers."

Though grammatically most straight sentences are simple, few compound, and even fewer complex, newsmen might pay more attention to what is known in English classes as the periodic sentence. The elements in American sentences are somewhat loosely tied, but not quite haphazard. By contrast, the periodic sentence builds from beginning to end, so the last element is the climax. That gives writing punch, like this: Mayor Jones paused over the document, frowned, and then, as his face and neck reddened, shouted, "Never!" Of course, putting an idea at the start of a sentence also can have impact: "Cut taxes" was the cry of most of those testifying.

Three common faults of newspaper sentences easily identified by the editor-teacher are the *clogged*, the *overburdened* and the *too-complex*.

The clogged sentence simply packs too much information between the capital letter and the period. Writing dense sentences used to be good style but is now old-fashioned. For example, no desk today should pass a sentence with this beginning:

> Jonathan Doakes, 41, of 6357 Harmondale Drive, a carpenter and part-time plumber, who told reporters he had never been in trouble before, and a companion, who gave his name as Samuel Smithson, 53, of 6359 Harmondale Drive, also a carpenter, were arrested today after what was, according to witnesses, a scuffle over the way another neighbor, Clyde Hendricks, 32, of 6358 Harmondale Drive, should build his fences.

The modern way is to rewrite, "Two carpenters were arrested today after a scuffle over the way another neighbor should build his fences." The specifics can wait.

The overburdened sentence, although like the clogged, is not so much packed with facts as overstuffed with ideas. The writer loads too much freight onto the sentence before he hits the period key.

> Like the legislature's redistricting plan of 1969, the proposed new constitutional amendment now before the Senate Judiciary Committee, and soon to go before the House Rules Committee, not only deals with the congressional district problem but also the issue of one-voter-one-vote, according to regulations set by a previous ruling of the Supreme Court.

Break it up, simplify.

The too-complex sentence resembles both the clogged and the overburdened. Its writer is following the dictum to get away from the simple Dick-saw-Jane sentence. It is good advice, especially for essays and editorials, but the newswriter can overdo by throwing in too many clauses and phrases.

> Since the recent outbreak of warfare and because of popular reaction to the news, especially in view of the fact that it came on the heels of revulsion about the pact of Vienna, the Communists and their satellites, not only in Eastern Europe but in much of Asia, have restricted travel by foreign newsmen who will now have to obtain stories from an official press bureau.

Again, break it up.

Writers of these three faulty types of sentences have in common the laudable attempt to pack a lot of information into a short space.

But an overconcentration of facts or ideas or grammatical style makes a story opaque. The antidote in each case is to lighten the load of each sentence. Even the most intelligent reader needs frequent periods to "catch his breath."

A fruitful suggestion for writing better sentences is summarized in the slogan, "One idea, one sentence." Elements in the preceding stories such as the carpenters' addresses, the old redistricting plan, or that Vienna pact should be cut away from the verbose illustrative sentences above. The main idea of each sentence then will stand out so the reader can grasp it quickly.

Editors of the *New York Times* have pushed the one-idea-to-a-sentence theme for several years. Their second-guessing bulletin, *Winners & Sinners*, has occasionally pointed up the value of the concept with illustrations from the paper. Here, for example, is one sentence which would be easier to follow if divided:

> Black nationalism is the dominant mood of the Negro masses in the United States today, according to James Farmer, who warns white liberals in his book, "Freedom—When?" that there will be no respite from demonstrations and other forms of direct action until full equality is achieved.

Here is another sinner from the *Times:*

> In Montreal, leaders of the American Bar Association killed Wednesday a resolution denouncing a key provision of the civil rights bill aimed at preventing discrimination in the selection of Federal jurors.

Of the second example the *W&S* editor commented: "The facts are all there, but the reader has to go to work on them. He has to take it from the bottom: The bill is against discrimination. Fine. But the resolution denounces this provision. Uh-uh. But wait a minute—the bar leaders have killed the resolution. So it's fine again, eh? In other words, the bar leaders took a stand in favor of preventing discrimination in the selection of Federal juries. Why not say it in some form similar to that?"

Words

The strength of sentences depends ultimately on the choice and arrangement of their words. The good editor becomes expert on these basic blocks. Instead of the vague, the abstract, and the unusual, he seeks words which are *direct, concrete,* and *familiar*—words which build vivid and accurate pictures for most readers.

Some editors prefer words of Anglo-Saxon background to those with Latin roots. Generally, pithy words are from Old English, flowery ones from the Romance languages (i.e., those descended from Latin, the language of the Romans). Actually, a combination of words from both streams often most effectively provides variation and texture. Accuracy and strength, as well as commonness, should guide word choice, and vitality in verbs is especially important.

Forms of "to be" are generally static—as in that clause—so editors prefer verbs which act, which suggest movement. One-syllable words often generate the most power. Reducing the sentence usually adds strength. Pare away weak or unnecessary adjectives and adverbs. (If this paragraph demonstrates its own preachments, it is because of vivid words like *roots, pithy, flowery, works, texture, static, guide,* and *pare.*)

Choice of the right word nowadays is complicated by rapid changes in language. Again, a number of guides are available. Published almost a decade ago, the third edition of *Webster's New International Dictionary* embodies mid-twentieth century language and so is available in most newsrooms today. But the third edition gives few value judgments on words. For a more regular, though more conservative evaluation of words, some editors prefer the second edition, compiled in the thirties. A good guide to modern American usage is the *Dictionary of Contemporary Usage* by Bergen and Cornelia Evans. Also valuable is the revision by Sir Ernest Gowers of the famous *Dictionary of Modern English Usage* of H. W. Fowler, a classic in England. Theodore Bernstein of the *Times*, quoted earlier, has three helpful books, the first based on *Winners & Sinners: Watch Your Language, More Language That Needs Watching,* and more recently, *The Careful Writer: A Modern Guide to English Usage.*

Commenting on the last book, literary critic Granville Hicks said that of the six guidelines Bernstein suggests for judging good usage, he preferred this one: *Observation of what makes for clarity, precision, and logical presentation.* Hicks points out that this rule prohibits some newer usages that obscure rather than clarify. While Hicks admits that the misuse of "like" for "as" will not greatly damage the language, he believes that the growing confusion of "infer" for "imply" does debase our common English coin. Such distinctions may seem picky. But effective writing depends upon careful and correct choices precisely at this level of language.

A final word on jargon

As we said before, jargon confuses more than clarifies. In medicine or law, to be sure, a specialized word may add precision. In education, argues Dr. James S. LeSure of the Connecticut Department of Education, jargon actually can confuse even educators. But teachers use phrases like "peer acceptance" and "group practice" because these seem to give them professional status, even though parents don't know what they are talking about. So Dr. LeSure wrote *Guide to Pedaguese*, "a handbook for puzzled parents" that may also help education writers.*

"When you get your degree you can't wear it around your neck to prove you're educated," urban reformer Saul Alinsky wrote in *Harper's* magazine, "so instead you use a lot of three and four-syllable words. Of course, they aren't any use at all if you really want to

*The U. S. Government Printing Office issues an inexpensive booklet with similar aims, *Gobbledygook Has Gotta Go* (1966).

communicate with people. You have to talk straight English, using a small word every time you can instead of a big one." Such advice is good not only for educators and sociologists but for reporters and editors. They communicate best when they use simple words in straight sentences in brief but well-organized paragraphs.

Theories of readability

In a computer age when so much of life is quantified, it is tempting to analyze and measure language in the search for better communication. Can English be approached scientifically? Can the clarity or interest of a piece of writing be weighed or measured? Yes and no. No calipers or scales exist to indicate accurately whether sentences convey their message well. But quantification of newspaper copy may help a writer analyze style.

What can be measured? The stylists and critics we have examined indicate the qualities we might hope to quantify: difficulty of words, complexity and density of sentences, use of clichés or jargon, strength of verbs, and so on. The problem with measurement is that many of these stylistic qualities defy objective judgment.

Readability theorists who search for objective measurements have centered on judging the difficulty of words and sentences, which is certainly a key consideration. This factor is measured in the "fog index" developed by Robert Gunning (explained in *The Technique of Clear Writing*) and in the "Flesch formula" described by Rudolf Flesch (in *The Art of Readable Writing* and other books). After study of these and other practical applications of readability theory, Dr. Jeanne S. Chall of Ohio State University identified four significant reliable measurements: vocabulary load, sentence structure, idea density, and human interest. The first two relate to the Gunning-Flesch work, and the third is associated with clogging and overburdening. We shall look at the fourth below.

The Flesch formula

In the late forties AP hired Flesch to advise on improving writing. So practical journalistic use was made of a "readability formula" he had devised. His scheme rests on two assumptions. First, the number of syllables in samples of 100 words each increases as the writing becomes more difficult. Second, the more short sentences in the samples the easier the reading. Actually, short words in short sentences can be hard going, but since the opposite is more often the case, the assumptions seem justified.

Starting with them, one can randomly choose a few samples from news stories, interpretive stories, or editorials. He counts the syllables and the number of sentences (to find average sentence length) and works out the Flesch score according to the mathematics or charts in Flesch's books. If the sentences average fifteen to eighteen words each and if there are 145 to 155 syllables in each sample, the writing scores as "standard" and is suitable for much newspaper writing. Such sentences are not very long, obviously, and such a vocabulary includes a great many one-syllable words. However, using more long words or making the sentences more complex (and therefore longer) will almost certainly make the writing more difficult.

Paring sentences to an average of twelve words each and vocabulary to 130 or 140 syllables per hundred words results in what Flesch rates as "easy." If news stories were written at this level—and few are—less-educated readers would doubtless grasp them more readily.

The chart in figure 15-2 gives a quick check of readability, according to the ideas of Flesch and Gunning. If the editor selects a random sample of 100 words of copy, he can count syllables and number of sentences and plot the coordinates, perhaps with help of an L-shaped cardboard. An editor should check several samples before making any generalizations about the paper, and he should consider hundreds of samples from different pages over a considerable period of time before determining the readability of his paper needs his special attention.

Fig. 15-2. Readability chart. Count the syllables in a 100-word sample of news copy and find that number on the horizontal line. Then count the sentences (to nearest quarter) in the same sample; find that number on the vertical line. The intersection of the coordinates (a cardboard cut in the shape of "L," as for picture editing, will help) identifies the simplicity or difficulty of the sample. The graph shows samples with the following counts plotted to indicate three major categories: Easy, Standard, and Hard (marked with E, S, and H, respectively).

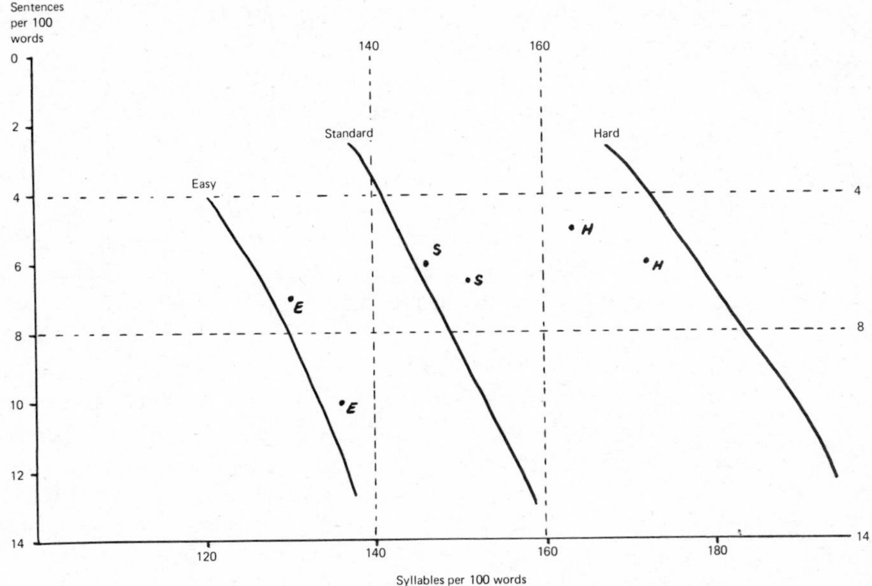

Applying the test

Using the Flesch method, two researchers compared news stories to editorials in several West Coast dailies. They found both forms difficult, but the news was actually less readable than the editorials! "The median readability level of news stories analyzed in this study indicates that most of them can be readily comprehended by only those people with a high school diploma or a college education."

Editors want copy which will, as these researchers say, reach "audiences from a wider range than that."[1]

Recognizing that some writing passes muster as "readable" but is still dull, Flesch later developed a "human interest" formula. The most important factor in these measurements are what he calls "personal words"—he, she, Mr. Brown, Susan, etc. He also counts, but gives less weight to, "personal sentences," which include quotations and direct address to the reader. Fortunately, news stories deal with people, so a degree of human interest "comes naturally." However, some writers tend to abstractions, especially in writing of such subjects as government finance or sociology. To counteract this, editors can remind reporters that they must bring human beings into their copy.

Assessing the audience

Being concerned to make news writing easier and more interesting does not mean an editor must seek the lowest common denominator of readership. True, he should provide some material, aside from sports and comics, which is clear even to poorly educated readers. And he should try to reach a broad readership. But some papers that have directed all content toward the "average" person have declined in circulation and general economic health. The successful papers of today continue to improve the quality of content a notch or two every few years. If a newspaper did choose stories for only a ninth grade audience, it would omit much information on science, the arts, serious economics, the inner workings of politics, and dozens of other subjects.

To argue that because the average *formal* educational level of a community is only 10.3 years the paper must be written for high school sophomores assumes that a person learns nothing after he leaves school. It also assumes that those with little schooling and little experience are newspaper readers. It is more realistic to assume that those above average in education and intelligence are the most avid readers. While still including news of interest for those who are not so lucky or concerned, the mix of content should emphasize news for them. Nonetheless, editors should insist that stories always are lively and clear, as well as fact-filled. Even the most intelligent reader, who is able to cope with a scholarly journal, may be pestered with distractions while reading his newspaper. Like everyone else, he must sometimes get the facts from his paper without much concentration. This means that the writing must be appealing and easy.

But Tom Wicker of the *New York Times* is right when he says, "Nobody yet ever made a writer out of a hack by setting up rules. . . . And to the man who tells me that every story can be written in 600 words, or 750, or whatever, I say that that is merely a rule; and I take my stand with Joseph Pulitzer, who said with a writer's exactness and a lawyer's flexibility that the prescription was 'terseness—intelligent, not stupid, condensation.'" Neither readability nor human interest concepts should be viewed as magic cure-alls. They can help newspapermen check on their talent for good copy, and no more. The good editor, as captain of his team, must above all continue to study overall story organization and the effective use of style.

16 Editorial management

Time and space are major problems for newspaper editors—the time of staff and the white space of newsprint. Money, a great deal of it, is needed to manage both of these, so the higher echelons of editors must also tackle budget questions. The managing editor's basic job is budget—budgeting of staff time, of news hole, and of money allotted to editorial. To administer this budget management relies on communications. Except for a few hours of reading and thinking, the managing editor spends most of his work-week communicating, in order to be in harmony with his organization and community. One of the ironies of newspapering is that, although the editor's business is communication, few are better with internal communications than are executives in any other business.

Internal communication

Newspapers use virtually every means of communication employed in modern social organizations. Staff members meet and confer in formal groups, then break up to meet and talk informally. Each editor talks individually with other staffers, chatting across his desk or theirs, or over the telephone with a police reporter at the jail, the stringer in the state, or the cub in trouble. Top editors drop in on sub-editors or look over a reporter's shoulder as he types; they casually chew over ideas with colleagues at lunch. Grouping desks by department in the newsroom facilitates communication. The grouping often leads to conversation that stimulates editorial effort and creativity.

Editors also communicate in writing. They send memos and notes. The smart chiefs post material on a bulletin board, teletype messages to outlying staffers, and distribute work plans, news budgets, and assignment sheets.

These are obvious ways editors communicate, but they might use them more effectively by taking time to ask themselves, apropos each message: What is the best way to communicate this? A general meeting? A quiet talk? A private memo? A note for the bulletin board?

Internal communication problems generate bureaucratic weaknesses. Any newspaper with more than three or four staffers, like any college with more than three or four professors, tends to become a little bureaucracy. Staffers complain about "too many meetings" or "so many memos I don't have time to read 'em all," as if humans somewhere managed organizations without them. Still, the good editor avoids the bureaucratic dangers of confusion, excessive complexity, and impersonal coldness. In the language of communications theory, he does not clog the channels with his messages until the output is only noise. An editor who keeps his communications brief, clear, warm, personal, and human will have a staff—and a newspaper—that reflects his effort.

Management style

Every editor inevitably develops a style of administration and so puts the stamp of his personality on procedure. Some editors are authoritarian, barking orders and pulling rank. Others are more democratic, discussing rather than dictating.

In college one used to hear much of developing a "winning" personality. The emphasis indicates that the successful leader likes and understands people—and knows how to persuade them to his purpose. But the fact is that, as in other lines of work, a fair number of martinets and neurotics gets into high editorial positions. For a while, at least, the wheels turn despite the friction and resentments. A few editors have used callousness to build a successful paper, but more have failed.

A newspaper manager ought to keep in mind that proud and talented reporters, editors, and photographers will resent being treated like drones. To bring them into the mainstream of decision-making usually means a better paper and a more satisfied staff. The paper then becomes "our paper," not merely "the paper."

Editors should make an extra effort to fit young men and women and their ideas into the operation, especially since today's college graduates have been on campuses during a period of ferment and independence. Young staffers probably have always complained that the management, usually middle-aged or above, is behind the times. Some of their criticism springs from youthful impatience, yet there is often a real lag as newspapers—and other institutions—cling to the old.

Put another way, newspaper executives must themselves try to be open, flexible. They should take pains to review their policies frequently. Some rules perhaps never were wise nor workable; now they hamstring and stultify. It is not unusual for a new staffer, hearing of a newsroom taboo, to mutter, "Who thought up that stupid rule?" If there is good reason for the policy, it ought to be explained. But editors must avoid defending outmoded standards with the cliché, "We've always done it that way."

Some flexibility and imagination are helpful also in the editorial managing of money. It is one thing to be economical and another to be parsimonious. Few things annoy a reporter or sub-editor more than to have the management pinch pennies in regard to taxi fares or ordinary newsroom supplies. One small newspaper chain even makes the staff furnish pencils. Such nickel-chasing damages staff morale and raises questions about the capabilities of management to manage anything.

The number of such moss-backed managers fortunately is declining. More and more newspaper plants are clean, attractive, and comfortable. Coffee, soft drinks, and sandwiches are available in a lunch room. Lighting is adequate. The noise is muffled and the work space is not crowded. Some newsrooms nowadays are even carpeted.

Budgeting the money

The top man on the editorial side—the executive editor or managing editor—has a certain number of dollars under his control per month or per year. How much control he wields can vary considerably. The publisher himself may hold the strings of the purse tightly. Or an executive editor, given virtually complete power over editorial budget, may choose to decentralize responsibility, sharing it with department heads such as the sports editor or the metropolitan editor.

In newsrooms across the country money questions generate most of the headaches among managing editors. They are not trained as accountants, and their rise through the news ranks probably indicates that figuring budgets is one of their least favorite tasks. On one hand, the managing editor must get the most good work for his salary dollar. On the other, he has to demand from the publisher or business manager the budget necessary for editorial excellence. Like a union official, he always seeks more money for his staff. To the extent he successfully gets a fair share of net income and wisely spends it, the managing editor produces the quality which creates a newspaper's reputation. His failure brings deterioration and decay so severe that even the casual reader notices.

If the chief editor represents all the editorial underlings—as a university dean may represent a school faculty and students in parlaying with top administration—he also serves as the representative of management. Reporters and department editors may feel he fronts for the publisher, as deans are accused of fronting for administrations to hold down faculty salaries or throttle students. He has a delicate role to play. He has to interpret the realities of publishing to a staff no more enthusiastic about budgeting than he is while having to convince everyone, above and below, that he is honest and fair.

Salaries and the Guild

The wicket is especially sticky in bargaining with the journalists' union, the American Newspaper Guild. The Guild's job is to convince all levels of management to give editors and reporters a better break in pay and working conditions. Steps to organize this union were taken in 1933, in the depths of the Great Depression, by newspaper columnist Heywood Broun. Since it is organized on industrial trade union principles, the Guild includes not only those employees in editorial but those in advertising, business, circulation, maintenance, and promotion. Membership hovers around 32,000, as new units open and big papers merge and die. Locals for papers in a hundred cities of the United States, Canada, and Puerto Rico now have agreements with major magazines and wire services. The Guild estimates its contracts cover about half the nation's newspaper circulation. Even though the managing editor may have been a member on his way up—and many top American editors have been in the Guild—he will often have to take part in union negotiations on the side of management.

The Guild is continuing pressure to raise the minimum pay for experienced reporters; The so-called "top minimum" of $200 a week was first adopted by the *Washington Post* in 1964, and it jumped in 1970 to $300. Though beginning reporters still start at about $125 a week on many papers, the Guild had locals in eighty-seven cities with $200 minimums written into their contracts by 1972. Moreover, both wire services had accepted minimums above $200. The 1969 Associated Press contract (signed after an eight-day strike, the first national strike in the Guild's history) provided the steps to a top minimum of $200 a week for newsmen during the contract period of 1969-1972. Other Guild concerns are underscored by the contract provisions for a cost-of-living increase, a boost in medical insurance payments, more vacations and holidays, and a breakthrough through toward a shorter workweek. Guild locals which already had the $200 minimum began to demand more money and other benefits, while other locals began trying to catch up. Either way management is always busy fitting demands to budget.

The managing editor can be crushed between the stones of management and staff in such dickering. But if he is strong he can mediate. The man of integrity will be believed when he levels with his staff about how far the publisher can go. At the same time he can press management to rememeber that not only the newspaper's reputation but its very financial strength rests on quality, which in turn depends upon competitive salaries.

The managing editor may not fret if he cannot get the money he wants for stenographers and copy boys. But he can bleed if he sees his best staffers leave for higher pay at other papers. If he needs two new men and persuades the publisher to give him $14,000 for salaries, he knows he can pay about $7,000 each and knows he will not be able to buy much experience or brains for that. But if he can get $24,000, he may dicker for one man in the $13,000 range and for another at around $11,000. Such salaries might attract a seasoned reporter even from a bigger paper, if the editor has the imagination to offer a degree of reportorial freedom, dynamic newspapering, and simple appreciation for work well done. The editor with clear goals and drive can attract writers who admire sharp leadership; but in the end even that editor needs dollars in his budget.

Budgeting the space

The budgeting of news space, like the budgeting of money, is a source of cooperation—and friction—between the business management and the editorial chiefs. As indicated in earlier discussions about news, the hole (the amount of space devoted to other than advertising) varies from day to day. The reading public may have little appreciation of the need to expand or contract the amount of editorial material as advertising sales go up or down, but every managing editor recognizes this fact of publishing life. One of his tasks is to plan and establish routines that can handle a quick change which may result from the unexpected sale—or loss—of one or two big ads.

At the same time, to be fair to his readers, the managing editor wants some stability in the size of the news hole. The publisher has cause to scream if the percentage of advertising drops to, say, 50 percent. He will go bankrupt if the news hole widens. But it is the managing editor who should scream if advertising goes up to 70 or 80 percent. There is no set proportion suitable for all papers, but the managing editor should get nervous about quality when the news hole drops much below a third. It takes planning and discussion day in and day out to maintain a satisfactory balance.

Practically, the number of columns to fill each day is more imporant to the editor than percentage. A stable or predictable number means he can avoid too much overset on the one hand and publication of too much dead time-copy on the other. A formula for adding columns as advertisements are sold is useful here. One paper with 170,000 circulation, for example, with a base of 122 columns, tries to add two editorial columns every time it adds two pages of new ads. The publisher of a paper with 140,000 circulation has agreed to give the editor a minimum of 136 columns for news every day.

A survey by the Associated Press Managing Editors Association showed that the range in news hole was from 70 to 130 columns on papers with less than 100,000 circulation. Bigger papers reported a range from 90 columns to 157. There appears to be no set formula, and plans vary considerably in ingenuity and flexibility, said John E. Leard, managing editor of the *Richmond* (Va.) *Times-Dispatch*, in reporting the study of sixty-four dailies. One paper with 148,000 circulation runs an average of 48 pages with 110 news columns, aiming at a 65-35 percentage break between ads and news hole.

Planning the news hole

Certainly this is one area where careful planning by the managing editor can bring better space control and therefore better financial control. Ken Weaver, when managing editor of the *Birmingham Eccentric*, has told how this Michigan weekly maintained a strict budget for each department and how this control related to careful planning of the news hole. On the basis of past ad sales, the paper calculated a news quota for each quarter of the year. This quota of column inches was then subdivided four ways to each of the paper's sections: general news and editorial page; society; "Arts of Living"; and general—schools, sports, etc. Since this is a weekly, the managing editor keeps daily charts to check the buildup of news toward the quota. For orderly composition of type, a daily must have a similar and perhaps faster copy control. Weaver said this system meant he knew for sure he had a certain amount of news space per quarter, unless the ad manager and he agreed on an adjustment somewhere along the line.

For subdivision of the news hole, the managing editor, probably in occasional consultation with other editors, decides priorities. Should sports have more space and comics less or vice-versa? One facet of subdivision is the purchase of syndicated material. Here the concerns of space and money intersect. The editor wants comics and columns which will add interest to his editorial mix. He knows they fill space cheaply, yet they make an easy expansion joint, too, if a big ad is sold or dropped. Still, he must avoid the temptation to dilute news coverage with economical space-fillers.

In analyzing his approach to space, E. E. Nichols, managing editor of the *Sacramento Union*, describes news as the meat and potatoes of his menu: "In an ordinary day of, say, 135 columns, the *Union* will devote roughly 30 columns to wire—and these totals include heads and art—20 to local news, 25 to sports, 13 to society, 8 to editorial page, 10 to comics, 16 to markets, 10 to columns, 2 or 3 to odds and ends. On food days we go to 150 columns with 15 columns devoted to food news." In very tight papers, the columns are held over. But since a good diet includes more than meat and potatoes, he considers a variety of syndicated material necessary to a good balance.

Normally the man carrying the title editor-in-chief or editor of the editorial page chooses the columnists for the editorial and "op ed" pages. He decides which columns should be run and, since they are often too long, what cuts should be made to fit them to available space. A symposium published by *Masthead*, journal of the National Conference of Editorial Writers, showed that nearly all editors buy more columns than they use and select those which are most original or on different subjects from what has been running.

Budgeting the people

More important for the editor than allotment of dollars and white space is his budgeting of time, for both his staff and himself. It is best if, from the start, the editor considers this budget question not in terms of hours and minutes, but of people who work for him. What are their wants and needs? What will satisfy and stimulate them as employees and as human beings working with other men and women?

Newsmen work on something more important than the manufacture of pickles or shirts, and the wise editor runs his shop so that the employees keep sight of this. Their feelings of significance ultimately give them their job satisfaction; and though good feelings cannot replace good pay they do contribute to a quality paper. Editors find ways to help staffers express themselves as individuals, to be creative: the photographer to get that special art shot, the reporter to dig into his exposé without fear of losing editorial support.

So the good editor operates as democratically as possible, turning decisions over to groups or committees. Such procedure introduces all the well-known shortcomings of democracy—delays, circumlocutions, slowness. But it also sparks spirit and creativity. One newspaper editor, reminded that the newsroom was shabby, let the Guild unit form a committee to recommend plans for redecoration. The committee members, excited about the task, suggested inexpensive changes that made the place attractive and convenient. Reporters and sub-editors alike felt that they had done well on a job normally considered management's baby.

An editor needs patience and wisdom to use this kind of cooperative approach. People are people, and committee operations are not always so sweet and sunshiny as some theorists suggest. Reporters and deskmen are sometimes selfish or ignorant and can make mistakes and overlook the obvious. A majority vote guarantees neither genius nor saintliness, and one bonafide neurotic can derail the best-intentioned editorial team. Still, the neurotic, and the selfish, and the ignorant, have to be dealt with, for staffs are built on earth rather than in heaven. If the editor keeps a sense of humor, he will be able to guide the fit, misfits, and the semi-fits of the newsroom with a helping hand rather than a threatening fist.

Of course the key editors must eventually promote the fit staffers, overlook the semi-fit, and fire the misfit. In these and other ways, they may undertake basic reorganization of their staff structure. But most of the time each editor has to learn how he can get the job done with the motley assortment already drawing paychecks.

Supervising the team

Since the managing editor is usually the major figure in the newsroom, it is necessary to look at supervision from his point of view. On the small paper the managing editor has fewer staffers to guide and must do much of the editing himself. Bonnie Brothers, managing editor of the *Spencer* (Iowa) *Daily Reporter*, describes her job as that of ringmaster in a circus. The only woman managing editor of an Iowa paper and of the nine papers in the Harris group, she says: "I am responsible for the content of the news columns, for the headlines, the layouts and the photography assignments. It is necessary for me to set deadlines, to see that my staff meets them and that I meet them myself."

The managing editor of a big paper has perhaps a half-dozen editors under him—two or three assistant managing editors, a city editor, a news editor, a Sunday editor, and so on. He may have to guide them as a group and at times move in to help one of them with his own supervision problems. On days when things are popping on the city desk, the managing editor may have to give all his time to bolstering it and let other editorial departments run themselves.

Sample managements

"Your time is limited," Edward L. Thomas, day managing editor of the *San Diego Union*, has observed. "Sometimes the news seems far away as you struggle with budgets, expense accounts, time cards that need signing, letters that need answering and the myriad other responsibilities of the managing editor." To manage the time problem, the *Union* has two managing editors, one for day and one for night. That gives the job more man-hours and means that each editor can look at every department more carefully than before.

Note the prominent role played at the *Union* by devices for communication among staffers:

> —The paper started a news conference of department editors the last Tuesday of every month. This system gives everyone an idea of the major upcoming stories.
>
> —Three or four days before the conference each department head submits his monthly news highlights, in writing, to the managing editor's office. This requires the editors to do some planning. Copies of the reports go to the department head, publisher, circulation manager, and other editors. At the meeting everyone discusses the plans in detail. Then top management explains policy and specific instructions, and the editors can question freely.
>
> —A monthly news budget grows out of this conference; a written weekly news budget outlining expected events is also prepared. And for most immediate supervision of news and staff, each department head also prepares a written *daily* news budget.

Thomas says this system means he does not have to peer over every editor's shoulder. If one desk or department ties up much of his day, the other editors go ahead routinely. They have the confidence to make their own decisions.

Thomas urges careful daily reading of the departmental messages and output in the newspapers. The managing editor can then discuss both good and bad points. Thomas continues:

> It is important for you to look at the wire service news budgets with these departments in mind. Instead of just thinking about Page One, you should back up your telegraph desk or news desk by calling attention of your department editor to a particularly good feature on the wires that day. We are constantly guiding special departments in the use of Copley News Service features, for instance. These come over the managing editor's desk before being routed to the appropriate department. In each case, unless we have specific orders, we avoid *ordering* a department editor to use a specific feature. We suggest that it is a good one for him to consider. Generally, he will agree. But this gives him a chance to say that he ran a similar feature two weeks ago or to offer some equally good reason for not using it. . . .
>
> Don't overlook the opportunity to liven up Page One with an offbeat sports, financial or women's page feature.

> . . . Encourage your sports, financial and women's editors to think in terms of offering features to general news. Get them to work closely with the city editor and the news editor on this.

"You can be helpful if you relay comments and criticisms from the outside about your paper," says John Dougherty, managing editor of the *Rochester* (N. Y.) *Times-Union.* "The boss always is feeling the public's pulse. You can help by making suggestions for improvement—many, many good ideas come from staffers."

Commenting from the writer's viewpoint, Tom Wicker of the *New York Times* has said that the editor must rely on the eyes and ears of his reporters.

> He may point [reporters] where he thinks they should go. He may send them back if they miss the target. He may see, with the sharp eye of his own knowledge and understanding, room for improvement and demand it. But he may not, in the long run, override or ignore the reporter's primacy of knowledge, intimacy of contact, vital instinct of truth, and considered expression of meaning. . . .
>
> [The] editor often can be blind to significance, overcome by the limitations and conditions the newspaper process so copiously imposes on him, and callous of his prime asset—the reporter.

Improvement and reorganization

The managing editor should continually review his operation for improvement. What new spot would excite and hold one of the better staffers? Which weak links need replacement? Is a basic reorganization needed?

Editorial hiring is still one of the soft spots of newspaper management. Too often it is hit-or-miss. An opening goes to a man who happens to drop into the office, or to one who persists, rather than to the best man available for the salary. As the good university dean watches promising instructors around the country and keeps files on the careers of men who may not be given an offer for five to ten years, the well-organized managing editor watches bylines on papers he can raid. He gets acquainted with reporters at newspaper meetings and Sigma Delta Chi conventions and on college campuses. When he loses a specialist in urban affairs or religion, he is able to pick knowledgeably from the best.

Increasingly, however, newspapers actively recruit in journalism schools. Often they are not searching for someone to hire upon graduation, but for a list of people who might be considered for jobs over the next few years.

The editor may promote from within, of course. Morale goes up when staffers see that the editor looks among them to pick a man when a better job opens among them. It may be that the would-be expert on urban affairs or religion is now writing obituaries or society notes. If the managing editor takes the time to chat with his men and women, he will know what their interests and talents are—and perhaps encourage the city editor to let some promising writer try out on a different subject.

Using this idea, the *San Diego Union* tried a woman's page "gal" out on general assignment. Her good work earned her a place on the city side. Even a paper with only 19,000 circulation, the *Delaware State News* of Dover, encourages reporters with special interests and so gets specialty reporting. Each reporter has an "enterprise" beat in addition to his regular news run. "On the side" one man covers leisure hours, night life, and so on; another "Sex and the Delawareans," including prostitution and the morals of military wives at home. "Everybody—the editor, managing editor, news editors, deskmen, everybody—has an enterprise priority," says Joe Smyth, managing editor.

Home-grown specialists

A good way for the editor with a tight budget to get specialists is to grow them on his own staff. He can go to a journalism school training in specialties or look for his man on another staff. But if he needs, say, an education editor, it may be best to try one or two of the thoughtful general assignment men on school topics and shape them into experts.

"Reviewing a few examples from our own list of specialists," said Earl J. Johnson, then vice president and editor of UPI, in supporting this idea in a 1965 talk, "I found that most of them started as all-around reporters. After mastering the discipline of that profession, they began to specialize because their own interest in special topics led them to qualify by intensive study. They were encouraged by their bosses, but the reporters themselves took the initiative."

In improving their editorial staffs, imaginative editors may want to emphasize particularly this development of specialists. Here they might take a tip from competing media in shaping goals and the staff to reach them. Recently, magazines devoted to specialized topics—travel, electronics, or boating, for example—have made the most spectacular circulation gains. "Public television," going beyond educational TV, is trying to put on programs to attract not a mass audience, but big segments of the population interested in special topics. Similarly, editors need not feel that every story must interest everyone. Some writers could well devote at least part of their time to coverage of medicine or psychology or other specialized topics of great interest to a segment of readers.

Fundamental changes

Sometimes more than shifting and upgrading of staffers is necessary. Fundamental reorganization may be required after careful study of the coverage. To grow in a changing environment, a newspaper has to change. If the suburbs are growing and circulation broadening, the staff must be reshaped to provide different or wider coverage. Are the slums festering and threatening the city's life? Then a reporting team, not just a police reporter, must cover the problem. Are staff leaders so busy or so unimaginative or so locked into routines that coverage is bland and uninspired? Then basic changes have to be made to release new blood and imagination.

If encouraged, good reporters and editors can pinpoint organizational flaws and suggest remedies. Dean I. William Cole, director of Northwestern's Urban Journalism Training Center, reports that scores of reporters taking this advanced program are impatient with the way newspapers are managed. Among their criticisms:

—The old beat system does not work on many urban stories, but involves a number of beats. This calls for some sort of team reporting approach.

—The city desk is a bottleneck because the city editor is expected to do the impossible. He does not have time to coordinate the local staff. He needs more assistants.

—City desks too often frustrate top management and the reporters. Top management knows that reporters are not doing a top notch job of anticipating stories and that too many stories are superficial and miss the point. When top management tries to change this, the city desk types just won't give an inch. They say, in effect, "This is the way I always did it and it worked for me, didn't it?"

Other basic managerial problems have been noted by Norman E. Isaacs, editor of the *Louisville Courier-Journal* and 1969-70 president of the American Society of Newspaper Editors. Speaking to a convention of Associated Press Managing Editors' Association, Isaacs said that managing editors take on too much work, crowding out time for imaginative thought or even for evaluating the day's paper. He continued:

> This leads to another serious failing. The chief task of a managing editor should be in training his key people. Yet if he doesn't even have time to himself, how can he train others? This lack of training down the line shows up in stereotyped thinking—with the overburdened managing editor the chief of the stereotyped clan.

To spread and rearrange the work and so solve such problems, David E. West, managing editor of the *Trenton Times* in New Jersey, reorganized his newsroom. He created the position of metropolitan editor and shifted the city editor to it; this man, a sort of assistant managing editor, works directly under West. Three editors of equal rank—a new city editor, a suburban editor, and a state editor—report to the new metropolitan editor, and they, in turn, each have a staff of reporters. Though West still lays out the front page and determines play of stories he now can devote more time to personnel problems and planning.

Even more extensive reorganization should be considered by some newspapers. The first job is to find the bottlenecks and outmoded routines and to work out an organizational plan that keeps the paper current and vital.

The editor's attitude

To supervise and reorganize effectively, top editors must have the standards or goals of the paper clearly in mind, for they are not merely managing but managing *to a purpose*. If perfection is impossible, then their target can be at least improvement. At the retirement of Lester Markel, long-time Sunday editor of the *New York Times*, a colleague recalled: "His mental set when approaching any job was not 'Is it good?' but 'What can I do to make it better?'" An editor must know where he wants the paper to go, and have the courage to drive it there.

Gardner (Mike) Cowles, president of the *Des Moines Register* and *Tribune* and editor-in-chief of Cowles Communications, Inc., complains that too many editors are "too careful, too cautious, too fearful of being controversial. To be a great editor, a man must be meaningfully involved in the important issues of his world; he needs *to care passionately*." Cowles advises young journalists:

> Dare to be unpopular. If you win a popularity contest, you probably aren't doing your job. You can and should be respected—but not necessarily popular. Always edit just a notch over the heads of your readers. They want to read a publication they can look up to and one which stimulates them to think—even if they are occasionally annoyed.

We need not further define goals here. They are analyzed and advocated in the chapters dealing with ethics, editorial imagination, policy, and the future of newspapers. The managing editor is—or should be — always working with his standards in mind, always reconsidering them, always checking whether the paper measures up.

Establishing priorities

So he establishes priorities. No paper can be all he would like, or even a very high proportion of it. Something has to give way, something has to be advanced. Editors must have the courage to focus on unpopular social issues but also to decide that no money or energy is available to ride out on this or that hobby horse, though important and influential and even highly moral forces press him. Wicker has compared the editor's task to the reporter's:

> If the reporter is supposed to get into his story the right things in the right order, no more and no less, to make you hear, to make you feel, to make you see, what he has understood—then the editor has the equally sensitive job of getting the right things in the right order, no more and no less, in the newspaper.

How well an editor succeeds depends first, then, on how clearly he sees and enforces the priorities that will take the paper to its goal.

As he does, so the editor communicates, not only facts or instructions but the *feel* of policy and aims and standards. Then he checks how well his communications are attended. At the end of the work day many an editor sighs at simply seeing the miracle of getting it out again. That sigh is both a confession and a profound self-criticism. The executive editor or managing editor somehow has to organize himself and his staff so that he has the time to evaluate as well as marvel at the daily miracle. He must not merely glance but read slowly—indeed, ruminate and contemplate. What values are coming across? Only as he seriously asks such questions, day after day, week after week, and strives to get them answered right, is the editor really dealing effectively with goals and standards. Perhaps the best title for top editorial administrator would not be executive or managing editor but evaluation editor.

Broadening leadership

High position and high standards combine to push the editor into leadership. He must lead his staff, but he also is sought to lead in the community and his profession. Precisely because his activities relate to the way he does his job in the office, every editor has to decide whether he will take on leadership roles in politics or community service. A few decades ago, editors ran for office and took party posts. Today only the unusual editor does. Hodding Carter, editor of the *Greenville* (Miss.) *Delta Democrat-Times*, is one who has become involved in many facets of his city's civic life, arguing that he is "first of all a citizen." Because his paper has a monopoly and locks into the city's economic life, he says, "I have no right to be the town scold without taking part in the town's life."

The argument against involvement is that the editor involved in controversy as a citizen has trouble maintaining the newspaper's objectivity on vital issues. On the other side, however, the editor who stands above community involvement may isolate himself from a penetrating understanding of the forces and yeasty ideas which are at work all around his paper.

However the editor resolves the dilemma of participation in the community, he has the duty to help provide leadership for the profession. He may attend the American Press Institute at Columbia University, may send staffers to a professional seminar at a nearby school of journalism, may accept election as secretary of a managing editors' association, or may work on a committee of the state or local Sigma Delta Chi. Irving Dilliard, a great editorial page editor of the *St. Louis Post-Dispatch*, has argued that a major characteristic of the good editor is "his devotion to the improvement of the professional group to which he belongs." Remembering such heroes of press freedom as John Peter Zenger and Elijah Lovejoy, the ideal editor "works year after year to protect it and to improve it." He speaks up against government interference and "goes to bed at night asking himself what he has done this day to help his republic and its press to rise." Practicing his preachments, Dilliard served as national president of Sigma Delta Chi in the forties.

In his professional service, the editor develops "contacts" who can help his paper in one way or another. But he also helps produce the professionalism and climate which make all newspapering better. No newspaper of quality can remain as an island washed all around by mediocrity and repression. At its best, professional leadership helps guarantee the survival of good newspapers in future generations.

The sharp editor, however, also establishes firm priorities for his own time. He does not spread himself too thin over community and professional needs. Finally, back at the paper, he has his main leadership job. Gardner Cowles links that leadership to the newspapers' peculiar role of public responsibility, unique in the media—a responsibility which includes serving as "the monitor and conscience of their communities and the nation."

An apathetic editor fails in that responsibility. He relies on the wire services and does no more that hope that reporters will bring in good stories from their beats to fill the columns. As a result, many issues are dull, news-thin, and weak in social responsibility. To counter that, Cowles suggests:

> Any real newspaper needs several good reporters and photographers who are not tied down covering spot news in the conventional sense, or covering a set beat, but who are free to dig out and work up material that is topical, but can be held for a week or a month until desperately needed on an otherwise dull news day. But this takes advance planning. It takes ideas. It takes imaginative leadership from the top editor running the news room.

17 Problems of policy

The *St. Louis Post-Dispatch*, each day in its masthead, carries this statement of policy by its founder:

THE POST-DISPATCH PLATFORM

> I know that my retirement will make no difference in its cardinal principles, that it will always fight for progress and reform, never tolerate injustice or corruption, always fight demagogues of all parties, never belong to any party, always oppose privileged classes and public plunderers, never lack sympathy with the poor, always remain devoted to the public welfare, never be satisfied with merely printing news, always be drastically independent, never be afraid to attack wrong, whether by predatory plutocracy or predatory poverty.
>
> Joseph Pulitzer
>
> April 10, 1907

Every newspaper should work out a clear and consistent concept of its aims and operations. The set of principles or guidelines for its procedures—the chart which sets its course—is called its policy. A newspaper policy may be Republican or Democratic, independent or non-partisan. It may range from liberal to conservative on social questions. And policy has a good many other facets, including the paper's attitude toward news, toward the community, toward reform.

Much of the policy is unwritten, carried in the heads of editors. Some points may be vague, some may be inconsistent. But it does offer a kind of "common law" which governs the way future decisions will be made.

The official policy of a newspaper is the publisher's responsibility. That is elementary, but there is so much obfuscation on the subject that the blunt statement of the object is necessary. Policy is not set by reporters, by the girls in classified advertising, by advertisers, by the unions in the composing room, by the professors at the local college, or by the subscribers in the best part of town. All of them may influence the publisher,* but ultimately he decides debatable policy issues.

In the American economy his power over policy rests on his ownership. Our system does not give control of the press to the state or co-operatives, much less to any interest group. As the man paying the piper calls the tune, the man or corporation that puts up the capital for a paper decides what it will say, and not say.

One indication of confusion on this point is the perennial tendency of some college editors to claim greater power of policy than others are willing to give them. In a private college individuals put up the capital on which the student paper ultimately rests, and in a state institution, the taxpayers provide most of the funds. But the locus of real power is obscured by talk of campus democracy, by the fact that students may subsidize the paper, and by the efforts of wise administrators to give editors maximum freedom. But if there is a libel suit, the institution, not the editor, pays. When student journalists don't like it that way, they quit, perhaps to start their own paper off campus. Then they meet the bills and pay for any libel suits, and they have a publisher's freedom to print and not to print, within the bounds of law and ethics. (Nor would they then, having put energy and money into their paper, probably be inclined to hand it over to just anyone to run as he pleased, without strings! It's not the nature of publishing—or ownership.) Though it is nice to get "something for nothing," there is no way to get the freedom to print as one pleases without paying in energy, money, and risk.

Because modern newspapers require substantial capital, only the well-to-do or rich can own one. It is possible to rent rooms and use a mimeograph to publish a free press, but that is not exciting today. It may be deplorable that wealthy families or impersonal corporations control our newspapers, but it is a reality to be faced in any discussion of press policy. Those who don't like it have no choice, short of changing the system itself, but to get out.

Lest the press picture appear hopelessly bleak, it should be added that most publishers are more interested in checking balance sheets than in advancing policies. They hand down word on policy. More often, they turn day-to-day policy over to men who will formulate policies they approve. When Col. "Bertie" McCormick was chief of the *Chicago Tribune*, a Northwestern University professor often asked *Tribune* editors whether memos instructed them to be anti-British or anti-labor. The teacher never found that the colonel gave such orders—the staff simply edited the paper on those lines because

* Some papers are co-operatively owned, and top staffers own stock in others; in these instances, the views of more than a single "publisher" obviously count. Moreover, in recent years there is a trend, notably in Europe, for staffs to participate democratically in policy-making, as faculty and students have similarly gained more influence on policies of universities. However, in a report made January 17, 1970, of a survey of a score of editors and publishers, *Editor & Publisher* disclosed that most of them opposed the idea of "staff control of newspaper policy."

they thought he wanted it that way. Sometimes, indeed, the true policy-maker of a paper is not so much the real-life publisher as a kind of newsroom phantom the editors visualize to represent the publisher's wishes.

The editor's role in policy

Though the publisher ultimately is responsible for policy and can change it, the top editors may have considerable influence in shaping it. Their first duty is to examine the phantoms for realities. They may find that the staff still worships sacred cows that the publisher himself slaughtered long ago. Changing conditions demand new policies, which editors can either make or suggest in hope of approval from the top. At minimum, they can try to influence the publisher to adopt the best policy. As policies prove unworkable or unwise, editors also can encourage the publisher to change them. The editor has special professional competence, after all, and a smart publisher will carefully consider his reasoned arguments. As an example, the managing editor of a paper in Rochester, New York, asked a copyeditor how he thought their paper could be improved. He replied that the paper printed almost no news about neighboring Canada, just across Lake Ontario. The editor agreed, and it became policy to give more attention to Canadian events.

It is possible that a strong and somewhat brash sub-editor will, in effect, change policy by making a switch in content on his own. The publisher may not notice it, or may even approve the change. He could grumble a little but not take the effort to order a reversal. He might be annoyed, of course, to the point of shifting the editor to a different job.

One troubling complication in this owner-policy situation is the ambiguity of absentee ownership, which today is widespread. At its worst, the absentee system means that the owners are interested only in the money a paper makes; management pinches pennies, lets editorial quality deteriorate, and adopts policies designed to save dollars rather than to better a community. At its best, however, absentee ownership may give dedicated professionals the authority to run a good paper.

William Randolph Hearst, Sr., personally sent editorials and orders through his whole chain of papers, and his editors everywhere reacted like bright puppets. But that is old-fashioned. Hearst papers under William Randolph, Jr., now have a much looser system. Gannett papers make such a point of autonomy that only recently has the term "chain" been used to describe them. They called themselves a "group" before. Looking back over his career at seventy-two, the president of the Knight Newspapers, John S. Knight, said: "We don't believe in having a central headquarters with teletype machines sending out editorials and instructions. Our papers are all run by the men in these respective cities. . . . Other than within the bounds of prudent management, we don't exercise any control over their discussions or policy." Local editors can learn readily to live with policy questions when they are decided by men with local roots, including themselves.

In looking at the publisher's role, it is also wise not to get too exalted a concept of what policy formation is. The publisher does not send down a code to some Moses. If he did, it could no more cover all cases than do the Ten Commandments, and, in any event, it would have to be interpreted by busy deskmen. The newspaper business is a pragmatic one. Let's say the publisher decrees the paper should be fair. Fine, but is it fairer to put in this news fact or leave it out? By repeatedly answering this question writers and editors form policy.

Or suppose a publisher orders that his paper support such-and-such a candidate. Professionalism decides how far the editors can go with such a policy, and if it is pushed too crassly, the paper—and the publisher's bank account—will suffer. In short, policy is not like a statue, which is formed once and for all; it is more like a hedge, which editors can prune and nurture.

Goals and policy

Policies stem from a newspaper's objectives. Where the goal is full and fair coverage, editors can develop specific policies to reach it. But if the aim is simply to make as much money as possible, other policies are required. In his book *Responsibility in Mass Communications* Wilbur Schramm lists six facets of the "emerging code of new responsibility." These are separation of editorials from news, accuracy, objectivity, balance, fairness, and reliability. Already, as ethical goals are envisioned, the outlines of a newspaper policy begin to emerge.[1]

To discover how editors and readers evaluate ideals, J. Daniel Hess gleaned nine newspaper attributes from the literature on social responsibility of the press. Dr. Hess surveyed 85 New York newspapermen and 194 Syracuse residents to see how they ranked these ideals. "Accurate" and "fair" took first and second place. "Ethical" and "adequate" ranked next.[2] The similarity to the Schramm listing is noteworthy. If such objectives are hard to reach, at least it is clear that some policies are more useful than others in the attempt. The five attributes ranked lowest were "interesting," "prompt," "profitable," "conservative," and "authoritarian," with almost no positive response for the last two. The judgments of editors and the public were remarkably similar.

The editorial mix

Magazines operate with what editors, borrowing from chemistry, call a formula. The term refers to the combination of ingredients—articles, photos, stories, cartoons, and so on—which regularly go into the publication. The shifting nature of the news makes it more difficult to stabilize a newspaper's formula or "recipe." A heavy admixture of foreign news may be best on one day; several local stories may demand treatment on the next. Nevertheless, the concept of a formula helps show how editors develop practices which reach policy goals. The serious paper has one editorial mix, the frivolous another. Descending from the heights of press ideals, we get to the practicalities of policy by considering three major ingredients—opinion, news, and entertainment.

Opinion

It is a truism that the American newspaper separates news and opinion, with the editors' views confined to the editorial page. Though the ideal may be violated, the policy remains sound. If editorial writers stay within the bounds of law and good taste, few questions are raised about their right to support or oppose candidates or programs. Whether the publisher sets editorial policy or hands the task to the editors of the page, decisions about the stands to be taken in these opinion columns are a keystone of the paper's overall policy.

Policy also has to be made for syndicated columns. Some editorial pages carry only columns which support the paper's own positions. A more common policy is to select columns which give "both sides." A vigorous, aggressive paper might, however, adopt a policy of selecting—even of finding and cultivating—columnists who will argue a wide variety of stimulating and nonconformist opinions. Vigorous leadership on the editorial page was advocated by Robert S. McCord, editor and publisher of the *North Little Rock* (Ark.) *Times*, in an article which won a Sigma Delta Chi writing award. Deploring that editors of many weeklies and small dailies include "no opinion, no interpretation, no comment," McCord declared such an editor "not only is cheating himself out of the fun of being a newspaperman but he is cheating his readers."

Guidelines also must be established for letters to the editor. One prominent editor threw away letters he disagreed with, but only after phoning or writing their authors to tell them off. This bizarre policy obviously angered many subscribers. A more sensible and common policy is to print as many letters as possible. Writers are thus encouraged to contribute. If at least a little of every literate contribution is used, the policy wins wider reader support.

Whether to insist on the writers' names on all letters is another policy matter. In a survey by the Pennsylvania Newspaper Publishers Association, 96 out of 128 publishers and editors said they had a policy of publishing letters without the name when anonymity was requested. But 42 said they were against such practice, arguing that anonymity encourages crank letters and lets writers vent spleen at the expense of others, including the newspaper.

News

If accuracy and fairness are desirable goals, independence is a leading virtue in policy on news. Selection of the news, as indicated already in discussions of news evaluation and journalism ethics, must be free from influence by editorial page policy, advertising pressures, or the biases of publisher or staffers.

Completeness and breadth of coverage are also important aims of news policy. Editors and publishers of papers outside the largest metropolitan centers sometimes complain when press critics hold up the thoroughness of the *New York Times* as an example. Though papers with smaller resources cannot offer such a wealth of news, the goal for even a paper of 50,000 should be coverage in breadth and depth of "all the news that's fit to print." By carefully selecting and editing news from local staffers and from the wires editors can cover world news with at least moderate thoroughness and local news with completeness and enterprise.

As we discussed in chapter 6, news policy should be to cover constructive as well as destructive events and trends. We indicated in the discussion of the relationship of Christian ethics to journalism that application of the Golden Rule might require more emphasis on the constructive. The outstanding ethical example of one Christian body's journalistic effort, the *Christian Science Monitor*, is enlightening on this point. The *Monitor* does not ordinarily print unpleasant items; as Christian Science emphasizes the basic goodness in the universe, the paper developed from this faith plays up the wholesome and plays down the bad. Christian Science views evil and sin, disease and suffering, as unreal. It follows that a newspaper founded on this view would print only news rooted in the real or true. So the *Monitor* usually does not print news of crimes or deaths or disasters. Evil is thwarted by its editors, and many newspaper readers wish that other journalists would follow the example.

No newspaper worthy of the name can ignore the popular concern with wars and urban violence; so, although trying to deal positively with such events, the *Monitor* makes the pragmatic compromise and does print news of these man-made disasters. This paper's general bias toward "good news," however, is wholly satisfactory only to members of this church and perhaps a few others, since most Americans probably want newspapers which give accounts of evil.

Commenting on the problem, Harry Ferguson of UPI argued that "when bad news is suppressed, worse news often results." People need to see the evil to correct it. "If you are opposed to teen-agers taking LSD and smoking marijuana and want to do something about it," he asks, "how are you going to accomplish anything unless you find out what's going on from newspapers, television, and radio?" UPI, he pointed out, carried an annual roundup of good news around the world; and papers all the time print the good news of weddings, births, and graduations as well as medical discoveries, the ends of wars, and so on.

Taking up Ferguson's comment, David Jacobs, assistant managing editor of the *Long Island Press* in Jamaica, New York, checked the good and bad news in his paper. He took a random issue, of thirty-six pages. The front page held three "particularly violent stories." But the tally of hard news showed 11 columns of "happy" or "good" news; 27 columns of "benign" or neutral news, and 10 columns of "bad" or violent news. Counting in women's and sports pages as largely good, he figured that only 10 of 278 columns were "bad"—yet circulation was soaring. Similarly, in a survey of the *Worcester* (Mass.) *Telegram and Gazette* for three weeks in 1969, state editor Sidney B. McKeen counted 4,308 column-inches of "good" news and 3,069 of "bad" (though he designated two-thirds of the total news neutral).

In 1969 a new weekly with 320,000 controlled circulation in the Denver area, *The Colorado Graphic*, came out with a policy of promoting "positive elements of community life." The managing editor explained that little space would go to crime or even general news but that emphasis would be "on food, shelter, clothing, recreation, health, education, welfare and worship"—another indication of editorial concern for "good news." The ideal of the *Monitor* does from time to time pick up a following.

Entertainment

It would be foolish for a newspaper to have a policy of "no entertainment," though some observers apparently feel that should be the goal. It is true that certain papers strive for mostly entertainment. On the other hand, in response to the disillusioning development of television as largely entertainment, some editors have felt that seriousness is the best competing policy. The policy of a paper on this score must, of course, be tailored to its readership. But, along with opinion and news, entertainment has a legitimate place; it has traditionally been a part of newspapers almost since they emerged from flysheets, and it should continue in any editorial formula. The question is how much of this leavening ingredient should be included?

Sometimes editors beg the question by contending that everything they print should be interesting—i. e., entertaining. That is neither possible nor desirable. Some important developments, such as crises in the gold market, are by their nature dull to ordinary readers. They can be explained clearly, and even interestingly. But it would be fatuous to twist these stories into entertainment.

Sometimes human fallibility dismisses as entertainment only that which does not fit its own tastes. Thus, male-oriented papers pontificate about eliminating women's-page frivolity, such as fashions, but never question the inclusion of features about professional football—for sports interest men and are therefore "important."

An honest, objective look at newspaper policy would include an analysis and categorization of what is proper to the editorial page, what is real news, and all the rest. "The rest" tends to be entertainment—comics, advice columns, sports, feature photographs, society items, and much of so-called "women's news." (Editors might differ as to whether cultural coverage—book reviews and music criticism, for example—are entertainment or a part of the news/opinion spectrum; but such features are part of a good mix.)

Sound policy would prescribe a balanced admixture of entertainment to keep the paper from dead seriousness or hopeless frivolity. (Since the *New York Times* is so often cited as quality journalism, it might be noted that its editors have consciously tried in the last decade to brighten its pages with material that must be categorized as entertainment, such as personality features and the humorous columns by Russell Baker. And while the *Times* carries no comic strips, the "serious" *Monitor* does.)

One guide to whether entertainment does its job is to check if a sizable part of the readership actually reads it. One sometimes senses, as his eye wanders over the two or three pages of cartoons in an out-of-town paper, that half of them might be omitted with little loss of circulation. From time to time editors do drop a comic and remark on how few complaints they get. Their policy might often be a bit more ruthless on rejecting the conventional if they really want to project a serious image. One editor of a paper with 13,000 circulation gave up *Little Orphan Annie* as she was descending to earth in a parachute—and only four readers complained.

Comic strips which are witty or satiric, like Walt Kelly's *Pogo* or Charlie Schulz' *Peanuts*, have almost disappeared. Readers apparently like the continued strip which replaces the old adventure serial. Some of these quite properly fit the budget as entertainment. However, editors might take a quizzical look at strips which dip into politics, some subtly, some crudely. The late Harold Gray often used *Little Orphan Annie* to present a right-wing view of the world, and Milt Caniff frequently turns to superpatriotism, if not militarism, in *Steve Canyon*. Editors who espouse such views should find a way to indicate these are cartoon-editorials, or perhaps even run such opinion strips on the editorial page.

The traditional political cartoon has a hallowed place in world journalism, and editors can both express opinion and win entertainment points by using more good cartoons. These, like other opinion, should go on the editorial page or perhaps in a spot like the upper front page, where tradition made the reader aware he is getting an editorial view.

The newspaper as public utility

In the somewhat mixed economy of the United States, the newspaper today fits somewhere between the old libertarian theory of maximum editorial freedom and the emerging theory of social responsibility. On the one hand, the editor does not make policy as does the puppet editor of *Pravda* in the Soviet Union. On the other, no matter how ardently Jeffersonians might wish it, he does not today have the freedom to be irascible and irresponsible, as did the editors when Jefferson was President. The role of the newspaper in the nuclear age must be thought out in new terms.

The image most appropriate for the American newspaper in the latter part of the twentieth century is probably that of public utility. The metaphor is imperfect but instructive. A telephone company or an electric corporation enjoys a monopoly that even free-enterprise enthusiasts rarely question. Though public commissions may control some aspects of the business, such as determining whether its rates are fair, the utility is relatively free to plan, purchase, and expand. Yet utility executives recognize that they must serve the whole community and cannot arbitrarily ignore any citizen, providing he keeps his bills paid. Similarly, the newspaper still enjoys many protections under the Constitution and by informal tradition. Yet it holds responsibilities both to the community and to individuals, no matter how odd their ideas may appear.

The public utility concept may help publishers and editors form policies which are realistic for this day. The newspaper, as public utility, is a business but not just any business. It has a trust, which might even be called sacred, to convey the information of a democratic society. Citizens have as much right to criticize how well it does this job as they have to criticize long-distance telephone service.

The newspaper is also a humanitarian enterprise, but not like the Red Cross. Rather, it is a business like the gas company, which serves people as it earns. The American Telephone and Telegraph Company may advertise as if its only goal in life were to bring cheery families together by wire, but ultimately it exists to produce profits for AT&T stockholders. The legitimate money needs of a newspaper should not be forgotten in fogs of humanistic rhetoric.

Businessmen publishers often sound hard-headed when they speak of their properties and profit and insincere when they carry on about their ideals. For their part, intellectual critics are inclined to be cynical about the business aspects of publishing and naive about the potential of our present newspaper system for humanity. Businessmen and intellectuals might find a common realistic ground if they recognize the modern newspaper as a public utility, requiring policies that produce profits and at the same time serve society well.

The consumer of newspapers, too, should examine his views with more care. Often a lay critic of the press demands fuller coverage, more courageous reporting, and less advertising, yet he might be the first to complain if his demands were met. He would most likely not read the wider coverage, would howl if a courageous reporter raked a little muck in his own back yard, and would object to paying a nickel more to help the paper reduce advertising.

Any editor, then, should not rush to accept the standards offered by critics. Human beings like to make lofty statements, but they often fail to match those statements with performance.

Three aims of policy

Let us, finally, consider how the concept of the public utility relates to policy aims. We have written above about such goals as accuracy and fairness, which define the newspaper's stance toward information. But related aims emerge from its dynamic role as public utility, and these have three overlapping phases or levels.

Community betterment

It would be difficult to find a publisher who would not say that his policy is to improve his community. That goal is minimal, but it is also a major challenge.

It will illustrate a paper's potential for community betterment if, in a seeming digression, we focus on an issue where most papers have failed and where many are still failing: their coverage of minority groups, and specifically of the Negro, Puerto Rican, and Mexican-American communities. During the sixties, editors met thorny problems in covering the so-called Black Revolution, and the growing discontent of Chicanos. Questions related to their freedom and equality will remain critical for a number of years.

Basic to the problem is the fact that until now almost all newspapers have been edited by whites for whites. Communities with "white schools" and "white churches" have also had "white newspapers," and Negroes quite properly have been bitter about a "white press." The black has been "the invisible man" to white society, including white editors and reporters. They simply don't see the world as a Negro reader does and often are blind to their blindness. An obvious illustration is the monopoly of society pages by white brides.* Don't Negro girls get married? The white press has been changing, but Negro and Puerto Rican leaders at a Columbia School of Journalism session on minority news coverage charged that papers in 1967 still ignored daily news in their communities, except for crime and disorder. The press has a distance to go before it becomes a truly representative press for a pluralistic society.

A traditional source of criticism has been labeling—Mexican, Puerto Rican, Negro, colored. Part of the trouble is the general problem of identification. When is one labeled an ex-convict, ex-G.I., former mental patient, student, Jewish leader, or Bircher? Somewhat cynically, editors argue that no group wants a member labeled when the news is bad but urges the labeling if the news is good. Traditions of discrimination make the problem especially acute for the Negro community. Stereotypes about the Negro and crime are reinforced when the Negro makes the newspaper only if he commits a crime, especially if he is identified not by his occupation, as the white violator probably would be, but by his race. Again, labeling is improving. Wire services handle labels more carefully than a decade ago, and news stories of sports, entertainment, and political successes are helping to improve the image of Negroes. But editors must still ponder whether a man's race is pertinent to a story, any more than his religion or his political party.† When it is important to the news that a person is a Catholic or a Negro or a Republican, then labeling may be justified; otherwise it is not.

The problem of stereotyping will remain severe since the struggle for Negro equality demands that attitudes change from disdain to acceptance. The same kind of stereotyping can be found in other areas. Students, for example, are often irritated by older people asking "what students think about" a certain issue. Students rarely can be so neatly catalogued—and neither can racial, religious, or even political groups.

Unimaginative newspapering easily falls into clichés, perhaps most readily in photographs—the child happily evading school or the coed studying in a bathing suit. With Negroes or other minority group members, the problem is sharpened by the fact that what the

* Sins of the press should not be exaggerated, however. For example, in the middle sixties, the *Banner-Herald* in Athens, Georgia, did begin to use pictures of newlywed Negro couples.

† In 1969, in the nation's capital, a unit of the American Newspaper Guild took the unusual step of protesting to the management of the *Washington Daily News* against its policy of recording the race of both victims and suspects in hold-ups, purse snatchings, and minor crimes.

insensitive newsman considers normal and harmless may be a touchy area with a minority. A New Brunswick, New Jersey, paper, for example, printed a picture of Negro children eating watermelon in a contest. Protest letters poured in, for the pictures reinforced the stereotype of the Negro as a happy, lazy, good-for-nothing watermelon-eater. It was a "cliché of bigotry," one writer protested. The editor asserted his innocence: there were no white children in the contest! But in his innocence, he had still erred, for he was insufficiently attuned to Negro sensibilities or he would have killed the picture. The truth of the smaller fact cannot outweigh the truth of the greater communication.

Riots and the rise of militant Black Power have made a touchy subject still touchier. News coverage reveals ethical questions: Why build up a few rioters as if they typified all Negroes? Why treat disturbances as if it were the good guys (police) against the bad guys? Why not get at causes and the big picture instead of just violence? Why promote militants with frequent interviews that could mislead the reader about their strength or popularity?

Since most readers of most papers are white, "the revolution" requires interpretive stories. This calls for specialists; ordinary reporters are no more qualified to cover racial issues than to cover international monetary negotiations or heart transplants. In *Race and the News Media*, a recent book edited by Paul L. Fisher and Ralph L. Lowenstein, it is proposed that reporters who cover racial news take additional in-service training, and that the best reporters be assigned to the police beat. They suggest also an increase in the number of Negro employees.

The news media were "the single most important factor helping to build tensions in some communities," according to a preliminary 1967 report of the Community Relations Service of the U. S. Department of Justice. Even if that charge lies heaviest on television, newspapers nevertheless have a responsibility to improve their handling of news in the race area. The challenge, this federal report said, is whether the newspaper "can do more than chronicle the fears and discomforts of whites caused by Negroes." Can the press mirror not only the violence and militance of minorities but also their anguish and poverty and struggle and success and bitterness?

In 1968 the National Advisory Commission on Civil Disorders charged that the mass media have failed "to report adequately on race relations and ghetto problems and to bring more Negroes into journalism." Thus, this presidential commission declared, the media "contributed to the black-white schism in this country."

Spurred by this report, the *Columbia Journalism Review* and the Anti-Defamation League of B'nai B'rith conducted a survey of 889 media outlets. Replies from almost half indicated a heartening concern on the part of newsmen to correct the false image of the Negro in America. Some respondents proposed that papers quote "average" Negroes as well as militants and seek "positive" stories about black accomplishments. Many reported they were trying to hire

Negro editorial workers. The survey revealed that Negroes constitute 4.7 percent of all newspaper employees.

Though black progress still may seem hopelessly slow, since 1967 the newspaper profession appears to have made several gains in handling race questions.

Crusades

The publisher and editor may crusade. It may be their policy to pick out evils to fight and grand goals for community struggle. By hammering in news stories and features and by hitting with editorials and cartoons, a newspaper can clean out the gamblers, build a civic center, get the city-manager plan adopted, or "run the crooks out of city hall."

Crusading easily slips into imbalance and unfairness, but it is exciting journalism. If crusading seems not so general or potent as a generation or two ago, the annual recognitions in the Pulitzer Prizes and the Polk and Sigma Delta Chi awards suggest that many papers still have crusading policies. To the crusader, merely giving the news is too slow a road to community betterment. And sometimes events are thrust upon a newspaper in such ways that the honest journalist is forced to look for the hidden facts if his paper is to meet its responsibilities. Recent Pulitzer Prizes indicate that several papers have plunged into what often would be unpopular frays to correct abuses which involve people's lives or fortunes.

In 1968, for example, the Gold Medal for public service was given by the Pulitzer Prize committee to the *Riverside* (Calif.) *Press-Enterprise*. The paper reported corruption in the handling of property and the estates of the Agua Caliente Indians. George Ringwald, a reporter, had dug up information that showed malfeasance in the handling of financial affairs for 100 Indians who owned 28,000 acres of land worth $50 million in Palm Springs. The estate was handled by court-appointed conservators and guardians under the supervision of the Superior Court of Riverside County, with the advice and consent of the Interior Department's Bureau of Indian Affairs. The newspaper reported how a judge had received $45,000 in fees for handling some Indian affairs and that another judge, in a former capacity, had been granted a quarter of a million dollars in fees for representing thirty-three Indians as their guardian.

A year before, Gene Miller of the *Miami Herald* had won a Pulitzer for local investigative reporting. His articles succeeded in freeing two persons wrongfully convicted of murder. He had done the work on two separate cases. In one, a woman had been sentenced to life imprisonment in Louisiana, and his stories proved that she was several hundred miles away at the time of the murder. In the same year the *Louisville Courier-Journal* received the Gold Medal for public service for its campaign to control strip mining in Kentucky. The mining had resulted in considerable stream pollution and had caused terrible erosion.

In these cases the newspapers probably did not make an extra nickel from circulation or advertising. It is also probable that the papers spent thousands of dollars to get the information. The Louisville case would have brought powerful and angry opposition from mine companies and some miners.

Leadership

Policy may also concern the newspaper's role in community leadership. This leadership is continuing, perhaps less intensely than the crusading burst, but in a more vigorous and directed fashion than that necessary for general community betterment. For example, take the perennial issue of schools: A paper may work for community betterment simply by giving thorough coverage of what is happening in local education. A crusading paper may go after the hide of the superintendent or try to get its candidates elected to the school board. But a paper oriented toward leadership might search out the opinions of teachers and parents, discuss alternate possibilities on its editorial page, and develop interpretive stories showing how similar communities have tackled similar problems.

A paper may operate on all three levels at different times, or even at the same time. Most of its effort may go to straight coverage and editorials which help the citizens themselves better their community. The paper may crusade on the high-school drug problem, while, simultaneously, its editors may move in and out of leadership efforts on pollution or street violence or international combats. A newspaper will be most effective, however, if the publisher and editors plan a coordinated policy small enough for the staff to handle yet big enough to make an impact.

The community agenda

In one vital aspect of policy, a newspaper cannot avoid contributing to the community's betterment or, perhaps, to its decline. The paper's policies influence what the citizens think about. Television and radio, ministers, professors, and clubs all have some part in picking out the big issues for local discussion, but the influence of the newspaper probably outweighs all of them. The paper establishes the agenda of concerns, as if it were chairman of a giant town meeting. If the paper prints a lot about muggings, the people worry about muggings. If it gives complete coverage to PTA meetings that deal with construction of new schools, the readers will be talking about new schools. Riots or pornography or peace activities or marijuana become public concerns or not as the paper covers or ignores them.

Especially through interpretive stories, the newspaper sets up the agenda of public discussion and action. If it does not cover, say, the desires or demands of the Negro community, it is difficult for community leaders to stir up public concern. If it does print such material, however, the issue is already of public concern. Editorial endorsement of a candidate or policy may be the kiss of death. But, unobtrusively, the policies of the paper work to change the community for better or worse; the staff simply establishes the agenda.

18 Newspaper editorial research

Research is the careful, organized investigation and analysis of a subject. A student researches when he digs for information to write a term paper. At a more complex level, when scientists create broad theories, construct specific hypotheses, and collect data which support or negate these they are doing research, with the aim to gain knowledge. So too on a newspaper, at a variety of levels and with a variety of methods, men and women conduct research which contributes to a better editorial product.

The library

Research need not be sophisticated or laborious to be useful to the editor. Even the staff of a small paper can develop research attitudes and habits which will lead to improvements.

An obvious place to start is the library of the paper. For generations good newspapers have kept morgues, where clippings are filed in envelopes for ready access. The librarian has typically been in charge of a few reference books; he also keeps bound volumes of the paper, a few other periodicals, and possibly some microfilms. His bailiwick is the traditional center for newsroom research.

Too often the library staff is small and its training inadequate. Too often the books are few and out of date. Good libraries and librarians require good budgets, so the first step for research improvement on a modern newspaper may simply be a financial commitment.

Library needs

To make the best use of the money, the editor should work closely with the head of the library. The librarian is an expert and wants a say in his department. And he appreciates assistance from the editorial staff, which too often ignores his problems.

If the librarian is not qualified, the editor may have to seek replacement. More likely, the editor will want to help the library staff already on the job. Sometimes schools of journalism have short courses which will give the needed training. Trips to see how other newspaper libraries solve problems are worthwhile. Perhaps a successful librarian from another paper which is not much bigger or wealthier could act as a consultant. Without infringing on the librarian's professional competence, the editors can guide and assist, much as they lead the business writer or the drama critic.

The editor also has a responsibility to see that the library is used. The copyeditors and others of the editorial staff should consult books and clippings to check accuracy and to get background and ideas. Perhaps even more important, they should try to get the specialized writers and the reporters in the habit of using the library resources. Sometimes this can be done simply by asking a reporter to check the clips on some aspect of a story he has turned in. Of course new editorial staffers should receive a brief orientation from the librarian, but an additional group session every year or so gives the librarian a chance to bring the whole staff up to date on the improvements he has introduced to help with their research.

Library resources

The librarian should be especially useful to the interpretive or investigative reporter, who, along with editorial writers, most deserves the title "researcher" on the newswriting staff. The clippings provide the depth reporter facts about previous events in the area he is checking. Books sometimes help. For example, if he is writing about the impact of imports on local industry or the growth of experimental theater in his section of the country, books that describe similar situations other places can provide valuable insights.

This reporter will want to visit the city and university libraries nearby for additional material, and one of the librarians may be able to get some vital book on loan from out of town. The librarian also should be able to help obtain copies of congressional hearings, reports of federal investigations, and the research and documents of state offices. Topics like price-gouging or welfare fraud are the concern of many editors, so the librarian can check other papers and get copies of relevant stories. Not least, the skills of the librarian should result in tips for lines of investigation. As the modern newspaper brings the librarian into status on the editorial team, he will develop experience in backstopping a number of different kinds of investigations and so provide special skill for future reporters.

Newspapers might consider setting up a human resources section, as have some public libraries. Here they would file, by subjects and with cross-references, the names of local men and women with special knowledge. Under the heading "Kenya," for example, might be the names of a teacher who spent two years there in the Peace Corps, an industrial executive who handles exports to Africa and Asia, a retired missionary from East Africa, and a university professor who specializes in African politics. Depth reporting, more and more requiring that the specialist seek interviews beyond the obvious, especially needs an up-to-date clearing house of experienced hands who collect Chinese art or did war relief work or once served on important national church committees.

A major development in newspaper library work is the recent establishment of the *New York Times* Information Bank, an interactive retrieval system. Data from the *Times Index* were the first to go into storage, but the bank now absorbs current data from additional sources. First used by the news and editorial departments of the paper, the system will eventually serve libraries, government agencies, and other newspapers. A *Times* report pictures how a story will be prepared during some future heat wave:

> The rewrite man walks over to a nearby typewriter-like device and types in: "Temperature—New York record high." The basic information on past hot spells appears immediately in front of him on a screen very much like a television tube. The rewrite man needs additional information so he types in a request for the original stories. Within seconds a high-speed printer located next to the teletypewriter prints out a hard-copy history of New York City heat waves as reported by the *New York Times*.

Besides having two or three reference books handy for daily work, an editor sometimes develops files of clips for his own use. If urban renewal or pop music is a special interest of his, the editor should keep his own folders. He should also encourage the specialized writers to build their own files; in their own fields, they can clip and collect more thoroughly than the librarian can or should. All such materials then can help, perhaps in copyediting or in their own writing, or maybe just in stimulating ideas for the staff to kick around.

Elementary behavioral research

The editor without specialized training in communications research may do some simple but useful investigations. However, a warning is needed. Newspapers have conducted unscientific polls before elections and have assigned reporters to man-in-the-street interviews on many subjects. Such features have human interest value and may be harmless, if editors are careful to point out they are playing a kind of game for fun, not promoting their findings as scientifically valid. Serious opinion research should be left in the hands of Gallup and the other professional pollsters (who developed their organizations from the desire of newspaper editors for more valid research about public attitudes). While amateurs should leave such broad research to those with proper training, there are some simple internal investigations where common sense suffices.

Ideally, the editor would discuss his research ideas with the staff of the research department. But usually there is no such department; if there is, it is often too busy to undertake all the research questions an alert editor might raise. Most of the time, then, the editor is on his own. As a first step he might, during office hours, take a course or two in the research techniques of communications, psychology, or sociology at a nearby university. Certainly, he would at least want to read a few books that provide elementary insights. (See Bibliography.) One does not have to be a statistician to know that 56 percent of the vote wins an election or that 95 percent foreign news on a front page is too high. Minimal self-education may save an editor from a serious error such as assuming that valid conclusions on readability can be drawn from calculating Flesch scores on two or three stories. Just as important, such research training will help the editor interpret the media research findings which come to his attention, including the countless "studies" now reported on news flow.*

What kind of rudimentary research, then, can an editor undertake? Front-page news is a good place to start. The editor may want to check hunches—that there are not enough humorous stories on page one, for example, or that there are too many from the state capital. It is no trick to set up a simple method to find out. He can establish categories such as local, area, state—or humorous, human interest, serious—depending on his focus. Then he categorizes, counts, and records the stories on page one every issue for a week or two, or every other front page for a month. When he strikes a total, finds an average, and discovers trends and patterns, he has a reasonably accurate picture of the choices editors have been making for the front page. Perhaps his emotions about the legislative correspondent were getting in the way and other editors had overruled his selection. Many questions remain, but at least he has some data, rather than mere impressions, to inform his thinking about future handling of front-page news.

Clearly, an editor would be foolish to make blanket accusations that there is too much capital news if he counts only during a period the legislature is in session. He should check pages throughout the year before he generalizes. Common sense should keep him from unwarranted conclusions—if he remembers to apply it.

Use of the news hole is also relatively easy to assess. What hunch—or hypothesis—does the editor want to check? Is too much or too little space going to pictures? Is the sports editor right when he gripes that he doesn't get as many columns as he used to? Again categories can be set up, and this time the column inches of stories put into each slot are measured and added, perhaps by a copy boy or an eager young reporter. The editor finds, say, that the average daily use of photographs in his paper last month was 130 column inches, or about 10 percent of his paper's average news hole. Is that too much or too little? Did papers with 15 to 20 percent of the news hole given to pictures really look better? His ruler points the way for evaluations and decisions.

Or perhaps measurement shows that, because of an unnoticed shift in advertising, the society editor is actually getting a full column a day more than allowed by the budget set up three years ago, and the sports editor averages 16 fewer column inches a day. The editor now has data for action.

*In March, 1970, a useful 11-page booklet, *How to Conduct a Readership Survey of Features,* was published by the News Research Center, American Newspaper Publishers Association, 750 Third Ave., New York, N.Y. 10017.

Reading ease and human interest levels of writing also can be checked, according to the theories discussed in chapter 15 on writing. Here again it is wise to establish categories first. Perhaps it is useful to know the average score for 500 samples drawn at random from the paper during the last month. It is more useful, however, if 100 samples each are calculated from wire copy, local news, editorials, sports copy, and business writing. Then the editor can make comparisons and suggest improvements. He may not be too bothered to discover that a college education is prerequisite to understanding the editorials. But he should be bothered if readability testing shows that an eighth grade graduate would find the sports coverage too difficult.

Some basic studies

While editors probably will want professional researchers to undertake their audience studies, a staff can and should learn about its region through its own digging techniques. At the Columbia Graduate School of Journalism, Prof. Walter B. Pitkin, a popular and sharp writer (*Life Begins at Forty*), required students to research thoroughly the circulation area of some small daily. Students wrote Chambers of Commerce, dug through Agriculture Department reports, and in other ways learned everything possible about their areas—the industries, employment levels, cultural activities, income, and so on. An editor might undertake this kind of research from time to time, to check his guesses and impressions about shifts in jobs, decline of dairying, or what not. Such inquiry yields not only story ideas but an understanding of the community his paper serves.

Editors should also make it a point to move outside their own professional and social circles and their own neighborhoods to talk with a cross-section of readers. "One of our top editors," says the research director of one large newspaper, "makes it a practice to make the rounds of the many neighborhood pubs to get the feel of the type of person who is a fairly large segment of his audience." Such down-to-earth "research" can usefully supplement the best computerized study of audience profile.

An editor's starting point for research is a need for more information. There is little point in measuring, questioning, and analyzing just for fun. Research is a problem-solving tool. So what is the problem? Does the editor want to know what cartoons are read or why kind of story dominates the Metro Page? Perhaps his problem demands research beyond his capacities—but often a simple method will give him a relatively accurate answer.

For example, Herbert E. Steinbach, managing editor, *Vidette-Messenger* in Valparaiso, Indiana, wanted to remodel the editorial page to increase readership. Inspired by a typography workshop at Southern Illinois University, he wrote to some thirty editors in surrounding states for editorial-page tearsheets. All but two responded. Steinbach checked the topics, the width of the columns, and the size of type. He then incorporated on his own page the best of what he found. It is an example of elementary research which many another editor could profitably follow.

Mass communications research

The field of mass communications theory and research, which in two decades has emerged from almost nothing to a place of great influence in journalism, refers to scientific investigation related to the mass media. As distinguished from a field such as research in journalism history, it is concerned with the way people act, that is, with their behavior. As a subdivision of the behavioral sciences, such as sociology and psychology, it focuses on people's attitudes and responses to papers and other media. Typically, it is quantitative—it measures and counts, in pursuit of objective knowledge; this tendency has been given a special push by the development of computers. Statistics help determine the significance of the calculations. If research generally is the careful investigation of a subject, then the researcher in mass communications scientifically studies the way humans act and react with the media—as journalists, decision-makers, readers, and so on. Even a study of news display or story content may be viewed as an effort to get at the way such communicators as editors act.

Several kinds of professional research are useful to newspaper editors, though at present many lack both the money and the time to use such help. Television executives, who depend on rating systems, are much more research-oriented, and magazine editors have shown more concern than newspapermen for scientific studies. Only ten or twelve newspapers have strong research departments, and most of them are concerned about research related to advertising. In short, it is a rare editor who can turn to his own research department with hope of real aid. Still, many editors can find useful information in research prepared for the business office, and through the seventies greater use of editorial research on newspapers is certain. Six areas of research are important to the editor: contents, effects and influence, reader interest, audience, graphics, and gatekeepers.

Content analysis

Research on content is similar to the rudimentary studies of front page and news hole discussed above. Content analyses can determine accurately the percentages of material on various topics, the balance of news on politicians, the number of times certain concepts are repeated in the news columns, even the number of prejudicial color words in so-called objective accounts. Such analyses help an editor ponder the quality of what is actually published.

Effects and influence

Attitude research is one of the most difficult and, unfortunately, one of the kinds least attempted. People are concerned about the influence of TV and comic book violence on listeners and readers, especially young ones. But the little solid research on the subject must compete with the many guesses by psychiatrists, pastors, disciples of Marshall McLuhan, and others. Newspapers seldom use such research, and yet from the editor's point of view this facet would probably interest him most. Do his editorials persuade? Do his news photos rouse? Do interpretive stories stimulate? An editor can ask his wife, his friends at lunch, and acquaintances at a tavern what they think, but such queries cannot carry the weight of thorough, objective research.

One vital question is whether the readers' perceptions of a story match the communicator's. One doctoral candidate discovered that a high proportion of readers took political cartoons to mean something different from what the cartoonist said he intended. Editors should know not only whether the reader reads but whether he gets the messages correctly!

Reader interest

Finding out what people actually read and what interests them is obviously important, so newspapers frequently judge readership by "reader traffic" stories. A researcher asks "did you happen" to read this, or that, and he can come up with percentages of those who "began" or "read most" of a particular story or ad. This gives a rough indication of whether readers were interested. Getting at the degree of interest is a subtle problem. Readers asked whether they were interested may misrepresent—or simply not remember clearly. And even if they do remember and are honest, past interest is not a sure guide to what will interest tomorrow.

Audience

Because advertisers want to know about readers and listeners, most corporate research dollars for communications research go into surveys of the audience. Countless studies tell how many readers are college graduates, own two cars, or buy more than a case of whiskey a year. Apart from commercial value, if a paper makes a good study of this kind for its advertising department, editors should peruse it for an understanding of their circulation area. It is important for them to know, for example, how many women and teenagers read the paper.

Graphics

Studies have been made of which type face and what column widths are optimum for easy or rapid reading. Graphic arts research overlaps with studies of effects and interest as researchers look into what head type pleases most or what ink colors demand attention. Unfortunately, a great deal of typographic expertise is traditional rather than based in sound research. One of the greatest editorial needs is for more studies of graphic arts.

Gatekeepers

In focusing on the people involved in communication, research looks not only at the receivers but the communicators, the senders of messages. Reporters, copyeditors, and sub-editors all control gates which regulate what part of the news flow gets into the paper, and where. So their perceptions, goals, and prejudices are important. An editor will be wary of testing his colleagues psychologically, but studies of gatekeepers in the media generally can give him clues to the strengths and weaknesses in his own organization.

One paper's range

No paper would be expected to go into all these and other possible types of research in any one year. However, a well-supported department may undertake a considerable variety, as indicated by these comments from the research director of a major Midwestern daily:

> The research work for an editor here consists of a wide range of activity. Many times I do confidential interviews with one to ten persons to provide the editor with feedback on certain editorial policies and company practices. . . .
>
> We do regular public opinion surveys and readership surveys of an elementary type for our editors. With our split-run facilities and with our "matched markets"—that is, equivalent groups with respect to certain demographics and behavior—we often test an editor's innovation in headlines, picture treatment, position in the paper—in general, the full line of subjects an editor wants to know about. . . .
>
> We also do group interviews. These are not scientific samples. They are collections of middle income housewives who meet with me and one of the women's department editors at a restaurant or clubhouse in the area and just talk about the newspaper. We've also had the teenagers in to our building for lunch. . . .
>
> An intelligent newspaper editor today realizes that he is isolated from his readers and from potential readers—and makes real effort to get feedback and information about the many segments of a newspaper audience. By now we know that there is an "aggregate of minorities" comprising what used to be called a "mass audience." These segments have different and similar interests with respect to news and feature material. Many times we point out to the editors that an item with an 8 percent "read all" readership is read by 90 percent of certain types of readers, or readers who read only a few items in the entire paper.

This director says he is also concerned abour researching the function of a newspaper. "Just because newspapers have been around for awhile," he adds, "and because the industry is the only one to be specifically protected by our Constitution, is no guarantee that they will be relevant to anyone except a hard core of intellectuals within ten years." He therefore tries to involve editorial and all other departments in considering problems—for example, training of personnel—so his paper can meet the changing communication situation.

This merges into what might be termed a seventh form of research —creative research. Some researchers feel that the most exciting kind of work is generating ideas for improving the paper, checking them out scientifically, and introducing them into routine practice.

Recent research findings

Journalism schools at major universities have been the chief source of useful newspaper research during the last decade. Individual newspapers have made good studies, but typically for internal use. Research by communications professors and graduate students, however, is published in psychology and sociology journals and notably in *Journalism Quarterly*. The following brief listing of some recent studies from *Journalism Quarterly* suggests both the variety of possibilities to editors:

Does direct competition of newspapers increase their sensationalism? At the University of Oregon, Dr. Galen Rarick and Barrie Hartman checked the news in the *Tri-City Herald* in Washington before, while, and after it had a competitor. They found that competition increased the number of stories which gave reward of vicarious pleasure immediately from 22 to 30 percent.

Do small afternoon dailies follow the newsplay of a big morning daily? Apparently not, according to a study of six North Dakota papers by Prof. Hanno Hardt and Michael White at the University of North Dakota. These dailies repeated 12 to 22 percent of the news stories in the morning *Minneapolis Tribune*, but the editors showed "a considerable amount of independence in the 'play' of national and international news."

How do reporters bat on accuracy? As part of the work for his M.A. at Stanford University, Fred C. Berry, Jr., asked persons mentioned in local news stories to check for accuracy. Slightly less than half of the stories got everything right. Misquotation was claimed of one-fourth of the stories, and other "errors of meaning" were often mentioned.

Do editorials and cartoons change opinion? After an experiment with 230 students, Del Brinkman of Kansas State University concluded that an editorial alone does change opinion. Teaming a cartoon with the editorial increases the effectiveness of the editorial, especially if both use the same argument.

Will wire copy be read more by those already getting such news or by those new to it? When the Ohio University student paper added wire copy, Profs. Guido Stempel III and Ralph E. Kliesch of that school checked to see who was reading it. Those exposed to two or more other media read much more of it than those with less exposure. However, the study proved the merit in adding wire copy, for of the students who read only their campus paper, two out of five read some telegraph stories.

Can an editor improve his mix of stories by learning his readers' preferences? Dr. Stempel studied the responses of Ohio adults who looked at thirty-eight categories of news subjects, and found eight kinds emerged as most significant, led by national politics, public health, and welfare. The degree of interest shown in economic news, for example, suggested that more be used in general news pages. Dr. Stempel noted that his research also suggested that an editor might do well to group stories on the same or similar subjects.

Do subheads help? From research for the Magazine Publishers Association, Prof. J. K. Hvistendahl of Iowa State University concluded that subheads are typographically useful because readers like them. But he made an experiment in which he slipped in some innocuous and even contradictory paragraph heads. Since about half the readers did not even spot the inaccurate subheads, he concluded most people pay little attention to them and that "time spent in preparing carefully written paragraph heads would appear to be wasted."

The practical side of research was underlined by Dr. Ernest Dichter of the Institute of Motivational Research: "Our newspaper studies show that as Americans become better educated and more sophisticated, they expect more from their newspapers." Among the pointers he suggested were these:

—Use stronger identification hooks. Readers want human identification with the news. "Too many newspapers have not learned the art of the novelist," so they present news as abstract historical event.

—Readers seek order out of chaos. While some papers admittedly oversimplify, Dr. Dichter said papers might serve as "a sort of optical lens that can reveal the overall significance, while at the same time showing close-ups of details that are often more emotional and human."

Chilton Bush, former journalism chairman at Stanford, issues a yearly book of abbreviated reports on research for the American Newspaper Publishers Association.* Another expanding source of information on current research is *Journalism Abstracts,* published each year for the Association for Education in Journalism; it contains brief accounts of findings in several hundred graduate theses.

A good continuing source of newspaper research is the column in *Editor & Publisher* by Jack B. Haskins, John Ben Snow Research Professor at the Syracuse University School of Journalism. Professor Haskins gives capsule reports on fruitful studies and sometimes puts together conclusions from several related studies over a period of time. For example, reporting an extensive review he made for the National Commission on Causes and Prevention of Violence, he saw little basis for valid generalizations about the amount of violence, either reported or portrayed, in the media. Editors who want to lead intelligently should keep in touch with the findings of the researchers as well as the hearsay of the newsroom.

* The four volumes of "News Research for Better Newspapers," published by ANPA Foundation, document the reading public's reaction to daily newspapers.

Theoretical vs. practical

Scientific endeavor generally involves a division between pure research and applied—between that which asks theoretical questions and that which seeks practical answers. Communications research has such a division between research-theoreticians and pragmatic professionals. In practical terms the split is largely between the universities and industry. Scholarly researchers tend to view working editors as unimaginative hacks who don't understand the basics of real communications, and newsmen tend to dismiss the "communicologists" or "chi square boys" as ivory-tower theoreticians who know little of the media and care less. In 1969 the ANPA Newspaper Information Service newsletter asserted that "of all the controversies in journalism being debated, the most unfortunate is the tug-of-war between professional newsmen and the campus."

Part of the clash results from the fact that newspaper publishers have shown less interest than other industrialists in R&D—research and development, a foundation stone of the modern corporation. At the same time, university administrations and faculty, concerned about research themselves and strongly skeptical of modern media, give the support of promotions and raises to journalism instructors who take the research path rather than practical working journalism in their careers. But to move rapidly to doctorate and significant research at an early age usually leaves little time for experience in the newsroom, so many prominent researchers have the barest professional credentials.

Bridging this psychological gap between newsroom and communications research lab is necessary if newspapers are to move ahead intelligently. Some educators have been pressing working newsmen to open their eyes to possibilities. Professor William R. Lindley, chairman of the Department of Journalism at Idaho State University, in a 1968 letter to *Editor & Publisher*, wrote that the ANPA summary of important research included such items as these which "no editor can afford to overlook":

> —One [study] tells of increasing readership by getting stories away from the inverted pyramid style, and heads away from the usual summary form.
>
> —Another indicates that TTS operators can set type 22.7 percent faster in 15-pica measure than in 11-pica measure.
>
> —With research-minded people revolutionizing the production end of newspapers, the lesson for the editorial departments is pretty clear.

Similarly, Prof. Roland E. Wolseley, long-time magazine chairman at Syracuse, warned New York State newspaper editors that thoughtless critics of research would be superseded, just as the buggy and the quill pen:

> Now it should be obvious that some of the researchers

are time-wasters, engaged in counting a lot of numbers to prove what we all know. . . . But any fair evaluation of the work of the majority, based on a careful reading of their reports in *Journalism Quarterly, Public Opinion Quarterly,* and other journals of the sort, shows that a considerable number of these brilliant scholars are making discoveries of importance. . . . I am myself not one of the research group; I cannot, therefore, be accused of defending my own clique. . . . Instead of worrying about whether the schools of journalism are devoting too much time to research in mass communications, the critics of those schools ought to catch up with the past and find out what is being learned.[1]

Research and tradition

Working newsmen might be more tolerant, and therefore more understanding, of many seemingly unethereal research projects if they tried to see the reason for abstruse theorizing. Theory is basic to scientific advance in other areas of study which are universally respected. Something can be said for the professional who wants practical findings—a study of whether readers liked this column, or research on the effects of that crusade. But it is not easy to fit such pieces into a bigger jigsaw picture of knowledge which is of wide application. It is this perspective the pure communications researcher seeks.

In history a Spengler or Toynbee speculates on the movement of events over a long period of time and relates data to his theories. Evolution is a biological theory which attempts to link and explain the interrelationship of data. No one would dream of trying shots to the moon or planets on the kind of hit-or-miss, shotgun research some newspapers use—any engineering advance is worked out with extreme care after the basic experimental and mathematical work. Communications researchers may make the obvious seem ridiculous with their talk of encoding and decoding, but they do so from a desire to establish fruitful patterns of thought or scientific models.

In all the behavioral sciences, methodology is vital to the accuracy of the findings which test the theories. Methods may loom so important that the social scientist becomes more interested in the gimmick or game than in what knowledge they produce. That such a researcher in journalism is open to justified skepticism should not blind the critic to the practical importance of good methodology. An illustration is the development of studies about how readers look at news and ads.

George Gallup, now famous as a pollster, did pioneer work in methodology and chose to report it in an article, "A Scientific Method for Determining Reader-Interest," in the March, 1930, *Journalism Quarterly.* He used a simple method of marking with a crayon the items which readers said they had read or seen in the paper. As he later adapted the method for IBM equipment, each item in the paper was marked with a serial number. The interviewer then noted the numbers of items seen, read in part, or read completely, and Gallup then could analyze the data that the machine quickly assembled from the interviewers' notes. Much more recently two researchers at the University of Minnesota, Roy E. Carter, Jr., and F. Gerald Kline, comparing the two methods, found each gave much the same result. So the way was cleared for return to Gallup's crayon method for research in outlying parts of Minnesota. The practical implications for editors and advertisers of such testing of methodology are obvious and considered worthwhile by the management of the *Minneapolis Star* and *Tribune,* which provided the money to conduct this study.[2] Now other research, such as eye-camera studies (movements of the eye recorded photographically to find what readers actually read), can add to development of theory and to conclusions about how people go through a paper.

Necessary research

On becoming research professor at Syracuse, Professor Haskins offered two cogent observations about the status and problems of newspaper research:

> The state of knowledge about newspapers is at a very primitive level. . . . Newspapers are still, for the most part, operating primarily on the basis of folklore and tradition, rather than on knowledge of causes and effects established by scientific procedures.
>
> Most research being done on newspapers misses the mark in one respect or another. In academic circles, more research attention is being devoted to other media and other aspects of communication than to newspapers. Of the newspaper research that is being done, most research that is scientifically sound is being done on trivial problems. Other academic research—both methodologically sound and dealing with important problems—is at an abstract and theoretical level, is rarely translated into terms that are meaningful to practitioners, and even more rarely applied to practical problems. Most research being performed by the newspapers themselves is for promotional purposes rather than to gain knowledge about improvement of the product.

To determine what publishers felt about the kinds of research needed, Haskins and Barry M. Feinberg surveyed publishers and other major decision-makers of newspapers. The leaders' views, obviously pertinent to the kinds of research the industry is likely to undertake, showed considerable concern about editorial research. "They believe," Haskins and Feinberg wrote, "that the most useful function of research is to solve long-range industry-wide problems, rather than either day-to-day problems or those peculiar to individual newspapers. Needed research should be carried out by cooperative industry-wide effort and by universities—rather than by individual newspapers."

But what kind of research? The largest group want research about people—readers, advertisers, and so on—rather than about machinery, profits, and other non-human factors. "Editorial product" was the largest category of the kinds of "people-oriented" research checked. Mechanical problems and personnel problems were seen as the two on which there is greatest need for information. Journalism education was fourth, research fifth, and "editing/content/selection" sixth in the "great needs" listing. The publishers, it is clear, are coming to want the kind of practical research which some universities have been attempting on newspaper editorial product.

Similarly, Richard H. Funsch, research manager of the *St. Petersburg Times,* emphasizes the need for more knowledge of readers: "The greatest single need in the area of newspaper research is for more and better audience data: who reads the paper, and why; what sort of person he is, and what does he want from his daily paper, and does he get it."

Planning the research

Planning by both the industry and the individual newspaper can help establish priorities for research; planning then clarifies what steps are appropriate to get the answers. Jack Haskins has devoted considerable time to study of all aspects of this planning process, and from his writings a neophyte researcher can get pointers on how to approach these problems. After evaluating the problems, he must check the knowledge already accumulated by others, then sift and evaluate existing evidence. Next Haskins suggests five steps for discovering more about the unsolved problems:

—Formulate some broad ideas and hypotheses pertinent to the problem.
—Reduce these to specific researchable questions.
—Formulate specific research designs to answer the questions.
—Conduct the research.
—Analyze and interpret the findings.

Finally, the researcher should communicate his findings to the professionals, the educators, and other researchers.

Following up the study of publishers reported above, Haskins listed research activities on two problem areas that had ranked high —personnel and editing. Here are his concerns which relate to editorial content and its effects on readers:

—Product improvement for *current readers.*
—Product improvement to attract *new readers.*
—Adjustment to changes and differences in readers.
—Competition for attention with other media and activities.
—General content selection, product improvement, editing.
—Quality control of the basic editorial product.
—Balance and social responsibility.
—Other editing and news problems

Haskins then proposed specific studies which would be of special interest to editors:

—"Effects of Increasing the Public's Familiarity with Newspaper Editors and Writers."

—"Motivation of Potentially Capable Negroes into Journalism Careers."
—"Effects of Newspaper Juvenile Coverage Variations on Juvenile Offenses."
—"Effects on Audience Size of Various Combinations of Newspaper Content."

Whatever general studies the industry may undertake, each individual paper also must establish its own priorities, a process most effective with some formal planning. Members of the Gannett newspapers group take a look ahead with loosely-organized committees. The *New York Times* has a committee to generate insights into problems of the future and a top-level management committee to act. Warren C. Engstrom, research director of the *Milwaukee Journal,* describes a good setup for planning to meet research needs:

> We formed a "what the reader wants" committee of editors, middle- to top-level executives and research people, to plan ahead to see what the audience is going to be like five years from now and what their entire life situation is with respect to newspaper reading. The committee has now been named the Product Development and Improvement Committee. We meet every Tuesday afternoon and bring in our homework—that is, projects of a research nature, position papers, etc. This even includes all the mechanical aspects of producing a newspaper; it includes circulation and advertising departments.

The value of research

A survey of editors

The authors surveyed members of the Council on Newspaper Research and Development in 1969 and received useful replies from a number who have an interest in editorial research. Several members indicated that they have done little or no editorial research or that all findings are confidential. But others shared ideas and reports which will be summarized briefly here.

Among the questions which yielded significant answers were these: What are the main things a managing editor or other editorial executive can hope to get from a good newspaper research department? What lines of research now appear most promising?

—We feel we can give editors sound guidance on where to go. As we make a study on one paper, we report it around. So we sort of spread the word and get other editors interested in getting answers to their questions about where they should go to please their readers better. (Richard L. Hare, research director, the Gannett newspapers.)

—For nearly a decade we have made periodic studies of the role of the three Toronto newspapers in people's lives and activities in Toronto. These studies have been useful in determining overall editorial policies but have not been used below an administrative editorial level. . . . As to future projects editorially, the direction taken depends very much on the managing editor. . . . Perhaps one of the first areas will be to find out how we can maximize readership. (Keith F. Bull, marketing research manager, *Toronto Star*.)

—One of the areas of great need and interest for newspaper research is the problem of attracting the "youth" reader. It's an area which we know very little about, and there are some studies in the planning stage which may reveal data in this area. (Glen H. Roberts, director of research, *Des Moines Register and Tribune*.)

—Most of our editorial research activities at the *St. Petersburg Times* and *Evening Independent* are directed toward providing editors with a better understanding of the reader they are attempting to serve. Such an endeavor attempts to go beyond the mere measuring of readership and reader demographics and go into the nature and makeup of the individual. In a retirement and tourist-oriented area such as St. Petersburg, it is felt our readers have many more different wants and needs than do those in other areas of the nation. Through our research activities an attempt is made to keep our editors in touch with these wants and needs. . . . (Richard H. Funsch, research manager, *St. Petersburg Times*.)

In these comments there is a common thread: research should find out more about groups of readers and their wants to help editors serve them better.

The Toronto Star

What specific findings have been made in studies by individual newspapers?

The *Toronto Star* conducts reader traffic studies (like those done since 1939 by the Advertising Research Foundation and published as the *Continuing Study of Newspaper Reading*.) The *Star* presents the findings of its studies in sticker-boxes on a reproduction of each page tested. For example, two boxes give the readership for a first page of the women's section, comprising several fashion pictures and a small amount of text. The research showed 94 percent of readers "looked at" the page and 67 percent "read something" on it; 65 percent "read some" of the editorial item and 28 percent "read most." "Read some" percentages inside the section included 47, 43, 76, and 46—so an editor can evaluate the relative pull of different kinds of copy. *Star* studies also show that the interest of male readers declines from the front page to last and that the interest of women increases in the same space, peaking, as might be expected, in the women's section.

Canadian Facts Co., Ltd., interviewed 1,520 individuals in Metropolitan Toronto for the *Star* and produced a bulky report on readers of the city's three papers. Using this study, the *Star* can show advertisers that 51,000 of its readers graduated from university, as compared to 30,000 of the *Telegram* and 48,000 of the *Globe and Mail.* This information on reader profile helps the editorial staffs of all three papers as well. Here is part of a table on the annual family income of female readers of the *Star*:

Income	Number of Readers (in thousands)
$5,000 - 5,999	50
6,000 - 6,999	43
7,000 - 7,999	49
8,000 - 8,999	26
Over $15,000	34

And the table on occupations of *Star* respondents includes this:

Occupation	Number of Readers (in thousands)
Managerial	48
School teachers	10
Clerical	107
Homemaker only	232
Retired	27

The study also showed each paper how many persons read it exclusively, where and how its readers traveled, how much they spent on housing, what investments and insurance they bought. With that knowledge both editorial and advertising staffs can improve their coverage.

The St. Petersburg Times

Such general information can help, but its application is limited by its generality, which is one reason that Mr. Bull of the *Star* recommends research on narrower editorial targets. Mr. Funsch of the *St. Petersburg Times* has come to the same conclusion: "A limited, specific study, especially when it is requested by the editor involved, has proven much more effective." His Florida paper had Suncoast Opinion Surveys conduct a three-day study of 538 residents in 1969 to learn more on the timing and duration of daily readership. Among the useful findings were these:

—Four of five *Times'* readers read it in the morning—but women are more likely than men to read it in the afternoon or evening.

—Nine of ten older readers read it in the morning.

—Readers spend an average of fifty-six minutes daily on the *Times*—but about half spend more than an hour.

—While some persons read the paper in one sitting, many others don't, picking it up and reading it at several times during the day, thereby affording news and advertising content multiple opportunities for exposure.

Other studies were made of the Sunday business pages and the

"Family Today" section. In response to the question "What sort of things do you like best about the *Times* business pages?" 30 percent said stock market reports, 11 percent said, in effect, that they "just like it all," and 9 percent favored general business coverage. Of the more than 25 percent who read the "Stock of the Week" column, 36 percent "like it." On a given weekday, the research showed, 53 percent of all *Times* readers will turn to the "Family Today." Ann Landers was the "most liked" feature, followed by food copy. "In rating 16 items or topics," the researchers concluded, "readers of the Family Today Section indicated they are most interested in reading more news about human interest stories, health, food and education; they are least interested in news about clubs, etiquette, beauty and child care."

The Iowans

The research department of the *Des Moines Register and Tribune* has published a thick book, *The Iowans,* giving results of a study based on a sample of 2,092 persons. Aside from information most pertinent to advertisers, such as the number of households with cars and TV sets, the study includes a number of items of interest to the editors:

One in four readers spends two hours or more on the *Sunday Register.* The largest block of city people reads the paper between 8 and 9 A.M. Sunday, while the largest group outside Des Moines reads it in the early afternoon. (One in five in both groups read it during the normal hours for church.) Eight percent of men read the morning daily at a restaurant and 18 percent read it at work. Twelve percent reading the evening paper get to it after midnight. A somewhat higher percentage of morning newspaper readers have high school and college educations, as compared to readers of the afternoon paper. Nine percent of total readers own mutual fund stock and 15 percent hold other stocks. High percentages had gone to Des Moines during the last year for the state fair or a show, for a visit with relatives, or for hospital care.

A case study

The Gannett newspapers, headquartered in Rochester, New York, have entered deeply into research the last decade, emphasizing what we have termed reader interest and audience research. Individual papers in this group use readership studies to find out how many men and women and boys and girls read various features. The Gannett papers have put even more emphasis, however, on asking readers what they like or would like to have.

Richard L. Hare, director of marketing and research, explained in an interview how research findings have helped the group shape new papers and reshape old ones. Since there are more than thirty papers in this group, scattered from Atlantic to Pacific, an interplay of research effort develops. What readers in one city say they want can be tried out there and, if it works, other papers can imitate. There is also a spill-over effect; that is, the smaller papers with low research budgets can use generally pertinent findings financed by their big brothers, saving their own limited money for research problems specific to their community.

Resources

The Gannett group undertakes all this activity with a small staff. This is possible because it buys research from established firms, especially Louis Harris and Associates, Carl J. Nelson Research, Opinion Research, Market Opinion Research, and Benson and Benson.

Hare, no "communicologist," is proof that useful research can be undertaken under the leadership of men with practical interests and training. Hare received his bachelor's degree in journalism at the University of Illinois and went to work from 1960 to 1964 with the Gannett paper in Danville, Illinois. He spent the next two years as an advertising representative in the group's New York State office and moved to the research job in 1966, meantime completing his master's in advertising at Illinois. In short, he came into research via advertising and marketing; but he has strong editorial interest and emphasized that the research companies employed by the papers bring a variety of experience from projects for many institutions.

Findings

Hare listed a number of findings of Gannett research which have been especially useful to the editors:

—Readers want local news. "They always want more local news, but what do they mean?" Gannett studies have sought a definition and have revealed that typical readers in the various cities are concerned about such issues as schools, local taxes, and transportation to and from work.

—Interest in business and finance is "on the upswing." Readers want this kind of news in both the big and small cities which Gannett has checked.

—Women are interested in much more than old-fashioned "society news." Their interests extend to family and their whole lives outside the home.

—Readers like to find the same feature in the same place every day. They like similar topics grouped. Findings support the idea of "packaging" related news and columns in pages or sections. People prefer four smaller sections to two bulky ones.

Checking a Gannett newspaper almost anywhere will show the influence of these findings. They have strong local coverage, considerable business news, family pages rather than society sections in the traditional sense, and strong, clearly defined departments and sections.

Applications

The papers in Rochester—the morning *Democrat and Chronicle* and the evening *Times-Union*—illustrate how research results can influence editors. Editorial changes were made following a research study in 1964; another study in 1967 indicated that the changes had been in the right direction. Local news is often played big on the front page, and a second front page (of a B Section) covers the local news on both papers.

The *Times-Union* kicks off one section with a page headed "Time Out," which combines such varied recreational fare as TV and music with interpretive sports material. (Hare said spot coverage by television has forced papers to move more into sports backgrounding.) Another section is headed "Family," with club news, fashions, "Dear Abby," and teen material. On the back page, following two pages of stocks, is the unique page heading "Money," including financial columns and local business news.

Both Rochester pages strengthened financial news, Hare said, because research showed stocks were widely held in this affluent city, where there is strong interest in local industry (e.g., Kodak, Xerox). So the *Democrat and Chronicle* has a whole section headed "Business." On the back of its local section is a "metro" page. Its women's section is headed "Feminique," with a local fashion column. On the back page is "People," with columnists Ann Landers, Evans and Novak, Art Buchwald, and other features, pictures and drawings. Editors of both Rochester papers have developed packaging with an eye to the special interests revealed in the studies of their audience. Another result of the 1964 findings was the launching of a local Sunday magazine section in Rochester.

In addition to readership studies, Gannett papers have done some work in polling. During political campaigns, for example, the Rochester morning paper conducts a poll of key districts. To provide a matching feature with research overtones, the afternoon paper has run texts of comments during interviews of small groups. For example, a group of law officers, teen-agers, and ordinary readers may discuss a topic such as civil unrest to give readers another approach to local public opinion.

Launching Today

When Gannett newspapers launched a Florida daily from scratch, they relied heavily on market research for guidance. They went to the Cape Kennedy area, on the hunch that the booming new population there needed a paper, and checked out banana-shaped Brevard County. Three small afternoon dailies were serving the area. The paper from Orlando had 50 percent coverage, according to Hare, but it arrived at many homes an hour after the head of the house had started his complicated drive to work.

Gannett researchers checked the population and found the people were a mobile group from larger cities, of above-average income, much younger and better educated than average. They expressed a need for a county-wide newspaper, for their local concerns were county problems—taxes, schools, roads. They wanted local shopping news and hints, along with articles on child care, fashions, stocks, and sports. A most telling question was what papers they had read in their former communities and what features they missed most.

Gannett launched *Today* in Brevard, making a point to get the paper to the home before the family head left in the morning. The editors followed Rochester findings, using several sections and packaging similar topics together. They started with seven-and-a-half columns on the front page—six wide columns and one 50 percent bigger than that—a format picked up soon by other Gannett papers. They emphasized local news; in fact, the team feared it had emphasized the local angle too much. But when the researchers went back into the field three days after the launching, they found that readers wanted even more local news. So the editors moved it from page three to the front page of a section. A typical copy of the paper today has these six sections: main, sports, local family, "Food Guide," and "Go" (travel).

Gannett researchers came back to the county six months later and again at the end of a year to see how *Today* was doing with readers. Bolstered thus by research, the paper grew from scratch in March, 1966, to over 50,000 circulation in three years—reaching more than three out of four households.

While Gannett papers profit from each other's research, Hare emphasized, each community's paper must solve its own peculiar problems. Travel sections were started both in Rochester and Brevard, for example; the one in Florida caught on, the other did not.

Growing fast, the Gannett group often applies research to existing papers which have been purchased. In such cases Hare designs a questionnaire with editors in the new location. Typically, they ask what features the readers like best in the present paper. A section of the questionnaire dealing with sports, for example, might ask readers which sports they are most interested in reading about, with a list including professional football, college basketball, bowling, tennis, fishing, and so on. For further definition, another section asks whether the paper under study carries the right amount with a form including this:

	Too much	**Too little**	**About right**	**Not sure**
Coverage of local college sports	______	______	______	______
Late scores	______	______	______	______
Auto racing news	______	______	______	______

etc.

A recent Gannett study in one city asked such questions in some 500 personal interviews and about 800 by telephone. When there is competition, Hare said, the researchers also check the competitor's rating on the various counts.

How does Hare relate his work to the various editors in the chain? Usually he sits down with a group of department heads at a paper and presents the proposed research. He takes suggestions for other topics for study. But above all he makes clear that the research is not a test of personnel, allaying fears that the researchers are out to "get" someone.

When the study is complete, the research team discusses the findings with the top management of the paper to determine "What can we do about it now?" Next the team takes the information to individual departments. Ten or more in editorial, including the managing editor, city editor, and other department editors, sit down to hear the findings and ask questions. Hare's experience is that editors are sometimes lukewarm about research. Sometimes they don't realize what it can do. In giving guidance, he feels he is selling the benefits of research and increasing interest.

Hare may tell an editor that the ratings of particular comics at other papers probably are sound for him too. He explains that Gannett is interested in helping with any local problem, no matter how small. This approach catches the editor's interest. From a research firm such an editor can get the counsel of a great deal of talent and experience, as well as statistics. Research, instead of complicating the editor's space problem when readers demand more, may ease his job. For example, some Gannett papers have reduced the amount of space given to stock market quotations because research has demonstrated they can get by with a smaller, selected list. This opens more space for other financial news which the readers want most.

The research attitude

As research catches on more and more in newspapers, it should influence editorial thinking at every level. The good researcher's emphasis on precision and thoroughness in fact-finding matches the newsman's traditional emphasis on care and accuracy. The editor who applies the attitudes of research to the editorial job will think in fresh ways, whether in a story involving statistics or in planning for revolutionary change in his whole operation.

Newspapers deserve many of the criticisms aimed at their handling of scientific data, for few editors and writers have adequate knowledge or concern about the methods of science. "I am often appalled, amazed, amused or horrified, when I read news accounts interpreting the weekly monetary statistics," Sherman Maisel, a governor of the Federal Reserve System, said recently at the University of Michigan. "Many stories present divinations that seem somewhat akin to the oracular portents produced by prior civilizations after a careful analysis of entrails, auspices or other odd indices."

Great care must be used by editors in handling public opinion polls. Scientific polling by Gallup and others has set back the pseudo-scientific "straw ballots" by individual papers, though some worthless newspaper polls survive as an anachronism. But when a politician or a party commissions scientific polls but releases only such results as they wish—and when they feel they will help most—newspapers have to be alert. Unfortunately they are sometimes fooled.

Editors play close poll figures as if they revealed a difference, when in fact they do not; the margin of error which wipes out their relevance is ignored more often than not. In the 1968 campaign, the percentages involving Nixon, Humphrey, and McCarthy in various "races" were often only one or two percentage points apart; since margins of error are always three to four points in such polls, these were meaningless spreads. That is, if Candidate X has 39 percent and Candidate Y has 37 or 38, Candidate Y may actually be ahead. Yet newspapers headline the "fact" that X is ahead.

Even the *New York Times* misrepresents in the polling field, according to Dr. Gerhart D. Wiebe, a public opinion scholar who is dean of the School of Public Communication, Boston University. He found "frequent serious defects" in *Times* reports of opinion research: "I have found headlines to be misleading, the customary buttressing of story themes with clarifying facts to be in error, and, if I am not mistaken, a supercilious approach to the field of public opinion research that raises questions as to the seriousness of the editors in their efforts to inform either themselves or their readers regarding this area." He illustrated with stories in which the paper had taken unscientific "polls" seriously, lumped sound polls with unscientific ones, and even had a reporter conduct an old-fashioned unscientific poll.[3]

Editors whose papers have research departments should check doubtful stories with their own experts, just as they check possible libel with their attorneys. Sometimes they can consult communications researchers, sociologists, psychologists, or statisticians at a near-by university. But for the best handling of scientific research there is no substitute for maximum know-how on the editorial staff itself. Editors of the future will be interested and educated in research. Already Mr. Bull of the *Toronto Star* notes that "the climate editorially is changing. New and younger men are rising to the top of the editorial ladder and they appear to be much more aware of the contribution marketing research can make."

Similarly, Mr. Engstrom of the *Milwaukee Journal* points out that in the past editors were supposed to know all about reader interest. "This intuitive genius was considered as the main requirement of a good editor," he says. "If he turned to a research person, it was considered a weakness on his part. This attitude has disappeared with the new breed of editors and publishers. They do not edit a newspaper with a slide-rule, but they have important questions to ask, and research provides this material."

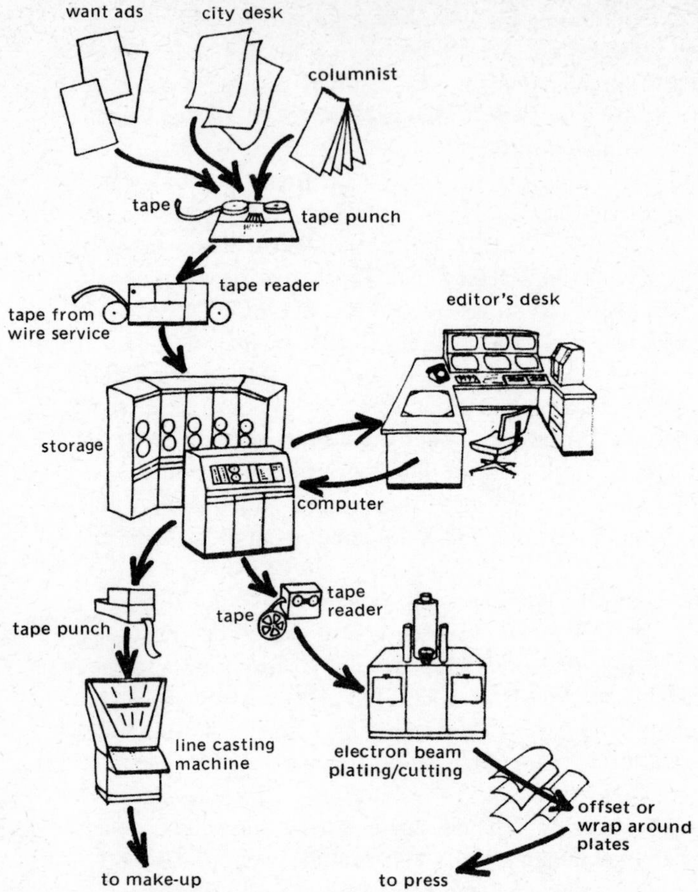

Fig. 19-1. Futuristic editing. A few years ago the Diebold Group visualized that editing in the 1970s would be done in this fashion, with consoles and light pencils.

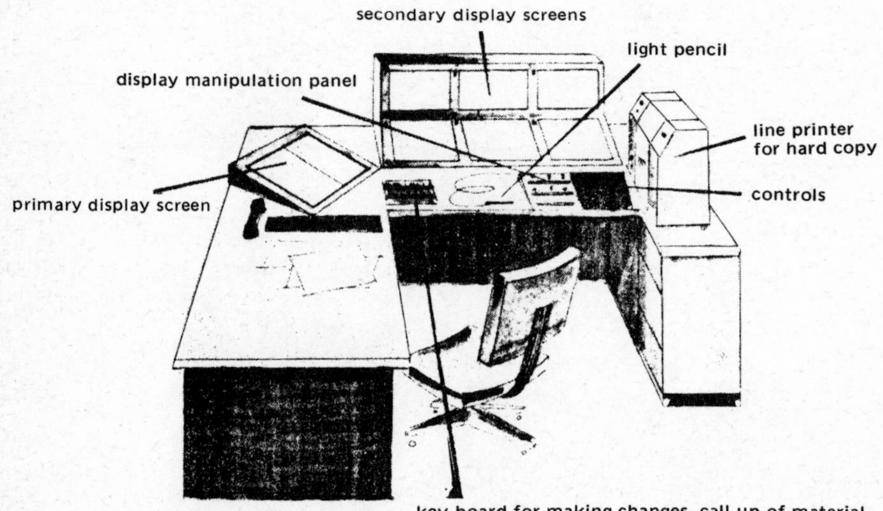

19 The future of newspaper editing

> The changing external conditions under which newspapers have published during the last 20 years have produced considerable ferment internally within the newspaper business. There has developed an attitude not merely of receptiveness to change, which at best is passive, but of making change happen—actively and positively. The publishers of daily newspapers are looking ahead. They have created '*a forward look in the daily newspaper business*.'
>
> —Stanford Smith, general manager,
> American Newspaper Publishers Association

To be ready for the future, a newspaper must plan for it. For concrete planning, an individual or a group probably has to be put in charge. The *New York Times* formed a temporary committee in the late sixties to see what should be done; its chairman, Lester Markel, Sunday editor at the time, came up with a report that, to be effective, a long-range plan must be coordinated and must have senior executives "fully committed" to it. As a result the *Times* named two committees—a group of executives to consider proposals and a permanent working committee to generate the ideals—the Committee on the Future. Topics which COMFUT researched or considered include characteristics of readers, new methods for getting information into the home, and predictions of the city's development. Even on a much smaller daily such a task force can make educated guesses to help the paper get ready for the future.

Identifying trends

A high priority for a newspaper's planners is to identify trends in its circulation area and in communications. For example, should editors take seriously the predictions of the late Bernard Kilgore, who was perhaps more responsible than any other of its editors for the phenomenal mid-century success of the *Wall Street Journal*? Kilgore saw four major kinds of newspapers in the future: giant regional papers, specializing in serious news; improved suburban papers with both local and broad coverage; small dailies and large weeklies heavy on community news; and specialized nationwide publications like the *Journal.* Events since the mid-sixties have underlined the reasonableness of those forecasts; and even late in the seventies the editors of an individual paper may fruitfully consider whether they are adjusting to the forces underlying the kinds of success predicted by Kilgore.

In another approach to trends, William B. Dickinson, managing editor of the *Philadelphia Bulletin* and a former president of the Associated Press Managing Editors Association, foresaw this "paper of 1976":

> The front page will give the reader, in condensed but readable form, all the news that is really new on any given day. . . . Really good, but highly compressed writing, will be necessary. A topflight staff will work furiously, and anonymously, before and during the hours of publication. There will be no jumps from page one. Instead, brief reference notes will key the reader to further information inside the paper.
>
> The headlines will reflect the importance of the news—and there will be at least one good picture, undoubtedly in color, on the page.
>
> The inside pages will supplement page one with background, interpretation, greater detail, editorial comment, columns and features. They will constitute, in effect, almost a daily magazine, designed to inform, entertain, even at times amuse, the reader. If the job is well enough done, our papers in 1976 will cut deeply into the ground now held by the weekly news magazines.
>
> Specialists—and they will be highly paid specialists—will deal with the advances in science, in medicine, in education, the problems of urban civilization and of government. . . .
>
> There will be scant space in the paper of 1976 for cheap crime, for iffy political stories, for water main breaks and two-alarm fires. Only really major crimes will rate separate coverage—the rest will be handled as sociology.
>
> The paper of 1976 will have fewer comics. . . . I think the women's pages of newspapers, as such, will have disappeared. . . . At least three areas certainly will be beefed up . . . amusements, books and travel. . . .
>
> The metropolitan newspaper of 1976 will have something in the nature of a planning board operating in the newsroom. The chief news executive will sit down each day for a time with several other executives who have had time to think, and they will apply their brains to deciding what to do tomorrow, next week, next month and even next year.

Such prognostications reflect themes on how economic, social, technical, and other forces will mold the press, as well as what readers of tomorrow will demand of papers. Will subscribers be better educated? Will they be too busy to read anything but the most digested accounts? Will they want more depth and detail than ever before?

Examining trends

Better educated readers

It is tempting to rub the crystal ball gently and predict a public ravenously devouring newspapers filled with meaty information on politics, economics, science, and the arts. Instead of being tied to concern over who won the Cub Scout citizenship award or whose fender was crumpled at Mulberry and Vine, the publisher then could "give them what they want"—quality.

A strong statistical case can be made for this kind of fantasy. Millions are going to college. A record number are working for advanced degrees. Young people have never been more alert to change and to their society. More quality newspapers should result from the current willingness of the general public, not merely the young, to buy serious books and subscribe to more and better magazines. And it is no longer unusual for people of modest means to have traveled extensively outside the United States.

But before we see Utopia in the crystal ball we ought to look at the reality that surrounds us. Although large numbers attend college we must realize that many reject the education offered there. They resist knowledge and retain their prejudices all four years of college. With their degrees they only settle somewhat comfortably, subscribe to the *Reader's Digest*, and spend hours each night watching whatever pops up on the television screen.

Despite educational advances and increased knowledge about the human personality, people seem no more able to be rational today than they could fifty years ago. We sometimes think of modern man as a rational being, forgetting that he is often a crucible of emotions. We easily switch from rational tolerance to irrational envy. We can even rationally build passion into hatred. Our reading can reduce our emotional prejudices, but it can also reinforce them. Formally-educated people, then, often are as full of fury, as narrow, and as ignorant on many subjects as the uneducated. Many persons with advanced degrees are uninterested in politics, government, and law, even though these subjects greatly influence their lives. Some do not even vote. Many who travel extensively gain little from it. They go abroad on American airplanes, stay at American hotels, go to American-style restaurants, and, with a few exceptions, speak only to fellow Americans or, showing their tolerance or insecurity, to the British.

But if a journalistic prophet cannot hope for a nation of highly intelligent people thirsting for information, he should not underestimate the public's interest and tastes. The papers that today underestimate change are sterile and listless, with declining or static circulations.

More thorough coverage

In general, the most financially successful publications have emphasized thoroughness in reporting the news. As we noted previously, papers like the *Washington Post, Los Angeles Times, Wall Street Journal,* and *New York Times* have enjoyed spectacular circulation gains. Smaller papers have enlarged their coverage by subscribing to the wire service provided by the *New York Times* or to such supplementary information as provided in the service offered by the *Washington Post* and the *Los Angeles Times*. These facts indicate that a growing public prefers to buy papers of breadth and depth. When the public supports such papers, advertisers are eager to buy space. The resulting victory is both journalistic and financial.

This kind of development almost certainly is going to spread. Success has many imitators, and as other publishers see how prosperous the quality papers have become, they too will improve their coverage. The public also can be expected to gradually increase its interest in public affairs. The better papers will de-emphasize spot news—the events of the day—in favor of long-range, in-depth reporting. This happened in the reporting of the Vietnam war. Many editors realized that readers were tired of skimming the daily reports from Saigon telling which military unit fired what in what region. So some papers summarize this spot news in three or four paragraphs on an inside page and devote the space to deeper reporting of the politics, economics, military strategy, health hazards, and refugee problems of the war.

Decreasing birth rate

Another trend for newspapermen to watch is population change. For years Americans have been used to the idea of a higher birth rate, which means more youth in the population. Before long, however, drops in the birth rate may alter the age ratios and, unless the percentage of youth going to college advances sharply, reduce university populations. The tendency may be to shift the focus to the old, a neglected minority growing in size due to medical advances.

But will this birth trend continue through the seventies? And if births increase again, will more and more young people get liberal educations which lead to newspaper reading? The sciences have been popular in college for at least a decade; but that trend has changed, at least temporarily, to the extent that science professors are concerned about getting enough quality students. Will the demands of a technological culture push more and more students into technical secondary education? Will such students give more emphasis to the social sciences and humanities than before? Newspaper planning committees will have to assess such questions, even though their answers today may not be correct tomorrow.

The rise of regional papers

The trend toward mechanization and automation within the newspaper plant itself does seem certain to continue. Some seers, on

Kilgore's tack, expect that developments in electronics and distribution will permit big, powerful, well-financed regional papers to drive out all but the biggest of today's metropolitan newspapers. These super-giants would cover the regional, national, and world news for various areas: one for New England, another for the Northwest, one for the South and Southwest, and perhaps two for the Midwest and the West. The community papers which today give local, regional, national, and world news would then print only local news. Readers would subscribe to both Big Paper and Little Paper.

If it goes as the optimists hope, the Big Paper will give superb coverage of its territory while the Little Paper examines thoroughly the events of its community. But things may not work out that way. Perhaps the Big Paper would become Big Brother, telling the readers only what some powerful person or group feels is safe for them to read. Since no other group could compete, there would be no antidote. The Little Paper, moreover, might do a poorer job than smaller papers do today, particularly if it takes its cues from the Big Paper.

On the other hand, the Little Paper might realize that its future lies with quality and would put out readable, pertinent material. A journalist might then find work on it satisfying because he would be helping readers learn about the problems of their community and thus become better citizens.

Even if the giant regional paper never emerges, some students of the press are concerned about the rapid moves toward chain ownership of American newspapers. It is true that some chains produce a better paper than the community had when the paper was locally owned. But the opposite of this occurs—for a chain may be interested only in skimming profits, with no feeling of responsibility to the dozens of communities where it owns papers. Or the newspaper may be owned by a conglomerate which also makes paper and radios, prints books, and operates TV stations. Some newspaper corporations are "going public"—selling their stock on the open market. The additional capital can help a newspaper update or expand its coverage. The danger is that stockholders interested in quick profits might oppose investment of capital and reinvestment of profits necessary to improve quality.

A changing physical world

Beyond trends of education, population and organization lies the perhaps still greater, more enigmatic, and essentially fresh problem of a rapidly changing environment—a new setting which is perhaps less sympathetic to the press and its freedom than in earlier American history. It is traditional to attack individual editors, but today many citizens attack the institutions of the media. Police have actually beaten newsmen and photographers—and won praise for it from many citizens. A press freedom review by the International Press Institute in Zurich in 1969 spoke of the "disquieting development" of popular attitudes against the press in the United States, Germany, France, Britain, and Brazil. It noted: "For the press of

America and elsewhere its own communication problem of reestablishing the trust of the readers may prove harder to solve than the technical and economic problems which beset it."

A changing political world

After becoming U.S. Ambassador to the United Nations, James Russell Wiggins, former editor of the *Washington Post,* pointed out in a talk at the University of North Dakota how press and society are moving away from consensus. Formerly, those with power differed about means, not ends, and a newspaper could serve varied views:

> Now I think it takes no seer to perceive that the age of consensus is ending or certainly will be ending in the seventies. I do not say that the characteristic daily newspaper will end with it; but I do say that it is going to be increasingly difficult to retain the confidence of a reader audience of infinitely more diverse views. The more that society divides into irreconcilable fragments, the more difficult it will be to maintain that universal credibility necessary both to general reader distribution and to advertising profitability in newspapers of general circulation.

Increasingly, Wiggins observed, reporters are more concerned to tell what they think about a speech than to report what the man said, and as this trend goes on, a newspaper may be able to hold one or two fragments of the divided audience "but it cannot hope to retain its credibility with all of them."

In recent years there have been numerous signs that newspapers are trying to understand new moods, as indicated by these *Editor & Publisher* reports:

Item: Of sixty-five society editors replying to a survey, thirty-six said they carry news and pictures of interracial marriages, only two said flatly "never," and others hedged.

Item: A New York newspaper group was challenged to follow the London *Mirror*, which grew to more than 5 million as its editor insisted it be edited for readers under thirty.

Item: Communications researcher Jack B. Haskins, in a report to the National Commission on Causes and Prevention of Violence, found a sample of editors considerably *underestimated* reader interest in such violent news as bombings, ambushes and forest-fire deaths.

It is now almost a cliché to observe that society is in ferment if not revolt. Many youth, especially, have demonstrated their desire for radical social change in the marches, riots, and sit-ins since the early sixties.

Whether the veterans returning from Southeast Asia will have an impact, in college and afterwards, like those back from World War II and Korea, is still pure guesswork. But editors are going to have to be ready for the wake following years of war, civil disobedience, student unrest and black revolution—and the wake of that wake. There is no prospect of a quiet, relaxing world during the lifetimes of young editors who plan the future of newspapers today.

The impact of technology

Shortly before his retirement as AP bureau chief in the New York state capital, Norris Paxton told an audience of editors, "If you want to go where the action and money are, learn about newspaper automation." And of computers he said, "If I were a young man entering journalism, I would woo these things." So experienced newsmen view the impact of mechanization on newspaper editing in the years ahead.

As already discussed, the technically minded envision the copyeditor of tomorrow sitting before a console on which a picture of copy appears. With an electronic pencil he will wave away the redundancies, the bad phrasing, and the misspelled words. The electronic box then will spew forth the corrected copy, which in some magical way will turn to print.* It sounds so easy that a copyeditor might imagine himself working about two hours a day, then returning to the old-fashioned pleasure of reading a paperback. In reality his work for the paper will no doubt take his full time on the job, but the work will be less mechanical and more intellectual.

Such change might take several directions and working editors will have to read and perhaps attend classes to understand the applications and problems of any system their papers adopt or consider. The neophyte looking to the future is under less pressure. He need only get an overview of the major possibilities in order to follow the trends reported in trade and professional magazines.

Automation and mechanization

First he should understand the distinction between automation and mechanization. *Automation* refers to a machine's production *on its own* according to instructions programmed into it beforehand. Obviously the writing, editing, and layout of newspapers requires too many minute by minute decisions for automation to go very far in this area soon. *Mechanization,* on the other hand, refers to a man's production *assisted by* a machine. Mechanization extends the human hand; automation extends the human brain. It is mechanization, not automation, which is usually being discussed in connection with the future technology of newspapers.

As the distinction implies, emphasis is necessarily on the mechanical or production side, rather than the editorial. The editor becomes involved because he has to adjust his operation to better production; lower production costs also give him more money for editorial. Unfortunately, as in so many areas since the industrial revolution, increased mechanization may bring stereotyped, monotonous, dull newspapers. Of course, if computers are developed that can write poetry or translate Russian, they would have the wit to write simple

*See footnote on p. 164.

news stories. The great newspaper of 2000, however, is hardly going to be built with a simple collation of related facts—and complex stories are something else again.

Predictions

What, then, are the imminent prospects for use of computers and more sophisticated mechanization? Ronald White, director of production and engineering for the Scripps-Howard Newspapers, has envisioned hooking the reporter's typewriter directly to the computer. It would store the copy temporarily during editing and then blend the desk's corrections into the original tape as it headed for type. As with TTS, the copyeditor might be discouraged from making many complicated changes, but the editing here would seem to be essentially the same as done by Ben Franklin.

In a much-quoted speech given in the early sixties to both the American Society of Newspaper Editors and the Magazine Publishers Association, an automation pioneer pictured a great change in editorial tools. Figure 19-1 illustrates this prediction by John Diebold, founder of the Diebold Group, Inc.:

> Editorial copy will be fed into a computer-like system upon arrival in your office—whether it comes in by wire, is typed in by a reporter, or is called up from the morgue.
>
> Copy will be manipulated electronically; displayed on TV screens that will be a part of every editorial desk; and dummied by manipulating the information on the screen with the use of light-pencils and light-erasers. . . .
>
> The editorial office of 1973 will differ greatly from the one in which you work today. At its heart will be an electronic information system connecting editorial desks, wire services, morgue, and electronic automation news library, and the composing room.[1]

Recent applications

One step toward such a "cathode-ray tube editorial terminal" was the recent development of the American Newspaper Publishers Abstracting Technique (ANPAT). The ANPA Research Institute created a computer program which can trim copy to any desired length. A 200-line wire story, for example, could be "computer-pencilled" in half. But ANPAT cuts only whole sentences and paragraphs, so no internal trimming or altering is possible. Noting the development, the American Newspaper Guild *Reporter* could joke about the day when editors are "replaced by transistors"—apparently confident that the automated console is not an imminent threat for union members.

From time to time other developments have brought such "automated" production closer. Unisetter, introduced by United Press International, provides automatic production of justified wire copy from TTS signals to offset newspapers. Harris-Intertype Corporation in 1968 marketed a cathode-ray tube phototypesetting system which composes complete pages of newspapers and magazines (cost:

$300,000 to $500,000). For average papers, however, the impact of the major mechanical features of Mr. Diebold's visions are unlikely before the eighties. Again, newness is essentially in mechanics; the editor must still solve the problems of selection, layout, and design.

It is perhaps more practical for most editors to look at the "future" which is already here on some papers; for the presumption is that more and smaller papers will be able to adopt these advances before long. The Perry Newspapers of Florida installed their first computer in 1962, and by 1965 their computers "began paying off handsomely," according to John H. Perry, Jr., president. Production was up 50 percent, the production payroll was down one-half, and many more people had been hired in editorial. The computers are used in bookkeeping and composing ads. An Electronic Retina Character Reader System, which accepts typewritten matter for a computer, facilitates typesetting. Changes and corrections are made on original copy in the conventional manner, and a typist at a special typewriter retypes the affected lines; these are fed into the Electronic Retina ahead of the copy, so that corrections are made before the copy is set.

In 1963 the Oklahoma City *Times* published the first paper with type justified entirely by computer. Computers have been used there, as elsewhere, to gather, tabulate and print out election returns. Charles L. Bennett, managing editor, feels that editors must use their imaginations to find other uses. For example, his paper was able to use the computer in an unusual piece of interpretation. The Oklahoma state legislature proposed a distribution formula for a new state sales tax, and the paper was able to figure out how much tax money each subdivision would receive—and publish it before the creators of the formula themselves knew exactly how it would work. Bennett says the computer also can be used to give the editor a running total of type committed that day and the space left, as well as an analysis of news selected so far. But then a copy boy with a pencil or an adding machine could do most of this.

Using new technology

A key question for the editor to consider is this: What problems can mechanization and automation solve for my paper? Usually the problems are those of production. This is the area where the critics say newspaper progress has been slow, and this is where costs must be trimmed. But some of the problems are editorial.

One perennial problem is fast recovery of material in the newspaper morgue or in other libraries. Because the computer now can retrieve information almost instantaneously, it holds the potential for vastly better-researched interpretive pieces. But the problem then, as now, will be for the writers to digest and synthesize the mass of facts. And there are certainly times, in the rush of deadlines, when the reporter who can "just see what the story looked like" would rather riffle through clips or the files than wade through pages of print-out from a computer.

Another problem is selecting the best mix of stories for the paper each day. Bennett indicates the computer could help. Perhaps. The difficulty here is the cafeteria-line nature of editing. Early in a morning or afternoon an editor has to select some stories and get them into type, before other stories are even written. The problem is really not one of sorting or retrieving, as those who speak of push buttons and magic screens sometimes imply, but of arranging a pleasing mix of entertaining and significant news. If printing processes are speeded up and computer storage of finished stories refined to give an editor until the last minute to make his choices, better mechanization could mean more careful evaluation and better selection.

Another problem, perhaps the biggest, is getting brighter writing, more imaginative copyediting, and a more penetrating understanding of the news generally. The claims that machines can help here are minimal. "Computers and all the rest of the new technology are not the central problem of the newspapers," Bennett said. "The central problem—and its answers—lies just as much as ever, and perhaps more than ever, within the minds of people."

Mechanization, after all, refers simply to tools. It is the men who use them who determine what art is produced. An offset newspaper can be duller than an old one set by hand, and a computerized newspaper could well be worse than a contemporary one.

The chairman of the ANPA Scientific Advisory Committee, Dr. Athelstan Spilhaus, dean of the Institute of Technology, University of Minnesota, has cautioned that newspapers are not so much in the newspaper business as in the *communications* business. Computers may help newspaper production. But the more pressing question is whether they will help newspapermen communitcate with readers—and each other.

Too often it is forgotten that a modern mechanism merely speeds up what can be done anyway. The computer is admired for its speed, a quality important in newspapering, but not all-important. And many things promised of automation can already be done if one finds it worthwhile. If a telegraph editor really wants to know how many stories he has sent to the composing room since 7 A.M., he can have a copyboy keep a tally—probably more cheaply than using a computer. Of course if the paper already has a computer, the editors should make maximum use of it. Bennett summarizes it well:

> Part of our task, so far as computers are concerned, is to find the jobs that they can do for us. This is as much the editor's and reporter's responsibility as it is the task of the production superintendent or data processing man. This means the editor must, first, become better informed about what computers are and what they can do. . . . Secondly, the editor must forget his traditional reluctance, his needs and problems with other departments. One characterisitc of this new age certainly is going to be a great deal of crossing over of normal "departmental lines." . . . The third requirement for editors is to enlist the understanding and help of the people in the news-

room. Their understanding will be vital if you ever expect to make new systems work. Their creative and imaginative thinking is essential if we are to get maximum use from the marvelous tools now available to us.

Problems of pay

While newspaper consolidation in recent decades has restricted opportunities for editorial workers, notable in New York City, the prospect is for more good openings in the rest of this century than colleges can fill. Some 3,500 new journalists are needed by daily newspapers each year just to fill esixting jobs, according to the Newspaper Fund, a nonprofit organization fostering such careers. About 100,000 workers have been added by papers in the last two decades, as increase of two for every five before 1950. This trend for qualified personnel promises to continue. The question is whether newspapers can compete in the job market for the brightest young people. That question is already crucial in some places where beginning school teachers, who had been notoriously underpaid, now get higher pay than seasoned reporters and copyeditors.

"If we refuse to pay starting salaries that are not competitive with even the teaching profession, we will abdicate our rights to the brightest and most talented newspaper newcomers," Cortland Anderson, editor of the now defunct *Suffolk* (N.Y.) *Sun,* wrote, "Yes, starting newspaper salaries are dramatically higher than they were even five years ago. But the same is true in teaching, general business, law, and whatever else you care to list. We talk about better and healthier newspapers of the future and, without pausing for breath, talk about making them that way with castoffs."

Publishers have long complained that, because the nespaper business is less profitable than many other industries, they cannot pay top salaries for editorial help. Are newspapers really hard up? As mechanization spreads and reduces production costs, talking poor-mouth becomes less and less honest. There is much evidence that newspapers could now afford to pay editors more. In recent years nespaper advertising revenues have been running at record highs—between 4 and 5 billion dollars. In 1965 the *Los Angeles Times* became the first newspaper to publish more than a million lines of ads. *Editor & Publisher,* in annual studies of an "average medium city newspaper," has reported operating revenues up faster than operating expenses, with increases in profits after taxes running 30 percent and more per year (the profits being more than half a million dollars annually). The newsroom staff can wonder if such figures indicate that more of the income should be distributed to personnel. Mechanization can increase the newsroom budget by reducing composing room costs.

Salaries for inexperienced newsmen have been going up, but still lag behind many other professions. The Newspaper Fund, which makes an annual check of salaries paid daily newsroom beginners with bachelor's degrees, reported the average figure at $132.39 for the Class of 1970, up 7.9 percent in a year. This was slightly lower than starting figures for all other media. Wire services were highest, with $147.19.

Management can cite frequent ads in *Editor & Publisher* that indicate many papers are paying $15,000 a year to experienced copyeditors. American Newspaper Guild figures at the start of 1972 revealed that the top eighty-seven union contracts paid reporters more than $200 a week, with copyeditors usually getting an extra 5 or 10 percent. The *Washington Post* contract calls for a minimum salary of $400 for experienced reporters in mid-1973. Other 1973 contracts provide for salaries of $360 at the *Washington Star,* $297 at the Honolulu papers, $310 at the San Francisco and San Jose papers, and $312.25 at the *Detroit Free Press.* Salaries for city editors, telegraph editors, or exceptional copyeditors are higher. This means that substantial numbers of newspapermen, who are not top editors, are making $20,000 a year.

While the biggest papers, under strong Guild pressure, have pushed salaries up in recent years, hundreds of medium-sized papers have lagged far behind. Staffs on these papers rarely belong to the Guild and the publishers have been content to pay experienced and capable newsmen between $160 and $200 a week. Sometimes ads in *Editor & Publisher* offer salaries as low as $125 a week for a demanding job. Low salaries in many medium and small newspapers cause bright young men and women to leave as soon as possible for bigger papers, TV, or public relations. This situation is disheartening, especially when a young person finds the smaller community appealing and would like to stay if he could make a moderately good income.

To be better, newspapers, both large and small, will not only have to increase prosperity but invest more in editorial talent. They will have to meet the competition. In public relations, salaries often top newspaper pay, $12,000 to $18,000 being common for men and women with limited experience. In spite of what some newspaper indeed, some public relations men say they like news work better but feel working standards are higher in the PR positions! Newspapers will attract and keep such men for responsible editorial posts in part by paying better but in part by embodying the integrity, the zeal for coverage, and the creative crusading which we advocate throughout this book.

Professional prospects

Equal opportunity

We have said that more Negroes should be working as newspaper editors. The same goes for the original Americans, Indians, and for hyphenated Americans who have sometimes but not often been on editorial staffs: Mexican-Americans, Chinese-Americans, Japanese-Americans, and so on. "Qualified" is sometimes used in connection with prospective employees from such minorities; the qualification may suggest hidden prejudice but it also points to the lack of educational opportunities for minority members. Recognizing this limitation, especially for blacks, newspapers and universities have been trying to provide scholarships and other incentives to train them, and hiring of Negroes is slowly going beyond tokenism.

Equality should also embrace women, who have too often been segregated to society pages and who rarely get into the executive positions they are qualified for. Research at the School of Journalism and Communications, University of Florida, indicates that a favorable change is underway. Harry H. Griggs reported that a study of *Editor & Publisher* ads showed one-fourth of them wanted males and 5 percent specified females. However, more than half the time when a woman was sought, it was for a newsroom job, not the women's page. A survey of seventy women on Florida newspapers showed that six out of ten rated their futures in newspaper work as outstanding to excellent. The Newspaper Fund reported 43 percent of all persons hired by newspapers in 1968 were women, compared to 30 percent in 1964.

Better professional practice in the future will also mean more careful use of resources. This will release money to hire the best staff and to help them use their time most efficiently, for poor newsroom planning diverts high-paid hours to run-of-the-mill phone calls, listings, and news bits. "The industry must begin to find methods of getting the routine done by relatively unskilled low salaried personnel or by machines," Dr. DeWitt Reddick, former dean of communications at the University of Texas, has written, "and thus establish a creative type of job for which high salaries can be paid." As those with high school or two-year college degrees prove themselves able, they can be recruited for higher levels of the profession and sent on for more training.

Educational background

The half-century debate between liberal-arts education and journalism school education for newspaper journalism promises to go on indefinitely. Without attempting to resolve that dispute, we can suggest that there will be a role for both kinds of education, as well as for a third type which has been emerging and which we will discuss below.

Editors need a liberal education in history, philosophy, art and other humanities.* Though critics of journalism schools are sometimes unaware of it, the student in such a school gets general education. He also receives not only training in skills, but an opportunity to apply his liberal training to practical problems involving ethics, creativity, reform, and integrity. Edward W. Barrett, former dean of the Graduate School of Journalism at Columbia University, outlined succinctly, in his presidential address to the Association for Education in Journalism, the ideal education for journalists of the future:

> The primary aim of education for journalism is the development of disciplines, arts, and attitudes of mind:
>
> The discipline of giving attention to the distasteful as well

* Miss Susan Tebbe, in a study of 117 managing editors on the West Coast, learned that 64 percent were college graduates; two-thirds of them had majored in journalism. In hiring, "managing editors do tend to prefer journalism majors. They also think that the journalism graduate should have had a broad education in other fields."[2]

as the appealing; the discipline of learning to gauge one's best effort to fit an allotted time span; the discipline of continuing self-education:

The art of expression that is lean, direct, precise, and deft; the art of grappling with a complex new subject, extracting information from inarticulate specialists, and synthesizing the findings faithfully and coherently; the art of recognizing fine points of accuracy and subtle gradations of meaning:

The attitude of profiting from criticism; and the attitude of approaching new problems with the open-mindedness and imagination that make solutions possible:

Above all, one seeks the attitude of ruthless fairness, of reporting what he dislikes as honestly as what he likes—in short, true intellectual integrity.

We have discussed the third form of emerging education, the importance for journalism of communications research and of automation. In addition to having both liberal education and professional knowledge of techniques and traditions, the future editor needs to understand the new technology and what it can do for newspapers. The ordinary journalism student must at least be aware of the new trends, but many serious students will want the specialized knowledge which comes from a master's degree or even a doctorate.

Practical research

This suggestion touches another live controversy of recent years between communications theorist-researchers and the newsroom oriented educators. Here again, as the newsman needs both skills training and liberal arts, he requires behavioral science as well. Some communications experts talk esoterically and impractically of computers, quantification, encoding, and information retrieval. And some have so little solid newspaper experience that they are more sociologists or psychologists than they will ever be media men. Nevertheless, some develop real knowledge, as distinguished from common sense guesses and prognostications the unwary sometimes mistake for "research," which will be invaluable to the future of journalists and journalism.

One important area has been little touched by even the "communicologists." That is the problem of news comprehension and retention. The newsman of the future ought to study seriously how people learn and why they forget. The most upsetting part of news work is that even superior reporting and editing draw only a few careful readers. Most skim the basics and then forget them within a few days. Perhaps educational psychologists could help a paper better serve its readers.

One way to help the reader remember is to repeat. Repetition has to be subtle, however, so the reader who does remember will not skip the story complaining, "I read this last week." The newspaper might use review techniques instead. For example, the "box score" reporting so common on the sports pages could be used more in the regular news pages.

A sizable number of papers already use this presentation for major votes in Congress. A boxed story may report that the Senate passed a measure forty-eight to forty-four, then list the votes of senators from the paper's circulation area. Other papers, before elections, list the voting record of home-based legislators. The wire services, during a big event, sometimes file an "at-a-glance" summary of the main facts. Much more of this kind of summation is needed. It is easy for readers to skim innumerable stories about a peace conference, a trial, or a strike without ever having a chance for a quick review. The box score approach offers this by reporting, on the peace conference, that Country A has made certain demands, Country B has made others, and they have agreed on Points 1, 3, and 4 but still disagree on Points 2 and 5. If one is wary of oversimplification this technique can serve as the kind of review that every student knows is so valuable before an examination.

Though some prophets foresee drugs as a way to improve man's learning and remembering capacities—"smart pills"—the budding editor should expect human beings of his future to be like readers today: ordinary persons who have to be lured into reading by good writing, pertinent material, and good typographical display.

Mid-career training

Because professionals can always learn more about these elements of journalism, the newspapers of the future must provide more training for men who have been on the job five years—or twenty years. Other professions now have in-service or mid-career training, and it should be a regular part of the professional press. It is possible that most good young newsmen in the next two decades will have a thorough formal education, and some will have advanced degrees. Yet they will eventually need refresher courses and classes in new techniques and ideas.

The Nieman fellowships at Harvard have provided a year of study for some thirty journalists each year for a generation. No degree is given; the student goes to classes of his choice and takes no examinations. More recently, special periods of study, less than a year, have been set up at Northwestern and Stanford for experienced journalists. The Washington Journalism Center was founded to give more training to young, relatively inexperienced newsmen. Other opportunities exist for studies lasting a few weeks or a month. The American Press Institute at Columbia University offers several seminars a year for specialized groups of working journalists. Some grants allow a journalist simply to read at a major library for several weeks. Many papers expect their top reporters to read for a few hours a day on company time to keep their minds attuned—and perhaps to dig up information for stories.

A few newspapers give staff members leaves of absence for study or travel. The academic sabbatical—a leave with pay—may be adopted by newspapers. Perhaps union contracts will some day give a newsman several weeks off every few years. In the early sixties the steelworkers' union obtained thirteen-week vacations for members after every five years of work. If this sort of vacation comes to newspapering, the journalist would be wise to use the time to improve his knowledge by reading, discussion, and travel—plus the refreshment of mind and body that a change can provide.

True professionalism for the newspaper of tomorrow, in short, rests in part on the encouragement of learning and fresh thought among professional journalists as well as journalism students.

Establishing trends

A leading newspaper does not merely reflect the polls and follow the trends. It establishes trends. The best newspapers of the future will not only report what happens in society but will consider what should happen and what will help to make it happen.

Newspapers could better their communities and their own relationships with them by spearheading improvement. This would involve responding to sound forces in the community and at the same time encouraging community members to press for advance. Communication between editors and readers may be most helpful if it is somewhat formalized; this requires new ventures, which range from "press councils" to revamped approaches towards the letters-to-the-editor tradition.

The press council idea has been debated for a generation, and most publishers oppose it, believing they and their staffs best know how to run a paper. A council of citizens would only get in the way. Yet such councils have been successful.

At Littleton, Colorado, several years ago Houstoun Waring, a well-known editor who spent a Nieman year at Harvard in the forties, decided to have breakfast each Sunday morning with two prominent citizens, who could express their feelings in a relaxed atmosphere. These meetings continued eight years. Then in 1967 two jointly-owned semi-weeklies in the Littleton area, the *Littleton Independent* and the *Arapahoe Herald,* appointed a ten-member press council to improve their own performance. The announcement said: "The critics may detect a bias in reporting or a failure to probe into some social situations. They may dislike the emphasis on one aspect of community life and sense a neglect in another field. The viewpoint of ten respected members of the Littleton trade territory will be brought to bear on the newspapers and their treatment of the news as well as socio-economic and cultural matters." Results within a year included the introduction of youth news and the brightening of pages by eliminating column rules. And an organization had emerged that might bring even more significant changes.

The Mellett Fund for a Free and Responsible Press provided funds to establish press councils, two in California and two in Illinois, in conjunction with universities. Three of these have continued as advisory groups after the experimental period, but the one at Redwood City, California, was discontinued after nine months. Of two additional special-purpose councils established at Seattle and St. Louis in the summer of 1968, only the one in Seattle survived.

This council, which local newspapers and TV stations paid to continue, included Black Panthers and a Negro judge and concentrated on the relation of the press and the black community.

Newspapers also might fruitfully view themselves as public defenders as well as the traditional watchdogs of government. In Sweden and New Zealand ombudsmen serve such a function. (An ombudsman is an official who receives and looks into complaints about the abuses or capricious acts of people in authority.) Radio station WMCA (New York) established what it called an electronic ombudsman to "serve as a catalyst between service agencies, both public and private, and the people, who often don't know where to turn for help." Some newspapers do the same thing with "Action Line" or "Hot Line." Readers send in their complaints of unfairness, cheating, or bias, and the paper tries to resolve the difficulty or simply provide information.

There also may be new approaches to public discussion. Newspapers have long had letters-to-the-editor, man-in-the-street interviews, and statements by experts. With better educated readers could a more advanced and meaningful kind of open forum be developed? Aside from the "combat page" previously discussed, a newspaper might, for example, pose important questions and then publish written contributions a certain day on a discussion page. The queries might range all the way from "Should the U.S. withdraw from Southeast Asia?" to "What is the most pressing educational problem in Ourtown today?" Perhaps the paper could first print essays by knowledgeable citizens to start the readers writing. Bonuses would perhaps help. One corner might be given to teen-age replies. Editors should use their imaginations to stimulate fresher kinds of public discussion than have already been used a generation or more.

As pointed out in the chapters, what the newspaper prints becomes the subject of community argument, and what it ignores may be ignored by the public. To help establish trends instead of always bending with them, the alert editor must mix his news to focus the citizens' attention. Does he make readers talk about TV stars? Or does he make them argue about new health hazards?

There is evidence that newspapers already are giving more serious attention to social issues, so editors who choose to push on in that direction are only furthering what appears to be a solid trend. The Associated Press Managing Editors Association has had a Content Committee at work, and a report indicated considerable change in the decade to 1967—a bigger change than most editors realized. According to the chairman, Fred Pettijohn of the *Ft. Lauderdale* (Fla.) *News,* papers had dropped few subjects in those ten years, but they had condensed a great deal of news, especially routine local stories. There were fewer meeting notices, and small fires, accidents, and crimes were de-emphasized by many papers. At the same time there was more emphasis on stories of social change. "Editors have added specialized writers and specialized materials in aerospace, air-water pollution, education, race relations, economics (including welfare programs), urban and city renewal, medicine, public affairs." More depth stories were being printed for readers of women's pages, and there was much more coverage of cultural events and the visual arts.

These are healthy trends, and they should continue through the seventies. Sharp editors who have social conscience will find and print the news in the future. Better means and better men for communicating important information to and from readers will enable a newspaper to provide better leadership for community and nation than ever before.

Appendix a: tips for copyeditors

Most editors-in-chief tell their copyeditors to "use words correctly." Good advice, of course, but hard to follow. What is correct? Who said so? What about new words not yet in dictionaries? Which dictionary is correct? Not only are there new words, but new meanings of old words, as with *hip, cool,* and *pot.*

Newspapers use a standard for the meanings of words. If they did not, the reader would be confused frequently by jargon, slang, and malapropism. Usually the standard is the big dictionary in the middle of the newsroom, even if the edition is twenty years old. Some supplement is needed, however, to cover words newly accepted into the written language. On the other hand, an editor should take care to avoid words or meanings that he thinks will appear for a short time and then pass into obscurity even as they are being listed in a new dictionary. Perhaps a good guide to word usage in a newspaper would be to cling to the old, so the meaning of language does not change every generation, but adapt to the new if it brings freshness and vividness to the language.

Editors should not only be alert to changing usage, they should spot redundancies, grammatical errors, and misleading language. To this end we offer the following tips on usage, grammar, and spelling.

Usage

The following words and phrases are often mistakenly used.

Actual fact or *true fact.* A fact is by definition true.

Advise, for *inform.* "He was *informed* [not *advised*] of his wife's illness and *advised* to call her doctor immediately."

Alternative, for *alternate.* "He had an *alternate* [not *alternative*] plan. It gave the voter a choice of *alternatives.*"

Alumna. One female graduate; the plural is *alumnae. Alumnus* means one male graduate; the plural is *alumni,* which also is the plural for a group including both men and women.

Amateur, for *novice.* A novice is a beginner; an amateur is one who works or plays for fun, not money; a *professional* works or plays for money. Because the professional is usually highly skilled, an amateur is sometimes complimented by being called "professional."

Amused, See *bemused.*

And etc. Etc. stands for *et cetera,* which means "and the rest" in Latin, so the "and" is redundant.

Anxious, for *eager.* "He was *eager* [not *anxious*] to try, but his mother was *anxious* for his safety."

Ask. In its varied forms it can often be dropped. "*Asked* what he thought about the game, he said he thought it was good" can be simply "He said he thought the game was good."

Author, as a verb. "He *authored* a text" should be "He wrote a text."

Baby girl (or boy) *is born.* Redundant, as no one is born fully grown.

Badly injured. No injury is good; say "severely injured."

Beautiful. The word involves a value judgment, and some crank is bound to disagree, especially over a "beautiful woman."

Bemused, for *amused.* Bemused means dazed, preoccupied, or confused.

Boat, for *ship.* Technically, boats are carried on ships; generally, a boat is a small vessel.

Bridegroom. See *groom.*

Broadcasted, as the past tense of *broadcast.* "The program was *broadcast* daily."

Brutal beating. No beating is gentle.

Collide. This verb refers to a bumping of two moving objects. "The car hit [not *collided with*] a telephone pole and then *collided* with another car."

Complected or *complexioned.* The noun *complexion* has no adjective form. "She is fair *complected* [or *complexioned*]" should be "She has a fair *complexion.*"

Completely destroyed. The "completely" is redundant.

Comprise means contain, embrace, or include. The whole *comprises* the parts.

Consensus of opinion. "of opinion" is redundant, as a consensus is a collective opinion.

Controversial usually is a waste word. "The crowd shouted down the controversial proposal" can be simply "The crowd shouted down the proposal."

Contusion. See *laceration.*

Critical, for *critical condition.* A sick person in *critical condition* is seldom *critical.*

Currently. Usually redundant if the sentence is in the present tense. "He is *currently* appearing in *Macbeth*" can be simply "He is appearing in *Macbeth.*"

Devout, for *religious. Devout* is an exceptionally high degree of devotion—too high for the layman to measure.

Different than, for *different from.* "Each house is *different from* [not *different than*] the one next to it."

Dove, for *dived. Dove* is the colloquial, not the written, past tense of *dive.* "He *dived* [not *dove*] from the side of the boat."

Due to, for *because.* "He was late *because* [not *due to*] the battery went dead. He had been *due to* meet us at noon."

Eager. See *anxious.*

Elderly. Be cautious about this word, as even persons of seventy-five may be sensitive about being called *elderly.*

Esquire, the honorable, and other undefinable titles should be omitted.

Etc. See *and etc.*

Fewer. See *less.*
Foreseeable future. Who can see into the future?
Forgotten. See *gotten.*
For the purposes of can be simply *for.*
Freak accident is a cliché. Let the facts show that it is peculiar.

Gauntlet, for *gantlet.* A *gauntlet* is a glove and can be thrown down; a *gantlet* is a form of punishment and can be run.
Gotten, for *got. Gotten* is the colloquial past participle of *get,* but *forgotten* is the regular past participle of *forget.* "He had *got* the man's address but had *forgotten* to get his age.
Groom, for *bridegroom.* "The *bridegroom* had recently been employed as a *groom* with Smith Stables."
Ground rules. Except in reference to baseball games, skip the "ground."

Half mast, for *half staff.* Flags may fly at half mast on a ship but at *half staff* ashore.
Hung, for *hanged.* "Spectators *hung* over the wall to see the murderer *hanged.*"

Inform. See *advise.*

Jewish rabbis. Rabbi is Jewish by definition.

Laceration, for *contusion.* A *laceration* is a cut; a *contusion* is a bruise.
Ladies, for *women.* All *ladies* are women, but not all *women* are ladies. So call all women *women.*
Less, for *fewer. Less* refers to a general quantity; *fewer* refers to the specific items that make it up. "*Fewer* dollars earned means *less* money to spend."
Located, for *situated. Located* means "found," and *situated* means "placed at." "He *located* the school, which was *situated* five miles from town." As in this example, even "situated" can often be dropped without loss of meaning.

Majority, for *plurality.* In an election, a *majority* is more than half the votes, and the *plurality* is the margin of victory. "Jones was elected by a clear *majority* (64%), rolling up a *plurality* of 115,000 votes."
Media, for *medium. Media* is the plural of *medium.* "Television is an important *medium* for a political candidate today."
Militant, for mere *protestor* or for *rowdy.* A militant is a fighter for a cause; a rowdy fights for selfish reasons. A *protestor* may be against violence entirely.
Monies, for *money. Money* is collective, so the plural is unnecessary.
More unique or *most unique. Unique* is an absolute, so cannot be modified.

Novice. See *amateur.*

Orientated, for *oriented. Oriented* is the proper past tense of *orient.*

Panic, riot, disaster, etc. should not be used unless the facts clearly indicate the need for strong words.

Per (in *per year, per day,* etc.). Skip the Latin; use *a* year, *a* day. *Per annum* is doubly unfortunate.
Plurality. See *majority.*
Presently, for *now. Presently* is a long word meaning *soon.*
Prior to should be simply *before.*
Professional. See *amateur.*
Protestor. See *militant.*

Raised, for *reared.* Children are *reared;* animals are *raised.*
Reason why is redundant.
Red-headed, for *red-haired.* Be accurate. Do you mean the scalp or the hair?
Religious. See *devout.*
Resides is a fancy way of saying *lives.*
Revert back is redundant.
Rowdy. See *militant.*

Ship. See *boat.*
Situated. See *located.*
Sudden explosion is redundant.
Superlatives (like eldest, fastest, biggest) should be handled with care. Often someone will be challenged to find something that surpasses your example.

The before a plural noun is usually unnecessary. "The voters filled the polling booths" could be simply "Voters filled the polling booths." Let your ear be your guide.
These kind should be *these kinds.*
Thusly should be *thus.*
To death is often redundant, as in "strangled to death" or "drowned to death."

Unaware of the fact that should be simply "unaware that."
Utterly, flatly, sheer, categorically, definitely, and many other such adverbs only pad most sentences.

Very should be used very seldom.

Whether or not, for *whether.* Because it implies an alternative, *whether* rarely needs to be followed by *or not.*
Wise is a bad general suffix. Other*wise* is fine, but health*wise,* automobile*wise,* tax*wise,* etc. smack too much of advertising shoptalk.

Grammar

Journalists often need review of these grammatical points.*

About may indicate approximation; *around* implies motion. "He weighs *about* 150 pounds and runs two miles *around* the track each day."
Adjective phrases should be hyphenated. "The *2-year-old* boy ran to the *sad-looking* man.

* Adapted from a section in *High School Journalism Today,* Gene Gilmore, ed. (Danville, Ill.: Interstate Publishers), 1967.

Adjectives referring to health or emotion. See *feel.*

Affect is a verb and means *to have influence. Effect,* as a noun, refers to a result. "His speech *affected* the audience deeply; the *effect* was a silence so profound one could hear the crickets outside the tent." As a verb, *effect* means *to bring about* or *accomplish.* "His work *effected* a cure." Note that as a verb *effect* is usually unnecessary. "His work cured her."

Agreement. A subject and its predicate, and a noun and its pronoun, should agree in number. "The *group* of boys *was* trying to break down the door. The *girls* inside *were* screaming in panic. The *group* lost *its* steam when the dean appeared and told the *boys* he had called *their* parents."

Among. See *between.*

Apostrophe (to indicate possession). See *possessives.*

Around. See *about.*

As. See *like.*

Beside refers to nearness; *besides* means *in addition to. "Besides* being sheriff he was dog catcher, so he built the dog pound *beside* the jail."

Between refers to two persons or things; *among* refers to three or more. "The power of government is divided *among* the legislative, judicial, and executive branches. The legislative power is divided *between* the Senate and the House."

Capitalization (in quotations). See *quotations.*

Commas setting off appositives or interrupters come in pairs. "John Smith, senator from Vermont will speak today" should be "John Smith, senator from Vermont, will speak today." And "The meeting, surprisingly enough went off on schedule" needs a comma after "enough."

Contrary-to-fact statements. See *subjunctive mood.*

Doubt, statements of. See *subjunctive mood.*

Effect. See *affect.*

Either pairs with *or; neither* pairs with *nor. "Either* he *or* I is at fault, but *neither* he *nor* I admits guilt." Note that both *either* and *neither* require singular verbs.

Farther refers to distance; *further* refers to thoroughness. "He wanted to check *further* on the flood damage, so he walked *farther* out onto the bridge."

Feel, when it refers to health or emotion, requires an adjective, not an adverb. "I feel bad about not calling him back." "I feel badly" would imply an impaired sense of touch. The same rule applies to *look, sound, smell,* and *taste.*

Gerunds coupled with a pronoun require that pronoun to be possessive. "I could watch *his dancing* for hours."

Hyphenation, of adjective phrases. See *adjective phrases.*

It's and *its. It's* is a contraction of *it is; its* is a possessive pronoun. *"It's* too bad the store lost *its* lease."

Lay and *lie*. *To lay* is a transitive verb and thereby takes an object; *to lie* is intransitive and thus takes no object.

Transitive: He *lays* bricks for a living.
He is *laying* the box on the counter.
Lay the box on the counter.
He *laid* the box down.

Intransitive: He *lies* in bed till noon.
He is *lying* in the sun.
Lie down for an hour or so.
He *lay* down to rest.
His head *lay* on the pillow.
He has *lain* there long enough.

Like is a preposition and requires an object; *as* is a conjunction and requires a following clause. "She looks *like* her mother, just *as* [not *like*] we thought." *Like* may be used as a conjunction in a simile. "He performed *like* Artur Rubinstein."

Look, when referring to health. See *feel*.

Neither. See *either*.

Nor. See *either*.

Or. See *either*.

Possessives. To form the singular possessive, in most cases, add an apostrophe and an "s." "The dog*'s* coat is glossy." To form a plural possessive, in most cases, add the apostrophe. "The dog*s'* coats are wet." If a word ends with an "s" sound, add only the apostrophe if it has more than one syllable. "Rabinowitz*'* book is well-written; Ross*'s* book is dull."

Prepositional object. When a pronoun is the object of a preposition, it should be in the objective case. "The decision was between *him* and *me*."

Quotations.

A quoted sentence needs only one capital:

"It is a difficult problem," Smith said, "but we can solve it."

Two quoted sentences require two capitals:

"The well is dry," she said. "We must get water elsewhere."

A quote within a quote takes single quotation marks:

"New devices let people 'hear' atomic explosions thousands of miles away," he said.

When quoted material continues for more than one paragraph, save the *ending* quotation marks for the end of the quoted material:

"The well is dry," she said; "we must get it elsewhere (no quotation marks).

"Maybe we can get it at the next farm."

Set and *sit*. *To set* is a transitive verb and thereby takes an object; *to sit* is intransitive and thus takes no object.

Transitive: He *sets* tile for a living.
He is *setting* plants in the garden.
Set the box on the table.
He *set* the box down.

Intransitive: He *sits* here regularly.
She was *sitting* in the chair.
Sit down, please.
He *sat* in front.
Have you *sat* there before?

Smell. See *feel*.
Sound. See *feel*.
Subjunctive mood. The subjunctive mood expresses wishes, doubts, or things contrary to fact. It requires a plural verb. "If he *were* seven feet tall, he would be on the basketball team for sure" (contrary to fact). "I wish I *were* old enough to be President" (wish). "He acts as if he *were* unable to speak" (doubt).

Taste. See *feel*.
Touch. See *feel*.

Were. See *subjunctive mood*.

Spelling

Reporters often misspell or confuse these words:

accommodate
advice, advise
allege
amateur
arctic
bridal, bridle
calendar
canceled
canvas, canvass
capital, capitol
category
cellar
cemetery
chauffeur
cite, site, sight
compliment, complement
conscious
coroner
corps, corpse
council, counsel
defendant
desert, dessert
emigrate, immigrate
flew, flu, flue
floe, flow
guerrilla
hemorrhage
judgment
knowledgeable
lessen, lesson
libel, liable
lose, loose
mantel, mantle
mileage
missile
Niagara
nickel
ordinance, ordnance
peaceable
penitentiary
personal, personnel
Philippines
plaque
prairie
precede, proceed
preventive
principal, principle
privilege
rhythm
separate
sergeant
sizable
soccer
sophomore
stationary, stationery
there, their
weird.

Appendix b: glossary

ABC. Audit Bureau of Circulations, which compiles statistics on *circulations.*

Ad alley. A section of the *composing room* for *makeup* of ads.

Add. The copy added to a story; also, one *take* or page of a story, such as "Add 1."

Ad side. The section of the business office where advertising is prepared; sometimes a synonym for *ad alley.*

Advance. A story written in advance of an event and held for *release;* also, a story written on a forthcoming event.

Agate. Five-and-a-half-*point* type, usually found only in classified advertising or lists.

Agate line. A measurement of advertising depth. Fourteen make one inch.

Air. See *white space.*

Alive. Usable copy or type.

Alley. A section of the *composing room.* See *ad alley.*

All in hand. The situation when all copy has been sent to the *composing room.* All pages for the *edition* are *closed* and "ready to roll."

All up. The situation when the *copyeditor* or reporter has finished his assigned work. The copy is all in type.

AM. A morning newspaper. AMs is the cycle sent by a wire service to morning newspapers.

A-matter. Copy set in advance of the *top* of a story, sometimes called *10-add* material because it is added to *lead* paragraphs of a story.

ANPA. American Newspaper Publishers Association.

APC. Wire service jargon for "appreciate."

Art. Any illustrative material, such as pictures, graphs, and sketches.

Ascender. The portion of a *lower case* letter rising above average letter height; contrast to *descender.*

ASNE. American Society of Newspaper Editors.

Astonisher. An exclamation point.

Audience research. The study of newspaper readers—their education, wealth, etc.

Back room. The *composing room;* usually on smaller papers where it adjoins the news room. Also called back shop.

Back shop. See *back room.*

Bad break. An unattractive or confusing division of type in a story of more than one column. A column may end with a period, giving the impression that the story has ended, or there may be a prominent *widow.*

Balloon. A device used in comic strips to make words appear to come from a character.

Bank. A part of a headline, sometimes called a deck or, if the lower part, a drop. It also means a storage place for stories or ads set in type.

Banner. A headline running across, or nearly across, the top of a page; also called streamer, line, ribbon.

Bastard type. Type that differs from the standard *point* system.

Beat. The area assigned to a reporter for his regular coverage—his run; also, an exclusive story, or scoop.

Ben Day. An *engraving* process that provides shading effects in line engravings. Editors use Ben Day mostly for borders on key stories.

BF. The abbreviation for *boldface.*

Binder. A small *banner* across an inside page. It sometimes shelters several related stories.

Bite. To cut a story so it fits the space allotted to it. The part cut is called a biteoff or a bite.

Biteoff. See *bite.*

Blanket. See *offset.*

Bleed. To run a *cut* right off the edge of a page; also, the cut so run. Sometimes a cut run to the edge of the outside column is erroneously called a bleed.

Blind ad. A classified ad which gives a box number instead of the advertiser's name.

Blind interview. An interview story which does not reveal the name of the source, referring to him as "an informed official," "an unimpeachable source," etc.

Blotter. A police department's record book.

Blow up. To enlarge printed or pictorial matter; the enlargement so made.

Body. The story itself, as distinguished from the headline and the illustration.

Body type. The type normally used for news stories. The size is usually 8-, 9-, or 10-*point.*

Boil or *boil down.* A *copyeditor*'s direction to reduce a story substantially.

Boiler plate. Editorial matter, usually *features* and pictures, mailed to small papers in *matrix* or metallic form.

Boldface. Dark or heavy type, as distinguished from *lightface;* sometimes called fullface. **This is boldface.**

Book. A group of several stories on the same general subject, usually from a wire service. See also *take.*

Border. The strips of type metal surrounding an ad, story, or headline.

Box. To enclose a story or headline with four *rules* to give it more prominence; also, such an enclosure.

Box-all. The instruction to put the headline, *body,* and, possibly, picture of a story in a single *box.*

Break. The division of a story continued from one page to another or from one column to another. Compare *jump, bad break, break-over, wrap, carryover.* Also, a story breaks when the event occurs or when the news becomes available to reporters.

Break-over. The part of a story continued to another page. The page where break-overs are placed is called the break-over page, carryover, or jump page.

Brite. A short, amusing feature story; short for page brightener.

Budget. The listing of stories expected by a wire service or by another news gathering group; also called news digest.

Bug. Any fancy typographic device used to break up areas of type, especially in headlines. Compare *dingbat.* Bugs are used with restraint by today's editors. The word also refers to the telegrapher's key and to the label of the International Typographical Union.

Bulldog. The newspaper's first *edition* of the day.

Bullet. A large black dot used for decoration, to separate sections of a story, or, at the left edge of a column, to mark each item in a series.

Bulletin. Important and often unexpected news. In wire service parlance only a *flash* is more important.

Bulletin-form. A wire service term for filing a story in short installments, or *takes.*

Bulletin precede. The latest facts of a story already set in type when the bulletin arrived. The precede is stuck in at the top of the story.

Bureau. A subsidiary newsgathering force placed in a smaller community, a state capital, or the national capital by a newspaper or wire service.

Business-office must. A story labeled "must" by the business office, which means the story cannot be omitted. Usually it is a page-one *box* promoting the paper itself.

C and lc. The abbreviation for *caps and lower case,* used to specify the conventional capitalizing used in ordinary writing; contrast to material marked "caps," which means the compositor should set every letter as a capital.

C and sc. The abbreviation for *caps and small caps,* used to set material all in capitals but with the pattern of *C and lc.*

Cablese. See *skeletonize.*

Canned copy. Prepared news or editorials sent by a *syndicate* or publicity organization.

Caps. The abbreviation for capitals; also, upper case. Every letter or a word so marked is capitalized. Compare *C and lc* and *C and sc.*

Caption. A headline appearing above a picture; now, through misuse, commonly a synonym for *cutline,* the words under a picture.

Carryover. See *break-over.*

Casting. A *plate,* usually an ad or picture, made by pouring molten type metal over a papier mâché *matrix.*

Casting box. The equipment used to cast a printing *plate* from a papier mâché *matrix.*

Catchline. See *guideline.*

Center. To place type in the center of a line.

CGO. Short for *can go over.* Copy that could be held for another day.

Chapel. A union local for printers, stereotypers, or pressmen.

Chase. A frame in which type is placed to make a page *form.*

Chi square. A test of statistical validity; used in communicatons research.

Circulation. The number of copies a paper sells in a particular *edition;* the department in charge of distributing the paper.

Circus makeup. A now rare *makeup* system which uses many large headlines scattered seemingly as random on a page.

City desk. The place where the city editor and his assistants, if any, work.

City editor. The editor in charge of the reporters covering news within a city and its environs. On smaller papers he also edits his reporters' copy.

City room. The news room, where reporters and editors work.

Clean copy. A story needing little editing.

Clean proof. A *proof* needing few corrections.

Clipsheet. A sheet of publicity material which its backers hope will be clipped and reprinted. AP and UPI, however, send filler material on a clipsheet.

Closed. A page *locked up,* ready for *stereotyping* and therefore not to be altered except in an emergency.

Col. The abbreviation for column.

Cold type. Print produced photographically or by a machine resembling a typewriter. Strips of paper so "printed" are pasted on a *dummy* and photographed, and a *plate* for an *offset* press is made from the negative.

Color. A story with human interest, often describing places and people in detail. But a "colored" story is a biased, or slanted, report.

Column inch. One inch of type one column wide; a standard measure of advertising space for smaller papers.

Column rule. A thin line separating columns.

Communicologist. A communications researcher; often used in derision.

Compose. To set type. See *compositor.*

Composing room. The mechanical department; in particular the place where type is *composed* and put into *forms.*

Composing stick. The small metal tray in which a *compositor* arranges type he is setting by hand.

Compositor. Someone who sets type professionally, either by hand or by machine.

Condensed type. Type narrower than the standard width of a particular type *face,* giving a squeezed appearance; contrast *extended type.*

Content analysis. A research method to analyze published material.

Copy boy. An errand boy in the news room. "Copy girls" perform the same duties.

Copy cutter. A *composing room* worker who cuts copy into various *takes* to facilitate quick typesetting. He also distributes copy to various *Linotype* operators.

Copydesk. A desk, frequently horseshoe-shaped, around which *copyeditors* sit to edit copy. The *slot man,* inside the horseshoe, is in charge.

Copyeditor. A person who edits copy; a copyreader.

Copyreader. See *copyeditor.*

Copy writer. A person who writes advertising copy.

Correspondent. A reporter who files stories from places outside the newspaper's city area. He may be on salary or may receive a flat fee or a per-inch rate. See also *stringer.*

Country copy. News from rural areas, often written by a part-time *correspondent*, or *stringer.*

CQ. An abbreviation for "correct"; used in copy but not as a symbol on *proof* or on a *mark.* See also *CX.*

Credit line. A line acknowledging the source for a story or picture.

Crop. To cut away parts of a picture to eliminate unwanted material or to make it a particular size.

Cut. To reduce a story's length; compare *bite.* As a noun, an *engraving* and therefore any *art.*

Cutline. Any explanatory material under a piece of *art.* Compare *caption.*

Cutoff rule. A horizontal line, the width of a column, used to separate material.

CX. An abbreviation for "correct." The editor puts this symbol on *proof* corrected in the newsroom, or on a *mark.* The symbols "X-correct" and "Krect" are also used for this purpose. All three abbreviations are used on edited copy to show the typesetter that something that might seem wrong is right. See also *CQ.*

Dateline. The words that give the story's origin and, often, the date on which the story was written, e.g., CHICAGO, Oct. 1 (UPI)–.

Dayside. The shift of day workers in the news room.

Dead. Copy or type that will not be used.

Dead bank. A storage area for *dead* type.

Dead stone. See *dead bank.*

Deck. See *bank.*

Descender. The portion of a *lower case* letter going below the baseline; contrast *ascender.*

Desk chief. The head of a particular desk.

Dingbat. Any typographical device used for decoration. Compare *bug.*

Dinky dash. A short dash used to separate items in a series.

Dirty copy. Matter for publication which is sloppy, full of corrections, and badly marked up; contrast to *clean copy.*

Display ad. All advertising except classified and legal.

District man. A reporter covering a particular district of a city or rural area.

Dog watch. See *lobster trick.*

Dope story. An interpretative story often based on background plus speculation.

Doublet. The repetition of some fact; also called doubleton.

Doubleton. See *doublet.*

Double-truck. A two-page layout, either news or advertising, which eliminates the margin, or *gutter*, between the pages.

Downstyle. A style with a minimum of capitalization. Contrast *upstyle.*

DPR. The telegraph symbol for Day Press Rate.

Drop. See *bank.*

Drop head. A headline with each line stepped (and so also called a step head):

President Says
Budget Deficit
Above Estimate

Drop line. See *drop head.*

Dummy. A diagram of a newspaper page used to show printers where stories, pictures, and ads are to be placed; occasionally called a map.

Dupe. A duplicate, usually a carbon copy; also, a story that appears twice in the same *edition.*

Ear. Either upper corner of the front page, often containing a slogan or a weather report.

Edition. Each *run* of a newspaper *issue.* There may be market editions, early editions, final editions, etc.

Editorial. Generally all the non-advertising and non-business material or operations of a newspaper; also, one of the opinion essays of the editorial page.

Electrotype. A copper-plated reproduction of type or *art;* usually used in advertising or book publishing.

Em. The square of the type size. An em in 12-*point* type is twelve points high and twelve points wide. Sometimes erroneously used to mean one-sixth of an inch; see *pica.*

En. Half an *em.*

End dash. A dash at the end of a story; usually about six *picas.* It is sometimes called a thirty-dash.

Engraving. A *plate* from which pictures and drawings may be printed; see *cut.*

Etaoin shrdlu. A *Linotype* operator sets these "words" to fill out a line he plans to throw away. The letters make up the first two vertical rows on a *Linotype.*

Exchange. A copy of a newspaper sent to another newspaper publisher as part of an agreement to exchange subscriptions.

Extended type. Type wider than the standard for a particular *face;* contrast *condensed type.*

Extra. A special, or extra, *edition* published because of spectacular news; now rare.

Eye camera. A camera specially arranged to record a reader's eye movements; used in research on *makeup.*

Face. A particular design of type; also, the printing surface of type.

Fake. A false story.

Feature. A story emphasizing the human interest or entertainment aspects of a situation; usually in narrative form. Also, material such as columns and comics brought from a *syndicate.* As a verb, it means to give prominence to a story; to emphasize a part of a story.

FF or *ff.* The abbreviation for fullface. See *boldface.*

File. To transmit a story by telephone, telegraph, or cable. As a noun, it refers collectively to the back issues of a paper; also, one day's production by a wire service.

Filler. Short stories, usually *time copy,* used to fill small spaces in the paper.

Fingernails. Parentheses; sometimes called toenails.

First-day story. The first published account of an event.

Flag. The newspaper's *nameplate* or *logotype,* often erroneously called the *masthead;* also, a *slug* or piece of paper inserted into printing *forms* to remind printers that a correction, *add*, or *insert* is required at that point.

Flash. The highest priority of news sent by a wire service; used rarely.

Flat-bed press. A press which prints from a flat surface.

Flimsy. Thin paper used for carbon copies; sometimes the carbon copy itself.

Flong. A cardboard-like sheet used for making the *matrix* in *stereotyping.*

Fluff. Inconsequential material.

Flush. The instructions to set type even, or flush, with a margin; "flush left" means flush with the left margin, "flush right" with the right margin.

Flush head. A headline whose lines are even on the left:

President Says
Budget Plan
'Unrealistic'

Folio. The line at the top of the page giving the page number, the name of the newspaper, the city of publication, and the date; also, a measure for legal advertising.

Follow. A story that *follows up* a *first-day* story; also, a *second-day* story; also, a story *shirt-tailed* to a similar, but more important, story.

Follow up. A story that gives the latest news of an event reported earlier.

Folo. An abbreviation for *follow.* Also see *folo copy.*

Folo copy. The order to set copy in type exactly as written.

Font. A set of a particular size and style of type.

Form. A *chase* filled with type.

Format. The physical appearance of a page, section, or book.

Four-color process. A printing process using four different engraving *plates,* each printing one color—black, red, blue, or yellow—to make natural-looking color.

Fourth estate. The public press.

Front office. The business office.

Fudge. A part of a press *plate* that may be removed or chiseled away so last-minute news, usually sports scores, can be inserted; also called a fudge box.

Fullface. See *boldface.*

Full line. Type that fills the line, making it both *flush* left and flush right; a line that has no room for spacing.

Future. A reminder of a forthcoming event. Such notes are put in a "future book" to be used in making reporting assignments. "Futures" are stories to be used within a few days or weeks.

FYI. The wire service abbreviation for "for your information."

Galley. A metal tray to hold type; also, about twenty inches of type.

Galley proof. A *proof* of a *galley* of type; used to check the copy for errors before it goes to press.

Ghost. A ghost writer; a person who writes stories or books for others' signatures.

Glossy. A shiny-surfaced photograph, best suited for *photoengraving.*

Goodnight. A wire service may end its *AMs* cycle with this word; an editor may call it out to a staffer, thereby indicating the staffer may leave for the day.

Graf. Short for paragraph.

Graveyard shift. The work period that covers the early morning hours; also called *lobster trick* or *dog watch.* Staffers on this shift may write and edit, but they are there primarily to cover emergencies.

Gravure. A process for printing from an indented surface. See also *intaglio* and *rotogravure.*

Gray out. A section of a page that has no typographical contrast, giving a gray appearance.

Green eyeshade. A somewhat sentimental term for an old-time newspaperman; refers to a former custom among deskmen of wearing green eyeshades.

Guideline. The first word or two of a headline, written at the top of the copy to identify it; also called catchline. It is sometimes confused with *slugline.*

Gutter. The margin between facing pages.

Hairline. An extra-thin *rule.*

Halftone. An engraving using small dots of varying depth to produce shaded effects, as in photos; contrast to *line cut.*

Handout. A press release.

Handset. Type set by hand.

Hanging indent. A headline with first line set flush left and other lines slightly and equally indented:

President Says
    Budget Plan
    'Unrealistic'

Head. Short for headline.

Head schedule. A sheet that displays headline types used by the newspaper; it includes the unit count for each type face so the editor can quickly figure how much space a word will take up in the headline. Popularly called the "hed sked."

Head slug. A *slug* which does not print, separating the headline from the story with blank space.

Head to come. The notice to the composing room that the headline will be sent after the story; abbreviated HTK or HTC.

Headwriter. A writer of headlines; usually a *copyeditor,* who writes the headlines for the story he edits.

Hed sked. Short for *head schedule.*

Hellbox. A container in the *composing room* for unwanted type.

Holdover. See *overset.*

Hole. See *news hole.*

House organ. A publication issued by a company primarily for its employees.

HTC or *HTK.* Abbreviations for *head to come.*

Human interest. The quality giving a story wide appeal. It often contains information on human foibles or oddities or heartwarming and sentimental matter.

Index. The summary of the contents or highlights of a paper; usually on page one.

Initial. A large capital letter at the beginning of an article or paragraph, common in magazines but sometimes used for magazine-style matter in newspapers.

Insert. Copy or type to be inserted into a story.

Intaglio printing. The *gravure* process that prints ink from a depressed surface.

Inverted pyramid. A headline form with each line centered and shorter than the preceding one:

President Reports
Deficit Plan
Today

Also, a news story with facts arranged in descending order of importance.

Issue. One day's newspaper, which may have several *editions.*

Ital. or *itals.* Abbreviations for *italics.*

Italics. Type with letters slanted to the right; used for cross references in this glossary. Contrast *roman* and *oblique.*

ITU. International Typographical Union, to which most printers (but not stereotypers or pressmen) belong.

Jim dash. A dash about three *picas* long, often used to separate a regular story and a *shirttail.*

Job. A commercial printing order.

Job press. A press used only for commercial printing.

Jump. See *break-over;* also, to continue a story. Compare *break.*

Jump head. The headline over the part of the story that was continued, or *jumped,* to another page.

Jump line. A line noting a story is continued (e.g., *Continued on Page 6*).

Jump page. See *break-over.*

Justify. To space out a column to make the type snug, or to space out a line of type so it is *flush* left and right.

Justowriter. A machine, basically like a typewriter, which sets *cold type.*

Kicker. A few words usually to the left and above a headline, to give it emphasis; sometimes it serves the same purpose as a *deck.*

Kill. To eliminate all or part of a story. Compare *mandatory kill.*

Label head. A headline, usually without a verb, that only labels the news and thus is listless (e.g., *List of Graduates*).

Late watch. See *lobster trick.*

Layout. A planned arrangement of stories and pictures on one subject; also, the whole typographical arrangement of a newspaper.

LC or *lc.* Abbreviations for *lower case.*

Lead (pronounced "led"). A strip of metal used to separate *slugs* of type. Strips are placed between paragraphs to justify a column.

Lead (pronounced "leed"). The first paragraph or two of a story; also, the story given number one position as the best of the day. Also, a *tip.*

Lead ("leed") *editorial.* The first, and most important, editorial.

Lead ("leed") *to come.* A device, used rarely, to indicate that the story's *lead* will come later. Compare *ten-add.*

Leaders ("leeders"). Dots or dashes to take the eye across a column; often used in tables.

Leftover. See *overset.*

Leg man. A reporter who gathers information and telephones it to a *rewrite man.*

Legibility. The quality of a type style which makes it easily and quickly comprehended or perceived; contrast *readability.*

Letterpress printing. The process by which ink is transferred to paper from a raised surface; the traditional method of printing.

Letter space. The insertion of thin spaces between letters to *justify* the line.

Library. A collection of clippings, newspaper files, and reference books; formerly called the morgue.

Ligature. One character of type that includes more than one letter (e.g., *fl* and œ). The initials of the wire services, such as AP and UPI, are also known as ligatures.

Linage. A measure of printed material based on the number of lines; also, the total amount of advertising over a given period of time.

Line. See *banner;* also, *agate line.*

Linecasting machine. A machine that casts line of type. Compare *Linotype.*

Line cut. An engraving which prints only black and white; also called line engraving. Contrast *halftone.*

Line gauge. A printer's ruler.

Lino. Short for *Linotype.*

Linotype. The brand name of a machine which sets hot type one line at a time; also a loose term for all similar machines.

Lithography. The process of printing from ink impressed on a sheet; also called photolithography. See also *offset.*

Live. Designation for type that will be used in the paper going to press.

Lobster trick. The shift on duty after the last *edition* of a morning paper has gone to press; the night shift of an afternoon paper. Sometimes called lobster shift, late watch, and dog watch. See also *graveyard shift* and *nightside.*

Local. A local news item; usually a *personal.*

Localize. To emphasize a local angle in a story.

Locked up. See *closed.*

Log or *logo.* Short for *logotype.*

Logotype. A one-piece line of type or a *plate* bearing a trademark, name, or frequently used phrase. A newspaper's *nameplate,* or *flag,* is a logotype.

Lower case. The small letters of type. The term originated with early type cases, which had the small letters near the bottom. Contrast *upper case.* See also *downstyle.*

Ludlow. A typecasting machine used for headlines or advertising. It casts *slugs* from *matrices* that are *handset.*

Magazine. An attachment on a *linecasting machine* for the storing of *matrices.*

Magazine style. See *upstyle;* also see *initial.*

Mail edition. An *edition* sent primarily to mail subscribers.

Makeover. To make a new page *plate* to correct an error or to include late news; also called replate.

Makeready. The series of *composing room* processes that prepare material for printing.

Makeup. To arrange type and pictures to produce a desired effect. The noun refers to the resulting design.

Makeup editor. An editorial employee stationed in the *composing room* to supervise the *makeup* of the paper.

Makeup rule. A thin piece of steel, shaped something like a protractor, used by printers in page *makeup.*

Mandatory kill. An order from a wire service to eliminate (*kill*) a story, probably because it has a serious error or is libelous.

Map. See *dummy.*

Mark. A story from one *edition* clipped and pasted on a sheet of paper to be marked for changes in the next edition–corrections, indications of inserts, adds, or new leads. Also called a markup or marker.

Marker. See *mark.*

Markets. A section of the paper that includes news of livestock, commodity, and stock markets.

Markup. See *mark.*

Masthead. A statement of the paper's name, ownership, subscription rate, etc., which often appears on the editorial page; often confused with *nameplate* or *flag.*

Mat. Short for *matrix.*

Matrix (plural: matrices). A die or mold from which type is cast. It can be papier mâché, from which the page *plate* is cast, or a brass die, from which lines of type are cast. Commonly referred to as mat.

Mat roller. The machine which squeezes the papier mâché matrix against the *form*, preparatory to making a page *plate.*

Measure. The length of a line of type, or the width of a column.

Media Records, Inc. A company that records data on newspaper advertising.

Milline rate. A method of measuring advertising rates in relation to *circulation.*

Monotype. A typecasting machine that sets each letter in a separate piece of metal.

More. A word placed at the end of a sheet of copy to indicate that the story has not ended.

Morgue. See *library.*

Mortice. An opening, usually rectangular, for the insertion of material, such as an opening in an *engraving* for a heading.

Must. An order from a superior that a certain story must run in the paper that day. See also *business office must.*

Nameplate. The *logotype* that carries the newspaper's name at the top of page one; also called *flag* and, wrongly, *masthead.*

NANA. North American Newspaper Alliance, a news *syndicate* specializing in feature stories.

National advertising. Advertising placed by an advertising agency, usually for a product sold nationally.

NEA. National Editorial Association, a group of weekly and small-daily editors; also, Newspaper Enterprise Association, a *feature* service.

New lead (pronounced "leed"). Also called new top. A fresh opening paragraph or two for a story. An editor may think the reporter's story basically sound but in need of a new *lead* to catch the reader's interest. Or the story may have been published earlier and need a new beginning; see also *second-day story.*

News digest. See *budget.*

News hole. The space in a paper allotted to news reports and illustration, the rest being given to advertisements, comic strips, etc.

New top. See *new lead.*

Nightside. The night shift of a newspaper. See also *lobster trick.*

Nonpareil. Six-*point* type.

NPR. The telegraph symbol for Night Press Rate.

Nutted. Type indented one *en.*

Obit. Short for *obituary.*

Obituary. A story reporting a person's death. For a well-known person, it is often written before he dies; the facts of his death are simply incorporated into the pre-written story of his life.

Oblique type. Slanted type, but without the handwritten appearance of *italics.* Contrast *roman.*

Off its feet. Type that does not quite stand vertically and therefore makes a poor impression on the paper.

Offset. A photographic method of printing. Copy is photographed and a *plate* made by "burning" light through the negative onto a sensitized sheet of thin metal. The part exposed to light, or "burned," absorbs ink while the rest of the plate rejects it. The plate, wrapped around a roller, transfers, or offsets, the ink to a rubber roller called a blanket, which actually imprints the paper.

Op ed or *opp page.* Abbreviations for "the page opposite"; usually the page devoted to columns and *features* and placed opposite the editorial page.

Overset. Set type that cannot be used because space is filled; called holdover or leftover if it can be used in the next issue.

Page proof. A *proof* (test printing) of a full page. Such proofs often are taken of the front page before it is made into a *plate.*

Patent or *patent insides.* Pre-printed material, usually on one side of a sheet so local news can be printed on the blank side; used rarely now, even on the smallest weeklies. Also see *readyprint.*

Perforator. A machine used to perforate a paper tape from which type can be set mechanically; also, a person who runs a perforator.

Personal. A one-paragraph item about minor family news; a kind of *local.*

Photocomposition. A photographic process to "set type." Actually, letters are formed on film which is photographically printed; then that print is photographed in the *offset* process to make a *plate.*

Photoengraving. See *engraving.*

Photolithography. See *lithography.*

Pi. Jumbled type, or, as a verb, to jumble type; past tense or adjective form is "pied."

Pica. Twelve-*point* type; also, a printer's measure–one-sixth of an inch. It is also called *pica em* or, wrongly, *em.*

Pica em. See *pica.*

Pick up. The instruction at the bottom of copy to tell the printer to pick up other type and add it to the story. In wire copy, it tells the editor where *adds, inserts,* etc. "pick up" into the story.

Pix. Short for pictures.

Planer. A wooden block pounded against type in *form* to make it level.

Plate. A *stereotype* page or an *offset* metal sheet from which newspapers are printed.

Platen press. A small *job press.*

Play. The typographical emphasis given a story, or the emphasis on a certain fact in a story. Facts or stories can be "played up" or "played down."

PM. An afternoon newspaper.

Point. A type measurement–one seventy-second of an inch. Hence, 72-point type is one inch high, 36-point one-half inch, etc.

Policy. The newspaper's position on how it handles news.

Policy story. A story that supports the newspaper *policy.*

Poll. A field study of opinion on an issue. It may be a scientific *public opinion survey* or merely unscientific guesswork.

PR. Public relations.

Precede. A *new lead* or story, taking precedence over a previous wire service transmission and usually intended to precede it. A *bulletin precede* could be set in type and placed ahead of the earlier story.

Pre-date. An issue printed before its announced date of publication. (Metropolitan morning papers put out an *edition* in the evening with the next day's date on it.)

Preferred position. An advertising term that refers to an advertiser's receiving a special place in the paper for his ads. Usually the advertiser pays extra for this preference.

Press agent. A person hired to get favorable publicity for an individual or organization.

Process color. A printing method that mixes primary colors optically to produce a full range of colors.

Proof. A test impression taken from type set and ready for printing. It allows errors to be spotted and corrections made before the paper goes to press. See also *galley proof.*

Proof press. A simple press used to make *proof.*

Proofreader. An employee in the *composing room* who reads and marks *proof* to make sure it conforms to copy.

Public opinion survey. A scientific study of the expressed attitudes of a representative sample of a population; often used before elections.

Public relations. The craft of issuing news of and creating a good image for an individual, agency, or firm; more professional and comprehensive than the work of a *press agent.* Often shortened to PR.

Puff, puffery. A publicity story or a story that contains unwarranted superlatives.

Puncher. A *teletype* operator.

Put to bed. See *all in hand.*

Q. and A. Copy including question-and-answer material, as in court testimony or a long interview.

Query. A question raised in a message to a wire service; also, a request by a freelance writer to see if a newspaper or magazine would be interested in a particular article.

Railroad. To send copy to the *composing room* with little or no editing; to put type into *forms* without *proofreading.*

Readability. The quality of copy which makes it easy to grasp; contrast *legibility.*

Reader interest. A type of research to determine the degree of appeal different materials have for the reader.

Readership. Research on the amount of newspaper copy which readers notice or read; also, the people actually reached by a publication, as distinguished from *circulation.*

Readout. A subsidiary headline that "reads out" (explains in more detail) from a *banner.*

Readyprint. Paper already partly printed with ads and *features,* so the rest of the space can be filled with local news and ads. See also *patent.*

Register. The correct placement or matching of *plates* in color printing so colors are exactly where they should be.

Release. The date and time at which a news source says information may be released to the public; also, a publicity handout; also, authorization for the use of a photograph.

Replate. See *makeover.*

Reprint. Published material that came from a previous issue or from some other source, such as a magazine.

Reproduction proof or *repro proof.* A fine *proof* on quality paper for use in preparing a *plate,* as in *offset.*

Retail advertising. Advertising placed by local merchants.

Retouch. To change a photograph, usually to improve it for *engraving,* by painting sections out (or in) with a small brush.

Revamp. To alter a story by shifting some of the paragraphs, but not by rewriting it. See also *rewrite.*

Reverse. Letters or *engravings* printed the opposite of normal, as white letters on a black background.

Reverse-6. The eye tends to scan the news page in a line resembling a reversed number 6.

Revise. A second, and presumably correct, *proof*–made after errors were noted on the first proof.

Rewrite. To write a story again, or to *revamp* a story from a wire service or from another newspaper; also, to write a story telephoned to the news room by another reporter. See also *rewrite man.*

Rewrite man. The reporter who takes facts from one or more reporters, usually by telephone, and writes the story; also, a reporter who revises stories written by other reporters.

Ribbon. See *banner.*

Rim. The outside edge of the *copydesk,* which is traditionally horseshoe-shaped.

Rim man. A *copyeditor,* so named because he sits on the *rim.*

Roman type. The common vertical type which is popularly contrasted to *italic* and technically to *oblique.*

ROP. Short for *run of paper.*

Roto. Short for *rotogravure.*

Rotogravure. An *intaglio* printing process using etching on copper and a rotary press; also, a section of a newspaper featuring photographs so printed.

Routing. Gouging metal from a *cut, casting,* or a page *plate* so only part of the surface will print.

Rule. A metal strip which prints a line dividing columns, stories, or sections of advertising; usually one or two *points* thick, but see also *hairline.*

Ruled insert. A story that accompanies another but is set off from it by *rules.*

Run. An *edition,* in the sense that the edition is "run"; also, a *beat.*

Run in. The instruction on copy to have material in tables or paragraphs run together without paragraphing.

Running story. A story–actually many stories–continued for several days or more.

Run of paper. An order meaning that an ad, picture, or story could go almost anyplace in the paper. Also, color printed by regular newspaper presses.

Sacred cow. A person or institution unethically deferred to by being given special news treatment.

Sans serif. See *serif.*

SAP. Occasionally used in messages to mean "soon as possible." The superlative SAPPEST is used humorously.

Schedule. A record of stories assigned or already processed.

Scoop. See *beat.*

Screen. A mesh through which pictures are rephotographed in making *engravings* or *cuts.* A fairly coarse screen is used in making newspaper cuts.

Second-day story. A story previously published but now carrying a *new lead* or some other revision to make it news. Also see *follow.*

Second front page. Usually the front page of a second section; also called split page. Sometimes page two or page three gets the name because it carries important news with little or no advertising.

Sectional story. A story received in pieces or sent to the *composing room* in sections; also, a story that would be of interest only to readers in a certain area.

See copy. The direction to *proofreaders* to check the *proof* against the copy.

Send down or *send out.* The direction to send copy to the *composing room.*

Separate. A story related to another and displayed separately, but usually nearby.

Series. Related stories, usually run on consecutive days.

Serif. A tiny finishing stroke or squiggle at the ends of letters in most type faces. A face with simple, square corners is called sans serif.

Set. To arrange type, either by hand or by machine, for printing.

Shirttail. Material added to a major story; also, a short *follow.*

Sidebar. A story that emphasizes one part of a main story and appears alongside it on the page.

Sidelight. A kind of *sidebar,* often dealing with a personality or one aspect of an event.

Side story. See *sidebar.*

Signature. An advertiser's name, often in distinctive type, in his ad; often printed from a *logotype.*

Skeletonize. To reduce copy by eliminating articles, some conjunctions, etc. in order to minimize cable tolls; now rarely done. The skeletonized language is called cablese.

Skyline. A line running above the *nameplate,* at the top of the page.

Slant. To emphasize a certain part or angle of a story; also, to distort the news. Compare *color.*

Slot. The inside of the horseshoe-shaped *copydesk;* occupied by the slot man, who directs the *copyeditors* sitting around the *rim.*

Slot man. See *slot.*

Slug or *slugline.* A mark on a story, usually one word like "blast" or "money," for identification as it passes through the news room and *composing room.*

Small caps. Capital letters smaller than the regular capitals of a particular type face; used almost exclusively in magazines and books, and rarely there. See also *C and sc.*

Soc. Short for society; sometimes "sox."

Solid. Lines of type set without space, or *lead,* between them.

Sox. See *soc.*

Space grabber. A publicity seeker.

Spike. A spindle, usually for unwanted copy; also, to eliminate, or *kill,* a story.

Split page. See *second front page.*

Split run. The dividing of a publication run into two or more slightly different versions, sometimes for research. For example, to check the effectiveness of a new ad, one version would have the new ad and one would have the old.

Spot news. Information about a specific, recent occurrence, as contrasted to a story about a trend or continually developing situation.

Spread. A prominent display, usually with *art.* Sometimes the large, multi-column head over the material is called a "spread head."

Squib. A short news item.

Standing. Material kept in type because often needed, such as a column heading or the *nameplate.* A headline used repeatedly, such as the head over baseball standings, is called a standing head or stet head.

State editor. The person who edits the news from the newspaper's *circulation* area outside the metropolitan region.

Step head. See *drop head.*

Stereotype. A cylindrical or semi-cylindrical *plate* of a page. A papier mâché *matrix* is squeezed against the original type to make a mold. Molten metal is poured over the mold to make the stereotype.

Stet. The abbreviation for "let it stand," written above crossed-out words to indicate that they should be set in type after all.

Stet head. See *standing.*

Stick. A rough measurement meaning about two inches of type. See also *composing stick.*

Stone. A metal- or marble-topped table for page *makeup.* See also *turtle.*

Straight matter. Regular editorial material set in *body type* without variations from convention.

Straight news. A story with only the bare facts, without *color* interpretation.

Streamer. See *banner.*

String. Newspaper clippings to be added up by or for a *stringer* to see how much he should be paid. The term comes from saving the clips on a string; as a verb it means to work as a stringer.

Stringer. A part-time reporter living outside the newspaper's central area. See also *correspondent.*

Style book or *style sheet.* A specific list of the conventions of spelling, abbreviation, punctuation, capitalization, etc. used by a particular newspaper or wire service.

Sub. A piece of copy that substitutes for something in a previous story.

Subhead. A headline, usually one line of *body type* in *boldface,* that appears every few paragraphs. It should describe the news in the paragraph or two following.

Symmetry. A style of page *makeup* that balances elements on the page so neither the top nor the bottom, the left nor the right, dominates.

Syndicate. A firm which sells and distributes columns, comics, *features,* and pictures. A wire service technically is a syndicate, but is rarely called by that name.

Tabloid. A newspaper half the size of a regular eight-column, twenty-one-inch newspaper. The dimensions usually are five columns by sixteen inches. Though some "tabs" are sensational, the term is not a synonym for *yellow journalism.*

Take. A section of copy, usually a page long, sent to the *copydesk* or to the *composing room.* See also *book.*

Tear sheet. A newspaper page sent to an advertiser as evidence that his ad was printed.

Telegraph editor. The person who supervises the editing of news from wire services; thus often called the wire editor.

Teleprinter. See *teletype.*

Teletype. A machine that automatically types out news coming from a wire service; also called teleprinter and ticker. It can be used to transmit, as well as receive, news.

Teletypesetter. An attachment to a *Linotype* so it can set type from a perforated tape; commonly referred to as TTS.

Ten-add. A method for sending details of a story to the *composing room* before sending the *lead.* The initial piece of copy (*take*) is labeled 10-add, the next 11-add, etc.

Think piece. An interpretative article.

Thirty. The end of a story; written "30."

Thirty-dash. See *end dash.*

Thumbnail. A *cut* half a column wide.

Ticker. See *teletype.*

Tie-back. A reference in a story to some previous event–to help the reader's memory.

Tie-in. A story or part of a story linked to some other event.

Tight. A situation of little or no room in the whole paper, in a particular story, or in a line. See also *tight line.*

Tight line. A line too crowded for proper spacing between words.

Time copy. Material always current and therefore timeless; can be run whenever convenient.

Tip. Information that may lead to a story.

Toenails. See *fingernails.*

Tombstone. To place similar headlines side by side so the reader tends to read from head to head rather than from head to story.

Top. The first few paragraphs of a story.

Top deck. The main part of a headline.

TR. The abbreviation of *turn rule.*

Trim. To reduce a story carefully.

Truck. See *turtle.*

Trunk. The main wire of a wire service.

TTS. The abbreviation for *teletypesetter.*

Turn column. A few papers continue column eight, page one, to column one, page two, and eliminate a *jump head.*

Turn rule. A direction to the printer to turn over a *slug* because an addition, *insert,* or correction will be made at that point. The slug then becomes a reminder, which must be removed before printing.

Turtle. A metal cart, often called a truck, used to transport page *forms* to the *mat roller;* often used as a *stone.*

Type high. Any material high enough to print. The standard height of type is .918 of an inch.

Typo. Short for typographical error.

Undated story. A story with no specific geographical focus, such as a war in the Near East, and therefore no specific dateline. The source of the story is printed at the top, such as "United Press International."

Under-dash material. Prepared stories, principally *obituaries,* ready for publication. When an event makes the story timely, first come a few paragraphs about the event, then a *jim dash* or *dinky dash,* and then the prepared material (under, or following, a dash).

Underline. See *cutline;* also *caption.*

Universal desk. A desk that handles copy from several departments of the paper, usually city, wire, and state.

Upper case. See *caps.*

Upstyle. A style that capitalizes more words than most papers do; also called magazine style. Contrast *downstyle.*

Urgent. A wire service designation for an important story, but less important than a *bulletin.*

WF. The *proofreader*'s mark for *wrong font.*

White space. The blank space, also called air, around heads, ad copy, and stories; left blank to make the printed material stand out.

Widow. A one- or two-word line at the end of a paragraph; usually unsightly if the last line of *cutlines* or the first line in a column. See also *bad break.*

Wild. Copy that may run on nearly any inside page. See also *run of paper.*

Wire editor. See *telegraph editor.*

Wirephoto. A system owned by Associated Press for transmitting pictures over wire.

Wrap. To place type in two or more columns under a multi-column headline. See also *break.*

Wrapped up. See *all in hand.*

Wrong font. The designation for a letter of type different from the style used in the story.

Xerography. A new process for printing with static electricity and without ink.

Yellow journalism. Sensational and often deliberately inaccurate reporting.

Citations

Chapter 1

1. Robert Root, "Syndicates," in *Journalism Tomorrow,* ed. Wesley C. Clark (Syracuse: Syracuse University Press, 1958), pp. 79-80.
2. Wilbur Schramm, *Mass Media and National Development* (Stanford: Stanford University Press, 1964), pp. 42-43.
3. W. H. Ferry and Harry S. Ashmore, *Mass Communications* (Santa Barbara, Calif.: Center for the Study of Democratic Institutions, 1966), p. 10.
4. Walter Gieber, "News Is What Newspapermen Make It," in *People, Society, and Mass Communications,* ed. Lewis Dexter and David White (Glencoe, Ill.: The Free Press, 1964), pp. 173-82.

Chapter 6

1. Lyndon Baines Johnson, *The Choices We Face* (New York: Bantam Books, 1969), pp. 135-36.
2. *Responsibility in Mass Communication* was republished in a revised edition by William L. Rivers and Wilbur Schramm (New York: Harper and Row, 1969).

Chapter 12

1. The quote from a Supreme Court ruling on "actual malice" is from Robert M. Bliss, "Development of Fair Comment as a Defense to Libel," *Journalism Quarterly* (Winter, 1967), 627-37.
2. Don R. Pember, "Privacy and the Press: the Defense of Newsworthiness," *Journalism Quarterly* (Spring, 1968), 14-24.

Chapter 13

1. Ira B. Harkey, Jr., *The Smell of Burning Crosses* (Jacksonville, Ill.: Harris-Wolfe, 1967), p. 45.
2. Richard T. Baker, *The Christian As a Journalist* (New York: Association Press, 1961), pp. 117-18.
3. Fred S. Siebert, et al., *Four Theories of the Press* (Urbana: University of Illinois Press, 1963), chapters 2 and 3.
4. For useful discussions of the report of the Commission on Freedom of the Press "twenty years after," see Edward Engbert's discussion in *The Center Magazine* (October-November, 1967), 22f., as well as the entire issue of the *Columbia Journalism Review* for Summer, 1967.
5. For details on successful operations of press councils in Redwood City, California, and Bend, Oregon, see William B. Blankenburg, "Local Press Councils: an Informal Accounting," *Columbia Journalism Review* (Spring, 1969), 14-18.
6. John C. Merrill, *The Press and Social Responsibility* (Freedom of Information Center Publication No. 001, University of Missouri, 1965), p. 2.
7. Karl Jaspers, *Philosophy Is for Everyman* (New York: Harcourt, Brace & World, 1965), p. 8.

Chapter 15

1. James Moznette and Galen Rarick, "Which Are More Readable: Editorials or News Stories?" *Journalism Quarterly* (Summer, 1968), 319-21.

Chapter 17

1. See the chapter on "Truth and Fairness" in *Responsibility in Mass Communications* (New York: Harper & Bros., 1957; rev. ed. by William L. Rivers and Wilbur Schramm, Harper and Row, 1969), pp. 217ff.
2. J. Daniel Hess, "An Inquiry into the Meaning of 'Social Responsibility,'" *Journalism Quarterly* (Summer, 1966), 325-27.

Chapter 18

1. Roland E. Wolseley, *Bulletin, New York State Society of Newspaper Editors,* April, 1964, pp. 5-8.
2. Roy E. Carter, Jr., and F. Gerald Kline, "An Experimental Study of Two Methods of Gathering Newspaper Readership Data," *Journalism Quarterly* (Spring, 1968), 118-122.
3. Gerhard D. Wiebe, "The *New York Times* and Public Opinion Research: a Criticism," *Journalism Quarterly* (Winter, 1967), 654-58.

Chapter 19

1. A fuller account of the speech by John Diebold on automation appears in *Quill* (November, 1965), 30-32.
2. Susan Tebbe, "Managing Editors and Journalism Education," *Journalism Quarterly* (Autumn, 1967), 555-56.

Bibliography

Editing, general

Bastian, George C., Leland D. Case, and Floyd K. Baskett. *Editing the Day's News*. New York: Macmillan, Fourth Edition, 1956.

Crowell, Alfred A. *Creative News Editing*. Dubuque: William C. Brown, 1969.

Garst, Robert F., and Theodore M. Bernstein. *Headlines and Deadlines*. New York: Columbia University Press, Third Edition, 1961.

Root, Robert. *Modern Magazine Editing*. Dubuque: William C. Brown, 1966.

Westley, Bruce. *News Editing*. Boston: Houghton Mifflin, 1953.

Typography

Arnold, Edmund C. *Ink on Paper*. New York: Harper & Row, 1963.

Arnold, Edmund C. *Modern Newspaper Design*. New York: Harper & Row, 1969.

Burt, Sir Cyril. *A Psychological Study of Typography*. Cambridge, England: Cambridge University Press, 1959.

Butler, Kenneth B. *Practical Handbook on Display Typefaces for Publication Layout*. Mendota, Illinois: Butler Type-Design Research Center, 1959.

Butler, Kenneth B., and George Likeness. *A Practical Handbook on Borders, Ornamentation and Boxes in Publication Layout*. Mendota, Illinois: Butler Type-Design Research Center, 1960.

Cogoli, John E. *Photo-Offset Fundamentals*. Bloomington, Illinois: McKnight & McKnight, 1960.

Dair, Carl. *Design with Type*. Toronto: University of Toronto Press, 1967.

Lewis, John. *Typography: Basic Principles*. New York: Reinhold, 1964.

Lieberman, J. Ben. *Printing as a Hobby*. New York: Sterling, 1963.

Tinker, Miles A. *Legibility of Print*. Ames: Iowa State University Press, 1963.

Photography and picture editing

Feininger, Andreas. *The Complete Photographer*. Englewood Cliffs, N.J.: Prentice-Hall, 1965.

Fox, Rodney, and Robert Kerns. *Creative News Photography*. Ames: Iowa State University Press, 1961.

Rhode, Robert B., and Floyd H. McCall. *Press Photography*. New York: Macmillan, 1961.

Sidey, Hugh, and Rodney Fox. *1,000 Ideas for Better News Pictures*. Ames: Iowa State University Press, 1956.

Writing and style

Baker, Sheridan. *The Practical Stylist.* New York: Thomas Y. Crowell, 1962.

Bernstein, Theodore M. *The Careful Writer.* New York: Atheneum, 1965.

Bernstein, Theodore M. *Watch Your Language.* New York: Atheneum, 1965.

Bryant, Margaret M., ed. *Current American Usage.* New York: Funk & Wagnalls, 1962.

Callihan, E. L. *Grammar for Journalists.* New York: Ronald, 1957.

Chall, Jeanne S. *Readability: An Appraisal of Research and Application.* Columbus: Ohio State University, 1958.

Copperud, Roy H. *A Dictionary of Usage and Style.* New York: Hawthorn, 1964.

Flesch, Rudolph. *The ABC of Style.* New York: Harper & Row, 1964.

Flesch, Rudolph. *The Art of Readable Writing.* New York: Harper & Bros., 1949.

Follett, Wilson. *Modern American Usage* (edited and completed by Jacques Barzun). New York: Hill & Wang, 1966.

Gowers, Sir Ernest. *Plain Words: Their ABC.* New York: Knopf, 1955.

Hayakawa, S. I. *Language in Thought and Action.* New York: Harcourt, Brace & World, 1964.

Klare, George R. *The Measurement of Readability.* Ames: Iowa State University Press, 1963.

Perrin, Porter G. *An Index to English* (Revised by Karl W. Dykema and Wilma R. Ebbitt). Glenview, Ill.: Scott, Foresman, Fourth Edition, 1968.

Strunk, William S., Jr., and E. B. White. *The Elements of Style.* New York: Macmillan, 1959.

Ethics and law

Ashley, Paul P. *Say it Safely.* Seattle: University of Washington Press, Third Edition, 1966.

Associated Press. *The Dangers of Libel.* New York, 1968.

Fisher, Paul L., and Ralph L. Lowenstein, eds. *Race and the News Media.* New York: Frederick A. Praeger, 1967.

Gerald, J. Edward. *The Social Responsibility of the Press.* Minneapolis: University of Minnesota Press, 1963.

Gross, Gerald, ed. *The Responsibility of the Press.* New York: Fleet, 1966.

Hale, William G. *Law and the Press.* St. Paul: West, Third Edition, 1948.

Haselden, Kyle. *Morality and the Mass Media.* Nashville: Broadman, 1968.

Lofton, John. *Justice and the Press.* Boston: Beacon, 1966.

Lyle, Jack, ed. *The Black American and the Press.* Los Angeles: Ward Ritchie, 1968.

MacDougall, Curtis D. *The Press and Its Problems.* Dubuque: Wm. C. Brown, 1964.

Phelps, Robert H., and E. Douglas Hamilton. *Libel and Slander.* New York: Macmillan, 1966.

Rivers, William L., and Wilbur Schramm. *Responsibility in Mass Communication.* New York: Harper and Row, Revised Edition, 1969.

Siebert, Fred S., Theodore Peterson, and Wilbur Schramm. *Four Theories of the Press.* Urbana: University of Illinois Press, 1963.

Wittenberg, Philip. *Dangerous Words.* New York: Columbia University Press, 1947.

Communication theory and research

Backstrom, Charles H., and Gerald D. Hursh. *Survey Research.* Evanston: Northwestern University Press, 1963.

Berlo, David K. *The Process of Communication.* New York: Holt, Rinehart and Winston, 1963.

Budd, Richard W., Robert K. Thorp, and Lewis Donohew. *Content Analysis of Communications.* New York: Macmillan, 1967.

DeFleur, Melvin L. *Theories of Mass Communication.* New York: David McKay, 1966.

Dexter, Lewis A., and David Manning White, eds. *People, Society, and Mass Communications.* New York: The Free Press, 1964.

Franzblau, Abraham N. *A Primer of Statistics for Non-Statisticians.* New York: Harcourt, Brace & World, 1958.

Haskins, Jack B., and Barry M. Feinberg. *Newspaper Publishers Look at Research.* Syracuse: Syracuse University School of Journalism, 1968.

Klapper, Joseph T. *The Effects of Mass Communication.* Glencoe, Ill.: The Free Press, 1960.

Nafziger, Ralph O., and David Manning White, eds. *Introduction to Mass Communications Research.* Baton Rouge: Louisiana State University Press, Second Edition, 1963.

Osgood, Charles. *Measurement of Meaning.* Urbana: University of Illinois Press, 1957.

Wright, Charles R. *Mass Communication.* New York: Random House, 1959.

Organization and management

Byerly, Kenneth R. *Community Journalism.* Philadelphia: Chilton, 1961.

Cranford, Robert J. *The State Editor and His Problems.* Lincoln: University of Nebraska Press, 1961.

Rucker, Frank W., and Herbert Lee Williams. *Newspaper Organization and Management.* Ames: Iowa State University Press, Revised Edition, 1969.

Sim, John Cameron. *The Grass Roots Press.* Ames: Iowa State University Press, 1969.

Tebbel, John. *Open Letter to Newspaper Readers.* New York: James H. Heineman, 1968.

Miscellaneous

Emery, Edwin. *The Press and America.* Englewood Cliffs, N.J.: Prentice-Hall, Second Edition, 1962.

Hohenberg, John. *The News Media: A Journalist Looks at His Profession.* New York: Holt, Rinehart and Winston, 1968.

Krieghbaum, Hillier. *Facts in Perspective.* Englewood Cliffs, N.J.: Prentice-Hall, 1956.

Peterson, Theodore, Jay Jenson, and William O. Rivers. *The Mass Media and Modern Society.* New York: Holt, Rinehart and Winston, 1965.

Rucker, Bryce W. *The First Freedom.* Carbondale: Southern Illinois University Press, 1968.

Waldrop, A. Gayle. *Editor and Editorial Writer.* Dubuque: William C. Brown, Third Edition, 1967.

Index

About the authors

Gene Gilmore has worked as an editor on papers ranging from the *Alma* (Mich.) *Record* (circulation 3,600) to the *Washington Post* (circulation 500,000). For eight years in between he was telegraph editor of the prize-winning *Gazette & Daily* in York, Pennsylvania. He started teaching in 1957 at Syracuse University and has been on the journalism faculty at the Urbana campus of the University of Illinois since 1963. His degrees are from the University of Michigan and Syracuse.

From 1968 until his death in June 1970, **Robert Root** taught comparative literature at Eisenhower College. He came to Eisenhower as a member of the charter faculty after sixteen years as a professor of journalism at Syracuse University. Before he began teaching, he had been a practicing journalist for twelve years. His experience included such positions as editorial writer for the *Des Moines Tribune,* special correspondent for the *Christian Science Monitor,* managing editor of *Leader's Magazine,* and part-time writer for the *Syracuse Post-Standard,* the *Rochester Times-Union,* the Associated Press, and the *New York Times.* His degrees were in humanities (PhD, Syracuse) and journalism (MA, Columbia). At his death the book had been in the proof stage, and his widow, Christine, has been vital in the final aspects of its production.